T0304702

Healthcare Management

Healthcare Management takes a look at international perspectives in healthcare management and the way regional priorities, national income, and social factors are crucial to effective healthcare services. Readers are provided the skills to address issues and solve problems as a healthcare manager by understanding and appreciating the complex interrelationships of global health provision. The book compares and contrasts different healthcare systems, examining the role of policymaking, health financing, healthcare beyond hospitals, leadership, risk management, and quality. A range of international case studies provide the opportunity to see how different theories work in practice. This comprehensive book is suitable for students and professionals undertaking healthcare management courses.

Alan Gillies is Professor of Healthcare Management at the International University of Applied Sciences in Germany. He also holds the titles of Honorary Professor at UCLAN in Preston in the UK and Doctor Honoris Causa at the Iuliu Hatieganu University of Medicine and Pharmacy in Cluj-Napoca, Romania.

Masters in Healthcare Management

This series is ideal reading for students undertaking postgraduate study in Healthcare Management. It covers the key topics, providing a strong grounding in theory while ensuring skills are provided for the journey into practice.

Healthcare Management
Global Perspectives
Alan Gillies

Healthcare Management

Global Perspectives

Alan Gillies

Routledge
Taylor & Francis Group

LONDON AND NEW YORK

Designed cover image: Credit: Jezperklauzen Creative #: 509171425

First published 2025
by Routledge
4 Park Square, Milton Park, Abingdon, Oxon OX14 4RN

and by Routledge
605 Third Avenue, New York, NY 10158

Routledge is an imprint of the Taylor & Francis Group, an informa business

© 2025 Alan Gillies

British Library Cataloguing-in-Publication Data
A catalogue record for this book is available from the British Library

ISBN: 978-1-032-76526-6 (hbk)
ISBN: 978-1-032-76525-9 (pbk)
ISBN: 978-1-003-47887-4 (ebk)

DOI: 10.4324/9781003478874

Typeset in Sabon
by Deanta Global Publishing Services, Chennai, India

This book is dedicated to my mother, Evelyn Gillies, 1934–2023

Contents

List of abbreviations and acronyms

Abbreviation	meaning
AB-NHPM	Ayushman Bharat–National Health Protection Mission
ACA	Affordable Care Act
AI	Artificial Intelligence
AL	Adaptive Learning (AL)
AMR	Anti-Microbial Resistance
ARR	Annual Rate of Reduction
ART	Antiretroviral Therapy
CAS	Complex Adaptive System
CAUTI	Catheter-Associated Urinary Tract Infections
CBA	Cost-Benefit Analysis
CDC	Centers for Disease Control
CDSS	Clinical Decision Support Systems
CE	Conformité Européene
CEN	European Committee for Standardisation
CENELEC	The European Committee for Electrotechnical Standardisation
CHC	Community Health Centre
CIHI	Canadian Institute for Health Information
CIRS	Critical Incident Reporting System
CMAJ	Canadian Medical Association Journal
CRM	Customer Relationship Management
CVD	Cardiovascular Disease
DALY	Disability-Adjusted Life Year
DAQI	Daily Air Quality Index
DCRA	The Dutch Colo-Rectal Audit
DDD	Defined Daily Doses
DICA	Dutch Institute for Clinical Auditing
DIN	Deutsches Institut für Normung
DNA	Deoxyribonucleic Acid
DRGs	Diagnosis-Related Groups
DSD	Differentiated Service Delivery
DSS	Decision Support Systems
EBM	Evidence-Based Medicine
EBP	Evidence-Based Practice
EC	European Commision

ECDC	European Centre for Disease Prevention and Control
EDL	Essential Diagnostics List
EEA	European Economic Area
EFQM	European Foundation for Quality Management
EHR	Electronic Health Record
EMA	European Medicines Agency
EML	Essential Medicines List
EN	European Norm
EU	European Union
FDA	Food and Drug Administration
FFS	Fee-for-service
FMEA	Failure Mode and Effects Analysis
GATT	General Agreement on Tariffs and Trade
Gavi	Global Vaccine Alliance
GBP	British Pounds
GDP	Gross Domestic Product
GDM	Gestational Diabetes Mellitus
GDPR	General Data Protection Regulations
GHI	Global Hunger Index
GP	General Practitioner
GST	Goods and Services Tax
HALE	Health-Adjusted Life Expectancy
HARP	Hospital Admission Risk Program
HF	Heart Failure
Hib	Haemophilus Influenza Type b (Hib),
HIPAA	Health Insurance Portability and Accountability Act
HMO	Health Maintenance Organisation
HPV	Human Papillomavirus
HR	Human Resources
HRQOL	Health-Related Quality of Life
IBRD	International Bank for Reconstruction and Development
ICD	International Classification of Diseases
ICDM	Integrated Chronic Disease Management
ICT	Information and Communication Technology
ICU	Intensive Care Unit
IDA	International Development Association
IHR	International Health Regulations
ILO	International Labour Organisation
IMR	Infant Mortality Rate (IMR)
IQ	Intelligence Quotient
ISO	International Standards Organisation
ISQua	International Society for Quality in Health Care
IT	Information Technology
JCI	Joint Commission International
JIT	Just in Time
KI	Kakwani Index
LEB	Life Expectancy at Birth
LMIC	Low- or Middle-Income Country

LMS	Laboratory Information system
MDR	Medical Device Regulation
MDSW	Medical Device Software
MIM PS	Minimal Information Model for Patient Safety
ML	Machine Learning
MOOC	Massive Open Online Course
MPI	Multidimensional Poverty Index
MRI	Magnetic Resonance Imaging
mRNA	Messenger RNA
NCD	Non-Communicable Diseases
NGO	Non-Governmental Organisation
NHI	National Health Insurance
NHIS	National Health Insurance Scheme (Ghana and Nigeria)
NHS	National Health Service
NICE	National Institute for Health and Clinical Excellence
NNS	Non-Nutritive Sweeteners
NOKC	Norwegian Knowledge Centre for the Health Services
NPSA	National Patient Safety Agency
NRLS	National Reporting and Learning System
OECD	The Organisation for Economic Cooperation and Development
OKR	Objectives and Key Results
OOP	Out-Of-Pocket
OTC	Over-The-Counter
PACS	Picture Archiving and Communication Systems
PACS	Picture Archiving and Communication Systems
PAS	Patient Administration Systems
PFI	Private Finance Initiative
PFM	Public Financial Management
PHI	Private Health Insurance
PIMS	Pharmacy Information Management Systems
PPM	Provider Payment Models
PPP	Public Private Partnership
PPS	Prospective Payment Systems
PROM	Patient-Reported Outcome Measure
QALY	Quality-Adjusted Life Year
QMS	Quality Management Systems
QOF	Quality and Outcomes Framework
RADAR	Results, Approaches, Deploy, Assess and Refine
RNA	Ribonucleic Acid
RT-PCR	Reverse Transcriptase Polymerase Chain Reaction
SAM	Suitability Assessment of Materials
SaMD	Software as a Medical Device
SARS	Severe-Acute-Respiratory
SARS-CoV-2	Severe-Acute-Respiratory-Syndrome-Related Coronavirus Strain 2
SDG	Sustainable Development Goal
SDI	Socio-Demographic Index
SDM	Social Distancing Measure
SHI	Social Health Insurance

SHIS	Statutory Health Insurance System
SIDS	Sudden Infant Death Syndrome
SiMD	Software in a Medical Device
SMS	Short Message/Messaging Service
SNOMED-CT	Systematized Nomenclature of Medicine Clinical Terms
SRH	Self-Rated Health
SSB	Sugar-Sweetened Beverages
SSDG3 GAP	The Global Action Plan for Healthy Lives and Well-being for All
SWOT	Strengths, Weaknesses, Opportunities and Threats analysis
TB	Tuberculosis
TOC	Theory of Change model
TRIPS	Trade-Related Aspects of Intellectual Property Rights
UHC	Universal Health Coverage
UK	The United Kingdom of Great Britain and Northern Ireland
UN	United Nations
UN-DESA	United Nations Department of Economic and Social Affairs
UNAIDS	The Joint United Nations Programme on HIV/AIDS
UNDP	United Nations Development Programme
UNESCO	United Nations Educational, Scientific and Cultural Organisation
UNFPA	United Nations Population Fund
UNICEF	United Nations Children's Fund
US	United States of America
USD	US Dollars
VA	The Department of Veterans Affairs
VAT	Value Added Tax
VHI	Voluntary Health Insurance
VR	Virtual Reality
WASH	Water, Sanitation and Hygiene Programme
WHA	World Health Assembly
WHO	World Health Organisation
WTO	World Trade Organisation

Foreword

I am reaching the end of my career, having worked in academia for almost 40 years and in health management for over 35 years.

In what is almost certainly my final academic role as Professor of Healthcare Management at the International University of Applied Sciences in Germany (IU), I have the privilege of teaching students from many different countries. In this role, I have become very conscious that most academic texts are very focused on the needs of the healthcare systems in Western Europe and North America.

In seeking to create a book that reflects a more global perspective, it is simply not possible to write a text that covers all aspects of healthcare management in all the different countries and healthcare systems around the world.

Therefore, this book takes a thematic approach to healthcare management and then seeks to illustrate its application with as wide a range of examples and case studies as possible. The key themes used to structure the book are the current state of health and healthcare, healthcare policy, healthcare financing, the healthcare industry, management and leadership, and information and innovation.

It's easy at my stage of career to be cynical. However, having refreshed my knowledge through the research I have carried out to determine the current state of the art at the time of writing, my view of the current state of health, healthcare, and our ability to manage it is a rather mixed picture.

On the one hand, I am depressed by:

- How many of the challenges we faced at the end of the 20th century remain;
- The inexorable rise in expenditure on healthcare in high-income countries that appears unsustainable as a result of stagnating economies and an ageing population;
- Ongoing health inequalities both between and within countries; and
- The failure of digital technology to deliver joined-up patient-centred care.

On the other hand, I am encouraged by:

- Progress in maternal and child health in lower-income countries;
- The speed of the global response to COVID-19 and a comparison with the Spanish Flu pandemic of 1919–20 that shows how far we have come; and
- The ongoing developments in preventative health, most recently the initial rollout of a vaccine against malaria.

Finally, I would like to thank all of the students and colleagues who have taught me so much over my career and especially the staff and students at the IU, who have rekindled my enthusiasm for teaching and writing.

Alan Gillies
May 2024

Section A

The current state of health and healthcare

1   The context

1.1 About this book

This book was written because the management of health and well-being is one of the two great global challenges facing the world today, alongside climate change. It was also written because attempting to teach students from across the globe made me realise that most of the textbooks in this area written in English present a very parochial world-view that readers outside of Europe and North America will find of limited relevance to their own situation. Hopefully readers from within Europe and North America will also find the global dimensions of interest!

The book is structured around a number of key themes:

- The current state of health and healthcare
- Healthcare policy
- Healthcare financing
- The healthcare industry
- Management and leadership
- Information and innovation

At the end of most sections, you will find a box with a case study or other material designed to reinforce what you have read. These are generally followed by a couple of questions designed to check if you have understood some of the key concepts from that section. All of these concepts are explained in the glossary of terms if you are unsure, in addition to the preceding section of the main text.

These are followed by a question or questions to think about. These don't come with answers, because the answers will be different for everybody. They are designed to help you reflect on what the preceding section means for you in your own situation and context. They may also be used by course tutors for group discussions.

1.2 The state of global health

1.2.1 *What the data says*

In 2023, the World Health Organization's (WHO's) World Health Statistics (WHO, 2023) reported that since the year 2000, global health had seen significant improvements, including halving child mortality, reducing maternal mortality, and lowering the incidence of infectious diseases. However, it also reported that progress had slowed since

DOI: 10.4324/9781003478874-2

2015, challenging the achievement of the Sustainable Development Goal (SDG) targets by 2030.

For example, in maternal mortality, the global maternal mortality ratio dropped by a third between 2000 and 2015, from 339 deaths per 100,000 live births to 227 deaths per 100,000 live births, representing a 2.7% average annual rate of reduction (ARR).

The total number of maternal deaths globally fell by 30% during the same period, from an estimated 447,000 deaths in 2000 to 313,000 deaths in 2015.

Such progress, however, has stalled since then. WHO (2023) estimates that 287,000 women lost their lives due to largely preventable causes related to pregnancy and childbirth in 2020 – equivalent to 223 deaths per 100,000 live births that year.

The COVID-19 pandemic resulted in 14.9 million excess deaths and exposed global health inequities. The pandemic also reversed positive trends in immunisation and the incidence of diseases like malaria. Additionally, WHO emphasises the threat of infectious diseases, especially in the context of antimicrobial resistance and highlights the ongoing impact of climate change on health. The demographic shift towards non-communicable diseases (NCDs) is a growing concern, with NCD deaths projected to increase by nearly 90% globally by 2048.

The Organisation for Economic Co-operation and Development (OECD) collates health data across 38 of the wealthier countries in the world. Some of the data takes a number of years to be collated.

At the end of 2023, the OECD reported the following data for life expectancy at birth from the countries that had supplied data for 2022.

The OECD collects a range of data sets relating to health. Figure 1.1 shows the percentage of the population reporting good or very good health in a range of European countries in 2022.

1.2.2 Health and healthcare

Healthcare is the means to achieve the end goal of the best health and well-being possible. The WHO constitution states: "Health is a state of complete physical, mental and social well-being and not merely the absence of disease or infirmity." An important implication of this definition is that mental health is more than just the absence of mental disorders or disabilities. (WHO, 1946).

Enhanced sanitation of water, food, and milk, decreased overcrowding, upgraded nutritional practices, and, in wealthier countries, the adoption of central heating using cleaner fuels were the key factors contributing to significant advancements in public health throughout the 19th and 20th centuries.

The World Bank suggests that more than half (56%) of the world's population – 4.4 billion inhabitants – live in cities. This trend is expected to continue, with the urban population more than doubling its current size by 2050, at which point nearly 7 of 10 people will live in cities (World Bank, 2023).

While rural citizens face specific health-related challenges, such as difficulties accessing healthcare due to transportation issues and availability concerns, the health impacts of inner-city living, including decay and crime, can be dramatic and interconnected with broader social issues. The health status of urban areas and their residents is shaped by a combination of political, socioeconomic, and environmental factors that influence health behaviours like exercise, diet, sexual lifestyles, and substance misuse.

Table 1.1 Life expectancy at birth in 2022 from those reporting data by the end of 2023

| Country | Life expectancy at birth | | |
	Female	Male	All
Argentina	78.6	72.2	75.4
Austria	83.5	78.8	81.1
Belgium	83.9	79.6	81.8
Brazil	76	69.6	72.8
Bulgaria	78.1	70.8	74.3
Chile	84	78.5	81.2
China (PRC)	81.2	75.5	78.2
Colombia	80.1	73.8	76.9
Costa Rica	83.5	78.3	80.9
Croatia	80.8	74.6	77.7
Czechia	82	76.2	79.1
Denmark	83.2	79.5	81.3
Estonia	82.4	73.7	78.2
Finland	83.8	78.7	81.2
France	85.2	79.4	82.3
Greece	83.3	78.1	80.7
Hungary	79.5	72.7	76.2
Iceland	83.4	81	82.1
India	68.9	65.8	67.2
Indonesia	69.7	65.5	67.6
Israel	84.9	80.9	82.9
Italy	85	80.9	83
Latvia	79.6	69.8	74.8
Lithuania	80.3	71.5	76
Luxembourg	85.3	80.9	83
Netherlands	83.2	80.3	81.7
Norway	84.2	81	82.6
Peru	74.7	70.1	72.4
Poland	81.3	73.5	77.4
Portugal	84.5	78.8	81.7
Romania	79.3	71.5	75.3
Slovak Republic	80.6	73.7	77.2
Slovenia	84.1	78.6	81.3
South Africa	65	59.5	62.3
Spain	85.9	80.4	83.2
Sweden	84.8	81.5	83.1
Switzerland	85.4	81.6	83.5

Negative environmental aspects of urban living, such as toxic buildings, proximity to industrial parks, and a lack of parks or green spaces disproportionately affect those already facing economic and social disadvantages due to the concentration of such factors in specific urban pockets of poverty and deprivation.

Urban residents may encounter elevated levels of air pollution. This has been linked to increased rates of cardiovascular and respiratory diseases. Individuals living in ageing

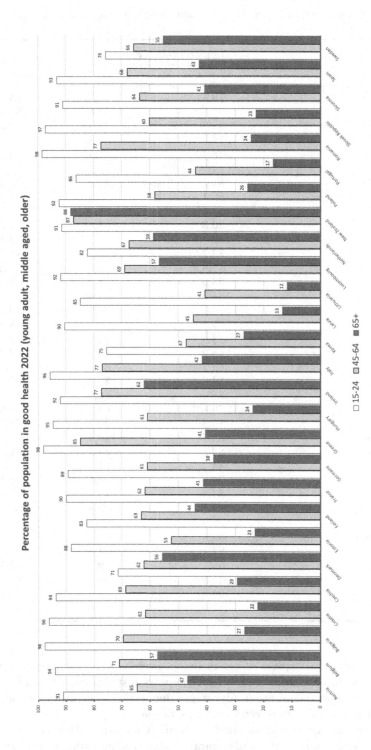

Figure 1.1 The percentage of young adults, middle-aged and older people reporting good or very good health in a range of European countries in 2022.

buildings and crowded, unsanitary conditions may also experience heightened levels of lead in their blood. Environmental factors like these are linked with higher incidences of asthma and allergies amongst other health risk factors (Manisalidis et al., 2020). These instances underscore the profound impact of the physical environment on health, as the places where people reside can expose them to detrimental factors.

Beyond the physical environment, the social environment can have a profound impact on the health of a population:

- socioeconomic position
- race and ethnicity
- social networks and social support
- working conditions

The world is profoundly unequal in financial terms. It is also profoundly unequal in terms of life expectancy and other indicators of health. There is little dissent from the argument that there is a correlation between these factors. Those with fewer material resources not only experience shorter lifespans but also contend with more health issues throughout their truncated lives.

For many years, it has been assumed that there was a causal link between the two, i.e., socioeconomic (dis)advantage produces health (dis)advantage. However, some authors have pointed out that studies using rigorous analytic methods have had trouble identifying a causal effect of education and, particularly, income on health. Such studies are most effective where there are a limited number of independent factors operating. Health on the other hand is influenced by many factors that are themselves inter-related and interdependent.

Mackenbach (2020) argues that countries with more advanced welfare states, such as the Nordic countries, do not exhibit smaller health inequalities. These nations have managed to achieve smaller income inequalities and lower poverty levels than most other European countries. However, their health inequalities remain as large as or even larger than those in other regions, primarily due to pronounced disparities in smoking, excessive alcohol consumption, and other health-related behaviours, suggesting that the welfare state may offer full protection comprehensively.

The role of race and ethnicity in health is a complex one. The factors that disadvantage members of specific racial groups are context-dependent and interact with other determinants such as poverty. To address these issues, Shannon et al. (2022) conducted an examination of five case studies to comprehend the impact of intersecting systems of oppression on health and wellbeing, as well as potential interventions. They found that whilst experiences of racism may vary in specific contexts, there are shared patterns in how racism operates to influence health and wellbeing. These include the influence of coloniality, the division and separation along evolving lines of identity and privilege, the institutionalisation of racism, both overt and covert forms of discrimination, and the pervasive violence associated with discrimination across various levels.

Frequently, health services fail to address these disadvantages or make them worse by a failure to understand the underlying causes of ill-health and impact on the way that these populations interact with services.

Several systematic reviews of the literature have suggested linkages between social support and health or service uptake in general, especially in relation to mental health (e.g. Terry and Townley, 2019) and that that negative impacts can be worse in specific population groups (e.g. McDonald, 2018). Findings in previous studies suggest that social support, which may be provided by a variety of individuals and services, plays an important role in promoting community integration and social networks for individuals with serious mental health challenges. The existing literature indicates that the relationship between mental health and social support is complex, emphasising the importance of social support in preventing mental health issues, sustaining positive mental health and aiding recovery from both moderate and severe mental health challenges (Bjørlykhaug et al., 2022).

Working conditions can have a profound impact on employees' health, both physically and mentally. Working environments may be polluted, exposing workers to toxins; working conditions may cause musculoskeletal problems ranging from back problems in manual workers such as miners working in cramped conditions to repetitive strain injuries in home office workers working in ergonomically unsuitable conditions. Work-based stress is a huge mental health issue and a major cause of sickness-based absence in office environments.

The enforced move to homeworking caused by the COVID-19 pandemic was heralded by many as a chance to improve the working conditions for many. However, a review by Wütschert et al. (2022) highlights the insufficient ergonomic working conditions experienced by home-based teleworkers. Despite employees attempting to implement ergonomic practices, organisational support is lacking. Management's limited awareness of ergonomics and its impact on workers' health further complicates the situation. The absence of clear regulations for home-based telework adds to the confusion, with varying interpretations of contractual requirements in different countries.

Additionally, teleworkers often fail to report health issues and medical expenses due to a lack of knowledge about their rights or differing motivations for working at home. Prolonged computer use, sedentary behaviour, and suboptimal ergonomic setups contribute to health complications, particularly musculoskeletal issues.

All of the research highlights that healthcare is just one of the determinants of health, and a smaller part than those involved with healthcare probably imagine. It also highlights that the different determinants of health are in a complex interrelationship that challenge assumptions about linear relationships between interventions and outcomes.

1.2.3 Knowledge review

Before you move on, can you define the following key concepts:

- (The wider) Determinants of health?
- Curative healthcare?
- Preventative healthcare?

1.2.4 Question to think about

How should a country allocate resources to maximise the health of their population – should they prioritise preventative or curative healthcare or wider improvements in people's living environment beyond healthcare altogether?

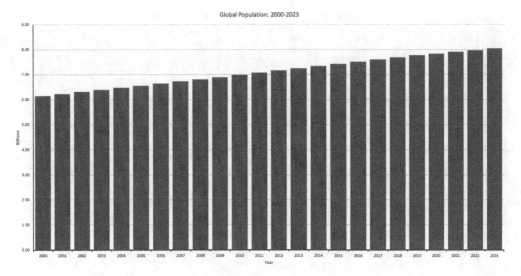

Figure 1.2 Global population 2000–2023. Graph created by the author from data by the United Nations. (United Nations Department of Economic and Social Affairs Population Division (UN-DESA), 2023).

1.3 Population as a driver of health

1.3.1 The global population

The global population continues to rise year on year, although the rate of growth has been decreasing since 1971 (Figure 1.2).

The overall trend appears to be a continuous increase. In 2023, the global population passed the 8 million mark. Also in 2023, and earlier than many had predicted, India, with a current population of around 1.37 billion, became the world's most populous country, ahead of China.

However, although the global population continues to rise, the rate of increase is slowing, albeit with a slight rise in 2022 and 2023 (Figure 1.3).

The growth rate reached its peak in the 1960s but has been on a decline since then, and this trend is expected to persist. While it took 12.5 years for the global population to increase from 7 billion to 8 billion, projections indicate that it will likely take 14.1 years to reach 9 billion and an additional 16.4 years to go from 9 billion to 10 billion.

Despite this slowdown, it is still expected that the world population will reach 10.2 billion by 2060. A significant portion, around three-quarters, of the world's population lives in countries where fertility is at or below the replacement level. The replacement-level fertility rate is often assumed to be 2.1 children, representing the number of births a woman would need to have in her lifetime to replace herself and the father. However, the specific fertility level required for long-term replacement varies among countries due to differing mortality rates.

Approximately, one-third of the global population lives in a country with a fertility rate close to replacement, including countries like India, Tunisia, and Argentina. Despite initial expectations that fertility would stabilise at replacement levels, it has continued to decline below replacement levels in many nations.

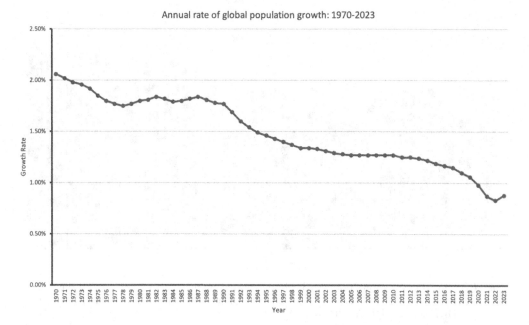

Figure 1.3 Global Population Growth Rate. 1970 to 2023 Graph created by the author from data by the United Nations (UN-DESA, 2023).

Around 15% of the world's population resides in countries with low fertility rates ranging from 1.6 to 1.8 children per woman. This group includes diverse countries, such as Brazil, Mexico, the United States, and Sweden. An additional 26%, or about one-quarter, lives in countries with very low fertility, defined as 1.5 children or fewer per woman. Examples of such countries include China, South Korea, and Spain.

Another 23% of the global population lives in countries with moderately high fertility, ranging from 2.3 to 5.0 children. This category encompasses a diverse range of countries like Papua New Guinea, Israel, and Ethiopia. Only about 4% of the world population, concentrated in Africa, resides in countries with very high fertility rates exceeding five children per woman. Notably, even in countries with very high fertility, the overall fertility is generally lower than it was in the past.

The overall global picture hides some significant regional differences and trends (UN-DESA, Population Division, 2019).

- Although the global population continues to rise, the population in 55 countries or areas is expected to shrink by at least 1% between now and 2050. Some of the largest decreases are expected in countries in Eastern Europe such as Bulgaria, Latvia, Lithuania, and Ukraine. This is due to low levels of fertility and, in some cases, high rates of emigration.
- The sub-Saharan African region is predicted to account for the majority of the increase in the world's population between 2019 and 2050, and the population of this region is expected to continue growing until at least 2100.

- Before the end of this century, the population in most Asian, European, and Central and Northern American countries is expected to peak and then start to decline.
- Although it is most likely that the global population will still be increasing in 2100, there is around a one-in-four chance that the world's population will peak and start to decline before 2100.

1.3.2 The ageing population

The global population is ageing and the number of people aged over 65 exceeds the number of children under 5 for the first time. By 2050, there will be more than twice as many over–65s as under–5s, and they will also outnumber adolescents and young adults in the 15–24 age range (UN-DESA, Population Division, 2019).

As fertility declines, there are proportionally fewer younger people and more older people. The share of the population at young ages has been declining. Today, 32% of people are 19 or younger. By 2060, that number is projected to slip to 26%.

As the share of young people declines, the proportion of people at older ages increases. Today, 10% of the world is 65 or older, and their share is projected to double to 20% by 2060.

As a result, the median age is changing. Today, the global median age is 32 (half the population is younger and half older). By 2060, however, the global median age is projected to climb to 39 years.

These general trends vary by country. Niger is the world's youngest country with a median age of 15 in 2023. Monaco, by contrast, is the oldest, with a median age of 56 in 2023.

Globally, the mean life expectancy at birth reached 72.6 years in 2019, and this has increased by more than eight years since 1990. This increase is expected to continue leading to an average of around 77.1 years in 2050. However, there are still wide variations between wealthy and poor nations. The lower life expectancy in the poorest countries is attributed to persistently high levels of child and maternal mortality. In some countries, deaths due to violence and HIV exacerbate the lower life expectancy (UN-DESA, Population Division, 2019).

In many countries where young-age mortality is already low, gains in life expectancy come from improving conditions at older ages. Canada, for instance, did not experience big declines in young-age mortality between 2000 and 2023, but its total life expectancy increased by an average of about four years, largely from reduced mortality at older ages.

For many other countries, however, life expectancy trends are driven more by dramatic declines in child mortality. In Niger, for example, child mortality declined from around 224 deaths of children under 5 per 1,000 births in 2000 to 103 deaths per 1,000 births in 2023. As a result, the country's average life expectancy at birth increased from 45 years in 2000 to 60 years in 2023. This trend is expected to continue and child mortality will drop to 45 deaths per 1,000 births by 2060. Life expectancy gains from reducing mortality at young ages make populations younger. As fewer children die, there are more children in the population.

While life expectancy is generally increasing, there are some exceptions. Many countries saw a decline in life expectancy due to the COVID-19 pandemic. Tables 1.2 and 1.3 show the 10 best- and worst-performing countries in terms of life expectancy at birth.

Perhaps surprisingly, there are some potential economic benefits to the age demographic in these poorer countries, derived from an effect referred to as the "demographic dividend."

Table 1.2 Life expectancy at birth for 10 best performing nations in 2020 (World Bank, 2022) Licence CC4.0

Country	1960	1980	2000	2020
Hong Kong SAR, China	66.96	74.67	80.88	85.39
Japan	67.67	76.09	81.08	84.62
Macao SAR, China	64.83	73.97	80.41	84.37
Singapore	65.66	72.19	77.95	83.74
Korea, Rep.	55.42	66.05	75.91	83.43
Channel Islands	70.74	73.44	79.04	83.24
Norway	73.55	75.67	78.63	83.21
Australia	70.82	74.33	79.23	83.20
Switzerland	71.31	75.46	79.68	83.10
Iceland	73.42	76.85	79.65	83.07

Table 1.3 Life expectancy at birth for 10 worst-performing nations in 2020 (World Bank, 2022) Licence CC4.0

Country Name	1960	1980	2000	2020
Guinea-Bissau	37.48	44.06	50.37	58.63
Africa Western and Central	37.21	46.37	49.22	58.45
Cote d'Ivoire	36.10	51.07	49.64	58.10
South Sudan	31.70	39.03	49.17	58.10
Somalia	36.98	44.73	50.87	57.70
Sierra Leone	31.57	40.19	39.44	55.07
Nigeria	36.98	45.33	46.27	55.02
Lesotho	47.92	56.70	47.69	54.84
Chad	38.02	44.79	47.71	54.51
Central African Republic	36.25	49.15	44.19	53.68

Recent reductions in fertility in most of sub-Saharan Africa, as well as in parts of Asia, Latin America and the Caribbean, mean that the population at working ages (25 to 64 years) is growing faster than in other age groups (UN-DESA, Population Division, 2019).

Nations that possess optimal conditions for demographic advancement are those embarking on a phase characterised by a healthy working-age population equipped with quality education, satisfactory employment opportunities, and a reduced ratio of young dependents. A lower number of children per family typically results in increased per-child investments, enhanced opportunities for women to participate in the formal workforce, and greater household savings for later stages of life. When these circumstances align, there is the potential for significant economic benefits at the national level, often referred to as a "demographic dividend."

To maximise the benefits from the demographic dividend, nations must strategically allocate their investments in crucial domains. The primary priorities include enhancing the capabilities of individuals and safeguarding their rights and freedoms to unlock their full potential. Providing young people with opportunities to acquire education and experience is paramount, especially in a competitive global job market that increasingly demands higher skills, education, and technical expertise.

South Korea: A case study in reaping benefits from the demographic dividend

The success of the "Asian Tigers," particularly South Korea, in leveraging demographic changes for economic growth is a striking example. South Korea underwent a swift transition from high to low fertility rates, accompanied by an impressive annual per capita GDP growth of 6.7% between 1960 and 1990. This transformation was the outcome of a multifaceted approach, encompassing population-focused policies, investments in reproductive health programs, education, and strategic economic initiatives.

The shift in South Korea's fertility rates is evident in population trends. Between 1950 and 1975, the fertility rate declined from 5.4 to 2.9 children per woman, indicating the start of the initiation of the transition. By 2005, the age structure reflected that of a mature population, with fertility plummeting to 1.2 children per woman. A key driver behind this transition was a proactive population policy, widely implemented across public and private sectors. Health services played a key role in this transition. Health centres were established to offer various services, but the most effective strategy involved field workers visiting homes, providing family planning information, and promoting contraceptive methods.

The government's family planning program aimed for 45% of married couples to use family planning, supported by initiatives like mothers' clubs in 19,000 villages. The societal recognition that having fewer children improved family life played a significant role in reducing fertility rates. Simultaneously, South Korea prioritised education, shifting from compulsory primary education to a production-oriented approach. By 1990, 97% of school-age children attended school, contributing to a well-educated population crucial for economic development.

South Korea's economic plans were comprehensive and evolved to take account of changing circumstances. Immediately after the Korean War, the economy centered on agriculture and fishing, but normalisation of relations with Japan brought capital infusion, strengthening various industries. Addressing unemployment through rural construction projects fostered a self-help attitude, contributing to national infrastructure development. Involvement in the Vietnam War further boosted manufacturing and infrastructure opportunities.

The demographic transition in South Korea resulted from well-timed changes, with deliberate population policies curbing growth and socioeconomic shifts impacting savings, investment, and women's roles. It showed the interrelationships between population, health, and economic development. (Gribble, 2012)

1.3.3 Knowledge review

Before you move on, can you define the following key concepts:

- Demographic dividend?

1.3.4 Question to think about

What is the age profile in your country? Do you have an ageing population or a potential demographic dividend? What are the implications for your healthcare system?

References

Bjørlykhaug, K. I., Karlsson, B., Hesook, S. K., & Kleppe, L. C. (2022). Social support and recovery from mental health problems: A scoping review. *Nordic Social Work Research*, 12(5), 666–697.

Gribble, J. N. (2012). *South Korea's demographic dividend* (p. 20036). Population Reference Bureau.

Mackenbach, J. P. (2020). Re-thinking health inequalities. *European Journal of Public Health*, 30(4), 615–615.

Manisalidis, I., Stavropoulou, E., Stavropoulos, A., & Bezirtzoglou, E. (2020). Environmental and health impacts of air pollution: A review. *Frontiers in Public Health*, 8, 14.

McDonald, K. (2018). Social support and mental health in LGBTQ adolescents: A review of the literature. *Issues in Mental Health Nursing*, 39(1), 16–29.

Shannon, G., Morgan, R., Zeinali, Z., Brady, L., Couto, M. T., Devakumar, D., ... Muraya, K. (2022). Intersectional insights into racism and health: Not just a question of identity. *The Lancet*, 400(10368), 2125–2136.

Terry, R., & Townley, G. (2019). Exploring the role of social support in promoting community integration: An integrated literature review. *American Journal of Community Psychology*, 64(3–4), 509–527. doi:10.1002/ajcp.12336.

UN-DESA. (2023). *Leaving no one behind in an ageing world world social report 2023*. UN-DESA.

UN-DESA, Population Division. (2019). *World population prospects 2019: Highlights (ST/ESA/SER.A/423)*. UN-DESA.

World Bank. (2022). *Life expectancy at birth*. The World Bank Data Bank.

World Bank. (2023). *Urban development update, Released: Apr 03, 2023*. World Bank.

WHO. (1946, November 1). Constitution of the world health organisation. *American Journal of Public Health*, 36(11), 1315–1323. PMID: 18016450

WHO. (2023). *World health statistics 2023: Monitoring health for the SDGs*. Sustainable Development Goals.

Wütschert, M. S., Romano-Pereira, D., Suter, L., Schulze, H., & Elfering, A. (2022). A systematic review of working conditions and occupational health in home office. *Work*, 72(3), 839–852.

2   An analysis of global health and healthcare

2.1 Strengths of global health and healthcare

2.1.1 Strengths of health and healthcare in Europe and Canada

The European and Canadian healthcare systems encompass a variety of models, but there are some similarities and general strengths. In this analysis, we will consider Canada alongside European nations because their healthcare systems have much more in common than say, Canada and the United States of America (US) (Martin et al., 2018). Most European countries have universal healthcare systems, ensuring that all citizens have access to essential healthcare services regardless of their ability to pay. This leads to more equitable access to care compared to systems based on private insurance.

Healthcare costs are often lower for individuals in European countries with publicly funded systems, as the burden of healthcare expenses is spread across the population through taxation or other funding mechanisms. This can alleviate financial strain on individuals and families, particularly during times of illness or injury.

European healthcare systems tend to prioritise preventive care and public health initiatives, aiming to reduce the incidence of illness and disease through education, screening programs, and early intervention. This can lead to better overall population health outcomes and lower healthcare costs in the long run.

Many European countries rank highly in terms of healthcare quality and patient outcomes. This can be attributed to various factors, including well-trained healthcare professionals, rigorous standards for healthcare delivery, and investments in medical research and technology.

European healthcare systems often provide comprehensive coverage for a wide range of healthcare services, including primary care, specialist care, hospital care, and prescription medications. This ensures that individuals can access the care they need without facing significant financial barriers (Marchildon et al., 2021).

The concept of solidarity is often emphasised in European healthcare systems, with the idea that healthcare is a fundamental human right and a collective responsibility. This fosters a sense of social cohesion and support for those in need of medical care, regardless of their socioeconomic status.

2.1.2 Strengths of health and healthcare in the US

The US healthcare system is the largest and costliest in the world, which does lead to some innate strengths. The US is a global leader in medical innovation, with a significant portion of the world's medical research and development conducted within its borders.

DOI: 10.4324/9781003478874-3

This innovation contributes to advances in medical technology, pharmaceuticals, and treatment modalities that benefit not only Americans but people worldwide.

The US healthcare system offers access to a wide range of specialised medical services and procedures, including advanced surgeries, specialised treatments for rare diseases, and cutting-edge therapies. Patients with the means to pay often have access to highly trained specialists and state-of-the-art medical facilities for complex healthcare needs.

In the US, patients typically have more freedom to choose their healthcare providers, treatment options, and insurance plans compared to systems with more centralised control. This flexibility can be appealing to individuals who prioritise choice and autonomy in their healthcare decisions, although those seeking lower premiums and signing up to health maintenance organisations have less choices.

The dominance of the private sector in the US healthcare system has led to innovation and competition in healthcare delivery, insurance products, and service offerings. This competition can drive efficiency, quality improvements, and consumer-focused innovations in healthcare.

Certain specialities within healthcare, such as cancer treatment, trauma care, and management of chronic conditions like HIV/AIDS, are among the best in the world. Leading academic medical centres and research institutions attract top talent and offer cutting-edge treatments.

The US healthcare system often adopts new technologies rapidly, such as electronic health records (EHRs), telemedicine, and medical devices.

Finally, the US healthcare system plays a significant role in global health initiatives, including funding medical research, supporting international aid programs, and providing expertise and resources during global health crises.

2.1.3 Strengths of health and healthcare in Asia and Australia

Healthcare systems across Asia vary widely in structure, financing, and effectiveness, but there are several strengths commonly found within the systems in this region. Many Asian countries have healthcare systems that deliver relatively high-quality care and outcomes at lower costs compared to their Western counterparts, for example, Singapore and Japan. This is often achieved through innovative approaches to healthcare delivery, such as leveraging technology, using community health workers, and emphasising preventive care.

These systems have adopted various innovative healthcare delivery models, including telemedicine, mobile health clinics, and community-based healthcare initiatives. These models help to extend healthcare access to remote and underserved populations, improve efficiency, and reduce healthcare disparities. They have also invested significantly in healthcare infrastructure, including the development of modern hospitals, medical facilities, and healthcare technology. This infrastructure supports the delivery of advanced medical care and contributes to improving healthcare access and outcomes.

Primary care is often prioritised as the foundation of Asian healthcare systems. This emphasis on primary care helps to promote early detection and management of health conditions, reduce unnecessary hospitalisations, and improve overall population health outcomes.

Some Asian countries integrate traditional medicine practices, such as traditional Chinese medicine, Ayurveda, and acupuncture, into their healthcare systems. This integration provides patients with a broader range of treatment options and enhances cultural competency in healthcare delivery.

Governments in many Asian countries demonstrate a strong commitment to improving healthcare access and quality through policy initiatives, funding allocations, and public health campaigns. This commitment often leads to improvements in healthcare infrastructure, workforce development, and health outcomes.

Several Asian countries, such as Thailand, Singapore, and India, have developed thriving healthcare tourism industries. These countries attract international patients seeking high-quality medical treatments at lower costs compared to their home countries, contributing to the economy and healthcare infrastructure development.

Community engagement and health education initiatives are prevalent in many Asian countries, promoting health awareness, disease prevention, and healthy behaviours. These initiatives empower individuals to take control of their health and play an active role in healthcare decision-making.

2.1.4 *Strengths of health and healthcare in Africa*

Although healthcare systems across Africa face numerous challenges, including limited resources, infrastructure deficits, and high disease burdens, there are also several strengths and positive aspects within these healthcare systems:

African healthcare systems have demonstrated resilience and adaptability in the face of significant challenges, including disease outbreaks, natural disasters, and humanitarian crises. Despite resource constraints, healthcare providers often find innovative ways to deliver care and respond to emergencies.

Many countries use community-based healthcare approaches to extend healthcare access to rural and underserved populations. Community health workers play a vital role in providing preventive care, health education, and basic treatment services, particularly in areas with limited access to formal healthcare facilities.

Traditional medicine practices are deeply ingrained in many African cultures, and some countries have integrated traditional healers into their healthcare systems. This integration recognises the importance of traditional medicine in addressing community health needs and promotes collaboration between traditional healers and modern healthcare providers.

African countries often prioritise public health programs aimed at disease prevention, immunisation, maternal and child health, and control of infectious diseases such as malaria, HIV/AIDS, and tuberculosis. These programs contribute to improving population health outcomes and reducing the burden of preventable diseases.

African healthcare systems benefit from collaboration with each other and with international organisations, donor agencies, and non-governmental organisations (NGOs) that provide financial assistance, technical support, and capacity-building initiatives. This collaboration helps strengthen healthcare infrastructure, improve healthcare delivery, and address health challenges on a regional and global scale.

Despite facing significant challenges such as understaffing, brain drain, and limited training opportunities, healthcare workers in Africa demonstrate resilience and dedication to their profession.

African countries have seen the emergence of innovative healthcare solutions leveraging technology, such as mobile health (mHealth) initiatives, telemedicine platforms, and health information systems. These solutions help overcome barriers to healthcare access, improve health service delivery, and empower patients to manage their health more effectively.

African healthcare systems often prioritise cultural competency and patient-centred care, recognising the importance of respecting cultural beliefs, values, and traditions in healthcare delivery. This approach fosters trust between healthcare providers and patients and improves health outcomes by addressing cultural barriers to care.

2.1.5   Strengths of health and healthcare in Central and South America

Many countries in Central and South America face numerous healthcare challenges, similar to those seen in African countries including limited resources, infrastructure deficits, and high disease burdens. However, many of these countries have made strides towards achieving universal healthcare coverage, ensuring that a significant portion of their populations have access to essential healthcare services. This is often achieved through government-funded or subsidised healthcare programs aimed at reducing financial barriers to healthcare access.

There is a growing focus on healthcare innovation and research in Central and South America, with efforts to develop new medical technologies, treatments, and interventions tailored to the region's specific healthcare needs. This innovation contributes to advancing healthcare quality, efficiency, and effectiveness in the region.

Their strengths often resemble those found in African countries including a focus on primary healthcare, community-based healthcare initiatives, and strong public health programs: cultural competency and traditional medicine integration and international collaboration and partnerships.

2.1.6   Knowledge review

Before you move on, can you define the following key concepts:

• Solidarity in healthcare?

2.1.7   Question to think about

What do you think are the greatest strengths of the healthcare system in your country?

2.2   Weaknesses in global health and healthcare

2.2.1   Weaknesses of health and healthcare in Europe and Canada

The European and Canadian healthcare systems are not without their weaknesses.

Many countries in this region are struggling with the issue of financial sustainability due to rising healthcare costs, ageing populations, and budget constraints. The increasing demand for healthcare services, coupled with limited resources, puts pressure on healthcare budgets and may lead to deficits or cuts in healthcare spending. Where systems are publicly funded, a stagnant economy and healthcare inflation exceeding general inflation squeeze the financial resources available in the face of increasing demands.

Despite efforts to achieve universal healthcare coverage, disparities in access to healthcare services persist across Europe. Vulnerable populations, such as migrants, minorities, and socioeconomically disadvantaged groups, often face barriers to accessing timely and quality healthcare, leading to health inequities and disparities in health outcomes.

In many European countries, long waiting times for certain healthcare services, such as elective surgeries, specialist consultations, and diagnostic tests, are a significant weakness. Prolonged waiting times can impact patient outcomes, quality of life, and patient satisfaction with the healthcare system.

Most European countries are experiencing shortages of healthcare professionals, including physicians, nurses, and allied health professionals. Workforce shortages can strain healthcare delivery systems, lead to increased workloads for existing healthcare workers, and compromise the quality and accessibility of healthcare services. Overworked staff still recovering from the excessive demands of the COVID pandemic will be more prone to work-based stress, absence due to sickness, and early retirements, further exacerbating the problem.

Many European healthcare systems are characterised by fragmentation, with multiple healthcare providers, insurers, and funding sources operating independently. This fragmentation can result in inefficiencies, duplication of services, lack of coordination between healthcare providers, and gaps in continuity of care, particularly for patients with complex healthcare needs. Within each system, there are usually many autonomous organisations tending to prioritise their own needs and interests.

The population in most European nations and Canada is ageing, leading to an increase in chronic diseases, such as cardiovascular disease, diabetes, and cancer. Addressing the healthcare needs of an ageing population and managing chronic diseases pose significant challenges for healthcare systems in terms of resource allocation, care coordination, and long-term sustainability and may require major organisational and cultural changes across the healthcare systems within these countries. The traditional medical model in these countries that values specialisation, especially within the medical profession, looks increasingly ill-suited to meeting the needs of an ageing population with multiple conditions and consequently complex needs.

While many European countries have adopted technologies, such as EHRs and telemedicine, challenges remain in integrating these technologies into routine clinical practice effectively. Limited interoperability between different health information systems, privacy concerns, and the self-interests of healthcare provider organisations are holding back the widespread adoption and use of healthcare technologies.

2.2.2 *Weaknesses of health and healthcare in the US*

The biggest weakness in the US healthcare system is its failure to achieve good health outcomes in spite of spending significantly more on healthcare per capita than any other country. These high, healthcare costs contribute to financial burdens for individuals, families, employers, and the government.

Unlike many other developed countries, the US does not have universal healthcare coverage. As a result, millions of Americans remain uninsured or underinsured, leading to disparities in access to healthcare services and poorer health outcomes, particularly among low-income and vulnerable populations, although the Affordable Care Act, popularly known as Obamacare, has succeeded in reducing the number of insured persons.

Minority populations, including Black, Hispanic, Native American, and immigrant communities, often face barriers to accessing timely and quality healthcare, resulting in higher rates of chronic diseases, lower life expectancy, and poorer health outcomes.

Like its European counterparts, the US healthcare system is characterised by administrative complexity, with multiple payers, billing systems, and regulatory requirements.

This complexity leads to administrative inefficiencies, high administrative costs, billing errors, and administrative burdens for healthcare providers, insurers, and patients.

Also like Europe, fragmentation of care is common in the US healthcare system, with patients often receiving care from multiple providers across different settings without adequate coordination. This lack of care coordination can result in gaps in care, medical errors, duplication of services, and poorer health outcomes, particularly for patients with complex healthcare needs.

The US healthcare system tends to prioritise specialty care over primary care, leading to a healthcare delivery model that focuses more on treating acute conditions and less on preventive care and chronic disease management. This imbalance contributes to higher healthcare costs, overutilisation of services, and poorer health outcomes.

Certain regions and populations in the US experience shortages of healthcare providers, including primary care physicians, mental health professionals, and specialists. These shortages can limit access to timely and quality healthcare services, particularly in rural and underserved areas, exacerbating healthcare disparities and barriers to care.

Despite advances in medical technology and healthcare delivery, concerns persist regarding healthcare quality and patient safety in the US. Medical errors, preventable hospital-acquired infections, medication errors, and disparities in quality of care contribute to adverse patient outcomes and undermine public trust in the healthcare system.

2.2.3 Weaknesses of health and healthcare in Asia and Australia

Healthcare systems in Asia and Australia, although diverse, share several weaknesses. Disparities in access to healthcare services persist within many countries in Asia and Australia. Rural and remote areas often have limited access to healthcare facilities, leading to barriers in accessing timely and quality care, particularly for marginalised and underserved populations.

The quality of healthcare services can vary widely across different regions and healthcare facilities in both Asia and Australia. While some urban centres and tertiary hospitals offer high-quality care with advanced medical technology and well-trained healthcare professionals, rural areas and smaller healthcare facilities may face challenges in maintaining consistent quality standards.

Infrastructure gaps, including shortages of healthcare facilities, medical equipment, and healthcare professionals, are common in many countries in Asia, particularly in low- and middle-income countries. These infrastructure deficits can limit healthcare access, hinder healthcare delivery, and compromise patient outcomes, especially during emergencies and public health crises.

Healthcare financing systems in Asia and Australia face challenges related to sustainability and equity. In some countries, out-of-pocket payments remain a significant source of healthcare financing, leading to financial hardship for individuals and families, particularly those with low incomes. Additionally, public healthcare financing may be insufficient to meet growing healthcare demands and address emerging health challenges.

Many countries in Asia and the poorer parts of Australia experience shortages of healthcare professionals, including physicians, nurses, and allied health professionals. Healthcare workforce shortages can strain healthcare systems, limit access to care, and compromise the quality of healthcare services, particularly in rural and underserved areas.

Asia and Australia face emerging health challenges such as non-communicable diseases (NCDs), infectious diseases, antimicrobial resistance, and ageing populations. Addressing these health challenges requires comprehensive strategies for prevention, early detection, treatment, and management, as well as investments in healthcare infrastructure, workforce development, and research.

Asia and Australia make up a culturally and linguistically diverse region, presenting challenges in delivering culturally competent and language-appropriate healthcare services. Healthcare providers can encounter barriers in effectively communicating with patients from different cultural backgrounds, leading to disparities in healthcare access, quality, and outcomes.

2.2.4 Weaknesses of health and healthcare in Africa

In spite of facing the heaviest disease burden, many countries in Africa have limited healthcare infrastructure and resources, resulting in inadequate access to essential healthcare services for large segments of the population, particularly those in rural and remote areas. Accessibility barriers include geographical remoteness, transportation challenges, and financial constraints, leading to disparities in healthcare access and utilisation.

Financing in Africa is often insufficient and unsustainable, with limited public funding allocated to healthcare and a heavy reliance on out-of-pocket payments by individuals, contributing to a reluctance to access healthcare services, and catastrophic spending plunging families into poverty, a problem seen in lower-income Asian and South American countries. Inadequate healthcare financing at a national level often hinders the expansion of healthcare infrastructure, acquisition of medical supplies and equipment, recruitment and retention of healthcare professionals, and provision of essential healthcare services.

Many countries in Africa face critical shortages of healthcare workers, including physicians, nurses, midwives, and other essential healthcare professionals. Healthcare workforce shortages are exacerbated by factors such as emigration of skilled healthcare workers, inadequate training and education programs, low retention rates, and challenges in attracting healthcare professionals to rural and underserved areas.

Healthcare infrastructure in Africa is often inadequate and poorly maintained, with shortages of hospitals, clinics, medical equipment, and essential supplies. Weak healthcare infrastructure limits the provision of basic healthcare services, emergency care, and specialised treatments, leading to delays in care, poorer patient outcomes, and increased mortality rates, particularly during public health emergencies and humanitarian crises.

Africa bears a significant burden of communicable diseases such as HIV/AIDS, malaria, tuberculosis, and neglected tropical diseases. Inadequate healthcare infrastructure, limited access to preventive measures, diagnostic tools, and treatments, and weak health systems exacerbate the impact of these diseases, contributing to high morbidity and mortality rates, particularly among vulnerable populations such as children, pregnant women, and people living with HIV/AIDS.

Weak health information systems hinder evidence-based decision-making, monitoring and evaluation of health programs, disease surveillance, and outbreak response efforts, impeding efforts to address health challenges effectively and allocate resources efficiently.

Health inequalities persist in Africa due to socioeconomic disparities, unequal access to education, clean water, sanitation, nutrition, and structural factors such as gender inequality and political instability. Addressing health inequalities requires a multisectoral approach that goes beyond the healthcare system to address the underlying social determinants of health and promotes equity in access to healthcare services and health outcomes.

2.2.5 *Weaknesses of health and healthcare in Central and South America*

Despite efforts to achieve universal healthcare coverage, inequities in access to healthcare services persist in Central and South America. Vulnerable populations, including indigenous communities, rural residents, and those living in poverty, often face barriers to accessing timely and quality healthcare, leading to disparities in health outcomes. Large rural and mountainous areas can be particularly challenging in terms of creating accessible and sustainable healthcare services.

These geographical challenges and a recent history of political instability in many countries exacerbate the weaknesses that Central and South American countries share with other low-income countries notably inequitable access to healthcare, financial constraints and high out-of-pocket expenses, infrastructure challenges, fragmentation of services, and weak governance and regulation.

Cancer is a prominent health challenge in Latin America and the Caribbean, contributing significantly to both disease prevalence and mortality rates. Annually, an estimated 1.5 million new cancer cases arise in the region, resulting in approximately 700,000 deaths. These figures correspond to incidence and mortality rates of 186.5 and 86.6 per 100,000 individuals, respectively. Notably, the primary cancer types in 2020 included prostate (15%), breast (14%), colorectal (9%), lung (7%), and stomach (5%). Lung cancer remained the foremost cause of cancer-related deaths (12%) though its prevalence varied across countries.

Trends indicate a decline in mortality rates for infectious-related cancers in many countries, while cancers associated with westernisation are generally increasing. Assuming current rates persist, the cancer burden is projected to escalate by 67% by 2040, resulting in 2.4 million new cases annually in the region. (Piñeros et al., 2022).

2.2.6 *Knowledge review*

Before you move on, can you define the following key concepts:

• Universal healthcare coverage?

2.2.7 *Question to think about*

What do you think are the greatest weaknesses of the healthcare system in your country?

2.3 Opportunities in global health and healthcare

2.3.1 *Opportunities in health and healthcare in high income countries*

In order to deal with the threats that they face, European nations and Canada must take advantage of opportunities to improve their effectiveness, efficiency, and quality of care.

Although these nations have made use of digital technology, there remain many more opportunities from technologies, such as telemedicine, mobile health apps, wearable devices, and health information exchanges, to improve healthcare delivery, improve access to care, and empower patients to manage their health more effectively. Integration of digital health solutions can enhance care coordination, enable remote monitoring, and facilitate communication between patients and healthcare providers. Quite basic technology can help information exchange between organisations to ensure that information follows the patient on their journey through the healthcare system, provided that the will is there from provider organisations to make this happen.

Data analytics and artificial intelligence (AI) can be used to derive greater insights from healthcare data, support clinical decision-making, predict disease outbreaks, improve diagnostic accuracy, and personalise patient care. On the management side, they can be used to optimise resource allocation and identify opportunities for preventive interventions and population health management.

There are opportunities in personalised medicine and genomics to tailor medical treatments and interventions to individual patients' genetic makeup, lifestyle factors, and disease risk profiles. Targeted therapies, predictive models, and personalised treatment plans can improve patient outcomes and reduce adverse drug reactions.

Population approaches can proactively address the health needs of diverse population groups, identify high-risk individuals, and implement preventive interventions at the community level. Risk stratification tools, care coordination protocols, and health promotion programs can improve population health outcomes and reduce healthcare costs.

Interprofessional and teamwork among healthcare professionals from different disciplines, specialties, and settings can help to deliver coordinated, patient-centred care and meet the needs of an ageing population with multiple health issues. Interdisciplinary education, team-based care models, and shared decision-making processes can help to optimise healthcare delivery and enhance patient satisfaction.

Value-based care models, payment reforms, and pay-for-performance incentives that prioritise healthcare outcomes, patient experience, and cost-effectiveness over volume-based reimbursement can incentivise desirable behaviours, drive change, and improve care coordination. In many cases, there are opportunities to make improvements by simply removing perverse incentives that encourage the wrong behaviours.

Targeted interventions, community outreach programs, and culturally competent care practices can address social determinants of health and can be used to promote health equity and reduce health disparities among different population groups, including ethnic minorities, socioeconomically disadvantaged communities, and rural populations.

Investments in preventive health and wellness programs that promote healthy lifestyles, disease prevention, and screening programmes for early detection of health conditions, vaccination campaigns, and health education campaigns all provide opportunities to reduce the burden of preventable diseases and promote well-being.

Many of the opportunities for healthcare in the US are similar to those in Europe and Canada. The US is particularly well placed to take advantages of technology-based opportunities such as electronic records, data analytics, and artificial intelligence. As a global leader in pharmaceuticals and genomics, the US is well-placed to take advantages in personalised medicine and novel forms of medication.

The success of the Affordable Care Act in reducing the number of uninsured citizens has shown that legislative change can deliver real progress towards universal health coverage in the US.

2.3.2 *Opportunities in health and healthcare in low- and middle-income countries*

In spite of the challenges facing low- and middle-income countries, there are significant opportunities for improving health and healthcare in these countries.

Investments in primary healthcare infrastructure, workforce development, and service delivery can strengthen the foundation of the healthcare system. Primary healthcare plays a crucial role in promoting preventive care, early detection, and management of common health conditions, reducing the burden on secondary and tertiary healthcare facilities. (Haque et al., 2020).

Investment in training, education, and retention of healthcare professionals, including physicians, nurses, midwives, community health workers, and allied health workers, expands healthcare workforce capacity, particularly in rural and underserved areas, to improve access to essential healthcare services and address healthcare workforce shortages.

These countries have the opportunity to miss out several generations of digital information technology. Telemedicine, mobile health (mHealth), and digital health technologies can all be used to extend healthcare access to remote and rural areas, facilitate remote consultations, and provide health information and support services via mobile devices. Mobile health applications, SMS messaging, and teleconsultation platforms can improve healthcare delivery, patient engagement, and adherence to treatment, even in areas with limited fixed line broadband networks.

Health information systems can drive evidence-based decision-making, disease surveillance, and health monitoring, and capturing local data can improve the local specificity of the evidence base.

Community-based health programs and outreach initiatives can reach underserved populations, promote health education, and deliver preventive and primary healthcare services at the community level. Empowering community health workers and volunteers can enable them to provide essential healthcare services, health education, and referrals to formal healthcare facilities.

Public-private partnerships between governments, private sector entities, NGOs, and international donors can leverage resources, expertise, and innovation for healthcare improvement initiatives. Public-private partnerships can support healthcare infrastructure development, healthcare service delivery, and capacity-building efforts in lower-income countries.

Implementing health financing reforms can improve the sustainability and equity of the financing of healthcare services, reduce out-of-pocket payments, and expand financial risk protection for vulnerable populations. Innovative financing mechanisms, such as social health insurance, community-based health financing schemes, and results-based financing approaches, can help to reduce out-of-pocket expenditure. In the longer term, social insurance or taxation-based financing can improve risk pooling and dramatically improve access to healthcare.

Prioritising health promotion, disease prevention, and public health interventions can address underlying determinants of health, reduce the burden of preventable diseases, and promote healthy behaviours and lifestyles. Implementing vaccination programs, maternal and child health initiatives, sanitation and hygiene interventions, and health education campaigns can contribute to improving population health outcomes.

Investments in research and innovation can help to develop context-specific healthcare solutions, technologies, and interventions tailored to the needs of lower-income countries. Supporting research collaborations, capacity-building initiatives, and technology transfer programs can accelerate healthcare innovation and address priority health challenges.

Global health partnerships, multilateral initiatives, and international collaborations to share knowledge, resources, and best practices for healthcare improvement can help to strengthen health systems, address cross-border health threats, and achieve sustainable development goals.

2.3.3 Knowledge review

Before you move on, can you define the following key concepts:

• Genomics?

2.3.4 Question to think about

What do you think are the greatest opportunities for the healthcare system in your country?

2.4 Threats to global health and healthcare

2.4.1 Global threats to health and healthcare

In the modern interconnected world, many threats to global health and healthcare are truly global in nature. While globalisation has facilitated economic growth and development, it has also increased the interconnectedness of populations, making it easier for diseases to spread across borders. Global travel and trade can accelerate the transmission of infectious diseases and facilitate the spread of antimicrobial resistance. Emerging and re-emerging infectious diseases, such as influenza, HIV/AIDS, Ebola, Zika virus, and most recently, the COVID-19 pandemic, pose a persistent threat to global health.

Climate change affects health directly through extreme weather events, natural disasters, and changes in infectious disease patterns. Indirectly, it impacts health by exacerbating food and water insecurity, increasing air pollution, and disrupting healthcare systems. Natural disasters such as earthquakes, tsunamis, and hurricanes and man-made disasters such as conflicts and humanitarian crises can have devastating effects on healthcare infrastructure, disrupt access to essential services, and exacerbate health problems.

The misuse and overuse of antibiotics and other antimicrobial drugs have led to the development of resistant strains of bacteria, viruses, parasites, and fungi, known as antimicrobial resistance. This makes infections harder to treat, increases healthcare costs, and leads to prolonged illness and death.

Chronic diseases, such as cardiovascular diseases, cancer, diabetes, and respiratory diseases, are the leading causes of death globally. Lifestyle factors, such as tobacco use, unhealthy diet, processed and fatty foods, physical inactivity, and harmful use of alcohol, contribute significantly to the burden of non-communicable diseases. As emerging economies and even low-income countries become more prosperous, these unhealthy lifestyles are spreading from traditionally higher-income countries to a much bigger group of countries. Even in low income countries, those with higher-than-average incomes aspire to many of these unhealthy habits.

Similarly, the majority of countries in the world have ageing populations increasing the level and complexity of demand for healthcare services. This trend increases demand for long-term care services, chronic disease management, and healthcare resources, putting pressure on healthcare systems whilst reducing the active workforce who represent the majority of funding in risk-pooled systems (Giusti et al., 2020).

2.4.2 Specific threats to health and healthcare in high-income countries

In addition to the general global threats to health and healthcare, higher-income countries face a number of specific threats which are greater in these countries. The demographic shifts towards an ageing population are greatest in high-income countries. Similarly, the prevalence of non-communicable diseases, such as cardiovascular diseases, cancer, diabetes, and respiratory diseases, is highest in high-income countries, where they are major contributors to morbidity and mortality. High-income countries have the highest rates of obesity and overweight population due to sedentary lifestyles, unhealthy dietary habits, and environmental factors such as food availability and accessibility. Obesity is associated with various health complications, including diabetes, cardiovascular diseases, and certain cancers.

Mental health disorders, including depression, anxiety, and substance abuse, are prevalent in high-income countries. Factors such as work-related stress, social isolation, economic inequality, and access to mental healthcare services all contribute to the burden of mental health issues.

Despite their overall prosperity, high-income countries often experience health inequalities based on socioeconomic status, ethnicity, gender, geography, and access to healthcare services. These disparities can result in differential health outcomes and access to healthcare, contributing to social and health inequalities. The most extreme example of this is found in the US, where these inequalities are exacerbated by a high, if reducing, number of uninsured people.

While access to antibiotics and other antimicrobial drugs is generally better in high-income countries, inappropriate use and over-prescription of these drugs contribute to the development of resistant strains of bacteria and other pathogens. Antimicrobial resistance poses a significant threat to healthcare in high-income countries, leading to increased healthcare costs, treatment failures, and mortality. Intensive farming can lead to high rates of veterinary use in these countries, further exacerbating the issue.

The demand for the implementation of technological advancements in high-income countries often fuelled by high patient expectations and the prevalence of advanced technology in other areas of life can lead to more rapidly rising healthcare costs.

2.4.3 Specific threats to health and healthcare in low-income countries

There are a range of threats that are either specific to or much greater for low-income countries. They often bear a disproportionate burden of infectious diseases such as malaria, tuberculosis, HIV/AIDS, diarrheal diseases, and neglected tropical diseases. Limited access to clean water, sanitation, and healthcare services all contribute to the spread of these diseases. For these reasons and others, maternal and child health remain major concerns in low-income countries, with high maternal and child mortality rates. Additional factors, such as inadequate access to prenatal care, skilled birth attendants, postnatal care, and nutrition, also contribute to poor maternal and child health outcomes.

Malnutrition, including undernutrition and micronutrient deficiencies, remains prevalent in low-income countries due to food insecurity, poverty, inadequate access to nutritious food, and poor feeding practices. Malnutrition contributes to stunted growth, impaired cognitive development, and increased susceptibility to infectious diseases and represents an ongoing threat to health and a burden on healthcare services.

Many low-income countries face challenges in providing accessible, affordable, and quality healthcare services to their populations. Barriers to healthcare access include geographical remoteness, lack of healthcare infrastructure, shortage of healthcare workers, and financial constraints. For individuals, high out-of-pocket expenses are a major threat to health well-being and household economic stability.

Healthcare systems in low-income countries often lack essential resources, including medical supplies, equipment, medicines, and trained healthcare personnel. Weak healthcare infrastructure, limited healthcare financing, and governance issues contribute to the inefficiency and ineffectiveness of healthcare delivery.

Climate change disproportionately affects low-income countries, leading to increased risks of vector-borne diseases, waterborne diseases, food insecurity, and natural disasters. Vulnerable populations in these countries often lack adequate resources to adapt to climate-related health risks.

Finally, in the face of a global shortage in the healthcare workforce, lower income countries lose out, as skilled staff emigrate in search of better prospects, remuneration, and lifestyles.

2.4.4 Knowledge review

Before you move on, can you define the following key concepts:

• Antimicrobial resistance?

2.4.5 Question to think about

What do you think are the greatest opportunities for of the healthcare system in your country?

2.5 National case study: strengths, weaknesses, opportunities, and threats in the Indian healthcare system

In 2023, India overtook China as the most populous country in the world. India is growing economically, achieving an annual average growth rate of over 5% over the last three decades, but the Indian healthcare system faces a number of challenges, including, according to Kumar (2023), "inadequate infrastructure, a shortage of healthcare professionals, urban-rural disparities, limited health insurance coverage, insufficient public healthcare funding, and a fragmented healthcare system."

The healthcare sector in India is worth $42 billion US dollars (USD). The National Health Policy of 2017 aimed to raise the percentage of Gross Domestic Product (GDP) spent on public healthcare to 2.5% by the year 2025. Total health expenditure, including both public and private sectors, is expected to account for 3.9% of the total GDP by 2025, but the percentage of health expenditure attributed to the public sector remains lower than most other developing and developed countries (Ghia & Rambhad, 2023).

Health insurance plays a crucial role in the Indian healthcare system, with individuals opting for various health insurance plans provided by public and private insurers.

2.5.1 Strengths of health and healthcare in India

Over the last 50 years, there have been significant improvements in the state of health of the Indian population. Selvaraj et al. (2022) report that "India's progress on reducing the infant mortality rate (IMR) is remarkable, from a high IMR of 88 per 1000 live births in 1990 to about 32 in 2020. Similarly, the maternal mortality ratio (MMR) declined from 556 in 1990 to 113 per 100,000 live births during 2016–2018." By 2020, life expectancy at birth had reached 69.6 years, an increase of 22 years over a 50-year period.

India has a rich tradition of alternative medicine, including ayurveda, yoga, naturopathy, unani, siddha, and homeopathy. These systems coexist with allopathic medicine and have their own institutions and practitioners. Since 2014, alternative medicine has been overseen by a federal Ministry of Ayurveda, Yoga and Naturopathy, Unani, Siddha, and Homeopathy.

India is one of the leading players in the global pharmaceutical and vaccine industries. It is the world's biggest supplier of generic medications. It is also the global leader in the production of measles and some other key vaccinations. The nation produces over 60% of the world's vaccinations and accounts for 20% of the worldwide supply volume.

2.5.2 Weaknesses of health and healthcare in India

There are wide regional variations and major disparities between rich and poor and urban and rural populations. Chawla (2023) notes that only 13% of rural residents have access to primary health centres, 33% to community health centres, and 9.6% to hospitals.

Private providers include hospitals, nursing homes, clinics, and diagnostic centers. Private hospitals range from small nursing homes to large, multi-specialty hospitals. There are specialty hospitals that focus on specific medical fields such as cardiology, orthopedics, oncology, and so on.

They play a significant role in providing healthcare services, especially in urban areas. Numerous private clinics and diagnostic centres offer outpatient services, including consultations, diagnostic tests, and minor treatments.

There is a wide range of public and private health insurance schemes. This fragmentation makes risk pooling less effective and will increase the cost of premiums. The first public insurance scheme was the Employees' State Insurance Scheme dating from 1948.

However, almost three-quarters (greater than 72%) of health expenditure in India is financed by individual households at the time of illness through out-of-pocket payments. More than half of this is spent on pharmaceuticals.

Almost 7% are reported to be pushed into poverty annually through catastrophic healthcare expenditure in order to meet out-of-pocket payments. (Ghia & Rambhad, 2023).

In spite of India's role in supplying the global pharmaceuticals markets, drugs are often expensive and inaccessible for the local population. More than half of the annual out-of-pocket expenditure on healthcare is spent on pharmaceuticals.

2.5.3 Opportunities in health and healthcare in India

Current health insurance schemes include:

- Private, for-profit schemes involve the collection of premiums from individual buyers.
- Public sector voluntary schemes are available, but their accessibility has been limited mainly to the middle class due to high premiums.
- Mandatory health insurance schemes cover specific groups, such as those employed in factories and central government employees, respectively.
- NGOs and community-based health insurance initiatives, provide coverage. supported by nominal premiums and government funding,
- Employer-based schemes are offered by employers to their staff, offering benefits like lump-sum payments, reimbursement of health expenses, medical allowances, or participation in group health.

The most recent government initiative is the Ayushman Bharat–National Health Protection Mission (AB-NHPM). Its goal is to provide health insurance coverage to 100 million families, totaling approximately 500 million beneficiaries. The focus is on individuals below the poverty line, identified through the 2011 Socio-Economic and Caste Census. All family members, regardless of number or age, are included.

Funding comes from both central and state government budgets, with central government providing a slightly larger share. Where states already have government-financed health insurance schemes, integration is planned.

AB-NHPM aims to cover 40% of India's population, potentially becoming the world's largest government-financed health insurance scheme. It offers secondary and tertiary care, including hospitalisation, with no cost to the patient, covering pre- and post-hospitalisation treatments. The coverage is portable across India, emphasising a fully digital and paperless system. (Gopichandran, 2019).

Although evaluation studies have started to appear, it remains too early to assess reliably the impact of AB-NHPM, partly due to its sheer scale and ambition. However, Kumar (2023) reports that by 2022, the program had established more than 115,000 health and wellness centres and more than 217,000 public health facilities.

To address local access to pharmaceuticals, the Free Drugs Service Initiative (FDSI) was launched in 2015 to provide universal access to free and quality medicines, irrespective of the ability to pay. Hannah et al. (2023) report that whilst progress has been made, there are significant variations. They report a range of challenges including:

- Inadequate demand forecasting
- fragmentation of procurement
- outsourcing procurement to agencies without technical competency
- an absence of compliance checks
- inefficient inventory management
- poor quality assurance mechanisms

In 2023, the Indian government produced new guidelines requiring doctors to prescribe generic drugs in an attempt to keep costs down, but the Indian Medical Association responded with concerns over quality assurance standards, citing recent cases of contaminated cough syrup manufactured in India but linked to the deaths of more than 300 children in other countries (Reuters, 2023).

Many private health outpatient insurances also cover pharmacy bills, and this may prove to be the most valuable benefit of such plans (Gambhir et al., 2019).

India is a leader in software with an annual market value in excess of 14 billion USD. Overall, the IT industry makes up 7.5% of India's GDP (Statista, n.d). The Ayushman Bharat–National Health Protection Mission seeks to use this expertise through eSanjeevani, the National Telemedicine Service of the Ministry of Health and Family Welfare. This platform, that emerged in 2020 as part of India's response to the COVID-19 pandemic, has been billed as the world's biggest telemedicine platform. It operates in two modes:

1. a provider-to-provider service that can be used by both patients and physicians from a health and wellness center
2. a patient-to-provider service which directly connects a patient to a provider from the patients' own homes (Balasubramanian, 2023)

The patient-to-provider service requires patients to register with the service. It then provides remote consultations and e-prescribing facilities. Bajpai and Wadhwa (2021) identify three principal challenges to the wider rollout of the service: abuse, a shortage of doctors and specialists, and access issues.

Without the requirement of any identity proof, the platform is open to abuse. Potential abusers may misrepresent their details and enter the platform without being traced back. The OTP verification process only serves to confirm if the mobile number is accessible to the patient at the time of registration.

Khanduja et al. (2021) report long waiting times due to the shortage of doctors.

Finally, the platform is solely video-based and requires patients to have a smartphone or laptop with internet connection. However, as of October 2019, around half of India's population is digitally excluded, which includes the individuals who either have feature phones with no internet connection or they do not have a mobile phone.

Before the COVID pandemic, India had emerged as a prominent medical tourism destination for overseas visitors. Whilst medical tourism has been hit by the COVID-19 pandemic, the Indian Government is seeking to make India the largest medical tourism destination in the world (Malhotra & Dave, 2022). India is particularly attractive because of the availability of an English-speaking workforce.

In 2021, the value of Indian medical tourism was estimated between USD 5–6 billion in 2021 (Financial Express, 2022).

The influence of medical tourism on the indigenous healthcare is hard to evaluate, and there is a shortage of academic evaluation studies. However, in a country where many citizens have little access to affordable and effective healthcare, the promotion of medical tourism raises legitimate ethical concerns.

2.5.4 Threats to health and healthcare in India

India faces many of the same threats to health and healthcare as other emerging economies such as:

- infectious diseases
- poor (but improving) maternal and child health

- malnutrition in sections of the population
- limited access to healthcare services
- weak healthcare systems
- climate-related health risks
- health inequalities

It also faces some particular challenges of its own. As countries develop economically, the burden of disease generally changes from communicable diseases, such as lower respiratory infections, diarrhoea and tuberculosis, to non-communicable chronic diseases. However, Ram and Thakur (2022) report that, in India "infectious diseases are still predominant, and non-communicable diseases are emerging without replacing the country's burden of contagious diseases." They highlight "diseases, such as dengue, malaria, typhoid, and tuberculosis" as still being prevalent in India and the country has the highest share of global prevalence of tuberculosis.

There is an ongoing challenge to deal with these infectious conditions, alongside new challenges such as COVID-19 whilst managing growing rates of long-term chronic conditions such as diabetes. Pradeepa and Mohan (2021) report that up to 77 million individuals had diabetes in India in 2019, and that this is expected to almost double by 2045. Further, they report that more than half of these individuals remain undiagnosed.

2.5.5 Knowledge review

Before you move on, can you define the following key concepts:

- Catastrophic healthcare expenditure?

2.5.6 Question to think about

What do you think is India's greatest need in terms of healthcare?

References

Balasubramanian, S. (2023). India is using technology to give 1.4+ billion people access to healthcare. *Forbes*.

Bajpai, N., & Wadhwa, M. (2021). *National teleconsultation service in India: eSanjeevani OPD* (ICT India Working Paper, No. 53). CSD Working Paper Series: Towards a New Indian Model of Information and Communications Technology-Led Growth and Development, Center for Sustainable Development, Earth Institute, Columbia University.

Chawla N (2023) Unveiling the ABCs: Identifying India's healthcare service gaps. *Cureus*, 15(7), e42398.

Financial Express. (2022, March). Medical value tourism in India: What makes the country a leading Medical Tourism Destination. *Financial Express*.

Gambhir, R. S., Malhi, R., Khosla, S., Singh, R., Bhardwaj, A., & Kumar, M. (2019). Out-patient coverage: Private sector insurance in India. *Journal of Family Medicine and Primary Care*, 8(3), 788–792.

Ghia, C., & Rambhad, G. (2023). Implementation of equity and access in Indian healthcare: Current scenario and way forward. *Journal of Market Access & Health Policy*, 11(1), 2194507.

Giusti, A., Maggini, M., & Colaceci, S. (2020). The burden of chronic diseases across Europe: What policies and programs to address diabetes? A SWOT analysis. *Health Research Policy and Systems*, 18, 1–7.

Gopichandran V. (2019). Ayushman Bharat national health protection scheme: An ethical analysis. *Asian Bioethics Review*, 11(1), 69–80.

Hannah, E., Basheer, N., Dumka, N., & Kotwal, A. (2023). Access to medicines in the Indian public health system – what works and what does not? A review of the national health mission common review mission reports (2007-2021). *Journal of Global Health Reports*, 7, e2023054. doi:10.29392/001c.84486

Haque, M., Islam, T., Rahman, N. A. A., McKimm, J., Abdullah, A., & Dhingra, S. (2020). Strengthening primary health-care services to help prevent and control long-term (chronic) non-communicable diseases in low-and middle-income countries. *Risk Management and Healthcare Policy*, 13: 409–426.

Khanduja, P., Goli, V., and Singh, S., (2021). Reimagining the Indian government's telemedicine platform user, Microwave Consulting, Blog, Feb 10, 2021.

Kumar, A. (2023). The transformation of the Indian healthcare system. *Cureus*, 15(5), e39079.

Malhotra, N., & Dave, K. (2022). An assessment of competitiveness of medical tourism industry in India: A case of Delhi NCR. *International Journal of Global Business and Competitiveness*, 17(2), 215–228.

Marchildon, G. P., Allin, S., & Merkur, S. (2021). *Health systems in transition* (3rd ed.). University of Toronto Press.

Martin, D., Miller, A. P., Quesnel-Vallée, A., Caron, N. R., Vissandjée, B., & Marchildon, G. P. (2018). Canada's universal health-care system: achieving its potential. *The Lancet*, 391(10131), 1718–1735.

Pradeepa, R., & Mohan, V. (2021). Epidemiology of type 2 diabetes in India. *Indian Journal of Ophthalmology*, 69(11), 2932–2938.

Piñeros, M., Laversanne, M., Barrios, E., de Camargo Cancela, M., de Vries, E., Pardo, C., & Bray, F. (2022). An updated profile of the cancer burden, patterns and trends in Latin America and the Caribbean. *The Lancet Regional Health–Americas*, 13, 100294

Ram, B., & Thakur, R. (2022). Epidemiology and economic burden of continuing challenge of infectious diseases in India: Analysis of socio-demographic differentials. *Frontiers in Public Health*, 10, 901276.

Reuters. (2023, January 24). Exclusive: WHO investigating links between cough syrup deaths, considers advice for parents. *Reuters*.

Selvaraj, S., Karan, K. A., Srivastava, S., Bhan, N., & Mukhopadhyay, I. (2022). *India health system review*. World Health Organisation, Regional Office for South-East Asia.

Statista. (n.d). *Software industry in India - statistics and facts*. Statista.

Thomas, S. V. (2009, April–June). The national health bill 2009 and afterwards. *Annals of Indian Academy of Neurology*, 12(2), 79.

3 The relationship between health and healthcare

3.1 Factors impacting on health

The health of a population is influenced by a wide range of factors, which are not a part of the healthcare system.

In the 1970s in the UK, an influential government-funded study, led by Sir Michael Marmot (Marmot et al., 1978), provided some of the first credible evidence of the strong relationship between socioeconomic status and health outcomes among British civil servants. Since then, the understanding of the impact of various factors, such as social, economic, behavioural, and environmental, on health has significantly advanced. It is now recognised that over 70% of health outcomes are influenced by factors beyond healthcare alone. The evidence suggests that the contribution of poverty to lost years of life is greater than smoking and obesity combined (McGinnis et al., 2002; Muennig et al., 2010).

In the US, McGinnis and Foege (1993) identified the "actual causes of death" like smoking, poor diet, and lack of exercise, and Galea et al. (2011) further assessed the mortality attributable to social determinants. Their estimates for the year 2000 revealed that around 423,000 deaths in the US were linked to poverty, 245,000 to limited educational attainment, 162,000 to inadequate socioeconomic support, and 119,000 to income inequality. Additionally, social and economic stressors significantly fuel what are termed "diseases of despair," such as suicide, alcohol abuse, and opioid addiction, inflicting immense suffering on countless American families and contributing to declines in life expectancy within certain demographic groups (Case & Deaton, 2015).

Factors beyond healthcare are known as the social determinants of health.

WHO (2024) defines the social determinants of health as "the conditions in which people are born, grow, live, work and age, and people's access to power, money and resources."

They list the following examples of the social determinants of health (Table 3.1), which can influence health equity in positive and negative ways.

Beyond the factors traditionally described as the social determinants of health, there are a further range of factors that impact upon health that are beyond healthcare.

Lifestyle choices and behaviours, such as diet, exercise, smoking, alcohol consumption, drug use, and sexual practices, have profound effects on individual and population health. Whilst external factors and education campaigns can influence these behaviours, in a free society, a degree of personal choice remains.

Genetic predispositions to certain diseases and individual biological factors influence individual susceptibility to illness and response to treatment. Whilst there is a growing awareness of this issue and an increasing ability to assess specific genetic risks, such

DOI: 10.4324/9781003478874-4

Table 3.1 Social determinants of health (after (WHO, 2024))

Social determinant	Description
Income and social protection	Socioeconomic status and income are determinants of health, linked to life expectancy, quality of life, and disease risk, with many diseases more prevalent in people from low socioeconomic status.
Education	Health literacy and education levels impact individuals' ability to understand and access healthcare services, adhere to medical advice, and make informed decisions about their health.
Unemployment and job insecurity	Unemployment is associated with a range of health risks and health inequalities caused both by the event of becoming unemployed as well as the reduced income, deprivation, and poverty due to being out of work. The risk of ill health increases as the duration of unemployment increases.
Working life conditions	Workplace conditions, occupational hazards, and access to healthcare benefits can all affect the health of workers and their families.
Food insecurity	A lack of regular access to enough safe, healthy, and culturally appropriate food is related to obesity, hypertension and hyperlipidaemia, diabetes, hypoglycaemia, chronic kidney disease, and frailty in the elderly.
Housing, basic amenities, and the environment	Living conditions, air and water quality, exposure to toxins and pollutants, access to green spaces, and housing conditions can all affect health outcomes.
Early childhood development	The first 1,000 days of life are becoming more well-recognised as important for the development of brain circuits that lead to linguistic, cognitive, and socio-emotional abilities, all of which are predictors of later-life labour market outcomes. This can also influence a person's overall well-being and functioning throughout their lifetime (Likhar et al., 2022).
Social inclusion and non-discrimination	Non-discrimination and social inclusion are fundamental to the mental health of the whole community. There is a recognised correlation between severe mental illness, low socio-economic status, and social exclusion.
Structural conflict	Structural determinants serve as the fundamental origins of health disparities, as they influence the nature of social determinants of health encountered by individuals within their localities and social circles. These determinants encompass governmental procedures, economic, and social regulations impacting wages, employment conditions, housing, and educational opportunities. They dictate whether essential health resources are equitably allocated across society or unfairly distributed based on factors such as race, gender, socioeconomic status, geographical location, sexual orientation, or other socially constructed identities.

techniques mostly remain inaccessible to citizens of low-income countries and poorer residents of wealthier nations.

Cultural beliefs, attitudes toward health and healthcare, and adherence to medical advice can vary widely among different populations and influence health outcomes. This can contribute to the differential effectiveness of both preventative and curative interventions between different communities.

Government policies related to healthcare, public health campaigns, vaccination programs, disease surveillance, and regulation of industries impacting health (e.g., tobacco and food) shape population health.

Strong social connections and support systems in tightly knit families or social networks can buffer against stress and improve mental and physical health outcomes. Conversely, loneliness and isolation can adversely affect mental and physical health outcomes.

Political stability, governance structures, economic development, and investment in social welfare programs all influence population health outcomes. Politically stable countries with limited economic inequalities tend to perform better in terms of population health.

Finally, trade policies, international travel, and globalisation can impact the spread of infectious diseases, access to healthcare resources, and environmental health standards.

These factors interact in complex ways and vary across different populations and geographic regions. Addressing health disparities and promoting population health often requires a multi-sectoral approach that addresses the root causes of health inequities.

Cardiovascular disease in Asia (after Zhao, 2021)

According to Zhao (2021), cardiovascular disease (CVD) is the leading cause of death in Asia, albeit with significant disparities between individual nations. The CVD mortality rates vary considerably, ranging from 810.7 per 100,000 population in Georgia to 39.1 per 100,000 population in Qatar, indicating a substantial 20-fold difference between the highest and lowest rates. CVD mortality rates differ even within regions, but Central and Eastern Asian countries generally exhibit higher rates compared to those in Southern and Southeast Asia.

Surprisingly, the lowest CVD mortality rate in Central Asian countries surpasses the highest rate among Southern Asian nations. Notably, high-income Asian countries like Japan and Israel demonstrate lower proportions of premature CVD deaths compared to many low- and middle-income Asian counterparts.

An unhealthy diet emerges as a significant risk factor for CVD in Asian nations, with a transition from traditional Asian diets to westernised diets observed in several countries. This shift is characterised by increased consumption of oil, animal-source foods, snacks, sugar, and sugar-sweetened beverages, alongside a decline in coarse grains and legumes consumption (Popkin, 2014).

Smoking remains a prevalent risk factor for cardiovascular health both globally and within Asia. Myanmar has the highest age-standardised smoking rate at 45.5%, contrasting with Oman's lowest rate of 9.6%. Although smoking prevalence is notably higher among men, it remains significant among women in several countries.

Obesity, primarily resultant from unhealthy lifestyles, emerges as an established risk factor for CVD and diabetes. The prevalence of obesity varies greatly across Asian countries, ranging from 37.9% in Kuwait to 2.1% in Vietnam. Western Asian countries typically exhibit higher obesity rates, while Eastern, Southern, and Southeastern Asian nations show relatively lower prevalence rates. However, due to the vast populations of countries like India and China, they contribute the highest absolute numbers of obese individuals.

Hypertension is prevalent in many Asian countries, contributing substantially to CVD deaths, particularly in regions where stroke is the dominant CVD type. Discrepancies exist in reported crude prevalence rates of hypertension, ranging from 19% to 28% in China, 11% to 29% in South Korea, and 17% to 42% in Japan. Despite improvements in the availability and accessibility of blood pressure measurement and antihypertensive medication, low awareness, treatment, and control rates of hypertension persist as the primary challenge in managing hypertension in most low- and middle-income Asian countries.

China, India, Japan, Indonesia, and Pakistan ranked among the top 10 countries with a substantial number of adults with diabetes in 2014, collectively representing 48% of global diabetes patients. Diabetes prevalence is increasing across all Asian regions.

However, the ageing population is the most important determinant of an increasing risk of CVD. The generally longer life span and lower birth rate in many Asian countries has led to changes in the age structure and increasing absolute numbers of older adults. The proportion of the population in Asia aged over 65 years in Asia was 4.8% in 2019, predicted to rise to 8.8% in 2020 and 17.8% in 2050, with an increase in absolute numbers more than doubling from 0.4 billion to 0.9 billion over this period.

3.1.1 Knowledge review

Before you move on, can you define the following key concepts:

• Social determinants of health?

3.1.2 Question to think about

What are the most significant factors beyond access to healthcare that impact upon your health and that of your family?

3.2 Prevention or cure?

Where possible, prevention of disease is almost always preferable to curing a disease.

Preventive measures, such as vaccinations, screenings, and lifestyle interventions, are normally more cost-effective than treating diseases once they have developed. Preventing diseases can reduce the burden on healthcare systems and lower overall healthcare costs.

Preventing diseases and injuries can lead to better health outcomes compared to treating them after they have occurred. For example, preventing chronic diseases through healthy lifestyle choices can significantly improve quality of life and reduce the risk of complications.

Prevention can reduce the physical, emotional, and financial suffering associated with illness or injury. By avoiding the onset of diseases or injuries, individuals can maintain their health and well-being and avoid the pain and discomfort associated with illness.

Many preventable diseases, such as heart disease, diabetes, and certain cancers, are closely linked to lifestyle factors such as diet, exercise, and smoking. Encouraging healthy behaviours and providing support for individuals to adopt healthier lifestyles can prevent the development of these diseases altogether.

Prevention measures, such as immunisation programs and public health campaigns, can have a significant impact on population health by reducing the incidence of infectious diseases and promoting healthy behaviours across communities.

Investing in prevention strategies can lead to long-term benefits for individuals, communities, and societies. By promoting health and well-being, prevention efforts contribute to a sustainable healthcare system and an overall healthier population.

Prevention of disease is a key part of the United Nations (UN) Sustainable Development Goals (SDGs) programme. Many of the targets set under SDG 3: Good Health and Well-being are linked to disease prevention and/or health promotion:

SDG 3: Good health and well-being targets linked to disease prevention and/or health promotion (after United Nations Department of Economic and Social Affairs (UN DESA), 2023)

3.1 By 2030, reduce the global maternal mortality ratio to less than 70 per 100,000 live births.

3.2 By 2030, end preventable deaths of new-borns and children under five years of age, with all countries aiming to reduce neonatal mortality to at least as low as 12 per 1,000 live births and under-5 mortality to at least as low as 25 per 1,000 live births.

3.3 By 2030, end the epidemics of AIDS, tuberculosis, malaria, and neglected tropical diseases and combat hepatitis, water-borne diseases, and other communicable diseases.

3.4 By 2030, reduce by one-third premature mortality from non-communicable diseases through prevention and treatment and promote mental health and well-being.

3.5 Strengthen the prevention and treatment of substance abuse, including narcotic drug abuse and harmful use of alcohol.

3.6 By 2020, halve the number of global deaths and injuries from road traffic accidents.

3.7 By 2030, ensure universal access to sexual and reproductive healthcare services, including for family planning, information and education, and the integration of reproductive health into national strategies and programmes.

3.8 Achieve universal health coverage, including financial risk protection, access to quality essential healthcare services, and access to safe, effective, quality and affordable essential medicines and vaccines for all.

3.9 By 2030, substantially reduce the number of deaths and illnesses from hazardous chemicals and air, water and soil pollution and contamination.

3.2.1 Disease prevention or health promotion?

Disease prevention encompasses targeted interventions at both population and individual levels, aiming to mitigate the impact of diseases and associated risk factors.

Primary prevention focuses on averting the onset of diseases, by addressing social and economic determinants, disseminating information regarding behavioural and medical risks, and implementing measures to mitigate these risks at personal and community levels.

It also includes initiatives such as nutritional supplementation, oral hygiene education, and clinical preventive services like immunisation for various age groups and protection against communicable diseases through vaccination or post-exposure prophylaxis.

Secondary prevention involves early detection leading to better prospects for favourable health outcomes. This can involve evidence-based screening programs to detect diseases at early stages or prevent congenital anomalies, as well as administering preventive drug therapies with proven efficacy during the initial phases of the disease.

While primary prevention initiatives can be implemented independently, secondary prevention relies on the capacity of broader healthcare services. Screening and early detection lose effectiveness if abnormalities cannot be promptly addressed within the healthcare system. A robust primary healthcare system with registered populations facilitates the organisation and delivery of accessible population-based screening programs.

Health promotion, on the other hand, empowers individuals to take control of their health and its determinants through health literacy campaigns and multisectoral actions to promote healthy behaviours. These efforts target the general community or populations at elevated risk of adverse health outcomes, addressing behavioural risk factors like tobacco use, unhealthy diet, physical inactivity, as well as mental health, injury prevention, substance abuse control, and sexual health.

While disease prevention and health promotion share similar objectives, they operate across different spheres. Disease prevention services predominantly operate within the healthcare sector, while health promotion activities often depend on intersectoral collaborations and address broader social determinants of health.

Impact of vaccinations on reducing childhood mortality in the 21st century (after Li et al., 2021)

According to Li et al. (2021), vaccine initiatives in low- and middle-income nations have prevented 37 million fatalities in the first two decades of the 21st century, with 36 million of these occurring in children under five years old. The research indicates that this success is anticipated to persist. By 2030, an additional 32 million deaths are projected to be averted by vaccination programs, with 28 million of those in children under five, assuming continuous progress.

Childhood vaccination efforts have expanded globally over the past two decades, significantly reducing diseases, such as measles, meningitis, and hepatitis, particularly in low- and middle-income countries. The study provides the most reliable estimates to date of the impact of childhood vaccinations on mortality.

The Vaccine Impact Modelling Consortium, comprising 16 research groups worldwide, produced estimates for 10 diseases, focusing on deaths prevented by vaccination across 98 low- and middle-income countries from 2000 to 2030, encompassing over two-thirds of the global population.

These diseases include hepatitis B, Haemophilus influenza type b (Hib), human papillomavirus (HPV), Japanese encephalitis, measles, meningitis A (Neisseria meningitidis serogroup A), pneumococcal disease (Streptococcus pneumoniae), rotavirus, rubella, and yellow fever.

Measles vaccination has had the most significant impact, preventing an estimated 33 million deaths from 2000 to 2019, with researchers expecting this trend to continue, potentially averting over 2.1 million deaths annually from 2020 to 2030.

Expanding HPV vaccination coverage in girls and increasing pneumococcal conjugate vaccine coverage are highlighted as key areas for additional gains, with potential to further reduce mortality, especially among children under five.

The study underscores the substantial public health benefits of vaccines and emphasises the importance of sustained investment in global vaccination coverage. The authors called for continued funding, political commitment, and strengthened health systems to maintain and enhance these achievements.

3.2.2 Knowledge review

Before you move on, can you define the following key concepts:

- Disease prevention?
- Health promotion?

3.2.3 Questions to think about

Do you know which disease you have been vaccinated against?

How many more might your children be vaccinated against?

3.3 Acute episodes versus long-term conditions

Managing long-term conditions is becoming increasingly important in healthcare. Long-term conditions are illnesses that cannot be cured. They can usually be controlled with medicines or other treatments. Examples include diabetes, arthritis, high blood pressure, epilepsy, asthma, and dementia.

Long-term conditions pose a significant threat to the health of the global population across all age groups, particularly as people grow older. Despite efforts to address public health concerns worldwide, there has been a continuous rise in chronic and non-communicable diseases, such as cancer, cardiovascular issues, and metabolic disorders, and a notable increase in mental health conditions. In 2010, chronic diseases accounted for 67% of deaths globally, a figure that climbed to 74% by 2019, with further acceleration observed during the COVID-19 pandemic and its aftermath. This trend is attributed partly to ageing demographics, lifestyle choices, and advancements in medical care, resulting in longer life expectancies.

In 2019, chronic conditions were responsible for 74% of all deaths worldwide, marking an increase from 67% in 2010. According to the Australian Institute of Health and Welfare (2022), nearly half of Australians (47%) have at least one chronic disease, with one-fifth experiencing two or more. Chronic diseases account for more than half (51%) of hospitalisations, and individuals from lower socioeconomic backgrounds and those residing in remote areas bear a disproportionately higher burden, with 90% of deaths and disease impacts falling on these demographics. These findings align with global trends observed in numerous countries.

Furthermore, mental health disorders, including addiction, are emerging as a growing challenge, constituting one-fifth of the global disease burden (Degenhardt et al., 2018).

Dementia is a significant and growing global health problem. Over 55 million individuals worldwide suffer from dementia, with over 60% residing in low- and middle-income nations and there are nearly 10 million new cases each year (WHO, 2017). Dementia arises from various brain-affecting diseases and injuries, with Alzheimer's disease comprising around two-thirds of instances. It ranks as the seventh leading cause of death and a significant source of disability and dependency among older individuals globally.

In 2019, dementia care cost 1.3 trillion US dollars, with about half of these expenses attributed to informal caregivers, such as family members and close friends, who provide an average of five hours of daily care and supervision. Women bear a disproportionate impact from dementia, facing higher disability-adjusted life years and mortality rates, while also shouldering 70% of caregiving responsibilities for those with dementia.

The reasons for the rapid rise in the numbers of cases of physical and mental long-term conditions globally is due to a number of interconnected factors:

- As life expectancy increases globally, there is a larger proportion of elderly individuals in the population. Many long-term conditions, such as cardiovascular diseases, cancer, dementia, and arthritis, are more prevalent in older age groups. Population growth and shifts in demographics, including declining birth rates and increased urbanisation, contribute to a larger population of older adults who are more prone to long-term conditions.
- Modern lifestyles characterised by sedentary behaviour, unhealthy diets, smoking, excessive alcohol consumption, and stress contribute to the development of chronic conditions such as obesity, type 2 diabetes, cardiovascular diseases, and certain cancers.
- Urbanisation is associated with changes in diet, physical activity patterns, exposure to pollution, and access to healthcare, which can influence the prevalence of long-term conditions.
- Economic development and globalisation have led to changes in dietary habits, increased consumption of processed foods, reduced physical activity, and higher levels of stress, all of which contribute to the rising burden of chronic diseases.
- Whilst advances in medical technology, early detection, and treatment have led to increased survival rates for acute illnesses and injuries, they have also resulted in a larger population living with long-term conditions.
- Genetic predispositions to certain diseases, as well as changes in the human microbiome and immune system, may also contribute to the development of long-term conditions.
- Global health challenges, such as infectious diseases (e.g., HIV/AIDS, tuberculosis) and environmental disasters (e.g., natural disasters, climate change), can exacerbate existing health inequalities and contribute to the burden of long-term conditions, especially in low- and middle-income countries.

In practice, whilst the balance of these factors will vary by countries, almost every country is facing multiple interconnected challenges in dealing with long-term conditions.

The Center for Medicare & Medicaid Services (2021) estimate that 90% of healthcare expenditure on the US is spent on chronic physical and mental health conditions.

Certain conditions cluster together more frequently than expected, with associations of up to three-fold, e.g., depression associated with stroke and with Alzheimer's disease, and communicable conditions such as tuberculosis (TB) and HIV/AIDS associated with diabetes and CVD, respectively. Clusters are important as they may be highly amenable to large improvements in health and cost outcomes through relatively simple shifts in healthcare delivery.

Healthcare expenditures greatly increase, sometimes exponentially, with each additional chronic condition with greater specialist physician access, emergency department presentations, and hospital admissions. The patient burden includes a deterioration of quality of life, out of pocket expenses, medication adherence, inability to work, symptom control and a high toll on carers. Long-term conditions can significantly impact individuals' quality of life, affecting their ability to work, engage in social activities, and perform daily tasks. Proper management aims to minimise symptoms, prevent complications, and enhance overall well-being.

Many long-term conditions are associated with preventable complications such as heart attacks, strokes, kidney failure, and amputations. Effective management strategies focus on preventing these complications through early detection, lifestyle interventions, and appropriate medical treatment. Longman et al. (2021) investigated preventable hospital admissions in New South Wales attributable to complications from long-term conditions. Of 323 admissions reviewed from a mixed urban and rural population, an expert panel found 148 to be preventable. However, the reasons for admissions were complex and variable, and no quick solutions were identified, although an absence of community-based services was often a contributory factor, especially in rural areas, Managing long-term conditions requires a holistic, patient-centred approach that takes into account individuals' preferences, values, and goals. This approach emphasizes shared decision-making, self-management support, and continuity of care to optimise health outcomes. Because long-term conditions often require care from multiple healthcare providers and across different settings (e.g., primary care, specialty care, community services), failures to place the patient at the centre of care can lead to increased complications, greater costs and poorer outcomes, and quality of life.

Integrated care models aim to coordinate and streamline services to ensure continuity of care and improve patient outcomes. Those integrated care models that place patients at the centre, rather than join up a series of interventions from variety of care providers are more likely to succeed.

Long-term conditions disproportionately affect certain population groups, including socioeconomically disadvantaged individuals, ethnic minorities, and those with comorbidities. Addressing health inequalities requires targeted interventions and tailored support for vulnerable populations. Many of the social determinants of health disproportionately affect vulnerable populations, and targeted interventions will have to look well beyond traditional health interventions to tackle the disproportionate adverse impacts of the social determinants of health amongst these populations.

Technological advancements, such as telemedicine, wearable devices, and digital health platforms, offer new opportunities for remote monitoring, self-management, and personalised care for individuals with long-term conditions. The technology offers the opportunity to monitor a patient's condition over a period of time, without the need for a physical consultation. If advice is needed, this can be provided remotely by a video consultation.

Strengthening primary healthcare services to help prevent and control long-term (chronic) non-communicable diseases in low- and middle-income countries (after Haque et al., 2020)

While previously more prevalent in high- and upper-middle-income nations, low-or-middle-income countries (LMICs) are now experiencing a greater impact from non-communicable long-term conditions. In low- and middle-income countries, long-term conditions currently contribute to 85–90% of premature deaths among individuals aged 30–69. These diseases pose significant challenges due to their high morbidity, mortality rates, and associated treatment costs, including those related to complications. Haque et al. (2020) advocate for the crucial role of primary healthcare services in preventing and managing long-term conditions, particularly in low- and middle-income countries, where healthcare infrastructure and hospital services may be strained.

Annually, approximately 40.5 million people worldwide succumb to long-term conditions, with around 13 million premature deaths occurring in individuals aged 30–69 from low- and middle-income countries. Currently, more than 75% (31.5 million) of global long-term condition-related deaths occur in these countries. Despite the World Health Organisation's prediction that the global burden of long-term conditions would rise to 80% by 2020, a disproportionate burden is expected to fall on low- and middle-income countries, with 70% of deaths occurring in these regions, half of which are premature.

Forecasts indicate a 17% average increase in long-term conditions globally over the next decade, with African nations facing a predicted 27% rise. In sub-Saharan Africa, long-term condition-related mortality rates have been steadily increasing, with countries like Malawi experiencing long-term condition-related deaths accounting for 28% of total fatalities. Challenges in data collection and analysis, coupled with political, social, and environmental issues, hinder effective policy implementation across the continent, leading to a failure to meet WHO recommendations.

Partly due to the large population, nearly 50% of long-term condition-related deaths currently occur in Asian countries, representing 47% of the global disease burden. In countries like India, long-term conditions are on the rise, particularly among individuals aged 45 and above. Indian data from 1990–2016 reveal an increasing prevalence of long-term conditions, notably cardiovascular diseases, respiratory disorders, and both types of diabetes.

Despite these challenges, progress is being made in several LMICs in implementing primary healthcare systems. Fourteen such countries have implemented large-scale primary healthcare programs, demonstrating significant advancements in public healthcare provision.

Moreover, studies highlight the effectiveness of community-based healthcare services, particularly when integrated with proper referral systems, supervised support, and medicine supply chains. In lower-income countries, Haque et al. (2020) argue that a primary healthcare approach is essential in preventing long-term conditions through comprehensive intersectoral collaboration and a focus on health equity.

3.3.1 Knowledge review

Before you move on, can you define the following key concepts:

• Long-term conditions?

3.3.2 Question to think about

Which are the most significant long-term conditions in your country at present?
Will that still be true in 10 years? 20 years?

3.4 Views of healthcare as a system

Healthcare operates as a system with entities, inputs, and outputs. There are a number of views that we can use to better understand how healthcare operates as a system and also to understand why sometimes it fails to do so.

3.4.1 View 1: Healthcare as an ecosystem

Healthcare may be viewed as an ecosystem with the patient and clinician at the centre of a number of layers (Figure 3.1).

The exact nature of the healthcare ecosystem and the business models used to organise and manage the relationships between the different stakeholders varies substantially in different countries and regions around the world.

At the centre of the ecosystem is the episode of care which is an encounter between a caregiver, typically a healthcare professional, and one in receipt of a care, generally known as a patient. This binary divide between purchasers and providers is reflected throughout the broader ecosystem. This encounter takes place in some sort of facility, either physical or virtual.

For the encounter to happen, there are a range of things that are needed, and these are provided by a range of suppliers, and these are funded by a variety of purchasing organisations.

The whole ecosystem requires planning, management, oversight, and evaluation. This may be carried out by a range of organisations.

At the centre of our ecosystem, the stereotypical episode of care is between a patient and a medical doctor. However, in practice, there are many variations on this stereotype. These days, the caregiver may be another healthcare professional, such as a nurse, paramedic, dentist, dietitian, or therapist. The caregiver may be a different type of professional such as a pharmacist or a counsellor.

Some commentators argue that developments in AI may soon mean that care is provided by AI systems without human intervention, but ethical concerns remain (Gillies & Smith, 2022). However, many people seeking advice turn to the World Wide Web or mobile phone apps for advice and act on what they find without referring to a healthcare professional. This use of technology is actually blurring the definition of what constitutes an episode of care.

The nature of healthcare episodes is certainly broader than treatment and may include advice, preventative interventions, or screening. As such, the recipient of care may not be ill as such and therefore may simply be a member of the public rather than a patient.

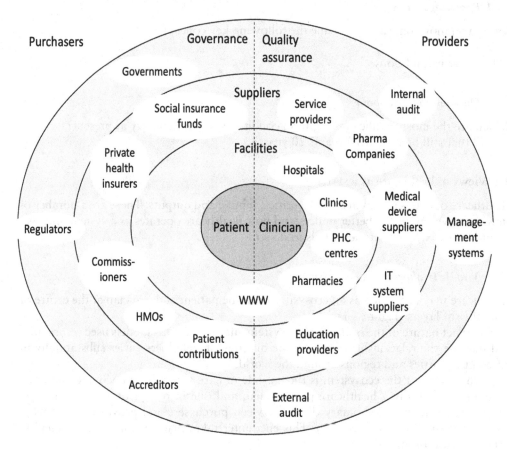

Figure 3.1 A schematic overview of the healthcare ecosystem.

In our traditional scenario, our episode of care takes place in a clinical setting, which may be in a hospital. clinic, health centre, or physician's office. In many countries, the occasions when a doctor will visit a patient in their home have declined. However, much care is still delivered by other health professionals and carers in patients' own homes or in residential care settings

In an attempt to increase access to services, care is being offered in an increasing variety of settings. The increased use of pharmacists for health advice, screening, and vaccinations means that care is provided in retail settings. The use of mobile imaging technology means that screening can be provided in any community setting, where the mobile facility usually in the form of a trailer can be set up.

Again, the increased adoption of digital technology is disruptive to the traditional ecosystem. A traditional episode of care may now be carried out over a video link or telephone call, and this has been adopted much more widely during and since the COVID-19 pandemic. Both parties may be participating from their own home, and the encounter effectively takes place virtually. Although convenient, there may be risks associated with the loss of non-verbal information available, or in some cases the inability of the professional to access the patient's health record.

There are more creative ways in which this type of technology may be used. For example, a local paramedic or primary care physician may access advice from a specialist who is located at a distance. And in settings where patients are a long way from any facilities, e.g., the Australian outback or Northern Canada, then it may be the only practical way for patients to access care.

Healthcare provider organisations that supply healthcare services take many forms.

Large care facilities such as hospitals are normally run as autonomous organisations. They may run as corporations, either as not for profit or for profit. In public healthcare systems, such as the UK and Canada, whilst public hospitals are part of the system, they operate with a high degree of financial autonomy. In Canada, the public hospitals are independent institutions incorporated under provincial Corporations Acts and are required by law to operate within their budget. In the UK, there are additionally hospitals providing paid for care run by private companies, some of whom are run for profit and others as not for profit.

In France, where healthcare is financed by social health insurance, almost two-thirds of hospital care is provided by publicly owned and managed hospitals. However, approximately one-sixth comes from non-profit sector hospitals (often connected to charitable or mutual organisations) and one-sixth from hospitals run for profit.

However, the episode of care is dependent upon a much wider range of suppliers. Drugs, medical devices, and Information Technology (IT) devices are all generally provided by for-profit businesses, albeit subject to significant levels of regulation in order to safeguard patients.

Many large hospitals have close links with education providers, such as universities and medical and nursing schools, since one of the largest supply needs of the sector is the availability of staff suitably qualified in medicine, nursing, allied health professions and other related disciplines. The cost of training this workforce is often met wholly or partially by public funding. Increasingly, students are being required to contribute a greater proportion of the cost of their training, often in the form of student loans. Where there is a high degree of public funding, there are increasing pressures to require professionals to repay this by giving a number of years to the public healthcare system, perhaps serving in areas where it is difficult to get doctors to locate their practice.

There are also ethical concerns about the number of doctors and other professionals working in wealthier countries whilst their home countries have a chronic shortage of suitably qualified staff.

On the purchase side, there are a number of organisational types whose purpose is to manage the supply of funding required to pay the suppliers of services and goods. Within an insurance-based system, whether private or social, there are organisations required to collect contributions, define the package of services to be offered, and distribute the funds for these services. Within a public system, these functions are carried out by public bodies, either at a national or local level.

An increasingly prevalent method of administering the distribution of funds, particularly is known as healthcare commissioning, which includes assessing needs, planning services, procuring services, and monitoring quality. In the English National Health Service (NHS), this is the primary mechanism for the distribution of funds through Clinical Commissioning Groups. The process of commissioning has evolved in the UK since the early 1990s, and there are increasing developments towards integrated commissioning of health and social care by joint commissioning with local authorities who have responsibility for social care (Kings Fund, 2019).

Within the private health insurance market in the US, a distinct type of insurance provider has emerged to carry out these functions, known as a health maintenance organisation.

A health maintenance organisation (HMO) is a network or organisation that provides health insurance coverage for a monthly or annual fee. It is made up of a group of medical insurance providers that limit coverage to medical care provided through doctors and other providers who are under contract to the HMO, who will negotiate the rates paid for particular services. These contracts mean that monthly premiums are able to be lower than alternative types of insurance but do with come with additional restrictions for premium holders.

The increased use of digital technology has also started to disrupt these traditional systems. Babylon Health started by offering a private general practitioner (GP) service directly to patients via their mobile phones in the UK, in return for an annual subscription, offering rapid access and guaranteed access. Although they have largely withdrawn from the UK provider market, they operate in the US, India, and around a dozen countries in South East Asia. In Africa, they were launched in Rwanda in September 2016 as Babyl in partnership with the Bill & Melinda Gates Foundation. By May 2018, Babyl was reported to have two million members, covering roughly 30% of Rwanda's adult population, and in January 2020, they reported one million completed consultations in Rwanda. Following this announcement, in March that year, they agreed to roll out Babyl to all Rwandans over the age of 12 through the government's community-based health insurance scheme, Mutuelle de Santé, which is switching from a model of funding based on fee-per-service to a capitation-based model. Regrettably, by 2024, Babylon Health had filed for bankruptcy globally.

The final layer of the health ecosystem is concerned with governance of the system as a whole. On the provider side, this is initially concerned with internal quality assurance by the suppliers to ensure that they are operating safely and within the parameters set by the purchasers, as well as any applicable laws and regulations that apply.

However, in some sectors, suppliers are required to demonstrate that their management systems comply with global standards often defined by the International Standards Organisation (ISO).

Typically, this will be based upon standards for management systems and a system of external or third-party audits to ensure compliance. For example, suppliers of medical devices are required in most jurisdictions to demonstrate compliance with ISO 130485:2016 (ISO, 2016):

> ISO 13485:2016 specifies requirements for a quality management system where an organisation needs to demonstrate its ability to provide medical devices and related services that consistently meet customer and applicable regulatory requirements. Such organisations can be involved in one or more stages of the life-cycle, including design and development, production, storage and distribution, installation, or servicing of a medical device and design and development or provision of associated activities (e.g., technical support). ISO 13485:2016 can also be used by suppliers or external parties that provide product, including quality management system-related services to such organisations.
>
> (ISO, 2016)

3.4.2 View 2: Healthcare as a patient journey

In this view, healthcare is seen from the patient's perspective as a journey, during which they interact with different players. Some of these interactions will be direct with healthcare providers, others will be less direct with their suppliers and funders.

Joseph and Borycki (2020) identified a number of different maps that can be used to describe the patients' journeys through the healthcare system:

- The Customer Journey where individual(s) are viewed as consumers of services or products;. it examines the relationship of an individual as a consumer of a particular service.
- The Experience Map where individual(s)' activities are viewed broadly and aren't organisation specific and can involve a variety of organisations; it examines the relationships of people interacting with multiple products and services while trying to satisfy their needs.
- Mental Model Diagrams where individual(s)' thought patterns and internal dialogue are observed and can be applied to an organisation or event; it examines the way an individual perceives an organisation.
- Service Blueprints that examine service processes, interactive touch points and provide a service overview
- Spatial Map where individual(s) and organisational perspectives and relationships are presented as models, and the goal is to examine the organisation holistically

The traditional organisational-based view of healthcare has led to a situation where too often patient care is discontinuous at organisational boundaries, leading to delays, loss of information with potentially serious consequences for patient safety and outcomes as well as impacting negatively on the immediate patient experience.

Attempts have been made to connect healthcare provider organisations better using technology to make the patient journey more seamless, but too often these have ended in failure (Campion-Awwad et al., 2014). Although these failures are often seen as technological failures, in practice, they are the victim of perverse incentives in the system, which do not reward healthcare providers for adopting a more patient-centred approach.

Joseph and Borycki (2020) argue that there is already evidence that using the patient journey as the primary view of healthcare can deliver benefits. How patients view their journey can directly impact recovery times and mortality rates. One effective approach to understanding this perspective is through the Mental Model mapping exercise, which can be framed within the stages theory proposed by Kübler-Ross (2009).

This theory outlines five common stages individuals may go through when confronted with illness or mortality: denial and isolation, anger, bargaining, depression, and acceptance. By understanding the patient's mental model as they progress through the continuum of care, organisations and clinical stakeholders can identify why certain gaps in care may affect the patient experience more severely than others. Recognising the complexities of the human psyche allows journey mapping designers to evaluate clinical workflows, healthcare processes, and interactions from a comprehensive patient-centric viewpoint.

Considering healthcare service delivery through the lens of each patient experiencing multiple and often overlapping journeys – such as illness, grief, life stage, and personal circumstances – can lead to positive patient care outcomes, reduced provider burnout, and heightened empathy in healthcare settings.

3.4.3 View 3: Healthcare as a complex adaptive system

As healthcare becomes more complex and there is an increasing recognition of the impact on health of factors beyond healthcare, healthcare is increasingly viewed as a complex adaptive system. The term complex adaptive system (CAS) is used in systems theory to describe a collection of individual agents or components that interact with each other and their environment, leading to emergent behaviours and properties that cannot be predicted from the characteristics of the individual agents alone. These systems are characterised by their dynamic, interconnected nature and their tendency to exhibit emergent, adaptive behaviour in response to changing conditions.

In healthcare, emergent properties arise from the interactions between various components such as patients, healthcare providers, facilities, treatments, and policies. These interactions give rise to outcomes and behaviours that are often unpredictable based solely on the individual components.

Healthcare outcomes do not always have a linear relationship with inputs or interventions. Small changes or interventions can lead to disproportionately large effects (positive or negative), and vice versa. For example, a minor adjustment in treatment protocols might significantly improve patient outcomes, or conversely, a slight oversight in medication dosage could lead to adverse effects.

Healthcare systems continually adapt and evolve in response to internal and external stimuli. This adaptation can occur at various levels, from individual patient care to organisational policies and healthcare delivery models. For instance, healthcare providers might adjust treatment plans based on new research findings or patient feedback.

Feedback loops are pervasive in healthcare systems, influencing behaviour, and outcomes. These loops can be reinforcing (positive feedback) or balancing (negative feedback). For example, positive patient outcomes may reinforce certain treatment approaches, while negative outcomes may prompt adjustments to treatment strategies.

Healthcare involves a wide array of stakeholders, including patients, caregivers, healthcare professionals, administrators, policymakers, and researchers. This diversity in actors, perspectives, and expertise contributes to the complexity of the system and provides resilience through redundancy.

Healthcare systems exhibit self-organising behaviour, with patterns and structures emerging spontaneously from the interactions of its components. This self-organisation can lead to the formation of healthcare networks, care pathways, and best practices that optimise patient care delivery.

Healthcare systems are characterised by dynamic networks of relationships and connections among various stakeholders and components. These networks enable information flow, resource allocation, and collaboration, but they also introduce vulnerabilities and dependencies.

Historical events, decisions, and contingencies can have lasting effects on healthcare systems, shaping their current structure and dynamics. Path-dependent processes can influence healthcare policies, practices, and organisational cultures over time.

This view can help managers understand unexpected outcomes and actions. However, it flies in the face of much traditional management that emphasises standardisation, consistency, and a linear relationship between actions and outcomes.

Using a CAS approach to help teams function more effectively after Hoogeboom & Wilderom (2020)

Hoogeboom & Wilderom (2020) used a CAS approach to examine how healthcare teams interacted and shared information. They found that found that team interaction patterns need to match their task environment.

They found evidence in their study that participative team interaction patterns were associated with a team's extensive sharing of information and, in turn, with team effectiveness in both routine and nonroutine task contexts. Especially in nonroutine task contexts, recurring team interaction patterns were found to be undesirable, with little information being exchanged amongst team members, and this rendered the team ineffective.

To be effective as a team, its members needed to be aware of the patterns in their team interactions so that they can move to or stay in a mode in which they share and use each other's information in the best possible way.

They argue that leaders of teams need to make themselves aware of the benefits of different interaction patterns. This will increase team participation and effectiveness in delivering their collective goals. Recurring interaction patterns among the team members lead to less collaboration and are to be avoided. Based on their results, the authors suggest that coaching guidance is especially important in restoring the effectiveness of knowledge-intensive work teams.

3.4.4 Knowledge review

Before you move on, can you define the following key concepts:

- Complex adaptive systems?

3.4.5 Question to think about

Looking at a recent interaction of you or a family member with your local healthcare system. How well did it meet your needs? Did it seem to be run to maximise the quality of your experience and outcomes, or for the benefit of the provider organisation?

References

Australian Institute of Health and Welfare. (2022, September 29). *Chronic condition multimorbidity.* AIHW, Australian Government.

Campion-Awwad, O., Hayton, A., Smith, L., & Vuaran, M. (2014). *The national programme for IT in the NHS - A case history, MPhil public policy 2014.* University of Cambridge.

Case, A., & Deaton, A. (2015, December 8). Rising morbidity and mortality in midlife among white non-Hispanic Americans in the 21st century. *Proceedings of the National Academy of Sciences of the United States of America, 112*(49), 15078–15083.

Center for Medicare & Medicaid Services. (2021, December 15). *National health expenditure data: Historical.* Center for Medicare & Medicaid Services.

Degenhardt, L., Charlson, F., Ferrari, A., Santomauro, D., Erskine, H., Mantilla-Herrara, A., ... Vos, T. (2018). The global burden of disease attributable to alcohol and drug use in 195 countries and territories, 1990–2016: a systematic analysis for the Global Burden of Disease Study 2016. *The Lancet Psychiatry*, 5(12), 987–1012.

Galea, S., Tracy, M., Hoggatt, K. J., Dimaggio, C., & Karpati, A. (2011, August). Estimated deaths attributable to social factors in the United States. *American Journal of Public Health*, 101(8), 1456–1465.

Gillies, A., & Smith, P. (2022). Can AI systems meet the ethical requirements of professional decision-making in health care? *AI Ethics*, 2, 41–47.

Haque, M., Islam, T., Rahman, N. A. A., McKimm, J., Abdullah, A., & Dhingra, S. (2020). Strengthening primary health-care services to help prevent and control long-term (chronic) non-communicable diseases in low-and middle-income countries. *Risk Management and Healthcare Policy*, 18(13), 409–426.

Hoogeboom, M. A., & Wilderom, C. P. (2020). A complex adaptive systems approach to real-life team interaction patterns, task context, information sharing, and effectiveness. *Group & Organization Management*, 45(1), 3–42.

ISO. (2016). *Medical devices — Quality management systems — Requirements for regulatory purposes*. International Standards Organisation.

Joseph, A. L., Kushniruk, A. W., & Borycki, E. M. (2020). Patient journey mapping: Current practices, challenges and future opportunities in healthcare. *Knowledge Management & E-Learning*, 12(4), 387–404.

Kings Fund. (2019, September 19). *What is commissioning and how is it changing?*. Kings Fund.

Kübler-Ross, E. (2009). *On death and dying* (40th ed.). Routledge.

Li, X., Mukandavire, C., Cucunubá, Z. M., Londono, S. E., Abbas, K., Clapham, H. E., ... Garske, T. (2021). Estimating the health impact of vaccination against ten pathogens in 98 low-income and middle-income countries from 2000 to 2030: A modelling study. *The Lancet*, 397(10272), 398–408.

Likhar, A., Baghel, P., & Patil, M. (2022). Early childhood development and social determinants. *Cureus*, 14(9), e29500.

Longman, J., Johnston, J., Ewald, D., Gilliland, A., Burke, M., Mutonga, T., & Passey, M. (2021). What could prevent chronic condition admissions assessed as preventable in rural and metropolitan contexts? An analysis of clinicians' perspectives from the DaPPHne study. *PLoS One*, 16(1), e0244313.

Marmot, M. G., Rose, G., Shipley, M., & Hamilton, P. J. (1978, December). Employment grade and coronary heart disease in British civil servants. *Journal of Epidemiology and Community Health*, 32(4), 244–249.

McGinnis, J. M., & Foege, W. H. (1993, November 10) Actual causes of death in the United States. *JAMA*, 270(18), 2207–2212.

McGinnis, J. M., Williams-Russo, P., & Knickman, J. R. (2002, March–April). The case for more active policy attention to health promotion. *Health Aff (Millwood)*, 21(2), 78–93.

Muennig, P., Fiscella, K., Tancredi, D., & Franks, P. (2010, September). The relative health burden of selected social and behavioral risk factors in the United States: Implications for policy. *American Journal of Public Health*, 100(9), 1758–1764.

Popkin, B. M. (2014). Synthesis and implications: China's nutrition transition in the context of changes across other low-and middle-income countries. *Obesity Reviews*, 15, 60–67. https://onlinelibrary.wiley.com/doi/pdfdirect/10.1111/obr.12120

Thomas, S. A., Browning, C. J., Charchar, F. J., Klein, B., Ory, M. G., Bowden-Jones, H., & Chamberlain, S. R. (2023). Transforming global approaches to chronic disease prevention and management across the lifespan: integrating genomics, behavior change, and digital health solutions. *Frontiers in Public Health*, 11, 1248254.

UN DESA. (2023). *The sustainable development goals report 2023: Special edition - July 2023.* UN DESA. © UN DESA.

World Health Organization. (2017). Global action plan on the public health response to dementia 2017–2025 WHO Geneva 7 December 2017.

World Health Organisation. (2020). *World health statistics 2020: Monitoring health for the SDGs, sustainable development goals*. World Health Organisation.

World Health Organisation. (2024). *Operational framework for monitoring social determinants of health equity*. Licence: CC BY-NC-SA 3.0 IGO. ISBN: ISBN 978-92-4-008832-0

Zhao, D. (2021). Epidemiological features of cardiovascular disease in Asia. *JACC: Asia*, 1(1), 1–13.

4 The impact of finance on health

4.1 The link between the income of countries and their health outcomes

The most common indicator for the wealth of a nation is GDP, which is defined as the total value of goods produced and services provided in a country during one year. In order to compare countries of varying populations, we need to consider the GDP per citizen or per capita to provide a measure of average wealth.

Health outcomes are measured using a wider variety of indicators. One of the most common is years of life expectancy at birth. In Figure 4.1, the GDP per capita is compared to the life expectancy at birth.

The life expectancy data come from the UN and the economic data from the World Bank and covers 190 countries (Our World In Data, 2022). The income is measured in international dollars at 2015 prices, a measure designed to adjust for inflation and for differences in the cost of living between countries.

The data show a moderate to strong correlation between GDP per capita and the life expectancy at birth, with a correlation coefficient of 0.73, meaning that most richer countries have a higher life expectancy at birth, although there are some interesting outliers that buck the trend. Although countries like Ireland, Singapore, and Luxembourg conform to the high-income long life norm, countries like Japan and Hong Kong (considered separately from mainland China) achieve higher life expectancies at lower income levels. China, although achieving lower life expectancy than the best performers, still outperforms expectations against its average income.

The distribution is characterised by a large tail at the lower end, where the poorest countries not only fail to reach the level of life expectancy expected for their income levels, but do so by a disproportionate margin. This effect is most pronounced in the five nations with the lowest recorded life expectancy: Somalia, Central African Republic, Lesotho, Nigeria, and Chad, of which Nigeria has a relatively higher income but the second lowest life expectancy.

In order to consider how much of this effect is due to healthcare, as opposed to other determinants of health, Figure 4.2 shows the relationship between life expectancy at birth and health expenditure per person. Once again, the life expectancy data come from the UN and the economic data from the World Bank and covers 190 countries, (Our World In Data, 2021) and the expenditure is measured in international dollars at 2015 prices.

This data are less widely available, so this comparison is based upon a group of 50 countries for which timely and relatively reliable data are available, and the data are approximately one year older. This makes precise comparison with the previous dataset less reliable. These indicators have a slightly weaker positive correlation of 0.67.

DOI: 10.4324/9781003478874-5

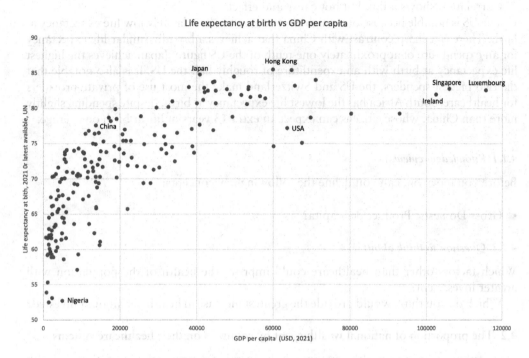

Figure 4.1 GDP per capita compared to the life expectancy at birth.

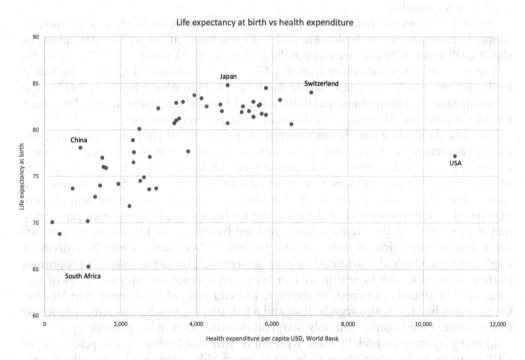

Figure 4.2 Healthcare expenditure per capita compared to the life expectancy at birth.

Correlation shows a link but not cause and effect.

The US is notable because of its high expenditure but its relatively low life expectancy at birth. There is a sharp contrast with China that achieves a broadly similar life expectancy for an expenditure of approximately one-tenth of the US figure. Japan achieves the highest life expectancy at birth with an expenditure of roughly half the US. It is also notable that the two biggest spenders, the US and Switzerland make the most use of private providers for healthcare. South Africa has the lowest life expectancy at birth, despite spending slightly more than China, whose citizens can expect an extra 13 years of life at birth on average.

4.1.1 *Knowledge review*

Before you move on, can you define the following key concepts:

- Gross Domestic Product per capita?

4.1.2 *Question to think about*

Which factors other than healthcare could improve the health of the population with greater investment?

Which do you think would provide the greatest increase in health per amount invested?

4.2 The proportion of national wealth spent by countries on their healthcare systems

One of the commonest health economic indicators is the proportion of national wealth spent by countries on their healthcare systems. This is a measure of the affordability of healthcare for countries.

Figure 4.3 shows the relationship between the percentage of GDP, as a measure of national wealth, spent on healthcare and life expectancy at birth. The percentage of global GDP spent on healthcare was 8.62% in the year 2000, rising to 10.89% by 2020.

The life expectancy data come from the UN and the economic data from the World Bank and covers 173 countries (World Bank, 2023; Our World In Data, 2022). The income is measured in international dollars at 2015 prices, a measure designed to adjust for inflation and for differences in the cost of living between countries.

The data show a low correlation between the percentage of GDP spent on healthcare and life expectancy at birth, with a correlation coefficient of 0.36, meaning that some countries spend a high proportion of their national wealth on healthcare without achieving longer lives for their citizens. Others spend a lower proportion of their income and achieve longer lives such as Japan and Singapore. Nigeria is an example of a country that spends a low proportion of their income on healthcare, but whose citizens enjoy only a proportion of the life expectancy realised by citizens of other countries investing a similar proportion of their national income on healthcare. Even the citizens of Zimbabwe, a country characterised by poor governance, investing a similar proportion of their national wealth in healthcare can expect on average an extra 6.5 years of life. Citizens of Indonesia can expect, on average, 15 extra years of life compared to Nigeria. On the other hand, Lesotho spends three and a half times as much of its national income on healthcare than Nigeria with only marginal improvements in life expectancy.

In many countries, especially those with publicly funded healthcare, the percentage of GDP spent on healthcare appears to be on an inexorable rising trend, and static economies and ageing populations are just two non-health factors that are predicted to continue this trend.

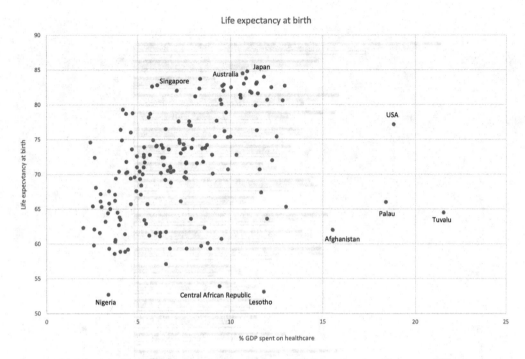

Life expectancy at birth

Figure 4.3 The relationship between the percentage of GDP spent on healthcare and life expectancy at birth by country.

Figure 4.4 shows the increasing percentage of GDP spent on healthcare in OECD countries in the years 2000, 2010, and 2019. 2019 is used instead of 2020 to avoid the distorting effect of the COVID-19 pandemic (OECD, 2024). In all countries, the trend is upwards.

One of the consequences of using this measure is that economic downturns can drive cutbacks and innovations in healthcare. This is often seen as the consequence of an increase in healthcare costs, when it is actually an increase in the affordability of healthcare. This is especially prevalent in healthcare systems funded by public schemes, primarily from taxation or universal social health insurance.

The onset of the global financial crisis in 2007 provided a significant disruption to the health system, originating externally, which severely impacted the availability of health resources, whilst creating an environment that impacts negatively on health. According to Mladovsky et al. (2012), this crisis posed three primary challenges for policymakers:

- Health systems require predictable sources of revenue with which to plan investment, determine budgets, and purchase goods and services. Sudden interruptions to public revenue streams can make it difficult to maintain necessary levels of healthcare.
- Cuts to public spending on health made in response to an economic shock typically come at a time when health systems may require more, not fewer, resources – for example, to address the adverse health effects of unemployment.
- Arbitrary cuts to essential services may further destabilise the health system if they erode financial protection, equitable access to care, and the quality of care provided,

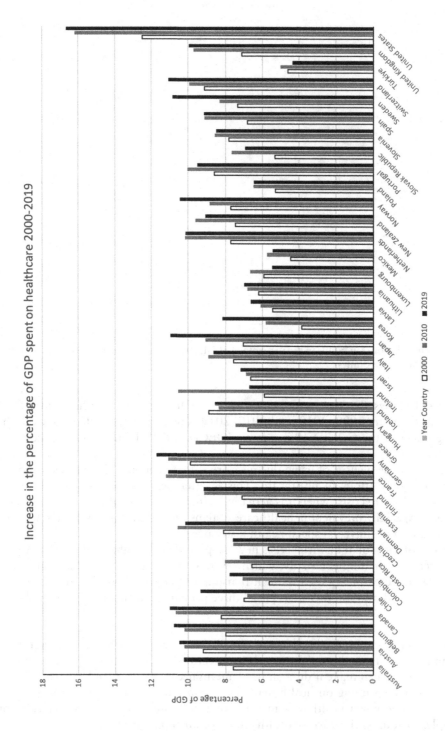

Figure 4.4 Rising proportion of GDP devoted to healthcare.

increasing health and other costs in the longer term. In addition to introducing new inefficiencies, cuts across the board are unlikely to address existing inefficiencies, potentially exacerbating the fiscal constraint (Mladovsky et al., 2012).

In 2009, the Regional Committee for Europe of the World Health Organisation (WHO) urged the member states to preserve universal access to effective health services during economic downturns.

Of the 53 nations making up the WHO European region at the time, just under one-quarter (13) increased the proportion of the government spending allocated to health and less than one-eighth reduced the proportion in the year following the crisis, but the impact was felt for much longer, and arguably, pandemic readiness was affected as late as 2020, when COVID-19 arrived, due to years of austerity and cost controls.

In the wake of the crisis, some countries cut national health budgets by over 20%. Rising unemployment reduced social insurance contributions in Bulgaria, Estonia, Hungary, and Romania. Finland implemented an economic stimulus package and saw an investment in the short term to protect government revenues in the longer term.

Various countries experienced different impacts on health budgets and policies, but almost universally trade-offs were made in policy decisions and the need to focus on enhancing value in the health system was emphasised.

The impact of the COVID-19 pandemic triggered a much bigger impact both on economic prosperity and on demand for healthcare. Whilst much of the response to the 2008 economic downturn was concerned with increasing economic efficiency, the greater impact of the COVID-19 pandemic following on from over a decade of economic austerity has led to significant innovations and the ongoing adoption of new methods of working beyond the pandemic.

Perhaps the most significant is the continued uptake of telemedicine, which rose to prominence during the pandemic but has been retained, because it is seen as a method of increasing productivity and access to medical staff, who are increasingly recognised as a scarce resource. Whilst this has predominantly been a feature of higher income countries, India is rolling out what may become the world's biggest telehealth project (Rajkumar et al., 2023), and Rwanda has introduced universal primary healthcare coverage and additional maternal health services using telemedicine (Nkurunziza et al., 2022).

Why Estonia's healthcare system was better equipped to deal with the financial crisis (after Mladovsky et al., 2012)

Certain countries, including the Czech Republic, Estonia, Italy, Lithuania, Republic of Moldova, and Slovakia, were better equipped to handle the financial crisis due to fiscal measures they had implemented prior to its onset. These countries had the ability to utilise reserves or implement other counter-cyclical measures to offset the decline in payroll tax revenues. This stands in contrast to countries like Hungary, where the healthcare system had already depleted its non-structural efficiency reserves by the time the financial crisis commenced, making it susceptible to a rapid erosion of healthcare goals.

For instance, Estonia, at the outset of the crisis, reduced public spending, including healthcare expenditure, as a strategic decision to meet the Maastricht criteria for Eurozone accession. Estonia's favourable economic conditions, characterised by low external debt and a minimal current account deficit, allowed for deficit financing as a feasible alternative.

Estonia's healthcare system demonstrated superior readiness for fiscal constraints compared to many neighbouring countries, primarily stemming from two factors. Firstly, a prior commitment to prioritise healthcare spending during economic downturns enabled the healthcare sector to accumulate reserves in its insurance fund, granting it a stronger bargaining position in budget negotiations with the Ministry of Finance. Consequently, transparent political discourse ensued regarding where and how much to allocate cuts. Secondly, Estonia's healthcare system had made appropriate investments in the sector prior to the crisis, enabling it to withstand delays in investment without compromising short-term healthcare objectives such as maintaining service quality.

However, the Estonian Health Insurance Fund supervisory board still attempted to ration the volume of care provided by deciding to increase maximum waiting times for outpatient specialists' visits from four to six weeks in March 2009. No other countries reported increasing waiting as an explicit policy response to the financial crisis.

4.2.1 Knowledge review

Before you move on, can you define the following key concepts:

• The affordability of healthcare (at a national level)?

4.2.2 Question to think about

If you were responsible for slowing the upward trend in the proportion of GDP spent on healthcare, what measures do you think you would prioritise? (This is a question you may like to reconsider when you have read the whole book to see if your view has changed.)

4.3 Health outcome measures

Life expectancy at birth is a relatively crude health outcome measure but its simplicity lends itself to global comparisons. Life expectancies can be calculated for any age and give the further number of years a person can on average expect to live given the age they have attained. In practice, raw life expectancy measures can be applied in two different ways: period life expectancy and cohort life expectancy.

Period life expectancy refers to the average number of years a person is expected to live, based on current mortality rates within a specific period. It provides a snapshot of expected lifespan at a particular point in time, as we have done so far in this chapter. It is calculated by examining the age-specific death rates in a given period (e.g., a year) and then projecting these rates into the future to estimate the average lifespan. It is normally used for broad comparisons across different populations or time periods.

Cohort life expectancy refers to the average number of years a group of individuals born in the same year is expected to live from a given point in time. It is calculated by following a specific birth cohort (a group of individuals born in the same year) over their lifetimes, tracking their mortality rates at different ages until the last member of the cohort dies.

It is useful for analysing changes in mortality patterns over time and for understanding how factors, such as advances in healthcare, lifestyle changes, or social conditions, impact the lifespan of a particular generation.

A useful method of assessing health outcomes is the quality-adjusted life year (QALY). The idea of QALY is simple: it assumes that a year of life lived in perfect health is worth 1 QALY (1 Year of Life × 1 Utility = 1 QALY) and that a year of life lived in a state of less than this perfect health is worth less than 1. To determine the exact QALY value, it is necessary to multiply the utility value associated with a given state of health by the years lived in that state. QALYs are therefore expressed in terms of "years lived in perfect health."

Half a year lived in perfect health is equivalent to 0.5 QALYs (0.5 years × 1 Utility), as is one year of life lived in a situation with utility 0.5 (e.g. bedridden) (1 year × 0.5 Utility) (Drummond et al., 2015).

Prieto and Sacristán (2003) critiqued the use of QALYs on both methodological and ethical grounds, but acknowledged their popularity, and that persists to this day.

Linked to the concept of QALYs is the concept of health-adjusted life expectancy (HALE). This is defined as the average number of years that a person can expect to live in "full health" by taking into account years lived in less than full health due to disease and/or injury (World Health Organisation, 2019). As with simple life expectancy, it can be calculated from any age, from birth onwards.

Figure 4.5 shows how the average healthy life expectancy at birth compares to the raw life expectancy at birth for each World Health Organisation region, with data

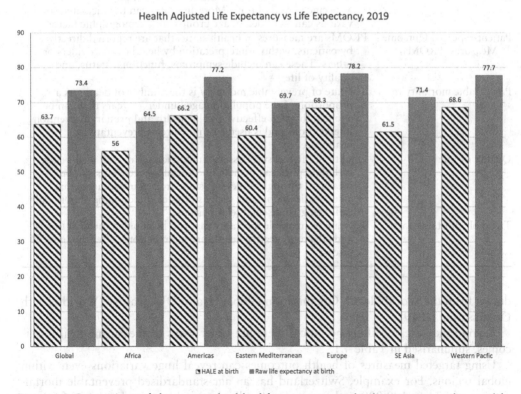

Figure 4.5 Comparison of the average healthy life expectancy at birth compares to the raw life expectancy at birth for each WHO region.

Table 4.1 Measures of health outcomes (or more often the lack of health outcomes)

Indicator	Description
Disability-adjusted life years (DALYs)	Disability-adjusted life years (DALYs) are a measure of overall disease burden, expressed as the number of years lost due to ill-health, disability, or early death. DALYs are calculated by taking the sum of the years of life lost due to dying early and the. years lost due to disease or years lived with disability/disease.
Disease-specific outcomes	For specific diseases or conditions, there may be specialised measures to assess outcomes relevant to that condition. For example, disease-specific symptom scales or clinical markers may be used.
Functional status	Functional status measures assess an individual's ability to perform activities of daily living, such as bathing, dressing, eating, and mobility. This can be particularly relevant for assessing the impact of chronic diseases or disabilities on a person's daily life.
Health-Related Quality of Life (HRQOL)	HRQOL measures specifically focus on how a person's health affects their quality of life. This can include aspects such as physical functioning, pain, mental health, and social relationships.
Morbidity rates	Morbidity refers to the prevalence or incidence of disease or illness within a population. Morbidity rates can be measured through surveys, medical records, or administrative data.
Mortality rates	This measures the number of deaths in a given population over a specific period of time. Mortality rates can be calculated for various causes of death, age groups, and demographic factors.
Patient-reported Outcome Measures (PROMs)	PROMs are measures of health status that are reported directly by patients, without interpretation by healthcare providers or others. These can include symptoms, functional status, and quality of life.
Preventable mortality rates	The rate of preventable mortality is the number of deaths as a proportion of the population aged under 75 years that can be avoided through effective public health and primary prevention interventions and is used as a measure of preventative healthcare.
Quality of Life	Quality of life measures assess an individual's overall well-being, including physical, mental, and social aspects. This can be measured through surveys or standardised instruments that assess various domains such as physical functioning, emotional well-being, and social relationships.
Treatable mortality rates	The rate of treatable mortality that can be avoided through timely and effective curative healthcare interventions, after the onset of disease.

drawn from the World Health Organisation Global Health Observatory (World Health Organisation, 2019).

Beyond measures of life expectancy, there are other ways of measuring health outcomes, summarised in Table 4.1.

Using targeted measures of health outcomes can reveal huge variations even within global regions. For example, Switzerland has an age-standardised preventable mortality rate of 83 per 100,000 and an age-standardised treatable mortality rate of 39 per

100,000. Latvia, at the end of the European scale has an age-standardised preventable mortality rate of 256 per 100,000 and an age-standardised treatable mortality rate of 149 per 100,000 (OECD Health Statistics, 2021).

Targeted measures like this are important for policymakers seeking to identify priority areas to address.

What does the US get for its high expenditure on healthcare? (after Mackinnon et al., 2023)

Mackinnon et al. (2023) compared health outcomes in the US with Australia, Canada, France, Germany, Japan, the Netherlands, New Zealand, Norway, South Korea, Sweden, Switzerland, and the United Kingdom (UK). They discovered that despite the United States having considerably higher healthcare expenditure per capita and as a percentage of GDP, it was the only country studied that lacks universal health coverage, a distinction unique among the countries studied. It has the lowest life expectancy at birth and experiences the highest rates of mortality from preventable or treatable conditions, as well as the highest maternal and infant mortality rates, along-side elevated suicide rates. The US has the highest proportion of individuals with multiple chronic conditions and an obesity rate nearly double the OECD average.

In 2020, the US recorded the highest infant mortality rate among the countries analysed, with 5.4 deaths per 1,000 live births, whereas Norway reported 1.6 deaths per 1,000 live births. Factors such as a high prevalence of caesarean sections, inadequate prenatal care, and socioeconomic disparities contributing to chronic diseases like obesity, diabetes, and heart disease, are all likely factors in the elevated infant and maternal mortality rates in the United States.

Although life expectancy at birth in the United States was 77 years in 2020, which is three years lower than the OECD average, it decreased further in 2021 despite being past the peak of the COVID-19 pandemic. Vaccination rates against COVID-19 in the US lag behind those of many comparator nations.

There are racial and ethnic disparities in life expectancy within the United States, with non-Hispanic Black Americans and non-Hispanic American Indians or Alaska natives experiencing life expectancies four and seven years lower, respectively, than non-Hispanic Whites. However, Hispanic Americans have a life expectancy higher than that of Whites and comparable to their racial peers in several other countries studied. Most surprisingly, Asian Americans, as a group, display a higher life expectancy than even the general population of Japan, who enjoy one of the highest life expectancies at birth of any country in the world.

The US has one of the lowest rates of practicing physicians and hospital beds per 1,000 population, and Americans have fewer physician consultations on average compared to individuals in most other countries.

The US does perform well in terms of preventive healthcare screening rates for breast and colorectal cancer, as well as influenza vaccination rates, which rank among the highest globally. The country also boasts a substantial number of Magnetic Resonance Imaging (MRI) scanners per capita, ranking second only to Japan. However, MRIs in the United States are notably more expensive than in other countries, with costs averaging 42% higher than those in the UK and 420% higher than those in Australia, contributing to higher overall healthcare spending.

The US is economically polarised in terms of household incomes, and this suggests that the social determinants of health, together with the failure to provide universal health coverage play a major role in the poor health outcomes.

4.3.1 Knowledge review

Before you move on, can you define the following key concepts:

- Preventable mortality?
- Treatable mortality?

4.3.2 Question to think about

What do you think the USA could do to improve its health outcomes? What barriers do you think might prevent this?

4.4 The impact of poverty on the broader determinants of health

Healthcare is only one factor impacting on the health of the world's population. Poorer countries show many other characteristics that are determinants of poorer health, and water quality and food issues are amongst those with the biggest impact. These countries are ill-equipped financially to deal with the additional healthcare costs arising from the consequential increased disease burden.

4.4.1 Water quality and sanitation

For example, water quality and sanitation can have a massive impact on the health of a population. Examples of the worst affected countries that show the link between poverty and poor water and sanitation include:

- Niger, where 54% lack access to clean water; Niger is the largest country in West Africa and among the world's poorest countries. Over 40% of Niger's population lives on less than $2.15 a day.
- Papua New Guinea, where 55% lack basic water services; This is exacerbated by the remote locations of communities spread among the country's 600 Asia Pacific islands.
- Democratic Republic of the Congo, where 54% lack basic water services; The Democratic Republic of the Congo is Africa's second-largest country and nearly 64% of Congolese live in extreme poverty, making it among the five poorest nations in the world.
- Ethiopia, where 53% lack basic access to clean water; Ethiopia has Africa's second highest population, and where the northern highlands often receive plentiful rainfall, but periods of severe drought and rainfall variability make water supplies unreliable especially for rural people, who make up 80% of the population (World Vision, 2023).

Angelakis et al. (2021) take a long-term historical view of the impact of clean water or its lack on health and life expectancy:

> *Overall life expectancy worldwide has almost doubled in the last 118 years, increasing from 31 years in 1900 to 72 in 2016 [67]. This has been particularly true for well-developed countries. A good European example is Finland, where an increase from 42.8 years in 1900 to 81.4 in 2018 was observed. This is the result of several factors, but water purification and a well-organised water supply system played a major role.*

In poorer parts of the world, major challenges remain, and improvements in water quality and sanitation may prove a more rapid and cost-effective route to health improvements than better healthcare.

According to the World Health Organisation (WHO, 2023), in 2021, over two billion people live in water-stressed countries, which is expected to be exacerbated in some regions as a result of climate change and population growth. In 2022, at least 1.7 billion people globally use a drinking water source contaminated with faeces. Microbial contamination of drinking water as a result of contamination with faeces poses the greatest risk to drinking water safety.

Diseases such as diarrhoea, cholera, dysentery, typhoid and polio can be transmitted by microbiologically contaminated drinking water, and this transmission is estimated to cause approximately 505,000 diarrhoeal deaths each year. In 2022, over one-quarter of the global population did not have access to a safely managed drinking water service – that is, one located on premises, available when needed, and free from contamination.

Clean water is covered by United Nations Sustainable Goal 6:

> By 2030, achieve universal and equitable access to safe and affordable drinking water for all and achieve access to adequate and equitable sanitation and hygiene for all and end open defecation, paying special attention to the needs of women and girls and those in vulnerable situations.

For this to be achieved, overall progress will need to be six times faster on drinking water, five times faster on sanitation, and three times faster on hygiene. At the current rate of progress, by 2030, two billion people will still be living without safely managed drinking water, 3 billion without safely managed sanitation, and 1.4 billion without basic hygiene services (UN-Water, 2023).

Clean water improvements in Shanghai (after Angelakis et al., 2021)

Angelakis et al. (2021) cite Shanghai in China as a modern example of improvements in sanitation leading to health improvements.

Since the 1980s, efficient water supply has become a goal of the Shanghai authorities.

This goal led to concrete improvements after the year 2000, when the required measures were taken and problems of "secondary pollution" due to water pipes and roof tank rust were solved, and at the same time, specific relevant jobs were created and promoted. The use of modern technology and standardised testing methods has gradually improved water quality and supply systems.

The latest "Urban City for Excellence" project is led by the "Shanghai Urban Master Plan" initiative. Water treatment enterprises, such as the "Shanghai State-Owned Drinking Water Company," have made significant improvements by leveraging computer network management, enhancing customer service, implementing efficient pipe network dispatching systems, and fortifying the development and utilisation of water supply information resources. At the same time, the city is undergoing water purification optimisation procedures and a new pipe network is geared towards pre-empting secondary pollution and leakage within distribution units, enhancing operational reliability, and fostering increased production and automation capabilities.

4.4.2 Hunger, diet, and food safety

Food plays a major part in global health. Malnutrition is an imbalance between the nutrients your body needs to function and the nutrients it gets and includes under- and overnutrition.

Around one-in-eight of the global population are malnourished. Whilst this marks a remarkable decline since the end of the Second World War, when almost half of the world's population was undernourished, nearly one billion people remain undernourished and over two billion not have consistent access to nutritious, safe, and sufficient food in 2022. At the same time, in high-income countries and increasingly in middle income countries, 1.4 billion are now overweight with 500 million of those classed as obese. Child malnutrition is high around the world. In 2021, 22.3% (148.1 million) children were stunted, 6.8% (45 million) were wasted, whilst 5.6% (37 million) were overweight (United Nations Children's Fund (UNICEF), 2023). Undernutrition, obesity, and micronutrient deficiencies are all associated with poverty and increase the burden of disease and associated healthcare costs.

The Global Hunger Index (GHI), compiled by a German non-profit organisation, ranks countries on a 100-point scale, 0 representing zero/no hunger. The GHI scores are based on four indicators. Taken together, the component indicators reflect deficiencies in calories as well as in micronutrients. Thus, the GHI reflects both aspects of hunger (undernutrition and undernourishment).

1. Undernourishment: the share of the population whose caloric intake is insufficient.
2. Child Stunting: the share of children under the age of five who have low height for their age.
3. Child Wasting: the share of children under the age of five who have low weight for their height.
4. Child Mortality: the mortality rate of children under the age of five (a reflection of the fatal mix of inadequate nutrition and unhealthy environments).

The 2023 GHI score for the world is 18.3, which is considered moderate. Globally, the share of people who are undernourished has increased to 9.2%. Improvements in global hunger have stagnated because of multiple factors such as the COVID-19 pandemic, the Russia–Ukraine war, and climate change.

The regions with the highest hunger levels in the world are South Asia and Sub-Saharan Africa. Each region has a GHI score of 27, indicating "serious" hunger.

The 2023 Global Hunger Index gives India, the most populous country in the world, a rank of 111 out of 125 countries. This indicates a hunger severity level of "serious" for the country. This also marks a fall from the previous year's rank of 107.

India's GHI score is 28.7 on a 100-point scale, where 0 is the best score (no hunger) and 100 is the worst. From 2000 to 2015, India made good strides in the GHI rank while from 2015, India has advanced on the GHI by only 0.5 points. Latin America and the Caribbean are the only regions in the world whose GHI scores have worsened between 2015 and 2023. On the other hand, China is among the top 20 countries that each have a GHI score of less than 5. The regions with the lowest GHI score are Europe and Central Asia, whose score of 6.0 is considered "low."

The health consequences of undernutrition include:

- Stunted growth and development: In children, undernutrition can impair physical and cognitive development, leading to stunted growth, delayed motor development, and lower intelligence quotient (IQ).
- Weak immune system: Undernutrition weakens the immune system, making individuals more susceptible to infections and diseases.
- Muscle wasting: In severe cases, undernutrition can lead to the breakdown of muscle tissue, causing weakness and loss of muscle mass.
- Organ damage: Chronic undernutrition can damage organs, such as the liver, kidneys, and heart, leading to long-term health complications.
- Immunity and wound healing: Immune function is also affected, increasing the risk of infection due to impaired cell-mediated immunity and cytokine, complement and phagocyte function. Delayed wound healing is also well-described in undernourished surgical patients (Saunders & Smith, 2010).

In addition, there are further consequences arising from deficiencies of specific essential vitamins and minerals. A deficiency of Vitamin A can cause vision problems, weakened immune function, and impaired growth and development. A deficiency of Vitamin D can lead to weakened bones, muscle weakness, and increased risk of fractures. Iodine deficiency is a cause of thyroid disorders and impaired cognitive development. Calcium deficiency, especially in older people, can lead to weakened bones (osteoporosis) and increased risk of fractures, and deficiency of iron can lead to anaemia, fatigue, weakness, and impaired cognitive function.

Undernutrition is a significant issue among elderly individuals during hospitalisation, posing a considerable healthcare burden globally (Bellanti et al., 2022). In hospitalised patients, malnutrition exacerbates health outcomes, increasing mortality, morbidity, infection rates, prolonging hospital stays, hindering response to medical interventions, and escalating healthcare costs (Correia et al., 2017). The rise in undernutrition-related illnesses among individuals with multiple health conditions is a pressing concern, influenced by both the aging population and advancements in healthcare. Notably, this demographic requires hospitalisation more frequently, with between 20% and 50% already undernourished upon admission. Alarmingly, nearly half of malnourished patients hospitalised for over a week either maintain or worsen their nutritional status. Furthermore, approximately one-third of patients with adequate nutrition before hospitalisation become undernourished during their hospital stay.

In 2019, globally, the prevalence of undernutrition was estimated at 16,835 per 100,000 population, with higher rates in females than males. Over the period from 2000 to 2019, there was a consistent annual decrease in undernutrition prevalence worldwide, albeit more pronounced in males. The burden of undernutrition-related disability-adjusted life years (DALYs) stood at around 50 million in 2019, with rates higher in females. However, there was a larger decrease in DALYs observed in males over the same period. Malnutrition-related DALY rates decreased annually across all regions, with the most significant reductions observed in South-East Asia and Africa. Additionally, undernutrition-related mortality showed an annual decline, with the highest age-standardised death rates observed in Africa. Lower income countries experienced higher undernutrition-related DALYs and mortality rates, with consistent reductions over the years (Chong et al., 2023).

Whilst undernutrition is on the decline globally, overnutrition leading to obesity is a growing problem globally. The health consequences from the excess intake of sugars and refined carbohydrates can contribute to the development of insulin resistance and type 2 diabetes. Overconsumption of high-fat and high-sugar foods can lead to obesity, hypertension, and elevated cholesterol levels, increasing the risk of heart disease and stroke. Overnutrition can disrupt the body's metabolic processes, leading to conditions, such as fatty liver disease and metabolic syndrome, and excess weight puts added stress on joints, leading to conditions such as osteoarthritis.

In 2019, there were an estimated 160 million disability-adjusted life years (DALYs) related to obesity globally, with a higher rate in males (2070 per 100,000 population) compared to females (1790 per 100,000 population). From 2000 to 2019, there was a 0.48% annual increase in age-standardised DALY rates related to obesity, with a larger increase observed in males than in females. Obesity-related DALYs varied across geographical regions, with the Eastern Mediterranean region having the highest rates and Europe the lowest. Trends in obesity-related DALYs also varied based on socio-demographic index (SDI), with higher SDI countries experiencing decreases and lower SDI countries experiencing increases. Overall, there were 5.0 million obesity-related deaths worldwide in 2019, with higher rates in males compared to females. From 2000 to 2019, the overall age-standardised death rate remained relatively constant, with increases observed in males and decreases in females. Projections suggest that obesity-related DALYs and mortality are expected to increase in the coming decade, with a widening gap between obesity and malnutrition burdens (Chong et al., 2023).

More than half (51%) of the global population will be living with overweight or obesity within 12 years unless prevention, treatment, and support improve, according to the World Obesity Federation (Mahase, 2023). This is up from 38% of the world's population in 2020.

In 2023, the federation reported that the economic impact of overweight and obesity on the world is set to reach $4.32tn annually by 2035. This represents nearly 3% of global GDP and is comparable with the impact of COVID-19 in 2020.

Obesity is no longer just a problem in higher-income countries. The impact on low and lower-middle-income countries will be an estimated $370 billion a year. The report found that 9 out of the 10 countries with the greatest expected increases in obesity globally were low or lower middle income, and all were either in Africa or Asia.

Poverty alleviation in Indonesia

The issue of poverty in Indonesia has worsened in recent times and remains unresolved. Efforts to alleviate poverty and inequality with their associated health consequences are complex, exemplified by the implementation of the Family Hope Program. The programme aims to break the cycle of intergenerational poverty by enhancing human capital accumulation, aligning with the UN SDGs.

The Family Hope Program is a conditional cash transfer programme launched by the Government of Indonesia in 2007. Since then, its beneficiary coverage has reached 10 million families with the goal of reducing intergenerational poverty. The programme is aimed at very poor families meeting set criteria and is the primary implementation mechanism. These criteria include having pregnant, postpartum, or under-five children, or children aged 5–7 not yet in school, among others (Parawangi & Wahid, 2023).

The programme has dual objectives: providing social assistance to meet basic needs, particularly in education and health and empowering poor households to escape poverty through health promotion and education encouragement. Funds disbursed are intended to facilitate access to education and health services, contingent upon children attending school and receiving immunisations, and pregnant women undergoing regular check-ups. An impact evaluation of the Family Hope program showed that after six years of investment it has significantly improved human capital development. However, it is not a replacement for employment and therefore has not assisted families to become self-sufficient in regards to their livelihoods (Cahyadi et al., 2018).

The majority of beneficiaries who created businesses encountered various obstacles throughout the business cycle.

- Many lack official business licenses, hindering their ability to expand into broader commercial markets. Out of the 69 small business owners surveyed by Huda et al. (2020), only five possessed a home industry business permit typically obtained through local assistance programmes facilitating permit applications. However, like most livelihood development initiatives, information dissemination about such programmes was insufficient, resulting in a lack of awareness among programme participants.
- Numerous small business owners attempt to sell their products to intermediary buyers but struggle to meet packaging, hygiene, and other essential consumer standards. This limitation primarily stems from a lack of resources, capital, and production knowledge necessary to compete effectively in their chosen markets. For instance, one cassava chip producer mentioned her inability to preserve chips for more than a week without an oil-absorbing machine, thereby restricting access to distant markets. Another business owners expressed frustration over her basic sewing machine's inability to meet buyers' demands for sophisticated stitching, rendering her uncompetitive in a saturated market.
- Most small business owners possess basic education levels and lack bookkeeping skills essential for monitoring their businesses' performance. Only 12% maintain written accounting records, with many relying on whether they can meet their basic needs as a gauge of profitability. Additionally, some entrepreneurs overlook

the fact that their children often consume their stock, failing to incorporate this into their assessments.

- Small business owners specialising in services typically acquire their skills informally and lack formal qualifications in their respective fields. Consequently, they struggle to compete with certified service providers and often resort to supplementary income sources, such as parking attendants or domestic work, to augment their earnings (Huda et al., 2020),

Parawangi and Wahid (2023) report that effective execution necessitates collective commitment and coordination to modify organisational behaviours, fostering an environment conducive to achieving social welfare objectives. While the programme holds promise in reducing poverty, several obstacles have hindered its implementation. Public misunderstanding and perceived discrimination in aid distribution, along with participant characteristics influencing program support or rejection, have provided challenges. Additionally, there have been concerns about misuse of assistance for electoral purposes.

Despite these obstacles, qualitative research suggests significant positive changes among Family Hope Program recipients in Makassar City, indicating the programme's potential for poverty reduction, with consequent health benefits and reductions in the disease burden and the consequential healthcare costs.

4.4.3 Knowledge review

Before you move on, can you define the following key concepts:

- Malnutrition?
- Undernutrition?
- Overnutrition?

4.4.4 Question to think about

Are you more at risk of under- or over-nutrition? What are the most likely health complications, especially later in life?

References

Angelakis, A. N., Vuorinen, H. S., Nikolaidis, C., Juuti, P. S., Katko, T. S., Juuti, R. P., ... Samonis, G. (2021). Water quality and life expectancy: Parallel courses in time. *Water*, 13(6), 752.
Bellanti, F., Lo Buglio, A., Quiete, S., & Vendemiale, G. (2022). Malnutrition in hospitalised old patients: Screening and diagnosis, clinical outcomes, and management. *Nutrients*, 14(4), 910.
Cahyadi, N., Hanna, R., Olken, B. A., Prima, R. A., Satriawan, E., & Syamsulhakim, E. (2018). *Cumulative impacts of conditional cash transfer programs: Experimental evidence from Indonesia*. National Team for the Acceleration of Poverty Reduction (TNP2K).
Chong, B., Jayabaskaran, J., Kong, G., Chan, Y. H., Chin, Y. H., Goh, R., ... Chew, N. W. (2023). Trends and predictions of malnutrition and obesity in 204 countries and territories: an analysis of the global burden of disease study 2019. *EClinicalMedicine*, 57, 101850.
Correia, M. I. T., Perman, M. I., & Waitzberg, D. L. (2017). Hospital malnutrition in Latin America: A systematic review. *Clinical Nutrition*, 36(4), 958–967.

Drummond, M. F., Sculpher, M. J., Claxton, K., Stoddart, G. L., & Torrance, G. W. (2015). *Methods for the economic evaluation of health care programmes*. Oxford University Press.

Huda, K., Hidayati, D., Tamyis, A., et al. (2020). *Strengthening economic opportunities for family hope program families: A summary Australia - department of foreign affairs and trade*. DFATSMERU Research Institute.

Inciong, J. F. B., Chaudhary, A., Hsu, H. S., Joshi, R., Seo, J. M., Trung, L. V., ... Usman, N. (2020). Hospital malnutrition in northeast and southeast Asia: A systematic literature review. *Clinical Nutrition ESPEN*, 39, 30–45.

MacKinnon, N. J., Emery, V., Waller, J., Ange, B., Ambade, P., Gunja, M., & Watson, E. (2023). Mapping health disparities in 11 high-income nations. JAMA network open, 6(7), e2322310-e2322310.

Mahase, E. (2023). Global cost of overweight and obesity will hit $4.32tn a year by 2035, report warns. *BMJ*, 380, 580.

Mladovsky, P, Srivastava, D. et al. (2012). Health policy responses to the financial crisis in Europe. World Health Organization. Regional Office for Europe. Health Evidence Network, European Observatory on Health Systems and Policies.

Nkurunziza, T., Williams, W., Kateera, F., Riviello, R., Niyigena, A., Miranda, E., et al. (2022). mHealth-community health worker telemedicine intervention for surgical site infection diagnosis: a prospective study among women delivering via caesarean section in rural Rwanda. BMJ Global Health,7(7), e009365.

OECD. (2024). Topics: Health spending and financial sustainability, Organisation for Economic Cooperation and Development, Paris.

OECD Health Statistics. (2021). *Health at a glance 2021: OECD indicators*. Avoidable Mortality (Preventable and Treatable).

Our World In Data. (2021). Life expectancy vs. health expenditure, 2021.

Our World In Data. (2022). Life expectancy vs. GDP per capita, 2022.

Parawangi, A., & Wahid, N. (2023). Poverty alleviation in the hope family program in makassar city. *Journal of Local Government Issues (LOGOS)*, 6(1), 49–62.

Prieto, L., & Sacristán, J. A. (2003). Problems and solutions in calculating quality-adjusted life years (QALYs). *Health and Quality of Life Outcomes*, 1, 80.

Rajkumar, E., Gopi, A., Joshi, A., Thomas, A. E., Arunima, N. M., Ramya, G. S., et al. (2023). Applications, benefits and challenges of telehealth in India during COVID-19 pandemic and beyond: a systematic review. BMC Health Services Research, 23(1), 7.

Saunders, J., & Smith, T. (2010). Malnutrition: Causes and consequences. *Clinical Medicine* (London, England), 10(6), 624–627.

UNICEF. (2023). *State of food security and nutrition in the world (SOFI) 2023*. UNICEF Data.

UN-Water. (2023). *Blueprint for acceleration: Sustainable development goal 6 synthesis report on water and sanitation 2023 the message: Key findings and recommendations*. United Nations.

World Bank. (2023). Life expectancy at birth total years - World Bank Open Data, principally drawn from United Nations Population Division. World Population Prospects: 2022, World Bank Group.

World Health Organization. (2019). *WHO methods and data sources for life tables 1990-2019*. WHO.

World Health Organization. (2023). *Drinking-water 2023*. World Health Organization.

World Vision. (2023). *10 worst countries for access to clean water*. World Vision.

5 COVID-19 The impact of a once-in-a-century event

5.1 The development of the pandemic

The COVID-19 pandemic was the largest global infectious disease event since the Spanish flu pandemic in 1918–20 that killed in excess of 50 million people globally (Johnson & Mueller, 2002). This compares to around seven million deaths attributed to COVID-19 by 2024. COVID-19 disease is caused by the Severe-Acute-Respiratory-Syndrome-Related Coronavirus Strain 2 (SARS-CoV-2) virus and is closely related to the first strain of the virus that caused the original Severe-Acute-Respiratory-Syndrome (SARS) epidemic in 2002.

The outbreak began in Wuhan China in December 2019. During the initial 50 days of the COVID-19 outbreak, despite its spread to additional countries beyond China, global concerns remained relatively low. The prevailing belief was that individuals in direct contact with the Wuhan seafood market were at the highest risk of infection. Consequently, countries neighbouring China and those connected to Wuhan via air travel were primarily seen as vulnerable. Notable among these were Taiwan, Australia, United Arab Emirates, Hong Kong, Japan, and Thailand.

December 1, 2019 marked the earliest recorded symptoms of COVID-19, according to Huang et al. (2020), although other sources suggest similar cases may have emerged as early as November. The first patient with symptoms resembling pneumonia was identified as a 55-year-old male from Hubei province. However, it wasn't until late December that Chinese authorities recognised the emergence of a novel virus, with symptoms predominantly originating from Wuhan. Reports indicate the first patient may not have been linked to the Wuhan seafood market, contradicting earlier assumptions.

By December 8, hospitals in Wuhan reported a steady increase in patients exhibiting pneumonia-like symptoms. While precautionary measures were implemented, the full extent of the outbreak remained unclear. By December 29, fear had begun to spread, particularly through social media platforms like WeChat, indicating a growing awareness of a new virus. Initial cases were traced back to the Huanan Seafood Wholesale Market, prompting concerns about the virus' origin and mode of transmission.

On December 31, Chinese authorities officially reported the presence of a new virus to the WHO, marking the beginning of international attention. Precautionary measures were taken, including quarantining affected individuals. By January 1, 2020, the Wuhan seafood market was closed indefinitely, emphasising its suspected role in the outbreak. Public awareness campaigns and sanitation efforts were initiated to contain the spread.

Following the identification of the virus as a novel coronavirus on January 7, efforts intensified to understand its characteristics and transmission dynamics. Initial genome

DOI: 10.4324/9781003478874-6

sequencing confirmed suspicions regarding the market's involvement in the outbreak. Concerns regarding human-to-human transmission grew, prompting global health organisations to issue guidelines and advisories.

By January 12, the first case outside China was confirmed in Thailand, challenging assumptions about the virus' origin. Efforts to track and contain the spread intensified, with neighbouring countries implementing screening measures. International collaboration facilitated the sharing of critical data for vaccine development and diagnostic testing.

Subsequent days saw a rise in reported cases, with Thailand and Japan confirming additional infections. Screening measures were expanded, and diagnostic testing protocols were developed. Despite efforts to contain the virus, estimates suggested a significant underreporting of cases, highlighting the need for comprehensive surveillance and response strategies.

As the outbreak continued to evolve, global health organisations emphasised the importance of collaboration and information sharing. Efforts to develop diagnostic tests and vaccines intensified, underscoring the urgency of addressing the pandemic collectively.

By January 17, cases outside China had risen, prompting heightened surveillance and response measures globally. While progress was made in understanding the virus's characteristics, challenges remained in containing its spread and mitigating its impact on public health (Allam, 2020).

In the WHO European Region, surveillance for COVID-19 was initiated on January 27, 2020. Surveillance efforts in the European Region were coordinated by the European Centre for Disease Prevention and Control (ECDC) and the WHO Regional Office for Europe. Data collected included demographics, travel history, symptoms, and clinical outcomes. By January 31, 2020, 47 laboratories across 31 countries, including 38 in 24 European Union and European Economic Area (EU/EEA) countries, had diagnostic capability for the SARS-CoV-2 virus that caused COVID-19.

As of February 21, 2020, there were 47 confirmed cases in the WHO European Region, with the first three cases reported in France on January 24. The first death occurred on February 15 in France. By February 21, cases had been reported in Belgium, Finland, France, Germany, Italy, Russia, Spain, Sweden, and the UK. Among these cases, 14 were infected in China, while 21 were infected in Europe, with 14 linked to a cluster in Germany and seven to a cluster in France.

The median age of cases was 42 years, with a higher proportion of male cases among those acquired in Europe compared to those in China. Hospitalisation was common, with delays in identifying index cases leading to longer times for locally acquired cases to be isolated. Symptoms included fever, cough, weakness, and others, with some cases being asymptomatic.

Laboratory confirmation of cases involved specific assays targeting SARS-CoV-2 genes, with various specimen types tested. As of March 5, the situation had rapidly evolved, with a large outbreak identified in northern Italy and a total of 4,250 cases reported across 38 countries in the WHO European region (Spiteri et al., 2020).

The first COVID-19 case identified in the United States was reported in January 2020, with the majority of initial COVID-19 cases linked to travel from high-risk countries or close contact with travellers. By late February, widespread community transmission of the virus was detected in the US, notably in Washington State, New York City, and Santa Clara County in California. However, it is believed that local transmission in the U.S. began earlier and was more extensive than initially realised. Outside of these early virus "hotspots," transmission of the virus largely went unnoticed due to limited testing until the second week of March. It is probable that large-scale events during this

period significantly accelerated early transmission, and subsequent interstate travel further fuelled the COVID-19 epidemic in the US (Zeller et al., 2021).

In Africa, the initial case of COVID-19 was reported on February 14 in Egypt, followed by Sub-Saharan Africa's first case on February 27 in Nigeria, more than a month
after the outbreak began in China. This delay allowed African nations to prepare for the
inevitable spread of the virus. Initially, most reported cases in African countries were
imported, but as the pandemic progressed, local transmission exceeded imported cases,
and the rate of infection accelerated.

By the end of August 2020, COVID-19 had been reported in 57 African countries,
the virus had infected over 1.2 million people and caused over 29,000 deaths across the
continent. The impact of the disease varied from one country to another. African nations
implemented a range of measures to prevent COVID-19 transmission following its noti-
fication from China, although the intensity of these efforts differed. Many countries in
Africa achieved positive outcomes due to aggressive interventions to combat the virus.
The majority of reported cases in 2020 originated from just four countries, with South
Africa alone accounting for half of them.

After peaking in June and July, the daily number of new COVID-19 cases in Africa
began to decline in August, although there were variations between countries. South
Africa, which reported the majority of cases, experienced a notable decrease in infections.
Similarly, Nigeria, Ghana, Algeria, and Kenya saw a significant reduction in COVID-19
incidence by the end of August 2020 (Haileamlak, 2020).

Across the world, during 2020, testing was very limited meaning that case numbers
are probably much higher than actually reported. Beaney et al. (2020) argue that excess
mortality during an epidemic outbreak can be taken as a proxy for COVID-19 mortality.

On this basis, by mid 2021, Karlinsky and Kobak (2021) found that excess global
mortality was 2 million since the start of the outbreak as opposed to the number of
deaths attributed to COVID 19 at that time which was 1.4 million.

What is COVID-19?

Coronavirus disease (COVID-19) is an infectious disease caused by the SARS-
CoV-2 virus. SAR-CoV2 is an RNA virus that is broadly distributed in humans
and other mammals. Shereen et al. (2020) demonstrated that as much as 96.2%
identical genome sequencing of SARS-CoV-2 with bat CoV RaTG13, leading to the
conclusion that bats are suspected as the key reservoir of the viruses.

Previously, a novel coronavirus (SARS-CoV) was responsible for SARS, a new
disease identified in 2002, which first occurred in Guangdong Province, China and
spread to 29 countries with 8422 cases and 916 fatalities. The newer virus had
the key property of being transmitted widely before symptoms appeared, making
COVID-19 much harder to control than SARS.

5.1.1 Knowledge review

Before you move on, can you define the following key concepts:

• Coronavirus disease (COVID-19)?

5.1.2 Question to think about

When did you first hear about COVID -19? Did you think it would be a serious threat?

5.2 National measures to control the pandemic

As the pandemic evolved, governments used different measures to seek to control the virus.

5.2.1 Lockdowns and social distancing measures

Social distancing measures (SDMs) are community-level strategies aimed at reducing interpersonal contacts within a community. These measures played a significant role in initially containing and later mitigating the spread of SARS-CoV-2. Common SDMs included restrictions on gatherings, closure of schools and workplaces, implementation of remote work arrangements, and more stringent measures such as lockdowns.

Murphy et al. (2023) conducted a review of 338 studies examining the impact of SDMs on SARS-CoV-2 transmission in community settings. Almost half of the studies assessed the effectiveness of stay-at-home orders, with 79% showing a substantial reduction in transmission. The main measure evaluated was the Rt (rate of transmission) of SARS-CoV-2 across different countries and demographics. Given variations in effectiveness across populations and over time, analysing experiences from multiple countries was valuable for understanding the average impact and variations worldwide. Further research is needed to explore factors influencing policy impact, such as changes in human behaviour over time. Additionally, interactions with individual protective measures warrant investigation.

Estimating the effects of individual interventions posed challenges due to the simultaneous implementation of multiple SDMs. High-quality randomised controlled trials were often impracticable, leading to reliance on observational evidence and modelling studies. Statistical models indicated that more stringent interventions like stay-at-home orders and restrictions on gatherings were most effective in reducing transmission. The combined effects of various SDMs, including school and workplace closures, proved highly successful in curbing community transmission, as evidenced by reduced circulation of other respiratory viruses during the COVID-19 pandemic.

Human mobility emerged as a useful indicator for assessing the impact of SDMs. Mobility data, often derived from public transportation or aggregated mobile device data, can reflect population movements and interactions. Reductions in mobility corresponded with SDM implementation, indicating reduced contacts. While some studies utilised mobility data to assess intervention effects, it was not consistently included in review searches. Mobility data could also gauge adherence to interventions and unintended changes in behaviour prompted by these measures.

While stringent SDMs incur societal costs, studies on unintended consequences, such as mental health impacts, were not within the review's scope. Nevertheless, considering unintended consequences, measures to reduce person-to-person contact within settings like schools and workplaces may be preferable to limit transmission while minimising adverse effects. More evidence is needed to identify the optimal combination of measures for these settings. Subgroup analyses and assessments of socioeconomic and cultural variations in SDM acceptability and feasibility are essential for future research. Overall, the combination of SDMs was effective in slowing or halting COVID-19 spread, though individual effects and optimal combinations remain uncertain. When planning for future pandemics, assessing the potential effectiveness and socioeconomic impacts of SDMs in the context of pathogen dynamics is crucial.

5.2.2 Masks

At the outset, many governments and the WHO initially held the belief that wearing masks offered little advantage. Nonetheless, some nations, such as Belgium, Czechia, and Poland, advocated for the general populace to adopt face coverings early in the pandemic. Some governments even facilitated this by distributing masks (like Switzerland and Finland) or by encouraging citizens to craft their own cloth masks (as seen in Belgium and Czechia). Conversely, certain countries, like the UK and France, adopted a more cautious approach, reserving limited mask supplies for healthcare and social care workers. Regional disparities in mask policies were evident in countries like Belgium, Germany, and Italy.

As evidence mounted regarding the efficacy of masks, particularly in controlling the spread of the virus, their usage became increasingly integrated into pandemic responses. However, enforcement and adherence to mask mandates still vary significantly across different regions and countries. While children have generally been exempt from mask-wearing requirements, the specific age exemptions differ between nations; for instance, in Spain, exemptions have been granted only to those under six years old, whereas Switzerland enforced mask requirements for individuals aged 12 and above (Rajan et al., 2022).

5.2.3 Testing

In contrast to some infectious diseases where infected individuals can be identified through observable symptoms, SARS-CoV-2 can be spread by seemingly healthy individuals who may not show symptoms or are in the pre-symptomatic stage. Therefore, detecting the presence of the virus through testing is crucial. There are two main types of tests used for this purpose: Reverse Transcriptase Polymerase Chain Reaction (RT-PCR), which amplifies the virus' RNA to detectable levels and rapid antigen tests, which provide immediate results akin to a pregnancy test. Each test has its own advantages and limitations. RT-PCR may detect viral RNA remnants even after the person is no longer contagious, while antigen tests may miss individuals with low virus levels. Both tests are influenced by the quality of sampling and are not interchangeable but rather serve specific purposes in different contexts.

Early in the pandemic, rapid genetic coding facilitated early virus detection, but the challenge was scaling up testing capacity. Some countries utilised existing laboratory infrastructure, while others initially relied on external testing facilities. Denmark, for instance, took time to expand its testing capacity, achieving maximum levels later in the year. Initially, testing was prioritised for symptomatic travelers and their contacts, but as community spread became evident, testing criteria expanded. However, capacity constraints led to testing being limited to certain groups, with priority given to those with severe symptoms and frontline workers.

As testing capacity increased, it encompassed a broader range of groups, including long-term care residents and contacts of confirmed cases. Besides individual testing, pooled RT-PCR testing and sewage sampling for virus surveillance were employed, particularly in low-prevalence settings. However, effective testing requires integration into a larger system, including reliable procurement and distribution of testing materials, efficient sample transportation, and robust laboratory capacity.

Accessing tests typically involves visiting testing centres or using home testing kits, with considerations for transportation and accurate sampling. While RT-PCR tests were initially predominant, rapid antigen tests became widely available later, especially for symptomatic testing in resource-limited settings. Some countries implemented mass screening using rapid antigen tests, although concerns about their sensitivity and sustainability have been raised. Focused use of rapid antigen tests, such as regular testing in specific workplaces or school outbreaks, appears more promising. However, effective testing must be accompanied by thorough contact tracing, isolation of cases, and support for vulnerable groups and key workers to ensure its effectiveness in controlling the spread of the virus (Rajan et al., 2022).

5.2.4 Contact tracing

Contact tracing is the process of identifying, assessing, and managing people who have been exposed to someone who has been infected with the COVID-19 virus. Effective contact tracing is essential for controlling disease transmission, yet many countries lacked sufficient capacity at the beginning of the pandemic. The World Health Organisation (WHO) defines contact tracing as the process of identifying, evaluating, and managing individuals exposed to a disease to prevent further spread. Critical components include community engagement, tailored planning, a trained workforce, logistical support, and real-time data analysis.

Traditionally, contact tracers were limited in number, often linked to specific health services such as tuberculosis or sexual health clinics. To meet the demands of the pandemic, countries adopted various strategies. Some redeployed existing health workers, including retirees, while others established new structures. For instance, Serbia mobilised 4,500 health workers, including 1,500 doctors, for contact tracing. In contrast, the United Kingdom outsourced contact tracing to private corporations, employing 18,000 individuals, with some lacking extensive training. However, concerns about performance led to a shift towards utilising existing local public health departments.

Germany and Austria used their existing infrastructure, with federal support for local health offices. They invested in digitising operations and recruiting additional tracers. Effective contact tracing involves both forward and backward tracing. Forward tracing identifies and isolates contacts of infected individuals, while backward tracing identifies the source of infection. However, contact tracing systems face challenges, including the need for trust-building, particularly in telephone or SMS-based systems.

Even well-established contact tracing systems can be overwhelmed during surges in cases, as seen in Germany. Therefore, contact tracing proved to be most effective for preventing outbreaks at the onset of the pandemic or suppressing them when infection rates were low.

Side-effects of the pandemic – the impact of isolation on children's mental health (after Panchal et al., 2023)

Panchal et al. (2023) conducted a review encompassing 61 studies focusing on the effects of lockdowns on the mental health of children and adolescents, primarily from Europe and Asia. Their analysis revealed a noteworthy increase in symptoms of depression and anxiety among children during lockdown compared to pre-lockdown levels. Additionally, various other negative outcomes, such as loneliness, psychological distress, anger, irritability, boredom, fear, and stress, were associated with the COVID-19 lockdown. The study highlighted specific groups at risk of mental health deterioration, including those with pre-existing mental health conditions such as eating disorders. Moreover, it was observed that new psychiatric conditions might emerge during lockdown, while individuals with pre-existing conditions could experience a resurgence of symptoms.

The prevalence of PTSD among children exposed to COVID-19 was found to be 3.2%, lower than that observed in previous pandemics. However, considering the delayed onset of PTSD symptoms, it is important to monitor its potential increase over time. The review emphasised the need for further research to assess the prevalence of PTSD and recommended preventive measures, including trauma-focused psychotherapy.

Among individuals with eating disorders, there was a significant reactivation of symptoms post-lockdown, particularly among those with low self-directedness and less adaptive coping strategies. The disruption of feeding routines during confinement likely contributed to this effect. Given the high mortality rate associated with eating disorders, the study advocated for increased utilisation of digital tools to support affected individuals during the COVID-19 pandemic.

Sociodemographic factors, such as older age and female sex, were found to influence the development of poor mental health outcomes during lockdown. Adolescents, in particular, experienced increased depressive symptoms, possibly due to the disruption of social interactions and peer relationships inherent in adolescence. Additionally, children and adolescents with neurodevelopmental disorders or special educational needs were identified as highly vulnerable groups, as they struggled to adapt to the sudden changes and lacked adequate support networks during lockdown.

The review emphasised the importance of identifying both risk and protective factors to develop effective clinical practices and public health strategies. Lack of routine, problematic internet usage, COVID-19 media exposure, and parental occupation in COVID-19–related roles were identified as risk factors. School closures were highlighted as a significant stressor for many young people, affecting their emotional well-being and access to support services. Excessive internet usage, particularly during isolation, was associated with psychological distress, underscoring the need for parents to limit screen time and model positive coping behaviours.

Encouraging alternative activities, such as listening to music, reading, and engaging in physical exercise, were recommended to mitigate the negative impact of lockdown on children and adolescents' mental health. Additionally, providing accurate and balanced information about COVID-19 and promoting social support were deemed essential in supporting their well-being during these challenging times.

5.2.5 Knowledge review

Before you move on, can you define the following key concepts:

• Contact tracing?

5.2.6 Question to think about

How were you restricted during the COVID-19 pandemic? How did it impact upon your life, health, and well-being?

5.3 Developing a vaccine to combat the vaccine

Following the identification of SARS-CoV-2 in China, Chinese researchers at Fudan University sequenced its genome (Wu et al., 2020). The genome sequence was rapidly made publicly available in GenBank. This sequencing effort spurred immune-informatics-based research into vaccines against SARS-CoV-2. Various researchers utilised immune-informatics to develop COVID-19 vaccine candidates. Concurrently, pharmaceutical companies began vaccine development to combat the virus.

Moderna was the first to initiate a clinical trial with mRNA-1273 in May 2020, followed by Pfizer with vaccine candidates BNT162b1 and BNT162b2 in collaboration with BioNTech. The Messenger RNA (mRNA) vaccines mRNA-1273 from Moderna and BNT162b2 from Pfizer received initial approval (Emergency Use Authorisation, EUA) from the USFDA and EMA at the end of 2020 or early 2021. By December 2022, at least 50 COVID-19 vaccine candidates had been approved by at least one country globally, with reports indicating that 201 countries were vaccinating their populations with approved COVID-19 vaccines.

The initial vaccines to gain approval were the Pfizer-BioNTech (BNT162b) and Moderna (mRNA-1273) mRNA vaccines. These two vaccines were approved by the EMA and FDA and granted EUA for use in the US and Europe. Pfizer-BioNTech received EUA from the USFDA on December 11, 2020 and from the EMA on December 21, 2020. Simultaneously, Moderna's mRNA vaccine received EUA from the USFDA on December 18, 2020 and from the EMA on January 6, 2020. Various vaccines have been approved globally, including CoronaVac, BBIBP-CorV, CoviVac, Covaxin, Oxford-AstraZeneca vaccine (ChAdOx1 nCoV-19), Sputnik V, the Johnson & Johnson vaccine, Convidicea, RBD-Dimer, and EpiVacCorona.

These approved vaccines fall into four categories based on the vaccine platform used:

- mRNA vaccines
- conventional inactivated vaccines
- viral-vector vaccines
- protein-subunit vaccines

Table 5.1 describes the different types of vaccines.

Among these, two mRNA vaccines, four conventional inactivated vaccines, four viral-vector vaccines, and two protein-subunit vaccines were approved for human use. The mRNA vaccines include Moderna and Pfizer-BioNTech, conventional inactivated vaccines include CoronaVac, Covaxin, BBIBP-CorV, and CoviVac, viral-vector vaccines include Sputnik V, the Oxford-AstraZeneca vaccine, the Johnson & Johnson vaccine, and Convidicea, and protein-subunit vaccines include RBD-Dimer and EpiVacCorona (Chakraborty et al., 2023).

Table 5.1 Types of vaccines

Vaccine type	Description
mRNA vaccines	mRNA vaccines work by introducing a piece of mRNA that corresponds to a viral protein. By using this mRNA, cells can produce the viral protein. As part of a normal immune response, the immune system recognises that the protein is foreign and produces specialised proteins called antibodies. Antibodies help protect the body against infection by recognising individual viruses or other pathogens, attaching to them, and marking the pathogens for destruction. Once produced, antibodies remain in the body, even after the body has rid itself of the pathogen so that the immune system can quickly respond if exposed again. If a person is exposed to a virus after receiving mRNA vaccination for it, antibodies can quickly recognise it, attach to it, and mark it for destruction before it can cause serious illness.
Conventional inactivated vaccines	Inactivated vaccines take a live pathogen and inactivate or kill it. This inactivated pathogen is then introduced to the human body. The inactivated pathogen is recognised by the immune system that will generate antibodies to create an immune response, but is not capable of causing disease. Multiple doses are often needed in order to build up immunity and offer full protection.
Viral-vector vaccines	Viral vector vaccines are made form a small section of a virus's genetic material. They use a harmless virus to deliver this material to the host's cells. The information about the antigen is delivered, which in turn triggers the body's immune response.
Protein-subunit vaccines	Subunit vaccines are made from a piece of a pathogen, not the whole organism, so they do not contain any live pathogens. Subunit vaccines only contain pieces of a pathogen, not the whole organism. The subunit is sufficient to be recognised by the immune system that will generate antibodies to create an immune response, but is not capable of causing disease.

What was the impact of vaccination on the COVID-19 pandemic (after Watson et al., 2022)?

The first COVID-19 vaccine outside a clinical trial setting was administered on December 8, 2020. According to Watson et al. (2022), based on official reports of COVID-19 fatalities, it is estimated that vaccinations prevented approximately 14.4 million deaths from COVID-19 across 185 countries and territories between December 8, 2020 and December 8, 2021. When using excess deaths as a metric for the true scope of the pandemic, this estimate increases to around 19.8 million deaths prevented, reflecting a global reduction of 63% in total deaths during the first year of COVID-19 vaccination (19.8 million out of 31.4 million). In countries participating in the COVAX Advance Market Commitment program, it was calculated that 41% of excess mortality (equivalent to 7.4 million deaths out of 17.9 million) was averted.

In low-income countries, it was projected that an additional 45% of deaths could have been prevented if each country had met the 20% vaccination coverage target set by COVAX. Furthermore, it was estimated that an additional 111% of deaths could have been averted if each country had met the 40% target set by the World Health Organisation by the end of 2021.

5.3.1 *Knowledge review*

Before you move on, can you define the following key concepts:

• mRNA vaccines?

5.3.2 *Question to think about*

Have you been vaccinated against COVID-19? How confident were you about the vaccination process?

5.4 Aftermath of the pandemic

The pandemic was the largest global health event for a hundred years. There are ongoing impacts for health, healthcare, the economy and the broader society.

The most immediate health impact were the millions of deaths attributable to COVID-19 itself. However, some of those affected by COVID-19 who survived have been left with long-term health issues, such as lung damage, heart problems, and neurological issues, typically described under the umbrella term of "Long Covid" (Callard & Perego, 2021). This has led to an increased ongoing burden on healthcare systems.

During the pandemic, many more routine healthcare activities were suspended or reduced leading to a backlog of activity and an increased severity of disease caused by delays of treatment.

Arsenault et al. (2022) reported on the impact of the pandemic on 31 health services across a range of countries including two low-income (Ethiopia and Haiti), six middle-income (Ghana, Lao People's Democratic Republic, Mexico, Nepal, South Africa, and Thailand) and high-income (Chile and South Korea) countries.

They examined the degree of maternal, new-born, child, and chronic disease care missed from April to December 2020. Of the countries studied, Haiti and Nepal had the largest estimated amount of missed maternal and new-born care, with 207 and 209 missed visits per 1,000 births, respectively. South Africa had the largest number of missed immunisations, with 266 fewer vaccinations per 1,000 births. Mexico had the largest estimated amount of missed hypertension and diabetes care (48 missed visits per 1,000 people). Throughout the first nine months of the pandemic, they estimate that a total of 130,431 fewer women gave birth in a health facility across Ghana, Haiti, Mexico, Nepal, and South Africa; 131,652 fewer children received their third dose of pentavalent vaccine across Chile, Ethiopia, Mexico, Nepal, and South Africa; and 4.6 million fewer people received care for diabetes across Chile, Haiti, Mexico, Nepal, South Africa, and Thailand. They also observed significant and sustained decreases in breast and cervical cancer screenings, a trend that has been observed globally.

TB case detection declined substantially in Ghana, Nepal, and South Africa, remaining below pre-COVID-19 levels by the end of 2020. This decline may be attributed to symptoms resembling COVID-19, leading individuals with TB symptoms to stay home or be misdiagnosed. The Global Fund estimates significant drops in TB and HIV testing in their supported countries, potentially resulting in untreated cases with far-reaching consequences. It remains uncertain if social distancing contributed to reduced TB or HIV transmission, though increased indoor time in crowded households could facilitate TB transmission.

Conversely, across four countries, the number of individuals receiving antiretroviral therapy (ART) remained largely unaffected during the pandemic. This resilience may be explained by differentiated service delivery (DSD) programmes, which decentralise care locations and adjust visit frequencies, thus ensuring continued ART provision even during lockdowns.

Malaria-related visits declined temporarily in Ghana and Thailand but rebounded to pre-pandemic levels by the end of 2020. Nevertheless, these disruptions could have led to increased malaria deaths, particularly if preventive measures, such as bed nets and insecticide spraying, were also affected.

Arsenault et al. (2022) observed significant declines in visits for diabetes or hypertension were noted across several countries. While some nations implemented strategies to maintain drug adherence, it remains unclear if these efforts were successful.

Reproductive and maternal healthcare showed relative resilience, with only Chile and Mexico's public sectors experiencing significant declines in contraceptive provision. Family planning visits saw minor declines in some countries despite disruptions in other services, likely due to increased demand for contraception amidst economic uncertainties.

Facility-based deliveries declined in several countries, possibly due to various factors such as hospitals converting to COVID-19 treatment centres and increased home births. Decreases in visits for children under five with diarrhoea and pneumonia were observed across reporting countries, possibly influenced by reduced incidence from social distancing and improved hygiene practices.

This reduction in screening and other preventative interventions will have an impact for years to come. For example, in England, delays in breast cancer diagnosis are expected to raise 5-year mortality rates by 8–10%, while Chile and Mexico face similar risks of increased breast cancer mortality over the next five years.

Lockdowns and social distancing measures have led to increased feelings of loneliness, anxiety, and depression. Arsenault et al. (2022) found that in-person mental health services experienced substantial declines in Chile and Mexico during the pandemic, although few countries reported on mental healthcare. Some nations, including Chile and Mexico, implemented digital mental healthcare platforms and telephone hotlines to mitigate the impact of reduced in-person care.

Alongside this increased demand as a consequence of the pandemic itself and the disruption of healthcare activities, the pandemic has placed an ongoing strain on healthcare systems.: Hospitals, other healthcare facilities and their staff were often at risk of being overwhelmed during the pandemic itself, and this has led to higher rates of staff burnout than before the pandemic.

Gambaro et al. (2023) undertook an online survey of healthcare workers involved in the COVID-19 pandemic in the Novara region of Italy, approximately one year after the end of the pandemic. They sought to evaluate the levels of burnout, anxious–depressive, and post-traumatic symptoms and the general health status of these workers.

They found that many of the workers demonstrated symptoms of burnout:

- 62% reported a poor state of general mental health
- 70% reported depressive symptoms
- 29% reported post-traumatic symptoms
- 16% reported symptoms of anxiety

On the economic front, the pandemic caused a global economic downturn, disruptions to supply chains, and a decline in national GDP. Many businesses closed or downsized, leading to widespread unemployment. Countries have shown a variable ability to recover economically, and vulnerable populations have been disproportionately affected. The World Bank reported that "global poverty increased for the first time in a generation, and disproportionate income losses among disadvantaged populations led to a dramatic rise in inequality within and across countries." (World Bank, 2022).

This has meant either less money for healthcare or an increasing proportion of GDP devoted to healthcare in 2023. Although the proportion spent by most countries reached an all-time high in 2020 at the height of the pandemic, it remains above pre-pandemic levels in most countries, and the medium-term trend is that most high-income countries will exceed the 2020 peak before the end of the 2020s.

Ongoing positive benefits from the COVID-19 pandemic

In spite of the massive challenges and disruptions caused by the COVID-19 pandemic, there have also been some positive ongoing benefits that have emerged:

- The pandemic has forced the healthcare sector to rapidly adopt and innovate new technologies, particularly in the areas of telemedicine, flexible working, and remotely managed self-care for patients. Shaver (2022) reported that "Telemedicine healthcare has grown in the United States since the beginning of the COVID-19 pandemic" but many of these advancements have persisted beyond the pandemic, and telemedicine is being rolled out in middle-to-low countries such as India and Rwanda as well as in higher income countries.
- Remote work has become more widely accepted and adopted by employers, leading to greater flexibility for employees and reduced commuting times and associated costs. This shift has the potential to increase job opportunities for individuals who may have previously been limited by geographical constraints. It can help provide health coverage to more remote areas, which have been traditionally been hard to reach. The same technology may also facilitate remote education for healthcare workers in low income countries, improving their capabilities and reducing the brain drain to richer countries (He et al., 2020).
- The pandemic has heightened public awareness of health and hygiene practices, such as handwashing, mask-wearing, and vaccination. These habits are likely to persist beyond the pandemic, leading to improved overall public health outcomes and a reduced transmission of infectious diseases. In Iraq, Othman et al. (2023) found that awareness by the hospital staff increased during the COVID-19 pandemic. They found that the rate of washing hands increased by 38% and the use of materials for cleaning hands by 46% for staff at a hospital in Sulaimaniyah City. As further evidence, water consumption increased by 135% in the hospital studied during the COVID-19 pandemic.
- During the pandemic, there was a significant reduction in global carbon emissions and pollution levels due to reduced travel and industrial activity. Zahid et al. (2022) report that during the pandemic, the concentration of particles 2.5 microns or less in diameter and the Daily Air Quality Index (DAQI) decreased

by about 7µg/m3 and 5-points in China, respectively. Similarly, in the Kingdom of Saudi Arabia, a 91% lower concentration of particles 10 microns or less in diameter was found in the air across nine cities. While some of these reductions may be temporary, there is growing awareness of the environmental impact of human activities, leading to increased efforts to adopt sustainable practices and reduce carbon footprints. In addition to raising awareness about climate change, it may increase efforts to improve air quality, with a corresponding reduction in respiratory diseases.

- Communities around the world have come together to support one another during the pandemic, with individuals and organisations offering assistance to those in need. This sense of solidarity and support has the potential to strengthen community bonds, foster a greater sense of empathy and resilience, and may go some way to reduce the mental health challenges that are a legacy of lockdown use to limit the spread of the virus. The pandemic has brought greater attention to mental health issues in general and the importance of prioritising mental well-being. There has been increased recognition of the need for accessible mental health resources and support services, leading to greater advocacy and investment in this area.

5.4.1 Knowledge review

Before you move on, can you define the following key concepts:

- Long COVID?

5.4.2 Question to think about

Do you see any health or societal benefits in your own setting that may be attributed to the impact of the COVID-19 pandemic or the measures taken to manage it?

References

Allam, Z. (2020). *The first 50 days of COVID-19: A detailed chronological timeline and extensive review of literature documenting the pandemic. Surveying the covid-19 pandemic and its implications: Urban health, data technology and political economy* (pp.1–7). Elsevier.

Arsenault, C., Gage, A., Kim, M. K., et al. (2022). COVID-19 and resilience of healthcare systems in ten countries. *Nature Medicine*, 28, 1314–1324.

Beaney, T., Clarke, J. M., Jain, V., Golestaneh, A. K., Lyons, G., Salman, D., & Majeed, A. (2020). Excess mortality: The gold standard in measuring the impact of COVID-19 worldwide?. *Journal of the Royal Society of Medicine*, 113(9), 329–334.

Callard, F., & Perego, E. (2021). How and why patients made long covid. *Social Science & Medicine*, 268, 113426.

Chakraborty, C., Bhattacharya, M., & Dhama, K. (2023). SARS-CoV-2 vaccines, vaccine development technologies, and significant efforts in vaccine development during the pandemic: The lessons learned might help to fight against the next pandemic. *Vaccines*, 11(3), 682.

Gambaro, E., Gramaglia, C., Marangon, D., Probo, M., Rudoni, M., & Zeppegno, P. (2023). Health workers' burnout and COVID-19 pandemic: 1-year after-results from a repeated cross-sectional survey. *International Journal of Environmental Research and Public Health*, 20(12), 6087.

Haileamlak, A. (2020). COVID-19 pandemic Status in Africa. *Ethiopian Journal of Health Sciences*, 30(5), 643–644.

He, S., Lai, D., Mott, S., Little, A., Grock, A., Haas, M. R., & Chan, T. M. (2020). Remote e-work and distance learning for academic medicine: Best practices and opportunities for the future. *Journal of Graduate Medical Education*, 12(3), 256–263.

Huang, C., Wang, Y., Li, X., et al. (2020). Clinical features of patients infected with 2019 novel coronavirus in Wuhan, China. *The Lancet, 395*, 497–506.

Johnson, N. P., & Mueller, J. (2002). Updating the accounts: Global mortality of the 1918-1920 "Spanish" influenza pandemic. *Bulletin of the History of Medicine*, 76(1), 105–115.

Karlinsky, A., & Kobak, D. (2021). Tracking excess mortality across countries during the COVID-19 pandemic with the world mortality dataset. *eLife*, 10, e69336.

Murphy, C., Lim, W. W., Mills, C., Wong, J. Y., Chen, D., Xie, Y., Li, M., Gould, S., Xin, H., Cheung, J. K., Bhatt, S., Cowling, B. J., & Donnelly, C. A. (2023). Effectiveness of social distancing measures and lockdowns for reducing transmission of COVID-19 in non-healthcare, community-based settings. *Philosophical Transactions. Series A, Mathematical, Physical, and Engineering Sciences*, 381(2257), 20230132.

Othman Ahmed, K., Hama Karim, P., Golukcu, F., Qarani Aziz, S., Sadeghifar, T., Hashim Noori, S., & Dana Bahaulddin, N. (2023). Impact of the Covid-19 pandemic on awareness, risk level, hand washing, and water consumption for hospital staff in Sulaimaniyah city of Iraq. *Journal of Studies in Science and Engineering*, 3(1), 13–29.

Panchal, U., Salazar de Pablo, G., Franco, M., et al. (2023). The impact of COVID-19 lockdown on child and adolescent mental health: systematic review. *European Child & Adolescent Psychiatry*, 32, 1151–1177.

Rajan, S., McKee, M., Hernández-Quevedo, C., Karanikolos, M., Richardson, E., Webb, E., & Cylus, J. (2022). What have European countries done to prevent the spread of COVID-19? Lessons from the COVID-19 Health system response monitor. *Health Policy* (Amsterdam, Netherlands), 126(5), 355–361.

Shaver, J. (2022). The State of Telehealth Before and After the COVID-19 Pandemic. Primary care, 49(4), 517–530.

Shereen, M. A., Khan, S., Kazmi, A., Bashir, N., & Siddique, R. (2020). COVID-19 infection: Emergence, transmission, and characteristics of human coronaviruses. *Journal of Advanced Research*, 24, 91–98.

Spiteri, G., Fielding, J., Diercke, M., Campese, C., Enouf, V., Gaymard, A., Bella, A., Sognamiglio, P., Sierra Moros, M. J., Riutort, A. N., Demina, Y. V., Mahieu, R., Broas, M., Bengnér, M., Buda, S., Schilling, J., Filleul, L., Lepoutre, A., Saura, C., Mailles, A., ... Ciancio, B. C. (2020). First cases of coronavirus disease 2019 (COVID-19) in the WHO European Region, 24 January to 21 February 2020. *Euro Surveillance: Bulletin Europeen sur les Maladies Transmissibles = European Communicable Disease Bulletin*, 25(9), 2000178.

Watson, O. J., Barnsley, G., Toor, J., Hogan, A. B., Winskill, P., & Ghani, A. C. (2022). Global impact of the first year of COVID-19 vaccination: A mathematical modelling study. *The Lancet Infectious Diseases*, 22(9), 1293–1302.

World Bank. (2022). *World development report 2022, Chapter 1. The economic impacts of the COVID-19 crisis*. World Bank.

Wu, F., Zhao, S., Yu, B., Chen, Y. M., Wang, W., Song, Z. G., ... Zhang, Y. Z. (2020). A new coronavirus associated with human respiratory disease in China. *Nature*, 579(7798), 265–269.

Zahid, F. D. B. M., Gambedotti, F., Gaze, S., Gould, N. K., & Walls, V. (2022). The impact of coronavirus-related lockdowns on air quality in England and Scotland. *Granite Journal*, 7(1). ISSN 2059-3791.

Zeller, M., Gangavarapu, K., Anderson, C., Smither, A. R., Vanchiere, J. A., Rose, R., Snyder, D. J., Dudas, G., Watts, A., Matteson, N. L., Robles-Sikisaka, R., Marshall, M., Feehan, A. K., Sabino-Santos, G., Jr, Bell-Kareem, A. R., Hughes, L. D., Alkuzweny, M., Snarski, P., Garcia-Diaz, J., Scott, R. S., ... Andersen, K. G. (2021). Emergence of an early SARS-CoV-2 epidemic in the United States. *Cell*, 184(19), 4939–4952.e15.

Section B
Healthcare policy

6 Policymaking and health policymaking

6.1 Why is policymaking complex?

6.1.1 What is policy?

A policy is a set of principles or guidelines that direct decision-making to follow a specific course of action in order to achieve a particular goal or goals. Policies are adopted by a wide range of organisations, including governments, political parties, businesses, or organisations, in order to shape and influence decisions and behaviours. Typically, policies are goal-oriented, focusing on addressing problems and proposing solutions. A policy may take various forms, including laws, regulations, contracts, procedures, administrative actions, incentives, guiding principles, or voluntary practices (Alla et al., 2017).

Policies are crafted by both the public and private sectors. In the private sector, internal policies are often developed to govern processes and services with the ultimate objective of achieving some form of gain, such as profit. However, private sector policies must be aligned with public laws and government regulations. Additionally, considering public opinion is crucial for the private sector, as unfavourable views could directly impact profitability.

Policymakers wield the authority to influence and are tasked with creating policies at various levels – local, national, regional, or international. It's important to note that policymakers are not solely limited to politicians; anyone capable of influencing policy is considered a policymaker.

6.1.2 Policymaking

The process of policymaking is an intricate one. It involves numerous participants, each with diverse roles, requirements, interests, and resources. Analysing policies is about allocating resources and understanding the reasons behind who receives what and its impact. Policies are implemented within a dynamic environment which can change during its implementation, so must be kept under constant review.

With the growing complexity of policymaking, global policymakers are making greater use of a variety of tools, techniques, and technologies to understand and influence the process. Crafting and executing policies often require addressing challenges within intricate systems, incorporating various personnel, institutions, and dynamic environmental factors. Additionally, it involves exploring ways to modify specific elements to achieve desired outcomes. However, because of the complex interrelationships between the many people and elements involved, there is a significant risk of unintended consequences or the desired outcome not being achieved.

DOI: 10.4324/9781003478874-8

It is important to understand the difference between "complex" and "complicated."

- Complicated challenges are usually technical in nature. They have linear, step-by-step solutions, and tend to be predictable. They can be solved by breaking them down into a series of steps. Each step can be taken in turn and when all the steps have been taken, you will have solved the overall problem. People with the right expertise can usually design solutions that are easy to implement. People with less expertise can be trained to follow a series of steps to address such challenges.
- Complex challenges are defined by the interrelationship between multiple players and factors. This means there is no linear route to a solution, and often a degree of trial and error is required. A key characteristic of systems of problems is that the whole is greater than and qualitatively different from the sum of its parts. There is no simple relationship between inputs and outputs and no simple cause and effect associated with interventions to address them.

Policymaking often assumes that the problems to be addressed are merely complicated rather than complex.

Saurin (2021) differentiates between the systems thinking needed to address complicated problems and complexity theory intended to deal with complex problems.

Systems thinking involves adopting a perspective that focuses on understanding various systems by modelling interconnections and causal links. This approach may be contrasted with reductionism, which concentrates on the properties of individual parts constituting a system rather than the whole.

Complexity theory represents a further step by applying of systems thinking specifically to complex systems. Complexity theory deals with dynamically interactive systems that remain open to their environment and therefore are incapable of complete description and control. Traditional systems thinking is better suited for complicated systems, those that are ultimately knowable and allow for a comprehensive, exhaustive description.

A technological artifact, like an electronic health records system, is a complicated system when considered in isolation. However, when such a system interacts with other technological systems and are embedded within a larger social ecosystem, they become integral parts of a larger complex system.

Complex and complicated problems during the COVID-19 pandemic

During the COVID-19 pandemic, there were frequent calls to "follow the science" when making decisions about how to manage behaviours. Developing a vaccine for COVID-19 was a complicated problem, amenable to science. It was possible to develop a vaccine by lots of clever people applying the science and, through a series of steps and the use of a huge amount of resources, arrive at a solution.

Managing human behaviours to minimise the spread of the virus was a complex and dynamic problem. This was qualitatively different, and no amount of science could derive policies guaranteed to solve the problem.

Once the vaccine had been developed, its deployment was also a complex problem. It necessitated the mobilisation, cooperation, collaboration, and coordination of numerous resources, individuals, and organisations. Each of these agents needed to act in specific ways within defined time frames. The deployment was also subject to further influences and challenges including corruption, incompetence, political motivations, financial challenges, scarcity of resources, and conflicting interests. As a result, vaccine rollouts did not always achieve their intended goals.

Although complexity in the policymaking process presents significant challenges, its impact can be mitigated. Improved governance, concerted efforts, consensus and collaboration, evidence-based information, well-qualified experts, and enhanced transparency can help to reduce these challenges and enhance the overall policymaking process. There are entire disciplines, such as project management, economics, and public management, that aim to offer theories, ideas, and techniques to enhance the policymaking process for better policy outcomes. However, it is important to remember that when addressing complex problems, whilst the goal of policymaking is to optimise the solutions, those solutions need to be dynamic and there is no single correct answer.

6.1.3 Knowledge review

Before you move on, can you define the following key concepts:

- Complex problems?
- Complicated problems?

6.1.4 Question to think about

Think about a range of problem of local health challenges. Are they complex, or merely complicated? What are the implications for policymakers?

6.2 The policymaking process

Policymaking is a process. Mickwitz (2021) suggests that this process should be considered in five stages:

- agenda-setting
- policy formulation
- decision-making
- implementation
- evaluation

Each of these stages contributes to the development, adoption, implementation, and evaluation of policies. Understanding this process is crucial for effective governance and addressing health and healthcare issues.

The first step in this process is agenda setting, a mechanism by which issues are brought to a government's attention. Problems in health and healthcare are identified, and stakeholders propose potential solutions (Hill & Varone, 2021). The government and public sector play a pivotal role in responding to public health needs promptly, marking the "why" of the policy.

The second phase is policy formulation. This involves considering, examining, and defining different policy options. Policymakers discuss and suggest potential solutions to mitigate problems identified during the agenda-setting stage. The selected policy must be an effective means of solving the problem in a viable and efficient way. Formulation involves analysing and determining alternative solutions, with a crucial consideration for political feasibility achieved through majority consensus and negotiation (Hill & Varone, 2021). Cost-benefit analysis (CBA) is a common method for assessing proposed policies, systematically predicting their social costs and benefits. It is imperative to ensure that potential policies do not exacerbate inequities in healthcare access, quality, and afford-ability, making this step integral to the "how" of the policy.

Health policy analysis, often considered the most challenging task in policymaking, defines and outlines the guidelines' purpose. It identifies similarities and differences in expected results and costs of competing alternative policies, elucidating interactions between institutions, interests, and ideas in the policy process. Conducting health policy analysis ensures a systematic process to choose the most effective and feasible policy to address the identified problem.

The third step is decision-making, where a course of action (or non-action) is adopted for future implementation. Developed guidelines must be adopted by the responsible body, with factors influencing agenda setting also affecting policy adoption. Strong stake-holder groups can use their political influence to decide which policy to adopt (Mongiello, 2016). Media, both traditional and social, plays a vital role in policy adoption. Objective and unbiased reporting can facilitate discussions on various policy options, with positive media bias increasing the likelihood of policy recommendations being adopted. This step emphasises the "who" of the policy.

The fourth stage of the policy cycle is policy implementation. This is the point at which the adopted policy is put into effect. Successful implementation depends on clear communication, avoidance of ambiguity, and integration of resources without causing widespread interference, competition, or conflict. Policies must be communicated clearly by policymakers to relevant managing bodies, and resources must be integrated within existing processes and institutions. Bureaucratic incompetence and scandals may compli-cate implementation, leading to delays or challenges in executing policies.

Policy evaluation is the process of monitoring and assessing results after policy imple-mentation and represents the final step. Continuous evaluation is necessary, although some policies that have become ingrained over time may not receive evaluation. Various criteria, including informal assessments based on anecdotes or stories and formal research providing empirical evidence, can be used for evaluation (Wollmann, 2017). Policy evaluation can occur at different times, such as during implementation or after to understand overall effectiveness. Despite numerous ways to evaluate policies, they are often not evaluated due to the time-consuming, costly, and complicated nature of formal and scientific research. Informal evaluation is more accessible but tends to be biased and subjective.

In policymaking, and particularly health policymaking, assessing policies can be chal-lenging. Some policies aim for broad conceptual goals subject to different interpretations, making evaluation complex. Policies may have multiple objectives that may not be com-patible, and evaluations often focus on whether the policy effectively addresses prob-lems. Process-focused evaluations consider the conditions for success rather than just the content-focused effectiveness. This step relates to the "what" of the policy, determining its success based on different perspectives.

**Implementing a policy of universal health coverage
in Ghana (after Agyepong & Adjei, 2008)**

In 2001, Ghana started to develop and implement a National Health Insurance Scheme (NHIS) as a more equitable and pro-poor health financing policy, aiming to replace out-of-pocket fees at the point of service use. By December 2006, 38% of the 21 million population had registered in the NHIS, and 21% were effectively protected from out-of-pocket fees. The government's vision was to ensure equitable and universal access to essential healthcare for all residents within five years. However, achieving universal health financial protection in a low-income country like Ghana presented technical and political challenges.

Universal health insurance coverage had mainly been achieved by wealthier nations, and Ghana faced obstacles due to its economic structure, with a significant non-formal sector and citizens in rural areas with limited access to services. Despite these challenges, Ghana was determined to pursue NHIS. Initially, the focus was on technical challenges, overlooking the political dynamics of social policy reform in a developing country.

The agenda-setting circumstances created a perception of a crisis and a need for change among political decision-makers, bureaucrats, and civil society. High-level decision-makers, including the president, were concerned about the success of the NHIS, driven by the need to fulfil a major election promise within a short time-frame. The urgency to demonstrate regime legitimacy and competence heightened the sense of insecurity, possibly influenced by Ghana's relatively new multiparty democracy.

Political decision-makers and researchers were eager for successful reform due to clear problems in the health sector. However, they seemed slower to recognise the political concerns, climate, and influences. Ghana's tradition of an independent, non-politicised civil and public service added complexity. Politicians sought to blur the lines between technical and political actors, favouring political associates perceived as loyal and responsive to the crisis.

The political associates, viewed as strong political loyalists, leveraged their political credentials over technical competence. This power imbalance raised concerns about potential conflicts of interest between personal financial gain and national progress. The blurring of independence between technical and political actors, while considered reasonable in a crisis decision-making situation, resulted in potentially avoidable implementation difficulties.

The Ghana experience highlights the importance of recognising and addressing political challenges alongside technical ones in health reform. Lessons learned include the need for scientific evidence on technical challenges, equipping decision-makers with skills to navigate political complexities, and maintaining a balance of power for effective policy goals. Despite achievements in Ghana's NHIS, understanding and planning for political challenges is crucial for successful health reforms in developing countries. This involves fostering a relationship of mutual trust and respect between technical, bureaucratic, and political actors without compromising scientific integrity.

6.2.1 Knowledge review

Before you move on, can you define the following key concepts:

• Agenda setting?
• Policy formulation?

6.2.1 Question to think about

Think of a major health policy initiative in your own country or region? Did it succeed or fail? Why do you think this was the case?

6.3 Health policymaking

The definition of health policy is linked to how health is defined. The WHO defines health as the state of physical, psychological, and social wellbeing, not merely the absence of illness, injury, or disease (WHO, 1984).

From this view of health, the WHO describes healthcare policy as "an articulation of objectives aimed at enhancing the health situation, the prioritisation of these objectives, and the primary direction for achieving them" (WHO, 1986, p. 86).

However, health is defined more simply by Oleribe et al. (2018) as the absence of illness or injury. Therefore, health policy can be understood in multiple ways. As policy is concerned with defining actions, definitions are generally focused on interventions They may encompass actions or inactions taken by both public and private sectors that impact public health, as well as all facets of the healthcare system. This includes, but is not limited to, policies concerning access to and availability of health services, healthcare service delivery, quality of healthcare services, funding arrangements, healthcare financing, and regulation of healthcare institutions.

Beyond the health sector, numerous policies aim to influence the practices and policies of non-health sectors to foster health and health equity. Initiatives like nutrition programmes and early childhood education programmes targeted at low-income communities exemplify such efforts. These activities seek to advance health equity and enhance the well-being of disadvantaged communities.

Social determinants of health refer to non-health related factors such as gender, race, socioeconomic status, education level, income level, employment status, occupation, and living conditions. These factors impact health directly and indirectly, potentially giving rise to various health risks (Saunders et al., 2017). Effectively addressing these determinants is essential for enhancing health and mitigating long-term health disparities. Globally, an increasing number of health policies are emerging based upon improving the social determinants of health, both within and outside the health system.

6.3.1 Types of health policy

Global health policy is a subset of health policy that concentrates on the global and national health systems, encompassing both healthcare and public health services. It also emphasises the allocation of resources among countries and organisations and the execution of plans and strategies to achieve health objectives. This form of policy governs the global framework responsible for shaping public health policy on a worldwide scale. When addressing global health issues, global health policy prioritises the health needs of people globally over the interests of specific countries, particularly those in the global North. An illustration of global health policy in action is the "Global Action Plan on Antimicrobial Resistance," designed to enhance coordinated global efforts against the increasing challenge of antimicrobial resistance (AMR) (WHO, 2021).

Healthcare services policy is a facet of health policy that centres on enhancing the delivery, accessibility, effectiveness, quality, efficiency, equity, and safety of healthcare services. A primary focus for many low to middle-income countries, such as Tanzania, has been the improvement of healthcare services through the primary healthcare system. In 2019, Tanzania initiated the universal health coverage programme, encompassing general outpatient and inpatient care, optical services, specialised surgery, pharmaceuticals, and orthopaedic services for the most underserved populations in the country (Bintabara, 2021).

Pharmaceutical policy is another branch of health policy concerned with the development, supply, and utilisation of medications within the healthcare system. It encompasses policies related to both brand name and generic drugs, biological products, vaccines, and natural health products. For instance, in Canada, the Patent Drug Price Review Board evaluates drug pricing and compares proposed prices with those in other countries to determine if they are "too high," requiring the manufacturer to submit a recommended price to the appropriate regulatory agency (Sketris et al., 2022).

Public health policy is a comprehensive term denoting the laws, regulations, actions, and decisions implemented in society to promote health and achieve specific health objectives. It is a multidisciplinary field involving various sectors such as healthcare, education, environment, and agriculture. Examples include vaccination policy, tobacco control policy, and breastfeeding promotion policy (Hill & Varone, 2021).

Public health policies include:

- *Food safety policies* aim to mitigate the risk of food-related illnesses. Public health officials formulate guidelines to ensure that only safe-to-consume food is available to the public, acknowledging the significant concern surrounding foodborne diseases.
- *Tobacco use policies* target the reduction of risks associated with tobacco consumption and smoking. Strategies may involve raising tobacco prices and establishing tobacco-free zones in communities to safeguard non-smokers from the adverse effects of second-hand smoke.
- *HIV policies* play a pivotal role in educating the public about HIV prevention, managing the virus, treatment options, and combating stigma. Initiatives, including enhanced access to testing, contraception, and medication, have been instituted to significantly diminish the impact and transmission of the virus in diverse communities.
- Alcohol policies seek to mitigate the harm caused by alcohol. Alcohol abuse is a major contributor to vehicular accidents, violence, sexual assault, and health complications, and these policies seek to tackle alcohol dependence and mitigate its adverse effects. Community-specific regulations, such as age restrictions on alcohol consumption and purchase, exemplify common measures to address alcohol-related issues.

Mental health policy is a relatively recent addition to health policy as it has been recognised that mental health services are often neglected compared to those aimed at physical illnesses. Governments, health departments, and ministries have been formulating visions, setting goals, and establishing action models. General objectives of mental health policy include promoting good mental health, preventing and treating mental disorders, rehabilitating those affected, developing services for individuals with mental health issues, and reducing stigma.

A large part of mental health policy is concerned with suicide prevention, which is a major cause of death in adults. WHO (2023) estimates that globally more than 700,000 people die due to suicide every year and that many more people attempt suicide. Suicide is the fourth leading cause of death among 15–29-year-olds, and it is a truly global problem, with over three-quarters of global suicides occurring in low- and middle-income countries.

In policy terms, target 3.4 of the Sustainable Development Goals, to reduce premature mortality from noncommunicable diseases by one-third by 2030, through prevention and treatment and promote mental health and well-being includes the suicide mortality rate as an indicator.

Another major part of mental health policy is concerned with helping those living with long-term mental health issues. Questions to be addressed include:

* how can positive mental wellbeing be promoted?
* how can the onset of mental ill-health be prevented?
* how can people needing support with their mental health be supported more quickly?
* how can the quality and effectiveness of treatment for mental health conditions be improved?
* how people living with mental health conditions be supported to live well?
* how can support for people in a mental health crisis and their carers/family be supported?

6.3.2 *The health policy triangle: A theoretical framework for evaluating health policy*

Walt and Gilson introduced the health policy triangle, as shown in Figure 6.1, in 1994 as an analytical tool for examining health policies (Zahidie et al., 2023).

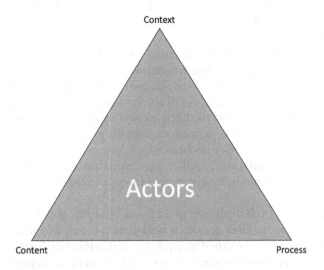

Figure 6.1 Walt and Gilson's health policy triangle.

This framework recognises the inherently political nature of the context in which health-related decisions are made, and it acknowledges that health policy choices can be influenced by socially implicit value judgments. Additionally, health policies themselves may be adjusted based on these social values and judgments. The triangle underscores the significance of considering power dynamics throughout the entire health policy process (Wollmann, 2017; O'Brien et al., 2020).

The "content" of the policy denotes the policy objectives, operational policies, regulations, guidelines, legislation, and more, with "context" referring to systemic factors such as social, economic, political, or cultural aspects. "Process" refers to how health policies are initiated, formulated, implemented, and evaluated. In the middle of the triangle lies the "actors" element, referring to influential individuals, groups, and organisations that affect or are affected by the health policy decision.

This framework can be applied both prospectively and retrospectively. While widely used in health policy research across diverse political and health systems globally, it is crucial to recognise that the framework offers a simplified representation of intricate interrelationships. Though valuable for systematically considering various factors influencing health policy, care is needed in its application since its lack of detail may result in confusion or oversimplification of the key health issues.

Sodi et al. (2021) utilised this framework to assess mental health policies and legislation in Ghana, Kenya, South Africa, and Zimbabwe in response to the heightened need for mental health services during the COVID-19 pandemic and other health emergencies. Employing this framework allowed them to identify strengths and gaps in existing mental health policies and provide recommendations for enhancing and strengthening these policies in future health crises.

Sodi et al. (2021) using Walt and Gilson's Policy Triangle Framework to evaluate mental health policy in four African countries

Sodi et al. (2021) used Walt and Gilson's Policy Triangle Framework to analyse the mental health policies of four African countries as part of an evaluation of mental health policy and system preparedness to respond to the COVID-19 and other health emergencies in these countries.

In line with the conceptual framework, they reviewed the role played by the different factors in shaping and influencing these mental health policies. The COVID-19 pandemic had immense psychological consequences ranging from anxiety among school children due to prolonged closure of schools, guilt and fear among healthcare workers, and grief complications due to restricted mourning activities. As the pandemic worsened, there were concerns raised about the preparedness of African healthcare systems to cope with the health and social consequences of COVID-19. Many African countries have struggled to put in place adequate policies, systems, and associated infrastructures to address the health and social needs of their citizens. There are doubts about the preparedness or even existence of mental healthcare policies and associated systems to help individuals and communities in Africa to deal with the psychological fallout of COVID-19.

The authors examined the preparedness of mental health legislation and policies in four African countries (namely, Ghana, Kenya, South Africa, and Zimbabwe) in responding to COVID-19 and other health emergencies. They found that the existing legislation and mental health policies that each of the four African countries have put in place appear adequate in so far as they enable psychology professionals to provide professional services to individuals, families, and communities under ordinary circumstances and during times of crisis. In terms of the Policy Triangle Framework, it appears that the shortage of psychology professionals (actors) and contextual and process factors are the key hindrances in the provision of psychological services during health emergencies.

Looking at the four countries, it appears that the historical legacies of colonialism and apartheid have continued to have a negative impact on the implementation of mental health legislation and policies. Some of the common problems in all these countries are inaccessibility of mental health services due to lack of prioritisation of mental health services and the failure to implement what is articulated in the policies, as well as low budgets for mental health services.

In Kenya, the biggest problem is failure to implement the available mental health legislations, meaning no regulation and funding of mental health services are available. In Zimbabwe, these kinds of problems are compounded by the current political and economic environment that hampers efforts by psychologists and other mental health professionals towards providing psychosocial support to the general population. The problems highlighted here have the potential to hinder mental healthcare systems in their effort to deal with health problems, including current and future health emergencies.

6.3.3 *Knowledge review*

Before you move on, can you define the following key concepts:

- Global health policy?
- Health policy?
- Mental health policy?

6.3.4 *Question to think about*

What are the key health policy challenges within your own country or region? What are the barriers to designing and implementing a successful policy?

6.4 Who are the stakeholders in health policy?

A stakeholder (Guise et al., 2021, p. 1) refers to any individual, group, or organisation participating in or impacted by a specific course of action (Guise et al., 2021, p. 1). Each stakeholder possesses distinct interests, requirements, and interpretations of health policy, underscoring the importance of engaging all stakeholders at an appropriate level.

In the realm of health policy, a stakeholder encompasses anyone intricately involved in or affected by the healthcare system, particularly those significantly influenced by potential reforms or changes to the system (Balane et al., 2020).

Stakeholders encompass a broad spectrum, including healthcare providers (such as physicians, pharmacists, nurses, nutritionists, midwives, and physiotherapists), patients and their families, as well as governmental and non-governmental organisations. Essentially, everyone holds a stake in health policy. The intricate interrelationships among stakeholders in the healthcare system and those involved in health policy arise due to varying interests, levels of influence, and degrees of power concerning specific policies.

Fundamentally, health policy revolves around managing stakeholders, as policies are crafted to meet their requirements and needs.

Stakeholder analysis consists of five steps:

- identifying all potential stakeholders
- categorising and prioritising them according to their interest or influence
- working out their needs, concerns, and expectations
- developing a plan to engage with them
- monitoring this engagement

Identifying stakeholders is an ongoing process, iteratively conducted throughout the policy development to ensure no stakeholder is overlooked. This is critical as the success and future of a policy hinge on stakeholders and their interpretations of it.

Stakeholder identification starts at the conception of a policy idea. During this phase, information about each stakeholder should be recorded in a stakeholder's register – a document delineating the stakeholders of a particular policy along with their interests, influence, and impact on the policy. Ideally, the stakeholder register should be completed early in the policymaking process to facilitate effective stakeholder engagement and management. The stakeholder register typically includes details such as names, titles, roles, power, interest, type of influence, requirements, expectations, contact information, and communication needs/frequency.

Various methods, including checking existing documentation, stakeholder benchmarking, interviews with experts, and brainstorming sessions, can be employed for stakeholder identification. Existing organisational assets, stakeholder engagement plans, and registers may be reviewed, and interviews with subject matter experts can provide valuable insights. Open-ended questions are recommended during expert interviews. Brainstorming sessions with teams or experts help gather information and identify stakeholders by considering direct or indirect involvement, potential impact, and gains or losses.

Stakeholder identification is an ongoing process that evolves as the policy progresses. New stakeholders may emerge, and some previously identified stakeholders may lose interest. Additionally, the power and interest of stakeholders can change over time, emphasising the need to continually monitor and update stakeholders' attributes.

6.4.1 *The power/interest grid*

The power/interest grid was first proposed by Mendelow (1991). It is a very commonly used tool in stakeholder management for categorising and prioritising them according to their interest or influence in the policymaking process, allowing for their effective management through the remaining steps in stakeholder analysis. Once all stakeholders involved in the policy process have been identified, they can be plotted on the grid based on the power and interest they hold regarding the formulated policy.

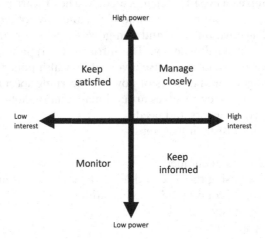

Figure 6.2 The power/interest grid.

Figure 6.2 provides a visual representation of the various strategies for segregating and subsequently prioritising identified stakeholders.

Stakeholders with both high power and high interest in the policy formulation, discussion, implementation, or evaluation are typically decision-makers and exert the most significant influence on project success. Managing their expectations closely becomes paramount.

Stakeholders possessing high power but low interest in the policy should be kept informed. Despite their lack of interest, maintaining their satisfaction is essential due to the influence they wield. However, caution is advised as these stakeholders, if dissatisfied, may leverage their power negatively, potentially hindering policy formulation or implementation.

Stakeholders with low power but high interest in the policy require consistent and timely communication to stay adequately informed. Regular interaction with these stakeholders is crucial to prevent major issues, as they can often provide valuable assistance during the policy process. Finally, stakeholders with both low power and low interest in the policy should be monitored, with communication kept to a minimum to avoid unnecessary engagement (Balane et al., 2020).

After stakeholders have been recognised and placed into categories, the subsequent phase involves understanding their requirements, concerns, and expectations. If there is pre-existing information or feedback, perhaps from prior projects, this can provide a beneficial starting point. In cases where information is lacking, conducting interviews, surveys, or focus groups with stakeholders can be instrumental in obtaining the necessary insights.

This stage emphasises the significance of attentive listening to stakeholders and striving to understand their viewpoints. Doing so helps to recognise potential risks or issues that might emerge. In addition, it guides decision-making processes to guarantee that the needs and concerns of stakeholders are appropriately acknowledged and addressed.

Based on this analysis, the fourth step is to develop a stakeholder engagement plan. This should outline how stakeholders will be engaged throughout the project or activity, how their needs and concerns will be addressed, and how their expectations will be managed.

The plan should also identify the methods and channels that will be used to communicate with stakeholders. It is also important to work out how often they'll be updated, and who is responsible for communicating with them, as most healthcare interventions occur in a dynamic environment.

For this reason, it is essential to monitor and evaluate engagement throughout the project or activity by tracking stakeholder feedback and checking on their levels of engagement. It may be necessary to adjust the engagement plan as required – such as if certain stakeholders feel they are not receiving enough updates.

Stakeholder engagement in the formulation of South Africa's Mental Health Policy and Strategic Framework

South Africa's Mental Health Policy and Strategic Framework originated from extensive policy consultations, including mental health summits held in 2012 across eight provinces: Eastern Cape, Free State, Gauteng, KwaZulu-Natal, Limpopo, Mpumalanga, North West, and the Western Cape. The culmination was a national mental health summit in April 2012, bringing together representatives from various sectors, such as research institutions, NGOs, the WHO, mental healthcare user groups, professionals, and government departments at national and provincial levels. Their collective input was sought for the draft policy.

Following the national summit, the task team appointed by the Minister of Health to organise it reconvened to incorporate feedback and finalise the policy, as documented in the final mental health policy. This process also involved the development of a strategic plan outlining priorities for implementation, leading to the promulgation of the Mental Health Policy Framework and Strategic Plan 2013–2020 in October 2013.

An evaluation by Marais et al. (2020) focused on stakeholder engagement, utilising semi-structured interviews as a retrospective process evaluation of the consultation. Two main sub-themes emerged from the interviews, highlighting the perceived impact of the national consultation summit and its influence on the final policy. Some participants viewed the summits as crucial signals of the government's commitment to mental health, endorsed by the WHO, even if the policy document saw limited substantive changes. Others had diverse perspectives on the degree to which inputs from the national summit influenced the final policy, with some noting specific recommendations included in the Strategic Plan appendix.

However, Marais et al. (2020) found that the mental health policy underwent no substantive changes after the consultation summits. The lack of systematic processes for capturing and transferring knowledge inputs between provincial and national levels was noted. Furthermore, there was no additional consultation on implementation priorities before finalising the policy, leading to concerns about local-level policy implementation. This missed an opportunity for greater involvement of service users in policy development.

In addition to inadequate service-user representation, the format of the consultation process hindered participant interaction and limited the incorporation of experiential knowledge. Several procedural aspects were identified as barriers to eliciting and transferring consultation contributions into policy. Recommendations for future policy consultations include adapting participatory processes to optimise participant knowledge use and increasing service-user participation.

6.4.2 *Knowledge review*

Before you move on, can you define the following key concepts:

- Stakeholder analysis?
- Power/interest grid?

6.4.3 *Question to think about*

List the different stakeholders in your country that might be involved with the health policy on child vaccinations in your own country, then classify, and plot them on the power/interest grid.

6.5 The role of the private sector in making health policy

The private sector, which we shall consider as those commercial organisations whose primary purpose is to make a profit, plays a key part in the healthcare of every country in the world. Entities within this sector primarily seek to generate profits for their shareholders, with profit and return on investment serving as its fundamental defining features. Even in instances where companies pursue objectives related to societal, environmental, or employee concerns, these goals are secondary and supplementary to the primary objective of profit generation. This may lead to concerns over conflicts between the profit motive and the need to maximise the health benefits to patients.

In practice, for-profit entities in the private sector are very diverse characteristics, ranging from small to large, and operating on domestic, multinational, or international scales. Within the health sector, examples of private sector components include private physician clinics, large group clinics, privately owned community pharmacies, pharmacy chains, generic drug manufacturers, major pharmaceutical companies, medical equipment suppliers, as well as private hospitals and nursing homes (Mackintosh et al., 2016).

When examining the private sector's role in health policy, we may wish to include non-profit organisations with legal status. These may comprise business associations, trade federations, advocacy groups (e.g., patient advocacy groups), academic organisations, research centres, and local or international non-governmental organisations (NGOs) involved in health policy processes. Although not motivated by profit, these organisations are often run on commercial lines, as they need to be self-sustaining and demonstrate their efficiency to their supporters and funders.

The private sector in health policy has significant influence because of its abundant resources and the capacity to achieve desired outcomes. These organisations contribute taxes to the government and often serve as significant employers, granting them influence over governmental decisions. Major pharmaceutical companies, particularly those with substantial profits and a large workforce, wield significant power. In practice, almost all of the pharmaceutical supply chain is made up of for-profit organisations. Companies in this, and other, sectors offer specialised knowledge crucial for government policy and regulation development. Consequently, both small and large private companies act as stakeholders in health policy, actively participating in debates. While governments typically formulate and implement public policy, the private sector is commonly directly or indirectly involved in this process (Szakonyi, 2021).

Public policy frequently impacts the private sector, prompting attempts by the latter to influence policies in line with its interests. This influence is exerted through various means, including financial contributions to politicians, political campaigns, and parties in the hope of gaining favourable consideration if these entities come to power (Verma, 2016).

Private companies may also engage in lobbying activities to support or oppose specific policies affecting their interests. For instance, tobacco companies have actively opposed tobacco control policies by discrediting scientific evidence, emphasising the economic significance of the industry, strengthening political connections, and consistently advocating for laxer tobacco control measures (Hird et al., 2021).

The interaction between interest groups from the private sector in health and policymakers is characterised by a spectrum ranging from confrontational to collaborative. However, there is some ambiguity in precisely defining these interrelationships, as most collaborative arrangements are described in diverse ways.

For instance, within the healthcare sector, certain associations may be termed coalitions, as seen in the relationship between the pharmaceutical industry and patient organisations. The pharmaceutical industry may share common interests with some patient groups, such as advocating for the inclusion of specific drugs in the government's essential drug lists. Nevertheless, these groups often find other arrangements more beneficial to them than forming an open coalition. Companies may assist in hiring, funding, and training staff for a particular patient organisation without explicitly endorsing a list of drugs. However, patient organisations also engage in lobbying and are well-equipped and funded for this purpose. Private sector interest groups in healthcare employ various means, with financial contributions for financing campaigns being a prominent approach (Giaimo, 2014). However, whatever the nature of these relationships, good governance is required for effective policymaking that is not unduly influenced by a few influential special interest groups (Sari, 2023).

Research institutes, commonly known as "think tanks," often serve as sources of political ideas; and in the policymaking process, while the distinction is not always clear, research institutes often play a more significant role than merely communicating policy ideas based on sound scientific evidence. They increasingly aim to shape these ideas into legislation that could be enacted by parliament and approved by the government. Successful endeavours in this regard often require forming alliances with other research institutes, as well as with parliamentary and administrative parties (Bermudez & Prah, 2022). Additionally, research institutes contribute policy ideas adopted by non-governmental stakeholder groups in their efforts to participate in the policymaking process. They also conduct policy analyses of legislation or existing programmes, and their reports can influence the legislative process and its content. Some research institutes operate independently while promoting policies closely aligned with specific stakeholders and political parties (Giaimo, 2014; Bermudez & Prah, 2022).

The term "lobby" historically refers to the area within parliamentary or congressional buildings where citizens meet to discuss policies and legislations with elected officials but it has become synonymous with making direct contact or communication with policymakers to discuss policies and exert influence. Lobbyists, employed by various individuals or privately owned companies, represent commercial interests and those of their clients.

Private healthcare organisations and interest groups frequently engage in lobbying efforts to sway health policy decisions impacting various aspects of healthcare, such as compensation, financing, licensing, research priorities, and oversight.

The dynamics of global health policymaking, after Bermudez and Prah (2022)

Bermudez and Prah (2022) conducted an empirical examination to explore the power dynamics within global health governance. The study involved the collection of around 75,000 tweets from 20 key global health actors between 2016 and 2020, using the Twitter API. The authors extracted the priorities from these tweets through topic modelling, and subsequently, they were compared with stated priorities from policy document content analyses.

The participants, comprising 20 global health actors, were identified based on a consensus from three peer-reviewed articles mapping global health networks. The tweets of each actor were collected in three-month intervals from November 2016 to May 2020. Policy documents and developmental assistance for health financial data for each actor were also collected for the same period.

The authors sought to prove the hypothesis that priorities in global health governance are based on the aggregation of individual explicit and implicit objectives. Explicit goals come in the form of mission statements, bylaws, and other founding documents. Implicit goals are priorities revealed from past decisions and behaviours.

Analysis of the tweets and other data showed that all 20 actors and the global health system collectively supported their hypothesis. Additionally, the authors found that funding organisations exerted compulsory power over channels of developmental assistance for health and the implementing institutions they directly fund. These funding organisations also possess influence over healthcare providers receiving developmental assistance health funding.

The correlation between the priorities of major funders and those of the funded institutions raises concerns. This gives significant power to large funders in determining the allocation of global health governance resources, limiting the funding of a broader range of health issues.

The study underscores issues of accountability, as funding organisations with outsized influence in priority setting may not be fully accountable for unfavourable outcomes. The limited involvement of implementing organisations, especially smaller local entities with close ties to target populations, in resource distribution decisions poses an additional concern. The authors conclude that global health governance structures can only lead to equitable health outcomes if major funding organisations collectively commit to goals of health equity and justice. The findings align with existing literature discussing the substantial influence of philanthropists and large funders on global health agenda setting, even without a clear ethical framework for decision-making.

As a specific instance, the authors suggest that whilst improvements were observed in HIV/AIDS, child health, and maternal health priorities between 2016 and 2020, the existing prioritisation process does not necessarily promote equity and justice in global health. Moreover, core health issues, such as horizontal health system improvements, were not found to be prioritised, potentially affecting the persistence of health inequities, and the current processes may limit the range of choices for health policies and programmes aimed at reducing inequities.

6.5.1 *Knowledge review*

Before you move on, can you define the following key concepts:

- Lobbying?
- Advocacy groups?

6.5.2 *Question to think about*

Think about a current health priority in your country or region. Which private sector organisations have an interest in how the issue is dealt with?

References

Agyepong, I. A., & Adjei, S. (2008). Public social policy development and implementation: A case study of the Ghana National Health Insurance scheme. *Health Policy and Planning*, 23(2), 150–160.

Alla, K., Hall, W. D., Whiteford, H. A., Head, B. W., & Meurk, C. S. (2017). How do we define the policy impact of public health research? A systematic review. *Health Research Policy and Systems*, 15, Article 84, 1–12.

Balane, M. A., Palafox, B., Palileo-Villanueva, L. M., McKee, M., & Balabanova, D. (2020). Enhancing the use of stakeholder analysis for policy implementation research: Towards a novel framing and operationalised measures. *BMJ Global Health*, 5(11), e002661.

Bermudez, G. F., & Prah, J. J. (2022). Examining power dynamics in global health governance using topic modelling and network analysis of Twitter data. *BMJ Open*, 12(6), e054470.

Bintabara, D. (2021). Addressing the huge poor–rich gap of inequalities in accessing safe childbirth care: A first step to achieving universal maternal health coverage in Tanzania. *PLos One*, 16(2), e0246995.

Browne, J., Coffey, B., Cook, K., Meiklejohn, S., & Palermo, C. (2019). A guide to policy analysis as a research method. *Health Promotion International*, 34(5), 1032–1044.

Giaimo, S. (2014). Interest groups, think tanks, and healthcare policy (1960s–present). In T. R. Oliver (Ed.), *Guide to U.S. health and healthcare policy* (pp. 375—392). Sage Reference/CQ Press.

Guise, V., Aase, K., Chambers, M., Canfield, C., & Wiig, S. (2021). Patient and stakeholder involvement in resilient healthcare: An interactive research study protocol. *BMJ Open*, 11(6), Article e049116.

Hill, M., & Varone, F. (2021). *The public policy process*. Routledge.

Hill-Briggs, F., Adler, N.E., Berkowitz, S.A., Chin, M.H., Gary-Webb, T.L., Navas-Acien, A., Thornton, P. L., & Haire-Joshu, D. (2021). Social determinants of health and diabetes: A scientific review. *Diabetes Care*, 44(1), 258.

Hird, T., Chamberlain, P., & Gilmore, A. (2021). Tobacco industry tactics to undermine tobacco control. In Tobacco Advisor Group of the Royal College of Physicians (Eds.), *Smoking and health 2021: A coming of age for tobacco control?* (pp. 136–149). Royal College of Physicians.

Mackintosh, M., Channon, A., Karan, A., Selvaraj, S., Cavagnero, E., & Zhao, H. (2016). What is the private sector? Understanding private provision in the health systems of low- income and middle-income countries. *The Lancet*, 388(10044), 596–605.

Marais, D. L., Quayle, M., & Petersen, I. (2020). Making consultation meaningful: Insights from a case study of the South African mental health policy consultation process. *PLoS One*, 15(1), e0228281.

Mendelow, A. (1991). *Stakeholder mapping*. Proceedings of the 2nd International Conference on Information Systems, Cambridge.

Mickwitz, P. (2021). Policy evaluation. In A. Jordan & V. Gravey (Eds.), *Environmental policy in the EU: Actors, institutions and processes* (4th ed., pp. 241—258). Routledge.

Mongiello, M. M. (2016). *Powerless in movement: How social movements influence, and fail to influence, American politics and policy*. University of Pennsylvania.

O'Brien, G. L., Sinnott, S.-J., Walshe, V., Mulcahy, M., & Byrne, S. (2020). Health policy triangle framework: Narrative review of the recent literature. *Health Policy Open*, 1, Article 10016.

Oleribe, O. O., Ukwedeh, O., Burstow, N. J., Gomaa, A. I., Sonderup, M. W., Cook, N., Waked, I., Spearman, W., & Taylor-Robinson, S. D. (2018). Health: Redefined. *The Pan African Medical Journal*, 30, Article 292.

Sari, A. R. (2023). The impact of good governance on the quality of public management decision making. *Journal of Contemporary Administration and Management (ADMAN)*, 1(2), 39–46.

Saunders, M., Barr, B McHale, P., & Hamelmann, C. (2017). Key policies for addressing the social determinants of health and health inequities, Health Evidence Synthesis Report 52, WHO Europe, Copenhagen.

Saurin, T. A. (2021). A complexity thinking account of the COVID-19 pandemic: Implications for systems-oriented safety management. *Safety Science*, 134, 105087.

Sodi, T., Modipane, M., Oppong Asante, K., Quarshie, E. N.-B., Asatsa, S., Mutambara, J., & Khombo, S. (2021). Mental health policy and system preparedness to respond to COVID-19 and other health emergencies: A case study of four African countries. *South African Journal of Psychology*, 51(2), 279–292.

Sketris, I., Bowles, S., & Manuel, R. (2022). Canadian public policies and practices related to drug prices, utilisation and expenditures. In Wertheimer, AI (ed.) *International drug regulatory mechanisms* (pp. 23–54), CRC Press. eBook ISBN9781003063858

Szakonyi, D. (2021). Private sector policy-making: Business background and politicians' behaviour in office. *The Journal of Politics*, 83(1), 260–276.

Verma, M. (2016). Role of the state in partnerships with the private sector. *Journal of Development Policy and Practice*, 1(1), 53-70.

Wollmann, H. (2017). Policy evaluation and evaluation research. In F. Fischer, G. J. Miller, & M. S. Sidney (Eds.), *Handbook of public policy analysis: Theory, politics, and methods* (pp. 393–404). Routledge.

WHO. (1984). *Health promotion: A discussion document on the concept and principles* (Summary report of the Working Group on Concept and Principles of Health Promotion, no. ICP/HSR 602 (m01)). WHO Regional Office for Europe.

WHO. (1986). *Healthcare policy*. WHO.

WHO. (2021). *Global antimicrobial resistance and use surveillance system (GLASS) report: 2021*. WHO.

WHO. (2023). *Suicide*. Factsheet published 28 August 2023. WHO.

Zahidie, A., Asif, S., & Iqbal, M. (2023). Building on the health policy analysis triangle: Elucidation of the elements. *Pakistan Journal of Medical Sciences*, 39(6), 1865.

7 Evidence in policymaking

7.1 Evidence-based policymaking

Evidence-based policymaking in healthcare involves the systematic use of rigorous and objective research evidence to inform the development, implementation, and evaluation of health policies and programmes. The aim is to ensure that policy decisions are grounded in the best available scientific evidence, promoting effective and efficient healthcare practices.

The key components of evidence-based policymaking in healthcare are:

- Rigorous research evidence
- Informed decision-making
- Transparent access to evidence
- Policy implementation and evaluation
- Consideration of context
- Interdisciplinary collaboration
- Continuous learning and improvement
- Communication and stakeholder engagement

The foundation of evidence-based policymaking is high-quality research evidence derived from well-designed studies, systematic reviews, and meta-analyses. This evidence should be obtained through robust research methodologies, such as randomised controlled trials, observational studies, or other appropriate study designs.

Policymakers use the accumulated evidence to inform their decision-making processes. This involves critically appraising and synthesising available evidence to understand the implications and potential outcomes of different policy options.

The process should be transparent, with policymakers having access to the evidence used to inform decisions. Transparency ensures accountability and allows stakeholders to understand the rationale behind specific policies.

Evidence-based policymaking extends beyond policy development to include the implementation and evaluation of policies. Policies should be implemented in a way that aligns with the available evidence, and their impact should be continuously assessed and adjusted based on ongoing evaluation.

While evidence plays a crucial role, policymakers should also consider the local context, values, and preferences of the population. The integration of evidence with contextual factors helps tailor policies to specific settings.

DOI: 10.4324/9781003478874-9

Effective evidence-based policymaking often involves collaboration between researchers, policymakers, healthcare practitioners, and other stakeholders. Interdisciplinary collaboration ensures that a diverse range of perspectives and expertise contribute to the decision-making process.

Evidence-based policymaking is an iterative process. Policymakers should be open to adapting policies based on new evidence and continuously seek opportunities for improvement.

Communicating evidence to various stakeholders, including the public, healthcare providers, and policymakers, is crucial. Engaging stakeholders in the policymaking process fosters support, understanding, and implementation of evidence-based policies.

Evidence-based policymaking in healthcare followed on from evidence-based medicine. The first article on evidence-based medicine was published in November 1992 (Evidence-Based Medicine Working Group, 1992), but the methods were not new; they were nearly a quarter-century old. Like its earlier iteration in 1978, the 1992 version of evidence-based medicine was developed and presented in the immediate context of medical education at McMaster University.

The acceptance of evidence-based medicine led to the adoption of the principles in other areas. In the UK, when the Labour Party took over the government in 1997, evidence-based policymaking was espoused as a means of moving away from ideology-based policymaking in favour of policies grounded in concrete and objective evidence (Arthur, 2017). Perhaps because of the link to evidence-based medicine, health policymakers were amongst the first to adopt the use of rigorously established and objective evidence.

The use of objective scientific knowledge, as opposed to fragmented, manipulated, or selectively chosen knowledge, is now widely deemed the most effective approach for achieving social goals (Arthur, 2017).

While affluent nations have predominantly facilitated health policymaking by incorporating evidence, low- and middle-income countries often encounter constraints as their healthcare systems still rely more on trial and error than evidence.

Nevertheless, the policymaking process does not consistently align with the straightforward logic of science. Health policy, vital for sustaining health systems, entails an intricate interplay among stakeholders possessing diverse perspectives, powers, interests, and agendas ((Cairney et al., 2019; Verboom et al., 2016).

This intricacy presents a challenge to the effective use of evidence in health policies and practices, particularly in low- and middle-income countries.

Despite these challenges, the incorporation of evidence in health policymaking is indispensable. It holds the potential to enhance the health policy process by pinpointing new agenda issues, assisting in decision-making regarding policy content and direction, and refining the assessment of policy impact. The role and utilisation of evidence in policymaking are subjects currently under examination, with a limited understanding of the comparative value of various types of evidence in shaping health decisions across diverse policy areas and scenarios.

Evidence-based medicine – an appropriate tool for evidence-based health policy? A case study from Norway by Malterud et al. (2016)

Norway adopted Evidence-Based Medicine (EBM) in 2004 through the establishment of the Norwegian Knowledge Centre for the Health Services (NOKC).

The NOKC, an independent government unit administered by the Norwegian Directorate of Health, aimed to enhance decision-making in health policy. Its establishment involved merging three existing health service research units and drawing on the expertise of researchers from the Norwegian branch of the Nordic Cochrane Centre. The NOKC's activities primarily focused on knowledge synthesis, including various types of systematic reviews, and monitoring through quality assessments and user satisfaction surveys.

The strategies employed by the NOKC for knowledge synthesis were explicitly drawn from EBM, with a conceptual perspective that promotes a balance between research evidence, experience-based knowledge, and patient values. An examination of NOKC publications, particularly systematic reviews, revealed a commitment to EBM standards, as well as a broader conceptual perspective emphasising the importance of patient values and preferences.

In 2014, a systematic examination by Malterud et al. (2016) of publications on the NOKC's website highlighted systematic reviews as the highest-ranked delivery format complying with EBM standards. The study aimed to explore the links and relations between EBM and Evidence-Based Practice (EBP) by focusing on activities related to knowledge synthesis. The sample selected for analysis included systematic reviews published between 2004 and 2013, reflecting the thematic areas of screening/diagnosis, treatment/medication/vaccination, prevention/psychosocial interventions, and initiatives within health and social services.

During the period of 2004–2013, the NOKC produced a total of 1,570 publications, with 151 systematic reviews representing 6–21% of its annual output. The highest proportion of systematic reviews was observed in the institution's early years, with a stable level since then. In 2012, 14 systematic reviews were published, covering various health areas, and the commissions came from government directorates, health professional trade unions, hospitals, and the Norwegian Cancer Society.

A qualitative evaluation of a subsample of systematic reviews from 2012 revealed a consistent rhetorical pattern in the conclusions, emphasising caution due to the quality or relevance of underlying documentation. The language used in the conclusions often expressed uncertainty, such as terms like "moderate," "low," or "very low quality" indicating the cautious approach in drawing conclusions. The analysis also highlighted the limited attention to contextual or qualitative matters in NOKC knowledge deliveries.

Malterud et al. (2016) raised concerns about the suitability of systematic reviews as universal tools for health policy decision-making. Despite the commitment to EBM values and methods, SRs, as the most valued format for knowledge delivery, demonstrated limitations in providing strong conclusions. The analysis suggested that the standardised and universal nature of EBM might not adequately address the complexity and context-specific nature of health policy decision-making.

The authors proposed that the EBM approach, with its restricted and simplistic view of scientific knowledge, might be inadequate for a government unit tasked with enhancing decision-making across a broad range of inquiries. The findings questioned whether the NOKC and similar institutions within the EBM movement, use too confined a range of tools for addressing too broad a range of inquiries.

They concluded that while EBM may be suitable for certain domains of inquiry, its application in health policy decision-making needs careful consideration. The limitations of EBM, especially in providing strong conclusions for complex interventions, raise questions about the potential consequences of "empty" knowledge deliveries and the impact on policy decision-making. Their study emphasised the importance of considering the context of interventions and advocated for a more nuanced and adaptable approach to knowledge provision in health policy decision-making.

7.1.1 Knowledge review

Before you move on, can you define the following key concepts:

- Evidence-based health policy?
- Evidence-based medicine?

7.1.2 Question to think about

Think about a major health policy initiative in your country or region. How strong is the evidence base behind the policy, in your view?

7.2 Sources of evidence

Health policymakers make use of various sources of evidence to inform their decisions. The choice of evidence sources depends on the nature of the policy issue, the available resources, and the context.

Scientific research and studies are usually published as articles in peer-reviewed journals: Policymakers often refer to published studies in reputable scientific journals. These studies are designed to provide rigorous and evidence-based insights into health-related issues. Their quality is checked by a process of peer review. Groups of studies may be summarised in systematic reviews and meta-analyses. Aggregated findings from systematic reviews and meta-analyses offer policymakers a comprehensive summary of existing research on a particular topic and can provide corroboration of findings from individual independent studies.

Government reports and publications, such as national health surveys, can provide valuable information on health trends, disease prevalence, and health disparities. Government health departments regularly commission their own research and publish reports on various health issues, outlining key statistics, trends, and policy recommendations.

International organisations, such as the World Health Organisation, World Bank, UNICEF, and other international organisations contribute to the evidence base through research, data collection, and the development of guidelines for health policies.

Both national and international organisations carry out Health Technology Assessments and economic evaluations. Health Technology Assessments of new medical technologies, treatments, or interventions help policymakers make informed decisions about adopting new healthcare practices, and economic evaluations, including cost-effectiveness analyses, help policymakers assess the financial implications and efficiency of healthcare interventions.

Clinical practice guidelines developed by medical and professional associations offer evidence-based recommendations for the diagnosis, treatment, and management of various health conditions. In other areas, policymakers may seek advice from expert panels or advisory committees composed of specialists in relevant fields to obtain expert opinions and recommendations. In addition, policymakers may undertake stakeholder consultations with healthcare professionals, patients, advocacy groups, and other stakeholders to understand diverse perspectives and the potential implications of policies.

Both the popular and specialist media can also contribute to policymakers' understanding of public concerns, emerging health threats, and the impact of policies on communities.

Gathering feedback directly from patients and the community provides insights into public preferences, concerns, and the potential impact of policies on different demographic groups.

Similarly, evaluation studies assessing the implementation and effectiveness of existing health policies can help policymakers understand what works and what needs improvement.

In practice, health policymakers often use a combination of these sources, recognising that a diverse evidence base enhances the robustness of decision-making and policy development. The integration of scientific evidence, real-world data, and input from various stakeholders contributes to more comprehensive and effective health policies.

7.2.1 Formal sources

Formal sources are sources that go through an extensive and rigorous review, assessment, and revision process before they are published. The credentials of each author on the source are evaluated and, when the source details are published, the authors' references are provided in addition to literature references and citations. Formal sources draw upon a range of different types of evidence.

7.2.2 Quantitative evidence

Quantitative research is the process by which numerical data are collected and analysed.

Quantitative research is based upon measurement. It may be used to assess patterns, find means, make predictions, test causality, and generate results that can be generalised to a wider population.

Table 7.1 lists the advantages and disadvantages of quantitative research.

There are a variety of types of research that are based upon quantitative data that may inform health policymaking.

- *Descriptive research* describes the characteristics of a population or phenomenon using surveys, observational studies, content analysis, e.g., a survey of a specific group of people to gather their perceptions of their health status.
- *Correlational research* examines the relationships between two or more variables using statistical techniques like correlation analysis, e.g., investigating the correlation between alcohol consumption and blood sugar levels.

Table 7.1 The advantages and disadvantages of quantitative research (after Edmonds & Kennedy, 2016; Rahman, 2020; Gelo et al., 2008)

Advantages	Disadvantages
Quantitative research relies on measurable data, which enhances objectivity and allows for replication of studies. This makes it easier to verify and reproduce results.	Quantitative research may not provide a deep understanding of the studied phenomenon, so complex concepts cannot be properly represented.
Quantitative data lends itself well to statistical analysis, providing researchers with the tools to identify patterns, relationships, and trends in the data.	Quantitative research relies on pre-determined variables and structured data collection methods, limiting the ability to adapt to unexpected findings or explore new aspects during the study.
The large sample sizes often associated with quantitative research allow for a higher degree of generalisability. Researchers can make inferences about the broader population based on the data collected.	The emphasis on numerical data may lead researchers to overlook important qualitative aspects, reducing the richness of the findings.
Quantitative methods are typically more precise and accurate when measuring variables. The use of standardised instruments and numerical data increases reliability.	The design of measurement instruments, such as surveys or tests, may introduce bias if not carefully constructed. This can impact the validity of the research.
Data collection in quantitative research is often more efficient, particularly when using surveys or experiments. This allows researchers to gather a significant amount of data in a relatively short time.	Many social phenomena are complex and multifaceted, making it challenging to capture all relevant aspects through quantitative measures alone.
Using formalised and established hypothesis testing methods means that research variables, predictions, data collection, and testing methods must be carefully reviewed and reported before reaching results.	Quantitative research heavily relies on the concepts of validity (whether a test measures what it intends to measure) and reliability (consistency of results). If these aspects are compromised, the entire study's credibility is at risk.
	Quantitative studies often use unnatural environments such as laboratories or do not consider historical and cultural backgrounds that can affect data collection and results.

- *Experimental research* seeks to establish cause-and-effect relationships by manipulating one or more independent variables and observing their effects on dependent variables, e.g., randomised controlled trials used to test the efficacy of new drugs. Example: Testing the impact of a new teaching method on student learning outcomes.
- *Quasi-experimental research* is. similar to experimental research but lacks random assignment of participants to groups. It uses methods, such as non-equivalent group designs and methods, based upon time-series designs. Because of its lower rigour, it would be used when randomisation is not an option.
- *Survey research* collects data from a sample of individuals using standardised questionnaires or interviews using structured interviews and questionnaires, e.g., a national survey to understand public opinions on a health policy proposal.

- *Longitudinal research* studies a group of participants over an extended period to observe changes or trends using data collection at multiple points in time, e.g., tracking the health status of a group of patients after surgery for particular cancer over several years.
- *Cross-Sectional research* collects data from a sample at a single point in time using surveys, observations, and experiments, e.g., analysing the health habits of different age groups in a specific community.
- *Causal-comparative research* seeks to identify causes or consequences of existing differences between groups by comparing groups that differ on an independent variable, e.g., investigating the impact of socioeconomic status on health status.
- *Meta-analyses* analyse and synthesise findings from multiple studies on a particular topic using statistical techniques to pool data from different studies, e.g., combining results from various clinical trials to assess the overall effectiveness of a medical treatment.
- *Simulation and modelling* creates mathematical or computer-based models to simulate real-world phenomena, e.g., simulating the spread of infectious diseases to assess the effectiveness of public health interventions.

In an ideal world, policy is based upon a range of evidence collected using a variety of methods.

7.2.3 *Qualitative evidence*

Qualitative research is based upon non-numerical data such as text, video, and audio. The data are collected and analysed with the aim of understanding concepts, opinions, or experiences, often within a specific context. Qualitative research is mainly used to gain in-depth insights into the problem or generate new ideas for the research in questions.

Qualitative research is used to understand how people perceive and experience the world (Smith & Smith, 2018; Hamilton & Finley, 2019).). There are many approaches to qualitative research, but they are flexible and tend to focus on gaining rich meaning in the interpretation of the data.

Common approaches include grounded theory, ethnography, action research, phenomenological research, and narrative research (Smith & Smith, 2018). Whilst these approaches have some similarities, they emphasise different goals and perspectives as detailed below:

- Grounded theory is used to collect extensive data on interesting topics and develop theories through induction.
- Ethnographic research is used by researchers who immerse themselves in groups and organisations to understand the cultures of the groups under observation.
- Action research is used by researchers and participants to jointly combine theory and practice to drive social change.
- Phenomenological research is used to study phenomena or events by explaining and interpreting the life experiences of participants.
- Narrative research gathers stories to understand how participants perceive and understand their experiences

(Tolley et al., 2016).

Whatever the approach, in qualitative research, a combination of data collection methods is preferred to triangulate the data. Methods may include:

- Interviews: conversations with participants to explore perspectives and experiences (e.g., in-depth interviews on social attitudes).
- Focus groups: facilitated group discussions to gather insights and opinions from multiple participants simultaneously (e.g., a focus group on treatment preferences).
- Observation: systematic watching and recording of behaviours in a natural setting (e.g., observing clinical consultations).
- Participant observation: actively participating in the setting being studied, collecting data while immersed in the context (e.g., joining a patient support group).
- Field notes: detailed written records of observations, reflections, and insights during qualitative research (e.g., field notes in ethnographic fieldwork).
- Document analysis: systematic examination of existing documents to gain insights into a phenomenon (e.g., analysing historical records).
- Content analysis: systematic analysis of text or media content to identify patterns or trends (e.g., analysing news articles on a specific policy issue).

Qualitative research holds significant value in the policymaking process. The insights derived from qualitative research, unlike those from quantitative methods, delve into the real-life experiences of stakeholders.

The approach offers a comprehensive understanding of policy contexts, shedding light on the intricate implementation processes. Furthermore, qualitative research contributes nuanced insights, especially beneficial for issues challenging to quantify (Green & Thorogood, 2018). Despite these advantages, policymakers often favour quantitative research, particularly randomised controlled trials (RCTs), regarded as the benchmark evaluation method (Murphy & Dingwall, 2017).

The advantages and disadvantages of qualitative research are shown in Table 7.2.

In reality, quantitative and qualitative research are different but complementary and a strong evidence base for policymaking can benefit from both as they answer different questions and have different characteristics:

- The main focus of quantitative research is on testing theories and hypotheses, whereas the main focus of qualitative research is on exploring ideas and gaining ideas.
- Quantitative research uses mathematical and statistical analysis, whereas qualitative research analyses data using summary, classification, and interpretation.
- Quantitative findings are mainly expressed in numbers, graphs, and tables; qualitative findings are mainly expressed in words.
- Quantitative research seeks to answer closed questions; qualitative research seeks to answer open-ended questions.
- Quantitative research emphasises testing, measurement, objectivity, and replicability; qualitative research emphasises understanding, context, complexity, and perceptions.

In health policymaking, a combination of qualitative and quantitative research methods, known as a mixed-methods approach, is often recommended to capitalise on the strengths of both approaches and provide a more comprehensive evidence base.

Table 7.2 The advantages and disadvantages of qualitative research (after Drisko, 2020; Mays & Pope, 2020; Smith, 2018)

Advantages	Disadvantages
Qualitative research allows for a deep exploration of complex health issues, providing a rich understanding of the experiences, perspectives, and contexts of individuals involved.	Findings from qualitative studies are often context-specific and may not be easily generalisable to broader populations, limiting their applicability.
Qualitative research helps policymakers to understand the cultural, social, and economic contexts that influence health-related behaviours and outcomes, making interventions more contextually relevant.	Qualitative research relies on interpretation, and findings may be influenced by the biases or perspectives of researchers, potentially introducing subjectivity.
Qualitative methods can uncover barriers and facilitators to health-related interventions, aiding policymakers in developing strategies that address specific challenges.	Qualitative research can be time-consuming and resource-intensive, requiring skilled researchers and extensive data analysis.
Continuous feedback from qualitative research enables policymakers to refine and improve health programmes based on real-world feedback, contributing to programme effectiveness.	Policymakers may prefer quantitative data for its numerical precision, and qualitative findings might be perceived as less straightforward or harder to quantify.
Qualitative approaches involve engaging with stakeholders, including communities and individuals, fostering a sense of inclusivity and ensuring that policies resonate with those directly affected.	Qualitative studies often involve smaller sample sizes compared to quantitative research, which may raise concerns about the representativeness of the findings.
Qualitative research is well-suited to explore unexpected or unanticipated outcomes, providing insights that may not be captured by quantitative methods alone.	In the real world, qualitative research is often unreliable due to uncontrolled factors that affect the data.

7.2.4 Mixed-methods research

Using mixed-methods research in health policymaking can offer a more comprehensive and nuanced understanding of complex health issues. By combining both qualitative and quantitative approaches, policymakers can leverage the strengths of each method to generate a more robust evidence base. (Stern et al., 2021).

Qualitative methods provide in-depth insights into the experiences, attitudes, and contexts of individuals, while quantitative methods offer statistical generalisability and numerical precision. The use of both qualitative and quantitative data allows for triangulation, where findings from one method can be cross-validated or corroborated by the other. This helps enhance the overall validity of the research.

Health policy issues are often multifaceted and complex. Mixed methods allow researchers to approach these questions from different angles, capturing both the breadth and depth of the issue. Quantitative data can provide generalisable findings, while qualitative data contributes to a contextual understanding. The combination ensures that research findings are applicable to a broader population while being sensitive to the specific contexts and nuances. Health policies often need to address real-world complexities. Mixed-methods research acknowledges and embraces this complexity, providing evidence that is more pragmatic for decision-making.

The inclusion of qualitative methods fosters stakeholder engagement, involving the voices of communities, individuals, and policymakers in the research process. This inclusivity increases the likelihood that research findings will be accepted and implemented.

A well-designed mixed-methods study with rigorous data collection and analysis processes enhances the credibility of the research. Policymakers are more likely to trust findings derived from a comprehensive research strategy that embraces multiple perspectives.

Whilst mixed-methods research can be resource-intensive, it optimises resource utilisation by ensuring that different types of data are collected to address different aspects of the research question, maximising the return on investment.

Schoonenboom and Johnson (2017) highlight seven critical dimensions for designing mixed-methods research, emphasising the importance of aligning design choices with research questions and purposes. Considerations of these dimensions will help researchers and policymakers bets exploit a mixed-methods approach.

The first dimension is purpose. There are many diverse purposes for which qualitative and quantitative methods may be combined, highlighting the need for alignment with research questions.

The second dimension focuses on the theoretical drive, as defined by Morse and Niehaus (2009). They distinguish between inductive and deductive approaches or a blend of both. Additionally, studies may be qualitatively or quantitatively driven or maintain an equal-status mix.

The third dimension deals with timing, addressing simultaneity (concurrent, sequential, or multiphase) and dependence, emphasising whether later components build upon earlier results.

The fourth dimension, the point of integration, is concerned with how and when the qualitative and quantitative components are brought together, a crucial aspect though not always explicitly stated in the design name.

The fifth dimension explores typological versus interactive design approaches, encouraging researchers to examine various design typologies to understand the field better. The authors suggest combining designs or constructing new ones when existing typologies do not align with research questions.

The sixth dimension addresses whether a design is fully specified during planning or allowed to emerge during the research process, highlighting the flexibility and interactive nature of research design.

The seventh dimension, complexity, underscores the need for embracing complex designs, including multilevel designs, as a means to effectively address research questions. The responsibility lies with researchers to learn how to construct, describe, and name mixed-methods research designs that align with their unique research questions and purposes, rather than fitting into pre-existing design categories. The emphasis is on a flexible and dynamic approach to research design, ensuring it evolves in response to the intricate nature of the research process.

7.2.5 Informal sources

Informal sources published by individuals or organisations may not contain author qualifications or citations, making it difficult to establish authority and often lack any process or rigor to evaluate the data and findings. Important emerging literature shows the role of informal knowledge in the planning of public health programmes, due to the fact that in some cases, researchers, public health professionals, and policymakers may need to make decisions about issues that are under-researched. In addition, due to the context-dependent nature of community-based health policy interventions, studies on the effectiveness of interventions may not be available (Kothari et al., 2015).

Grey literature is an umbrella term for various types of literature that is not formally published through traditional academic publishing channels and usually not peer-reviewed. This type of literature may be produced by government agencies, non-profit organisations, industry groups, think tanks, and other entities outside the commercial or academic publishing sphere. Grey literature includes a wide range of materials that are not easily accessible through conventional databases or indexing systems. Specific examples include government reports, (non-peer reviewed) conference papers and proceedings, working papers, technical reports, non-governmental organisation (NGO) reports, policy briefs, and newsletters and magazines.

Grey literature is valuable for several reasons. It often provides timely information, covers niche topics, and offers insights into ongoing research or policy discussions. However, since grey literature may not undergo the same rigorous peer-review process as formally published literature, researchers should critically assess the quality and reliability of the information it contains. It may be published to promote the interests of a specific stakeholder.

Despite its informal nature, grey literature plays a crucial role in the dissemination of knowledge and can contribute significantly to research, especially in applied fields and policy-related contexts.

Other informal sources of evidence can include blogs and social media posts, podcasts, letters and emails, and videos on social media platforms.

7.2.6 Hierarchies of evidence

The hierarchy of evidence is a framework for ranking evidence to be used in health policymaking. The hierarchy of evidence (or level of evidence) is a top-down approach used to rank the relative strength of scientific research results. The hierarchy of evidence serves as a structured framework for evaluating the strength of research findings, particularly in the context of health policymaking. This top-down approach, established since the late 1970s, prioritises various research methods based on their validity and reliability (Canadian Task Force on the Periodic Health Examination, 1979).

Over 80 different hierarchies have been proposed, considering factors such as study design (e.g., randomised controlled trials) and measured endpoints (e.g., survival or quality of life). Large-scale epidemiological studies generally hold a consensus as strong evidence.

While randomised controlled trials (RCTs) are often considered the best evidence in clinical studies, systematic reviews are frequently deemed the highest-quality evidence in policy research, often referred to as the "gold standard" since they represent the distillation of multiple RCTs. A typical hierarchy of this type is shown in Figure 7.1

Criticism of the hierarchy of evidence has emerged in the 21st century (Tugwell & Knottnerus, 2015). Critics argue that it overlooks the value of qualitative studies and that even systematic reviews, considered the gold standard, have limitations and flaws (Bigby, 2008).

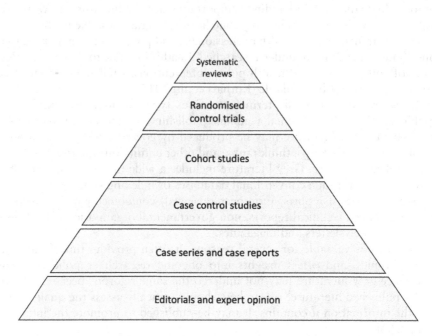

Figure 7.1 A classical hierarchy of evidence (after Canadian Task Force on the Periodic Health Examination, 1979).

The concept of the "quality" of evidence is defined as the confidence in the estimation of the effect supporting a specific recommendation. This definition underscores the need for judgment by the research team, considering the specific context of use. Systematic reviews, which do not make recommendations, require a different definition for the quality of evidence, focusing on the confidence that the effect estimate is accurate.

Research rigour is another crucial aspect, involving components like credibility, transferability, dependability, and conformability. Credibility assesses the reliability and appropriateness of a research report. Transferability focuses on the ability to apply research results or methods to different groups. Dependability concerns the consistency and reliability of research results, emphasising thorough documentation of research procedures. Conformability involves the objectivity of data collection and analysis, requiring agreement among independent individuals about the accuracy and relevance of data. Overall, these components contribute to building trust in research results, ensuring consistency in methods over time and providing an accurate representation of the studied population.

Using evidence to formulate policy on advice to parents to prevent sudden infant death syndrome (after Jullien, 2021)

Despite the success of several preventive campaigns started in the 1990s targeting modifiable risk factors related to sudden infant death syndrome (SIDS), it remains a leading cause of infant mortality in high-income countries.

Current guidance from the UK National Institute for Health and Clinical Excellence (2015) advises healthcare professionals to:

- "Recognise that co-sleeping can be intentional or unintentional. Discuss this with parents and carers and inform them that there is an association between co- sleeping (parents or carers sleeping on a bed or sofa or chair with an infant) and SIDS."
- "Inform parents and carers that the association between co-sleeping (sleeping on a bed or sofa or chair with an infant) and SIDS is likely to be greater when they, or their partner, smoke."
- "Inform parents and carers that the association between co-sleeping (sleeping on a bed or sofa or chair with an infant) and SIDS may be greater with parental or carer recent alcohol consumption, or parental or carer drug use, or low birthweight or premature infants."

Similar guidance is provided by the American Academy of Pediatrics (AAP) and is endorsed by both the WHO and CDC.

Jullien (2021) conducted a literature review up to the end of 2020 and found the following key evidence for the advice given (Table 7.3).

7.2.7 Knowledge review

Before you move on, can you define the following key concepts:

- Quantitative research?
- Qualitative research?
- Hierarchy of evidence?

7.2.8 Question to think about

How often when you have heard health advice has the evidence been explained to you? If it was, did it make sense to you?

7.3 Paradigms in policy research

Paradigms serve as fundamental theoretical approaches for observing and comprehending the world, playing a crucial role in shaping the methodology adopted by researchers. Historically, the most significant and contrasting paradigms have been the positivist and naturalistic paradigms.

Table 7.3 Key evidence for advice to parents to prevent sudden infant death syndrome (after Jullien, 2021)

AAP Policy recommendation	Evidence
To reduce the risk of SIDS, infants should be placed for sleep in the supine position (wholly on the back) for every sleep period by every caregiver until one year of age.	Consistent findings across the world and decreasing trend on the incidence of SIDS in countries that have implemented the "Back to Sleep" recommendations support the hypothesis that the supine position for sleep protects against SIDS; supine position does not increase the risk of choking and aspiration.
Firm surfaces should always be used: the mattresses must be firm and maintain their shape even when covered with the sheets, so that there are no gaps left between the mattress and the crib railing. Adjustable sheets and specific bedding should be used.	Soft sleep surface has consistently been reported as a risk factor for SIDS. A case-control study conducted in the US among 260 SIDS cases and 260 matched living controls showed an association between soft sleep surface and a higher risk of SIDS.
Other loose accessories, such as blankets, quilts and pillows, cushions, soft objects and neck pendants, should be kept away from the infant's sleep area.	Several publications pointed out that soft objects (pillows, pillow-like toys, quilts, comforters, sheepskins) and loose bedding (blankets, nonfitted sheets) can cause the obstruction of an infant's external airways, leading to an increased risk of suffocation, rebreathing, and SIDS.
Avoid overheating and avoid the head to be covered while sleeping.	Overheating has been identified as a risk factor for SIDS, especially when the head is covered. Several studies had shown that overheating (including external temperature and the child's clothes) was associated with an increased risk of SIDS, but it is difficult to provide any specific room temperature recommendation as the definition of overheating varies across studies.
The crib in the parents' bedroom is the safest place. Recommend against co-sleeping if father or mother are tobacco smokers, have drunk alcohol, or anxiolytic, antidepressant, or hypnotic drugs have been used and in case of extreme exhaustion.	There is a lack of evidence to determine the balance between harm and benefits of bed-sharing among infants without other risk factors associated (parental use of tobacco or alcohol), taking breastfeeding into consideration. However, there are specific circumstances that have been shown to substantially increase the risk of SIDS including: when one or both parents are smokers, even if they are not smoking in bed; when the mother smoked during pregnancy; when the infant is younger than four months of age, regardless of parental smoking status; when the infant is born preterm and/or with low birth weight; or when the parent has consumed alcohol and/or illicit or sedating drugs.
Unless contraindicated, mothers should breastfeed exclusively or feed with expressed milk (i.e., not offer any formula or other nonhuman milk-based supplements) for six months.	Breastfeeding is a clear protective factor for SIDS based on a systematic review that included 18 case control studies.

(Continued)

Table 7.3 (Continued)

AAP Policy recommendation	Evidence
Recommend against tobacco smoking to parents, especially to the mother during pregnancy, although also after delivery. Don't allow anybody smoking in the infants' presence.	Maternal smoking is an independent risk factor for SIDS. This association has been found independently for both maternal smoking during pregnancy and after birth, from several studies.
Avoid the prenatal and postnatal use of alcohol and illegal drugs.	The use of alcohol or illicit drugs during prenatal (periconceptional and gestational) and postnatal periods has been associated with an increased risk of SIDS [2, 4]. Similarly, to smokers, the risk increases when an alcohol or drug user share the bed with the infant.

The positivist or experimental paradigm is linked to scientific methods and research, emphasising quantitative approaches. By contrast, the naturalistic paradigm is commonly connected to specific domains like social anthropology and sociology and associated with the use of qualitative research methods.

7.3.1 *Positivism*

Positivism originated in the 19th century and gained prominence with the work of Auguste Comte, who is often considered the founder of positivism.

It relies on observable and measurable phenomena. It values empirical evidence derived from sensory experience and experiments. It emphasises the application of the scientific method in research. The positivist paradigm is based upon formulating hypotheses, conducting experiments or empirical observations, and analysing data to draw conclusions.

Positivism seeks objectivity in the study of social and natural phenomena. It aims to eliminate personal biases and subjective interpretations, emphasising the importance of verifiable and replicable results. This often involves the collection and analysis of quantitative data, using statistical methods to identify patterns and relationships.

Positivism seeks to establish causal relationships between variables. It aims to identify the cause-and-effect relationships underlying observed phenomena.

Positivism is particularly influential in the natural sciences, where its emphasis on empirical observation and the scientific method has been successful, and it has been a powerful influence on the development of evidence-based medicine. However, it has been critiqued for its limitations in addressing complex social phenomena, leading to the development of alternative paradigms, such as interpretivism and critical theory, in the social sciences, and these paradigms have often been cited as alternatives to positivism when dealing with the complex problems faced by health policymakers.

Positivism relies on hypothetical deduction to verify a priori hypothesis, usually expressed in a quantitative manner, in which causality and the functional relationship between explanatory factors (independent variables) and outcomes (dependent variables) can be derived (Park et al., 2020).

Ontology, in philosophy and theoretical discussions, refers to the branch of metaphysics that explores the nature and existence of being or reality. Within the positivist view of the world, there is one concrete reality. Further, this one reality can be understood, identified, and measured.

Positivism argues that knowledge can and must be developed objectively without the value of researchers and participants affecting its development. Knowledge is true when properly developed, meaning it is certain, realistic, and accurate. For this to occur, there must be an absolute separation between research participants and researchers in order for the truth to develop "correctly." In addition, the two units are separated by adhering to strict protocols to reduce research bias.

Positivism places a strong emphasis on objectivity, leading to the rejection of individual subjective experiences and values, including those of both research participants and researchers themselves (Park et al., 2020). This necessitates researchers to maintain objectivity during data collection, refraining from interaction with participants and avoiding involvement in the experiment. Achieving such objectivity is relatively straightforward in certain contexts, such as experimental physics conducted in a vacuum, where external factors are excluded from the study. However, attaining objectivity is more challenging in other domains. For instance, social science research utilises empiricism, relying on rigorous research protocols to minimise researcher bias (Park et al., 2020).

Positivist methodologies stress the importance of conducting research in controlled environments where variables can be manipulated. In the social sciences, researchers often create somewhat artificial settings to minimise external factors beyond the research variables (Lindenfeld, 2022). In its purest form, positivism directs research towards examining descriptive or causal relationships between variables, akin to practices in the natural sciences. Consequently, the positivist paradigm prioritises experimental designs, including quasi-experimental designs. The outcomes of these experiments serve to validate or refine existing theories and may generate new hypotheses and avenues for further research (Lindenfeld, 2022).The main goal of the positivist experiment is to isolate and control the effects of all factors and examine only the variables of interest.

Research within the positivist paradigm focuses on meticulously monitoring potential threats to internal validity and devising study designs that enable control over confounding factors. Positivism underscores the significance of maintaining internal validity and addressing confounding variables to ensure the robustness of research tests. Additionally, positivism emphasises the necessity of a sufficient sample size to guarantee statistical power and a meaningful effect size. Determining an appropriate sample size and consequently ensuring power and effect size is achieved through the application of suitable statistical tests (Park et al., 2020).

In contrast to other research paradigms that may not prioritise the importance of a large study sample, positivist researchers contend that having an adequately large sample is pivotal. This is because it enables the utilisation of a statistical principle to select appropriate study designs, determining a "priori virtual effect size." In simpler terms, a larger sample size allows researchers to ascertain the actual "potential size of the difference" between the intervention group and the control group The greater the sample size, the lower the statistical uncertainty, leading to more dependable and reliable results (Park et al., 2020).

The complexity of many health policy problems means that designing studies to gather evidence using a positivist paradigm is often impossible, and other approaches are needed.

7.3.2 *Interpretivism*

Interpretivism is a research paradigm or philosophical approach that emphasises the subjective and context-dependent nature of reality. Unlike positivism, which seeks to uncover universal laws governing phenomena through objective observation and measurement, interpretivism acknowledges that reality is socially constructed and shaped by individual experiences and perspectives. (Pulla & Carter, 2018).

Interpretivism recognises that individuals interpret the world based on their unique experiences, values, and cultural backgrounds. It emphasises the importance of understanding and exploring these subjective interpretations.

As a consequence, interpretivist research often relies on qualitative methods such as interviews, participant observation, and content analysis. These methods allow researchers to delve into the meanings, perspectives, and experiences of individuals within a specific context.

The interpretivist paradigm emphasises the importance of studying phenomena within their natural context. Researchers seek to understand the social and cultural context in which individuals operate to gain insights into the meaning-making processes.

Designers of interpretivist research often take a holistic approach, considering the interconnectedness of various factors and recognising that the whole is more than the sum of its parts. They will acknowledge and reflect on their own biases, assumptions, and influence on the research process.

Interpretivist research often makes use of inductive reasoning, where theories and explanations emerge from the data rather than being imposed a priori, and then tested.

Interpretivism is commonly employed in social sciences, humanities, and qualitative research settings where the goal is to understand and interpret the meanings and lived experiences of individuals and groups. It contrasts with positivism, offering an alternative perspective that is particularly suited to exploring complex, subjective, and contextually rich phenomena.

Interpretivist approaches may be welcomed by health policymakers dealing with complex social problems but are likely to treated more sceptically by medical doctors and scientists embedded in the scientific tradition with its emphasis on objectivity and generalisation.

7.3.3 *Knowledge review*

Before you move on, can you define the following key concepts:

* Positivism?
* Interpretivism?

7.3.4 *Question to think about*

Think of a key health policy issue in your country or region. If asked to investigate the issue, would you adopt a positivist or an interpretivist approach?

7.4 Health policy analysis

Thus far, we have considered the gathering of evidence in order to create new health policies. Just as important is how evidence is used to make or change policies based on how well they are meeting their goals. Health policy analysis is a collective term for the evidence-based creation and evaluation of health policies.

It aims to understand the development, implementation, and impact of policies related to health and healthcare. Health policy analysts use various methods to assess policies, identify their strengths and weaknesses, and provide evidence-based recommendations for improvement.

Health policy analysis is an interdisciplinary field based on economics, political science, sociology, epidemiology, and biostatistics.

Health policy analysts examine the process of policy formulation, looking at how policies are developed, drafted, and shaped. This involves understanding the political, economic, social, and cultural factors that influence policy decisions. Their analysis extends to the implementation phase, assessing how policies are put into practice. This involves studying the roles and responsibilities of different stakeholders, the allocation of resources, and the operational challenges encountered during implementation.

They assess the impact of policies on health outcomes, healthcare delivery, and various population groups. This includes examining whether the intended objectives are achieved and identifying any unintended consequences. They explore how policies affect equity and access to healthcare services. They assess whether policies contribute to disparities in health outcomes and access to services among different demographic groups.

Health policy analysis often involves economic evaluation, examining the financial implications of policies. This includes assessing the cost-effectiveness of interventions, budgetary considerations, and potential economic impacts. It may also include the legal and ethical dimensions of health policies, ensuring that they align with established legal frameworks and ethical principles. This may involve assessing issues related to patient privacy, informed consent, and human rights.

Health policy analysis must take account of the perspectives of various stakeholders, including policymakers, healthcare providers, patients, advocacy groups, and the general public. Engaging stakeholders helps ensure that policies reflect diverse interests and concerns.

Browne et al. (2019) frames the scope and purpose of health policy analysis in terms of a number of key questions:

- What has happened thus far as a consequence of this policy?
- What is happening now as a consequence of this policy?
- Why have these consequences happened?
- What will the consequences of policy alternatives be in the future?
- What would the consequence of doing nothing be in the future?
- What is the value of the consequences of different particular options based not just on cost, but also utilisation, satisfaction, health outcomes, and so on?

And finally, based upon the answers to these questions: What should be done in the future?

Health policy analysis may be undertaken at the clinical, administrative/managerial or legislative level. A typical task at the clinical level might be to develop, implement, and evaluate clinical guidelines. At the administrative/managerial level, it might be used to assess the implementation of policies such as accreditation. At a legislative level, it may be used to assess development, implementation, and evaluation of banning smoking in public places (Browne et al., 2019).

7.4.1 Conducting health policy analysis

Seven steps to conduct health policy analysis have been proposed by the likes of Fischer et al. (2017) and Morgan (2017).

1. Define the context/state of the problem
2. Analyse the actors/stakeholders
3. Develop policy options
4. Project the outcome and potential impact (cost, benefit, etc.)
5. Apply evaluative criteria
6. Evaluate and weigh the outcome
7. Make decisions based on the evidence

Step 1 – Clearly articulate the context or identify the existing problem
During the initial phase, it is crucial to precisely define the nature of the problem and identify the specific population affected. Examining the historical evolution of the issue provides a comprehensive understanding of the context, facilitating a more in-depth analysis of the root causes, which can be explored through root-cause analysis.

Step 2 – Evaluate the actors and stakeholders
This stage involves a thorough analysis of all potential stakeholders with vested interests in the policy under consideration. After this analysis, their levels of interest and influence are identified and plotted on a power/interest grid to determine optimal strategies for managing and engaging with them.

Step 3 – Formulate policy alternatives
This step uses a comparison of best practices and benchmarks. Soliciting input from stakeholders is essential at this juncture to build consensus and garner support from those who can facilitate progress. Approaches such as incentives, information dissemination, and the introduction of new programmes can be considered.

Step 4 – Anticipate outcomes and potential impacts
This phase involves assessing the anticipated outcomes and potential impact of the proposed policy, considering factors like benefits for the population and community (e.g., health outcomes), costs, ethical and equity considerations, as well as administrative and organisational feasibility. Various stakeholders' perspectives also play a significant role in this evaluation.

Step 5/6 – Apply evaluative criteria/Evaluate and prioritise outcomes
In this step, researchers establish a decision matrix based on specific criteria. This matrix, which visually compares various options, is created by determining key decision-making criteria and assigning weights to each criterion.

Table 7.4 Example of how to use a sample decision matrix

Scenario: Policymakers want to develop a policy to decrease the prevalence of underage drinking among youth.

Criteria (relative weight)	Policy option 1: Increase taxation on alcohol (Score 1–10)	Policy option 2: Eliminate access of youth to alcohol through asking for ID, etc. (Score 1–10)
Population benefit	10	10
Cost	6	8
Ethics/equity	6	6
Organisational	7	7
Feasibility	8	6
Stakeholders	7	9
Total	44	46

Step 7 – Make evidence-based decisions

This final step involves making decisions based on the best option identified in the decision matrix. Once the decision is made, it is shared with stakeholders. Subsequently, the policy will need advocacy, implementation, and evaluation. Table 7.4 gives an example to illustrate a sample decision matrix.

Based on the above matrix, the second policy option may be considered to be the better option.

7.4.2 *Knowledge review*

Before you move on, can you define the following key concepts:

• Health policy analysis?

7.4.3 *Question to think about*

Use Browne et al.'s (2019) six questions to examine a current health policy in your own country.

How well is the policy working?

7.5 Evidence in a complex world

Despite all the information already mentioned about the importance of the use of the best evidence in policymaking, as well as the various types and sources of evidence, it is important to note that there are limitations.

7.5.1 Problem complexity

Much of the evidence gathered by researchers is from a positivist. As has been discussed, health policy problems are often complex in nature and therefore, this type of evidence can only go so far in providing policies and delivering solutions. Evidence generated within an interpretivist world-view is often context dependent, and so this may limit its use in other contexts.

For this reason, policymakers should be cautious in their use of prior evidence. Practical measures that can be adopted to ensure that the policy is appropriate in the context where it will be applied include:

- Use pilot programmes to test policy interventions on a smaller scale before full-scale implementation. This allows for adjustments based on real-world feedback and early results.
- Establish mechanisms for ongoing monitoring and evaluation to assess the impact of the policy from the start. Use quantitative and qualitative data to determine whether the intended outcomes are being achieved.
- Create feedback mechanisms to continuously collect information during policy implementation. Use this feedback to make necessary adjustments and improvements as you go.
- Recognise that health policy is an evolving process. As new evidence emerges, be willing to adapt and refine policies accordingly.
- Clearly communicate the evidence supporting the policy to various audiences, including the general public, healthcare professionals, and policymakers.
- Invest in training programmes to build the capacity of healthcare professionals, policymakers, and community members. This helps ensure effective implementation and sustainability of health policies.
- Empower stakeholders to feedback, report unexpected outcomes and challenges and to suggest changes.
- Ensure that the leaders of the policy have an overall view to prevent changes made in one part of the implementation creating unexpected challenges elsewhere.

All policies must be dynamic and respond to both changes in the operating and external environments and in unforeseen outcomes.

7.5.2 Unavailability of the evidence needed

In certain instances, obtaining the most suitable evidence for shaping and executing a specific policy can be either impracticable or actually impossible. This challenge is particularly pronounced when introducing novel management strategies and technologies (Malekinejad et al., 2018). In such situations, the absence of established knowledge, often coupled with insufficient organisational data, can hamper the policymaking process, diminishing the likelihood of favourable outcomes (Malekinejad et al., 2018).

Moreover, another constraint arises from the swiftly evolving management landscape, surpassing the pace of scientific and empirical knowledge generation relevant to policymaking contexts beyond the present day. Technology is increasingly disruptive to the status quo, leading to more complex and dynamic environments.

Faced with these challenges, policymakers may be forced to rely on the available evidence but treat the ongoing policy as a prototype, exploring what might or might not be effective.

For example, during the early stages of the COVID-19 pandemic, limited evidence existed on the optimal approaches to managing such a crisis, leaving governments and policymakers worldwide were uncertain about the most effective strategies for containment (Cairney, 2021).

7.5.3 The gap between researchers and policymakers

There is often a cultural gap between researchers and policymakers. Much of the evidence has traditionally been generated by scientific researchers, whilst health policymakers are often from a social science perspective.

The scientists may regard policymakers as lacking in the skills to find and evaluate scientific evidence and expect the policymakers to upskill themselves in the required skills which takes a lot of time and effort. Without these skills, policymakers tend to be limited by confirmation bias, meaning they only see evidence to support their personal experiences and judgments.

However, from the policymakers' perspective, they may regard evidence from within the positivist paradigm as too limited to meet their needs in creating policies to tackle complex social problems and look for other types of evidence which the scientists will regard as lacking rigour.

The relationship between researchers/scientists and policymakers has historically been a "complicated" relationship, which is subject to a permanent paradox (Gollust et al., 2017). Policymakers are constantly seeking empirical data, evidence, facts, and authoritative explanations on which to base their policies in order to justify their decisions based on scientific evidence (Gollust et al., 2017). However, the communication between researchers and policymakers is almost always limited to the communication of evidence by researchers, leaving the explanations, interpretations, and judgments associated with the policy process to the policymakers. In addition, the literature clearly highlights that the use of evidence in policymaking is limited (Gollust et al., 2017; Uzochukwu et al., 2016). This "gap" between research and policy/politics can be traced back to the gap of communication and understanding between these two parties, which renders a lot of research pointless and purposeless (Uzochukwu et al., 2016).

In order to address this gap, it is necessary for scientific researchers to learn more about each other's world views and respect each other's positions to gain maximum benefit from the relationship between researchers and policymakers.

7.5.4 Bias and conflicts of interest

Research bias arises when a researcher, whether intentionally or unintentionally, skews the entire research process towards specific outcomes by introducing systematic errors into the sample data. Essentially, it involves manipulating the systematic aspects of research to achieve a particular result.

A type of bias associated with scientific evidence and its subsequent utilisation in policymaking or decision-making at any level is the conflict of interest. Although there is no consistent definition of conflict of interest, it revolves around the apprehension that competing interests could influence research methods, data interpretation, and conclusions. Instances of conflicts of interest in research typically occur when it is perceived that a researcher prioritises their obligations and responsibilities over their personal interests. These conflicts can be realistic, potential, or perceived, encompassing both monetary and non-monetary interests (Romain, 2015).

In severe cases, conflicts of interest can contribute to scientific misconduct, impede the training of scientists, delay the dissemination of research results, jeopardise human health and the environment, and misguide decisions in the realm of social science. Government-sponsored research, whether direct or indirect, significantly contributes to policymaking. However, the perceived preference of a government agency for a specific type of study can influence how the study is conducted, potentially leading to biased results. Policy researchers, seeking to align with government priorities, often tailor their research capabilities accordingly, although the topics and formats may be influenced by the donor's priorities (in this case, the government).

Similarly, concerns arise when research is funded by private donors, such as pharmaceutical companies, regarding potential conflicts of interest and their impact on the quality of produced evidence. Nonetheless, privately funded clinical research is crucial because involvement from non-governmental, privately owned organisations provides researchers with resources – financial, equipment, technological – that may be unavailable through government funding.

Rahman-Shepherd et al. (2021) identify three broad types of conflict of interest in health policymaking.

- The first form of conflict of interest arises when policymakers or regulators assume dual roles, leaving their (primary) professional decisions susceptible to influence from other connections involving financial, social, or familial bonds with the institutions or industries under their regulatory purview. For instance, individuals who own pharmaceutical companies or have family ties to such owners often hold decision-making authority in drug regulatory agencies responsible for formulating and implementing policies regarding drug quality and ethical marketing practices. Consequently, influential decision-makers have incentives to shape new policies or allocate resources in a manner that safeguards the sales of medicines, thereby protecting their financial interests or those of their associates.
- The second type of conflict of interest is rooted in concealed financial associations between licensed and unlicensed healthcare providers. Due to financial transactions from informal to formal providers, the latter may publicly advocate for stricter regulation of the informal healthcare sector while clandestinely leveraging their influence to impede policies restricting informal practices. As an example, doctors and pharmacists may illicitly lease their professional licenses to establish drug shops and clinics where less qualified attendants, often lacking the necessary credentials, deliver services. Policies aimed at addressing improper healthcare delivery by unqualified providers in such establishments would potentially diminish a revenue source for doctors and pharmacists, leading to their covert resistance.
- The third type of conflict of interest emerges when policymakers are swayed to pursue a course of action more likely to garner political support rather than aligning with public health evidence. Policymakers are aware that implementing or enforcing regulations to govern private healthcare provision could be unpopular due to dependencies on the sector's contributions, potentially jeopardising their careers. For instance, the formidable challenge faced by policymakers in numerous countries relies on unlicensed medicine sellers to provide access to essential medicines in under-resourced areas. Policies aimed at reducing service provision by private providers, including those lacking proper training and delivering substandard care, are often avoided due to concerns that they might expose gaps in healthcare that the public sector should address.

Various measures can be taken to mitigate conflicts of interest, including requiring researchers to disclose any such conflicts in their publications and implementing effective management strategies to minimise their development. However, conflicts of interest continue to be a legitimate concern and a potential limitation in the use of research in policymaking.

Preventing and managing conflict of interest in nutrition policy (after Ralston et al., 2021)

The World Health Organisation (WHO) recently devised a proposed tool aimed at aiding member states in preventing and managing conflicts of interest in nutrition policy. Ralston et al. (2021) analysed the responses from an online consultation to examine how stakeholders from various sectors comprehend conflicts of interest and how they employ this concept to shape the terms of the commercial sector's involvement in health governance.

Using a thematic framework informed by framing theory, they categorised submissions from 44 member states, international organisations, NGOs, academic institutions, and commercial sector entities, The respondents' alignment with the tool revealed two overarching frames: a "collaboration and partnership" frame endorsing multi-stakeholder approaches and a "restricted engagement" frame emphasising core tensions between public health and food industry actors.

The responses to the WHO tool showcased divergent conceptualisations of conflicts of interest and their implications for health governance. While most member states, NGOs, and academic institutions strongly supported the tool, commercial sector organisations criticised it as inappropriate, unworkable, and incompatible with the SDGs.

The commercial sector respondents promoted a narrow, individual-level understanding of conflict of interest, considering it adequately addressed by existing disclosure mechanisms, and perceived the WHO tool as unduly limiting the scope for private sector engagement in nutrition policy. In contrast, health-focused NGOs and several member states embraced a more expansive understanding of conflicts of interest, recognising broader tensions between public health goals and commercial interests, along with associated governance challenges. These submissions mostly welcomed the tool as an innovative approach to preventing and managing such conflicts, although some NGOs advocated for the broader exclusion of corporate actors from policy engagement.

Ralston et al. (2021) argue that the WHO tool for preventing and managing conflicts of interest in nutrition policy stands as a crucial innovation in global health governance, providing a framework to assess and manage potential conflicts between public health goals and the interests of the commercial sector and other external actors. They say that it represents a significant development in global health, extending the consideration of conflicts of interest beyond tobacco control in the context of NCD governance and offering member states guidance in safeguarding their nutrition goals amidst engagements with non-state actors.

To fully realise the potential of the WHO tool, they propose that a strategic approach is necessary to learn lessons from efforts to test its applicability across diverse country contexts, building upon the initial experience of Brazil. Additionally, they argue that there is a clear need to enhance research efforts to better support such a process, addressing the contested and confusing concepts highlighted in the submissions analysed here. Analyses of initiatives to implement the WHO tool could also contribute to the limited empirical studies on preventing and managing conflicts of interest in health policy contexts.

Their analysis shows that submissions on the WHO tool also demonstrate how differing stances on conflicts of interest are integral to understanding broader debates surrounding the role of commercial sector actors in nutrition policy and global health. These debates often hinge on somewhat oversimplified binary categories of partnership with or exclusion of commercial entities. Governance innovations like the tool offer the potential to move beyond a blanket acceptance or rejection of partnership, identifying specific actors and forms of engagement where conflicts of interest can be managed to protect public health nutrition goals.

In this context, the tool may serve as a valuable reference point for member states, officials, and policymakers seeking to prevent collaborations deemed inconsistent with their nutrition goals, particularly amidst pressures to pursue partnerships or accept offered funds or support. A critical aspect of defining appropriate terms of engagement with the private sector in nutrition policy is the need to differentiate between actors within the "food industry," a broad category that groups together diverse entities, hindering efforts to distinguish between those actors whose economic interests can and cannot be substantively aligned with public health goals.

Finally, they claim that there is an urgent need for the development of a more detailed typology of conflicts of interest that can be operationalised and applied in diverse policy contexts.

7.5.5 Knowledge review

Before you move on, can you define the following key concepts:

- Conflict of interest?

7.5.6 Question to think about

Think about a health policy initiative in your country or region. Who are the stakeholders, and what do you perceive to be their conflicts of interest?

References

Arthur, J. (2017). *Policy entrepreneurship in education: Engagement, influence and impact.* Routledge. ISBN 9781138214606.

Bigby, M. (2008). The hierarchy of evidence. In H. C. Williams, M. Bigby, A. Herxheimer, L. Naldi, B. Rzany, R. P. Dellavalle, Y. Ran, & M. Furue (Eds.), *Evidence-based dermatology* (2nd ed., pp. 34–37). John Wiley & Sons.

Browne, J., Coffey, B., Cook, K., Meiklejohn, S., & Palermo, C. (2019). A guide to policy analysis as a research method. *Health Promotion International*, 34(5), 1032–1044.

Cairney, P. (2021). The UK government's COVID-19 policy: What does "guided by the science" mean in practice?. *Frontiers in Political Science*, 3, 624068.

Cairney, P., Heikkila, T., & Wood, M. (2019). *Making policy in a complex world*. Cambridge University Press. ISBN 9781108679053

Canadian Task Force on the Periodic Health Examination. (1979). Task force report: The periodic health examination. *Canadian Medical Association Journal*, 121(9), 1193–1254.

Drisko, J. W. (2020). Qualitative research synthesis: An appreciative and critical introduction. *Qualitative Social Work*, 19(4), 736–753.

Edmonds, W. A., & Kennedy, T. D. (2016). An applied guide to research designs: Quantitative, qualitative, and mixed methods. Sage Publications.

Evidence-Based Medicine Working Group. (1992). Evidence-based medicine. A new approach to teaching the practice of medicine. *JAMA*, 268, 2420–2425.

Fischer, F., Miller, G. J., & Sidney, M. S. (Eds.). (2017). *Handbook of public policy analysis: Theory, politics, and methods*. Routledge. ISBN 9781315093192

Gelo, O., Braakmann, D., & Benetka, G. (2008). Quantitative and qualitative research: Beyond the debate. *Integrative Psychological and Behavioral Science*, 42(3), 266–290.

Gollust, S. E., Seymour, J. W., Pany, M. J., Goss, A., Meisel, Z. F., & Grande, D. (2017). Mutual distrust: Perspectives from researchers and policymakers on the research to policy gap in 2013 and recommendations for the future. *INQUIRY: The Journal of Healthcare Organisation, Provision, and Financing*, 54, 0046958017705465.

Green, J., & Thorogood, N. (2018). *Qualitative methods for health research* (4th ed.). SAGE. ISBN 9781526448804

Hamilton, A. B., & Finley, E. P. (2019). Qualitative methods in implementation research: An introduction. *Psychiatry Research*, 280, 112516.

Jullien, S. (2021). Sudden infant death syndrome prevention. *BMC Pediatrics*, 21(Suppl. 1), 320.

Kennedy, J. (2016). Why have the majority of recent polio cases occurred in countries affected by Islamist militancy? A historical comparative analysis of the political determinants of polio in Nigeria, Somalia, Pakistan, Afghanistan and Syria. *Medicine, Conflict and Survival*, 32(4), 295–316.

Kothari, A., Boyko, J. A., & Campbell-Davison, A. (2015). An exploratory analysis of the nature of informal knowledge underlying theories of planned action used for public health-oriented knowledge translation. *BMC Research Notes*, 8, Article 424.

Lindenfeld, D. F. (2022). *The transformation of positivism: Alexius Meinong and European thought, 1880–1920*. University of California Press. ISBN: 9780520307544. First published 1980.

Malekinejad, M., Horvath, H., Snyder, H., & Brindis, C. D. (2018). The discordance between evidence and health policy in the United States: The science of translational research and the critical role of diverse stakeholders. *Health Research Policy and Systems*, 16, Article 81.

Malterud, K., Bjelland, A. K., & Elvbakken, K. T. (2016). Evidence-based medicine–an appropriate tool for evidence-based health policy? A case study from Norway. *Health Research Policy and Systems*, 14, 1–9.

Morgan, M. G. (2017). *Theory and practice in policy analysis: Including application in science and technology*. Cambridge University Press. ISBN 978-1-107-18489-3

Morse, J. M., & Niehaus, L. (2009). *Mixed method design: Principles and procedures*. Left Coast Press.

Murphy, E., & Dingwall, R. (2017). *Qualitative methods and health policy research*. Routledge. ISBN 9781315127873

Park, Y. S., Konge, L., & Artino Jr, A. R. (2020). The positivism paradigm of research. *Academic Medicine*, 95(5), 690–694.

Pope, C., & Mays, N. (Eds.). (2020). *Qualitative research in health care* (pp. 111–134). Wiley-Blackwell. ISBN:9781119410836

Pulla, V., & Carter, E. (2018). Employing interpretivism in social work research. *International Journal of Social Work and Human Services Practice*, 6(1), 9–14.

Rahman, M. S. (2020). The advantages and disadvantages of using qualitative and quantitative approaches and methods in language "testing and assessment" research: A literature review. *Journal of Education and Learning*, 6(1), 102–112.

Rahman-Shepherd, A., Balasubramaniam, P., Gautham, M., Hutchinson, E., Kitutu, F. E., Marten, R., & Khan, M. S. (2021). Conflicts of interest: An invisible force shaping health systems and policies. *The Lancet Global Health*, 9(8), e1055–e1056

Ralston, R., Hill, S. E., da Silva Gomes, F., & Collin, J. (2021). Towards preventing and managing conflict of interest in nutrition policy? an analysis of submissions to a consultation on a draft WHO tool. *International Journal of Health Policy and Management*, 10(5), 255.

Romain, P. L. (2015). Conflicts of interest in research: Looking out for number one means keeping the primary interest front and center. *Current Reviews in Musculoskeletal Medicine*, 8(2), 122–127.

Schoonenboom, J., & Johnson, R. B. (2017). How to construct a mixed methods research design. *Köln Z Soziol*, 69(Suppl. 2), 107–131.

Smith, B. (2018). Generalizability in qualitative research: Misunderstandings, opportunities and recommendations for the sport and exercise sciences. *Qualitative Research in Sport, Exercise and Health*, 10(1), 137–149.

Smith, R., & Smith, L. (2018). Qualitative methods. In L. McConnell & R. Smith (Eds.), *Research methods in human rights* (pp. 70–93). Routledge.

Stern, C., Lizarondo, L., Carrier, J., Godfrey, C., Rieger, K., Salmond, S., ... Loveday, H. (2021). Methodological guidance for the conduct of mixed methods systematic reviews. *JBI Evidence Implementation*, 19(2), 120–129.

Tolley, E. E., Ulin, P. R., Mack, N., Robinson, E. T., & Succop, S. M. (2016). *Qualitative methods in public health: A field guide for applied research*. John Wiley & Sons.

Tugwell, P., & Knottnerus, J. A. (2015). Is the "Evidence-Pyramid" now dead? *Journal of Clinical Epidemiology*, 68(11), 1247–1250.

Uzochukwu, B., Onwujekwe, O., Mbachu, C., Okwuosa, C., Etiaba, E., Nyström, M. E., & Gilson, L. (2016). The challenge of bridging the gap between researchers and policymakers: Experiences of a health policy research group in engaging policymakers to support evidence informed policy making in Nigeria. *Globalisation and Health*, 12(1), Article 67, 1–15.

Verboom, B., Montgomery, P., & Bennett, S. (2016). What factors affect evidence-informed policymaking in public health? Protocol for a systematic review of qualitative evidence using thematic synthesis. *Systematic Reviews*, 5, 1–9.

8   Public health policy

8.1 The role of public health

8.1.1 What is public health?

According to the World Health Organisation (WHO), "Public health refers to all organised measures (whether public or private) to prevent disease, promote health, and prolong life among the population as a whole. Its activities aim to provide conditions in which people can be healthy and focus on entire populations, not on individual patients or diseases."

The concept of public health, much like the broader idea of health itself, is challenging to define comprehensively. Despite efforts to establish a clear and uncontested definition, various approaches highlight different facets of public health.

In a definition, that has subsequently proved to be influential, Acheson (1988) defined public health as:

> the science and art of preventing disease, prolonging life, and promoting human health through organised efforts and informed choices of society, organisations, public and private, communities and individuals.

This definition emphasises the population's health, future orientation, and the need for collective action across sectors.

Public health is not confined to the activities of the public health workforce but extends to societal efforts addressing various health-related issues. The challenge lies in maintaining disciplinary identity while acknowledging the plurality and breadth inherent in population health. Public health is inherently interdisciplinary in nature as it deals with both factors that impact on health and well-being such as vaccination programmes and those dealing with the social determinants of health. This requires leveraging civil society and, in some cases, the private sector. Public health must embrace a broader notion that aligns multiple disciplines and perspectives for effective outcomes. Interdisciplinary initiatives have historically contributed to significant public health achievements, such as controlling infectious diseases and reducing transportation-related injuries.

Public health has a key role as the foundation of prosperity. Addressing emergencies like pandemics has a positive return on investment in economic terms, alongside the health benefits. Health is intricately linked to all policies, and public health must advocate for its integration into decision-making processes. The global challenges posed by issues like inequality, climate change, and sustainable development goals require

DOI: 10.4324/9781003478874-10

transformative societal change, making public health a crucial player in advancing a health-in-all-policies agenda.

Public health is a multifaceted concept encompassing the science and art of promoting population health through organised efforts. The challenges lie in defining it comprehensively without losing focus, engaging diverse sectors, and adapting to the evolving landscape of healthcare. Public health's importance is underscored by its role in emergencies, positive return on investment, and the potential to impact health profoundly through social spending decisions. As the world grapples with complex issues, public health emerges as a key player in driving transformative societal change for the betterment of health and well-being.

Recently, the term population health has become popular and in some discussions seems to have superseded "public health." Whilst the champions of this term have been very clear that there is a difference between the two terms, they do not agree on the nature of that difference.

The use of the term "population health" dates back to at least as early as 1990, when Evans and Stoddart (1990) described the population health approach as a framework characterised by a broad definition of health that recognised determinants outside the healthcare system and explicitly acknowledged trade-offs between investing in healthcare and investing in other social goods. Kindig and Stoddart (2003) defined population health more literally as "the health outcomes of a group of individuals, including the distribution of such outcomes within the group."

Champions of the term "population health" often make a special effort to distinguish it from public health. However, they differ on how this may be done. Some posit that public health has a greater focus on government and does not sufficiently recognise the role of the healthcare system in health (i.e., the argument is that public health is primarily government oriented and not biomedical enough).

By contrast, others argue that population health has a broader view of the drivers of health than public health because public health remains tied to service provision and to its more powerful sister, medicine or in other words that public health is too biomedical and personal service oriented to really encompass the role of broader societal factors. (Stoto, 2013).

8.1.2 *What does public health do?*

Public health encompasses a wide range of activities and interventions aimed at promoting and protecting the health of populations, with a focus on prevention, health promotion, and addressing the underlying determinants of health. The principal activity types are summarised in Table 8.1.

The health benefits from a non-health development programme in Vietnam (after International Renewable Energy Agency, 2018)

The Biogas Programme for the Animal Husbandry Sector in Vietnam, established in 2003, aimed to create a commercially viable biogas market to enhance sustainable lighting, heating, and cooking services in rural areas. Over the years, it has facilitated the construction of nearly 250,000 domestic biogas digesters, addressing waste management challenges from the growing livestock population and improving living conditions for over 1.2 million people.

Table 8.1 Public health activities

Category	Activity examples
Disease prevention and control	• Public health professionals work to prevent the spread of infectious diseases through measures such as vaccination programs, surveillance, and outbreak investigations. • They develop and implement strategies to control and manage the impact of existing diseases, including the promotion of healthy behaviours and lifestyle changes.
Health promotion	• Public health initiatives focus on promoting positive health behaviours and lifestyles among individuals and communities. This may involve campaigns to encourage physical activity, healthy eating, and smoking cessation. • Education and awareness programs are designed to empower people with information to make informed choices about their health.
Environmental health	• Public health addresses environmental factors that can affect health, such as air and water quality, sanitation, and exposure to hazardous substances. • Efforts are made to prevent and mitigate the impact of environmental hazards on public health.
Health policy and advocacy	• Public health professionals engage in policy development and advocacy to influence laws and regulations that impact health. This includes advocating for measures like smoking bans, seatbelt laws, and access to healthy foods. • They work to ensure that health considerations are integrated into various policies and decision-making processes.
Health surveillance and research	• Monitoring and analysing health data is a crucial aspect of public health. Surveillance systems track the prevalence of diseases, identify trends, and guide public health interventions. • Research in public health contributes to the development of evidence-based practices and policies. This includes epidemiological studies, clinical trials, and health services research.
Emergency preparedness and response	• Public health plays a critical role in preparing for and responding to emergencies, including natural disasters, disease outbreaks, and other public health crises. • Planning, coordination, and communication are key components of public health emergency response efforts.
Social determinants of health	• Public health recognises that social, economic, and environmental factors significantly influence health outcomes. Efforts are made to address social determinants, such as income inequality, education, and housing, in order to improve overall health.
Community engagement	• Public health initiatives often involve working closely with communities to understand their unique health needs and challenges. • Engaging communities in the planning and implementation of health programs ensures cultural competence and increases the likelihood of successful outcomes.
Global health initiatives	• Public health extends beyond national borders, with a focus on addressing global health challenges such as infectious diseases, maternal and child health, and access to healthcare in resource-limited settings.

The technology employed involves biogas digesters that produce both biogas and bio-slurry. Biogas is utilised for household cooking, livestock feedstock, and electricity production, supporting activities such as egg hatching, rice wine production, and tofu making. The bio-slurry serves as a fertiliser, enhancing crop yields and quality. The popular brick-made fixed-dome digester model requires minimal maintenance, can be built with local materials, and is constructed by local masons. Additionally, there are composite biodigesters in the supply chain, offering faster installation, reduced labour needs, and suitability for areas with high water levels.

Financially, the program was initiated by the Dutch government and the Vietnamese Ministry of Agricultural and Rural Development, with SNV Netherlands Development Organisation as the technical advisor. Costs were initially covered by the Dutch government, Vietnamese provincial governments, and farmers themselves. Energising Development became the primary donor in 2013, and funds are now also generated from carbon certificate sales. A flat-rate subsidy of approximately USD 50 per digester was provided to incentivise households, with recent shifts towards results-based financing replacing household subsidies.

The program, currently in its final phase until 2020, has contributed to the development of a commercial domestic biogas sector in Vietnam. The approach emphasises long-term commitment, tailored incentives, and local capacity building to maximise socio-economic and environmental benefits in the promotion of a sustainable biogas market.

The program has a direct health benefit as a result of reduced indoor air pollution.

The programme has been calculated to have averted approximately 27,700 DALYs (disability-adjusted life years) and 750 premature deaths. In addition, the economic benefits are associated with a positive impact on the health of the population.

8.1.3 *Knowledge review*

Before you move on, can you define the following key concepts:

- Public health?
- Population health?

8.1.4 *Question to think about*

What public health interventions have you seen recently? How successful do you think they have been?

8.2 Public health policymaking

Public health policy refers to the decisions, plans, and actions undertaken by governments and other stakeholders to address public health issues and improve the overall health of a population. These policies are formulated based on scientific evidence, public health research, and a consideration of the social, economic, and environmental factors that influence health outcomes. Public health policies aim to prevent and control diseases, promote health and well-being, and address the broader determinants of health in a population.

Public health policies are developed through a systematic process that involves identifying health issues, setting goals and objectives, and determining the most effective strategies to achieve those goals. Policymakers should consider input from public health experts, researchers, community members, and other stakeholders during the formulation stage.

Public health policies should be evidence-based. However, it is subject to same challenges as other areas of health policy. Some areas of public health policy, such as those dealing with disease outbreaks, are amenable to traditional scientific evidence and research from epidemiological studies, clinical trials, and quantitative health surveillance. Traditionally, public health professional education is highly focused around numerical methods.

However, other aspects, for example, those dealing with human behaviour and the social determinants of health may require a more interpretivist approach and a broader range of evidence.

8.2.1 Key areas of public health policy

Disease prevention and control has always been a primary goal of public health, and the COVID-19 pandemic has focused the minds of many governments in this area. Although policies often focus on preventing the spread of infectious diseases through measures such as vaccination programs, screening, and outbreak response, they may also include regulations related to food safety, sanitation, and environmental health to reduce the risk of diseases.

Public health policies promote positive health behaviours and lifestyles. This may involve educational campaigns, community programs, and regulations aimed at encouraging healthy habits such as physical activity, nutrition, and smoking cessation.

Where education and influencing behaviours are insufficient, policies may involve the creation and enforcement of laws and regulations that impact health. For example, in a review of the 10 great public health achievements of the 20th century, the US Centers for Disease Control argued that each of them was influenced by a policy change with a legal basis such as seat belt laws or regulations governing permissible workplace exposures.

Policies may impact on healthcare and its providers. In particular, public health policies may address issues related to healthcare access, affordability, and quality including the expansion of healthcare services, health insurance reforms, and initiatives to improve the healthcare workforce. Such policies may have to deal with ideological issues about whether public health policies must recognise the influence of social, economic, and environmental factors on health outcomes. As such, some policies may aim to address social determinants of health, such as education, housing, and income inequality, to improve overall health, rather than tackle the causes of ill-health directly.

Policies should guide the development of plans and strategies for responding to public health emergencies, including natural disasters, disease outbreaks, and other crises. Fauci and Folkers (2023) argue that most countries were insufficiently prepared for the COVID-19 pandemic and that lessons need to be learnt and incorporated into future public health policies in this area, including:

- early, rapid, and aggressive action is critical in implementing public health interventions and countermeasure development
- global information sharing and collaborations are essential for a successful response to a pandemic
- already existing infrastructure should be leveraged for the rapid and effective performance of clinical trials

Effective public health policies often involve collaboration with communities. Policymakers should engage with community members to understand their unique needs, incorporate local perspectives, and increase the likelihood of successful policy implementation.

Some public health policies cannot be addressed solely within national borders. Policymakers may need to participate in global health initiatives and collaborate with international organisations to address issues such as infectious diseases, maternal and child health, and access to essential medicines.

8.2.2 Making public health policy

Public health policy impacts upon the lives of citizens and may seek to restrict their freedoms with the goal of keeping them healthy. For this reason, almost all public health policies whether enshrined in law or not are seen as political in nature.

Bambra et al. (2007) identify at least four widely used definitions of politics:

- Politics as government
- Politics as public life
- Politics as conflict resolution
- Politics as power

Politics as government is primarily associated with the art of government and the activities of the state. Politics as public life takes the view that politics is primarily concerned with the conduct and management of community affairs. Politics as conflict resolution emphasises the expression and resolution of conflicts through compromise, conciliation, negotiation, and other strategies. Politics as power views politics as the process through which desired outcomes are achieved in the production, distribution, and use of scarce resources in all the areas of social existence (Bambra et al., 2005).

Politics and public health policy are inter-related because generally public health policies are implemented through the mechanism of politics. Each of these different views of politics may be encountered in public health policymaking. It is enacted by governments, part of public life, requires conflict resolution between different interests and the exercise of power to achieve its stated goals.

Politics is focused on process, whereas policy is generally focused on content. It is about the science and process of governing and can thus be described as "power-based" whereas most policymakers would describe their policies as "evidence-based."

Perhaps for this reason, there is a considerable gap between what research shows is effective and the policies that are enacted and enforced. The process of influencing policy development through research typically involves an extended period of communication and interaction. The complexity of the research–policy interface is heightened by the characteristics of scientific information, which is often extensive, varies in quality, and

Table 8.2 Barriers to implementing effective public health policy (after Brownson et al., 2009)

Barrier	Example
Lack of value placed on prevention	Only a small percentage of most government healthcare expenditure is allocated to public health activities.
Insufficient evidence base	Many of the issues addressed by public policy are complex in nature and therefore the evidence available may be of limited use.
Mismatched time horizons	The need to align public health agendas with political timescales may limit the effectiveness of both evidence gathering and implementation.
Power of vested interests	Many of the unhealthy lifestyle choices addressed by public health are the source of large profits for commercial organisations who will defend their interests.
Researchers isolated from the policy process	The research and policymaking communities are distinct researchers may not be incentivised to, or interested in, thinking about through the policy implications of their work.
Policymaking process can be complex and messy	Evidence-based policy occurs in complex systems and social psychology suggests that in the face of the unsuitability of traditional scientific evidence, decision-makers revert to relying on habits, stereotypes, and cultural norms.
Individuals in any one discipline may not understand the policymaking process as a whole	Organisations tend to compartmentalise staff, leading to a failure in interdisciplinary interactions.
Practitioners lack the skills to influence evidence-based policy	Much of the formal training in public health (e.g., masters of public health training) is focused on statistics and epidemiology and contains insufficient emphasis on broader policy-related competencies.

is not readily accessible to policymakers. Numerous models describe how research influences policymaking, with many transcending a simplistic linear model in favour of more nuanced and indirect pathways, resembling a gradual process of "enlightenment." These non-linear models acknowledge that research evidence may have comparable, or even diminished, importance compared to other factors influencing policy, such as policymakers' values and the influence of alternative sources of information, including anecdotes and personal experiences.

Table 8.2 summarises the barriers to implementing effective public health policy.

Brownson et al. (2009) proposed that evidence-based policy can be conceptualised as a continuum spanning three domains – process, content, and outcome.

1. The process domain seeks to understand approaches to enhance the likelihood of policy adoption. Policymakers may use key informant interviews, surveys, and case studies to understand the lessons learned from different approaches and key players involved in state health reforms.

2. The content domain seeks to identify specific policy elements that are likely to be effective through systematic reviews and content analyses to synthesise the research

evidence available.Developing model laws on tobacco that make use of decades of research on the impacts of policy on tobacco use.

3. The outcome domain seeks to document the potential impact of policy   through surveillance systemsand natural experiments tracking policy-related endpoints.

Recognising and identifying key factors that inform the policy process is also critical to furthering evidence-based policy. Policymaking is complicated and the factors that inhibit or facilitate the process are equally complex.

There are very distinct stages or strands that, when woven together, strengthen the odds of a policy being adopted.

The first strand is the problem – agenda setting and how certain problems or conditions come to be regarded as problems worthy of governmental intervention.

The second strand is policy – the alternative policy approaches that may be taken to address those problems (Kingdon, 2003).

The third strand, politics, recognises those factors both inside and outside government that influence the policymaking process. Public policies must be not only technically sound, but also politically and administratively feasible (Kraft & Furlong, 2019).

Barriers to Sugar-Sweetened Beverage (SSB) taxation in Australia (after Dry and Baker (2022) and Sainsbury et al. (2020))

Overweight and obesity is a major public health issue facing Australia, along with many other high-income countries.

Findings from the 2017–18 National Health Survey revealed a troubling trend in Australia, indicating that 67% of adults were either overweight or obese, signifying an 11% surge since 1995 (Lung et al., 2019). More alarming is the escalating rates of overweight and obesity in children, rising from 21% in 1995 to 25% in 2017–18 (Lycett et al., 2023). In 2013, Australia ranked as the fifth most obese country among OECD member countries (Australian Bureau of Statistics, 2016). Dietary shifts, particularly the excessive consumption of sugar, have been identified as a probable factor in the obesity rise and associated non-communicable diseases. This has led the Australian government to contemplate a range of regulatory measures aimed at curbing sugar intake.

One significant yet underutilised strategy for obesity prevention is the imposition of taxes on sugar-sweetened beverages (SSBs), given their substantial contribution to excess added sugar intake (World Health Organisation, 2016). Globally, 43 state and federal jurisdictions had implemented an SSB tax by October 2019 (World Cancer Research Fund International, 2018). Research has substantiated the effectiveness of these taxes in reducing SSB consumption (Colchero, 2017). Paradoxically, despite this global trend, both major political parties in Australia have steadfastly rejected the idea of introducing an SSB tax. They argue that efforts to prevent obesity should prioritise health education to empower individuals in making healthier food choices.

While Australian governments, spanning the political spectrum, have employed fiscal and regulatory measures for public health concerns, especially in tobacco control, there has been a notable absence of specific fiscal measures addressing obesity and diet-related chronic diseases. For instance, an Australian Labor Party government introduced tobacco plain packaging legislation, prohibiting trademarks and other distinguishing features on cigarette packs (Australian Government, 2011). It also implemented a 70% tax increase on "ready-to-drink" alcoholic beverages to safeguard adolescents from binge drinking (Gilmore et al, 2020). However, no government has adopted specific fiscal measures targeting obesity and diet-related chronic diseases. The Coalition introduced a broad-based Goods and Services Tax in 2000, imposing a 10% value-added tax on most packaged food and non-food products in Australia (Kaplin and Thow, 2013). While not designed for public health purposes, healthy foods like fresh fruit and vegetables, fresh meat, and milk are exempt from this tax (Kaplin and Thow, 2013).

Despite substantial evidence supporting the effectiveness of an SSB tax and its acceptability among the majority of the population, Australia is far from embracing such a policy as a solution to the challenges of sugar overconsumption and obesity. The paper emphasises the critical need for a nuanced understanding of the political dynamics hindering the implementation of crucial public health measures, offering insights that could inform advocacy efforts not only within Australia but also in other regions grappling with similar health challenges.

Barriers identified include fragmented public health advocacy efforts, industry interference, inadequate pressure for change from civil society, and neoliberal ideologies.

8.2.3 Knowledge review

Before you move on, can you define the following key concepts:

• Politics?

8.2.4 Question to think about

Can you think of a public health policy in your country or region that has been blocked because of political or commercial vested interests?

8.3 Public health policy implementation

Implementing public health policy is a complex process that involves navigating various challenges. These challenges can arise from social, political, economic, and logistical factors.

8.3.1 Political challenges

Frequent changes in political leadership and policy priorities can disrupt the continuity of public health initiatives. Shifting political landscapes may lead to alterations or abandonment of existing policies, hindering long-term planning and implementation. Different political ideologies will emphasise different aspects of public health activity.

McCartney et al. (2019) examined studies in the literature concerning the impact of political economy on population health. They found limited evidence, but based upon the evidence available concluded that nations adopting social democratic welfare policies and higher public spending generally exhibit enhanced overall population health. However, the correlation between the type of welfare state and health disparities remains unclear. Societies with systemic discrimination, such as race-based voting restrictions in the United States, show that political inclusion reduces health inequalities. Health disparities tend to rise with neoliberal state restructuring, and privatisation adversely affects workers' mental health.

They found robust evidence indicating that income inequality independently influences self-rated health (SRH) and mortality, with greater income inequality being detrimental. While there is some lower-quality evidence suggesting that economic recessions harm mental health, SRH, and mortality, the generalisability of these findings was unclear. Limited evidence indicated that fair trade policies positively impacted well-being and child health.

Expansions of health insurance coverage in countries lacking a comprehensive universal system were generally linked to health improvements, especially for lower-income groups. Similarly, increased primary care availability, augmented public health spending, and conditional cash transfers tied to healthcare engagement in some low-income countries had positive effects on population health. Housing rent assistance and enhancing physical housing infrastructure, particularly for low-income and cold-home dwellers, were shown to improve health. Regeneration programs' impact was mixed in high-income countries, with no evidence of a clear positive health outcome. Workplace health and safety policies and the prohibition of driving under the influence of alcohol were found to enhance health. Microfinance initiatives within low-income countries were associated with lower infant and maternal mortality, particularly among those in poverty. Lastly, compulsory education extensions were linked to reductions in subsequent mortality rates.

Public health activities tend to be given a lower priority than curative healthcare activities, unless the agenda is shifted by an emergency such as the COVID-19 pandemic. This can lead to resource constraints that may impede the effective implementation of public health policies. These constraints are not limited to financing, but typically also include shortages of healthcare professionals and inadequate infrastructure, all of which can limit the scope and reach of interventions.

8.3.2 *Communication and misinformation*

Public health policies may sometimes face resistance or opposition from individuals or interest groups who may disagree with the measures being proposed. Misinformation and lack of public awareness can contribute to scepticism and resistance.

The term infodemic has been coined to mean "an overabundance of information – some accurate and some not – that makes it hard for people to find trustworthy sources and reliable guidance when they need it," to categorise some of the common features of rumours, stigma, and conspiracy theories during public health emergencies (WHO, 2020).

Social media may be used to circulate misinformation that is false or inaccurate information spread in ignorance or disinformation that is false information which is deliberately intended to mislead.

Public health emergencies are challenging times for individuals and communities. It is essential for pandemic preparedness policies to include measures to effectively handle rumours, combat misinformation and conspiracy theories, and alleviate fear and stigma towards affected individuals and locations. International health agencies, such as the WHO, acknowledge rumours, stigma, and conspiracy theories as evolving threats to pandemic preparedness and control. Consequently, they advocate for systematic monitoring and implementation of control measures.

Islam et al. (2020) identified various purported "cures" for COVID-19 circulating on social media.

- "Eating garlic can cure coronavirus"
- "Drinking bleach may kill the virus"
- "Drinking alcohol may kill the virus"
- "Gargling vinegar and rose water or vinegar and salt may kill the virus in the throat"
- "Drinking cow urine and cow dung can cure coronavirus"
- "Silver solution for coronavirus treatment"
- "Wearing warm socks, mustard patches, and spreading goose fat on one's chest as treatment"
- "Keeping throat moist, avoid spicy food and taking vitamin C may prevent the disease"
- "Avoiding cold or preserved food and drinks, such as ice cream and milkshakes, may prevent infection"
- "Spraying chlorine all over your body can prevent coronavirus infection"
- "Sesame oil can prevent coronavirus infection"
- "Granite bath can prevent coronavirus infection"
- "Sea lettuce can prevent coronavirus infection"
- "Vitamin C intake can prevent coronavirus infection"
- "Vitamin D can prevent coronavirus infection"
- "Eating Centella asiatica may prevent coronavirus infection"
- "Drinks containing mint or white willow and spices like saffron, turmeric, and cinnamon would strengthen the lungs and the immune system against the virus"
- "Rinse mouths with saltwater solution to prevent infection from the new virus outbreak"
- "Do not hold your thirst because once your membrane in your throat is dried, the virus will invade into your body within 10 minutes"
- "Applying petroleum jelly around your nostrils will protect against dangerous air pollutants"
- "Do-it-yourself coronavirus detection test"
- "Cannabis boosts immunity against the novel coronavirus"
- "Frequently washing clothes can reduce transmission"

Policies that aim to regulate industries, such as tobacco or food, may face resistance from powerful interest groups. Economic considerations and lobbying efforts can influence policy decisions and impede effective implementation. Such groups may also use a variety of means to provide misleading information or counter messages not aligned with their vested interests.

8.3.3 *Cultural sensitivities*

Socioeconomic and cultural differences within a population can pose challenges to policy implementation. Strategies that do not consider the cultural context or fail to address disparities may not be effective or may face resistance from specific communities.

Cultural sensitivity may be characterised in terms of two dimensions: surface and deep structures.

Surface structure entails aligning intervention materials and messages with the visible, external characteristics of a target population. This may include using elements such as people, places, language, music, food, locations, and clothing that are familiar to and preferred by the target audience. Surface structure assesses how well interventions integrate with a specific culture.

Deep structure involves the inclusion of cultural, social, historical, environmental, and psychological factors that impact the target health behaviour within the proposed population. While surface structure generally enhances the "receptivity" or "acceptance" of messages, deep structure imparts significance. The techniques for developing culturally sensitive interventions draw from social marketing and health communication theory.

Social marketing uses marketing principles to create, communicate, and deliver value in order to influence target audience behaviours that benefit broader society as well as the target audience. One major aspect of social marketing is using audience insights to understand the key drivers that will lead to changing a certain behaviour.

Seneres (2023) identified five steps in social marketing in public health as part of researching and developing an effective social marketing campaign aimed at increasing COVID-19 vaccination rates among American Indian and Alaska Natives in the Southeastern United States:

1. Identify the problem and the goal for behaviour change
2. Identify the target audience
3. Understand the audience's perceptions and values
4. Develop a strategy built on audience insights
5. Disseminate through appropriate channels

Effective communication is crucial for successful policy implementation. In addition to cultural sensitivities, challenges in health literacy, language barriers, and ineffective communication strategies can all impede public understanding and compliance with recommended measures.

8.3.4 *Structural barriers*

The structures in place to manage and implement public health policy can themselves provide barriers to implementation. For example, in countries with fragmented healthcare systems, coordination and collaboration among different healthcare entities may be challenging. Lack of integration can lead to gaps in service delivery and hinder the achievement of comprehensive health outcomes. In some cases, public health measures can be perceived to be in direct competition for resources with curative health services, either due a limited global budget allocation or payment mechanisms that reward healthcare providers for activity that perversely disincentivise health prevention.

Similarly, overly complex policies and bureaucratic hurdles can slow down the implementation process. Streamlining policies and minimising bureaucratic obstacles are essential to ensuring timely and efficient execution.

8.3.5 Emergency preparedness and response challenges

Implementing policies during public health emergencies, such as pandemics or natural disasters, poses unique challenges. Rapid decision-making, resource mobilisation, and effective communication become critical but may be hampered by the urgency of the situation. In times when no obvious challenge exists, preparedness may be given a lower priority, leading to inadequate arrangements being in place when an emergency arises.

Valuable lessons were gleaned from the SARS epidemic in 2003, during which the Chinese government delayed crucial information regarding a new infectious outbreak in Guangdong province. Subsequent to that epidemic, the World Health Organisation's (WHO) Member States revisited the International Health Regulations (IHR) in 2005 (WHO, 2005), which were eventually adopted by the World Health Assembly. These regulations were intended to be implemented globally by mid-2007, binding governments to disclose essential information about identifying and detecting new disease outbreaks, irrespective of the causative agent. This mechanism led to China promptly sharing information and the viral genome of SARS-CoV-2 during the COVID-19 outbreak.

Regrettably, in the context of the COVID-19 pandemic, although China rapidly reported in accordance with the 2005 IHR, not all countries responded immediately. Governments failed to swiftly recognise the threat posed by COVID-19, and in some countries, health systems were unprepared to cope with such emergencies. This is despite the commitments made by all countries' delegates in 2005 during the approval of the revised IHR and their renewed pledge in 2015 at the highest political level of the UN SDG. SDG 3, focusing on health, specifically outlines in target 3.D that countries should enhance their capacity for "early warning, risk reduction, and management of national and global health risks" (UN General Assembly, 2015). The lack of a strong commitment to translate international resolutions into a well-financed plan for health emergencies leaves countries highly vulnerable to pandemics. In an interconnected world, health issues often transcend national borders. Coordination between countries and adherence to international guidelines can be challenging, especially when dealing with global health threats

To oversee countries' strategic preparedness for emergencies, two instruments were developed: the WHO's IHR Core Capacity Monitoring Framework and the Joint External Evaluation process. However, both tools primarily assess the coordination between Public Health and Security authorities, lacking a measurement of how interventions are executed and their effectiveness. Additionally, the IHR heavily relies on self-reporting data, lacking an external review mechanism due to higher costs, resulting in limitations in speed and frequency (Villa et al., 2020).

Addressing these challenges requires a collaborative and adaptive approach. Successful policy implementation often involves stakeholder engagement, community involvement, continuous evaluation, and the flexibility to adjust strategies based on evolving circumstances. Additionally, addressing the social determinants of health and fostering equity can contribute to more effective and sustainable public health interventions.

> **The impact of misinformation during the COVID-19 pandemic (after Islam et al., 2020)**
>
> Rumours, social stigma, and conspiracy theories all possess the potential to erode trust within communities towards governments and international health agencies.
>
> Rumours may disguise themselves as credible strategies for infection prevention and control, posing significant risks if prioritised over evidence-based guidelines.
>
> For instance, a widely circulated myth suggested that consuming highly concentrated alcohol could disinfect the body and eliminate the virus, leading to approximately 800 deaths, 5,876 hospitalisations, and 60 cases of complete blindness, as individuals ingested methanol as a supposed cure for coronavirus.
>
> Similar misinformation caused 30 deaths in Turkey, while in Qatar, two individuals ingested harmful substances like a surface disinfectant or an alcohol-based hand sanitiser after exposure to COVID-19 patients. In India, 12 people, including five children, fell ill after consuming liquor made from toxic Datura seeds, driven by a belief propagated on social media that Datura seeds provide immunity against COVID-19.
>
> Beyond individuals falling prey to misinformation, documented cases exist of organisations adopting inappropriate and misguided practices. In South Korea, a church using a spray bottle with contaminated water led to over 100 infections among attendees. Instances of such practices were also noted in other orthodox churches globally, though the specific number of infections linked to these practices remains undocumented.
>
> Stigma and fear of discrimination may have contributed to healthcare-associated infections in South Asia. Individuals with COVID-19 concealed their symptoms or exposure histories when seeking medical help, resulting in healthcare workers treating patients with inadequate personal protective equipment, leading to healthcare-associated infections in Bangladesh.
>
> The fear of stigma caused people to avoid screening, potentially spreading the disease further. Throughout the pandemic, there were numerous reports of verbal and physical abuse against those involved in healthcare activities. Stigmatised individuals face social avoidance, rejection, poor health-seeking behaviour, and even physical violence.
>
> The stigma associated with COVID-19 patients, driven primarily by contagion fears, led to the denial of patient admission in hospitals in Uganda. The escalating number of COVID-19 cases, coupled with a shortage of healthcare workers and resources, resulted in violence not only against healthcare workers but also against healthcare facilities.

8.3.6 *Knowledge review*

Before you move on, can you define the following key concepts:

- Disinformation?
- Misinformation?

8.3.7 Question to think about

Where do you get your information from? How trustworthy are your sources? How sceptical are you about the information that you read?

8.4 The relationship between public health and healthcare

The relationship between public health and healthcare is one of interdependence. While public health focuses on preventing and addressing health issues at the population level, healthcare provides individualised care and treatment. A comprehensive and effective health system requires the integration of both, with collaboration and shared goals to achieve optimal health outcomes for individuals and communities.

Table 8.3 compares and contrasts public health and healthcare.

Lurie and Fremont (2009) compared medicine and public health to trains running on parallel tracks, each with windows facing opposite directions and observing the same landscape. Those on the medical train focus on individual trees, noting subtle differences in size, colour, age, and health. Meanwhile, those on the public health train see the forest, observing populations of similar trees growing together and facing common challenges. Despite their potentially complementary perspectives, they argue that the lack of communication and coordination between medical and public health professionals, along with fragmented data systems, hinders efforts to improve care, personal health, and population health.

Healthcare in high income countries is making increasingly slow, progress in enhancing healthcare quality and outcomes and is facing increasing financial pressures. With a demographic in these countries of an ageing population and an increasing proportion of patients with multiple long-term conditions, quality often remains unacceptably low, especially for chronic disease and especially for those from ethnic minority and/or low-income groups. The current model of healthcare delivery, emphasising brief encounters with physicians or calls from disease managers, is often seen as inadequate. Patients are typically treated as isolated individuals, overlooking the impact of community characteristics on their health (Lurie et al., 2008).

Health providers, driven by financial constraints, often categorise populations broadly by demographics and administrative criteria and to not consider the communities in which individuals live.

Sparse information about the communities from which members originate, typically presented in tables and charts, frequently conceals concentrations or "hotspots" of substandard care prevalent in specific neighbourhoods. Even in comprehensive "medical homes" equipped with electronic medical records, physicians lack the tools to pinpoint clusters of patients and understand the impact of local community characteristics on their health (Ruder et al., 2009).

From the public health perspective, data available to professionals is often less than ideal. Although health departments may have detailed demographic information, health indicators and their distribution within jurisdictions are often less detailed and provide insufficient granularity to be useful. Information about chronic disease risk factors and burdens is typically available only at the county level or higher, and public health officials may lack access to data from users of the broader healthcare system.

In essence, fragmented clinical and public health data, along with gaps in data sharing, result in each group lacking pertinent and actionable data to optimise the health of the populations they serve. This disconnect leads to divergent views of problems, risks

Table 8.3 Public health and healthcare, after Lurie and Fremont (2009)

Feature	Public health	Healthcare
Scope and focus	Public health has a population-focused perspective, aiming to prevent diseases, promote health, and address the social, economic, and environmental determinants of health. It involves interventions at the community and societal levels, emphasising health promotion, disease prevention, and overall well-being.	Healthcare, on the other hand, is primarily concerned with the diagnosis, treatment, and management of individual health conditions. It involves the provision of medical services, including clinical care, surgeries, and pharmaceutical interventions, with a focus on individual patients.
Prevention vs. treatment	Public health is oriented towards preventive measures, such as vaccinations, health education, and policy interventions that address the root causes of health issues. It aims to reduce the incidence of diseases and improve overall health outcomes at a population level.	Healthcare primarily deals with the treatment and management of existing health conditions. It involves the delivery of medical services, surgeries, medications, and therapies to individuals seeking care for specific health problems.
Population-level impact	Public health initiatives have a broad impact on entire populations. Strategies may include implementing public health campaigns, advocating for policies, and conducting interventions that reach large segments of the community to improve health outcomes on a societal scale.	Healthcare services operate at the individual level, providing personalised care to patients based on their unique health needs. While healthcare contributes to the well-being of individuals, its impact on populations is often indirect through the collective health of individuals.
Collaboration and integration	Both public health and healthcare systems need to collaborate for a comprehensive and effective health system. Integration involves coordinating efforts to ensure seamless transitions between preventive measures, early detection, and treatment. Public health strategies can inform healthcare practices, and healthcare services contribute to the success of public health interventions	
Health system strengthening	Public health efforts contribute to the strengthening of health systems by addressing broader determinants of health, promoting equity, and advocating for policies that create supportive environments for health.	Healthcare services are a vital component of the health system, providing essential medical care and responding to the health needs of individuals. Effective healthcare contributes to the overall resilience and responsiveness of the health system.
Emergency preparedness and response	Public health plays a crucial role in preparing for and responding to public health emergencies, such as pandemics, natural disasters, and disease outbreaks. This involves coordination, planning, and implementing strategies to protect and support communities.	Healthcare services are on the front lines during emergencies, providing immediate medical care, managing surge capacity, and collaborating with public health agencies to mitigate the impact of crises on individual and community health.

misinformed decision-making, and restricts opportunities to integrate community and public health efforts with individual patient care.

This gap between medicine and public health contrasts with collaborative approaches in basic science research, such as genomics and proteomics, where shared efforts across disciplines accelerate growth and disseminate knowledge (Hottes et al., 2023).

Similar breakthroughs are occurring in the social sciences, with information technologies facilitating the integration of data about neighbourhood environments, population characteristics, and associated health outcomes, highlighting the importance of community-level factors in healthcare.

Childhood vaccinations in Europe: Public health measures or healthcare? (After OECD, 2020)

All European Union member states have implemented childhood vaccination initiatives aimed at reducing the transmission of various infectious diseases and associated fatalities. However, there is variability in the number and types of mandatory or recommended vaccines across these countries. Family physicians are the primary providers of child vaccination rates, with good access through frequent interactions with parents and children with other illnesses or attending check-ups. All vaccines must be administered by regulated professionals. Within Europe, there are wide variations in who can administer vaccines. While medical practitioners and nurses can do so everywhere, some countries also permit pharmacists to administer them in an attempt to broaden access.

In recent times, certain regions in Europe have witnessed a significant resurgence of vaccine-preventable diseases, attributed in part to declining vaccine coverage driven by anti-vaccine campaigns. To address these concerning trends, the European Commission has consistently urged increased efforts and collaboration to combat vaccine hesitancy. This emphasis on improving vaccination coverage is especially critical in the aftermath of the COVID-19 pandemic to prevent additional strain on healthcare systems.

The containment measures implemented during the COVID-19 outbreak led to a substantial decrease in the spread of communicable diseases like measles between March and August 2020. However, the sustainability of these reductions depends on the elevation of vaccination coverage. The pandemic has also disrupted routine vaccination programs in some countries due to concerns about virus exposure and restrictions on movement, impacting children's access to immunisation services.

Measles vaccination is a part of all national childhood vaccination programs in Europe, while hepatitis B vaccination has been incorporated into an increasing number of countries, though not yet in most Nordic countries and Hungary. The World Health Organisation (WHO) has recommended achieving a minimum coverage of 95% for children with two doses of measles-containing vaccine and three doses of the hepatitis B vaccine by 2020.

In 2018, the average across EU countries showed that 94% of one-year-old children received at least one dose of measles vaccination. However, half of the EU countries had not yet reached the target of 95% coverage. Measles outbreaks occurred in several countries, even in those that had previously eliminated endemic transmission. In 2019, WHO declared that Albania, the Czech Republic, Greece, and the United Kingdom had lost their measles elimination status due to continuous transmission. The highest number of measles cases from March 2019 to February 2020 were reported in France, Romania, Italy, Bulgaria, and Poland, with most cases among unvaccinated individuals, including infants below the age of one.

For hepatitis B, an average of 93% of one-year-old children received vaccination in 2018 across EU countries where this vaccine was part of the national immunisation program. Several countries surpassed the 95% target, including Malta, Portugal, Belgium, Cyprus, the Slovak Republic, Greece, Latvia, Luxembourg, and Italy. However, Austria, Bulgaria, Germany, Montenegro, and Switzerland had less than 90% coverage. Most Nordic countries, except Sweden, lack data on childhood vaccination rates for hepatitis B since this vaccine is not yet included in the general infant vaccination program but is provided to high-risk groups.

8.4.1 Knowledge review

Before you move on, can you define the following key concepts:

- The relationship between public health and healthcare?

8.4.2 Question to think about

If you were responsible for decisions about allocating resources to public health or curative healthcare services, which would you prioritise and why?

References

Acheson, E. D. (1988). On the state of the public health [the fourth Duncan lecture]. *Public Health*, 102(5), 431–437.

Australian Government. (2011). *Tobacco plain packaging act (Cth)(Austl.) No. 148, 2011.* Australian Government.

Australian Bureau of Statistics (2016). Australian Health Survey: Consumption of added sugars, 2011-12. cited in Sainsbury, E., Magnusson, R., Thow, A. M., & Colagiuri, S. (2020). Explaining resistance to regulatory interventions to prevent obesity and improve nutrition: a case-study of a sugar-sweetened beverages tax in Australia. Food Policy, 93, 101904.

Australian Institute of Health and Welfare. (2017). *A picture of overweight and obesity in Australia 2017.* Cat. no. PHE 216. Australian Institute of Health and Welfare.

Bambra, C., Fox, D., & Scott-Samuel, A. (2005). Towards a politics of health. *Health Promotion International*, 20(2), 187–193.

Bambra, C., Fox, D., & Scott-Samuel, A. (2007). A politics of health glossary. *Journal of Epidemiology and Community Health*, 61(7), 571–574.

Brownson, R. C., Chriqui, J. F., & Stamatakis, K. A. (2009). Understanding evidence-based public health policy. *American Journal of Public Health*, 99(9), 1576–1583.

Cabaj, J. L., Musto, R., & Ghali, W. A. (2019). Public health: Who, what, and why? *Canadian Journal of Public Health = Revue canadienne de santé publique*, 110(3), 340–343.

Centers for Disease Control and Prevention (CDC). (1999). Ten great public health achievements--United States, 1900-1999. MMWR. *Morbidity and Mortality Weekly Report*, 48(12), 241–243.

Colchero, M. A., Rivera-Dommarco, J., Popkin, B. M., & Ng, S. W. (2017). In Mexico, evidence of sustained consumer response two years after implementing a sugar-sweetened beverage tax. *Health Affairs*, 36(3), 564–571.

Dry, T., & Baker, P. (2022). Generating political commitment for regulatory interventions targeting dietary harms and poor nutrition: A case study on sugar-sweetened beverage taxation in Australia. *International Journal of Health Policy and Management*, 11(11), 2489–2501.

Evans, R. G., & Stoddart, G. L. (1990 [1982]). Producing health, consuming health care. *Social Science & Medicine*, 31(12), 1347–1363.

Fauci, A. S., & Folkers, G. K. (2023). Pandemic preparedness and response: lessons from COVID-19. *The Journal of Infectious Diseases*, 228(4), 422–425.

Gilmore, W., Chikritzhs, T., McManus, H., Kaldor, J., & Guy, R. (2020). The Association between the Australian Alcopops Tax and National Chlamydia Rates among Young People-an Interrupted Time Series Analysis. *International Journal of Environmental Research and Public Health*, 17(4), 1343.

Hottes, A. K., Blumenthal, M. S., Mondschein, J., Sargent, M., & Wesson, C. (2023). *International basic research collaboration at the US department of defense: An overview* (p. 146). RAND National Defense Research Institute.

International Renewable Energy Agency. (2018). *South-Eastern Asia case studies, case study 1 biogas program in Viet Nam*. International Renewable Energy Agency.

Islam, M. S., Sarkar, T., Khan, S. H., Kamal, A. H. M., Hasan, S. M., Kabir, A., ... Seale, H. (2020). COVID-19–related infodemic and its impact on public health: A global social media analysis. *The American Journal of Tropical Medicine and Hygiene*, 103(4), 1621.

Kaplin, L., & Thow, A. M. (2013). Using economic policy to tackle chronic disease: options for the Australian Government. *Journal of Law and Medicine*, 20(3), 604–620.

Kindig, D., & Stoddart, G. (2003). What is population health?. *American Journal of Public Health*, 93(3), 380–383.

Kingdon, J. W. (2003). *Agendas, alternatives, and public policies* (2nd ed.). Addison-Wesley Longman Inc.

Kotler, P., & Lee, N. (2008). *Social marketing: Influencing behaviours for good* (3rd ed.). Sage Publications.

Kraft, M. E., & Furlong, S. R. (2019). *Public policy: Politics, analysis, and alternatives*. CQ Press. ISBN: 9781452202747.

Lung, T., Jan, S., Tan, E. J., Killedar, A., & Hayes, A. (2019). Impact of overweight, obesity and severe obesity on life expectancy of Australian adults. *International Journal of Obesity*, 43(4), 782–789.

Lurie, N., & Fremont, A. (2009). Building bridges between medical care and public health. *JAMA*, 302(1), 84–86.

Lurie, N., Fremont, A., Somers, S. A., Coltin, K., Gelzer, A., Johnson, R., ... Zimmerman, D. (2008). The national health plan collaborative to reduce disparities and improve quality. *The Joint Commission Journal on Quality and Patient Safety*, 34(5), 256–265.

Lycett, K., Frykberg, G., Azzopardi, P. S., Cleary, J., Sawyer, S. M., Toumbourou, J. W., ... Olsson, C. A. (2023). Monitoring the physical and mental health of Australian children and young people: a foundation for responsive and accountable actions. *Medical Journal of Australia*, 219, S20–S24.

McCartney, G., Popham, F., McMaster, R., & Cumbers, A. (2019). Defining health and health inequalities. *Public Health*, 172, 22–30.

OECD. (2020). *Childhood vaccinations | Health at a Glance: Europe 2020*. European Centre for Disease Prevention and Control.

Ruder, T., Gresenz, C. R., & Lurie, N. (2009). *Ambulatory care sensitive hospitalisations and emergency department visits in baltimore city. 2009* (RAND Peer-Reviewed Technical Report TR-671-ALS), Rand Corporation, Santa Monica, CA.

Sainsbury, E., Magnusson, R., Thow, A. M., & Colagiuri, S. (2020). Explaining resistance to regulatory interventions to prevent obesity and improve nutrition: A case-study of a sugar-sweetened beverages tax in Australia. *Food Policy*, 93, 101904.

Seneres, G. (2023). *Case study: Using social marketing to improve public health, school of public health*. University of Michigan.

Stoto, M. A. (2013). *Population health in the Affordable Care Act era*. Academy Health.

United Nations General Assembly. (2015). *Transforming our world: The 2030 agenda for sustainable development* (Resolution A/RES/70/1). United Nations.

Villa, S., Lombardi, A., Mangioni, D., Bozzi, G., Bandera, A., Gori, A., & Raviglione, M. C. (2020). The COVID-19 pandemic preparedness... or lack thereof: From China to Italy. *Global Health & Medicine*, 2(2), 73–77.

World Cancer Research Fund International. (2018). *Building momentum: Lessons on implementing a robust sugar sweetened beverage tax*. World Cancer Research Fund International.

World Health Organisation. (2005). *The international health regulations* (3rd ed.). World Health Organisation.

World Health Organisation. (2016). Taxing sugar-sweetened beverages could reduce childhood overweight and obesity in the Western Pacific Region. 22 September 2016 News release, WHO Western Pacific, Manila, Philippines.

World Health Organisation. (2020). *Coronavirus disease 2019 (COVID-19): Situation report, 73*. World Health Organisation.

9   Global health policy

9.1 Globalisation

Globalisation is a term used to describe how trade and technology have made the world into a more connected and interdependent place. The term has also come to represent the economic and social changes that have come about as a result. It is not new; it has its origins in international trade that dates back over 2,000 years from early examples like the development of an ancient network of trade routes across China, Central Asia, and the Mediterranean used between 50 BCE and 250 CE, known as The Silk Road. Even at this stage, trade ideas and customs were exchanged.

Another key aspect of globalisation is the role played by technology. Even at this early stage, new technologies played a key role. Innovations in metallurgy resulted in the development of coins; improvements in transportation led to the construction of interconnected roads among major empires; and enhanced agricultural output enabled the increased exchange of food between different regions. In addition to the trade of Chinese silk, Roman glass, and Arabian spices, concepts like Buddhist beliefs and the techniques of paper-making were also disseminated through these interconnected networks of trade.

In the modern world, it refers to the increasing integration of economies around the world, particularly through the movement of goods, services, and capital across borders. In the contemporary era, globalisation denotes the growing interconnectedness of world economies, particularly through the cross-border movement of goods, services, and capital. Additionally, it encompasses the transnational flow of people (labour) and knowledge (technology). The concept also encompasses broader aspects such as cultural, political, and environmental dimensions. The term "globalisation" gained prominence in the 1980s, coinciding with technological advancements that facilitated quicker and more efficient international transactions in both trade and finance. Other innovations, such as a massive growth in the use of standardised shipping containers, led to a massive drop in the cost of transporting manufactured goods, opening up opportunities for manufacturing in cheaper locations. Essentially, globalisation extends the reach beyond national borders of market forces that have historically operated at various levels of human economic activity, whether in village markets, urban industries, or financial centres.

Globalisation has been credited with a rapid expansion in the global economy. In current US dollars, the World Bank estimates that global GDP per capita has risen from $2,587 per head in 1980 to $12,744 per head in 2022.

The level of digital connectedness measured as the percentage of the global population connected to the Internet has grown from zero in 1990 to 63% in 2021 (World Bank, 2024).

DOI: 10.4324/9781003478874-11

Steger et al. (2023) characterise this rapid growth as "neoliberal globalisation" and highlight the key role of multinational media corporations who used the newly emerging online communication channels to promote the benefits of growing consumption and rapidly developing technology. They also point to a number of global setbacks which they argue have started to challenge the view that everybody wins in a globalised world starting with the global financial crisis of 2008, leading to the emergence of populist political leaders like Trump in the US in the 2010s and culminating in the Global COVID-19 pandemic at the start of the 2020s.

At the same time, the technology that has made a major contribution to globalisation continues to evolve and is now starting to disrupt some of the very foundations of globalisation. Steger et al. (2020) describe the global interchange of intangible things and processes as disembodied globalisation. They include the sharing and transmission of ideas, language, visuals, meanings, knowledge, sounds, data, electronic texts, software programmes, and innovative digital assets like blockchain-encoded cryptocurrencies. Since the inception of the information and communication revolution in the 1990s, numerous activities in these realms have manifested as electronic transactions within cyberspace.

As the worldwide movement of people, goods, and institutions lags behind the expansion of digital networks and the intensification of electronic connectivity, the rising prominence of intangible flows within the global system starts to impact its neighbouring structural components. For instance, 3-D printing has revolutionised the global trade of goods, traditionally based on global value chains – a facet of tangible globalisation – by evolving it into regional and local networks of exchange reliant on digitally facilitated on-demand production as close to the end market as feasible.

Conventional strategies like outsourcing and offshoring, which were at the heart of tangible globalisation, have become unsettled and, in some cases, reversed and localised as the emerging intangible globalisation makes reshoring an appealing choice for numerous companies. Likewise, the service sector is undergoing transformation as digital globalisation increasingly converts physically present workers located miles away into virtual tele-migrants through new collaborative software tools and electronic project management platforms.

9.1.1 Globalisation and health

The most obvious impact of globalisation on health is the increased international flows of people. At the end of the 20th century, the number of people travelling by air was nearly 2.6 billion (Hobsbawm, 2007, p. 86). By 2019, a year before the outbreak of COVID-19, the International Civil Aviation Organisation's statistics estimated that the total number of passengers carried on scheduled services was now 4.5 billion (ICAO, 2020).

This level of travel facilitates the spread of a virus, such as COVID-19, especially a virus like COVID-19, which is often infectious before the onset of distinctive and obvious symptoms. This makes it much harder to contain than viruses such as SARS-CoV, more commonly known as SARS that caused an outbreak in 2003. The 2003 virus is estimated to have killed less than 800 people globally from almost 8,100 cases (World Health Organisation, 2004). This compares with estimates of 550 million cases of COVID-19, resulting in 6.5 million confirmed deaths (Steger et al., 2023). Whilst greater mobility will have contributed to the difference in impact, the different nature of the viruses is a much bigger factor.

COVID-19 is more easily transmitted than SARS. One possible explanation is that the amount of virus, or viral load, appears to be highest in the nose and throat of people with COVID-19 shortly after symptoms develop. In SARS, viral loads peaked much later in the illness. This indicates that people with COVID-19 were likely to transmit the virus earlier in the course of the infection, just as their symptoms are developing but before they begin to worsen, making it much harder to detect.

However, globalisation has had many other impacts on health and healthcare. As with broader economic aspects, there have been positive and negative impacts.

The rise in income of citizens globally has enabled many to pay for healthcare for the first time. Increased national incomes have provided greater funds for governments to invest in healthcare systems. Reduced manufacturing costs have helped to make cheaper pharmaceuticals and middle income countries such as India have established indigenous pharmaceutical manufacturing, particularly for generic drugs, that are out of patent protection.

Globalisation encourages collaboration among countries, leading to joint efforts in addressing global health issues. This includes coordinated responses to pandemics, sharing research findings, and pooling resources for the development of new treatments and vaccines. It has facilitated the dissemination of health-related information and advancements in medical technology enabling faster sharing of knowledge, improved diagnostics, and better treatment options.

Increased mobility has been a mixed blessing. Patients can now access medical services globally, seeking treatment in countries with advanced healthcare facilities. This has led to increased competition among healthcare providers, potentially improving the quality of services. However, health tourism can be a headache for regulators.

Globalisation allows for the movement of healthcare professionals across borders, facilitating the transfer of medical expertise and skills to regions with shortages of healthcare workers. However, this has led to many developing countries experiencing a "brain drain" as healthcare professionals migrate to developed nations in search of better opportunities. This exacerbates healthcare workforce shortages in some regions.

This is one way in which globalisation has exacerbated health inequalities. While some countries and regions benefit from advanced healthcare technologies and resources, others struggle with limited access to basic healthcare services.

In addition to inequalities in access to human capital, the gap between low- and high-income countries has widened under globalisation, and this is reflected in the resources available to provide healthcare. The commercialisation and globalisation of healthcare can lead to the prioritisation of profit over public health. Private healthcare providers may focus on treatments that are financially lucrative rather than addressing essential public health needs and focus on markets where there are more patients willing and able to pay higher prices.

Globalisation contributes to environmental degradation, which, in turn, can affect public health. Climate change, pollution, and the depletion of natural resources can lead to health problems such as respiratory diseases, malnutrition, and waterborne illnesses.

Globalisation has helped multinational fast food brands to spread to even poorer countries. In Ghana, where millions still live in poverty in spite of general improvements in income, the fast food franchise KFC is becoming commonplace and its rising popularity amongst local people coincides with increased instances of obesity. By 2016, 25% of Ghanaian adults were clinically obese, compared to 5.5% in 2005.

Impact of globalisation on life expectancy at birth (after Labonté et al., 2011)

An innovative econometric exercise carried out as background research for the Commission on Social Determinants of Health, using data from 136 countries, compared trends in life expectancy at birth (LEB) over the period 1980–2000 with those that would be predicted based on a counterfactual in which trends in all the relevant variables remained at the 1980 value or continued the trend they followed over the pre-1980 period.

The results of this simulation indicated that, on a worldwide basis, over the period 1980–2000, globalisation cancelled out most of the progress towards better health (as measured by LEB) that occurred as a consequence of diffusion of medical progress.

9.1.2 *Knowledge review*

Before you move on, can you define the following key concepts:

- Globalisation?
- Disembodied globalisation?

9.1.3 *Question to think about*

How has the increased mobility of healthcare staff under globalisation impacted your country or region? Is it a net benefit or loss?

9.2 World Health Organisation and other governmental health agencies

9.2.1 *World Health Organisation*

The World Health Organisation (WHO) operates as a specialised agency of the United Nations (UN), dedicated to promoting global health, preventing and controlling diseases worldwide, and responding to health emergencies. The primary objective, as stated in the WHO Constitution, is to achieve the highest possible level of health for all people.

The UN's health objectives include ensuring universal access to quality healthcare, safeguarding vulnerable populations from disease outbreaks and promoting healthy lifestyles. Collaboration with member states involves the development and implementation of health policies, alongside the provision of financial and technical assistance to countries in need. Despite the UN's impactful role in global health, there are areas for improvement, such as responding more efficiently to disease outbreaks and addressing non-communicable diseases like obesity and heart disease.

The WHO was established in 1948. It functions as the UN's specialised health agency, leading and coordinating international health activities. Currently, 194 nation-states (all UN members except Liechtenstein, Cook Islands, and Niue) are WHO members. Additionally, various non-governmental organisations (NGOs) participate in the governance of WHO as non-voting associate members. The Director-General, serving a renewable five-year term, leads the WHO Secretariat, accountable to the World Health Assembly (WHA).

The WHO operates globally with over 8,000 staff in 149 country offices, and its structure includes six regional divisions with respective headquarters. The WHO's governance rests with the WHA, comprising ministers of health and other representatives, convening annually to decide international health policy, approve programmes, and budget. The Executive Board advises the WHA and consists of 34 technically qualified members elected for three-year terms.

The WHO's Constitution, adopted in 1946, outlines crucial principles guiding its policies, emphasising health as a human right, the role of health in peace and security, and addressing unequal development. The WHO's objectives involve directing international health efforts, assisting governments in strengthening health services, eradicating diseases, promoting health research, and setting international standards for pharmaceuticals.

Over the years, the WHO has played a pivotal role in combating infectious diseases, neglected tropical diseases, and non-communicable diseases. Embracing the principles of universal health coverage (UHC), the WHO aims to ensure that individuals, households, and communities receive needed healthcare without financial hardship. The organisation continues to evolve, adopting new initiatives to strengthen health systems globally and address contemporary health challenges. The International Health Regulations (IHR) exemplify the WHO's regulatory role, with internationally binding regulations aiming to prevent and control the cross-border spread of diseases, adapted to globalisation and infectious disease dynamics.

The introduction to the WHO's Constitution states that

- the enjoyment of the highest attainable standard of health is a human right
- the health of all peoples is a key foundation of peace and security
- unequal development in the promotion of health and control of disease presents a common danger to all
- healthy development of the child is of basic importance and that the ability to live harmoniously in a changing total environment is essential to such development
- it is necessary for the benefits of medical, psychological, and related knowledge to be extended to all people
- governments have a responsibility for the health of their people

(WHO, 2020, p. 1).

In practical terms, the functions defined for the WHO include the responsibility to

- act as directing and coordinating authority in international health
- assist governments in strengthening health services
- advance work to eradicate epidemic and other diseases
- promote and conduct research in the field of health
- establish international standards for pharmaceutical and similar products

(WHO, 2020, pp. 2–3).

The WHO has been actively involved in global health campaigns, such as the worldwide eradication of malaria initiated in 1955, followed by the "Roll Back Malaria" initiative in 1998. Notably, the organisation successfully eradicated smallpox between 1966 and 1980, leading to the universal abolition of vaccination.

The WHO promotes breast-feeding. In addition to its elimination of smallpox, it has launched campaigns against tuberculosis, malaria, poliomyelitis, and AIDS. It fights against tobacco-smoking through the adoption of the Framework Convention on Tobacco Control. One of its current challenges is to identify new threats by new or re-emerging diseases and initiate or recommend effective action against them (Beigbeder, 2017).

The WHO has also played a crucial role in disease control programmes, exemplified by the Onchocerciasis Control Project (OCP) launched in 1974. The project, concluded in 2002, achieved its objectives in 10 of the 11 African countries it covered, focusing on vector control and later incorporating the distribution of medication.

The WHO's engagement in combating HIV/AIDS began with the establishment of the Global Programme on AIDS in 1987. The organisation has been a key sponsor of the Joint United Nations Programme on HIV/AIDS (UNAIDS) and has initiated projects such as the HIV Vaccine Initiative and the Access to Quality HIV/AIDS Drugs and Diagnostics project.

Addressing new health threats, the WHO established the Global Outbreak Alert and Responses Network to ensure swift technical assistance reaches affected states during outbreaks like Ebola, Severe Acute Respiratory Syndrome (SARS), and Avian influenza. The organisation continues to seek to adapt to emerging health challenges, collaborating with various stakeholders and networks, including scientific institutions, UN agencies, and humanitarian NGOs.

One major obstacle encountered by the WHO is the interconnection between health and factors such as politics, economics, social dynamics, and culture. It is dependent on funding from national governments, most notably the US, where support for the WHO has waxed and waned in recent years. The WHO has limited direct influence on these elements, posing a significant challenge in its efforts to address global health issues.

9.2.2 UNICEF

UNICEF, or the United Nations International Children's Emergency Fund, is a specialised agency of the United Nations (UN) dedicated to promoting the well-being and rights of children worldwide. Established on December 11, 1946, UNICEF operates in over 190 countries and territories, providing humanitarian assistance, healthcare, and education to children and mothers in need.

The organisation works to ensure that every child has access to basic necessities, including nutrition, clean water, sanitation, healthcare, and education. UNICEF is guided by the principles of the Convention on the Rights of the Child, striving to protect children from exploitation, violence, and discrimination.

UNICEF collaborates with governments, non-governmental organisations (NGOs), relies on donations from governments, agencies and individuals. It has evolved from primarily an emergency response organisation to the UN's primary development agency working with children.

During 2022, UNICEF:

- ran malnutrition prevention programmes reaching over 356 million children
- ran programmes to detect and treat wasting that reached over 182 million children
- vaccinated 77.9 million children against measles and led the COVAX vaccine programme delivering 977.8 million COVID-19 vaccine doses across 143 countries

- provided basic sanitation services for 26 million people and clean water for over 30 million people (UNICEF, 2023)

9.2.3 UNAIDS

UNAIDS, or the Joint United Nations Programme on HIV/AIDS, is a specialised agency of the United Nations dedicated to addressing the global HIV/AIDS epidemic. Established in 1996, UNAIDS serves as a coordinating mechanism for the UN's efforts to combat HIV/AIDS and works towards achieving global targets for prevention, treatment, care, and support related to the virus.

UNAIDS brings together various UN agencies, including WHO, UNICEF, the United Nations Development Programme (UNDP), the United Nations Population Fund (UNFPA), the United Nations Educational, Scientific, and Cultural Organisation (UNESCO), the International Labour Organisation (ILO), the World Bank, and the World Food Programme (WFP), amongst others. The programme's collaborative approach involves coordinating the efforts of these organisations to provide a comprehensive and effective response to the HIV/AIDS pandemic.

The mission of UNAIDS includes promoting global leadership, advocating for the rights of people living with HIV/AIDS, mobilising resources, and supporting countries in developing and implementing strategies to prevent the spread of the virus, provide care and support for affected individuals, and ensure access to treatment. UNAIDS also works towards reducing the stigma and discrimination associated with HIV/AIDS and promoting policies that protect the rights of individuals affected by the virus.

Despite some notable successes, there has been some criticism of UNAIDS. Specifically, "the creation of new UN agencies to address specific global diseases as they arise is a less desirable strategy than improving the effectiveness of existing institutions" (Condon & Sinha, 2009, p. 285).

9.2.4 The Global Fund

The Global Fund is a worldwide movement to defeat HIV, TB, and malaria, which started in 2002. The Fund states that they "raise and invest 4 billion US dollars a year to fight the deadliest infectious diseases, challenge the injustice that fuels them and strengthen health systems in more than 100 countries. They place a high priority on uniting world leaders, communities, civil society, health workers and the private sector in support of their goals as well as seeking to challenge the existing power dynamics to ensure affected communities have an equal voice in the fight and an equal chance at a healthy future.

Countries where the Fund invests take the lead in determining where and how to best fight the three diseases and present funding applications for review by different Global Fund structures. Country ownership allows them to tailor their own response, considering their political, cultural, and epidemiological context (Montagu, 2021).

The Fund has set out a Five Year Strategy for the years 2023-2028. The Strategy's primary goal is to end AIDS, tuberculosis, and malaria, with a particular focus on making catalytic investments and leveraging innovations to spur faster progress in reducing new infections, addressing structural barriers and building equity, sustainability, and lasting impact. The new Strategy puts people and communities at the centre of the Fund's work. The objectives of the Strategy are designed to leverage the core strengths and comparative advantages of the Global Fund.

The Strategy seeks to:

- maximizing people-centred integrated systems for health to deliver impact, resilience, and sustainability
- maximizing the engagement and leadership of the most affected communities to leave no one behind
- maximizing health equity, gender equality, and human rights
- mobilizing increased resources

The Fund is a global example of a Public Private Partnership; Currently, 94% of its funding is from the public sector. The Fund draws on pledges from a wide range of governments around the world. The remaining funding comes from the private sector, foundations, and innovative financing initiatives.

The Global Fund raises much of its funding in three-year cycles known as replenishments. During a replenishment, governments, private sector donors, and foundations pledge resources to meet the Global Fund's needs. The Fund is entering its Seventh Replenishment cycle, covering the period 2023-2025, seeking at least 18 billion US dollars to fight HIV, TB, and malaria and build stronger systems for health that will also reinforce pandemic preparedness.

As of January 2022, private sector and non-governmental partners have contributed more than 3.6 billion US dollars to the Global Fund, with the largest commitments originating from the Bill & Melinda Gates Foundation, which initially provided seed funding. In addition to financial contributions, these partners actively engage in various ways, such as resource mobilisation, delivery innovation, innovative finance, and advocacy, thereby enhancing the impact of Global Fund activities.

The Fund employs innovative financing techniques, exemplified by (RED), a collaboration with renowned brands and organisations. Through (RED)-branded products and services, corporate giving to the Global Fund is triggered, resulting in a substantial contribution of US$700 million to combat AIDS in Africa.

Philanthropic investment funds with innovative structures allow diverse contributors, including investors, foundations, and philanthropic leaders to pool resources effectively. These pooled funds are designed to coordinate and distribute financial support efficiently to Global Fund-backed health programmes, leveraging both financial resources and expertise.

The Debt2Health programme by the Global Fund transforms debt repayments into investments in health. Through "debt swap" agreements, implementing countries invest in disease-fighting programmes or health system strengthening, leading creditor countries to cancel owed debt.

Blended finance strategies integrate Global Fund grants with financing from various sources, including development finance institutions. Loan buy-downs are employed to enhance domestic financing, expedite prevention investments, and scale up services. The Global Fund is investing 40 million US dollars to assist India in securing a 400 million loan from the World Bank to combat tuberculosis, expanding collaborations with institutions such as the World Bank, Asian Development Bank, and Inter-American Development Bank.

Results-based financing is integral to the Fund's approach, involving disbursement after achieving pre-agreed results at specific milestones. This model has been supported in countries like the Solomon Islands, El Salvador, and Rwanda. Outcome-based financing, encompassing social impact bonds, has also been employed to direct investments towards programmes with effective social outcomes in the fight against diseases, including a social impact bond in South Africa addressing HIV in adolescent girls and young women.

The success of the Global Fund, which has saved 50 million lives by the end of 2021, is largely attributed to effective partnerships and collaborative programmes with its diverse range of supporters.

In countries where the Global Fund invests:

- 23.3 million people were receiving lifesaving antiretroviral therapy, up from 21.9 million in 2020. The percentage of people in need of antiretroviral therapy who received it has significantly increased over the past decade, from 23% in 2010 to 75% in 2021.
- AIDS-related deaths have been reduced by 70% since the Global Fund was founded in 2002 and new infections have been reduced by 54%. In the absence of prevention measures and antiretroviral drugs, deaths would have increased by 240% and new HIV infections by 158% in the same period.
- TB deaths (excluding people living with HIV) since the Global Fund was founded two decades ago have been reduced by 21% as of 2020, while new TB cases (all forms) have dropped by 5%. In the absence of TB control measures, deaths would have increased by 121% and TB cases by 35% in the same period. In 2020, the number of deaths from TB rose for the first time in a decade. But since then, TB programmes have started to recover.
- Malaria deaths have reduced by 26% between 2002 and 2021. The incidence rate has declined by 28% and the mortality rate by 47% since 2002. In the absence of malaria control measures, deaths would have increased by 84% and malaria cases by 70% in the same period.

(Global Fund, 2023)

9.2.5 The Global Vaccine Alliance (Gavi)

Gavi is based in Geneva, Switzerland. Gavi was founded in 2000. Like the Global Fund, Gavi is also as a public-private partnership. It has the aim of improving access to vaccinations and vaccines in the poorer countries of the world (Zerhouni, 2019).

Gavi supports immunisation programmes in individual countries in close cooperation with them. The countries develop applications, which are subject to a rigorous evaluation process within Gavi's internal governance structures. The processes are carried out in close cooperation with the relevant UN organisations, in particular the WHO and UNICEF. Because Gavi operates with five-year funding cycles, it can negotiate long-term contracts with the relevant industry.

As with the Global Fund, many individual countries and private organisations participate in the funding. In the last funding cycle, the Bill & Melinda Gates Foundation emerged as the second largest donor behind the United Kingdom Government and ahead of the US Government (Zerhouni, 2019).

Gavi emphasises transparency and measurement of progress and has defined a comprehensive set of indicators shown in Table 9.1.

Table 9.1   Gavi Indicators and performance (Gavi, 2022)

Indicator category	Indicator	Performance
Mission indicators	M.1 Under-five mortality rate	The under-five mortality rate in the 57 lower-income countries supported by Gavi fell from 57.5 to 55.7 deaths per 1,000 live births between 2020 and 2021.
	M.2 Future deaths averted with Gavi support	The cumulative number of deaths averted from 2000 through 2022 is more than 17.3 million.
	M.3 Future disability-adjusted life years (DALYs) averted with Gavi support	By the end of 2022, more than 121 million future DALYs had been averted by Gavi-supported vaccinations since the Gavi 5.0 strategic period began in 2021.
	M.4 Reduction in zero-dose children	In 2022, there were 10.2 million zero-dose children in the 57 lower-income countries supported by Gavi, down from 12.4 million in 2021.
	M.5 Unique children immunised through routine immunisation with Gavi support	Countries immunised more than 68 million unique children with Gavi-supported routine vaccines in 2022.
	M.6 Economic benefits generated through Gavi-supported immunisations	More than 220.5 billion US dollars economic benefits in the countries we support have been generated through Gavi-supported immunisations since Gavi began in 2000.
Vaccine goal strategy indicators	S1.1 Breadth of protection	The 57 Gavi-supported countries increased breadth of protection by 5% in 2022 to 56%.
	S1.2 Vaccine coverage	Among Gavi57 countries, PCV3 coverage has increased from 56% in 2019 to 70% in 2022.
	S1.3 Rate of scale-up of new vaccines	Coverage of MCV2 and yellow fever vaccine were both under the target of 90% relative coverage, with a decline in 2022. PCV3 and rotaC both exceed the benchmark.
	S1.4 Vaccine introductions	In 2022, 16 new routine introductions took place against a target of 15.
	S1.5 Country prioritisation of vaccines	No evidence available
	S1.6 Measles campaign reach	In 2022, 70.2% of children aged under five previously unvaccinated against measles received an MCV dose among countries conducting a Gavi-supported preventive MCV campaign, up from 37.3% in 2021.
	S1.7 Timely detection of and response to outbreaks	In 2022, the proportion of globally supported outbreak responses which met the timely detection and response criteria was 18%, a decline from 28% in 2021.

(Continued)

Table 9.1 (Continued)

Indicator category	Indicator	Performance
Equity goal strategy indicators	S2.1 Geographic equity of third dose of diphtheria-tetanus-pertussis-containing vaccine (DTP3) coverage	Geographic equity of DTP3 coverage remained at 62% in 2022, down from 67% in 2019.
	S2.2 DTP drop-out	DTP drop-out increased overall in Gavi57 countries, from 6% in 2019 to 7% in 2021, before declining back to 6% in 2022.
	S2.3 Coverage of first dose of measles-containing vaccine (MCV1)	There were moderate delays/challenges in 2022, leading to a mixed picture.
	S2.4 Immunisation sessions conducted	In 2022, Gavi-supported countries reported 17.2 million immunisation sessions were conducted, with 9.6 million taking place in fixed site facilities and 7.6 million in outreach facilities.
	S2.5 Stock availability at facility level	In 2021, the reported average full stock availability of DTP-containing and measles-containing vaccines across the 57 Gavi supported countries was 71.6%.
	S2.6 Expanded Programme on Immunisation (EPI) management capacity	No evidence available
	S2.7 Implementation of tailored plans to overcome demand-related barriers	No evidence available
	S2.8 Addressing gender-related barriers to immunisation	No evidence available
Sustainability goal strategy indicators	S3.1 Co-financing fulfilment	Most Gavi-eligible countries have been able to maintain or increase domestic resources for co-financing of Gavi-supported vaccines in 2022.
	S3.2 Preventing backsliding in Gavi-transitioned countries	No decline – target met
	S3.3 Vaccine introductions in Gavi-transitioned countries and never Gavi-eligible countries	No evidence available
Healthy markets goal strategy indicators	S4.1 Healthy market dynamics	Gavi's ongoing market shaping efforts and collaborations with manufacturers helped ensure that 10 vaccine markets exhibited acceptable levels of healthy market dynamics, compared with a record 11 markets in 2021.
	S4.2 Incentivise innovations	The Vaccine Innovation Prioritisation Strategy (VIPS) is making progress.
	S4.3 Scale up innovations	Two new products with improved characteristics are newly offered in 2022.

9.2.6 *Knowledge review*

Before you move on, can you define the following key concepts:

• Public-private partnerships?

9.2.7 *Question to think about*

Why do you think pharmaceutical companies will engage with programmes like Gavi and The Global Fund?

9.3 Private philanthropy in global health

The Bill & Melinda Gates Foundation is the largest private philanthropic foundation in the world. It invested over 7 billion US dollars to development projects in 2022.

Of this, $1.66 billion was spent on global health projects "to reduce the burden of infectious disease and the leading causes of child mortality in developing countries" and a further $1.89 billion went on development projects, focused on "improving the delivery of high-impact health products and services to the world's poorest communities and helping countries expand access to health coverage" (Gates Foundation, 2022). For comparison, the overall budget is slightly higher than the 2022 share of UNICEF's four-year budget of $23.3 billion for 2022–2025 and higher than WHO's planned expenditure in 2024–25 of $6.83 billion.

Harvey et al. (2021) highlight five concerns about this kind of large-scale private philanthropy:

1. By actively seeking remedies for intricate social issues, entrepreneurial philanthropy inevitably broadens the influence of affluent entrepreneurs beyond economic realms into the social and political domains (Aschoff 2015). This exacerbates the "empowerment gap" between influential decision-makers and ordinary citizens who already feel marginalised by elites and the wealthy (Callahan, 2017, p. 9).
2. Critics argue that the encouragement of this process through generous tax breaks on charitable giving adds insult to injury, augmenting the power of private foundations labelled by Reich (2016, p. 67) as "the most unaccountable, non-transparent institutional form" in democratic societies. Horvath and Powell (2016, p. 116) raise questions about the role of entrepreneurial philanthropy in reshaping government, positioning itself as a preferred provider of public goods, thereby undermining democracy and creating tension with the foundational ideal of equality (Pevnick, 2016, p. 227).
3. Entrepreneurial philanthropy not only diminishes support for government spending on social goods and services (McGoey, 2015, p. 8) but also unfairly places the burden of alleviating poverty on the poor themselves by promoting self-help poverty action, neglecting the recognition of poverty as a consequence of capitalist dynamics (Kohl-Arenas, 2015).
4. By financing market-based solutions to social issues, entrepreneurial philanthropists worsen the situation by reinforcing the structural determinants of poverty (Herro & Obeng-Odoom, 2019).

5. Entrepreneurial philanthropists directly benefit from their supposed generosity by expanding market reach, creating new profit opportunities, and legitimising extreme income and wealth inequalities (Aschoff, 2015; Eikenberry & Mirabella, 2018).

Karlan and List (2020) assessed the reputation and impact of the Foundation through two randomised fundraising appeals and a survey experiment involving a representative sample of US residents.

The study revealed that a matching grant from the Bill & Melinda Gates Foundation yielded better results compared to a matching grant from an anonymous donor. Furthermore, the research demonstrated that a matching grant from the Bill & Melinda Gates Foundation performed better than having no matching grant at all. Both of these findings persisted a year later, extending beyond the conclusion of the matching grant opportunity. The survey experiment also indicated that simply identifying the Bill & Melinda Gates Foundation as a major donor to a project increased the likelihood that individuals perceived the project as high quality.

However, this association was observed only when defining perceived quality as a binary variable, not a continuous one. The researchers suggested that this result regarding perceived quality provides consistent, though not conclusive, evidence that the Bill & Melinda Gates Foundation is encouraging more donations due to a quality signal rather than simply attracting attention or mimicking celebrity endorsements.

Examples of leveraged funding and collaborative initiatives

The Gates Foundation's played a key role in creating Gavi in 2000. They provided $750 million in seed funding and about $4 billion in funds overall. The group only got off the ground because the Foundation used their money to bring in the World Bank, UNICEF, the World Health Organisation, and others as allies and to raise money directly from governments. The US government, for instance, threw in another $2.2 billion on top of the Gates Foundation's $4 billion.

A World Health Organisation report estimated that between 2000 and 2013, Gavi provided 440 million immunisations and averted six million deaths. The investment of $4 billion combined with the Gates' political influence has led to a total budget up to 2020 closer to $18 billion. Similarly, the formation of the Global Fund is as much about bringing together the key players and seeking matched funding as the investment of funds.

The Foundation played a convening and angel-funding role in creating an organisation that now established, effectively subsists on funding from governments. Here the total spending is even greater: the Global Fund had approved $49 billion in total funding for on-the-ground projects by summer 2019, of which $18 billion came from the US government and less than $3 billion from the Foundation directly.

9.3.1 Knowledge review

Before you move on, can you define the following key concepts:

* Philanthropy?
* Leveraged funding?

9.3.2 Question to think about

Has the private Gates Foundation been more successful in bringing about collaboration in the 21st century than established agencies like the UN and WHO? Why?

9.4 Other governmental global agencies impacting on global health

9.4.1 World Bank

The World Bank plays a significant role in the global health arena, with its involvement dating back to the 1950s and expanding notably in recent decades. The organisation provides financial support through loans and grants for health programmes in developing nations, along with offering technical assistance. In 1979, the World Bank established the Health and Nutrition Fund for global health. A pivotal moment occurred 30 years ago when the World Bank released its World Development Report 1993, titled "Investing in Health," which presented crucial health data and insights on global healthcare development. This report appealed to higher-income countries to increase investments in healthcare for lower-income countries.

Over the years, the World Bank has become a crucial participant in healthcare discussions, particularly in low- and middle-income countries, contributing to the strengthening of health systems and health financing. The organisation actively participates in the technical working groups of health ministries in these countries, collaborating with various donor organisations. Despite its primary mandate of providing funding for reconstruction and development in individual countries, the World Bank is unique among international institutions in that voting rights are tied to capital subscriptions, leading to perceptions of it being an instrument of high-income countries.

Despite occasional criticism, the World Bank remains closely engaged with politically influential finance ministries in recipient countries. Globally, it is a major source of funding for health initiatives, offering loans, grants, and technical assistance through the International Bank for Reconstruction and Development (IBRD) and the International Development Association (IDA). The World Bank's support in health financing has contributed to improved access to essential health services and better health outcomes in numerous countries. In recent years, the organisation has focused on promoting transparency and accountability in health spending, along with exploring innovative financing mechanisms. Collaborating with partners, the World Bank aims to assist countries in building the necessary capacity and systems to achieve Universal Health Coverage (UHC).

**The World Bank as a source of evidence for
national and global health policymakers**

The World Bank conducts and publishes a lot of research which can be a valuable resource on health policy matters. For example, they published a report on the economic burden of COVID-19 infections amongst healthcare workers in the first year of the pandemic in Kenya, Colombia, Eswatini, and South Africa (Wang et al., 2023). It concluded that healthcare workers faced a higher likelihood of infection and complications leading to death compared to the general population.

In Kenya, they were nearly 10 times more likely to be infected, and in two provinces of South Africa, the risk was 7–8 times higher. In Colombia, infection rates did not vary significantly between healthcare workers and the rest of the population, resulting in a lower burden.

The economic impact of infection was most significant in countries with low healthcare worker density and severe staff shortages. The major costs were associated with secondary infections and excess maternal and child deaths.

Overall, COVID-19 infections among healthcare workers incurred substantial socio-economic costs. The report estimates that each healthcare worker infection cost $10,000 in Colombia, equivalent to 1.5 times the Gross Domestic Product (GDP) per capita. In Kenya, the cost was estimated at almost $34,000, or 18 times GDP per capita, and in Eswatini, it was assessed at almost $36,000, equivalent to 9 times GDP per capita. As a percentage of annual health expenditure, the total burden associated with HCW infection and death amounted to 1.5% in Colombia, with the highest ratio in Western Cape, South Africa, at 8.4%.

In the wake of the COVID-19 pandemic, the World Bank announced significant funding programmes to health rebuild national economies and healthcare systems in 2020. A $14 billion aid package was directed through the International Finance Corporation, the Bank's private sector financing branch. This was criticised because of their lack of expertise in building public health systems and evidence pointing to the drawbacks of public–private partnerships in health, Accepting these loans from the World Bank burdened countries with additional debt payments, potentially diverting funds from health systems.

The remaining $6 billion was designated to directly support healthcare and facilitate new rapid procurement methods for the bulk purchase of medical supplies (Kentikelenis et al., 2020).

9.4.2 *The World Trade Organisation*

The WTO precursor General Agreement on Tariffs and Trade (GATT), was established by a multilateral treaty of 23 countries in 1947. The treaty aimed to break down barriers to free trade across the world. It is one of the foundations of the subsequent globalisation in trade. Between 1947 and 1986, the GATT continued to operate for almost half a century as a semi-institutionalised multilateral treaty regime on a provisional basis. Between 1986 and 1994, there were a series of negotiations known as the Uruguay Round leading to the establishment of an organisation known as the World Trade Organisation, which continued to oversee the General Agreement on Tariffs and Trade and a range of other international treaties on international trade.

Two of these additional treaties impact on global healthcare policy in particular.

The General Agreement on Trade in Services (GATS) is a treaty of the World Trade Organisation (WTO) that came into force in 1995. (World Trade Organisation, 1994a).

Its objectives were to create a reliable and predictable system of international rules for trade in services and to facilitate the progressive liberalisation of services markets.

Barlow et al. (2022) conducted a systematic review focusing on the health impacts of trade policies, examining evidence from 2016 to 2020. The review encompassed 21 methodologically robust articles, revealing that child mortality tended to decrease following trade reforms. However, negative trends were observed in worker health, with deteriorating conditions noted, along with an increase in the supply of sugar, ultra-processed food, tobacco, and alcohol following trade reforms. Moreover, there was an uptick in drug overdoses post-trade reforms compared to periods preceding the reforms. The associations, however, displayed considerable variation across different contexts and socio-economic characteristics. The researchers concluded that trade policies exhibit diverse effects on health and health determinants, with substantial variations across contexts and socioeconomic groups.

The Agreement on Trade-Related Aspects of Intellectual Property Rights (TRIPS) is an international agreement among all members of the World Trade Organisation (WTO, 1994b). It plays a pivotal role in terms of access to medicines in low- and middle-income countries. TRIPS mandates WTO member states to ensure strict protection of intellectual property rights, requiring enforceable patents for a minimum of 20 years (Art. 33), with limited exceptions to exclusive rights.

Using the Exceptions in TRIPS to enable universal access to HIV/AIDS medications

The Millennium Declaration of 2001 established the objective of achieving universal access to HIV/AIDS treatment for all those in need by 2010. This commitment was reiterated in the Political Declaration on HIV/AIDS, emphasising the flexibilities within the TRIPS Agreement to enhance treatment accessibility. The World Health Organisation (WHO) Global Strategy and Plan of Action on Public Health, Innovation, and Intellectual Property encouraged governments to utilise the full range of flexibilities outlined in the TRIPS Agreement.

Within the TRIPS agreement, WTO Members retained essential policy options, flexibilities, and safeguards. These include the discretion to determine the grounds for issuing compulsory licenses and when to order government use, permitting various forms of parallel imports, applying general exceptions, and utilising transition periods for developing countries, with a longer, extendable transition period specifically for least developed countries.

Some governments have leveraged the exceptions available within TRIPS. In July 2007, Rwanda became the first country to declare its intention to use the WTO's August 30, 2003 decision to import a generic fixed-dose combination of antiviral therapies from a Canadian generic manufacturing company. The Brazilian Government, employing the threat of compulsory licensing, successfully negotiated substantial price reductions for key antiviral drugs between 2001 and 2006. In late

2006 and early 2007, Thailand issued compulsory licenses for several pharmaceutical products.

While the use of TRIPS exceptions to provide cost-effective access to HIV antivirals remains contentious, it is a crucial tool for low-to-medium income countries with high HIV rates to combat the disease and achieve the goals of universal access.

9.4.3 Knowledge review

Before you move on, can you define the following key concepts:

*   The General Agreement on Trade and Tariffs (GATT)?

9.4.3 Question to think about

How far should the intellectual property rights of pharmaceutical companies be protected to ensure sufficient funds for future investment and a return on the investment of shareholders?

9.5 Sustainable Development Goals (SDG)

The Sustainable Development Goals consist of 17 global objectives that have been unanimously embraced by all member states of the United Nations. These goals serve as a comprehensive plan to attain a more prosperous and sustainable future for everyone. Building upon the earlier Millennium Development Goals (MDGs), which aimed to eradicate extreme poverty by 2015 and were unanimously adopted through the Millennium Declaration at the 2000 Millennium Summit, the Sustainable Development Goals were established in 2015. The target for their achievement is set for 2030, focusing on realising human rights for all, promoting gender equality, empowering women and girls, eliminating poverty in all its forms worldwide, and putting an end to global hunger. The Sustainable Development Goals "recognise that ending poverty and other deprivations must go hand-in-hand with strategies that improve health and education, reduce inequality, and spur economic growth – all while tackling climate change and working to preserve our oceans and forests." (United Nations, n.d.).

The 17 Sustainable Goals are as follows:

Goal 1: No Poverty
Goal 2: Zero Hunger
Goal 3: Good Health and Well-Being
Goal 4: Quality Education
Goal 5: Gender Equality
Goal 6: Clean Water and Sanitation
Goal 7: Affordable and Clean Energy
Goal 8: Decent Work and Economic Growth
Goal 9: Industry, Innovation, and Infrastructure
Goal 10: Reduced Inequality

Goal 11: Sustainable Cities and Communities
Goal 12: Responsible Consumption and Production
Goal 13: Climate Action
Goal 14: Life Below Water
Goal 15: Life on Land
Goal 16: Peace and Justice Strong Institutions
Goal 17: Partnerships to Achieve the Goal

Although Goal 3 explicitly relates to health, many of the others relate to social determinants of health, and many of the goals are inter-related.

Within SDG 3, there are nine distinct targets (WHO, n.d.):

3.1. By 2030, reduce the global maternal mortality ratio to less than 70 per 100,000 live births.
3.2. By 2030, end preventable deaths of new-borns and children under five years of age, with all countries aiming to reduce neonatal mortality to at least as low as 12 per 1,000 live births and under-five mortality to at least as low as 25 per 1,000 live births.
3.3 By 2030, end the epidemics of AIDS, tuberculosis, malaria, and neglected tropical diseases and combat hepatitis, waterborne diseases, and other communicable diseases.
3.4. By 2030, reduce by one-third premature mortality from noncommunicable diseases through prevention and treatment and promote mental health and well-being.
3.5. Strengthen the prevention and treatment of substance abuse, including narcotic drug abuse and harmful use of alcohol.
3.6. By 2020, halve the number of global deaths and injuries from road traffic accidents.
3.7. By 2030, ensure universal access to sexual and reproductive healthcare services, including for family planning, information and education, and the integration of reproductive health into national strategies and programmes.
3.8. Achieve universal health coverage, including financial risk protection, access to quality essential healthcare services, and access to safe, effective, quality and affordable essential medicines, and vaccines for all.
3.9. By 2030, substantially reduce the number of deaths and illnesses from hazardous chemicals and air, water and soil pollution, and contamination.

The significance of the SDGs is that almost all major global players in health and development incorporate SDG indicators within their evaluation frameworks.

At the halfway point towards 2030, progress towards these targets is behind schedule, the lag exacerbated by the COVID-19 pandemic. The World Health Organisation (2023) emphasised the need for greater collaboration to accelerate progress. The Global Action Plan for Healthy Lives and Well-being for All (SDG3 GAP) is a set of commitments, signed by 13 multilateral agencies, to strengthen collaboration and alignment with country priorities in health. While the SDG3 GAP agencies are committed to strengthening collaboration and providing more streamlined support to countries, lessons learned since 2019 show that nation states can also do more to incentivise collaboration and fully leverage the SDG3 GAP at the country level.

Progress towards SDG3 targets in the Americas (after PAHO, 2023)

Before the onset of the COVID-19 pandemic, advancements towards achieving SDG 3 targets displayed positive trends in certain aspects but were insufficient and varied across countries in the Americas.

While the majority of SDG 3 indicators in the Americas exhibited a modest improvement in their regional averages, there was no significant reduction in inequality. For instance, the mortality rate from prioritised chronic diseases decreased from 14.8% in 2015 to 14.2% in 2019 (SDG 3.4.1), but the absolute disparity between more and less developed countries remained at 6%. Conversely, mortality from road traffic injuries (SDG 3.6.1) declined from 15.8 per 100,000 inhabitants to 15.3 during the same period. Despite this improvement, the absolute gap widened from 5.3 to 7.8.

However, certain SDG 3 indicators not only experienced an upward trend at the regional level but also witnessed an increase in inequality between more and less developed countries, indicating a setback. For example, the suicide mortality rate rose from 8.4 per 100,000 population in 2015 to 8.9 in 2019, with the gap between more developed and less developed countries expanding from 4.9 to 7.3 during the same timeframe.

9.5.1 Knowledge review

Before you move on, can you define the following key concepts:

• Sustainable Development Goals?

9.5.2 Question to think about

Can the Sustainable Development Goals be viewed as a success if only some of the targets are met?

References

Aschoff, N. (2015). *The new prophets of capital*. Verso Books.
Barlow, P., Sanap, R., Garde, A., Winters, A., Mabhala, M. A., & Anne-Marie Thow, A.-M. (2022, May 1). Reassessing the health impacts of trade and investment agreements: A systematic review of quantitative studies, 2016–20. *The Lancet: Planetary Health*, 6(5), E431–e438, Open Access Published: May, 2022.
Beigbeder, Y. (2017). *The world health organisation: Achievements and failures*. Routledge.
Callahan, D. (2017). *The givers: Wealth, power, and philanthropy in a new gilded age*. Vintage.
Condon, B. J., & Sinha, T. (2009). *Global lessons from the AIDS pandemic: Economic, financial, legal and political implications*. Springer.
Eikenberry, A. M., & Mirabella, R. M. (2018). Extreme philanthropy: Philanthrocapitalism, effective altruism, and the discourse of neoliberalism. *PS Political Science & Politics*, 51(1), 43–47.
Gates Foundation. (2022). 2022 Annual Report, Bill & Melinda Gates Foundation, Seattle, WA.

Gavi. (2022). Annual progress report 2022.

Harvey, C., Gordon, J., & Maclean, M. (2021). The ethics of entrepreneurial philanthropy. *Journal of Business Ethics*, 171, 33–49.

Herro, A., & Obeng-Odoom, F. (2019). Foundations of radical philanthropy. *VOLUNTAS: International Journal of Voluntary and Non-profit Organisations*, 30, 881–890.

Hobsbawm, E. (2007). *Globalisation, democracy, and terrorism*. Little Brown.

Horvath, A., & Powell, W. (2016). Contributory or disruptive: Do new forms of philanthropy erode democracy? In R. Reich, C. Cordelli, & L. Bernholz (Eds.), *Philanthropy in democratic societies* (pp. 226–243). University of Chicago Press.

Howden-Chapman, P., Siri, J., Chisholm, E., Chapman, R., Doll, C. N., & Capon, A. (2017). *SDG 3: Ensure healthy lives and promote wellbeing for all at all ages. A guide to SDG interactions: from science to implementation* (pp. 81–126). International Council for Science.

ICAO. (2020). The world of air transport in 2019 (annual report).

Karlan, D., & List, J. A. (2020). How can bill and melinda gates increase other people's donations to fund public goods?. *Journal of Public Economics*, 191, 104296.

Kentikelenis, A., Gabor, D., Ortiz, I., Stubbs, T., McKee, M., & Stuckler, D. (2020). Softening the blow of the pandemic: Will the international monetary fund and world bank make things worse?. *The Lancet Global Health*, 8(6), e758–e759.

Kohl-Arenas, E. (2015). *The self-help myth: How philanthropy fails to alleviate poverty (Vol. 1)*. University of California Press.

Labonté, R., Schrecker, T., Packer, C., & Runnels, V. (2011). The growing impact of globalisation for health and public health practice. *Annual Review of Public Health*, 32(1), 263–283.

McGoey, L. (2015). *No such thing as a free gift: The Gates Foundation and the price of philanthropy*. Verso.

Montagu, D. (2021). The provision of private healthcare services in european countries: Recent data and lessons for universal health coverage in other settings. *Frontiers in Public Health*, 9, 636750

Pevnick, R. (2016). Philanthropy and democratic ideals. In R. Reich, C. Cordelli, & L. Bernholz (Eds.), *Philanthropy in democratic societies* (pp. 226–243). University of Chicago Press.

Reich, R. (2011). Toward a political theory of philanthropy. In P. Ilingworth, T. Pogge, & L. Wenar (Eds.), *Giving well: The ethics of philanthropy* (pp. 177–195). Oxford University Press.

Reich, R. (2016). Repugnant to the whole idea of democracy? On the role of foundations in democratic societies. *PS: Political Science & Politics*, 49(3), 466–472.

Steger, M. B., Benedikter, R., Pechlaner, H., & Kofler, I. (2023). *Globalisation*. University of California Press.

Steger, M. B., & James, P. (2020). Disjunctive globalisation in the era of the great unsettling. *Theory, Culture & Society*, 37(7–8), 187–203.

The Global Fund. (2023). *Results report: 2023*. The Global Fund.

UNICEF. (2023). *Annual report 2022*. United Nations Children's Fund (UNICEF), May 2023. ISBN: 978-92-806-5461-5

United Nations. (n.d.). *The 17 goals, department of economic and social affairs*. Sustainable Development.

Wang, H., Zeng, W., Munge Kabubei, K., Rasanathan, J., Kazungu, J., Ginindza, S., Mtshali, S., Salinas, L. E., McClelland, A., Buissonniere, M., Lee, C. T., Chuma, J., Veillard, J., Matsebula, T., Chopra, M. (2023). *The economic burden of SARS-CoV-2 infection amongst health care workers in the first year of the pandemic in Kenya, Colombia, Eswatini, and South Africa*. Washington, DC: World Bank. License: CC BY-NC 3.0 IGO.

World Bank. (2024). *Data bank*. World Bank.

World Health Organisation. (2004). *Summary of probable SARS cases with onset of illness from 1 November 2002 to 31 July 2003*. WHO.

World Health Organisation. (2019). *Global action plan for healthy lives and well-being for all (SDG3 GAP)*. WHO.

World Health Organisation. (2020). *Basic documents* (49th ed.). The Constitution of the World Health Organisation.

World Health Organisation. (2023). 2023 Progress report on the Global Action Plan for Healthy Lives and Well-being for All What worked? What didn't? What's next? WHO Geneva. ISBN 978-92-4-007337-1.

World Health Organisation. (n.d.). *Targets of sustainable development goal 3*. World Health Organisation.

World Trade Organisation. (1994a). *General agreement on trade in services*. World Trade Organisation.

World Trade Organisation. (1994b). *Agreement on trade-related aspects of intellectual property rights*. World Trade Organisation.

Zerhouni E. (2019). GAVI, the Vaccine Alliance. *Cell*, 179(1), 13–17.

Section C
Healthcare financing

10 Health financing systems

10.1 Health financing functions

10.1.1 Health financing systems

The goal of health financing systems is to maximise the quality and quantity of health-care within the available resources. In practice, resources are always finite, so there are always compromises to be made. At the same time, maximising the return on the resource invested can reduce the compromises and choices needed to be made. Financial incentives within the system drive behaviours of healthcare providers, suppliers, and the behaviour of individual clinicians and patients.

The implications of health financing go far beyond accounting. It acts as a crucial factor in advancing or impeding the goal of universal health coverage, especially in lower-income countries. Its effectiveness lies in enhancing the reach of services and providing financial safeguards. Currently, a significant number of individuals are unable to access healthcare due to financial constraints, while others, despite paying out-of-pocket, receive substandard services. Strategic health financing policies, when carefully formulated and implemented, have the potential to tackle these challenges. For instance, payment structures and contracts can serve as incentives for better coordination of care and improved service quality. Moreover, the timely and sufficient allocation of funds to healthcare providers is essential in ensuring adequate staffing levels and the availability of necessary medications for patient treatment.

The functions of a health financing system are to collect revenues, pool resources, and purchase health services within the scope of a health system (Evans et al., 2023). A country's approach to health financing plays a critical role in determining if there will be adequate funding available to support the delivery of essential health services, especially to the most vulnerable.

Revenue raising is a health financing function that involves the identification and mobilisation of funds to support all activities that are necessary to deliver healthcare (WHO, 2010). The three types of funds that can be mobilised for health are government, domestic private sources, and external sources. The government collects taxes, transaction fees, and insurance premiums. Institutions and individuals contribute to domestic funding through the payment of user fees, insurance premiums, donations, and out-of-pocket spending. Funding for health can also come from overseas grants and donations, which are categorised as external sources. In recent years, countries' funding for health services are largely contributed by taxes, insurance, and out-of-pocket spending.

Key to maintaining equity and protecting vulnerable is the concept of risk pooling. Risk-pooling is the "accumulation and management of revenues in such a way as to

DOI: 10.4324/9781003478874-13

ensure that the risk of having to pay for healthcare is borne by all members of the pool and not by each contributor individually." The larger degree of pooling, the less people will have to bear the health financial risks (Ahangar et al., 2018).

Individuals within a population encounter varying risks of falling ill. Combining these diverse risk levels ultimately leads to an averaging effect across the population, achieving a balance within the health system. The greater the pooling of funds, the more extensive the system's ability to address a broad spectrum of health risks within the population.

Provider payment mechanisms are the methods by which purchasers of healthcare pay providers for the services they provide. They create incentives or signals that influence the behaviour of healthcare providers (Kazungu et al., 2018).

Purchasing of healthcare is just one step in the broader procurement process. Procurement within the realm of health financing involves strategically distributing resources to address a variety of population health needs. It entails determining the payment methods for healthcare providers, ensuring that citizens can access high-quality essential health services. The process of procuring health services necessitates a delicate balance between the interests of the population, healthcare providers, and the primary payer, typically the government. Within this context, the payer establishes a payment mechanism with healthcare providers, creating a mutually agreed-upon funding flow to ensure providers are compensated for meeting the healthcare needs of the population.

Governments, within the confines of their health budgets, allocate resources based on their prioritisation of health activities. To make health services available to the public, a combination of provider payment mechanisms is deployed. This diverse approach creates various incentives aimed at facilitating the delivery of care at an acceptable standard. Governments leverage their authority, utilising tools like regulation or contracting, to implement these provider payment mechanisms. When appropriately designed and executed, the government's procurement function can, for instance, encourage proper referral and coordination of care, along with other measures to ensure the provision of high-quality health services. By aligning incentives with the timely disbursement of funds and accountability measures, health facilities are guided to assure patients of the availability of adequate staff, medicines, and supplies to meet their needs, while maintaining the sustainability and profitability of health facility operations.

10.1.2 Strategy options

There are a number of strategy options used to finance healthcare. Each strategy has advantages and disadvantages, depending on the country's situation. In general, the combination of strategies along the health financing functions fall into four models of health financing systems (Gabani et al., 2023):

1. National health service
2. Social health insurance
3. Private insurance
4. Out-of-pocket expenditures

There is no single perfect strategy, and typically, a combination of approaches is necessary. Therefore, governments are entrusted with the responsibility of determining the optimal mix of strategies to meet the needs of their citizens, support healthcare providers, and achieve health system objectives. The evaluation of health financing strategies should be dynamic, relying on timely information to facilitate adjustments. This ensures that, while maintaining financial risk protection, citizens can access health services efficiently and equitably.

The health financing system is intricately linked to broader government planning, budgeting, and financing systems. Consequently, mobilising resources for health services must take into account the overall development and economic priorities of the country. The journey toward achieving healthcare goals for the population must align with the broader values and aspirations of the citizens. On a global scale, governments are expected to uphold and safeguard the right to health for their people, making a crucial contribution to the realisation of SDGs as outlined by the United Nations in 2015 (United Nations, 2015).

UHC is SDG Target 3.8. UHC ensures that all people and communities receive the full spectrum of health services, from health promotion to prevention, treatment, rehabilitation, and palliative care, across the life course that they need and of sufficient quality to be effective while also ensuring that the use of these services does not expose the user to financial hardship.

The resource requirements that make health services accessible to all citizens depend on the prevailing disease profile, population profile and dynamics, health system capacity, and economic condition, among others. Thus, while the funding needs vary across jurisdictions, all countries aiming for timely access to essential health services must have a well-functioning health financing system that is able to raise revenues, pool risks, and purchase the necessary health services to produce their desired results. In practical terms, this means that countries are able to analyse their situation, determine what changes need to be made, and what kind of policies must be in place to direct actions. Realistically, the lowest-income countries face some of the biggest challenges to financing universal health coverage.

In many of these countries, there is a high incidence of catastrophic health expenditure. Catastrophic health expenditure occurs when medical spending of a household exceeds a certain level of capacity to pay, often in response to a sudden unexpected illness. It is measured as the frequency of events where a household's out-of-pocket expense for health services exceeds a threshold (typically 10% or 25%) of consumption or income, resulting in financial hardship. In addition to causing serious financial hardship for whole households, the threat of catastrophic hardship can prevent people seeking healthcare leading to deterioration in their health or even death from essentially treatable conditions.

Eze et al. (2022) conducted a literature review examining over one million households across 31 countries in Sub-Saharan Africa. The combined annual occurrence of catastrophic health expenditure was found to be 16.5%, affecting one in six households, using a threshold of 10% of the total household expenditure. The highest and lowest incidence rates were observed in central and southern Sub-Saharan African countries, respectively. Despite an initial decrease in the first decade of the 21st century, a trend analysis revealed an increase in catastrophic health expenditure incidence in Sub-Saharan Africa between 2010 and 2020. Individuals affected by diseases such as noncommunicable diseases (e.g., HIV/AIDS and tuberculosis) generally experienced higher incidence rates.

The perception of health within a country's population and the shaping of political agendas can be significantly influenced by socio-political realities. For example, in a context where health is strongly acknowledged as a human right, there is an expectation for the government to play a more prominent role in executing the three health financing functions of collecting revenues, pooling of resources and risks, and purchasing of health services . On the opposite end of the spectrum, when health is viewed as a commodity that individuals are required to pay for, the private sector predominantly determines the terms of healthcare access for specific population groups.

However, the majority of countries fall somewhere in between these extremes: citizens anticipate their nations to uphold the right to health, while the private sector plays a supplementary role in areas where governments may face limitations in resources.

UHC cannot be attained without proper measurement, monitoring, and evaluation. Since a health financing system provides a critical role for UHC, its performance can generate insights about progress. In particular, health financing functions are expected to reduce financial barriers. Thus, the contribution of health financing functions are generally assessed by the extent of financial hardship that citizens experience as a result of healthcare utilisation.

The main consideration in this regard is the use of out-of-pocket payments by patients at the time of healthcare utilisation. When out-of-pocket payment becomes a dominant source of funding to access health services, it presents an automatic barrier for most people. It changes the way people seek care, as this decision can impact the overall financial status of individuals.

Even in wealthier countries, citizens may be expected to contribute to services that are funded either only partially or not at all from pooled resources. This may act as a barrier to service utilisation and result in poorer outcomes.

Co-payments for dental services in Japan

For example, Cooray et al. (2020) looked at the impact of a 30% co-payment on dental services in Japan. From the age of 70, this is reduced to 20%. They found that the co-payment discount policy increases oral health service utilisation among older citizens and argued that the co-payment should be reduced amongst younger citizens to encourage participation in cost-effective preventative dentistry.

10.1.3 Knowledge review

Before you move on, can you define the following key concepts:

• Catastrophic health expenditure?
• Risk pooling?
• Universal health coverage?

10.1.4 Question to think about

In your own healthcare system, which parts of healthcare require out-of-pocket expenditure?

Does this influence your utilisation of these services?

Are there consequences for your wealth or your health?

10.2 Revenue raising

10.2.1 Sources of revenue

Revenue raising is the collection of funds from various sources for the purpose of funding healthcare activities. In practice, in almost all cases, there is a combination of different mechanisms. For individuals to avail themselves of health services, there must be sufficient funding to ensure the availability of necessary resources at the point of care, including diagnostic tools, medications, and skilled healthcare professionals. Health service financing can be derived from various channels. Domestic resources are generated through government revenues and private sources, encompassing institutions and individuals. External funding for health is also possible through avenues such as overseas development assistance, grants, or donations.

Governments generate revenue through a variety of methods such as taxes, fees, and insurance. Some of these may be collected specifically to fund healthcare, others as general taxation, in which case the funds will be in competition with other government priorities.

Table 10.1 summarises the key methods by which governments raise revenue to cover healthcare costs.

Where healthcare financing does not come from government contributions, it may be paid for by individuals at the time of treatment. However, this comes with a high risk of catastrophic expenditure. Insurance is the commonest method to prevent this, when government coverage is not provided. Typically, this may be individual private health insurance where individuals and families often purchase private health insurance plans to cover medical expenses or employer-sponsored health insurance. Many employers provide health insurance as part of their employee benefits. This can cover a significant portion of the population, especially in countries where employer-sponsored insurance is common. Even in countries like Canada, where many citizens are proud of their publicly funded healthcare system, pharmaceuticals for the working population are mostly provided by employer-sponsored health insurance.

Not-for-profit organisations, including charities and foundations, may contribute to healthcare financing by providing funds for medical services, research, and public health initiatives. This may be complemented by donations and philanthropic contributions from individuals, corporations, and foundations. These funds may be directed towards specific medical research, treatment programs, or community health initiatives.

At a national level, low-to-middle income countries may receive financial assistance from international organisations or other countries to support their healthcare systems, especially in regions with limited resources.

The balance between public and private financing can differ based on the healthcare model adopted by a particular country.

The World Health Organisation (2023) argues that domestic public funds are increasingly recognised as an essential component of a high-performing, sustainable and equitable health financing system that can drive progress towards UHC and that a reliance on out-of-pocket payments is associated with inefficiency, regressivity, and impoverishment. In almost all cases, public funding maximises risk pooling, reduces the risk of catastrophic expenditure and maximises equity and the opportunities to deliver on the UN SDGs.

Therefore, the World Health Organisation (WHO) advocates that nations should ensure that government funding at least covers essential health services guaranteed

Table 10.1 Principal methods by which governments raise revenue to support healthcare costs

Source	Details
Taxation	Governments often finance healthcare through taxation. This can include income taxes, value-added taxes (VAT), or corporate taxes. Additional taxes may be targeted at goods deemed harmful to health, such as such as tobacco, alcohol, or sugary beverages, to disincentivise consumption as well as raise revenue.
Social health insurance	Many countries, particularly in Europe, operate social health insurance systems, where citizens contribute to a health insurance fund. These contributions may be mandatory, and the funds collected are used to cover the costs of healthcare services. Social health insurance is often designed to ensure that everyone has access to essential health services.
Mandatory health contributions	In certain systems, governments may impose compulsory health contributions on individuals or employers. These contributions are earmarked for healthcare and are kept separate from general taxes. Employers may be required to contribute on behalf of their employees, and individuals may also make direct contributions.
User fees and co-payments	Governments may implement user fees or co-payment systems, requiring individuals to pay a portion of the cost for healthcare services at the point of use. This can help generate revenue and, in some cases, may also be a strategy to manage healthcare demand.
Donor funding	In addition to domestic sources, governments may receive external funding from international donors, non-governmental organisations (NGOs), or other countries. This funding can come in the form of grants, loans, or aid specifically allocated for healthcare projects or improvements.
Private health insurance	Some governments encourage or require citizens to purchase private health insurance. In these cases, individuals or employers pay premiums to private insurance companies, and the insurance coverage helps offset the cost of healthcare services. In other systems, Governments incentivise the uptake of private health insurance by tax reliefs.
Investment income	Governments may earn revenue through investments such as returns on investments in financial markets. This income can contribute to overall government revenue, which may be allocated to healthcare.

under UHC. To adhere to this recommendation, a government must accurately estimate the cost of UHC and progressively increase its share of the total health expenditure over time. The significance of bolstering government financial support for health services rests on two key aspects. By exercising the state's authority within reasonable limits, a country can enforce prepayment collection from citizens and make payment mandatory.

10.2.2 Prepaid health contributions

Prepaid health contributions are made in advance of the actual need, and in a well-designed financing system, a prepaid approach is preferable. This allows citizens to plan and set aside a predetermined amount, preventing a situation where they must pay more than they can afford when the need arises. Consequently, elevating the government's share of the overall cost of health services aligns with the objective of reducing out-of-pocket expenses.

Compulsory payments orchestrated by the government enhance risk pooling and foster population solidarity around health services, as individuals are obligated to contribute financially, irrespective of their use of health services. Both prepaid and compulsory features enable a government to plan for the utilisation of these contributions with a long-term perspective. This approach increases the likelihood of government funding being predictable and stable, thereby supporting long-term planning. Although centrally mobilised revenue is generally recommended for its efficiency, governments must ensure the implementation of policies and regulations that ensure equity.

Revenue collection strategies should enhance financial access for low-income households, incentivise individuals with lower incomes to seek care, alleviate financial burdens, prevent the exacerbation of poverty, enable income cross-subsidisation, and enhance the quality of services. The International Monetary Fund argues for tax reform as a mechanism to help countries achieve this and cited the experiences in five countries (Akitoby, 2018).

Case study: Is Canada's archetypal universal access healthcare system funded through taxation?

Canadians often assert their difference from their United States neighbours and none more so than by highlighting difference in their healthcare systems.

Canadians aspired to universal healthcare provided through general taxation for many decades. This culminated in the passing of The Canada Health Act 1984, (Government of Canada, 1985) which is often regarded as enshrining into law, Canadian citizens' right to access healthcare free at the point of need.

In practice, the Act is concerned with the method of payment for healthcare, and states that:

> The purpose of this Act is to establish criteria and conditions in respect of insured health services and extended healthcare services provided under provincial law that must be met before a full cash contribution may be made. (Government of Canada, 1985, section 4, page 5)

Provided these criteria are met, the Federal Government is then required to make a cash transfer to the provinces to cover an agreed proportion of the cost of healthcare. The criteria are public administration, comprehensiveness, universality, portability, and accessibility (Government of Canada, 1985, section 7, page 5).

In practice, the healthcare services covered by the Act cover hospital care and physician services, but significantly not the cost of pharmaceuticals outside of hospitals. This leads to a situation where only about 70% of health spending is publicly funded through taxation, with citizens funding the rest through insurance or direct payments (Canadian Institute for Health Information (CIHI), 2019).

Whilst this is much less than the US, where 51% is contributed by private contributions, it is significantly more than the UK National Health Service where 20% comes from private sources (CIHI, 2019).

10.2.3 Knowledge review

Before you move on, can you define the following key concepts:

- Social health insurance?
- Co-payments?

10.2.4 *Question to think about*

In your own healthcare system, how much of healthcare is funded from revenue collected by the government? Which publicly funded services require a contribution at the point of use?

10.3 Risk pooling

Risk pooling is concerned with combining and sharing the financial risks associated with healthcare expenses among a large group of individuals. Health funding models, whether taxation-based, social-, or private-insurance-based, operate on the principle of risk pooling. Insurance companies collect premiums from policyholders, and in return, they cover the costs of medical care based on the terms of the insurance plan. Similarly, national governments collect taxes from citizens and use the income to provide healthcare services.

The goal is to distribute the financial burden of healthcare costs across a broader population, reducing the impact on any single individual or family.

The key benefits from risk pooling are:

- Individuals contribute to a common pool through insurance premiums or other financing mechanisms. By doing so, they collectively share the financial responsibility for covering healthcare costs.
- Healthcare expenses can be unpredictable and sometimes result in significant financial burdens, especially in the case of major illnesses or emergencies. Risk pooling helps protect individuals from the potentially catastrophic financial consequences of high medical bills.
- Healthy individuals who may not require extensive medical care at a given time contribute to the pool alongside those who are currently facing health challenges. This cross-subsidisation allows resources to be allocated to those in need, creating a balance in financial contributions.
- Risk pooling promotes fairness by ensuring that the costs of healthcare are distributed more equitably across the population. Those who are healthier at a particular point in time contribute to the pool, knowing that they may benefit when their health needs increase.
- From the perspective of both individuals and the healthcare system, risk pooling provides a level of stability and predictability. It helps individuals plan for potential healthcare expenses, and it allows the healthcare system to manage financial risks more effectively.
- Adverse selection occurs when individuals with higher health risks are more likely to seek insurance coverage, potentially leading to imbalances in the risk pool. Risk pooling mechanisms often include strategies to mitigate adverse selection, such as mandatory enrolment or risk adjustment mechanisms.
- By spreading the financial burden across a larger population, risk pooling contributes to increased access to healthcare services. Individuals are more likely to seek necessary medical care when they know that the costs are shared among a larger group.
- The World Health Organisation argues that risk pooling is essential for the delivery of UHC and the UN SDGs.

When the whole population is included within the revenue collection model, the pool expands, and the pools encompass a more varied mix of health risks among their members, as individuals with varying levels of health risk are included.

This may be achieved through either compulsory or automatic coverage. Compulsory coverage requires a specific contribution from or on behalf of the individuals covered. On the other hand, automatic coverage is determined by a person's residency or citizenship, and the funds are drawn from non-specific taxation.

Overall, risk pooling is a foundational concept in health financing, playing a crucial role in making healthcare more accessible, affordable, and sustainable for individuals and communities.

Four different methods of risk pooling after Mathauer et al. (2020)

Mathauer et al. (2020) identify four different methods of risk pooling:

1. *Shifting to compulsory or automatic coverage for everybody.* Some low- and middle-income countries, such as Chile, Mongolia, and Rwanda, have adopted mandatory contributory coverage for individuals in the informal economy. In contrast, countries like Ghana and Vietnam face challenges in covering a middle segment of individuals outside the formal sector who are not categorised as poor or vulnerable. Despite official mandates for enrolment, enforcement becomes problematic, leading to non-participation in contributory schemes, especially for the partially subsidised missing middle group. Gaps in automatic or compulsory coverage contribute to certain population groups lacking coverage, resulting in higher out-of-pocket expenses and a subsequent financial burden, leading to reduced utilisation of services.
2. *Merging of existing fragmented pools.* The merging of pools increases the number of pool members and their health needs and risk and reduces administrative costs because duplication of tasks is reduced. Merging may also enhance the purchasing power of the pool and hence the potential to purchase health services more strategically for gains in efficiency and equity. Various countries, such as Kyrgyzstan, the Republic of Moldova, and Ukraine, have addressed fragmentation and overlap at national and provincial levels by vertical merging; that is, elevating the level of pooling to higher levels of government.
3. *Cross-subsidisation of pools* may be used when different pools have members with lower revenues and higher health risks. More affluent segments of the population may resist the consolidation of pools due to concerns about having to financially support less privileged groups. Nevertheless, countries such as Indonesia, South Korea, Turkey, and Vietnam have successfully implemented such reforms. In each case, the amalgamation of pools augmented risk diversity within the combined pool, a key step toward reducing disparities in health service access.
4. *Harmonisation across different pools.* In this approach, discrete populations are maintained but pseudo-pooling is achieved through the harmonisation of terms of benefits, payment methods, and contribution rates. This approach was deployed in Colombia and has also been tried in India.

10.3.1 Knowledge review

Before you move on, can you define the following key concepts:

*   Compulsory healthcare coverage?
*   Automatic coverage?

10.3.2 Question to think about

In the healthcare system where you live, is risk pooling applied? If so, how?

Table 10.2   The key principles of resource allocation in healthcare

Need-based allocation	Resources should be allocated based on the healthcare needs of the population. This involves prioritising interventions and services that address prevalent health issues and contribute to the overall well-being of the community.
Cost-effectiveness	Efficiency is crucial in resource allocation. It involves maximising the health outcomes achieved with the available resources. Cost-effectiveness analysis helps in evaluating the benefits of healthcare interventions relative to their costs.
Equity	Ensuring fair and equal access to healthcare is a fundamental principle. Resource allocation should aim to reduce disparities in health outcomes and guarantee that vulnerable or marginalised groups have adequate access to essential services.
Utilitarian approach	This approach seeks to maximise overall societal well-being. Resources are allocated to interventions that provide the greatest overall benefit to the population, even if this means sacrificing some individual benefits.
Priority to preventive care	Emphasising preventive measures can be more cost-effective in the long run by reducing the incidence of diseases and the need for expensive treatments.
Public participation	Involving the public in decision-making processes can contribute to more democratic and transparent resource allocation. Understanding the preferences and values of the community is vital in shaping healthcare policies.
Evidence-based resource allocation	Allocating resources based on scientific evidence helps ensure that interventions and treatments are effective and have a proven impact on health outcomes.
Emergency and essential services	Allocating resources to emergency and essential healthcare services is a priority to address immediate health needs and ensure the basic health requirements of the population are met.
Continuous evaluation and adaptation	Healthcare systems should be dynamic, with continuous evaluation of resource allocation strategies. This allows for adjustments based on changing health needs, technological advancements, and evolving societal priorities.
Local context	The optimal allocation of resources may vary based on cultural, economic, and political contexts. Ethical considerations can play a significant role in shaping healthcare policies and resource allocation strategies, and these will be influenced by the local context.

10.4 Resource allocation

Resource allocation is the assignment of the available human, intellectual, and financial resources across different healthcare activities, programs, and services. It ensures that the correct amount of funding is assigned to the priority areas in healthcare, particularly with reference to UHC. It is considered as the determination of support across the spectrum of promotive, preventive, curative, rehabilitative, and palliative health services.

Within a given resource availability, the approach to its allocation can influence the attainment of health goals; proper allocation can optimise the population health outcomes. This can happen when allocation is done fairly according to a defined prioritisation process. A prioritisation process can be systemically used to inform allocation according to population need, availability of services, cost, capacity of the health system, effectiveness of intervention, and other criteria.

Fair allocation through prioritisation can also guide the efficient and equitable distribution of resources in a given population. The allocation process can also be defined based on the funding sources. For example, government revenues are usually allocated for long-term, historical, and needs-based investments, whereas compulsory collection from individuals can be allocated according to health risks In terms of equity, the allocation of health funding must influence the supply side to cater to the needs of people experiencing lower income while providing incentives to this same group to make use of the services.

The allocation of resources cannot be a static decision but a dynamic, ongoing process. Guided by information about underutilisation or overutilisation of health services, resources can be moved, for example, from supporting services that are underutilised to others that are higher in demand. Crises, such as the COVID-19 pandemic, may also create a need for diverting resources. Decision-makers must balance immediate emergency needs with long-term priorities.

Table 10.2 highlights the key principles that are used to allocate resources for healthcare.

Resource allocation for healthcare in rural China

In many countries, there is a challenge in allocating healthcare resources between rural and urban areas as well as between different regions. Ao et al. (2022) investigated the equity of access in the Chinese healthcare system. They used data from the China Health Statistics Yearbook, the China Health Yearbook, and the China Statistical Yearbook between the years 2004 and 2021 to determine a number of indices of resource density and equity.

They found that following an extended period of reform and growth, China's rural three-tier healthcare service system has undergone significant transformation. This study reveals that the most rapid development is observed in county and county-level city medical and health institutions. While the quantity of institutions in township hospitals is decreasing, there is an increase in both bed numbers and personnel. The outlook for village clinics is less favourable, marked by a decline in healthcare resources and persistent widening gaps. This situation is attributed to the highly dispersed healthcare service system, a lack of interaction between market mechanisms, and the consolidation of administrative villages.

They also found that village clinics exhibit greater institutional fairness, whereas county-level facilities and township hospitals show more equitable distribution of beds and personnel. There is an uneven geographical distribution of healthcare resources between the eastern and central regions compared to the western region, but the intra-regional distribution of beds and personnel in the west and central regions is superior to that in the eastern region. Intra-regional differences carry more significance than inter-regional disparities, and fairness based on population distribution surpasses that of geographical area allocation.

This type of analysis can inform future resource allocation to redress inequities.

10.4.1 Knowledge review

Before you move on, can you define the following key concepts:

- Need-based allocation?
- Evidence-based resource allocation?

10.4.2 Question to think about

In the healthcare system where you live, do you think that the resources allocated to healthcare are distributed equitably and efficiently?

10.5 Service provision

The delivery of health services involves coordinating resources, healthcare professionals, medications, and equipment to provide necessary services that address people's health needs.

The provision of healthcare services is traditionally classified in a number of ways.

1. *Nature of health services.* The OECD classifies services under the headings of health promotion, preventive services, curative services, and rehabilitative and palliative services (OECD, 2017). Health promotion activities extend to a broader range of public health services, including disease surveillance and population-level disease control. Medicine tends to be organised around clinical specialties and they fit well within this classification but may lead to less than holistic treatment, and this is a challenge where there is an ageing population with multiple and complex health needs.
2. *Recipients of health services.* Health services may be categorised based on recipients, either directed at individuals or communities in general. Individual-based services are directly linked to a specific patient (e.g., health consultations), while population-based services aim to benefit a target community (e.g., health campaigns). Traditionally, population-based health services have been treated as public health services. In some systems, this leads to them being linked with non-health function such as housing and sanitation. This has some advantages but may limit their access to health resources, especially data and evidence.
3. *Complexity of health services.* Health activities are organised into levels indicating the complexity of services, including (1) primary care/first-level hospital care, (2) second-level hospital care, and (3) specialty/third-level hospital care. There is evidence that

the quality of outcomes of surgical procedures is linked to number of patients treated. This can lead to centralisation in specialist centres, where geographical proximity and convenience must be weighed against potential risks and outcomes.

4. *Location of provision.* Services may be located within hospitals in which case they may be differentiated by those requiring an overnight stay, or those leaving hospital the same day. Alternatively, they may be located in a clinic or doctors' offices or by a healthcare professional visiting the patient home. The growth of telemedicine has disrupted the traditional boundaries within this classification. Inpatient care is expensive and may place the patient at an increased risk of infection. The increased availability of less invasive treatments has facilitated the growth of day-case and outpatient treatments, and the reduced proportion of inpatient care.

5. *Ownership of healthcare institutions.* Healthcare institutions can be owned by governments or private entities, which may be for-profit or non-profit. Ownership of healthcare providers is independent of the source of financing. In many public systems, such as the UK NHS, private providers are used to increase capacity and eliminate bottlenecks and waiting times. There may be cost implications of this shift.

6. *Types of healthcare providers.* This encompasses the type of healthcare institutions (e.g., primary care facilities, clinics, and hospitals) and the type of healthcare workers (e.g., doctors, nurses, midwives, healthcare professionals, and non-professional volunteers). The type of institution and role of the treating professional can have significant implications for the cost and quality of healthcare services. Trends to diversify the staff and providers and use technology to treat patients remotely are driven by a desire to control costs without compromising quality and outcomes.

7. *Provider payment mechanisms.* The link between service provision and payment for healthcare institutions can be structured to enhance overall system efficiency. Depending on the complexity of health services, providers can be paid per service, a fixed rate per patient, or with a set annual budget. Different provider-payment mechanisms incentivise different behaviours. Sometimes, changing the provider-payment mechanisms can have unintended consequences, or encourage providers to game the system.

It may not be enough to simply provide one model of service delivery. Often the greatest need exists amongst populations who are difficult to reach and reluctant to engage with formal health service provision. Targeting healthcare services at vulnerable and hard-to-reach populations involves implementing strategies that address barriers to access and ensure that these populations receive the necessary care.

Establishing strong connections with local communities is essential. Engagement with community leaders, advocates, and influencers is needed to build trust and awareness. Outreach programs can bring healthcare services directly to the communities, through mobile clinics, community health fairs, and door-to-door campaigns.

Healthcare providers need to be trained to understand and respect the cultural nuances of the populations they serve. This includes language proficiency, cultural sensitivity, and awareness of cultural practices related to health. Overcoming the stigma and discrimination associated with seeking healthcare services in particular groups may require specific interventions. This is particularly important for populations facing discrimination based on their health conditions, ethnicity, or other factors.

Telehealth services and technology can reach populations in geographically remote or underserved areas. This may include virtual consultations, mobile health applications, and telemedicine initiatives or a combination of these.

Partnerships and collaboration can be invaluable. There may be opportunities to collaborate with local organisations, non-profits, and community-based groups that already have established connections with the target populations. Religious institutions, schools, and community centres may help to reach individuals who may not access traditional healthcare settings.

Flexible service delivery models such as home healthcare, school-based clinics, or workplace health programs may reach populations where they are more accessible.

Health literacy programs may empower individuals with the knowledge and skills to make informed decisions about their health. These may include educational workshops, accessible health information, and community training programs.

Finally, flexible scheduling and extended hours for healthcare services may help to address the diverse and often challenging schedules of vulnerable populations.

By combining these strategies, healthcare providers and policymakers can work towards breaking down barriers and ensuring that vulnerable and hard-to-reach populations receive the healthcare services they need. Tailoring approaches to the specific needs and circumstances of these populations is crucial for successful outreach and impact.

Access to and utilisation of youth-friendly sexual and reproductive health services in sub-Saharan Africa

Ninsiima et al. (2020) looked at providing youth-friendly sexual and reproductive health services in sub-Saharan Africa. Despite international agreements addressing adolescents' sexual and reproductive health and rights, access to and utilisation of these services among youth/adolescents in low- and middle-income countries remain inadequate, posing a significant hindrance to progress in this domain. In a comprehensive database search that identified 23,400 studies, a subsequent full-text screening revealed that 20 studies from seven countries met the inclusion criteria and were incorporated into the final review.

The review disclosed that prevalent barriers obstructing access to health services were primarily structural, encompassing negative attitudes and lack of skills among health workers. Additionally, individual barriers emerged from low levels of knowledge among youth/adolescents. Conversely, factors facilitating utilisation included sustained community involvement, outreach initiatives, school health education, recreational activities, and the provision of free or reduced-cost services for those facing financial constraints. These facilitators were identified as strategies to enhance utilisation and grant youth access to health services, promoting sustainability.

While global guidelines advocate for standardised and quality adolescent health services, the study found the current services to be highly fragmented, poorly coordinated, and inconsistent in terms of quality. Although pockets of excellent practices were identified, overall, services required significant improvement to align with existing guidelines. The review underscored the importance of educating and training youth/adolescents about the reproductive health services available at youth-friendly centres and involving them in the design and implementation of interventions tailored to their needs.

The authors concluded that stakeholder interventions should prioritise intensive training of health workers and establish standardised quality implementation guidelines in clinics to deliver services in accordance with the preferences and needs of youth.

10.5.1 *Knowledge review*

Before you move on, can you define the following key concepts:

*   Palliative health services?
*   Population-based health services?

10.5.2 *Question to think about*

In the community where you live, who are the patients with significant health needs that are difficult to reach? How might you encourage them to utilise services that are provided?

10.6 Public-private partnerships

A public–private partnership (PPP) is an agreement between one or more public and private entities, usually of a long-term nature, which reflects mutual responsibilities in the promotion of common interests.

As of 2022, there were roughly 600 major PPPs in the healthcare sector, focusing on infrastructure. These projects include those in various stages of development, construction, or already functioning, such as health centres and hospitals. Europe has the most with approximately 60% of these initiatives, followed by the United States at 15%, the Asia Pacific region at around 10%, Latin America at 5%, and the rest of the world the remaining 5% (Abuzaineh et al., 2018).

In addition to infrastructure, some major health programmes are funded as public-private partnerships including the Global Fund (to fight AIDS, tuberculosis, and malaria) and Gavi.

In its initial decade, the Global Fund distributed over $19 billion, offering grants for initiatives targeting the three diseases in 151 countries. By 2013, the organisation, in addition to allocating $10 billion for HIV/AIDS-related efforts, emerged as the world's largest supporter of harm-reduction programmes for individuals using drugs. It also became the foremost external contributor to TB programs on a global scale (Hanefeld, 2014).

According to Abuzaineh et al. (2018) common reasons for the public sector to pursue PPP are:

*   requirement for new or updated infrastructure
*   financial constraints (capital and cash flow)
*   necessity to improve health service quality and efficiency

- need for new skills or services

The same authors suggest that the private sector pursues PPPs because of the

- opportunity to access new markets at lower risk profile
- potential for revenue growth and increased market share
- contribution to the public good and associated reputational benefits
- diversification of investment and service delivery profile

There was widespread adoption of the model in the UK in the early 21st century to assist with the rebuilding of older hospitals under the Private Finance Initiative (PFI). The rationale for the use of PFI was alleviating the immediate financial burden on the UK government and taxpayers to finance major public-sector projects, allowing much more rapid infrastructure renewal. PFIs were also intended to transfer some of the risks associated with a project from the public sector to the private sector.

However, in the UK, there has been major criticism of the extent to which these benefits have been realised and how much risk was retained by the public sector.

A new hospital for Liverpool, England – a cautionary tale from the UK

Liverpool University Hospitals NHS Foundation Trust needed to build a complete new hospital for the city. Work began in February 2014 when the private developer Carillion initiated the construction of the Royal Liverpool with a planned completion date of March 2017. However, Carillion faced a number of problems, leading to over a year's delay. The Royal Liverpool project encountered numerous challenges, starting with the discovery of asbestos in the ground in May 2014, just three months after Carillion began work. This led to a series of claims for delays and additional costs. The situation worsened in December 2016 when a construction worker found cracks in the concrete beams, prompting investigations and further setbacks. Carillion's subsequently declared bankruptcy in January 2018. Following 10 months of attempting to salvage the PFI project, it was eventually abandoned in October 2018. Another eight months passed before remedial work commenced in June 2019, with Laing O'Rourke replacing Carillion as the main contractor. The completion required three years of remedial efforts, including cladding replacement, significantly surpassing the initially projected three-year construction period.

The estimated construction cost of the Royal Liverpool escalated from £350 million to £724 million as of January 2020, according to the government agency responsible for ensuring value for money in public projects. Their report highlighted various issues faced during the construction period, including structural concerns, safety issues, and non-compliance with fire regulations.

The new Liverpool University Hospitals NHS Foundation Trust finally opened at the end of September 2022.

10.6.1 Knowledge review

Before you move on, can you define the following key concepts:

- Public–private partnership?
- Private finance Initiative?

10.6.2 *Question to think about*

Are you aware of any public–private partnerships operating in your country? How successful have they been?

References

Abuzaineh, N., Brashers, E., Foong, S., Feachem, R., & Da Rita, P. (2018). *PPPs in healthcare: Models, lessons and trends for the future*. PWC.

Ahangar, A., Ahmadi, A. M., Mozayani, A. H. M., & Dizaji, S. F. (2018). Why are risk-pooling and risk-sharing arrangements necessary for financing healthcare and improving health outcomes in low and lower-middle-income countries? *Health*, 10(1), 122–131.

Akitoby, B. (2018, March). Raising revenue. *Finance and Development, International Monetary Fund*, 55(1), 18–21.

Ao, Y., Feng, Q., Zhou, Z., Chen, Y., & Wang, T. (2022). Resource allocation equity in the china's rural three-tier healthcare system. *International Journal of Environmental Research and Public Health*, 19, 6589.

Canadian Institute for Health Information. (2019). *National health expenditure trends, 1975 to 2019*. CIHI.

Cooray, U., Aida, J., Watt, R. G., Tsakos, G., Heilmann, A., Kato, H., Kiuchi, S., Kondo, K., & Osaka, K. (2020). Effect of co-payment on dental visits: A regression discontinuity analysis. *Journal of Dental Research*, 99(12), 1356–1362.

Evans, D. B., Kurowski, C., & Tediosi, F. (2023). Health system financing. In Raviglione, M. C. B., Tediosi, F., Villa, S., Casamitjana, N., and Plasència, A. (eds.). *Global health essentials* (pp. 291–295). Springer International Publishing.

Eze, P., Lawani, L. O., Agu, U. J., Amara, L. U., Okorie, C. A., & Acharya, Y. (2022). Factors associated with catastrophic health expenditure in sub-Saharan Africa: A systematic review. *PLos One*, 17(10), e0276266.

Gabani, J., Mazumdar, S., & Suhrcke, M. (2023). The effect of health financing systems on health system outcomes: A cross-country panel analysis. *Health Economics*, 32(3), 574–619.

Government of Canada. (1985). *Canada healthact* (R.S.C., 1985, c. C-6). https://laws-lois.justice .gc.ca/PDF/C-6.pdf

Hanefeld, J. (2014). The global fundto fight AIDS, tuberculosis and Malaria: 10 years on. *Clinical Medicine* (London, England), 14(1), 54–57.

Ifeagwu, S. C., Yang, J. C., Parkes-Ratanshi, R., & Brayne, C. (2021). Health financing for universal health coverage in Sub-Saharan Africa: A systematic review. *Global Health Research and Policy*, 6, 1–9.

Jowett, M., Kutzin, J., & World Health Organisation. (2015). *Raising revenues for health in support of UHC: Strategic issues for policy makers* (No. WHO/HIS/HGF/PolicyBrief/15.1). World Health Organisation.

Kazungu, J. S., Barasa, E. W., Obadha, M., & Chuma, J. (2018). What characteristics of provider payment mechanisms influence healthcare providers' behaviour? A literature review. *The International Journal of Health Planning and Management*, 33(4), e892–e905.

Mathauer, I., Vinyals Torres, L., Kutzin, J., Jakab, M., & Hanson, K. (2020). Pooling financial resources for universal health coverage: options for reform. *Bulletin of the World Health Organisation*, 98(2), 132–139.

Ninsiima, A. B., Michielsen, K., Kemigisha, E., Nyakato, V. N., Leye, E., & Coene, G. (2020). Poverty, gender and reproductive justice. A qualitative study among adolescent girls in Western Uganda. *Culture, Health & Sexuality*, 22(sup1), 65-79.

OECD. (2017). Classification of healthcare functions (ICHA-HC). In *OECD/Eurostat/WHO, A system of health accounts 2011: Revised edition* (pp. 71–120). OECD. 70985-7-en.pdf?expires =1676164467&id=id&accname=guest&checksum=74132FA46A419EFCE561A59EE44C0F8F

Saugat Pratap, K. C., Sharma, S., Pandey, A. R., & Baral, S. C. (2023). Nepal health financing in light of federalism and pandemic. *Perspectives in Public Health*, 143(5), 249–251.

Syafinaz, I., Haslinda, N., Juni, M. H., & Aljaberi, M. (2018). Health care provision and equity. *International Journal of Public Health and Clinical Sciences*, 3(4), 1–14.

Tang, L., Shen, Q., & Cheng, E. W. (2010). A review of studies on public–private partnership projects in the construction industry. *International Journal of Project Management*, 28(7), 683–694.

United Nations. (2015). *Transforming our world: The 2030 agenda for sustainable development*. United Nations.

WHO. (2010). *The world health report: Health systems financing: The path to universal coverage: Executive summary* (No. WHO/IER/WHR/10.1). World Health Organisation.

WHO. (2023). *Leveraging public financial management for universal health coverage in the WHO South-East Asia region: A regional synthesis report*. World Health Organisation. ISBN: 978-92-9021-086-3

11 Revenue collection

11.1 Taxes

Taxes are collected by governments through various means. They provide the resources that constitute the government budget. In countries where the government provides the majority of the health services, these are often funded by taxes from the general population. Revenue from taxation used for healthcare links the amounts paid to ability to pay rather than clinical need and avoids the risk of catastrophic health expenditure.

Taxes are predictable sources of health revenue, as these are enforced by law and regularly collected within the government's financing cycles. As long as the economic performance of the country is moving as expected, the proportion of the budget intended for health is typically stable and may grow according to the government's priorities. Health services are often funded largely through general tax in high-income countries.

Taxes may be collected directly or indirectly.

11.1.1 Direct taxation

Direct taxes are taxes that are imposed directly on individuals or entities and cannot be transferred to another party. These taxes are typically levied on income, wealth, or profits. The burden of direct taxes falls directly on the person or entity that is subject to taxation. Here are what direct taxes include:

- *Income tax* is the first recorded levying of tax linked to income was in the UK in 1798 to help pay for the Napoleonic wars. Although billed as a temporary measure, it has become one of the most common forms of direct taxation. Individuals are required to pay a percentage of their income to the government.
- *Corporate (or corporation) tax* is a tax imposed on the profits of businesses. It is levied on the income earned by companies and is usually calculated as a percentage of their net profits.
- *Wealth tax* is a tax on the net wealth of individuals or businesses. This may include assets such as real estate, investments, and other valuable possessions.
- *Property tax* is levied on the value of real estate properties owned by individuals or businesses. It is usually imposed by local governments.
- *Capital gains tax* is applied to the profits earned from the sale of assets such as stocks, real estate, or other investments.

DOI: 10.4324/9781003478874-14

Direct taxes can be gathered based on income generated either within the formal business sector or the informal business sector. The formal sector comprises registered businesses and their workforce, offering a more anticipated and dependable source of taxation. Businesses are required to submit accounts and then pay taxes based upon the income they have generated. Formally employed individuals also contribute mandatory taxes, automatically deducted from their wages by their employers.

Conversely, the informal sector encompasses those engaged in contractual services, seasonal work, or less regulated industries like independently operated farms, fisheries, online ventures, and various personal services. The collection of taxes from the informal sector poses greater challenges for governments necessitating additional administrative measures to enhance compliance. As a result, in countries characterised by a substantial informal sector, often the case for low-income nations, raising government revenues becomes more complex. Such countries exhibit a lower percentage of government revenues relative to the gross domestic product (GDP).

11.1.2 Indirect taxes

Indirect taxation is paid by consumers through the prices of goods and services. Unlike direct taxes, which are levied on income, profits, or wealth, indirect taxes are applied to the production or sale of goods and services.

There are a number of types of indirect taxes. Sales tax is imposed on the sale of goods and services. The rate may vary depending on the jurisdiction. Similarly, Goods and Services Tax (GST) is a consumption tax applied to the supply of goods and services, and it is paid by the final consumer. Value Added Tax (VAT) is calculated slightly differently because it is based upon the value added at each stage of the production and distribution chain. The end consumer ultimately bears the tax, but those earlier in the supply chain only pay tax on the value that they add to the product or service, hence the name.

Other specific indirect taxes include excise duties that are imposed on specific goods, often those considered harmful or non-essential, such as tobacco, alcohol, or gasoline. The taxes are included in the price of these goods and are often justified in terms of paying for the additional burden that their consumption imposes on the healthcare system. There are also customs duties levied on goods imported or exported between countries and usually collected at the border.

Sin taxes on sugary drinks – after Popkin and Ng, S. W. (2021)

Duties imposed on harmful goods are sometimes known as sin taxes. In recent years, some countries have imposed taxes on sugary drinks.

Excess sugar consumption is a major cause of obesity and the increasing risk of type 2 diabetes, hypertension, liver and kidney damage, heart disease, and some cancers. Additionally, high-caloric beverages offer little caloric compensation, so reducing their consumption lowers obesity risk. The goal of these specific taxation measures is primarily to reduce consumption and change the behaviours of both consumers and manufacturers rather than to provide a large income stream.

In the United Kingdom, the Sugar Drinks Industry Levy, which operates on multiple tiers depending on sugar content, has led to significant changes in formulations and consumer choices, resulting in the emergence of new low-calorie beverage options. In Portugal, previous studies indicate a decrease in sugar content in beverages and a decline in sales.

There may be other consequences. There is evidence that sugar reduction policies will and have resulted in the introduction of beverages with both sugar and non-nutritive sweeteners (NNSs) (Bandy et al., 2020).

The consumption of NNS is increasing in high-income nations, but the future trend in low- and middle-income countries, where diet beverage consumption is currently minimal, remains uncertain. For example, a study in Mexico (Colchero et al., 2016) showed a shift towards water consumption In low-income countries; limited studies suggest only a slight increase in the consumption of NNS-sweetened beverages, but this may change with the implementation of high tax rates on sugar-sweetened beverages (SSBs) or ultra-processed foods.

Currently, there is no global consensus on the long-term health implications of extended and/or higher doses of NNS intake. The scarcity of information regarding the types and amounts of NNS used in our food supply makes it difficult to study these questions, but it may be prudent to proceed with caution to avoid replacing the harm caused by excess sugar with other as yet unknown harms from NNSs.

11.1.3 Progressive vs regressive taxation

One of the most important characteristics of a taxation system is whether it is progressive, proportional, or regressive. This determines its equity and fairness, although different people may have different views of the most equitable solution:

- *Progressive tax* is a taxation system where higher-income groups contribute a greater percentage of their income, in contrast to low-income groups.
- *Proportional tax,* on the other hand, applies a uniform percentage across all income brackets.
- In a *regressive tax* system, the burden is higher for low-income individuals, as it takes a larger percentage of their income compared to high-income individuals.

Figure 11.1 provides a schematic representation of the different types of taxation.

Direct taxes can be designed to be progressive, proportional, or regressive, depending on how they are structured. In many countries, income taxes are often designed to be progressive, with higher-income individuals paying a higher percentage of their income in taxes. However, the specific structure of direct taxes can vary widely between different jurisdictions.

As of 2023, Countries such as Mongolia and Kazakhstan impose flat taxes of 10%, and Bolivia and Russia have a 13% flat tax rate. In the United States, at the Federal level, there is progressive income tax system. Income is taxed on a graduated scale at rates that range from 10% to 37%. However, 11 states (Colorado, Illinois, Indiana, Kentucky, Massachusetts, Michigan, North Carolina, New Hampshire, Pennsylvania, Tennessee, and Utah) have a flat rate of income tax.

Rostampour and Nosratnejad (2020) measured the progressivity of the taxation regimes of a number of countries using the Kakwani index (KI) that was originally

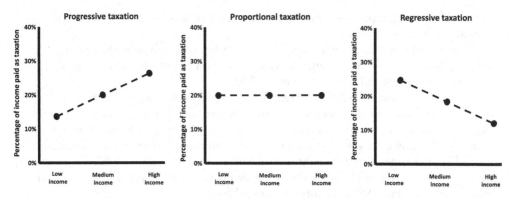

Figure 11.1 A schematic representation of the different types of taxation; in practice, the trends are unlikely to be linear.

devised to measure the progressivity of tax systems, but is increasingly used to measure the examine the equity of government healthcare provision. This was a literature review, so the data were historical and should be treated with some caution. The direct and indirect tax system was studied in Uganda, Malaysia, Ghana, China (Gansu), and China (Heilongjiang). The value of the KI for direct tax was positive in three countries: Uganda, Malaysia, and Ghana. The direct tax system was thus found to be progressive there. Nevertheless, the value of KI was negative in China (Gansu) and China (Heilongjiang), and the direct tax system was regressive in these two regions.

Indirect taxes are generally regressive, because they take a proportionally larger share of income from lower-income individuals compared to higher-income individuals. This is because everyone, regardless of income level, pays the same tax rate on the purchased goods or services. Indirect taxes are a significant source of revenue for many governments and play a crucial role in funding public services and infrastructure.

Indirect taxes are popular with government because they are easy to collect. Although they are regressive, it may be argued that people have an option to buy the goods and services and therefore there is an option to pay. This is especially true in countries where basics such as food are exempt from such taxes. Where they are applied as excise duties to goods that harm health notably alcohol and tobacco, they may be justified as being needed to offset the cost of the associated harm and incentivising a healthier lifestyle. In most European countries where VAT is levied, the tax is included in the price, making the tax largely invisible.

Case study: Italy (after OECD & European Observatory on Health System and Policies, 2021)

Italy's healthcare system is primarily funded through general government taxation, with each region being responsible for organising and delivering healthcare services through both public and private providers. The central government allocates tax revenues for healthcare, establishes the benefits package, and oversees the system's operation. Regions manage healthcare delivery through local health units and public as well as accredited private hospitals. This structure remained intact during the COVID-19 pandemic, although there was some centralisation of leadership and administrative authority for the national pandemic response.

With a population of 59.1 million, Italy boasts the highest life expectancy in the European Union (EU) after Switzerland, reaching 84.0 years in 2023. Overall, Italy offers good access to high-quality healthcare, but weaknesses in the system were exposed during the COVID-19 crisis, such as underinvestment in the healthcare workforce and infrastructure.

Italy has relatively few hospital beds but a longer average length of stay compared to other EU countries. The number of hospital beds per 1,000 population remained stable at 3.2 between 2014 and 2019, well below the EU average of 5.3. There are significant regional disparities, with southern regions having lower capacity than northern regions. Despite stable bed numbers, there has been a notable decrease in hospital discharges, with Italy ranking third lowest in the EU in 2019. Health spending per capita in Italy was 8.7% of GDP in 2019, lower than the EU average of 9.9%, although public spending increased sharply in 2020 due to the pandemic.

The healthcare financing system in Italy has some regressive aspects, meaning it can be inequitable, especially when health costs are uniform regardless of household income. In 2019, public spending accounted for 74% of total health expenditure, lower than the EU average of 80%. Out-of-pocket payments by households constituted 23% of expenses, while voluntary health insurance (VHI) played a minor role, covering only 3% of the total (de Belvis et al, 2022).

Outpatient care represented the largest category of health spending in 2019, followed closely by inpatient services. Italy spent less per capita on both outpatient and inpatient care compared to the EU average. Pharmaceuticals and medical devices accounted for a significant portion of health expenditure. Long-term care, although increasingly important due to Italy's ageing population, received less funding per capita compared to the EU average. However, spending on prevention in Italy surpassed the EU average both in percentage terms and per capita.

11.1.4 Knowledge review

Before you move on, can you define the following key concepts:

* Progressive taxation?
* Regressive taxation?
* Indirect taxation?

11.1.5 Question to think about

Do you think that progressive taxation is a fairer means of taxation than proportional taxation? Why?

11.2 Social insurance contributions

Social health insurance funds operate differently in different nations, but the different systems share common characteristics. They are common in Europe in countries such as Germany, France, and the Netherlands. There are also models in other countries such as the Vajpayee Arogyashree scheme, a social health insurance scheme implemented in 2010, in Karnataka, a state in India, focused on increasing access to tertiary care for households below the poverty line (Sood & Wagner, 2018). At the start of 2014, the Indonesian Government launched its National Social Health Insurance Scheme, which aimed to provide health coverage for all Indonesians, with the government paying the modest premiums for lower-income citizens. Significant progress was made in the early years, but WHO (2023) reports that progress has stalled. Indonesia reduced the number of citizens facing catastrophic out-of-pocket health spending of at least 25% of household consumption from 0.9% in 2017 to 0.4% in 2018. Indonesia's UHC service coverage index (SCI),[1] which had increased slowly from 42 in 2010 to 56 in 2019, decreased again to 55 in 2021.

Within a social health insurance model, people pay contributions to non-governmental bodies, separate from the tax system, with a significant proportion of social health insurance revenue coming from employers and employees. However, the governance of SHI may be retained within the Ministry of Health or as a component of a wider social protection funding mechanism. The effectiveness of Social Health Insurance (SHI) as a funding source depends upon the government's ability to manage costs. This hinges on the contractual agreements established with healthcare providers and the government's influence on ensuring appropriate utilisation by its members.

Contributions are compulsory, and everyone is entitled to the same set of services and treatments. Social insurance funds differ from private insurance schemes because they accept everyone, regardless of age or health status. To enable this, contributions are pooled and adjusted so that insurers can cover the health needs of their enrolled population (Thorlby, 2023). As a funding source, SHI is expected to provide all of the benefit entitlements of its covered members within the parameters of benefit utilisation. Each SHI system specifies the type of population that can be covered, including how dependents will be considered.

One of the most attractive features of SHI as a method of financing healthcare is its message of fairness and social solidarity as a means to improve equity in health financing, link to its extensive risk pooling. In addition to financial pooling risks, there is also pooling across income groups where higher income households support lower income households. Typically, the premium payment structure is progressive along salary bands. SHI aims to cover lower income households that may not always have good access to health services.

Historically, systems based on social insurance collected funds from employed people and their employers to offer coverage primarily to the working population. Over time, the scope of coverage has expanded to encompass individuals of all ages, irrespective of their employment status. In most countries with social health insurance, the financing of healthcare has evolved to include both taxes and contributions. This has been due to extending coverage beyond those employed and an attempt to prevent an adverse financial burden on businesses and working-age individuals, particularly in light of an ageing population.

For example, in France, contributions from employment-based social health insurance constituted 33% of insurance revenues in 2021. The remaining funds were sourced from designated income taxes and levies on alcohol, tobacco, pharmaceuticals, and private insurance companies. In the Netherlands, individuals aged 18 and older are mandated to pay a premium directly to an insurer. Additionally, those of working age make employment-based contributions through the tax office. An additional 13% of the overall healthcare expenditure is funded through general taxation in the Netherlands. This allocation provides subsidies for individuals with low incomes who may struggle to afford insurance premiums and supports preventive services such as screenings and vaccinations. In Germany, approximately 10% of the total health expenditure is covered by general taxation.

Social health insurance funds provide a prescribed range of services and may require co-payments for some services, not deemed to be essential. In France, more than 95% of the population opts for complementary private insurance, selecting from a pool of 439 providers as of 2019. This insurance primarily covers user charges associated with a wide array of health services within the public system. Since 2000, the government has implemented a series of reforms to make private insurance more accessible, particularly for those with lower incomes. Up until 2019, individuals with low incomes and those slightly above the poverty line were shielded from charges through two schemes funded by a tax on insurance companies. One of these schemes, a voucher programme, had only been utilised by a quarter of eligible individuals by 2015, with research indicating that the administrative complexities of the application process posed a significant barrier. Although the schemes have since been merged, 5% of the French population did not have private insurance in 2019. A survey conducted in the same year, encompassing over 150,000 respondents, revealed that a quarter of participants had refrained from seeking healthcare in the previous 12 months, with financial barriers being the most commonly cited reason (Thorlby, 2023).

As well as complementary private insurance to cover contributions, citizens may opt for supplementary insurance to provide additional services beyond the scope of their social insurance package. The addition of supplementary insurance can lead to a complex array of choices. In 2015, the Dutch healthcare regulator estimated approximately 6,000 different combinations of options available in both the primary and supplementary insurance markets. Between 6% and 7% of individuals switch social insurance plans annually. As of 2019, half of the population had never changed their insurance plans since the introduction of insurance market reforms in 2006.

On the plus side, SHI is generally regarded as a predictable, stable, and easy source of health revenue; the collection of SHI from citizens is generally straightforward, as they can see the health benefits they can see the services they receive for their premiums. There is a more direct link between their contributions and these services than in a general taxation system where contributions go into a larger pot from which healthcare must compete with other funding demands. The flow of funds from the insurance agency to the service delivery point can either be made directly or through a third-party provider. Also, insurance agencies can decide to have their own health facilities, which can also facilitate a predictable funding flow.

However, a social insurance system may be more expensive to run than a system funded from taxation. The OECD (Mueller et al., 2017) identified that social insurance systems, particularly those where insurers compete, tend to have higher administrative costs than systems managed by central governments. In 2021, 1% of the UK's Government-funded spending on the public healthcare system was on governance and administration, compared with 3.6% in France, 3.9% in Germany and 3.2% in the Netherlands.

SHI is not an efficient way to cover preventive and chronic care, which is a much-needed service among people with a lower income. It is also a weak mechanism to fund services that require multidisciplinary coordination, as well as those closely intertwined with public health services.

Case study: Germany

In Western European countries, including France and Germany, SHI schemes are common. For example, Germany's health system has been based on a SHI system longer than any other country (OECD & European Observatory on Health Systems and Policies, 2021). In Germany, health insurance is compulsory. For most employed people, this takes the form of SHI; for those with an income above a fixed threshold or self-employed people, they can opt out of SHI coverage and enrol in PHI as an alternative. In practice, almost 90% of people are covered by SHI, and the rest – except for the 0.1% of the population who have no health insurance – are covered by PHI.

Germany is a federal state, and responsibility for healthcare is shared between federal and state bodies. The federal government defines only the legal framework. There is the Federal Joint Committee, consisting of representatives from associations of sickness funds, physicians, dentists, and hospitals, as well as independent members, that makes decisions on SHI benefits, reimbursement systems, and quality assurance.

The states (Bundesländer) are responsible for decisions about hospital planning and investments in public health and medical education. In 2019, Germany spent 11.1% of its GDP on health, which was the highest share in the EU along with France. More of this comes from public finances than in other EU countries, and one reason for this is the coverage of dental care for adults.

In return for this high level of funding, Germany has the highest number of hospital beds per population in the EU and a higher-than-average number of physicians and nurses per population. The proportion of financing from OOP payments in 2019 was 3% below the EU average at 12.7%. About one-third of this is used for long-term care, because SHI usually covers only around 50% of total costs for long-term care delivered in institutions.

Although life expectancy at birth in Germany (81.1 years in 2020) has increased by almost three years since 2000, most of this gain occurred between 2000 and 2010. There is still a substantial gender gap in life expectancy in Germany. At birth, women can expect to live 4.7 years longer than men. The preventable mortality rate has remained fairly stable since 2011, in contrast to many other EU countries where it has fallen. The leading causes of preventable mortality in Germany are lung cancer, alcohol-related diseases, ischemic heart disease, and chronic lower respiratory diseases, which contribute to 57% of preventable deaths in total.

The mortality rate from treatable causes (i.e., deaths that could be avoided through timely and effective healthcare) is 85 deaths per 100,000 of the population. This is below the EU average but worse than other comparable Western European countries, such as France, the Netherlands, Spain, and Italy, which suggests that healthcare expenditure may not be deployed optimally (OECD & European Observatory on Health Systems and Policies, 2021).

11.2.1 *Knowledge review*

Before you move on, can you define the following key concepts:

* Social health insurance?
* Complementary health insurance?

11.2.2 *Question to think about*

What do you think are the advantages and disadvantages of a social health insurance financing model over a system funded from general taxation?

11.3 Private insurance contributions

Almost all national healthcare systems draw on private contributions towards the cost of healthcare, and much of this funding is derived from private healthcare insurance funds (Figure 11.2).

The public-sector share of total health spending is deemed to be the total of expenditures for government schemes and compulsory health insurance.

This includes employer and employee social health insurance contributions in the European countries where these are compulsory and make up the majority of healthcare funding. Private insurance expenditures are not included, even when they are compulsory and this explains the ranking of the US.

Private contributions come through both individual payments at the point of delivery care or through private insurance schemes. Where the care is covered by insurance, it may be paid directly by the insurer or paid by the recipient who is then reimbursed by the insurer. This reimbursement may be for the whole cost or partial. Where reimbursement is partial, this may be because the insurer requires an excess to be paid by the insured in the event of a claim or because the insurer may cap their contribution, and the insured may select a more expensive provider.

As shown, the US has the highest overall health costs measured in both dollar terms and as a share of GDP, as well as one of the highest shares of healthcare costs funded by private contributions. In practice, public spending in the US on healthcare is similar to other countries, but out-of-pocket and private spending are higher than most.

In spite of this, the US has the lowest life expectancy and highest suicide rates among the 11 OECD nations. It has the highest rates of chronic disease and obesity, the highest rate of avoidable deaths and amongst the highest number of hospitalisations from preventable causes. There are less physicians per head of population and they make fewer visits per patient than in most OECD countries (Tikkanen et al., 2020).

On the positive side, the US is strong in preventative medicine and in its use of technology such as MRI. It has the one of the highest rates of breast cancer screening among women aged 50 to 69 and is second only to the UK amongst OECD countries in vaccinating the over-65s against influenza (Tikkanen et al., 2020).

Because of the high cost of healthcare in the US and the overall level of performance, writers in other countries (and some in the US) feel that private health insurance is an inefficient way to fund healthcare.

The Kings Fund (2017) has identified five different ways in which private health insurance is used to fund healthcare, which are summarised in Table 11.1.

Public and private revenues of healthcare financing schemes for OECD countries with comparable data, 2017

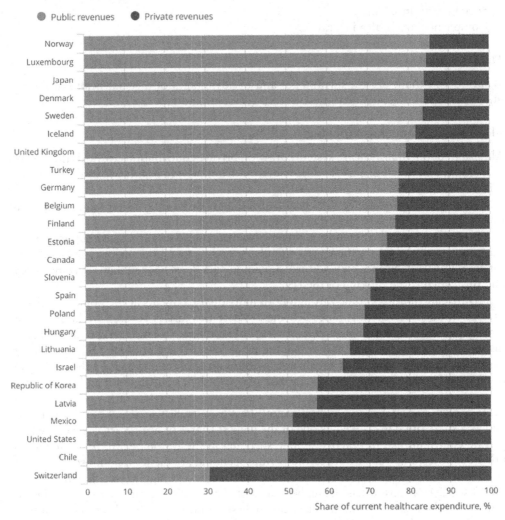

Figure 11.2 Proportion of healthcare expenditure from public sources (Office for National Statistics, 2019), Open Government Licence.

In lower income countries without universal government health coverage or social health insurances schemes, private health insurance offers one way of reducing the risk of catastrophic health expenditure. However, the lower level of risk pooling that is associated with schemes based on universal coverage means that, for many citizens, premiums are too high to be affordable.

According to Mhazo et al. (2023), Zimbabwe has one of the highest rates of private health insurance (PHI) expenditures as a share of total health expenditures in the world but this is primarily a function of history and politics. Population coverage remains

Table 11.1 Five different ways in which private health insurance is used to fund healthcare. Source: The Kings Fund (2017).

Cover type	Description	Practical examples
Dominant or primary cover	Private insurance is the dominant means of funding healthcare.	Private health insurance dominates the US healthcare system although in practice, public funds still provide half of the healthcare financing in that country. In Switzerland, private health insurance is compulsory, although many insurers are not-for-profit businesses.
Duplicate cover	Duplicate cover occurs when private health insurance provides access to services, which are also available in the publicly funded system. This may offer faster access to services and greater choice to those who can pay.	This is used in countries such as the UK and Australia. The premiums may be subsidised by governments in the belief that they reduce pressure on the public system, but the UK abolished such tax reliefs in 1997, and more recently, they have been scaled back in Australia. Canada does not permit the provision of duplicate services within the country, although citizens may access them in the US.
Complementary – or "additional" cover	In countries where government or social insurance schemes provide the majority of healthcare funding but citizens are expected to make a contribution, private health insurance may be used to complement the main scheme by covering the costs of co-payment.	In France. for example, this type of insurance is held by approximately 85% of the population to cover the cost of statutory co-payment charges.
Supplementary cover	Under supplementary cover, private insurance is used to cover the cost of those items not covered by the publicly funded care or social insurance funds.	In Canada, private insurance is used to cover the cost of those items not covered by the Canada Health Act (1985), principally prescription drugs because only medications administered in hospital are covered by public funding but dental and optical care are also beyond the scope of the Act.
Substitutive cover	Where substitutive cover is available, citizens have the right to opt out of public schemes and cover the cost of their care through a private insurance scheme. It is normally highly regulated to prevent it from destabilising the public system.	In Germany, citizens have the right to opt out of public schemes and cover the cost of their care through a private insurance scheme.

dismally low because PHI enrolment is generally limited to a small number of privileged individuals. Wealth and employment status has replaced institutionalised racism as the basis for access to enrolment. For the remainder of the population, OOP expenditure remains the primary mechanism for financing healthcare with catastrophic consequences especially amongst poorer citizens.

In a middle-income country like India, Purohit (2023) reports that 47% of citizens rely on private healthcare providers but only 17% have private health insurance leaving almost a third of the poorest citizens reliant on out-of-pocket expenditure with its associated risks and challenges.

Members of private health insurance (PHI) mutually share health risks across the policyholders. Risks may arise from factors like baseline health status, age, or occupational exposure. Essentially, individuals in better health within the insurance scheme bear the financial burden of health services used by those who require more coverage under the insurance. However, unlike social health insurance schemes, private insurance companies will calculate individual premiums based upon calculations of an individual risk profile. This may be bespoke to individuals or calculated by adding supplementary premiums for pre-existing conditions or to take account of unhealthy lifestyles or behaviours, such as smoking, that increase the likelihood of illness. If the risk is deemed too high, the insurer may refuse to insure an applicant, an option not open to universal public coverage schemes or social health insurers.

Due to the typically high premium costs, PHI companies target individuals with higher incomes, resulting in a smaller segment of the population being covered. In countries with social health insurance (SHI) systems, particularly in high-income countries, PHI may be utilised as a supplementary benefit once SHI has been fully utilised subject to regulatory restrictions.

Like social insurance, private insurance faces challenges that can impact the adequacy of its funding from its premiums. They may offer incentives and discounts to encourage policy holders to adopt healthy lifestyles and avoid risky behaviours. They may also engage in "cream skimming," biasing enrolment toward individuals with lower health risks.

Similar to social insurance schemes, private insurance contributes a stable and predictable income flow to the health system, enabling the pooling of out-of-pocket spending as a prepaid expense. However, since private insurance targets a specific population, its funds are not as extensive as those generated by government facilities. The income-related targeting of PHI may lead to further fragmentation of risk pools as insurers compete to attract healthier members, potentially excluding those who need insurance the most.

Private insurers must choose between being more selective about whom they insure to reduce their outgoings and increasing their pool of policyholders to increase income and spread the risk.

The role of Private Health Insurance (PHI) in the US

Healthcare in the United States is provided by publicly- and privately-owned facilities. The providers are funded by for-profit and not-for-profit insurers. The federal government supplies funds through a diverse range of programmes.

Medicare covers individuals aged 65 and above and certain individuals with disabilities. Veterans and those with low incomes are covered by Medicaid and the Children's Health Insurance Program. At the state level, oversight and funding are provided for local coverage and safety net programmes. The primary means of coverage is private insurance, the burden of which falls mostly on employers. The proportion of individuals lacking insurance has dropped to approximately 10% of the population from 16% in 2010, following the enactment of the significant Affordable Care Act. Both public and private insurers formulate their own coverage plans and cost-sharing structures, operating within the framework of federal and state regulations (Tikkanen et al., 2020).

The United States does not have universal health insurance coverage, with just over 10% of citizens not having coverage in 2021, down from just under 10% in 2019 (OECD, 2021).

The Affordable Care Act, also known as ACA, was enacted in 2010 and marked a significant expansion of the government's involvement in healthcare financing and regulation. The major components of the law's coverage expansions, which took effect in 2014, were as follows:

- Mandating most Americans to have health insurance or face a penalty (the penalty was later removed).
- Allowing young people to stay on their parents' private health plans until they reach the age of 26.
- Establishing health insurance marketplaces, or exchanges, that offer premium subsidies to individuals with lower and middle incomes.
- Expanding Medicaid eligibility in certain states with the assistance of federal subsidies.

As a result of the ACA, approximately 20 million people gained health coverage, leading to a decline in the percentage of uninsured adults aged 19 to 64 from 20% in 2010 to 12% in 2018 (Collins et al., 2019).

In 2018, private health insurance spending comprised 34% of the total health expenditures. For 67% of Americans, private insurance serves as their primary health coverage. Among private insurance plans, 55% are employer-sponsored, while 11% are individually purchased from for-profit and not-for-profit carriers (Tikkanen et al., 2020).

Employers commonly collaborate with private health plans to administer benefits, offering coverage to both employees and their dependents, often providing a selection of different plans to choose from. Premiums are typically shared between employers and employees, though in some cases, employers cover the full premium amount.

With the implementation of the Affordable Care Act (ACA), a federal marketplace called HealthCare.gov was established, enabling individuals to purchase primary health insurance or dental coverage from private plans. States also have the option to set up their own marketplaces.

In 2019, more than one in three Medicare beneficiaries opted for coverage through a private Medicare Advantage health plan. Medicaid beneficiaries may receive their benefits through private managed care organisations, which receive capitated payments, usually adjusted for risk, from state Medicaid departments.

Managed care enrolment is common, with more than two-thirds of Medicaid beneficiaries being enrolled in such programmes (Jacobson & Parmet, 2018).

The ACA requires plans for individuals and firms (with 50 or fewer employees) to cover 10 "essential health benefits": "visits to the doctor, emergency services, hospitalisation, maternity and new-born care, mental health services and substance use disorder treatment, prescription drugs, rehabilitative services and devices, laboratory services, preventive and wellness services and chronic disease management paediatric services, including dental and vision care" (Healthcare.gov, 2023).

11.3.1 *Knowledge review*

Before you move on, can you define the following key concepts:

• Duplicate cover?
• Supplementary health insurance?

11.3.2 *Question to think about*

What do you think are the advantages and disadvantages of a private health insurance financing model over a social health insurance financing model?

11.4 Out-of-pocket payments

Payments made by individuals when they avail themselves of healthcare services across various care levels and from diverse healthcare providers are referred to as out-of-pocket (OOP) payments (WHO, 2023). These payments may take the form of cost-sharing or informal payments, provided they are not reimbursed by the health system to the recipient. Such payments can originate from the household level, encompassing income, savings, or loans. Catastrophic OOP health spending reduces households' ability to purchase other necessities such as food, shelter, clothing, or education, and in turn has the potential to cause further health problems such as malnutrition.

In countries with limited capacity to generate public funding for healthcare, OOP spending plays a crucial role as a funding source for healthcare activities. However, as these funds flow directly from individuals to providers, they lack the ability to influence service prices. This situation creates little motivation for healthcare providers to curb unnecessary demands for health services. In environments where price regulation is deficient and individual health needs continue to rise, healthcare costs tend to escalate, leading to inefficiencies in service delivery.

OOP payments are often regressive because charges at the point of care are typically fixed and seldom vary based on household income. Consequently, the move towards fair and equitable health financing involves reducing the reliance on OOP spending. Additionally, out-of-pocket spending is associated with catastrophic health spending, defined as individuals paying more than 40% of their household disposable income for health services (OECD, 2009). Fear of catastrophic health spending act as a barrier to citizens accessing healthcare (Nakovics et al. 2020). Due to its characteristics, OOP expenditure emerges as the least predictable funding source for health service.

WHO argues that deriving a high proportion of healthcare from OOP expenditure is the most significant barrier to achieving UHC by 2030, UN SDC Target 3.8. WHO (2023) states that "improvements to health services coverage have stagnated since 2015, and the proportion of the population that faced catastrophic levels of out-of-pocket (OOP) health spending has increased."

The global proportion of individuals residing in households allocating over 10% of their household budget to out-of-pocket (OOP) health expenses has consistently risen since the turn of the century reaching 12.6% in 2015 and 13.5% by 2019, from a baseline of 9.6% in 2000 and over the same period, the estimated number of people facing such substantial OOP health spending increased by 76%, from 588 million in 2000 to 1.04 billion in 2019 (WHO, 2023).

The percentage of the global population experiencing impoverishing OOP health spending at the extreme poverty line actually reduced by 80% between 2000 and 2019, declining from 22.2% to 4.4%. However, during the same period, the rate of impoverishing OOP health spending at the relative poverty line increased by 42%. For those living in poverty or near poverty, any level of OOP health spending can lead to financial hardship, even if it accounts for less than 10% of their household budget, given their lower financial capacity.

Impoverishing OOP health spending at the extreme poverty line is concentrated in Low-Income Countries (LICs) and Lower-Middle-Income Countries (LMICs) with higher poverty rates. Conversely, there is no strong correlation between impoverishing OOP health spending at the relative poverty line and a country's income level. LMICs witnessed the most significant increases in the proportion of the population facing impoverishing OOP health spending at the relative poverty line. Within countries, financial hardship is more prevalent among those living in rural areas, multi-generational households, male-headed households, or households headed by individuals under 60 years old.

In 2019, the total global population experiencing catastrophic spending, impoverishing health spending at the relative poverty line, or both (i.e., any form of financial hardship) was estimated at two billion people (WHO, 2023).

Case study: Nigeria

Nigeria has a high burden of OOP healthcare expenditure. With a population of over 215 million people, Nigeria has the highest population of all countries in Africa. The 2019 Sustainable Development Goals (SDGs) index ranked Nigeria at 159th among 162 countries. With 53.5%ent of the population living on less than the equivalent of $1.9 a day in 2021, poverty is prevalent (Statista, 2022).

The responsibility for healthcare in Nigeria is shared between the federal, state, and local governments. Delivery is shared between public and private providers. Access to government healthcare services can be difficult, especially in rural areas, and the use of traditional medicine (TM), as well as complementary and alternative medicine (CAM) has increased significantly in recent years. There are many healthcare challenges, and these have been exacerbated by political instability and tensions. As a result, there has been limited political will and resources to address these challenges, leading to a deterioration in the accessibility and quality of healthcare services.

The federal government's role is mostly limited to coordinating the affairs of the university teaching hospitals with their associated tertiary healthcare facilities. This leaves the state governments to manage the secondary healthcare provided through district general hospitals and the local government to focus on primary healthcare delivered through dispensaries. Although primary care delivery is the responsibility of local government, it is regulated by the federal government. The high proportion of healthcare funded by OOPs is a major issue for Nigerians, with the associated risks of catastrophic health costs for households or a failure to access care. Only about 3% of Nigerians surveyed by the government in 2018 had any form of health insurance. Of these, most had employer-based coverage and privately purchased insurance was rare (Statista, 2022). Ninety-seven percent of people without insurance have to pay for medicine OOP, which is often "expensive and difficult to afford. In 2019, on average, healthcare made up 6% of Nigerian household spending, with higher figures in rural areas than in urban zones" (Statista, 2022).

Over 20 years ago, Nigeria established the Nigerian National Health Insurance Scheme (NHIS), which was officially launched in 2005. The goal of the NHIS was to provide financial risk protection for citizens and reduce the high proportion of OOPs. The scheme was created using a number of programmes with a mixture of SHI for employed citizens, community-based health insurance, PHI, and voluntary health insurance. The NHIS' objective of ensuring access to quality health services for all Nigerians was, at the time, seen as a positive step toward achieving UHC.

However, the NHIS has had little impact in practice. Nearly 90% of the total private health spending are OOP expenditures, and the majority of all health spending is financed directly by households without insurance. As a very regressive way of funding healthcare, there is no mechanism to use OOP payments to deliver equitable and quality healthcare for citizens. Onwujekwe et al. (2019) assert that OOP payments should be completely eradicated, or at least substantially reduced, by better health financing mechanisms to enable equity and UHC, which is an internationally recognised human right. Nigeria committed to UHC through the National Health Act of 2014. However, global agencies have highlighted the lack of data on available resources for health, the cost and use of health services, and the performance of frontline providers as barriers to planning and advocating for additional investments in health (Hafez, 2018; World Health Organisation, 2023).

11.4.1 Knowledge review

Before you move on, can you define the following key concepts:

- Extreme poverty line?
- Relative poverty line?

11.4.2 *Question to think about*

In countries with a very high level of out-of-pocket healthcare expenditure, what measures may be feasible to start to reduce this level?

Note

1 The Universal Health Coverage (UHC) Service Coverage Index is measured on a scale from 0 (worst) to 100 (best) based on the average coverage of essential services including reproductive, maternal, new-born and child health, infectious diseases, non-communicable diseases, and service capacity and access (WHO, 2023).

References

Australian Bureau of Statistics (2016). Australian Health Survey: Consumption of added sugars, 2011-12. cited in Sainsbury, E., Magnusson, R., Thow, A. M., & Colagiuri,S. (2020). Explaining resistance to regulatory interventions to prevent obesity and improve nutrition: a case-study of a sugar-sweetened beverages tax in Australia. Food Policy, 93, 101904.

Bandy, L. K., Scarborough, P., Harrington, R. A., Rayner, M., & Jebb, S. A. (2020). Reductions in sugar sales from soft drinks in the UK from 2015 to 2018. *BMC Medicine*, 18(1), 1–10

Canada Health Act. R.S.C. (1985). c. C-6. https://laws-lois.justice.gc.ca/eng/acts/c-6/

Colchero, M. A., Popkin, B. M., Rivera, J. A., & Ng, S. W. (2016). Beverage purchases from stores in Mexico under the excise tax on sugar sweetened beverages: Observational study. *BMJ*, 352, 1–9.

Collins, S. R., Bhupal, H. K., & Doty, M. M. (2019, February). Health insurance coverage eight years after the ACA: Fewer uninsured americans and shorter coverage gaps, but more underinsured. The Commonwealth Fund.

Commonwealth Fund. (2020). *U.S. Health care from a global perspective, 2019: Higher spending, worse outcomes* (p. 10021). The Commonwealth Fund.

de Belvis, A. G., Meregaglia, M., Morsella, A., Adduci, A., Perilli, A., Cascini, F., Solipaca, A., Fattore, G., Ricciardi, W., Maresso, A., & Scarpetti, G. (2022). Italy: Health system review. Health Systems in Transition. 24(4), i–203.

Hafez, R. (2018). *Nigeria health financing system assessment*. World Bank Group.

HealthCare.gov. (2023). *Health* maintenance organisation *(HMO), U.S. Centers for medicare & medicaid services* (p. 21244). 7500 Security Boulevard.

Jacobson, P. D., & Parmet, W. E. (2018). Public health and health care: Integration, disintegration, or eclipse. *The Journal of Law, Medicine & Ethics*, 46(4), 940–951.

Kings Fund. (2017). *How health care is funded, part of how should the NHS be funded?* Kings Fund London.

Mhazo, A. T., Maponga, C. C., & Mossialos, E. (2023). Inequality and private health insurance in Zimbabwe: history, politics and performance. *International Journal for Equity in Health*, 22(1), 1–13.

Mueller, M., Hagenaars, L., & Morgan, D. (2017). *Administrative spending in OECD health care systems: Where is the fat and can it be trimmed? in OECD (2017), tackling wasteful spending on health*. OECD Publishing.

Nakovics, M. I., Brenner, S., Bongololo, G., Chinkhumba, J., Kalmus, O., Leppert, G., & De Allegri, M. (2020). Determinants of healthcare seeking and out-of-pocket expenditures in a "free" healthcare system: Evidence from rural Malawi. *Health Economics Review*, 10, 14.

Office for National Statistics. (2019). *Healthcare expenditure, UK Health Accounts: 2019*. ONS, London.

Onwujekwe, O., Ezumah, N., Mbachu, C, Obi, F., Ichoku, H., Uzochukwu, B., & Wang, H. (2019). Exploring effectiveness of different health financing mechanisms in Nigeria; What needs to change and how can it happen? *BMC Health Services Research*, 19(661), 1–13.

Organisation for Economic Co-operation and Development (OECD). (2009). Burden of out-of-pocket expenditure. In *OECD, health at a glance* (pp. 146–147). OECD Publishing.

Organisation for Economic Co-operation and Development (OECD). (2021). *Health at a glance 2021: OECD indicators*. OECD Publishing.

Organisation for Economic Co-operation and Development (OECD) & European Observatory on Health Systems and Policies. (2021). *Germany: Country health profile 2021*. OECD Publishing.

Popkin, B. M., & Ng, S. W. (2021). Sugar-sweetened beverage taxes: Lessons to date and the future of taxation. *PLoS Medicine*, 18(1), e1003412.

Purohit, B. C. (2023). *Economics of public and private healthcare and health insurance in India*. Taylor & Francis.

Rostampour, M., & Nosratnejad, S. (2020). A systematic review of equity in healthcare financing in low-and middle-income countries. *Value in Health Regional Issues*, 21, 133–140.

Sood, N., & Wagner, Z. (2018). Social health insurance for the poor: Lessons from a health insurance programme in Karnataka, India. *BMJ Global Health*, 3(1), e000582.

Statista. (2022). *Health in Nigeria: Statistics and facts*. https://www.statista.com/topics/65 75/health-in-nigeria/

Thorlby, R. (2023). *Social health insurance: Be careful what you wish for*. The Health Foundation.

Tikkanen, R., Osborn, R., Mossialos, E., Djordjevic, A., & Wharton, G. A. (2020). United States of America, Country Profiles, Commonwealth Fund.

World Health Organisation (WHO). (2017). *Tracking universal health coverage: 2017 global monitoring report*. World Health Organisation.

World Health Organisation (WHO). (2021). *Nigeria: Annual report 2021: Making people healthier*. World Health Organisation.

World Health Organisation (WHO). (2023). *Tracking universal health coverage: 2023 Global monitoring report*. WHO. ISBN: 978-92-4-008037-9

12 Models of payment to providers

12.1 Provider payment models (PPMs)

PPMs are the mechanism that define how healthcare providers are paid. Their characteristics provide incentives and disincentives that will drive provider behaviours.

They may be classified according to how providers are paid, when they are paid, and if they are paid by the number and type of services, and how the services are costed.

Payment to providers may be fixed or vary according to the services rendered. Under fixed models, providers receive the same amount from the purchaser whatever services are provided. In contrast, under a variable payment system, providers are compensated according to the actual number of services provided. In such cases, payment may be made per item of service, patient, day, case, or a combination of a set of factors.

Alternatively, PPMs may be classified according to the timing of the payment in relation to when a service has been rendered. In a retrospective payment system, providers are paid after they deliver treatment or care, whereas prospective payment systems pay providers before a service is carried out, with a previously determined set rate or total budget.

12.2 Fee-for-service as a provider payment model

Fee-for-service (FFS) is a remuneration model where healthcare providers charge separately for each service rendered, leaving the purchaser responsible for covering the provider's specified fees. Under this system, there exists a motivation for healthcare providers to engage in activities reimbursed by the purchasers, often linked to enhanced financial returns.

Purchasers can exploit this by offering increased compensation for prioritised health services. Consequently, healthcare providers may find themselves rationalising the execution of activities for which reimbursement is higher, potentially leading to a concentration on services with elevated payment rates.

In terms of Payment and Performance Management (PPM) characteristics, fee-for-service is characterised as variable, retrospective, and calculated per service item performed during a consultation. Healthcare providers receive payments through diverse channels, including patients making direct out-of-pocket payments immediately after receiving services. In this model, healthcare providers are remunerated on a per-service basis, predetermined by a fixed price.

In practice, fee-for-service PPM allows healthcare providers to receive payments from various sources, providing flexibility. The primary aim of fee-for-service is to compensate

DOI: 10.4324/9781003478874-15

healthcare providers for the expenses associated with delivering necessary patient care tasks. Consequently, purchasers can use fee-for-service as a tool to motivate providers to prioritise specific tasks, for example, after decades of capitation-based payments to family doctors. The United Kingdom's National Health Service (NHS) introduced additional incentives in the 1990s to encourage specific activities such as cervical screening, blood pressure checks, and childhood immunisations (Gillies, 1998). Fee-for-service is particularly effective when purchasers seek to manage the overall activity of healthcare providers while finding it costly to closely monitor all sub-activities or processes leading to desired performance, as seen in diagnostic and patient management procedures at the primary level or general practice An acknowledged advantage of fee-for-service is the ability for purchasers to compensate healthcare providers on a per-activity basis, fostering motivation to align efforts with payor requirements. However, a drawback is the potential for providers to focus primarily on tasks that are measured and rewarded, possibly diverting attention from other critical responsibilities.

Within fee-for-service, a provider's income correlates with the number of services performed, incentivising providers to influence patients to request services that may not be essential, leading to supplier-induced demand. For example, physicians may create a perception that more diagnostic tests equate to better care quality, prompting patients to request additional tests.

Table 12.1 provides a summary of the advantages and disadvantages of fee-for-service as a model of payment to providers:

Table 12.1 The advantages and disadvantages of fee-for-service as a model of payment

Advantages of fee-for-service	Disadvantages of fee-for-service
Incentivising desired activities: Fee-for-service allows purchasers to incentivise healthcare providers to prioritise specific health services. By assigning higher reimbursement for priority services, purchasers can influence provider behaviours	*Focus on measured tasks:* There's a risk that healthcare providers may focus primarily on tasks that are measured and rewarded, potentially neglecting other important aspects of patient care.
Flexibility in payment methods: Healthcare providers can receive payments through various means, such as direct payment from patients, reimbursement from insurance companies based on treatment provided, or government reimbursement based on agreed-upon rates.	*Supplier-induced demand:* Providers may be motivated to encourage patients to request services that may not be essential, leading to unnecessary diagnostic tests or services. This phenomenon is known as supplier-induced demand.
Provider efficiency: The set price per service encourages providers to be more efficient in delivering patient care, as they are compensated for each activity conducted.	*Potential overutilisation:* The system may lead to overutilisation of services, as providers may be motivated to perform more services to increase their income, even if they may not be essential for patient care. In inpatient care settings, this may take the form of extending a patient's length of stay longer than necessary to maximise reimbursement.

Case study: Fee-for-service as a cost-control mechanism in Japan

In Japan, the adoption of UHC incorporates an FFS model as one of the key components in its social insurance systems. A notable aspect is that over 98% of the Japanese population is encompassed by the statutory health insurance system (SHIS), supplemented by a distinct public social assistance program designed for individuals facing poverty, covering the remaining 1.7%. Mandatory enrolment in an SHIS plan is required for all citizens and residents. The SHIS comprises two essential types of compulsory insurance, as outlined by Matsuda (2020):

- Employment-based plans: These cater to the working population.
- Residence-based insurance plans: Designed for unemployed individuals aged 74 and under and all adults aged 75 and older.

For the second type of insurance, predominantly funded through taxes, the government establishes a uniform fee for physician services. This fee schedule undergoes biennial updates and is subject to negotiation with key stakeholders, primarily involving the government and the Japan Medical Association. To ensure effective price control, physician fees are determined based on government expenditure targets and predefined budgetary limits.

In Japan, the government directly participates in healthcare negotiations. In anticipation of universal health insurance in 1958, the country consolidated diverse fee schedules into a unified one to address discrepancies in access arising from different insurers paying varying prices to physicians. The achievement of universal access in Japan is seen as dependent on establishing consistent prices for comparable services.

The Ministry of Health, Labour, and Welfare in Japan is responsible for setting prices and overseeing the medical profession. While the ministry wields considerable power in the centralised system, the health budget is ultimately determined by the prime minister, and the ministry is focused on controlling costs. The global budget is influenced by officials from both the Ministry of Health, Labour, and Welfare and the Ministry of the Economy and Finance.

The Central Social Insurance Medical Council, situated within the ministry, revises the fee schedule biennially, incorporating inputs from diverse stakeholders. Increases in payments to physicians often coincide with reductions in the pharmaceutical budget, with pharmaceutical companies contributing to higher physician fees. Unlike the American Medical Association's committee, the council is an integral part of the Ministry of Health, Labour, and Welfare.

Japan's healthcare system involves open meetings with various stakeholders, such as the media, pharmaceutical industry, and the public. Despite the importance of the Central Social Insurance Medical Council, the primary relationship is between the ministry and the Japan Medical Association. Primary care physicians take a leading role in the Japan Medical Association and receive more favourable compensation compared to specialists. In contrast to many countries, Japanese specialists are less politically active due to their employment in hospitals and university clinical departments (Gusmano et al., 2020).

12.2.1 Knowledge review

Before you move on, can you define the following key concepts:

- Fee-for-service?
- Variable payment system?

12.2.2 Question to think about

As a patient, based on the care that you or your family have received, have you seen evidence of treatment driven by specific incentive payments? If so, did you think it was a good thing?

12.3 Capitation as a Provider Payment Model

Capitation is a type of payment where the amount of remuneration is based on the number of people on a patient list, which defines the population that will be served by a healthcare provider. The primary objective of a capitation system is to manage the cost of care for primary or basic interventions, often deliverable at the lowest level of the health system.

The capitation fee per patient can be standardised across all individuals listed, or it may be adjusted based on the risk level or profile of specific patient types within the list, such as by age and sex. Policies governing capitation fee amounts are typically designed to guide healthcare providers in serving a desired patient mix within their designated list.

In practice, capitation may be combined with additional payments for patients with specific conditions requiring more care or with fee-for-service to incentivise some procedures; e.g., health prevention or promotion, although in theory, the fixed amount allocated per patient on the list should incentivise physicians to prioritise preventive care, which generally requires fewer resources compared to curative services (Gillies, 1998).

A capitation PPM offers significant leverage in organising a healthcare team and system around a designated patient list, typically within a specific catchment area. The system also encourages the establishment of long-term relationships between healthcare providers and individuals on the list. Consequently, patients can receive more consistent care from their designated general practitioner. In the context of service delivery, a capitated provider payment mechanism aims to guide patients through the primary care level, reducing unnecessary resource utilisation at higher care levels, which is then reserved for more complex health conditions.

Pott et al. (2023) carried out a systematic review of the impact of prospective payment systems (PPS) including capitation on quality of care based on 64 studies and concluded that based on evidence on mortality, readmission, complications, discharge disposition and discharge destination, there was no conclusive evidence of a positive or negative impact of PPS on the quality of care.

Dzampe (2023) looked at the impact of capitation on introduction of capitation into a mixed payment system for healthcare services in the Ashanti region of Ghana. They found that outpatient visits were approximately 35% lower following the introduction of capitation. However, they found no corresponding significant change in inpatient outcomes, such as the in-hospital death rate or the length of hospital stay, which they used as a proxy indicator for the severity of illness. They suggest that this means that the observed reduction in outpatient visits may be in unnecessary or low-value visits, especially in primary care.

Furthermore, providers are likely to avoid unnecessary service utilisation when reimbursement is solely based on capitation.

Healthcare providers stand to increase their income with a growing number of individuals on their list, often up to a cap defined by the purchaser. This creates an incentive for physicians to engage in activities that generate demand, enrol more patients in their clinics, and foster long-term relationships with these patients. These long-term relationships positively impact the quality of care provided.

Providers remunerated by capitation are sometimes accused of "cream skimming." This refers to choosing patients for some characteristic(s) other than their need for care, which enhances the profitability or reputation of the provider. Under capitation or other fixed payment schemes, this often means choosing patients that are less ill or likely to need less provision. A simple example would be primary care physicians refusing to register new patients over a certain age. Within a publicly funded system, governments or social insurance providers can effectively ban such practices by requiring providers not to discriminate.

However, without appropriate controls, providers compensated through capitation may establish a system where they selectively choose relatively healthy individuals for their list or make it challenging for patients with complex health conditions to join.

The impact of capitation on costs at the Avenue Hospital, Nairobi

Ochieng (2019) used retrospective data from the Avenue Hospital's EHR system to compare reimbursement costs using capitation and fee-for-service models paid to four Kenyan insurance companies.

The reimbursement costs were compared among comparable illnesses in patients attending the outpatient department, examining 3,694 patient visits within a six-month timeframe. The analysis used the average costs for treating diseases, involving a comparison between the mean capitation costs and mean fee-for-service payments. The data were extracted, organised, and filtered using Excel, followed by analysis through pivot tables and pivot charts. Descriptive analysis was employed to obtain means and percentage counts, which were then presented in tables and bar graphs. The findings indicated that capitation costs were 7.8% lower than the mean costs associated with the fee-for-service model. This difference proved to be statistically significant for three out of the four illnesses examined, with hypertension being the only exception. The study's outcomes confirmed that capitation-based health cost payments were more economical than those under the fee-for-service model.

This suggests that in this context capitation provided as a more cost-effective form of insurance compared to fee-for-service schemes. The study only looks at reimbursement costs. It does consider longer-term outcomes with their potential for additional costs and/or benefits or the impact on clinical decision making.

12.3.1 Knowledge review

Before you move on, can you define the following key concepts:

- Prospective payment models?
- Cream skimming?

12.3.2 *Question to think about*

Would you rather be treated by a primary care physician remunerated by capitation or fee-for-service? Would your view be different if you were personally footing the bill as opposed to the government or an insurance provider?

12.4 Global budget as a Provider Payment Model

The global budget PPM operates by imposing an annual spending limit and specifying an acceptable level of services to be achieved within the allocated funding. This limit can be established using historical input costs or anticipated service volume. Hospitals receive reimbursement based on their adherence to expected activities, outputs, or outcomes rather than the actual incurred costs. Any exceeding of anticipated costs becomes the responsibility of the hospitals to absorb as a loss.

This model is typically employed in health systems where the government has the authority to transfer financial risk to hospitals. Global budgets pose challenges for hospitals with limited management capacity. It is usually implemented as a response either to a significant economic downturn or a significant increase in expenditure incurred under a fee-for-service model.

Effective prevention and management of funding deficits, as well as the handling of patient waiting lists, are essential for hospitals adopting the global budget payment model. Cost control measures implemented to stay within the budget may lead to prolonged waiting times, necessitating vigilant monitoring to prevent harm to patients.

The use of global budgets reflects governmental priorities in controlling spending for facility-based health services and encourages hospitals to provide services in a cost-efficient and clinically effective manner. While hospitals have flexibility in determining their approach to achieve efficiency within the budget, implementing a strict budget ceiling can be politically challenging, and some hospitals may seek additional funds even after reaching their ceilings.

The parameters used to set the budget ceiling introduce their own risks. Setting the ceiling based on input activities may incentivise hospitals to increase inputs but refer patients elsewhere quickly, resulting in an overall under-provision of services. Conversely, if the volume of services is the basis for the budget ceiling, hospitals may increase the number of services per patient to meet the volume requirement while promptly referring new patients to other facilities.

Global budget as a PPM in Taiwan

Global budget was adopted as PPM by Taiwan's healthcare sector in 2002 in response to significant financial challenges. Taiwan's National Health Insurance (NHI) scheme offers almost universal coverage and aims to ensure equal access to healthcare across the different socioeconomic levels of the population.

Yang et al. (2021) reported that following the introduction of global budgets, there was significant reform in Taiwan's healthcare sector. They reported improvements in the financial efficiency of hospital resource allocation. Since the NHI system in Taiwan allows all insured individuals complete freedom of choice among hospitals, strong competition can encourage hospitals to enhance both productivity and financial efficiency. The Ministry of Health and Welfare restricted the establishment or expansion of hospitals in regions with abundant medical resources to balance medical resource allocation among urban and rural districts. After the introduction of global budgeting, resource allocation in healthcare became more efficient and prevented waste, especially in the metropolitan areas with existing abundant healthcare resources. In contrast, remote districts, with less hospital-based resources demonstrated increased productivity and financial efficiency, with more hospitals being established to close the gap in healthcare between urban and rural districts.

Liu et al. (2019) looked at the impact on the quality of care of the introduction of the general budget PPM. Specifically, they looked at the differences in health service utilisation, healthcare expenditures, and quality of care provided to patients with unexplained fever before and after global budget implementation in Taiwan. They found that the quality of care improved, at the expense of increased length-of-stays and incremental total costs for patients with unexplained fever. This specific clinical case shows trends at odds with the global case and suggests that the impact of the global budget varied according to the clinical speciality and was both heterogeneous and complex.

12.4.1 *Knowledge review*

Before you move on, can you define the following key concept:

• Global budget?

12.4.2 *Question to think about*

How might a hospital change their priorities if a global budget PPM is introduced?

12.5 Pay-for-performance as a Provider Payment Model

Pay-for-performance is a type of PPM that ties renumeration to clinical effectiveness and quality indicators. It is often used in conjunction with other payment models, such as capitation or fee-for-service, to address their weaknesses. Pay-for-performance can target cost reduction in addition to clinical and quality objectives, and the incentive structure is influenced by various factors, including the intervention characteristics, existing incentives in the payment system, organisational capacity, patient characteristics, and market dynamics.

While pay-for-performance can effectively encourage hospitals and their staff to participate and improve clinical care in organisations with a strong culture of quality, its impact may be influenced by the dominant payment system. The additional incentive can lead to patient selection, increased focus on rewarded activities, and a wider performance gap between high-performing and struggling providers. Therefore, the outcomes of pay-for-performance can be mixed and depend on its design and interaction with the dominant payment mechanism.

Nevertheless, pay-for-performance offers the potential for providers to be motivated in delivering effective clinical care and meeting quality indicators.

Case study: The Quality Outcomes Framework in English general practice

The Quality Outcomes Framework is an example of pay-for-performance used in English general practice alongside capitation to incentivise primary care physicians to carry out prevention and promotion activities.

The Quality and Outcomes Framework (QOF) was implemented in 2004 as part of a new NHS GP contract, with the intention of financially incentivising general practices for adhering to evidence-based care standards. It followed on from previous more piecemeal incentives. While pay-for-performance models are found elsewhere, QOF was one of the largest in scope, ambition, and cost.

Initially, up to 25% of general practice income was tied to QOF performance. Recently, the funds allocated to QOF have been increasingly challenged by the demands of urgent care and immediate patient needs but also on preventing, diagnosing early, and managing long-term medical issues, such as cardiovascular disease, diabetes, and chronic lung diseases, which significantly contribute to poor health, multimorbidity, reduced quality of life, NHS workload, and mortality.

During the COVID-19 pandemic, the NHS understandably shifted its focus to urgent care, given the unavailability of options like vaccination. However, as these options have become available, there is a renewed need for the NHS to prioritise high-quality care for long-term conditions. The pandemic period witnessed a decline in patients starting treatment for conditions like high blood pressure, and death rates in England exceeded expectations, partly due to increased deaths from conditions such as cardiovascular disease. These public health challenges underscore the importance of the QOF, especially its components focused on secondary prevention and managing chronic conditions.

Majeed and Molokhia (2023) argue that recent evidence demonstrates that patients meeting QOF targets for type 2 diabetes management experience lower rates of death, emergency hospital admissions, retinopathy, and amputation. These findings highlight the QOF's potential as a powerful tool for secondary prevention, resulting in improved health outcomes for patients and reduced strain on other parts of the NHS. They also argue the QOF supplies crucial data for healthcare quality measurement, essential for planning services, addressing health disparities, and ensuring value for public investment in NHS primary care. The structured data entry required for QOF also facilitates its use in clinical research, as witnessed during the COVID-19 pandemic.

On the other hand, a systematic review by Forbes et al. (2017) argues that there is insufficient evidence to support the idea that the QOF effectively enhances care and outcomes for individuals with long-term conditions. In fact, the QOF might have adverse effects. When practices attain maximum or nearly maximum points within the system, which is the case for most practices, there is limited incentive for them to further enhance their performance. It is probable that the QOF steers practices and professionals away from delivering high-quality primary care that falls outside the QOF framework. Additionally, the QOF fails to motivate practices to enhance care for patients with the most intricate needs in primary care, as these individuals are more likely to be exempted from the scheme. Elevating the achievement thresholds could backfire, as there is evidence indicating that it results in increased exception reporting, creating the appearance of higher achievement without a genuine escalation in the desired activities. There is also evidence that whilst QOF has increased data quality around specific indicators, this is at the expense of other data.

Concerns over cost and the lack of effectiveness of the scheme led to the abandonment of a similar scheme in Scotland in 2016, and its withdrawal has been discussed in England as well. It is noticeable that many of those arguing for its retention do have a significant financial incentive.

12.5.1 *Knowledge review*

Before you move on, can you define the following key concepts:

- Pay-for-performance (as a type of PPM)?

12.5.2 *Question to think about*

What are the advantages and disadvantages of pay-for-performance as a PPM?

12.6 Diagnosis-Related Groups (DRGs) as a Provider Payment Model

DRGs are a PPM based on the diagnoses and procedures performed on patients.

The DRG system categorises patients into groups based on similar clinical conditions and resource requirements. It is primarily used in the United States and several other countries as a method of payment for inpatient hospital services. The key stages of the method are summarised in Table 12.2.

The DRG system provides a standardised approach to reimburse hospitals based on the resources used for patient care. It promotes efficiency by incentivising hospitals to manage costs and deliver effective care within the predetermined payment structure. Additionally, DRGs facilitate data analysis, research, and benchmarking across healthcare facilities to monitor quality of care and resource utilisation patterns.

The DRG PPM is intended to reward hospitals that improve cost efficiency. However, it also has downsides. Patients that have different clinical conditions may be classified within the same case rates when they present almost similar factors according to the DRG formula. This can motivate hospitals to select the relatively easier or simpler clinical cases within a category rather than the more difficult ones that could become more complex.

The use of DRGs can also lead to hospitals classifying patient conditions into higher DRG types upon admission to maximise income. Finally, since the cost being controlled boils down to individual case management, the overall cost to the hospitals may be difficult to control when there are no limiting terms in admitting patients.

Table 12.2 The key stages of the DRG method (after Mathauer & Wittenbecher, 2013)

Stage	Description
1 Patient admission	When a patient is admitted to a hospital, their medical records and clinical information are collected, including the primary diagnosis, secondary diagnoses, and procedures performed during their stay.
2 DRG assignment	The hospital assigns a specific DRG code to the patient based on their diagnoses and procedures. Each DRG has a unique payment weight assigned to it, which represents the average cost associated with treating patients in that group.
3 Cost calculation	The payment weight is multiplied by a standardised base rate or hospital-specific rate to determine the reimbursement amount for that particular DRG. The base rate is adjusted by factors such as geographic location, teaching status of the hospital, and the presence of specialised services.
4 Reimbursement calculation	The reimbursement amount is calculated by multiplying the payment weight by the base rate. For example, if a DRG has a payment weight of 1.5 and the base rate is $10,000, the reimbursement for that case would be $15,000.
5 Payment and adjustments	The reimbursement amount may be subject to certain adjustments, such as additional payments for outliers (cases with exceptionally high costs) or specific conditions that require additional resources. These adjustments aim to account for variations in patient severity and treatment complexity.
6 Coding accuracy and audits	Accurate coding and documentation are crucial for appropriate DRG assignment and reimbursement. Hospital coders review medical records to ensure the diagnoses and procedures are coded correctly. Periodic audits may be conducted by government or private payers to verify the accuracy of coding and compliance with reimbursement rules.

Lessons from nine national case studies: Bredenkamp et al. (2019)

Bredenkamp et al. (2019) argue that DRGs are deployed in the expectation of increased efficiency and sustainability. They looked at nine countries (US, Australia, Thailand, The Kyrgyz Republic, Germany, Estonia, Croatia, China, and The Russian Republic) that had introduced DRGs and argue that for increased efficiency and sustainability to be achieved requires careful design, complementary reforms, and consideration of process and politics.

They highlight a number of lessons from the implementation of DRGS in these countries:

- Clarity of objectives and expectations to prevent the DRG implementation becoming an end in itself rather than the means to an end
- Ensure that there is an implementation team who have the ability and authority to do what is needed
- Start by adopting an existing grouping classification – it can always be adapted to local needs later
- Involve providers in the calculation of cost weightings to achieve consensus and provide appropriate incentives to encourage the desired behaviours
- Ensure that there is a hard budget ceiling to prevent cost escalation

---

- Use a phased implementation to allow for lessons to be learnt and adjustments to be made
- Involve all relevant stakeholders and ensure that communications are inclusive and transparent to establish and maintain buy-in
- Continue to monitor and fine-tune the DRG model even after it is fully established – healthcare and the environment in which it operates is both complex and dynamic

---

12.6.1 *Knowledge review*

Before you move on, can you define the following key concepts:

- Diagnosis-Related Groups?

12.6.2 *Question to think about*

Do you think that the advantages of the DRG approach outweigh the disadvantages?

12.7 The role of deductibles, coinsurance, and co-payments in Provider Payment Models

Deductibles, coinsurance, and co-payments constitute various patient payment mechanisms (PPMs) directly tied to individuals. This contrasts with other PPM types where institutional funders play a more predominant role, negotiating agreements with healthcare providers. In coinsurance and co-payment scenarios, patients contribute a portion of the cost for each healthcare service in collaboration with a third party.

- A deductible is the amount paid by the patient for healthcare services before their health insurance begins to pay.
- Coinsurance is a percentage of the bill for services paid for by the patient after they have paid the deductible amount. Patients normally agree to coinsurance in order to keep their premiums down.
- A co-payment is a fixed amount paid for a healthcare service or procedure by the patient, usually when they receive the service. Co-payments may be required in taxation funded, social insurance or private insurance systems. In social insurance or taxation funded systems, patients may take out additional private insurance to cover co-payments in some systems.

In private systems, co-payments may be tiered, where the amount paid is linked to the type (and cost) of care received. If a health insurance plan offers tiered co-payments, the lowest fees will be for office visits to a primary care physician, physician's assistant, or nurse practitioner. For a visit to urgent care or to see a specialist, such as a cardiologist or an immunologist, the payment will be a little higher. The most expensive co-payments will be associated with visits to the emergency room.

The practice of utilising deductibles and various cost-sharing measures has a history tracing back to the late 1940s in the United States. In the US, two primary types of deductibles exist within the healthcare system. The first type, a conventional and wide-spread model, is offered by health maintenance organisations, preferred provider organisations, and point-of-service plans, both for individuals and families. The second type involves high deductible health plans, which provide higher deductible amounts and greater premium discounts (Mirian et al., 2020).

Since January 2008, the Netherlands has enforced a mandatory deductible plan. Additionally, individuals have the option to choose a voluntary deductible plan alongside the compulsory one. To offset the increased financial risk, those insured receive premium discounts.

Switzerland has an annual mandatory deductible for insured individuals, who are also required to cover 10% of charges exceeding their deductibles as a co-payment. Various options are available, including selecting higher deductible amounts in exchange for greater reductions in premiums for insured individuals. In Germany, deductibles have been offered by health social insurance companies since 2007, presented in the form of optional tariffs.

The principal aim of imposing a deductible is to prevent moral hazard by reducing the use of unnecessary healthcare services. Moral hazard is a change in health behaviour and consumption of health services because of insurance coverage. Koohi Rostamkalaee et al. (2022) define it both as an increase in demand for health services or a decrease in preventive care due to insurance coverage. According to the theory of moral hazard, by lowering the price of care, health insurance and third-party payers encourage the consumer to consume more care than when they consume at the market price, the implication is that this additional consumption is unnecessary (Doran & Robertson, 2009).

Although reduction in the use of healthcare services due to implementation of deductibles can potentially prevent moral hazard and consequently lead to cost savings, this can encourage people not to use essential healthcare services with preventive aspect, and this, in turn, may endanger people's health in the medium and long term and also lead to greater long-term cost.

In a systematic review of the impact of cost-sharing on medications in the US healthcare system, Fusco et al. (2023) found that the majority of publications examined found that, regardless of disease area, increased cost-sharing was associated with worse adherence, persistence, or discontinuation, and that studies evaluating reducing or eliminating cost-sharing found that total costs did not rise.

Case study: Co-payments in Vietnam

In 1998, Vietnam introduced a health insurance cost-sharing plan through co-payments, and this approach has undergone several modifications since then (The Government of Vietnam, 2005). The current co-payment rates vary, with certain groups, such as children under the age of six, members of impoverished households, recipients of monthly social insurance allowances, and war veterans, enjoying a 0% co-payment rate. Others, including members of near-poor households, pensioners, and those receiving monthly working capacity loss allowances, face a 5% co-payment rate. The remaining individuals are subject to a 20% co-payment rate.

A study conducted by Truong et al. (2023) used survey data from three Vietnamese provinces to explore the impact of co-payment exemption on self-reported health.

The findings of their research strongly indicate that exempting individuals from co-payments has a positive influence on self-reported health. The authors contend that while cost-sharing can effectively reduce pharmaceutical costs, its detrimental effects on health could negate these cost savings.

Another implication is that co-payment exemptions could serve as a tool for the government to enhance the overall health of specific covered groups. In Vietnam's health insurance system, vulnerable populations like children under six, the impoverished, and those receiving monthly social insurance allowances receive co-payment exemptions, potentially contributing to improved health outcomes. Truong et al. (2023) propose that if the government aims to enhance the health of other targeted groups, implementing co-payment exemptions remains a viable option.

Their results suggest that co-payment exemptions positively impact the self-reported health of individuals with middle and high incomes but do not affect those with the lowest incomes. They propose that the lack of responsiveness among the lowest-income group may be attributed to the lower co-payment rate that is applied to this population.

12.7.1 Knowledge review

Before you move on, can you define the following key concepts:

- Deductible?
- Co-payment?

12.7.2 Question to think about

Why do you think that Fusco et al. (2023) found that studies evaluating reducing or eliminating cost-sharing found that total costs did not rise?

References

Bredenkamp, C., Bales, S., & Kahur, K. (Eds.). (2019). *Transition to Diagnosis-Related Group (DRG) payments for health: Lessons from case studies*. World Bank Publications.

Doran, E., & Robertson, J. (2009). Australia's pharmaceutical cost sharing policy: Reducing waste or affordability?. *Australian Health Review*, 33(2), 231–240.

Dzampe, A. K., & Takahashi, S. (2023). *Financial incentives and health provider behaviour: Evidence from a capitation policy in Ghana*. Health Economics.

Forbes, L. J., Marchand, C., Doran, T., & Peckham, S. (2017). The role of the quality and outcomes framework in the care of long-term conditions: A systematic review. *The British Journal of General Practice: The Journal of the Royal College of General Practitioners*, 67(664), e775–e784.

Fusco, N., Sils, B., Graff, J. S., Kistler, K., & Ruiz, K. (2023). Cost-sharing and adherence, clinical outcomes, health care utilisation, and costs: A systematic literature review. *Journal of Managed Care & Specialty Pharmacy*, 29(1), 4–16.

Gillies, A. C. (1998). Computers and the NHS: An analysis of their contribution to the past present and future delivery of the national health service. *Journal of Information Technology*, 13(3), 219–229.

Government of Vietnam, The. (2005). *Decree 63/2005/NĐ-CP on health insurance principles (Nghị định số 63/2005/NĐ-CP. Ban hành điều lệ bảo hiểm y tế).* Government of Vietnam.

Gusmano, M., Laugesen, M., Rodwin, V., & Brown, L. (2020). Getting the price right: How some countries control spending in a fee-for-service system. *Health Affairs*, 39(11), 1867–1874.

Koohi Rostamkalaee, Z., Jafari, M., & Gorji, H. A. (2022). A systematic review of strategies used for controlling consumer moral hazard in health systems. *BMC Health Services Research*, 22(1), 1–12.

Liu, K. S., Yu, T. F., Wu, H. J., & Lin, C. Y. (2019). The impact of global budgeting in Taiwan on inpatients with unexplained fever. *Medicine*, 98(37), e17131.

Majeed, A., & Molokhia, M. (2023). The future role of the GP quality and outcomes framework in England. *BJGP Open*, 7(3). BJGPO.2023.0054. doi:10.3399/BJGPO.2023.0054

Mathauer, I., & Wittenbecher, F. (2013). Hospital payment systems based on diagnosis-related groups: Experiences in low- and middle-income countries. *Bulletin of the World Health Organisation*, 91(10), 746–756A.

Matsuda, R. (2020). The Japanese health care system. In R. Tikkanen, R. Osborn, E. Mossialos, A. Djordjevic, & G. Wharton (Eds.), *2020 International profiles of health care systems*. The Commonwealth Fund.

Mirian, I., Kabir, M. J., Barati, O., Keshavarz, K., & Bastani, P. (2020). Deductibles in health insurance, beneficial or detrimental: A review article. *Iranian Journal of Public Health*, 49(5), 851–859.

Ochieng, T. B. (2019). *A comparison of capitation and fee for service provider payment mechanisms and their effects on cost of healthcare: A case study of the Avenue Hospital, Nairobi* (MBA Thesis). Strathmore University.

Pott, C., Stargardt, T., & Frey, S. (2023). Does prospective payment influence quality of care? A systematic review of the literature. *Social Science & Medicine*, 323, 115812.

Truong, T. A., Le, L., & Pham, K. N. (2023). *The impact of co-payments on self-reported health: Evidence from rural vietnam.* SSRN 4645329. https://ssrn.com/abstract=4645329

Yang, S. W., Chu, K. C., & Kreng, V. B. (2021). The impact of global budgeting on the efficiency of healthcare under a single-payer system in Taiwan. *International Journal of Environmental Research and Public Health*, 18(20), Article 10983.

13 Efficient government health spending

13.1 Government health expenditure

In publicly funded systems, there is an expectation that greater expenditure will lead to better health outcomes. Since there is always more that can be done and spent, this leads to pressure on governments to spend more on healthcare, who must balance this expenditure against expenditure in other areas and the need to keep taxes down to manageable levels.

Figure 13.1 shows the percentage of GDP devoted to healthcare through government schemes or compulsory public schemes, typically social health insurance in 2022 in OECD countries:

The standout country is the United States with the highest percentage of government expenditure, in spite of some of the poorest health outcomes amongst OECD countries and a large contribution from private contributions in addition to the public expenditure.

At the other extreme is Singapore, with an average life expectancy higher than any European Union (EU) country at just over 84 but a health expenditure of less than half the EU average, just 4.1% of the GDP in 2023.

In order to achieve the expected outcomes outlined in the SDGs, lower-income countries need to significantly boost their health spending. In practice, this investment must come from government expenditure.

However, Sri Lanka, classified as a lower middle-income nation, is an example of how a strong public commitment to healthcare and careful attention to how health investments are allocated can deliver positive health outcomes from relatively low spending (1.6% of GDP in 2023). Sri Lanka has successfully increased life expectancy and eliminated malaria, filariasis, polio, and neonatal tetanus (Rajapaksa et al., 2021). Sri Lanka significantly outperforms its peers on major health indicators, such as in reducing child and maternal mortality rates and in life expectancy at birth is 77 years and still rising.

It is essential to note that merely increasing government spending on health does not guarantee improved health outcomes. For instance, if citizens believe that public resources allocated to basic health services are sufficient, they might redirect their private resources elsewhere, potentially contributing to unhealthy practices. Additionally, when increased public spending does not target the prevalent health issues or is diverted to specialised services rather than community-level infectious disease control, the investment becomes ineffective.

Considering health spending as part of overall societal investment planning is crucial to ensure that healthcare services are accessible, especially when other necessary infrastructure elements, like roads and transportation, are lacking for certain population

DOI: 10.4324/9781003478874-16

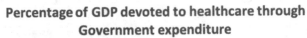

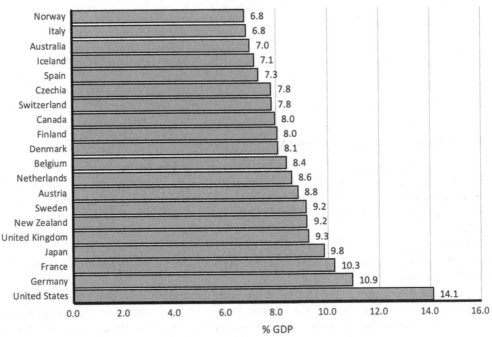

Figure 13.1 The percentage of GDP devoted to healthcare through government schemes or compulsory public schemes in 2022 in OECD countries. Source data (OECD, 2023)

groups. In low-income countries, basic infrastructure, such as provision of clean water, can have a greater and more cost-effective impact on healthcare than enhancing healthcare services.

While increasing health spending is crucial, efficiency in resource utilisation is equally important to achieve desired outcomes. Research by Greene (2004) suggests that improving efficiency with existing resources could enhance a country's health outcomes by up to 20%. Within a country, efficiency measures can reduce hospital costs (Puig-Junoy, 2000), and geographic considerations also play a role in healthcare delivery efficiency. However, there may be conflicting demands on the ethical grounds of equality of access (Hofmann, 2022).

Governments can enhance spending efficiency through reducing waste. Compared to many other countries, Saudi Arabia's healthcare expenditure as a percentage of its gross domestic product (GDP) is relatively high; therefore, there is resistance to increasing government healthcare expenditure. In the face of such resistance, efficiency becomes a key consideration with the goal of maximising patient care and outcomes while optimising resource utilisation. Efficiency may be considered as technical efficiency that ensures effective use of resources within healthcare facilities or allocative efficiency that involves strategic resource allocation for better population health (Alshehri et al., 2023). In Saudi Arabia, 75.8% of assessed public hospitals were found to be technically inefficient. The average efficiency score was 0.76, indicating that these hospitals could have reduced their inputs by 24% without compromising the provision of health services (Alatawi et al., 2020). One of the key factors in the Saudi system was extended lengths of stay. Reducing the length of stays is a common method of improving technical efficiency in hospitals in many countries.

The International Monetary Fund (2018) highlights the need for tax reforms to maximise income for public services including health. Governments that have a clearly defined mandate for change have a powerful advantage. Georgia undertook a comprehensive tax reform after experiencing a high level of dysfunction that led to a revolution International Monetary Fund (2022). Similarly, Ukraine witnessed tax reforms following the catalyst of the 2004 Orange Revolution, and Liberia initiated reforms after the conclusion of the civil war in 2003. While a clear mandate is crucial, it is not sufficient: high-level political commitment and engagement from all stakeholders are also needed.

A straightforward tax system with a limited number of rates is essential for promoting taxpayer compliance, as exemplified by the case of Georgia. In fragile states, the focus should initially be on simplifying taxes, procedures, and structures. Simplifying tax systems and legislation is especially crucial in weak states lacking basic institutions such as security and a well-functioning judicial system such as Liberia's after its civil war reforms.

Reducing exemptions can help to simplify the tax system and increase revenue by broadening the tax base. Many countries experience significant revenue losses due to poorly designed exemptions. The reduction of exemptions featured prominently in the reform efforts of several countries, such as Guyana's comprehensive exemption reform.

VAT has proven to be an effective method to boost revenue. Countries imposing this tax tend to generate more revenue than those that do not. Georgia, for example, increased revenue from VAT by streamlining its refund mechanism. Guyana successfully introduced a VAT in 2007, facing challenges in preparatory work but achieving success through a broad-based approach with a single rate.

Excise and sales tax increases can quickly raise revenue without fundamentally altering the tax system. For instance, Guyana increased fuel excise taxes in 2015 during an economic slowdown, while Liberia broadened its goods and services tax scope and raised excise taxes on alcoholic beverages and cigarettes.

A holistic approach to modernising tax institutions is needed. In the countries examined, revenue administration reforms covered legal, technical, and administrative measures, including changes in management, governance, and human resources. Large taxpayer offices were established to focus compliance efforts on major taxpayers, and information management systems were modernised for improved compliance and anti-corruption efforts. Additionally, countries updated registration, filing, and payment management processes and enhanced audit and verification programmes through a risk-based approach.

While governments possess the authority to mandate fund collection for health services, there are limitations on the extent to which taxes or compulsory contributions can be imposed on citizens. This is heavily dependent on the overall economic conditions of the country. Moreover, government funds are also required for other priority activities, such as social services, education, and defence.

Case study: Singapore high life expectancy in return for low expenditure

The national health expenditure in Singapore is expected to be 4.09% of GDP by 2023, down from 4.47% of GDP in 2016 (OECD, 2023).

Between 2009 and 2016, the government's share of health expenditures increased from about 32% to 41% due to increased public subsidies, which are intended to help reduce out-of-pocket costs.

Correspondingly, the out-of-pocket share of health expenditures fell from 43% to 31%. Singapore's average annual healthcare inflation was 2.6%, compared to 2.3% for all goods and services, between 2007 and 2017.

Private health insurance premiums are subsidised by the government on the basis of income. In addition, working-age persons pay higher premiums so that older residents can have lower premium increases.

The government provides various other subsidies to help make care more affordable:

At public hospitals, patients can obtain a subsidy by choosing a ward with fewer amenities. For example, patients admitted to C-class wards, which are rooms with eight beds, receive a subsidy of up to 80% of their hospital bill for that admission. In contrast, A-class single occupancy rooms are not subsidised. Clinical care is not affected by ward class.

Primary care visits at public clinics, known as polyclinics, are subsidised up to 75%, with different charges based on residency status.

Specialist outpatient care visits can be subsidised up to 75%, depending on the patient's income level and residency status.

Emergency services at public hospitals are subsidised equally for all.

Means tested subsidies are also provided to patients requiring intermediate and long-term care after hospital discharge, as well as to community-dwelling elderly individuals needing assistance with daily living.

Patients who wish to obtain additional coverage for private hospitals or care in private wards in public hospitals can purchase private insurance. The most common coverage is through Integrated Shield Plans, which are available only to citizens and permanent residents. As of 2017, 68% of citizens and permanent residents had one of these plans (Tikkanen et al., 2020). Whilst Singapore provides a very positive example of an efficient healthcare system with exceptional outcomes, it should be noted that it has a very small population by global standards, and it may not provide scalable solutions for other countries.

13.1.1 Knowledge review

Before you move on, can you define the following key concepts:

- Technical efficiency (in hospitals)?
- Allocative efficiency (in hospitals)?

13.1.2 *Question to think about*

Why do you think Singapore can deliver strong health outcomes in return for a relatively low government investment in healthcare and overall low expenditure, even when private contributions are included?

13.2 Fiscal space for health

Fiscal space is defined as the capacity within a government's budget that allows it to allocate resources for a specific purpose without putting the sustainability of its financial position or the stability of the economy at risk. The concept emphasises the need for fiscal space to be either pre-existing or deliberately created to make additional resources available for meaningful government expenditures. To create fiscal space, a government can take various measures such as increasing taxes, securing external grants, reducing less essential expenditures, obtaining resources through borrowing (from citizens, foreign lenders, or the banking system), and expanding the money supply. However, it is crucial to execute these actions without compromising macroeconomic stability and fiscal sustainability. This involves ensuring that the government has the capacity, both in the short and long term, to finance its desired expenditure programmes and meet its debt service obligations.

In developing and emerging market nations, the issue of fiscal space may appear more immediate compared to advanced economies due to the urgent expenditure needs at present. However, even for lower-income countries, there are longer-term considerations to address to ensure flexibility in responding to unforeseen fiscal challenges. For instance:

> Countries reliant on substantial foreign resources for a specific sector, like healthcare, might encounter future spending requirements resulting from the sector's expansion, potentially pre-empting a portion of future domestic budgetary resources.

The macroeconomic situation of a country may be adversely affected by foreign resource inflows, such as aid, leading to challenges like an increase in the real exchange rate and a decrease in international competitiveness. Excessive aid dependency may necessitate limitations on such inflows. Consequently, a foreign-funded expansion in a specific sector, such as education, could impose constraints on the availability of foreign resources for other sectors.

Resource inflows might finance a government activity, like pension reform, creating a liability in the form of uncertain future pay-outs in terms of both magnitude and timing.

In 2006, Heller et al. identified five avenues for expanding fiscal space for health:

(i)   increasing revenue
(ii) reprioritising expenditure
(iii) borrowing
(iv) using seigniorage
(v)   mobilising external resources

The World Bank developed this concept in 2010 into five pillars for expanding fiscal space for health in low- and middle-income countries (LMICs):

(i)   economic growth
(ii) budget prioritisation
(iii) earmarking certain revenues
(iv) improving the efficiency of health spending
(v)   utilising external resources(Tandon & Cashin, 2010)

Empirical studies conducted in approximately 40 countries since the formulation of this framework have revealed that the macro-fiscal performance of an economy is a crucial factor influencing the increase in public funding for health. Moreover, evidence suggests that reallocating a larger share of the budget to health can substantially augment resources in the health sector, particularly in situations where initial allocations are low. While earmarked revenues offer comparatively fewer resources overall for the sector, the efficiency component, the fourth pillar in Tandon and Cashin's model, has yielded mixed results regarding the extent to which efficiency gains can be converted into additional resources for the health sector. Country experiences indicate that efficiency gains do not automatically translate into an increased health budget; rather, effective public financial management (PFM) systems are necessary to retain and redirect these gains toward priority health needs.

Enhanced financial management policies and tools within the health sector can also carve out space in the sector's budget, especially in publicly funded systems. Inadequate PFM acts as a constraint on fiscal discipline and hinders the realisation of fiscal space potential. A growing body of evidence underscores the impact of PFM processes on public spending, particularly health expenditure. Notable examples include delayed, incomplete, and misaligned budget releases in many LMICs, significantly constraining the actual budget available for the health sector. Conversely, effective PFM rules, such as consistent fund releases and flexibility in reallocating funds across budget lines, are likely to enhance the prospects of maximising the existing budget for health.

Asamani et al. (2022) apply the concept of fiscal space to the healthcare workforce in Sub-Saharan Africa. They define fiscal space for the health workforce as

> *the ability of governments to direct resources towards health workforce investments without unduly compromising the short- to- medium ability of the government in other functions or substantially crowding out expenditure in other areas of the health sector or other sectors.*

They find that 20 countries in Eastern and Southern Africa in 2021 had a cumulative fiscal space of 12.179 billion US dollars for employing health workers in the public sector, which under a business-as-usual fiscal growth would likely be an increase of 28% by 2026; even under the most optimistic scenarios, the cumulative fiscal space for the countries would increase by 38% in 2026. They advocate for increased investment in the healthcare workforce to at least match the overall increase in fiscal space, calculating a 10-fold return on such an investment.

Case study: The five pillars of fiscal space applied to Cambodia at the time of the global downturn of 2008 (Tandon & Cashin, 2010)

In 2008–2010, in Cambodia, the majority of health spending in the country was out-of-pocket and this posed a significant barrier for the poor to access essential services. Furthermore, public sector wages were low, which is one factor behind poor quality of care. Therefore, there was a need for additional fiscal space for health – the need to improve public sector services and provide better access and financial protection for the poor.

Prior to the downturn of 2008, Cambodia had experienced high economic growth rates, which it has sustained for nearly a decade. Real per capita income in the country more than doubled between 1997 and 2007 through a disciplined economic development approach combined with integration into the global economy. Cambodia saw a rapid shift of jobs from agriculture to manufacturing, a demographic transition, and migration from rural to urban areas. Economic growth in the country translated into better public services and led to significant reductions in poverty rates as well as improvements in health and education. Driven largely by this sustained economic growth, real per capita government health expenditures in the country increased from 13 billion US dollars to 31 billion US dollars over 1997–2007.

In 2008, Tandon and Cashin reported Cambodia's prospects for fiscal space under the five pillars as follows:

- *Macroeconomic conditions:* Moderate GDP growth rates reduced from 8 to 4.8% due to global economic crisis. Revenues as % of GDP projected to remain at 12% but not likely to translate into fiscal space for health.
- *Re-prioritisation of health in the government budget*: Limited. The government reached its commitment to allocate 11% of the budget to health, and it is expected to remain at this level through 2011.
- *Health sector-specific resources:* Limited. Social health insurance is being discussed but is a longer term plan. No discussions of earmarked taxes.
- *Health sector-specific grants and foreign aid*: Moderate. ODA for health is 22% of total health spending and has been on an upward trend.
- *Efficiency gains:* Good. Inefficiencies in the public finance system prevent resources from being allocated to programmes in the health strategy and reaching service providers.

Figure 13.2 shows how healthcare expenditure in Cambodia has grown within the fiscal space before, during, and since the global downturn in 2008.

13.2.1 Knowledge review

Before you move on, can you define the following key concepts:

- Fiscal space?

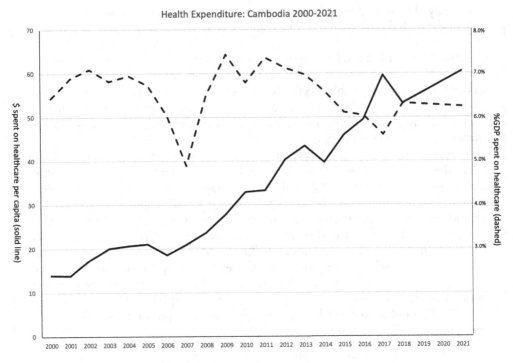

Figure 13.2 Healthcare expenditure in Cambodia in US dollars and the percentage of GDP.

13.2.2 Question to think about

How do you think the COVID-19 pandemic impacted on the fiscal space for healthcare expenditure in low-to-middle income countries and in higher income countries?

13.3 Improving public sector management

The WHO advocates for government control of healthcare to maximise equity, increase risk pooling, and to maximise the chances of achieving UHC in line with UN SDG 3.8. To make best use of the fiscal space that can be created for healthcare, governments need to look for innovations in the management of public sector healthcare that can be leveraged to achieve improvements.

Efficient public sector management and the corresponding institutional capacity are essential for the effective utilisation of public funds. In cases where the mechanism for public sector management is weak, it results in inadequate planning, budgeting, oversight, and regulation, negatively impacting the accessibility and effectiveness of basic essential health services.

As public resources are directed towards enhancing investments for UHC, it is crucial to concurrently implement measures to reduce inefficiencies in public sector management (Banzon & Mailfert, 2018). The reduction of inefficiency is instrumental in ensuring that public spending translates into improved access to health services. Enhancing efficiency within public sector management can be achieved through measures such as empowering health system organisations with greater autonomy within a specified governance framework. Providing government staff with the necessary capacity and autonomy in decision-making, while operating within an accountability system, is vital.

Simplifying the structure of health budgets to minimise complexity facilitates easier management. Among OECD countries, diverse measures have been adopted to enhance public sector efficiency, including decentralisation, fostering competition, optimising workforce structures, strengthening the budget process, and incorporating results-based management.

Since the 1980s, the UK Government has used targets to drive improvements in public services. Davies et al. 2021) explored the historical use of targets by the UK government, particularly in the context of new public management theory. They found that targets have improved the specific areas they aimed to address, such as reducing hospital waiting times, e.g., the four-hour waiting time target in Accident & Emergency departments led to a 14% reduction in deaths within 30 days, particularly benefiting patients with time-sensitive conditions like strokes. However, some of these achievements were partly due to gaming the system. In hospitals, data were manipulated, leaving patients waiting in ambulances, and some appointments were cancelled that feature in explicit targets.

They argued that targets appear effective at raising minimum standards but less so at driving excellence, so, for example, they had a significant impact on the longest waiting times, while in education, the elimination of school league tables in Wales didn't affect the top-performing schools. They also identified negative, sometimes unforeseen consequences of targets. They found that targets can lead to prioritising easy wins, neglecting critical issues, and manipulating data for short-term achievements. They may restrict the ability of frontline staff to use professional judgment, creating a demotivating environment, and that the bureaucratic burden of complying with targets can overwhelm frontline workers and policymakers, diverting attention from direct support to people.

Public sector management encompasses public financial management systems a critical component for countries aspiring to achieve UHC. This system involves the "institutions, policies, and processes that govern the use of public funds" (Cashin et al., 2017, p. 3). A well-aligned public financial management and health financing system enables less fragmented public revenues, the linkage of public revenues to a predictable budget, and the connection of the budget to timely disbursement and accountability processes.

Garcia-Escribano et al. (2022) underscore the importance of allocating a larger portion of government expenditure to Universal Health Coverage (UHC) for greater efficiency, particularly in lower middle-income countries. The study also identifies inequity as a source of inefficiency, emphasising the need for improved access to health services to reduce resource wastage in the health sector. Corruption in government spending is highlighted as a contributor to inefficiencies, especially in low- and middle-income countries. While increased efficiency in government spending can enhance health outcomes without additional funds, there is a limit to what can be achieved without a concurrent increase in funding for UHC.

Globally, the most important health targets are the UN SDGs. Part of the problem with using targets to drive improvements in public sector management is the way in which different targets compete for government resources. Although not all the UN SDGs are directly health-related, the economic, social and environmental spheres of sustainable development impact upon health and therefore the health-related targets. Even the target of universal healthcare is only a means to the end of improving global health.

Van Vuuren et al. (2022) argue that "hardly any information exists on what is needed for achieving all SDGs together accounting for the linkages between SDGs and possible synergies or trade-offs."

To overcome the conflicts between targets and take account of the interrelationships, Biggeri et al. (2019) proposed the use of an enhanced version of the "Integrated Sustainable Development Index" (I-SDI), designed to consider trade-offs and synergies within and between goals across the economic, social, and environmental aspects of sustainable development. Additionally, recognising the diversity within goals, they introduced a new index by applying the method both within and between goals. By considering heterogeneity within and between goals, across economic, social, and environmental dimensions, and by capturing synergies and trade-offs among indicators, their study revealed significant variations resulting scores and rankings. This provides a more adaptable and integrated measure to guide policymakers and effectively monitor overall progress.

The broader lesson here is the importance of recognising the complexity of delivering improvements in healthcare and population health. Nearly all effective interventions must recognise the need for a multifaceted approach and be aware of the possibility of unintended consequences and unforeseen confounding factors.

There is also a need to recognise the multiple benefits that may be achieved when considering both the business case before investment and the return on that investment post-implementation.

The relationships between the SDGs, fuel-based lighting and reducing child and maternal mortality

Goal 7 of the UN SDGs is concerned with sustainable energy.

- Target 7.1: By 2030, ensure universal access to affordable, reliable, and modern energy services.
- Target 7.2: By 2030, increase substantially the share of renewable energy in the global energy mix.

At first glance, this may seem to have little direct impact on healthcare. However, Mills (2016) reports that whilst there is no global estimate of burn-injuries attributable to fuel-based lighting, more than 95% of deaths worldwide from all types of burns occur in the low- and middle- countries. The mortality rate is five times higher in low- and middle-income populations in Africa than in high-income countries in Europe.

The use of kerosene-based lighting has been associated with a higher-than-expected rate of still births (Stachel, 2013) attributed to air pollution and, in spite of the lack of studies, there is anecdotal evidence of injuries and death caused by accidental fires during childbirth lit candlelight or kerosene lamps.

Therefore, the introduction of off-grid solar energy not only contributes to the renewable energy goals but to health-related targets.

Bisaga et al. (2021) argue that electricity access in Rwanda has increased steadily over the last decade. In 2009, approximately 9% of households had access to electricity compared to 55% in 2020, including 15% by the use of off-grid solar energy schemes. They argue that the off-grid solar energy sector in Rwanda benefits performance contributing to 16 out of the 17 SDGs.

13.3.1 *Knowledge review*

Before you move on, can you define the following key concept:

• Gaming the system?

13.3.2 *Question to think about*

Where do improvements in economic, social, and environmental conditions in your country deliver improvements in health outcomes?

13.4 Decentralising healthcare governance

Decentralising healthcare governance is a public sector policy reform aimed at providing increased autonomy to lower administrative levels, when delivering health services. The essence of decentralised governance in health involves transferring planning, management, and decision-making authority from the national level to sub-national entities, such as regional, state, or district/municipal levels. This shift can encompass various governmental functions, including the allocation of central funds and human resource recruitment for health services, with some functions remaining centralised while others being decentralised. The degree of centralisation or decentralisation fluctuates over time based on the prevailing political circumstances.

It is important to separate decentralising governance from decentralising healthcare services. The factors driving the centralisation or decentralisation of care services themselves are driven by clinical factors as well as economics (Sreeramareddy & Sathyanarayana, 2019).

In high-income countries like the US, UK, Spain, and Italy, the decentralisation of health services has been part of broader fiscal decentralisation efforts, where federal authority is devolved to sub-national entities, granting autonomy to regional and local authorities.

In contrast, many low- and middle-income countries (LMICs) have embraced health service decentralisation primarily in response to the international promotion of the primary healthcare approach by organisations like the World Health Organisation (WHO) and the United Nations Children's Fund (UNICEF). The implementation of decentralisation varies across countries, depending on their political and administrative structures. Several Southeast Asian countries, including India, Nepal, and Bangladesh, have acknowledged decentralisation in principle through their constitutions and policy frameworks. However, the actual implementation has been limited due to factors, such as the absence of committees, boards, or local governments in some areas, reluctance from central authorities, and resistance from health staff.

The condition of health service decentralisation is complex and not a straightforward reform, as it involves uncertainties regarding which functions should be decentralised, who initiates the process, and at which administrative levels decentralisation should occur. Studies on the effects of decentralised public governance tend to focus on government size, quality, economic growth, with limited attention to population health outcomes and health systems performance.

Decentralisation's potential impact on health outcomes involves governance, a key building block of health systems. Improved governance is thought to enhance health system performance, ultimately leading to better access and utilisation of healthcare services.

Decentralisation allows for local decision-makers to have more authority, potentially aligning priorities better with local needs, increasing accountability to communities, and building local institutional capacity. The logic model suggests that community participation in decision-making is a pathway through which decentralisation improves access to healthcare.

However, decentralisation may also have negative consequences, such as inadequate funding by local governments, increased workloads for frontline health workers, potential mismanagement of funds, and poor service management if local managers lack sufficient capacity and training. The success of decentralisation in improving health outcomes depends on various factors, including institutional capacity and accountability mechanisms.

Case study: Decentralisation in Belgium

In Belgium, both federal and regional authorities are responsible for health policy. Federal authorities are responsible for:

- the general legislative framework of the health system
- regulation of compulsory health insurance
- ambulatory care budgets
- hospital budgets and programming standards
- pharmaceuticals and their price controls
- regulating the health professions

Regions and local authorities are responsible for:

- health promotion and prevention
- organisation of primary care and palliative care
- maternal and child healthcare
- social services and community care
- financing hospital infrastructure and medical equipment
- establishing hospital licensing standards

Belgium operates a social health insurance system funded by contributions from employers, employees, social insurance, taxes, and out-of-pocket expenditures. The country's health services feature a high degree of freedom of choice for both patients and providers, with remuneration primarily based on fee-for-service payments.

Martens et al. (2021) contend that the decentralisation of healthcare in Belgium has led to a fragmentation of decision-making power, undermining efforts towards integrated care. Van Belle et al. (2023) argue that reform attempts are highly politicised, emphasising the need for a comprehensive restructuring of the governance structure to enhance Belgium's health system. To guide this process, they propose six interconnected principles.

1.   Sense-making in building a shared long-term vision:

Establishing a long-term vision requires moving away from entrenched positions. All stakeholders must acknowledge the necessity of governance reform for the success of any health policy initiative. Key unifying narratives include addressing persistent health inequity and ensuring the health system's sustainability and resilience.

2.   Foster mind shifts required for health governance reform:

Underlying social values and societal dispositions play a crucial role in health system complexity. Emphasising values like social accountability, responsiveness, equity, sustainability, equitable resilience, and bottom-up intersectoral action calls for a more inclusive approach. Involving primary care stakeholders is key to creating and implementing a common vision at the local level.

3.   In a polycentric field, meta-governors are required:

The current complex federal system necessitates clear allocations of mandates, roles, and responsibilities. More importantly, the appointment of neutral, stable meta-governors operating beyond short-term and party-political goals is crucial. This may involve rethinking the roles of existing agencies or creating new mechanisms and agencies to facilitate coordination and ensure accountability.

4.   Clarify and strengthen accountability:

The lack of transparency of the current Belgian health governance system requires active management to increase accountability to citizens. Meta-governors are needed for this, backed by a robust legislative framework. Special attention is needed to provide an active voice to underserved groups.

5.   Pro-actively manage power dynamics at the local level:

Given Belgium's predominant medico-centred culture, the composition and capabilities of the overarching Care Council (ZorgRaad) in the Primary Care Zone are pivotal. Adequate funding is needed to provide a well-resourced team, enabling the Care Councils to not function as local meta-governors initiating innovations, beyond their current coordinating role.

6.   (Co-)create a health management information and learning system:

It is essential to establish a system that involves all stakeholders, including patients, citizens, healthcare, and social care workers. This system, linking local, regional, and national levels, should support decision-making processes across all levels of the healthcare system.

13.4.1 *Knowledge review*

Before you move on, can you define the following key concept:

• Decentralising healthcare governance?

13.4.2 Question to think about

Do you know how decentralised healthcare governance is where you live, and which level of governance is responsible for which services?

References

Alatawi, A. D., Niessen, L. W., & Khan, J. A. (2020). Efficiency evaluation of public hospitals in Saudi Arabia: An application of data envelopment analysis. *BMJ Open*, 10(1), e031924.

Alshehri, A., Balkhi, B., Gleeson, G., & Atassi, E. (2023). Efficiency and resource allocation in government hospitals in saudi arabi: A casemix index approach. *Healthcare (Basel, Switzerland)*, 11(18), 2513.

Asamani, J. A., Kigozi, J., Sikapande, B., Christmals, C. D., Okoroafor, S. C., Ismaila, H., ... Mwinga, K. (2022). Investing in the health workforce: Fiscal space analysis of 20 countries in East and Southern Africa, 2021–2026. *BMJ Global Health*, 7(Suppl. 1), e008416.

Banzon, E., & Mailfert, M. (2018). *Overcoming public sector inefficiencies toward universal healthcare, the case for national health insurance systems in Asia and the Pacific* (ADB Sustainable Development Working Paper No. 53). Asian Development Bank.

Belle, S. V., Michielsen, J., Cornu, T., Martens, M., & Marchal, B. (2023). The tale of nine belgian health ministers and a multi-level fragmented governance system: six guiding principles to improve integrated care, responsiveness, resilience and equity; a response to the recent commentaries. *International Journal of Health Policy and Management*, 12, 7848. https://doi .org/10.34172/ijhpm.2022.7848

Biggeri, M., Clark, D. A., Ferrannini, A., & Mauro, V. (2019). Tracking the SDGs in an 'integrated' manner: A proposal for a new index to capture synergies and trade-offs between and within goals. *World Development*, 122, 628–647.

Bisaga, I., Parikh, P., Tomei, J., & To, L. S. (2021). Mapping synergies and trade-offs between energy and the sustainable development goals: A case study of off-grid solar energy in Rwanda. *Energy Policy*, 149, 112028.

Cashin, C., Bloom, D., Sparkes, S., Barroy, H., Kutzin, J., & O'Dougherty, S. (2017). *Aligning public financial management and health financing: Sustaining progress toward universal health coverage* (Health Financing Working Paper No. 4). World Health Organisation.

Davies, N., Atkins, G., & Sodhi, S. (2021). *Using targets to improve public services*. Institute for Government.

Dubas-Jakóbczyk, K., Domagała, A., Zabdyr-Jamróz, M., Kowalska-Bobko, I., & Sowada, C. (2023). The 2021 plan for hospital care centralisation in Poland–When politics overwhelms the policy process. *Health Policy*, 129, 104707.

Garcia-Escribano, M., Juarros, P., & Mogues, T. (2022). *Patterns and drivers of health spending efficiency* (Working Paper No. 2022/48). International Monetary Fund.

Greene, W. (2004). Distinguishing between heterogeneity and inefficiency: Stochastic frontier analysis of the World Health Organization's panel data on national health care systems. *Health Economics*, 13(10), 959–980.

Heller, P. (2006). The prospect of creating 'fiscal space' for the health sector. *Health Policy and Planning*, 21(2), 7579.

Hofmann, B. (2022). Ethical issues with geographical variations in the provision of health care services. *BMC Medical Ethics*, 23(1), 127.

International Monetary Fund. (2018). *Five country cases illustrate how best to improve tax collection*. IMF.

International Monetary Fund. (2022). *First review under the stand-by arrangement and request for modifications of performance criteria and structural benchmarks* (IMF Country Report 22/389). IMF.

Martens, M., Danhieux, K., Van Belle, S., et al. (2021). Integration or fragmentation of health care? Examining policies and politics in a Belgian case study. *International Journal of Health Policy and Management*. doi:10.34172/ijhpm.2021.58.

Mills, E. (2016). Identifying and reducing the health and safety impacts of fuel-based lighting. *Energy for Sustainable Development*, 30, 39–50.

Puig-Junoy, J. (2000). Partitioning input cost efficiency into its allocative and technical components: An empirical DEA application to hospitals. *Socio-Economic Planning Sciences*, 34(3), 199-218.

Puig-Junoy, J. (2000). Partitioning input cost efficiency into its allocative and technical components: An empirical DEA application to hospitals. *Socio-Economic Planning Sciences*, 34(3), 199-218.

Rajapaksa, L., De Silva, P., Abeykoon, A., Somatunga, L., Sathasivam, S., Perera, S. Fernando, F., De Silva, D., Perera, A., Perera, U., Weerasekara, Y., Gamage, A., Wellappuli, N., Widanapathirana, N., Fernando, R., Wijesundara, C., Seneviratne, R., & Weerasinghe, K. (2021). *Sri Lanka health system review*. World Health Organisation Regional Office for South-East Asia.

Sreeramareddy, C. T., & Sathyanarayana, T. (2019). Decentralised versus centralised governance of health services. *The Cochrane Database of Systematic Reviews*, 2019(9), CD010830.

Stachel, L. (2013). Isha's dream – lighting up lives in Sierra Leone. *WeCare Solar*. http://wecaresolar.org/ishas-dream-lighting-up-health-care-in-sierra-leone/ [Accessed June 13, 2014]

Tandon, A., & Cashin, C. (2010). *Assessing public expenditure on health from a fiscal space perspective* (HNP Discussion Paper 56053). World Bank, Washington, DC.

Tikkanen, R., Osborn, R., Elias Mossialos, E., & Djordjevic Wharton, G. A. (2020). *International health care system profiles*. Commonwealth Fund.

van Vuuren, D. P., Zimm, C., Busch, S., Kriegler, E., Leininger, J., Messner, D., ... Soergel, B. (2022). Defining a sustainable development target space for 2030 and 2050. *One Earth*, 5(2), 142–156.

Section D
The healthcare industry

14 Healthcare as an industry

14.1 The healthcare industry

14.1.1 The size of the industry

Healthcare is one of the largest industry sectors in the world. It made up 18% of the value of the US economy and 11% of the value of the EU economy in 2023. Whilst the share of the economy in other countries is lower, the overall global figure approached 10% of global GDP in 2020. In the EU, the percentage of the economy devoted to healthcare is more than six times greater than the percentage spent in the defence sector.

The healthcare industry is one of the world's biggest employers. In 2020, the global workforce stock was 29.1 million nurses, 12.7 million medical doctors, 3.7 million pharmacists, 2.5 million dentists, 2.2 million midwives, and 14.9 million additional occupations, totalling 65.1 million health workers in all (Boniol et al., 2022). However, they are becoming a scarce resource.

By the year 2030, the global healthcare sector is projected to require approximately 80 million additional workers to fulfil the growing demand, with around 18 million of them necessary for low-income countries.

Presently, 83 countries in sub-Saharan Africa, Southeast Asia, South Asia, and Oceania fall short of meeting the basic standard of having 23 skilled health professionals per 10,000 people.

Despite the escalating need for healthcare professionals, there is an emerging trend where doctors and nurses express intentions to reduce their working hours. In the United States, one in four physicians and two in five nurses state their plans to exit the field of medicine. The United Kingdom may already be witnessing this trend, as evidenced by the increase in the attrition rate for hospital workers from 18% in 2019 to 26% in 2021, with approximately one-in-six hospitals reporting critical staffing shortages in 2019, even before this increase.

In the US, Shen et al. (2024) report that they found "a substantial and persistent increase in healthcare workforce turnover after the pandemic," and they go on to suggest that this "may have long-lasting implications for workers' willingness to remain in healthcare jobs."

We shall consider the industries operating in the healthcare market under four broad headings:

• Healthcare services and facilities
• Pharmaceuticals

DOI: 10.4324/9781003478874-18

- Manufacturers of medical devices, digital technologies, equipment, and hospital supplies
- Medical insurance, medical services, and managed care

14.1.2 Knowledge review

Before you move on, can you define the following key concepts:

- scarce resources?

14.1.3 Question to think about

How may the growing shortage of skilled healthcare professionals be addressed in an equitable way?

14.2 The major sectors in the healthcare industry

14.2.1 Healthcare services and facilities

The global healthcare services market experienced a growth from $7.5 trillion in 2022 to $7.98 trillion in 2023. The Russia-Ukraine war has resulted in economic sanctions on multiple nations, a rise in commodity prices, supply chain disruptions, and inflation affecting various markets worldwide. Despite the fact that the war has disrupted the potential for global economic recovery from the COVID-19 pandemic, the healthcare services market is anticipated to exceed 10 billion USD by 2028.

Other sectors such as pharmaceutical manufacturers and medical device suppliers generate over two trillion USD of business, and the global private health insurance market is worth a further 2.1 trillion USD in 20121, forecast to grow to 3.8 trillion USD by 2030.

All of the sectors of the healthcare business are forecast to show healthy growth for the foreseeable future and to maintain or grow their market share relative to other business sectors.

The healthcare services market encompasses revenues generated by entities offering human healthcare services, such as medical and diagnostic laboratory services, dental services, nursing care, residential substance abuse and mental health facilities, and other healthcare services. The market value includes the worth of associated goods sold by the service provider or integrated within the service offerings.

Hospitals provide medical, diagnostic, and treatment services to both inpatients and outpatients. They are often the focus of most attention not least because they account for most of the expenditure. However, their focus is generally on acute health events, and most healthcare relates to longer term issues or prevention.

In the UK, for example, most healthcare interactions occur in primary care settings. In addition to General Medical Practitioners, in primary care settings, care may be provided by a wide range of healthcare professionals including nurses, pharmacists, physiotherapists and other physical therapists, dentists, opticians and optometrists, psychologists, counsellors, and nutritionists and dietitians, in a variety of settings.

Nursing services provide residential or ambulatory care as needed for patients with needs defined by age, long term conditions, and physical and mental disability.

Healthcare providers organisations that supply healthcare services take many forms.

Large care facilities, such as hospitals, are normally run as autonomous organisations. They may run as corporations either as not for profit or for profit. In public healthcare systems, such as the UK and Canada, whilst public hospitals are part of the system, they operate with a high degree of financial autonomy. In Canada, the public hospitals are independent institutions incorporated under provincial Corporations Acts and are required by law to operate within their budget (Government of Canada, 2022). In the UK, there are additionally hospitals providing paid for care run by private companies some of whom are run for-profit and others as not-for profit.

In France, where healthcare is financed by social health insurance, almost two-thirds of hospital care is provided by publicly owned and managed hospitals. However, approximately one-sixth comes from non-profit sector hospitals (often connected to charitable or mutual organisations) and one-sixth from hospitals run for profit (Ridic et al., 2012).

In Switzerland, although financing is entirely through private health insurance, the largest hospitals are publicly owned.

This mixed ownership is reflected in other types of facilities irrespective of the source of funding. In 2019, in the UK, there were 332 million consultations within General Practice, and this had increased by 8.9% by 2022, without taking into account COVID-19 appointments (UK Parliament, 2022), which makes up the vast majority of NHS consultations. UK GP surgeries are private businesses, owned either by the partners or by external businesses, and run for profit, although those run by the partners do not have shareholders to remunerate. Concern has been raised about the increasing number of practices sold to external for-profit businesses often from the US and the implications for patient care (Cowling et al., 2017).

However, the episode of care is dependent upon a much wider range of suppliers. Drugs, medical devices, and IT devices are generally provided by for-profit businesses, albeit subject to significant levels of regulation in order to safeguard patients.

Many large hospitals have close links with education providers such as universities and medical and nursing schools, since one of the largest supply needs of the sector is the availability of staff in suitably qualified in medicine, nursing, allied health professions, and other related disciplines. The cost of training this workforce is often met wholly or partially by public funding. Increasingly, students are being required to contribute a greater proportion of the cost of their training, often in the form of students. Where there is a high degree of public funding, there are increasing pressures to require professionals to repay this by giving a number of years to the public healthcare system.

14.2.2 *The pharmaceutical industry*

The pharmaceutical industry develops, produces, and markets drugs and other treatments, licensed for use as medications. They can often deliver better health outcomes at lower costs than other methods by preventing or reducing the consequences of disease and eliminating the need for expensive and invasive alternatives such as surgery.

Pharmaceuticals play a crucial role in the provision of health services. In the year 2021, the global consumption of pharmaceuticals amounted to about 3,665 billion defined daily doses (DDD), according to IQVIA (2022). Considering our current global population of approximately eight billion people, this implies that every individual, from infants to seniors, regardless of location, consumes an average of 1.3 doses of pharmaceuticals per day. Over the past five years, there has been a 2.9% annual increase in pharmaceutical usage, primarily fuelled by growth in emerging markets such as Brazil, Indonesia, Mexico, and South Africa (IQVIA, 2022).

The pharmaceutical industry manufactures medications to address a wide range of medical conditions. According to projected global expenditure for 2026, the four primary areas of pharmaceutical usage are oncology (cancer), immunology (autoimmune conditions), antidiabetics (diabetes), and neurology (conditions impacting the nervous system such as epilepsy and Parkinson's disease). Oncology is anticipated to have the highest global spending in 2026 at $306 billion, followed by immunology ($178 billion), antidiabetics ($173 billion), and neurology ($151 billion) (IQVIA, 2022).

However, when prioritising therapy areas based on the volume of use, defined by defined daily doses, rather than global sales, the landscape shifts. Cardiovascular issues (heart and blood vessels), diabetes, kidney disease, and musculoskeletal disorders (muscles and bones) emerge as dominant areas in both emerging and developed markets (IQVIA, 2021).

Because of the potential for harm alongside the considerable benefits, the sector is subject to a high degree of regulation regarding the patenting, testing, safety, efficacy and marketing of drugs.

The pharmaceutical sector includes:

- prescription drugs for treatment or prevention
- OTC drugs for other purposes such as pain management
- vaccines for prevention of disease
- generic drugs, providing cheaper drugs once patents have expired
- food supplements and vitamins
- support services such as packaging and labelling services

Pharmaceutical companies are often criticised for the high price of new and especially of novel treatments but bringing a new drug to the market is an expensive business and many potential drugs do not get that far.

On the other hand, they are generally able to demonstrate healthy profits and significant growth in recent years.

By the end of 2021, the total global pharmaceutical market was valued at about 1.42 trillion USD, which represents around a 450% growth over the last 20 years (Mikulic, 2021). The sector employs in excess of five million staff around the world.

14.2.3 Medical devices, digital technologies, and other equipment

The global medical devices market was worth nearly 456.8 billion USD in 2020 and is expected to exceed 863 billion USD by 2030 (Business Research Company, 2024). There are more than 34,000 medical technology companies in Europe alone.

Medical devices vary from simple aids such as walking sticks to complex MRI scanners. Because of the potential risk to patient care, medical devices are highly regulated. The degree of regulation is based upon the classification of risk.

Digital technology is playing an increasing role in healthcare. Technology such as monitoring or scanning equipment are classified as medical devices. However, there are other digital technologies, such as electronic patient record systems, which are associated with the management of patient care. Zion Market Research (2022) reports that the global electronic health records market was worth around 29.4 billion USD in 2021 and is estimated to grow to about 42.2 billion USD by 2028.

At-home monitoring systems could alleviate the increasing demand resulting from a growing elderly population. For example, integrating technologies like smartwatches with remote sensors and monitors enables the ageing population to stay in their homes, reducing emergency room visits and enhancing both mental health and the quality of care. Consequently, the global market for remote monitoring devices is projected to experience substantial growth, reaching over $101 billion by 2028, up from approximately 30 billion USD in 2021, at an annual rate of 18.9% (Fortune Business Insights, 2022).

Deloitte (2023) anticipates a rise in the shipment of consumer health and wellness wearable devices to nearly 440 million worldwide by 2024. This increase includes smartwatches targeted at and bought by consumers, as well as medical-grade wearables, often referred to as "smart patches," prescribed by healthcare professionals and available over the counter. The increasing comfort of healthcare providers with these devices contributes to this trend.

Whilst virtual health services gained prominence during the pandemic, applications targeting mental health are growing in popularity amongst mobile users. Apps play a significant role in managing mental health conditions like anxiety or depression, complementing traditional therapies by providing access to mental health professionals through live chat, video, or telephone. These apps can also promote general well-being by encouraging behaviour changes such as mindfulness and meditation (Roffarello & De Russis, 2023).

The mental health app landscape is extensive, with approximately 20,000 apps available. Many developers are forging collaborations with other online services and apps like Snapchat and Bumble, expanding their consumer reach. Deloitte (2023) predicts continued growth in global spending on mobile mental health applications, which surged by 32% annually, reaching 269 million USD in the first 10 months of 2020 from 203 million USD during the same period in 2019, with an expected annual increase of around 20%.

The increased use of digital technology has also started to disrupt traditional healthcare delivery systems, including systems aimed at low-income countries designed to provide cost-effective methods of achieving universal healthcare coverage.

Babylon Health started in the UK, but they also operate in the US, India, and around a dozen countries in South East Asia. In Africa, they launched in Rwanda in September 2016 as Babyl, in partnership with the Bill & Melinda Gates Foundation. By May 2018, Babyl was reported to have two million members, covering roughly 30% of Rwanda's adult population, and in January 2020, they reported one million completed consultations in Rwanda. Following this announcement, in March that year, they agreed to roll out Babyl to all Rwandans over the age of 12 through the government's community-based health insurance scheme, Mutuelle de Santé, which is switching from a model of funding based on fee-per-service to a capitation-based model . Whilst this illustrates the possibilities of digital technology, the New Times (2024) reported that Babylon Health, operating as Babyl in Rwanda, had recently ceased its operations in the country. The development follows the permanent closure of Babylon Health's U.S. operations, resulting in the laying off of 94 employees. This illustrates the risks associated with a country becoming dependent upon a single private provider.

14.2.4 Medical insurance and managed care

The value of the global private health insurance market is estimated at over two trillion USD in 2021 and is expected to reach 3.79 trillion USD by 2030, growing at an annual growth rate of around 6.8% during this decade (Skyquest, 2022).

One of the key driving factors that will drive the health insurance market in this decade is the ageing population. A large proportion of the elderly population suffers from one or more chronic diseases, such as heart disease, cancer, type 2 diabetes, or arthritis, and this increases the demand for health insurance policies among this age group. Furthermore, the adoption of sedentary lifestyles among the adult population is increasing the patient pool with various chronic diseases.

Although these factors have traditionally been seen in high-income countries, many middle-income countries are also now showing populations and this will lead to similar trends. The percentage of the global population aged 65 and above is expected to rise from 10% in 2022 to 16% in 2050, and the world's population of people aged 60 years and older will double to 2.1 billion over the same period.

North America is currently the dominant region in the global health insurance market. In the US, government initiatives to provide low-cost Medicare and Medicaid insurance, as well as increase the population covered by healthcare policies, are expected to continue to drive regional growth. Furthermore, the high cost of medical products in this region, as well as favourable healthcare reimbursement policies, support market growth. In Canada, although healthcare services are provided by the government and parallel private provision is banned, pharmaceutical costs for working adults are covered by private insurance, and this is a growing market.

However, the Asia Pacific market is expected to be the fastest-growing market due to the increasing penetration of private providers in this region and the increasing launch of schemes by central and state governments.

In addition, the ageing population and rising prevalence of chronic diseases and densely populated countries, such as China and India, will support market growth.

At the other end of the market, the limited penetration of insurance companies in the emerging markets of Latin America, and the Middle East and Africa are expected to account for lower market shares during the 2020s.

Private health insurance in China (after Wu & Ercia, 2020)

Private health insurance was introduced in China during the economic reforms of the 1980s, with the government viewing it as a potential financial source for the health system and a means to address gaps in the existing social health insurance system. The expansion of private insurance was seen as a way to provide coverage for individuals unable to access social insurance and to complement and supplement coverage for those already covered by social insurance plans. Initially limited to corporate customers, demand for private insurance increased from the mid-1990s, leading to the emergence of more commercial insurers.

Over the years, the private insurance market in China has experienced rapid growth in terms of total aggregate premium income. Government officials aimed to create a mutually reinforcing relationship between social and private insurance, with private insurance filling gaps in social coverage and social expansion boosting the private insurance market. Initiatives such as tax incentives for employers and individuals purchasing private insurance were introduced to encourage uptake.

Despite this growth, there are ongoing debates regarding the effectiveness of private insurance in achieving universal health coverage.

One argument against the effectiveness of private insurance in expanding coverage is its reliance on individuals' willingness and capacity to pay, potentially leaving low-income populations without coverage. Risk-rated premiums could make coverage unaffordable for certain groups, exacerbating inequities. The private insurance market is also susceptible to market failures, including moral hazard and adverse selection. Moral hazard may lead to suboptimal care and increased costs, while adverse selection can result in inaccurate premium setting based on average risks, favouring those with above-average health risks.

Wu and Ercia (2020) found that private insurance coverage prevalence increased since 2000, but commercial insurers' income from private insurance increased disproportionately, indicating an upmarket movement in China's private insurance market. Many private insurance plans are bundled with other products, potentially inflating the costs attributed to private insurance premiums without a proportional increase in coverage.

The distribution of private insurance in China appears to favour affluent urban and eastern areas, indicating unequal access. Limited selling agencies, information availability, and poor connections in less affluent areas, makes private insurance less effective for low-income populations. Implementing private insurance as a means to improve universal health coverage faces challenges in expanding coverage while ensuring equity.

The profitability of the private insurance market in China is still uncertain, leading commercial insurers to hesitate in expanding business to attract less affluent populations. Government subsidies or tax breaks may aid expansion but may disproportionately benefit more affluent groups. Additionally, affluent regions may introduce additional subsidies, exacerbating inequalities in accessing private insurance across the country. Therefore, achieving effective universal health coverage through private insurance in China requires addressing challenges related to coverage expansion and equity protection.

14.2.5 *Knowledge review*

Before you move on, can you define the following key concepts:

• Moral hazard?

14.2.6 *Question to think about*

How can private health insurance companies be incentivised to make their products more equitable? Why might this not be desirable?

14.3 The ethics of healthcare as a market

Running healthcare as a commercial market raises several ethical concerns, as it introduces market dynamics into an essential service that involves the well-being and lives of individuals. These ethical concerns may be seen at an individual level or affecting groups within the population of a single country or whole countries of regions.

14.3.1 Conflicts of interest

The involvement of for-profit entities in healthcare can create conflicts of interest, where decisions about patient care, treatment options, or medical research may be influenced by financial considerations rather than the best interests of patients or public health.

Ethical concerns may arise when patients, driven by financial constraints or lack of information, make healthcare decisions without fully understanding the implications. Informed consent becomes challenging in situations where financial considerations play a significant role in treatment choices.

The commercialisation of healthcare can impact the traditional physician-patient relationship. Physicians may face pressures to meet financial targets or prioritise revenue-generating procedures, potentially compromising the trust and integrity of the doctor-patient relationship.

In the United States, it is commonplace for physicians to receive financial payments from the pharmaceutical industry. Mitchell et al. (2021) conducted a systematic review of 36 studies of prescribing practice, encompassing 101 distinct analyses. The objective was to assess whether physicians' receipt of payments from the drug industry correlated with their prescribing practices. Among the 101 individual analyses examined, 89 revealed a positive correlation.

They found that such payments were linked to an increase in prescribing the pharmaceutical company's specific drug, heightened prescription costs, and an increase in the use of branded drugs. The observed association between industry payments and physician prescribing remained consistent across all studies that explored this relationship. Additionally, findings regarding temporal patterns and dose-response indicated a likely causal connection.

Corruption occurs when a conflict of interest is exploited for personal gain. Bozhenko (2022) suggests that global fraud and corruption costs the world's healthcare system average of about 455 billion USD annually or 6.2% of the total budget. He argues that the COVID-19 pandemic has further exacerbated the challenge of transparency, accountability, and oversight mechanisms in the healthcare sector.

Since the onset of the pandemic, there has been a surge in incidents involving bribery to secure preferential access to medical services, tests, and equipment, as well as attempts to evade quarantine. Additionally, the falsification of medical drugs has become more prevalent due to heightened demand and limited supply (GRECO, 2020). On average, approximately 6% of citizens in European Union countries resorted to paying bribes for access to medical services, while 29% relied on personal connections.

Transparency International (2021) suggests that amongst EU countries, the level of bribery in the field of healthcare was the highest in Romania (22%), Bulgaria (19%), Lithuania (19%), and Hungary (18%).

14.3.2 Access inequality

In a market-driven healthcare system, access to medical services may be influenced by an individual's financial means. Those with higher incomes might have better access to quality healthcare, potentially leading to inequalities in health outcomes. This raises ethical questions about fairness and social justice. However, larger inequalities are likely to arise from inequalities in the social determinants of health. Inequalities may arise both within and between countries.

In a government-led healthcare system, the healthcare system is a means to reduce the inequalities caused by social determinants such as income, race, gender, and neighbourhood deprivation. In a healthcare system driven by profit, providers and insurers are likely to actively seek the wealthier clients, reinforcing the health inequalities.

However, a study of European national health systems by Baeten et al. (2018) concluded that inequalities in access to healthcare cannot be demonstrated to be linked to the model of health system funding. They categorise health systems into three models, depending on how they are funded: Government-funded national health systems, social health insurance, and systems based on private health insurance funds. They found well-performing countries amongst all three models. They suggest that the performance of systems in terms of safeguarding access is related to the country-specific details of the organisation of healthcare provision and the way in which vulnerable groups are protected from user charges within each of the systems, rather than the funding system.

However, the private insurance funds in this study are operating in Lithuania, Netherlands, and Switzerland. They are subject to a high degree of government regulation. The private health insurance premiums are mandated and directly paid by the insured members to the insurance company on an individual basis or are paid by the employer and deducted from the salary of the employee or may be paid by unemployment insurance. Premiums are, as a rule, not related to income. In principle, insurers must accept all applicants. In both Lithuania and the Netherlands, all persons covered by the same insurer pay the same premium regardless of age, gender, and health status (Baeten et al., 2018). Thus, in these countries, although health funding is derived from private health insurance funds, they do not operate a free market.

14.3.3 Profit motives vs. patient welfare

Treating healthcare as a market commodity can lead to the commodification of health, where medical services are viewed as products to be bought and sold. Critics argue that this commodification undermines the intrinsic value of health and healthcare, potentially eroding the ethical foundations of the medical profession.

When healthcare becomes a commodity, there is a risk that profit motives may take precedence over patient welfare. Pavlakis and Roach (2021) argue that:

As long as healthcare is considered a commodity instead of a basic right, it will be susceptible to market forces and to efforts to maximize profit. Our entrepreneurial healthcare system all but ensures that patients with more resources will receive different care than other individuals

Ethical conflicts may arise when decisions about treatment and care are influenced by financial considerations rather than what is in the best interest of the patient.

- Pharmaceutical companies may influence healthcare providers to over-prescribe certain medications that are more expensive or have a higher profit margin, even if they may not be the most effective or necessary for the patient and the review by Mitchell et al. (2021) supports the view that this is actually occurring.
- Some healthcare providers or facilities may perform unnecessary medical procedures solely for financial gain. This can include surgeries, diagnostic tests, or treatments

that are not medically justified but contribute significantly to the provider's revenue. Choonara and Eyles (2016) report on instances in the US, Brazil, and elsewhere including unnecessary caesarean sections and colonoscopies.

- Insurance companies may deny coverage for necessary treatments or medications to maximise profits, leading to delays or denials of care for patients. This can happen through strict coverage policies or high out-of-pocket costs.
- Healthcare facilities may cut corners on staffing levels, training, or resources to reduce costs, potentially compromising the quality of patient care. For example, inadequate nurse staffing levels could lead to patient neglect or errors. Inadequate levels may be in terms of absolute numbers or in terms of experience, since more experienced staff are more expensive. Aiken et al. (2018) found that a 10% increase in the proportion of professional nurses amongst care personnel responsible for frontline nursing care was associated with 11% lower risk of mortality after general surgery and 10% lower risks of poor hospital ratings from patients.
- Pharmaceutical companies may manipulate or selectively report clinical trial data to make their drugs appear more effective or safer than they actually are, prioritising profits over providing accurate information to healthcare professionals and patients. Selective reporting may not always be motivated by a deliberate desire to mislead but in a study of 471 publications. Salandra (2018) found that the odds of selective reporting are higher for industry-funded studies than for publicly-funded studies.
- In a market-oriented healthcare system, there may be a tendency for healthcare providers to prioritise services that are more profitable over those that are essential for public health. This can result in a skewed distribution of resources and an ethical dilemma regarding the allocation of healthcare resources. Alpern et al. (2019) highlight cases where drugs have been withdrawn in spite of ongoing patient need due to the manufacturer deeming to be insufficiently profitable.

14.3.4 Affordability and financial barriers

Healthcare costs in a market-driven system can be prohibitive, leading to financial barriers that prevent individuals from seeking necessary medical care. Ethically, there are concerns about individuals being denied access to essential services based on their ability to pay. Vulnerable groups, such as the uninsured, low-income individuals, and marginalised communities, may face heightened ethical challenges in a market-driven healthcare system. The potential neglect of these populations raises concerns about justice, equity, and the ethical obligation to care for the most vulnerable. A further inequity arises because OOP expenditures for maternal healthcare in private health facilities are much higher than in public health facilities (Ladusingh et al., 2018).

In countries where there is little public provision, the burden of healthcare costs often falls on out-of-pocket expenses. The combination of low income, unexpected expenditure, and weak cost-controls in such systems can lead to catastrophic expenditure, which in turn, leads to vulnerable people either avoiding accessing care or facing bankruptcy sometimes for whole family groups Figure 14.1 compares the percentage of household income devoted to OOP healthcare expenditure with the GDP per capita in 2019. Whilst there is a wide distribution, there is a greater incidence of high OOP expenditure in lower income countries.

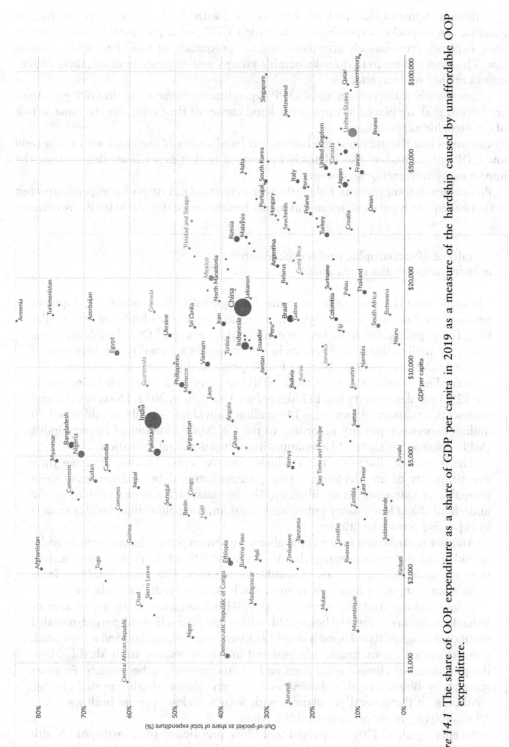

Figure 14.1 The share of OOP expenditure as a share of GDP per capita in 2019 as a measure of the hardship caused by unaffordable OOP expenditure.

Although countries like the United States and Switzerland have some of the highest absolute out-of-pocket expenditures, their high GDP per capita means that for many these expenses are relatively affordable and the percentage of GDP per capita remains low. This does not mean that for vulnerable groups within these countries, these expenditures are not problematic.

Countries where the percentage of OOP expenditure is highest and the GDP per capita are lowest, that are placed at the top left-hand corner of the graph, are the most at risk of catastrophic expenditure.

Countries like Rwanda near the bottom left hand corner of the chart with a relatively low GDP per capita but also relatively low out-of-pocket expenditure demonstrate the impact of a government-run system.

Private health insurance can reduce the worst effects of out-of-pocket expenditures but without adequate regulation, it can still render healthcare unaffordable for many citizens.

Prevalence of catastrophic health expenditure in India (after Swetha et al., 2020)

Although India is a prominent economic force globally, its economic development has not been matched by developments in healthcare and the health of the population. The population in India bears a considerable burden of OOP health expenses, primarily attributable to deficiencies in public healthcare quality, the high cost of private healthcare, and the absence of widespread health insurance coverage.

According to estimates from the UNDP, the percentage of people living below the $2.15 per day poverty line in India reduced to 10% in 2021. However, this still represents a substantial number – 140 million individuals – while an additional 70 million experience poverty according to the UN Multidimensional Poverty Index (MPI), considering factors like malnutrition, education, and sanitation.

The impact of diseases on individuals extends beyond health, affecting their overall quality of life, depleting savings, accumulating debt, and rendering them incapable of managing future illnesses. The financial strain is exacerbated by the underfunded and low-quality public health system, compelling individuals to resort to expensive private healthcare.

Another contributing factor is the absence of protective measures, such as widespread health insurance coverage, leaving less than 10% of the population insulated from the financial implications of healthcare expenses. This unpredictability leads to an annual impoverishment of approximately 3.3% of India's population.

A longitudinal study by Swetha et al. (2020) conducted in an urban area of Bangalore city, involving 350 households with a one-year follow-up period, revealed significant insights. Based upon a simple random sampling method and a pre-tested, semi-structured questionnaire administered in interviews, the study shed light on the prevalence of chronic conditions and healthcare-seeking behaviours. Previous research by Bhojani et al. indicated an 8.6% prevalence of self-reported chronic conditions in the general population, with 80.6% seeking private healthcare and 19.4% relying on government health services.

Swetha et al. (2020) discovered a 14.9% prevalence of catastrophic health expenditure, with over 85% of these cases linked to one or more chronic diseases.

Notably, they established a statistically significant association between socio-economic status and catastrophic health expenditure.

In response to these findings, Swetha et al. (2020) advocate for alleviating the financial burden of high healthcare expenses through enhancements to the government healthcare system, provision of free medications for chronic disease patients, and improvements in insurance scheme benefits.

14.3.5 Knowledge review

Before you move on, can you define the following key concepts:

- Conflicts of interest?

14.3.6 Question to think about

Which healthcare services are funded by out-of-pocket expenditure in your country or region? How affordable are they? Have you or your family ever avoided seeking treatment because of the cost?

14.4 Environmental sustainability in the healthcare industry

The healthcare sector, while essential for addressing health needs, is not immune to sustainability challenges. Environmental sustainability in healthcare refers to the responsible management of natural resources to fulfil current healthcare needs without compromising the ability of future generations to meet theirs.

Several key environmental sustainability issues exist within the healthcare sector.

14.4.1 Energy consumption and carbon footprint

Healthcare facilities are energy-intensive, leading to a substantial carbon footprint. Healthcare facilities consume energy to provide lighting, power medical equipment, heat water, and supply heating and air conditioning. Hospitals consume more energy than other non-residential buildings per square metre of floor space, partly because they are in use 24 hours a day.

Globally, however, there are major differences in energy consumption in healthcare:

- Close to one billion people in low- and lower-middle-income countries are estimated to be served by healthcare facilities without reliable electricity or with no electricity access at all.
- Electricity is needed to power critical and life-saving medical devices as well as the most basic services such as lighting, communications and clean water supply. Electricity is crucial for the availability and reliability of essential health services, as well as for bettering health, with outcomes such as safe childbirth, vaccination, diagnostic capacity, and emergency response.

- In low- and lower-middle-income countries of South Asia and sub-Saharan Africa, approximately 12% and 15% of healthcare facilities, respectively, have no access to electricity.
- In sub-Saharan Africa, only half of hospitals have reliable electricity access and the energy access challenge is higher for healthcare facilities in remote and rural areas.

(World Health Organisation, 2023)

High energy consumption contributes to greenhouse gas emissions, exacerbating climate change. Brown et al. (2012) found that health-related emissions in England and the US account for 3% and 8% of total national emissions, respectively.

Efforts to reduce energy use through energy-efficient technologies and renewable energy sources are crucial for sustainability. Many of the parts of the world, where electricity is needed for healthcare, have climates where renewable energy is plentiful, but the World Bank estimates that USD 4.9 billion is urgently needed to bring healthcare facilities in 63 low- and middle-income countries up to a minimal or intermediate level of electrification to ensure that all the essential health services are covered.

Sustainable electrification of healthcare facilities in low income countries (after Soto et al., 2022)

Soto et al. (2022) investigated how electricity can be provided sustainably and affordably in low-income countries. Operational lighting constitutes 19% of hospital energy consumption, and various alternatives have been proposed to reduce energy usage, incorporating more efficient technologies and renewable energy sources. Energy-efficient suggestions encompass enhancing the quality of luminaires and employing lighting modelling before construction. The implementation of high-quality luminaires, like LEDs, can cut energy consumption by approximately 50% compared to fluorescent lighting. Lighting modelling can estimate the required light for each space and time, facilitating mechanisms to reduce energy consumption before construction (Olatomiwa et al., 2018).

Effective lighting is crucial in healthcare institutions for safe medical procedures and night-time access to services. Inadequate illumination impacts safety and maternal mortality rates. Providing minimal light and electric power to surgical equipment, as suggested by Olatomiwa et al. (2018), could potentially reduce maternal mortality by 70%. Integrating renewable energy into buildings is paramount, especially in regions like Europe, where the building sector accounts for 40–45% of total energy consumption.

Healthcare facilities rely on diverse equipment, including communication systems, crucial for efficient information management and patient transfers. In areas with a shortage of healthcare workers, solar energy can sustain communication equipment, facilitating systems like telemedicine to enhance service efficiency.

Telemedicine has proven effective in overcoming barriers in developing countries, addressing issues like geographic access, availability, and affordability. Refrigeration is vital for healthcare institutions, especially for supplies requiring proper storage. Improper refrigeration practices lead to vaccine inefficacy, and low-cost renewable energy systems, such as solar energy, can offer refrigeration solutions in areas lacking reliable electricity (Sandoval Aguilar, 2022).

Sterilisation is crucial in preventing infections in healthcare facilities, and without stable electricity, non-WHO-approved methods are employed. Roughly 50–60 million people worldwide suffer from wounds, with 20% of patients developing postoperative infections (Ouedraogo & Schimanski, 2018). Electricity is essential for medical equipment, and studies have shown that using electric incubators in Kenyan health institutions reduced neonatal death rates from 40% to 28% (Ouedraogo & Schimanski, 2018). Additionally, renewable energy sources, like solar energy, can provide reliable energy to medical equipment, ensuring prompt emergency responses.

The opportunity to electrify healthcare facilities for the one billion global citizens who do not currently have access to facilities with electricity is a major opportunity to improve healthcare sustainably, consistent with both Sustainable Development Goal 7, which seeks to ensure access to affordable, sustainable, and modern energy for all, and Goal 3 on health.

14.4.2 *Waste generation*

Healthcare generates significant amounts of waste, including hazardous and non-hazardous materials. Healthcare waste is composed of sharps, heavy metals, pharmaceutical, infectious waste, genotoxic waste, chemical waste, anatomical and pathological, and pressurised containers. Proper waste management, recycling, and the adoption of reusable materials can help mitigate this issue.

European Union legislation separates healthcare waste into the following three categories of materials:

- waste that poses a risk of infection
- waste that is a chemical hazard
- medicines and medicinally contaminated waste containing a pharmaceutically active agent

In practice, almost 85% of waste generated by healthcare activity is considered 'non-hazardous waste' and the remaining 15% is labelled as 'hazardous' (Kenny & Priyadarshini, 2021).

The escalating volume of healthcare waste has led to an increase in disposal practices such as landfilling, composting, and the preferred method of incineration. However, these disposal methods have been associated with significant environmental and human health issues. Incineration, for instance, poses risks of emitting pollutants like acid gases, oxides of nitrogen, metals, particulate matter, and sulphur, with adverse effects on the respiratory and endocrine systems, contributing to chronic diseases and cancers.

The impact of healthcare waste disposal practices is influenced by various factors, including waste type, classification, segregation mechanisms, and waste management techniques. Compliance with advanced technological and legislative guidelines, such as those provided by the European Community, is crucial to ensuring clean and safe incineration processes. Conversely, improper healthcare waste disposal, often due to factors like lack of facilities, equipment, education, training, or regulation, has disastrous effects on the environment and human health.

Notably, healthcare waste disposal involves not only healthcare settings but also patients who contribute significantly. Improper disposal of medications by adults can lead to unsafe pharmaceutical compounds entering the environment, posing health risks to the general public.

Efforts have been made to adopt "greener" and "safer" healthcare waste disposal methods, including autoclaving, microwaving, and steam auger. However, these methods come with challenges and are often complementary rather than replacements for conventional techniques. The limitations in managing large volumes of waste and the lack of widespread availability hinder their effectiveness. Despite initiatives for waste management education and "green hospital" practices, serious problems and safety issues persist.

The growing global population, increased lifespan, and the rise in chronic diseases contribute to a surge in healthcare waste production, emphasising the need for improved waste management. The existing disposal methods are limited in addressing the global healthcare waste problem, necessitating a deeper understanding of the barriers to innovation and improved technologies. The extent of the damaging effects of healthcare waste disposal methods remains widely underestimated, highlighting the urgent need for a better understanding and global change to mitigate both health and environmental consequences.

In their review, Kenny and Priyadarshini (2021) conclude that although there are many innovations under investigation in healthcare waste management, few so far have proved able to demonstrate scalable improvements in this literally growing problem.

Disposal of biomedical waste in India (after Thakur et al., 2021)

The World Health Organisation and the Indian Government, under the biomedical waste (BMW) (Management & Handling) Rules 1998, categorised biomedical waste as the second most hazardous type of waste, after only radioactive waste. Strict policies have been established to treat it as special waste (Hsu et al., 2008).

Developing countries, such as India, encounter significant challenges in effectively implementing healthcare waste management policies. State Pollution Control Boards in India have identified a major challenge: the lack of budget allocation by hospital administrations for waste management activities (Hsu et al., 2008). Another obstacle in establishing a healthcare waste management system is the employment of unskilled and illiterate workers handling infectious waste, putting their lives at risk and sometimes recycling the waste without proper chemical treatment (Ho, 2011).

A WHO report in 2012, encompassing 22 developing countries, including India, revealed that approximately 18% to 64% of healthcare establishments poorly manage healthcare waste (Zhang et al., 2013).

14.4.3 *Water use and pollution*

Water is inextricably linked to healthcare. Failure to provide access to clean water creates a major disease burden.

Every year:

- There are 1.7 billion cases of diarrhoea among children younger than five years.
- An estimated 446,000 children younger than five years die from diarrhoea, mostly in low- and middle-income countries. This contributes to 9% of the 5.8 million deaths of children under five.
- There are three million cases of cholera leading to an estimated 95,000 deaths.
- There are 11 million cases of typhoid fever leading to an estimated 129,000 deaths.

Universal access to safe drinking water, adequate sanitation, and hygiene has the potential to reduce the global disease burden by 10%. All cholera deaths are preventable (Center for Disease Control, 2022).

Healthcare facilities need large amounts of water for various purposes, including patient care, sanitation, and facility maintenance. Water scarcity and the environmental impact of water usage are growing concerns. Implementing water-saving technologies and adopting water-efficient practices are crucial for sustainable water management.

However, this picture of potentially unsustainable water consumption by healthcare facilities in high income countries contrasts sharply with the situation in LMICs, where Cronk and Bartram (2018) reported that:

- 50% of facilities lack access to piped water
- 33% of facilities lack adequate sanitation
- 39% of facilities lack soap for handwashing
- 39% of facilities lack adequate infectious waste disposal

Work towards improving facilities in line with SDG6 under the global WASH programme led by UNICEF.

In addition to providing access to clean water and conserving its use of water, the healthcare sector also must consider the impact of its disposal of waste and contaminated water. Healthcare relies on various chemicals, including pharmaceuticals and cleaning agents. Improper disposal and the release of these substances into water bodies can lead to water pollution and harm ecosystems. sustainable procurement practices and the use of environmentally friendly alternatives are essential for reducing chemical-related environmental impacts. Improper disposal of pharmaceuticals and the excretion of active substances by patients can result in the presence of pharmaceutical residues in water bodies. This can have adverse effects on aquatic ecosystems and potentially lead to the development of antibiotic-resistant bacteria. Proper disposal methods and improved wastewater treatment are needed to address this issue.

Water pollution in Portugal and the role of hospitals (after Morin-Crini et al., 2022)

Water pollution in Portugal has been extensively monitored according to a review by Sousa et al. (2018). Since 2015, several research groups have conducted extensive monitoring of pharmaceuticals. In the Tejo estuarine waters, a comprehensive study focused on 66 human and veterinary pharmaceuticals from seven therapeutic groups, revealing antibiotics, β-blockers, antihypertensives, lipid regulators, and anti-inflammatories as the therapeutic classes in over 90% of samples (Reis-Santos et al., 2018).

A separate year-long monitoring study targeting 23 pharmaceuticals in Tejo and Mondego Rivers (Pereira et al., 2020) identified a site in the Tejo River with comparable concentrations of diclofenac, gemfibrozil, and bezafibrate. Pharmaceuticals were detected in 27.8% of the samples, with the highest frequencies and mean concentrations found in selective serotonin reuptake inhibitors, anti-inflammatories, and antibiotics. The study confirmed the influence of wastewater treatment plants on rising mean concentrations downstream and highlighted the impact of lower river flow rates on increasing frequencies and concentrations. Although risk quotients were found to be excessive for only two pharmaceuticals, the authors emphasised the ecotoxicological pressure, particularly during water scarcity in drought periods, posing a risk in rivers located in the Iberia region.

A study conducted in Lisbon's drinking water supply system investigated 31 pharmaceuticals in surface waters from Tejo and Zêzere Rivers, detecting 15 and 10 pharmaceuticals, respectively. Caffeine, erythromycin, acetaminophen, sulfadiazine, sulfapyridine, sulfamethoxazole, carbamazepine, and atenolol were quantified in both rivers, while propranolol, sulfamethazine, gemfibrozil, indomethacin, ibuprofen, diclofenac, and naproxen were found in the Tejo River. Nimesulide was determined only in the Zêzere River. Despite the quantification of these pharmaceuticals, the study suggested that exposure to residual pharmaceuticals in drinking water was improbable.

Cytostatics, a class of environmental relevance due to increasing cancer incidence and cytostatic consumption, were investigated in river water samples. From seven cytostatics studied, mycophenolic acid was the only one detected in Uíma, Douro, and Leça Rivers (Santos et al., 2018).

In a separate study analysing 27 pharmaceuticals, including antibiotics and psychiatric drugs in Douro and Leça Rivers (Fernandes et al., 2020), higher frequencies and concentrations were reported in the Leça River. Notably, six antibiotics were found, with azithromycin registering the highest concentration and fluoxetine being the most frequently detected pharmaceutical. Interestingly, none of the studied antibiotics were detected in the Douro River samples. Concurrent monitoring studies focusing on pharmaceuticals and other compound classes, such as pesticides, have been conducted in recent years. For example, a monitoring programme in four rivers (Ave, Antuã, Cértima, and Leça) reported spatial and temporal variations of 39 priority substances and contaminants of emerging concern, some of which are included in European directives.

14.4.4 Knowledge review

Before you move on, can you define the following key concepts:

- Environmental sustainability in healthcare?

14.4.5 Question to think about

How far do higher income countries have a responsibility to help fund sustainability in lower-income countries given that all countries exist within an interlinked global ecosystem?

References

Aiken, L. H., Ceron, C., Simonetti, M., Lake, E. T., Galiano, A., Garbarini, A., ... Smith, H. L. (2018). Hospital nurse staffing and patient outcomes. *Revista Médica Clínica Las Condes*, 29(3), 322–327.

Alpern, J. D., Dunlop, S. J., & Stauffer, W. M. (2019). Broken drug markets in infectious diseases: Opportunities outside the private sector?. *PLoS Neglected Tropical Diseases*, 13(4), e0007190.

Baeten, R., Spasova, S., Vanhercke, B., & Coster, S. (2018). *Inequalities in access to healthcare: A study of national policies 2018*. European Social Policy Network (ESPN), European Commission Directorate-General for Employment, Social Affairs and Inclusion, Directorate C — Social Affairs, B-1049 Brussels

Bhojani, U., Thriveni, B. S., Devadasan, R., Munegowda, C. M., Devadasan, N., Kolsteren, P., & Criel, B. (2012). Out-of-pocket healthcare payments on chronic conditions impoverish urban poor in Bangalore, India. *BMC Public Health*, 12(1), 1–14.

Boniol, M., Kunjumen, T., Nair, T. S., Siyam, A., Campbell, J., & Diallo, K. (2022). The global health workforce stock and distribution in 2020 and 2030: A threat to equity and 'universal' health coverage?. *BMJ Global Health*, 7(6), e009316.

Bozhenko, V. (2022). Tackling corruption in the health sector. *Health Economics and Management Review*, 3(3), 32–39.

Brown, L. H., Buettner, P. G., & Canyon, D. V. (2012). The energy burden and environmental impact of health services. *American Journal of Public Health*, 102(12), e76–e82.

Business Research Company, The. (2024). *Healthcare services global market report 2023*. Business Research Company.

Center for Disease Control. (2022). *Global water, sanitation, & hygiene (WASH) facts, centers for disease control and prevention*. National Center for Emerging and Zoonotic Infectious Diseases (NCEZID), Division of Foodborne, Waterborne, and Environmental Diseases at CDC. Data reviewed May 31, 2022

Choonara, S., & Eyles, J. (2016). Out of control: Profit-seeking behaviour, unnecessary medical procedures and rising costs of private medical care in South Africa. *BMJ Global Health*, 1(1), e000013.

Cowling, T. E., Laverty, A. A., Harris, M. J., Watt, H. C., Greaves, F., & Majeed, A. (2017). Contract and ownership type of general practices and patient experience in England: Multilevel analysis of a national cross-sectional survey. *Journal of the Royal Society of Medicine*, 110, 440–451. doi:10.1177/0141076817738499 pmid:29096580

Cronk, R., & Bartram, J. (2018). Environmental conditions in health care facilities in low- and middle-income countries: Coverage and inequalities. *International Journal of Hygiene and Environmental Health*, 221(3), 409–422.

Deloitte. (2023). *Global health care Outlook, 2023 global life sciences Outlook*. Deloitte.

Fortune Business Insights. (2022, February). *Remote patient monitoring devices market size, share & COVID-19 impact analysis*. Fortune Business Insights.

GRECO. (2020). *Corruption risks and useful legal references in the context of COVID-19*. GRECO.

Government of Canada. (2022). *Canada's health care system*. Government of Canada/ Gouvernement du Canada.

Fernandes, M. J., Paíga, P., Silva, A., Llaguno, C. P., Carvalho, M., Vázquez, F. M., & Delerue-Matos, C. (2020). Antibiotics and antidepressants occurrence in surface waters and sediments collected in the north of Portugal. *Chemosphere*, 239, 124729.

Ho, C. C. (2011). Optimal evaluation of infectious medical waste disposal companies using the fuzzy analytic hierarchy process. *Waste Management*, 31(7), 1553–1559.

Hsu, P. F., Wu, C. R., & Li, Y. T. (2008). Selection of infectious medical waste disposal firms by using the analytic hierarchy process and sensitivity analysis. *Waste Management*, 28(8), 1386–1394.

IQVIA. (2021). *Global medicine spending and usage trends: Outlook to 2025*. IQVIA.

IQVIA. (2022). *The global use of medicines 2022: Outlook to 2026*. IQVIA.

Kenny, C., & Priyadarshini, A. (2021). Review of current healthcare waste management methods and their effect on global health. *Healthcare (Basel, Switzerland)*, 9(3), 284.

Ladusingh, L., Mohanty, S. K., & Thangjam, M. (2018). Triple burden of disease and out of pocket healthcare expenditure of women in India. *PLoS One*, 13(5), e0196835.

Mikulic, M. (2021). *Pharmaceutical market: Worldwide revenue 2001-2021*. Statista GmbH.

Mitchell, A. P., Trivedi, N. U., Gennarelli, R. L., Chimonas, S., Tabatabai, S. M., Goldberg, J., … Korenstein, D. (2021). Are financial payments from the pharmaceutical industry associated with physician prescribing? A systematic review. *Annals of Internal Medicine*, 174(3), 353–361.

Olatomiwa, L., Blanchard, R., Mekhilef, S., & Akinyele, D. (2018). Hybrid renewable energy supply for rural healthcare facilities: An approach to quality healthcare delivery. *Sustainable Energy Technologies and Assessments*, 30, 121–138.

Ouedraogo, N. S., & Schimanski, C. (2018). Energy poverty in healthcare facilities: A "silent barrier" to improved healthcare in sub-Saharan Africa. *Journal of Public Health Policy*, 39, 358–371

Pavlakis, S., & Roach, E. S. (2021). Follow the money: Childhood health care disparities magnified by COVID-19. *Pediatric Neurology*, 118, 32–34.

Pereira, A., Silva, L., Laranjeiro, C., Lino, C., & Pena, A. (2020). Selected pharmaceuticals in different aquatic compartments: Part I—Source, fate and occurrence. *Molecules*, 25(5), 1026.

Ridic, G., Gleason, S., & Ridic, O. (2012). Comparisons of health care systems in the United States, Germany and Canada. *Materia Socio-medica*, 24(2), 112–120.

Reis-Santos, P., Pais, M., Duarte, B., Caçador, I., Freitas, A., Pouca, A. S. V., … & Fonseca, V. F. (2018). Screening of human and veterinary pharmaceuticals in estuarine waters: A baseline assessment for the Tejo estuary. *Marine Pollution Bulletin*, 135, 1079–1084.

Roffarello, A. M., & De Russis, L. (2023). Achieving digital wellbeing through digital self-control tools: A systematic review and meta-analysis. *ACM Transactions on Computer-Human Interaction*, 30(4), 1–66.

Salandra, R. (2018). Knowledge dissemination in clinical trials: Exploring influences of institutional support and type of innovation on selective reporting. *Research Policy*, 47(7), 1215–1228.

Sandoval Aguilar, R. (2022). *Small solid-state refrigeration development for use with solar power for medical supply storage*. Texas Christian University Fort Worth.

Santos, M. S., Franquet-Griell, H., Alves, A., & Lacorte, S. (2018). Development of an analytical methodology for the analysis of priority cytostatics in water. *Science of The Total Environment*, 645, 1264–1272.

Shen, K., Eddelbuettel, J. C., & Eisenberg, M. D. (2024, January). Job flows into and out of health care before and after the COVID-19 pandemic. In *JAMA health forum* (Vol. 5, No. 1, pp. e234964–e234964). American Medical Association.

Soto, E. A., Hernandez-Guzman, A., Vizcarrondo-Ortega, A., McNealey, A., & Bosman, L. B. (2022). Solar energy implementation for health-care facilities in developing and underdeveloped countries: Overview, opportunities, and challenges. *Energies*, 15, 8602.

Sousa, J. C., Ribeiro, A. R., Barbosa, M. O., Pereira, M. F. R., & Silva, A. M. (2018). A review on environmental monitoring of water organic pollutants identified by EU guidelines. *Journal of Hazardous Materials*, 344, 146–162.

Skyquest. (2022). *Global health insurance market size, share, growth analysis, industry forecast 2023-2030* (Report ID: SQMIG40N2008). Skyquest.

Swetha, N. B., Shobha, S., & Sriram, S. (2020). Prevalence of catastrophic health expenditure and its associated factors, due to out-of-pocket health care expenses among households with and without chronic illness in Bangalore, India: A longitudinal study. *Journal of Preventive Medicine and Hygiene*, 61(1), E92.

Thakur, V., Mangla, S. K., & Tiwari, B. (2021). Managing healthcare waste for sustainable environmental development: A hybrid decision approach. *Business Strategy and the Environment*, 30(1), 357–373.

The New Times (2024). Babyl Rwanda reportedly ceases operations Thursday, August 15, 2024, Kigali, Rwanda.

Transparency International. (2021). *Global corruption barometer European Union 2021. Citizens' views and experiences of corruption*. Transparency International.

UK Parliament. (2022). *The future of general practice, fourth report of session 2022–23, House of Commons Select Committee on Health*. UK Parliament.

World Health Organisation. (2023, August 31). *Factsheet: Electricity in health-care facilities*. WHO.

Wu, R., Li, N., & Ercia, A. (2020). The effects of private health insurance on universal health coverage objectives in China: A systematic literature review. *International Journal of Environmental Research and Public Health*, 17(6), 2049.

Zhang, H. J., Zhang, Y. H., Wang, Y., Yang, Y. H., Zhang, J., Wang, Y. L., & Wang, J. L. (2013). Investigation of medical waste management in Gansu Province, China. *Waste Management & Research*, 31(6), 655–659.

Zion Market Research. (2022). *EHR industry trends, analysis & forecast report*. Zion Market Research.

15   Hospitals and their management

15.1 What hospitals do

Patients are the service users of hospitals, even if they are not necessarily direct payers when funding comes from the government or insurance funders. In such cases, patients still pay for the services indirectly through their taxation or insurance premiums.

As we have seen in the previous unit, patients are at the centre of the healthcare ecosystem. Generally, when they need to access healthcare, they go on a journey with a number of episodes of care provided by different healthcare providers. The type and number of episodes of care will vary according to their needs. A typical patient journey is shown schematically in Figure 15.1.

In most healthcare systems, primary care acts as a gatekeeper to the rest of the healthcare system. Patients generally start their journey by accessing primary care, traditionally a primary care physician, but nowadays, perhaps a telephone advice service, walk-in centre or telemedicine service.

If their problem, is not too severe, it may be dealt with within primary care, typically with medication or simply advice. If the patient needs further treatment, they will generally be referred to a hospital for a planned admission. In emergency situations, they may be sent to hospital as an unplanned admission, and this may also happen without the intervention of primary care in emergency situations such as an accident or life-threatening acute health event, e.g., stroke or heart attack.

15.1.1 Unplanned hospital admissions

Planned admissions are easier for hospitals to manage. Because of the variations in the numbers and severity of unplanned admissions, hospitals must have sufficient capacity to deal with peaks in demand for unplanned emergency admissions. Without this, delays occur in the emergency department, leading to poor quality of care, and potentially severe consequences for patient outcomes when optimum treatments for life-threatening and life-changing conditions are time-dependent.

One solution to managing unplanned urgent admissions is the triage system. The primary goal of triage is to allocate medical care efficiently and effectively, ensuring that the most critically ill or injured patients receive immediate attention.

When a patient arrives at the emergency room, they are initially greeted by a triage nurse or healthcare professional. The triage nurse asks the patient about their symptoms, medical history, and the reason for their visit. This quick assessment helps identify potentially life-threatening conditions that require immediate attention.

DOI: 10.4324/9781003478874-19

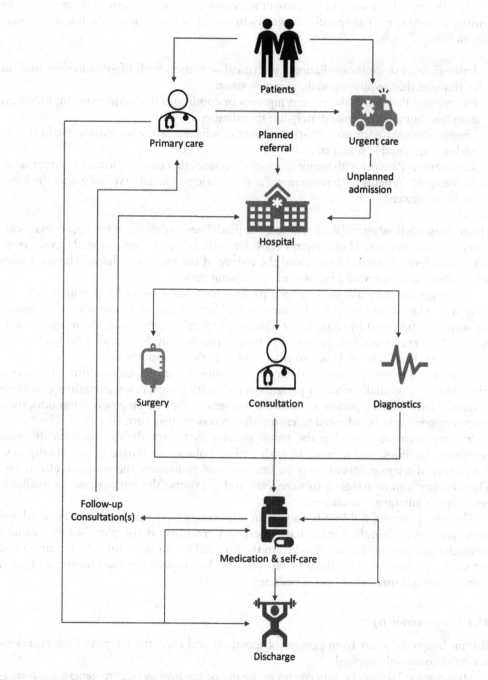

Figure 15.1 Schematic of a patient journey.

After the initial assessment, the patient is assigned a triage category that indicates the priority of their care. The specific categories may vary between hospitals, but they generally include:

- *Immediate (resuscitation)*: Patients in critical condition with life-threatening injuries or illnesses that require immediate intervention.
- *Emergency*: Patients with severe symptoms or conditions that require prompt medical attention but are not immediately life-threatening.
- *Urgent*: Patients with non–life-threatening conditions but who require medical care within a reasonable timeframe.
- *Semi-urgent*: Patients with minor illnesses or injuries that can wait longer for treatment.
- *Non-urgent*: Patients with non-emergency conditions who can typically wait the longest for treatment.

Triage nurses follow established protocols or guidelines to determine the appropriate category for each patient. These criteria consider various factors such as vital signs, symptoms, pain level, medical history, and the nature of the injury or illness. The guidelines help ensure consistency and fairness in prioritising patients.

The triage category assigned to each patient determines the order in which they will be seen by a healthcare provider. Patients in the "Immediate" or "Emergency" categories are seen first, followed by those in the "Urgent," "Semi-urgent," and "Non-urgent" categories. However, waiting times can still vary depending on the overall workload, availability of medical staff, and the severity of other patients' conditions.

Triage is a dynamic process, and patients' conditions can change over time. Therefore, triage nurses continually monitor patients in the waiting area, reassessing their condition at regular intervals. If a patient's condition worsens or they develop new symptoms, their triage category may be adjusted to ensure they receive timely care.

It's important to note that the triage process may vary slightly between different healthcare facilities, and in times of high patient volumes or during mass casualty incidents, special triage protocols may be implemented to manage the situation effectively. The ultimate aim of triage is to save lives and maximise the efficient use of available resources in emergency situations.

The next potential hold-up for a patient who enters hospital as an unplanned admission may occur when their immediate emergency treatment is complete but they cannot be discharged and need to be admitted to the hospital for longer-term care. Finding a bed for such a patient relies on there being sufficient bed capacity in the hospital and good information to know where spare beds are available.

15.1.2 Intervention types

Within hospitals, apart from general observation and care, three types of interventions are most commonly applied.

Diagnostics: Diagnostic procedures make use of medical devices to generate information to help doctors and other healthcare professions make decisions about care. This may vary from a simple procedure such as taking a patient's temperature or measuring their blood pressure to a three-dimensional MRI scan.

Consultations: These are the times when the doctors interact with the patients combining diagnostic results with their own observations, the patient's own observations, and medical history. Based on these, the doctors is likely to arrive at a decision which may include further interventions, continuing with existing treatments, or discharge from the hospital.

Surgery: One of the possible interventions is surgery. Surgery is more expensive and riskier than most other interventions, so its use must be justified by balancing the risks against the benefits to the patients. Even when its use is the best solution for the patient, the extent of the surgery should be kept to a minimum to achieve the desired results. General anaesthetics also carry a significant risk and should be minimised with local anaesthesia used when this is an appropriate alternative.

Once a patient leaves the hospital, they are likely to need follow-up care either at the hospital or in primary care.

15.1.3 *Planned hospital admissions*

To effectively manage planned hospital admissions, most hospitals will use a set of processes built around a computerised patient administration system. In practice, many hospitals computerised their patient administration systems before digitising their clinical records.

Hospital administrators and staff need to plan for anticipated admission numbers by forecasting and allocating appropriate resources. This includes estimating the number of expected admissions, determining bed availability, and ensuring sufficient staffing levels. Adequate planning helps prevent overcrowding and allows for the timely admission of patients.

Prior to admission, patients should undergo a comprehensive assessment to gather essential information about their medical history, current condition, and any special needs they may have. This assessment may involve medical tests, consultations with specialists, and evaluations by healthcare professionals. Gathering this information in advance helps in determining the appropriate level of care and facilitates a smoother admission process.

Effective bed management is crucial for planned admissions. It involves monitoring bed availability, ensuring proper utilisation of existing beds, and coordinating with different departments within the hospital. Bed management systems or software can assist in tracking bed occupancy, predicting discharges, and facilitating patient flow.

Adequate staffing is essential to handle planned admissions efficiently. This includes ensuring the availability of doctors, nurses, technicians, and other healthcare professionals required for patient care. Additionally, hospitals need to ensure the availability of necessary medical equipment, supplies, medications, and support services to meet the anticipated demand.

Efficient communication and coordination between various hospital departments are vital for managing planned admissions. Effective channels of communication must be established to facilitate the seamless flow of information between admitting departments, nursing units, diagnostic facilities, and other relevant areas. Clear protocols and guidelines should be in place to ensure smooth transitions during the admission process.

Providing patients with clear instructions and information about their admission process, including what to expect, necessary preparations, and any specific requirements, can help reduce anxiety and confusion. Patient education materials, pre-admission clinics, or dedicated personnel who guide patients through the admission process can be beneficial in ensuring a positive patient experience.

Proper documentation and information systems are crucial for managing planned admissions effectively. EHRs and other hospital information systems help track patient information, medical history, test results, and treatment plans. Accurate and up-to-date documentation facilitates continuity of care and enhances communication among healthcare providers.

Planning for the patient's discharge and designing any necessary follow-up care should start early in the admission process. This involves coordinating with the healthcare team to develop a post-discharge plan, arranging necessary support services or equipment, and ensuring appropriate follow-up appointments. Effective discharge planning helps optimise bed utilisation and ensures a smooth transition for patients to the next phase of their care.

By implementing these elements and establishing efficient processes, hospitals can effectively manage planned admissions, enhance patient care, optimise resource utilisation, and improve overall operational efficiency. However, an increasing number of surgical interventions, especially when planned in advance are being carried out as day cases with the patient not staying in hospitals overnight in order to reduce the resources needed and hopefully improve outcomes for the patients.

The HARP initiative to reduce unplanned admissions to the Royal Melbourne Hospital (after Wan et al., 2021)

In Australia, the Victorian State Government allocated $150 million towards the development of the Hospital Admission Risk Program (HARP), aiming to implement chronic disease management initiatives tailored to specific chronic conditions. HARP offers comprehensive care coordination and disease-specific input for individuals dealing with intricate and chronic conditions, necessitating intensive and complex care coordination. The primary objective of HARP is to prevent hospital admissions by establishing connections between tertiary care, community support systems, and general practitioners for ongoing patient management.

The HARP care plan involves direct collaboration between the HARP care coordinator, the individual, their GP, various healthcare professionals, and community support services. Acting as a central point of contact, the HARP care coordinator organises, refers, and coordinates services to enhance self-management and foster independence, enabling individuals to reside at home and autonomously manage their conditions. The assignment of an individual to a specific HARP care coordinator and involvement of other multidisciplinary HARP staff are determined by the individual's specific conditions and needs.

Research conducted by Wan et al. (2021) revealed that participants in all HARP chronic disease management programmes exhibited the highest rates of unplanned hospitalisations, bed days, and total hospital costs in the three months preceding HARP enrollment. However, these metrics decreased during the HARP intervention. Conversely, post-HARP intervention, hospitalisation rates, bed days, and total hospital costs were higher compared to the pre-intervention period. Individuals enrolled in chronic heart failure and chronic respiratory programmes demonstrated the lowest survival rates.

The reduction in unplanned hospitalisation rates and bed days during the HARP intervention, compared to the three months before HARP enrolment, demonstrates the effectiveness of the programme in mitigating potentially avoidable unplanned readmissions. Conversely, the increased unplanned hospitalisation and bed days in the three months before HARP enrollment underscore the integrated and intensive care needs of the individuals during that period.

15.1.4 Knowledge review

Before you move on, can you define the following key concepts:

- Triage?

15.1.5 Question to think about

- How do patients gain access to hospitals in your country?
- What are the barriers to accessing hospitals in your country?

15.2 Strategic management in hospitals

Hospitals are large complex organisations with many functions, all of which need managing. At the heart of their activity is the care of patients, but in order to achieve this goal, they have to carry out many functions, including the principal functions described in Table 15.1.

Each of these functions requires an operational plan and day-to-day management but there also needs to be an overall plan which ensures that the hospital knows where it is going, how it is going to get there, and enables senior leaders to monitor progress and ensure that the hospital is moving in the right direction – all of these in a dynamic external environment.

This is the purpose of strategic planning.

15.2.1 Mission, values, and vision

The starting point is reaching a consensus on the purpose of the hospital. At its heart is patient care, but there may be other purposes: patient education, growing knowledge through research, training the next generation of healthcare professionals, and in a profit-making hospital, proving a profit to the shareholders. This purpose is usually expressed as a mission statement, which should be a succinct statement of not more than one or two sentences. Although mission statements have been regarded sceptically in some circles, the alternative is generally worse. Without a clear agreed statement of purpose, any strategic planning is built on shaky foundations.

A brief mission statement can be accompanied by value statements expressing core beliefs regarding issues such as patient care, interaction with the community, and how members of the hospital work together to achieve common goals.

The vision statement describes where the hospital should be aiming to get to. It should be broad and descriptive rather than detailed, and it should be about the end point, not the way to get there.

Table 15.1 Hospital functions

Function	Description
Staffing and human resources	Hospitals require a diverse workforce, including doctors, nurses, technicians, support staff, and administrative personnel. Management needs to ensure proper staffing levels, recruit and hire qualified individuals, provide ongoing training and professional development, and manage employee performance.
Financial management	Hospitals must manage their financial resources efficiently. This includes budgeting, financial planning, billing and coding, revenue cycle management, cost control, financial reporting, and compliance with regulatory requirements.
Quality assurance	Maintaining high-quality patient care is essential. Hospital management should implement quality assurance programmes, develop and enforce clinical protocols and guidelines, monitor patient outcomes, collect and analyse data, and continuously improve processes to enhance the quality of care.
Operations management	Hospital management should oversee daily operations, including patient flow, scheduling, facility maintenance, supply chain management, inventory control, and equipment maintenance. Infection control and bed management play a direct role in patient care and outcomes.
Information technology	Hospitals rely heavily on technology for medical records, billing, communication, and diagnostic tools. Management must ensure the effective implementation, integration, and security of information systems, as well as stay updated with technological advancements.
Regulatory compliance	Healthcare is subject to various regulations and standards to ensure patient safety, privacy, and ethical practices. Hospital management must stay informed about applicable laws and regulations, develop policies and procedures, and ensure compliance with regulatory bodies.
Risk management	Hospitals face potential risks such as medical errors, malpractice claims, cybersecurity threats, and emergencies. Management should implement risk management strategies, conduct risk assessments, develop disaster preparedness plans, and promote a culture of safety.
Community relations and partnerships	Hospitals often engage with the local community, government agencies, insurers, and other healthcare providers. Management should foster positive relationships, engage in community outreach, collaborate with stakeholders, and seek partnerships to enhance healthcare services.

15.2.2 Models and tools for strategic management and planning

Strategic planning for a large healthcare organisation is a complex process. The starting point is a clear understanding of the current state of the organisation, and there are a range of models and tools available to help managers construct a formal model of their organisation.

Model 1: The balanced scorecard

The balanced scorecard is one of the commonest strategic planning models, designed to give managers a holistic overview of their organisations' operations (Trotta et al., 2013). It is a comprehensive strategic performance evaluation framework that offers a complete perspective of an organisation's performance by taking into account various dimensions.

Table 15.2 The four perspectives of the balanced scorecard

Perspective	Description
Financial	This perspective focuses on performance measures that focus on the organisation's financial health and sustainability. Typical indicators would be revenue growth, profitability, return on investment, and cost control. These measures provide insights into how well the organisation is achieving its financial objectives.
Customer	The customer perspective emphasises the organisation's ability to meet customer needs and expectations. It involves metrics related to customer satisfaction, loyalty, retention, and market share. By understanding and measuring customer satisfaction, organisations can identify areas for improvement and enhance their competitive position. A healthcare organisation has a complex variety of customers from funders such as insurance companies or governments to patients and their families. A key factor is that the funding may not come directly from the consumer of services.
Internal processes	This perspective is focused upon delivering value to customers by reviewing critical processes and operations. It involves identifying key processes and measuring their efficiency, quality, and effectiveness. Metrics may include cycle time, error rates, productivity, and innovation. By optimising internal processes, organisations can enhance their overall performance and deliver better outcomes.
Learning and growth	The learning and growth perspective focuses on the organisation's ability to develop and leverage its intangible assets, including human capital, information systems, and organisational culture. It includes metrics related to staff satisfaction, skills development, knowledge management, and technology utilisation. Investments in learning and growth enable the organisation to build capabilities and adapt to changing environments.

It surpasses financial metrics and integrates non-financial indicators to evaluate an organisation's advancement towards its strategic objectives. The balanced scorecard takes into account four key perspectives: financial, customer, internal processes, and learning and growth, as described in Table 15.2.

The balanced scorecard works by translating an organisation's strategic objectives into specific performance indicators within each perspective. These indicators are typically selected based on their relevance to the organisation's strategy, their measurability, and their ability to drive desired outcomes. Once the indicators are defined, targets or benchmarks are set for each indicator to provide a basis for performance evaluation.

Regular monitoring and measurement of the chosen indicators allow organisations to track their progress and identify areas that require attention and improvement. The balanced scorecard enables a more comprehensive and balanced assessment of performance than alternatives which are focused solely upon financial aspects, as it considers both financial and non-financial aspects that are critical for long-term success. For healthcare organisations, where the primary goal should arguably be patient outcomes and financial performance merely a means to deliver more and better care, this is particularly significant.

By using the balanced scorecard, organisations can align their various strategic initiatives and performance measures with their overall objectives. For not-for-profit and public healthcare organisations, they may place a higher priority on patient outcomes than hospitals run for profit who must balance returns to investors with their broader goals. The approach promotes a balanced approach to decision-making, encourages cross-functional collaboration, and provides a clear framework for evaluating and improving performance in a holistic manner.

A balanced scorecard may be summarised in terms of a strategy map: whilst this does not contain the full details of a balanced scorecard, it does provide a strong visual summary particularly useful for communicating the balanced scorecard to staff and other stakeholders:

Model 2: Objectives and Key Results

As its name implies, the Objectives and Key Results (OKR) model involves the process of converting broader organisational goals into specific objectives and monitoring the corresponding key results (Niven et al., 2016).

Typically, the process starts between three and five attainable objectives with the corresponding results that should flow from each of them. The process can be described in terms of a five-step process, as shown in Table 15.3 (Niven et al., 2016):

Table 15.3 The five steps of the OKR model (after Niven et al., 2016)

Step	Description
Set the strategic objectives	Begin by identifying the high-level strategic objectives that the organisation aims to achieve. These objectives should align with the organisation's mission, vision, and long-term goals. For example, strategic objectives could focus on enhancing patient outcomes, improving operational efficiency, expanding healthcare services, or fostering innovation.
Define Key Results	Key Results are measurable outcomes that indicate progress towards the objectives. Each objective should have a few (typically 3–5) Key Results associated with it. These results should be specific, quantifiable, time-bound, and challenging yet achievable. Key Results should provide a clear indication of success and reflect the desired impact of achieving the objectives.
Step Cascade Objectives and Key Results	Once the strategic objectives and corresponding Key Results are established at the organisational level, cascade them down to different departments, teams, or individuals within the organisation. Align the objectives and Key Results at each level so that they contribute to the achievement of higher-level strategic objectives. This ensures alignment and focus throughout the organisation.
Define initiatives and actions	Identify the initiatives and actions that need to be taken to drive progress towards each Key Result. These initiatives should outline the specific steps, projects, or programmes that will be implemented to achieve the desired outcomes. Assign responsibilities and establish timelines for each initiative to ensure accountability and progress tracking.
Regular monitoring and review	Monitoring and reviewing progress is crucial for OKRs. Establish a system to track Key Results on a weekly or monthly basis. This can be done through meetings, dashboards, or performance management tools. Regular check-ins allow for course correction, identification of challenges, and celebration of achievements. If progress is not on track, it provides an opportunity to reassess strategies and take corrective actions.

Table 15.4 Examples of how the Objectives and Key Results model can be used in a hospital. Adapted from Niven et al. (2016)

Sample objective	Linked Key Results
Improve patient outcomes	Reduce hospital-acquired infections (HAIs) by 20% within the next year.
	Increase the percentage of patients with controlled chronic conditions (e.g., diabetes, hypertension) by 15% in the next six months.
	Decrease the average length of stay for specific procedures (e.g., hip replacement, cardiac surgery) by 10% within the next quarter.
Enhance patient experience	Achieve an overall patient satisfaction score of 90% or higher in the next year based on surveys.
	Reduce wait times in the emergency department by 20% within the next six months.
	Increase the percentage of patients who receive personalised care plans upon discharge by 15% within the next quarter.
Optimise operational efficiency	Achieve a cost reduction of 10% in supply chain management within the next year.
	Improve bed turnover time by 15% in the next six months.
	Increase the utilisation rate of operating rooms to 80% within the next quarter.
Enhance staff engagement and development	Increase employee satisfaction scores by 10% based on annual surveys within the next year.
	Implement a professional development programme for staff, ensuring that 80% of employees participate in at least one training or skill-building activity within the next six months.
	Reduce employee turnover rate by 15% within the next quarter.
Strengthen community engagement	Establish partnerships with three local community organisations to provide health education programmes within the next year.
	Increase the number of community health screenings conducted by the hospital by 20% within the next six months.
	Implement a volunteer programme, aiming to have 50 volunteers actively engaged in hospital initiatives within the next quarter.

Table 15.4 shows some examples of how this could be used within a healthcare organisation such as a hospital.

It is possible to use the OKR process as part of developing a balanced scorecard, specifically to help develop metrics for measuring change and success.

Model 3: Theory of Change (TOC)

The Theory of Change (TOC) model is another strategic planning framework that is designed to help healthcare organisations articulate their long-term goals, map out the necessary actions, and identify the anticipated outcomes and impact of their initiatives (Mayne, 2017, 2023).

It can be described in terms of seven steps, illustrated in Figure 15.2.

The Theory of Change model provides a comprehensive framework for healthcare organisations to think strategically, map out their desired outcomes, and design their

Figure 15.2 The seven steps of the Theory of Change model.

interventions and strategies accordingly. It helps hospitals identify the logic behind their strategic plans, understand the causal relationships, and ensure that their actions are aligned with their ultimate goals.

When strategic planning model is implemented, there are a range of tools and additional resources that can be used to assist in the implementation. One of the commonest is the SWOT Analysis

Tool 1: SWOT analysis

A SWOT analysis is a strategic planning method used to evaluate and analyse the internal strengths and weaknesses, as well as the external opportunities and threats, of an organisation, business, project, or individual. It involves identifying and assessing the factors that can positively or negatively impact the entity or endeavour under consideration. It provides a structured framework for assessing the current situation and determining the potential for success or failure (van Wijngaarden et al., 2012). It is generally represented visually as a 2 x 2 matrix.

Typically, in order to carry out a SWOT analysis, individuals or teams typically brainstorm and gather information in each of these four categories. This may involve internal assessments, market research, competitor analysis, customer feedback, and industry insights. Once the data are collected, the analysis helps identify areas for improvement, strategic directions, potential risks, and competitive advantages.

The SWOT analysis is most often used as a starting point in strategic planning, assisting with formulating strategies, making informed decisions, setting goals, allocating resources, and if necessary being done again to help organisations adapt to changing circumstances. It can provide a comprehensive overview of the internal and external factors that impact an organisation, facilitating a more holistic understanding of its position in the market.

- *Strengths* are the internal attributes, resources, qualities, and assets possessed by an organisation that provide it with a competitive edge over others. These can encompass elements such as a well-established brand reputation, highly skilled workforce, cutting-edge technology, exclusive products or services, dedicated customer base, streamlined processes, or solid financial stability. Identifying strengths helps an organisation understand its competitive advantages.
- *Weaknesses* are the factors internal to an organisation that place it at a disadvantage compared to others. Weaknesses may be areas requiring improvement or challenges that hinder progress. Examples may include a lack of resources, outdated technology, poor management, limited market presence, low customer satisfaction, or high operating costs. Recognising weaknesses allows an organisation to address or mitigate them.
- *Opportunities* are external factors or situations that have the potential to benefit an organisation. Opportunities arise from market trends, new drugs or treatments, changes in regulations, emerging technologies, customer needs, or gaps in the competition. By identifying and capitalising on opportunities, an organisation can expand, innovate, or gain a competitive edge.
- *Threats* are external factors that could potentially harm an organisation's performance or hinder its goals. Threats may include increased competition, economic downturns, changing consumer preferences, new regulations, disruptive technologies, supplier or vendor issues, or geopolitical risks. Understanding threats helps an organisation to proactively minimise risks through contingency planning and strengthening where necessary.

Tool 2: Porter's Five Forces

Porter's Five Forces is a framework developed by Porter (1980). This tool is designed to analyse the competitive dynamics and attractiveness of an industry. The model helps identify the underlying forces that shape an industry's competitive structure and influence the profitability of the organisations within it. In the healthcare sector, the emphasis on profitability will not be relevant in public and not-for-profit organisations, but even here, the tool can be used to maximise financial efficiency. The language of this model emphasises the dynamic nature of the operating environment and the relationships between factors.

There are the five forces in Porter's framework (Porter, 1980):

1. *The threat of new entrants* measures how difficult it is for new businesses to break into an established industry and compete with existing firms. Barriers to entry include high capital requirements, economies of scale, government regulations, proprietary technology, or strong brand loyalty. Industries with high barriers are generally less threatened by new entrants.
2. *The bargaining power of suppliers* examines the suppliers' ability to influence their pricing and the terms on which they supply goods and services to their customers. Suppliers gain power when they are few in number, provide unique or critical inputs, or have established strong relationships with their customers. Strong supplier power can limit the profitability of firms within the industry. Suppliers here include

pharmaceutical companies and medical device manufacturers, as well as organisations supplying or representing the interests of the workforce.

3. *The bargaining power of buyers* measures the buyers' ability to influence the pricing and the terms on which they obtain goods and services from their suppliers. Buyers gain power when they are few in number, purchase in large quantities, have access to alternative suppliers, or can easily switch to substitutes. Strong buyer power can put pressure on industry profitability as buyers demand lower prices or better terms. Buyers here are the funders of healthcare provision, typically governments, private insurance companies, social health insurance funds, or patients themselves.

4. *The threat of substitute products or services* assesses how readily customers can obtain alternative products or services that meet their needs. The factors that influence this include price-performance trade-offs, switching costs, and customer loyalty. Industries facing a high threat of substitutes may experience reduced profitability. Disruptive technologies may facilitate the transfer of services typically carried out in a hospital into the home, or surgery may be replaced by new pharmacological interventions.

5. *The intensity of competitive rivalry* assesses the competitiveness of the existing marketplace. Factors influencing competitive rivalry include the number of competitors, industry growth rate, product differentiation, cost structure, and exit barriers. Intense rivalry can lead to price wars, reduced profits, and increased marketing efforts. This factor depends on the nature of the healthcare system in the country of operation – some are competitive, others collaborative or even monopolistic or publicly owned.

By analysing these five forces, organisations can gain insights into the competitive dynamics of the healthcare system within their setting and make informed strategic decisions. The framework helps identify opportunities and threats, assess the attractiveness of different services, determine competitive strategies, and allocate resources effectively.

Tool 3: PESTLE analysis

PESTLE analysis is another strategic planning tool (Visconti, 2012). PESTLE is an acronym made up of:

- P: Political
- E: Economic
- S: Social
- T: Technological
- L: Legal
- E: Environmental

In the specific case of a hospital, the political factors will include regulatory requirements requirements, changes in healthcare policies, the impact of government policy on funding for healthcare services and any changes in budget allocations, and may also include the stability of the political environment,

Economic factors will be focused upon the hospital's financial stability and its ability to provide quality healthcare within budget constraints, but this can be influenced by the overall economic health of the region and any changes in reimbursement policies.

Social factors include the age distribution, population growth, and cultural diversity in the catchment area, public awareness, attitudes towards health, wellness, and preventive care, and lifestyle trends and their impact on healthcare needs and services.

Technological factors include the adoption of new medical technologies, equipment, and advancements in medical treatments; the implementation of electronic health records (EHRs) and other health information technologies such as those facilitating telehealth services and remote patient monitoring.

Legal factors include adherence to healthcare laws, regulations, and accreditation standards, the legal implications related to medical malpractice and patient rights and the need to comply with data protection laws and patient confidentiality.

Environmental factors include those that have a direct and immediate impact on public health and healthcare demand alongside the longer-term issues of sustainability in hospital operations and readiness for climate-related events that could affect healthcare services.

A SWOT analysis of China's COVID-19 prevention and control strategy (after Wang & Wang, 2020)

In a SWOT analysis of China's COVID-19 prevention and control strategy, Wang and Wang (2020) identified the following strengths:

• The medical and health system is gradually improving
• China's health emergency system has improved dramatically since SARS in 2003
• Quick and effective cooperation in the joint prevention and control of various departments

However, they also found the following weaknesses:

• Cases of COVID-19 developed in many regions within a short period
• The COVID-19 epidemic coincided with the spring festival, complicating epidemic prevention and control measures
• China is a vast country with a huge population
• Lack of relief materials and human resources
• Health emergency discipline is underdeveloped
• The public became flustered and lacked awareness leading to rumours spreading

They identified the following opportunities:

• New exploration of the pneumonia epidemic
• Further improvement and inspection of the emergency health system
• Opportunities for education in infectious diseases

Together with the following threats:

• Unknown source of the pneumonia outbreak at the start of the COVID-19 epidemic
• The impact of COVID-19 on public daily life, work, and psychology
• The impact of COVID-19 on the national economy

They were able to make recommendations for how to develop a strategic plan for recovery from their analysis.

15.2.3 Knowledge review

Before you move on, can you define the following key concepts:

- Mission statement?
- Vision statement?

15.2.4 Question to think about

Which technologies in life sciences and information technology are most likely to be disruptive in healthcare in the next decade?

15.3 Service management in hospitals

Most hospitals are large complex organisations offering a wide range of services to a large patient population with varied and often complex needs.

They need to develop service plans that align with the healthcare needs of their target population. This involves identifying the range of services to be provided, determining the appropriate service mix and designing care pathways and workflows to optimise patient flow and resource utilisation.

To implement their plans, hospitals must establish standardised processes for delivering healthcare services. This includes defining clinical protocols and guidelines, implementing evidence-based practices, ensuring efficient patient scheduling and registration, and coordinating multidisciplinary care teams to provide comprehensive and coordinated care.

Plans must include robust quality assurance and patient safety systems. This involves monitoring and measuring clinical outcomes, implementing quality improvement initiatives, conducting patient satisfaction surveys, promoting infection control measures, and fostering a culture of safety among staff.

To measure actual performance against their plans, hospitals need to establish performance metrics to assess the effectiveness and efficiency of their services. Key performance indicators may include measures such as patient wait times, length of stay, readmission rates, surgical outcomes, infection rates, and financial indicators. Regular monitoring and analysis of these metrics allow for identification of areas for improvement and the implementation of corrective actions.

Service quality is about meeting or exceeding patient needs and expectations. This must be done whilst taking into account their preferences and values. It includes ensuring timely access to services, respectful and compassionate treatment, effective communication, and active involvement of patients in their care decisions. However, different aspects may be in conflict. For example, the best outcomes may require costlier treatments and better outcomes may require greater interventions which may increase temporary pain and discomfort.

Hospitals need to work with patients to achieve the best outcomes and assist them to make informed decisions about their own care. This involves providing information about their health condition, treatment options, and self-care instructions. Enabling patients to make an informed decision is a legal minimum requirement. Empowering patients further with knowledge and involving them in shared decision-making can enhance patient satisfaction and outcomes.

As well as planning to meet the needs and expectations of individual patients, hospitals need to align service plans with the healthcare needs of their target population. This involves identifying the range of services to be provided, determining the appropriate service mix, and designing care pathways and workflows to optimise patient flow and resource utilisation. Determining the most effective outcomes for the whole population may cause conflict with meeting the needs of individual patients or bring into direct conflict the competing needs of different patients or patient groups. Service plans inevitably represent a compromise and there may be conflicts between preventative and curative treatments, long term conditions and care for acute episodes, and health promotion and treatment of illness.

Service planning includes establishing standardised processes for delivering healthcare services. This includes defining clinical protocols and guidelines, implementing evidence-based practices, ensuring efficient patient scheduling and registration, and coordinating multidisciplinary care teams to provide comprehensive and coordinated care. These processes also provide a foundation for performance management and quality assurance.

Hospitals use performance metrics to assess the effectiveness and efficiency of their services. Key performance indicators may include measures such as patient wait times, length of stay, readmission rates, surgical outcomes, infection rates, and financial indicators. Regular monitoring and analysis of these metrics allow for identification of areas for improvement and the implementation of corrective actions. Quality assurance and patient safety systems involve monitoring and measuring clinical outcomes, implementing quality improvement initiatives, conducting patient satisfaction surveys, promoting infection control measures, and fostering a culture of safety among staff.

The service plan is not static. Hospitals need a culture of continuous improvement. This involves conducting regular audits, soliciting feedback from patients and staff, conducting root cause analyses for adverse events, and implementing quality improvement initiatives based on data-driven insights.

15.3.1 Hospital service management and complexity

Traditionally, hospital service management has been treated as a linear problem. Managers break down the overall system into individual components and determine the required inputs and desired outputs for each component. Then they represent the whole as a summation of all the components. This approach ignores the interrelationships and dependencies between the components of the overall plan.

Increasingly, managers are recognising the need to acknowledge the inadequacy of this approach and the need to acknowledge the role of complexity:

> Complexity has been defined as "a dynamic and constantly emerging set of processes and objects that not only interact with each other, but come to be defined by those interactions" (Cohn et al., 2013, p. 42)

Complex systems exhibit fuzzy boundaries, with their interacting agents operating based on internal rules that are not always predictable (Plsek & Greenhalgh, 2001). These systems also have the capacity to adapt, interact, and co-evolve with other systems. It is important to note that complexity is not solely a characteristic of interventions but a fundamental feature of the system(s) involved. Whether an intervention is simple, consisting of a single unchanging active element, or complex, involving multiple interacting components, the environment where the intervention is implemented will inevitably need to make adjustments to accommodate it.

For example, a clinical intervention, aimed at preventing type 2 diabetes and its context, such as a deprived and diverse inner-city community with limited recreational facilities, numerous fast-food outlets, and existing faith-based community support programmes, are interconnected and mutually influential (Greenhalgh & Papoutsi, 2018).

Braithwaite et al. (2018) contrasted approaches based on traditional implementation science with approaches based on complexity science.

They found that traditionally, tasks are seen as specific: for example, getting evidence into clinical practice in an understandable way whereas complexity science sees the task as context dependent. In order to manage complexity, this suggests tailored solutions and iterative processes.

Theoretical assumptions are traditionally seen as heterogeneous and diverse, leading to numerous theories, frameworks, and models, By contrast, the core assumptions of complexity science are deemed to apply across all complex systems. In practical terms, this means that an understanding of complexity features, such as interconnection, emergence, uncertainty, and unpredictability, must be added to traditional theoretical frameworks.

Implementation science emphasises standardised interventions that are generalisable, whereas complexity science argues that they need to be adapted to meet the contextual needs to take account of complex interventions and settings. Further, the context is an integral part of the system.

One of the threats to traditional thinking from complexity is that it argues that the traditional foundations of evidence-based practice movement, statistics, and the scientific methods are insufficient and may not be applicable once the context is included within the system.

Incorporating complexity science into service planning is intended to help managers understand the context in which they operate, the relationships among agents, and how rules and governance structures emerge.

By anticipating a range of possible outcomes, the goal is to avoid as many unintended negative consequences as possible and maximise the chance of delivering in a sustainable manner; potentially through the adaptation of the intervention to different settings.

Helping to understand how a healthcare team works using complex adaptive systems (CAS) principles (after Pype et al., 2018)

Pype et al. (2018) carried out an interview study with 21 palliative home-care nurses, 20 community nurses, and 18 general practitioners in Flanders, Belgium. A two-step analysis used the CAS principles as a coding framework for interview transcripts, followed by an identifying patterns in the codes for each CAS principle.

They found that the teams interviewed exhibited characteristics of both Complex Adaptive Systems (CAS) and traditional plan-and-control systems. CAS principles are identified in team members' daily interactions, with principles such as team autonomy and the influence of attractors being particularly prevalent. The study suggests that in clinical situations with clear procedures, teams operate in a plan-and-control manner. However, under conditions of uncertainty, teams function as CAS, necessitating adaptive approaches.

CAS principles were identifiable in team members' perceptions of day-to-day interactions, and each principle was exhibited across different professional backgrounds. The structuring principles, such as team autonomy, attractors, team history, and openness to the environment, significantly shaped the way the team operated.

They also found that the healthcare team functioned in line with CAS principles based on members' perceptions of daily interactions.

They explored the factors facilitating or hindering information flow and expertise sharing. They identified CAS principles such as internalised basic rules and attractors, relating to professional and interprofessional identity. They described the relationship between patient care quality and preserving professional relationships as a "balancing act."

The study provides insights into the way the teams function based on complexity science, and it demonstrates how recognising the complex nature of team dynamics enables greater insights to be gathered.

15.3.2 *Knowledge review*

Before you move on, can you define the following key concepts:

- Linear management?

15.3.3 *Questions to think about*

- When you or a friend or family member use a healthcare service, what characteristics do you associate with a good quality service?
- When you or a friend or family member use a healthcare service, what characteristics do you associate with a poor quality service?
- How many of these do you think directly influence the long-term health outcomes?

15.4 Financial management in hospitals

Financial management in hospitals is concerned with both sides of a balance sheet: money in or funding, and money out or expenditure. In a public or not-for-profit hospital, financial management is about maximising service provision whilst ensuring the expenditure does not exceed funding available. In a for-profit hospital, the goal is to ensure that funding exceeds expenditure so that profit can be made. In such cases, the system relies either on external regulation or customer choice to ensure that the health outcomes are met. Hospitals with good services and outcomes will attract more paying patients, but regulation of the market may be needed to ensure that over health needs are met across a region or population.

There are several main funding sources for hospitals. Funding models will vary depending on the country, healthcare system, and specific hospital. Most hospitals rely on a combination of funding sources to sustain their operations and deliver healthcare services to their communities.

Many hospitals receive funding from government sources, such as national or regional healthcare systems. In this model, the government allocates funds to hospitals based on various factors like the number of patients served, services provided, or a predetermined budget. These funds may be drawn from general taxation or social health insurance contributions.

In countries like the United States, hospitals receive funding from government programmes like Medicare and Medicaid. Medicare provides health coverage to elderly and disabled individuals, while Medicaid offers coverage to low-income individuals. Hospitals bill these programmes for services provided to eligible beneficiaries.

Either as an alternative or in addition to government funding, hospitals may receive payments from private health insurance companies. These payments are typically made on behalf of individuals who have insurance coverage. Hospitals negotiate contracts with insurance companies to determine payment rates for various services.

In both of these cases, it is important to recognise that funding is independent of ownership. In other words, public hospitals may receive public or private funding, and so may privately owned hospitals, dependent upon the funding model operating in their country of operation.

Hospitals can generate revenue through direct payment from patients. These fees can include charges for services, treatments, surgeries, diagnostic tests, and other medical procedures. The amount charged is typically based on the hospital's fee schedule or negotiated rates with insurance companies. In some cases, these fees may be top-ups or co-payments in addition to other sources.

Some hospitals receive funding through charitable donations from individuals, foundations, corporations, or community organisations. These funds can be used to support specific programmes, research initiatives, capital projects, or provide financial assistance to patients in need.

Academic medical centres and research hospitals often secure funding through grants from government agencies, non-profit organisations, and pharmaceutical companies for specific purposes. These funds support medical research, clinical trials, and the advancement of healthcare knowledge and innovation.

Some hospitals have associated foundations that raise funds through various means, including fundraising events, campaigns, and community outreach. These foundations provide financial support for hospital projects, equipment purchases, community health initiatives, and other healthcare-related programmes.

In certain healthcare systems, hospitals may use cross-subsidisation, where revenue generated from profitable services or departments is used to subsidise less profitable or unprofitable areas. This helps ensure the provision of essential but financially challenging services. This is sometimes used to justify public hospitals offering priority services to patients paying either directly or through private health insurance.

Crucial to effective financial management for hospitals is the provider payment mechanism, which determines how hospitals are financially reimbursed for activity. We have seen the different provider payment mechanisms in the section on health financing.

15.4.1 Controlling costs

Effective financial management requires cost control as well as income maximisation. However, if cost cutting is overzealous, then patient care and their outcomes may suffer.

Healthcare organisations must balance expenditures with outcomes. However, there is not a simple linear relationship between expenditure and excellent patient care.

Hospitals costs are many and varied. They may be fixed or variable.

Fixed costs are those that remain constant regardless of the level of activity in the hospital, such as rent, salaries of permanent staff, insurance premiums, and administrative expenses. Variable costs by contrast fluctuate with the level of activity or the number of patients treated. Examples include medical supplies, medications, utilities (like electricity and water), and certain types of staffing costs (e.g., overtime payments).

Costs may be incurred directly or indirectly. Direct costs are those that can be directly attributed to a specific patient or department. These may include the cost of medical procedures, diagnostic tests, medications, and supplies used for individual patients. Indirect costs, also known as overhead costs, are incurred for the overall functioning of the hospital and are not directly attributable to specific patients or departments. Examples include administrative salaries, facility maintenance, and general utilities.

A specific type of indirect costs are capital costs. These are the expenses related to acquiring and maintaining physical assets such as medical equipment, buildings, and infrastructure. They will often include elements for depreciation and interest on loans for equipment or facility purchases.

The key to cost containment without compromising patient outcomes is eliminating unnecessary expenditure and reducing waste.

Standardising contracts is a useful approach to cost management for hospitals. When hospitals deal with numerous vendors and protocols, there is a risk of wasting money and compromising the quality of care. Point 4 in W. Edwards Deming's 14 points for management (Deming, 2018) advises organisations seeking improvement to put an end to the practice of awarding business solely based on the price tag. Instead, they are advised to focus on minimising the overall cost and on establishing long-term relationships of loyalty and trust by moving towards having a single supplier for each item or service. Examples of areas where contracts can be bundled include waste management, catering, and environmental services.

Examining patient flow is another important aspect of cost in healthcare. Establishing a standardised process for the movement of patients around a hospital can reduce costs save time and improve the patient experience and outcomes. Specifically, it can:

- Reduce delays and wait times
- Improve room turnaround times
- Utilise staff resources effectively
- Maximise occupancy for hospital beds

As an example of a single supplier relationship, using a single specialised patient transportation provider and establishing a long-term relationship can help to develop optimised patient flows, with the potential to reduce bottlenecks and maintain a smooth patient experience while lowering costs.

When it comes to healthcare staff, getting rid of staff should be a last resort. By recruiting individuals who align with the organisational culture, retaining excellent staff, and optimising scheduling, hospitals can build a team that is committed to delivering more for patients and the organisation.

Keeping existing staff and reducing turnover helps to manage costs. Recruitment is expensive and time-consuming. Improving job satisfaction and fostering a positive work environment will improve staff retention. Loyalty will be encouraged by providing proper job training, which not only ensures staff members being competent in their roles but also encourages them to stay with the organisation, contributing to long-term cost reduction.

Staff retention will also be improved through recognition of good work by publicly acknowledging teams and celebrating accomplishments; this has a measurable impact on engagement and ultimately contributes to better retention rates.

In order to make the best use of the available staff resources, hospitals should analyse staffing requirements at different times to optimise a scheduling strategy based on trends and demand.

Finally, there may be clinical needs that may be undiagnosed but consuming resources. For example, addressing malnutrition can be crucial in cost management, as preventable readmissions due to untreated malnutrition can result in significant financial burdens for hospitals. During the year 2000, in the UK, approximately 70–80% of malnourished patients entered and left the hospital without receiving any treatment for their malnutrition, and their discharge summary did not include any mention of the diagnosis (Kelly et al., 2000).

In such cases, it is essential to accurately code malnourished patients for malnutrition to improve patient health and generate funds that would otherwise be missed (Lean & Wiseman, 2008).

Malnutrition in German hospitals (after Volkert et al ., 2019)

Prior to a study by Volkert et al. in 2019, many previous studies had shown a high prevalence of malnutrition in German hospitals.

Their study focuses on malnutrition prevalence at the individual and structural levels in German hospitals. Various definitions of malnutrition are employed due to the lack of a gold standard, including Body Mass Index (BMI), nursing staff assessments, unintentional weight loss, and food intake. Nurses' assessments reveal 12% of patients as malnourished and 12% at risk, while BMI classifications vary based on criteria, ranging from 5% to 17%. Unintentional weight loss is reported by 42% of patients in the last three months, with different criteria hindering direct comparisons between studies.

Food intake emerges as a key criterion for malnutrition, with 20% reporting consuming only half as much as usual. Lack of appetite, nausea, and dissatisfaction with food quality are cited as reasons. In 2018, 7% of patients reported being prohibited from eating, emphasising the need for critical evaluation and avoiding skipped meals due to surgeries or exams. Lack of support with eating is reported by only a few, but it is suggested that many patients requiring help might be unable or unwilling to express this need.

On the structural level, nutrition teams in German hospitals are limited despite being deemed essential for nutritional care. While 58% of participating wards claim to have nutrition teams, it is suggested that these figures may be influenced by selective participation. Routine screening for malnutrition is frequent in Germany (88% in 2018), but only 50% weigh patients at admission, and 25% implement clinical nutrition without guidelines. Fortified food usage is low at 7%.

The study concludes that malnutrition is a significant health concern in German hospitals, affecting up to a third of patients depending on criteria. Nutritional infrastructure, including trained staff and routines, is not standardised, with only 10% of hospitals having a dietitian. The study calls for representative data to assess nutritional infrastructures accurately and recommends measures to improve nutritional care in hospitals for prevention and treatment of malnutrition.

The study highlights the issue of malnutrition in Germany and suggests that as in other European countries, this is a major area for improvement with the potential for better health outcomes and cost savings.

15.4.2 Knowledge review

Before you move on, can you define the following key concepts:

- Cost containment?

15.4.3 Questions to think about

- When you or a friend or family member have used a hospital, what evidence of efficient use of resources have you seen?
- When you or a friend or family member have used a hospital, what evidence of wasteful use of resources have you seen?
- How many of these do you think directly influence the long-term health outcomes?

15.5 Customer management in hospitals

In reality, hospitals have multiple customer groups. The primary customers are the patients, but hospitals also need to manage relationships with funders and the broader community.

Measuring the satisfaction of patients regarding the service they receive is challenging. Services are abstract and varied, and may be evaluated in terms of both their outcomes and the quality of the user experience during the process. This dual evaluation can lead to diverse interpretations and judgments, influenced by both the service provider and the individual using the service. The SERVQUAL model is a widely used framework for assessing and measuring service quality across a wide range of industries.

It was developed by Parasuraman, Zeithaml, and Berry in the late 1980s and has since become a prominent tool in the field of service management and marketing (Parasuraman et al., 1998). The model helps organisations understand customer perceptions of service quality and identify areas for improvement.

Its use in health services has been explored by Pena et al. (2013). They evaluated the users' view of the quality of an ambulatory ophthalmological service by the National Health System in Belo Horizonte (MG) in Brazil and also the quality of health services in the public and private networks in Ribeirão Preto-SP.

SERVQUAL is an abbreviation of Service Quality, and it consists of five dimensions, summarised in Table 15.5 below.

Table 15.5 Dimensions of SERVQUAL. Table adapted by Gillies from Parasuraman et al (1998)

Dimension	Description
Tangibles	This dimension refers to the physical aspects of the service, including the appearance of facilities, equipment, personnel, and any other tangible elements associated with the service delivery. It assesses the level of professionalism, modernity, cleanliness, and overall physical appearance.
Reliability	Reliability refers to the ability of the service provider to perform the promised service accurately and dependably. It involves aspects such as delivering the service as promised, meeting deadlines, and maintaining consistency in service quality over time.
Responsiveness	Responsiveness focuses on the willingness of service providers to help customers and provide prompt assistance. It includes attributes such as the willingness to listen to customers, timely response to inquiries or complaints, and the overall willingness to go the extra mile to meet customer needs.
Assurance	Assurance refers to the knowledge, competence, and courtesy of service providers and their ability to inspire trust and confidence in customers. It encompasses aspects such as the expertise of employees, their ability to convey trust and confidence, and their capacity to handle customer inquiries or concerns.
Empathy	Empathy refers to the caring, individualised attention, and personalised service provided to customers. It involves understanding and addressing customer needs and concerns, as well as providing a supportive and empathetic environment.

Funders are also customers because they are paying for the services provided. They may be the patients, but are typically governments, social insurers, or private insurance companies.

Managing relationships with funders requires proactive communication, alignment of goals, evidence-based outcomes, relationship building, stewardship, compliance, and collaboration. By effectively managing these relationships, hospitals can secure ongoing financial support, foster long-term partnerships, and ensure sustainable healthcare delivery. Therefore, hospitals need a strategy to manage their relationships that describes how they will achieve effective relationships. The elements of such a strategy are summarised in Table 15.6.

Hospitals need to foster strong relationships with the communities they serve in order to improve health outcomes in the local community, increase patient satisfaction, and a deeper sense of trust and partnership between the hospital and the community. A hospital that is trusted and attractive to the local community may also prove attractive to good staff and enhance staff retention. Contrawise, a hospital that is not highly regarded locally may find it difficult to attract and retain good staff.

Hospitals need to be proactive in community engagement and outreach by participating in local events, hosting health fairs, organising educational programmes, and offering health screenings. By being visible and accessible, hospitals can demonstrate their commitment to the community's health and well-being.

Hospitals can establish partnerships with local community organisations, non-profits, schools, and government agencies. Such relationships can provide hospitals with useful

Table 15.6 Content of strategy to manage relationships with funders

Element of Strategy	What needs to be done
Open and transparent communication	Establishing open lines of communication with funders is crucial. Hospitals should proactively engage with funders, providing regular updates on their operations, financial performance, and strategic initiatives. Transparency in financial reporting and accountability builds trust and strengthens the funder-hospital relationship.
Alignment of goals and objectives	Hospitals should ensure that their goals and objectives align with those of their funders. By understanding the funding organisation's mission and priorities, hospitals can tailor their strategies and initiatives to align with the funder's expectations. This alignment enhances the likelihood of continued financial support.
Demonstrating impact and outcomes	Hospitals need to demonstrate the impact of their programmes and services on the community and population they serve. By collecting and presenting data on outcomes, patient satisfaction, quality metrics, and cost-effectiveness, hospitals can showcase their value proposition to funders. This evidence-based approach reinforces the funder's confidence in the hospital's ability to deliver effective and efficient care.
Grant writing and proposal development	When seeking grant funding, hospitals should invest in developing well-crafted grant proposals. This includes conducting thorough research on the funding organisation's priorities, aligning the proposal with their specific requirements, and clearly articulating the intended outcomes and the hospital's capacity to deliver results. Writing compelling narratives and demonstrating the potential for positive impact increases the chances of securing funding.
Relationship building	Hospitals should invest time and effort in building strong relationships with funders. This can involve regular meetings, attending funder events, and participating in collaborative initiatives. Engaging in dialogue and understanding the funder's expectations, challenges, and long-term strategies fosters a mutually beneficial partnership.
Stewardship and recognition	Recognising and appreciating the support of funders is vital. Hospitals should acknowledge funders' contributions publicly, through avenues such as press releases, annual reports, and events. Regularly updating funders on the progress of funded projects and sharing success stories demonstrates good stewardship of resources.
Compliance and accountability	Hospitals must adhere to the terms and conditions set by funders. This includes complying with reporting requirements, budgetary guidelines, and any specific regulations or restrictions imposed by the funding organisation. Demonstrating financial responsibility, transparency, and adherence to regulatory standards builds trust and credibility with funders.
Collaboration and partnerships	Hospitals can strengthen their relationships with funders by actively seeking opportunities for collaboration and partnership. By working together on shared initiatives, such as community health programmes or research projects, hospitals can leverage their expertise and resources alongside the funder's support to achieve common goals. Collaboration enhances the value proposition and demonstrates a commitment to collective impact.

intelligence about the health of the local population and any significant local health issues. Collaborative initiatives can address community health needs, promote preventive care, and support social determinants of health. By working together, hospitals can maximise their impact on the community and develop long-term relationships.

Hospitals may create patient and family advisory groups comprised of community members and patients. These groups provide a platform for community members to voice their concerns, provide feedback on hospital services, and participate in decision-making processes. Involving the community in shaping healthcare services fosters a sense of ownership and promotes patient-centred care.

In response to specific local needs, hospitals can develop and implement health education programmes that target specific community health needs. These programmes can focus on preventive care, chronic disease management, healthy lifestyles, and promoting healthcare literacy. By empowering the community with knowledge and skills, hospitals contribute to better health outcomes and may be able to focus their own clinical resources on more critical areas.

Hospitals need to provide culturally sensitive care that respects and addresses the diverse needs of the community. This involves training staff to understand and appreciate cultural differences, providing interpretation services, and ensuring that healthcare practices are inclusive and respectful of diverse backgrounds and beliefs. The community themselves can be involved in educating and informing staff.

Hospitals can implement volunteer programmes that engage community members in meaningful ways. Volunteers can provide support to patients and their families, assist with community outreach efforts, and contribute to the overall patient experience. Volunteering opportunities create a sense of community involvement and ownership.

Hospitals can demonstrate their commitment to the community and the environment by adopting sustainable practices, reducing waste, and implementing environmentally friendly initiatives. Engaging in corporate social responsibility activities, such as community clean-up events or fundraising for local causes, showcases the hospital's commitment to the community's well-being beyond healthcare services and reinforces the relationship between health and the physical environment.

For all of these activities to be effective, open and transparent communication with the community is vital. Hospitals should regularly communicate updates, health information, and community impact reports through various channels, including websites, newsletters, social media, and community forums. This helps build trust, improves understanding, and promotes community involvement.

Case study: The use of SERVQUAL to assess the role of quality service delivery in client choice for healthcare in two hospitals in Ghana (after Aikins et al., 2014)

In a study conducted by Aikins et al. (2014), the focus was on assessing patient satisfaction at two hospitals in the densely-populated and rapidly-expanding urban hub of the Brong Ahafo Region in Ghana. The study aimed to compare a public hospital, Bechem Government Hospital, with a private hospital, Green Hill Hospital, by employing the SERVQUAL Model, a methodology used previously in Singapore to evaluate hospital service quality.

At Bechem Government Hospital, the primary reasons for attendance were identified as easy access (54%), good customer service (35%), and good infrastructure

(11%). The frequency of visits varied, with 7% visiting weekly, 36% monthly, and 57% quarterly. While 21% preferred alternative healthcare options, a significant 79% preferred Bechem Government Hospital. Factors contributing to poor healthcare quality at this public hospital included poor customer service (81%), health professionals' refusal of postings (84%), inadequate staff (69%), and insufficient funds (68%).

Reliability was considered crucial, with 62% agreeing that the hospital acted on its promises. Employee responsiveness received mixed responses, with 44% agreeing that employees respond quickly. Factors such as system expansion, availability of medicine, and modern equipment were positively rated by respondents, identifying various aspects influencing healthcare quality.

At Green Hill Hospital, primary reasons for attendance were easy access (67%), good customer service (31%), and good infrastructure (2%). Inadequate staff (56%) and insufficient funds (44%) were noted as main factors contributing to poor service delivery, with untrained staff ranking lowest. The hospital was perceived to act on its promises by 85% of clients. Positive ratings were also given for the availability of medicine (89%) and the need for improved and upgraded equipment (88%).

Comparing the two hospitals, Bechem Government Hospital faced challenges with inadequate staff (69%) and poor customer service (81%). In contrast, Green Hill Hospital had a higher percentage of respondents identifying inadequate staff (56%) and financial constraints (44%) as contributing factors. Reliability was rated highest at Green Hill Hospital (85%) compared to Bechem Government Hospital (62%), suggesting a stronger commitment to promises. Green Hill Hospital also excelled in responsiveness, with 57% easily obtaining information compared to Bechem Government Hospital's 44%.

In terms of assurance, both hospitals had high ratings for skilful and knowledgeable staff, with Green Hill Hospital at 57% and Bechem Government Hospital at 56%. Empathy levels were similar, with Green Hill Hospital at 56% and Bechem Government Hospital at 57%. Overall, the study emphasised that patient satisfaction is influenced by multiple factors, including accessibility, customer service, reliability, responsiveness, and the availability of resources and equipment.

15.5.1 Knowledge review

Before you move on, can you define the following key concepts:

- The SERVQUAL model of customer service quality?

15.5.2 Questions to think about

- Do local hospitals in your area visibly seek to communicate and engage with the community? How?
- Do local hospitals in your area enjoy a good relationship with the community? Why?

References

Aikins, I., Ahmed, M., & Adzimah, E. A. (2014). Assessing the role of quality service delivery in client choice for healthcare: A case study of bechem government hospital and green hill hospital. *European Journal of Logistics Purchasing and Supply Chain Management*, 2(3), 1–23.

Braithwaite, J., Churruca, K., Long, J. C., Ellis, L. A., & Herkes, J. (2018). When complexity science meets implementation science: A theoretical and empirical analysis of systems change. *BMC Medicine*, 16(1), 63.

Cohn, S., Clinch, M., Bunn, C., & Stronge, P. (2013). Entangled complexity: Why complex interventions are just not complicated enough. *Journal of Health Services Research & Policy*, 18(1), 40–43. doi:10.1258/jhsrp.2012.012036

Deming, W. E. (2018). *Out of the crisis*. MIT Press.

Greenhalgh, T., & Papoutsi, C. (2018). Studying complexity in health services research: Desperately seeking an overdue paradigm shift. *BMC Medicine*, 16(1), 95.

Kelly, I. E., Tessier, S., Cahill, A., Morris, S. E., Crumley, A., McLaughlin, D., et al. (2000). Still hungry in hospital: Identifying malnutrition in acute hospital admissions. *Quarterky Journal of Medicine*, 93, 93–98

Lean, M., & Wiseman, M. (2008). Malnutrition in hospitals. *BMJ* (Clinical research ed.), 336(7639), 290.

Lopes, J., Farinha, L., Ferreira, J. J., & Silveira, P. (2018). Does regional VRIO model help policy-makers to assess the resources of a region? A stakeholder perception approach. *Land Use Policy*, 79, 659–670.

Mayne, J. (2017). Theory of change analysis: Building robust theories of change. *Canadian Journal of Program Evaluation*, 32(2), 155–173.

Mayne, J. (2023). Assumptions in theories of change. *Evaluation and Program Planning*, 98, 102276.

Niven, P. R., & Lamorte, B. (2016). *Objectives and key results: Driving focus, alignment, and engagement with OKRs*. John Wiley & Sons

Novak, K. (2003). The WTO's balancing act. *The Journal of Clinical Investigation*, 112(9), 1269–1273.

Parasuraman, A., Zheitmal, V. A., & Berry, L. L. (1998). SERVQUAL: A multipleitem scale for measuring consumer perceptions of service quality. *Journal of Retailing*, 64(1), 12–40.

Pena, M. M., Silva, E. M., Rizatto Tronchin, D. M., & Melleiro, M. M. (2013). The use of the quality model of Parasuraman, Zeithaml and Berry in health services. *Revista da Escola de Enfermagem da USP*, 47(5), 1227–1232. doi:10.1590/S0080-623420130000500030

Plsek, P. E., & Greenhalgh, T. (2001). The challenge of complexity in health care. *BMJ*, 323(7313), 625–628.

Porter, E. M. (1980). *Competitive strategy*. The Free Press and Macmillan.

Pype, P., Mertens, F., Helewaut, F., & Krystallidou, D. (2018). Healthcare teams as complex adaptive systems: Understanding team behaviour through team members' perception of interpersonal interaction. *BMC Health Services Research*, 18, 1–13.

Trotta, A., Cardamone, E., Cavallaro, G., & Mauro, M. (2013). Applying the balanced scorecard approach in teaching hospitals: A literature review and conceptual framework. *International Journal of Health Planning and Management*, 28, 181–201.

UK Parliament. (2022, September 30). Research and development spending: Pharmaceuticals. *House of Lords Library*.

van Wijngaarden, J. D., Scholten, G. R., & van Wijk, K. P. (2012). Strategic analysis for health care organizations: The suitability of the SWOT-analysis. *The International Journal of Health Planning and Management*, 27(1), 34–49.

Visconti, R. M. (2012). *PPP versus traditional healthcare procurement in Italy: Assessing value for money with PESTLE and SWOT analysis* (p. xviii). Universita Cattolica del Sacro Cuore.

Volkert, D., Weber, J., Kiesswetter, E., Sulz, I., & Hiesmayr, M. (2019). Nutritional situation in German hospitals—Results of the nutrition Day project 2018. *Ernähr. Umsch*, 66, 204–211.

Wan, C. S., Mitchell, J., & Maier, A. B. (2021). A multidisciplinary, community-based program to reduce unplanned hospital admissions. *Journal of the American Medical Directors Association*, 22(6), 1331-e1.

Wang, J., & Wang, Z. (2020). Strengths, Weaknesses, Opportunities and Threats (SWOT) analysis of China's prevention and control strategy for the COVID-19 epidemic. *International Journal of Environmental Research and Public Health*, 17(7), 2235.

16 Primary healthcare provision

16.1 Primary healthcare

16.1.1 Primary care

Historically, primary care was defined as part of the Alma–Ata declaration from the international conference on primary healthcare:

> *Primary healthcare is essential healthcare based on practical, scientifically sound, and socially acceptable methods and technology made universally accessible to individuals and families in the community through their full participation and at a cost that the community and country can afford to maintain at every stage of their development in the spirit of self-reliance and self-determination*
>
> (WHO, 1978)

However, the WHO has kept the definition under review, and its modern definition is:

> *Primary healthcare is a whole-of-society approach to health that aims at ensuring the highest possible level of health and well-being and their equitable distribution by focusing on people's needs and as early as possible along the continuum from health promotion and disease prevention to treatment, rehabilitation and palliative care, and as close as feasible to people's everyday environment,*
>
> (WHO and UNICEF, 2018)

Since the launch of the Sustainable Development Goals, primary healthcare has been at the heart of efforts to achieve the required outcomes.

WHO (2023) estimates that an effective approach to primary healthcare can effectively deliver 90% of the interventions necessary for achieving universal health coverage and 75% of the anticipated health improvements outlined in the Sustainable Development Goals. This has the potential to rescue 60 million lives and enhance average life expectancy by 3.7 years by the year 2030.

In order for this potential to be realised, significant investment and development in primary healthcare needs to be prioritised. The International Symposium on Quality Primary Health Care Development (2023) identified 11 specific areas for development to deliver the potential of primary healthcare:

- fulfil political commitment and accountability
- achieve "health in all policies" through multisectoral coordination

DOI: 10.4324/9781003478874-20

- establish sustainable financing
- empower communities and individuals
- provide community-based integrated care
- promote the connection and integration of health services and social services through good governance
- enhance training, allocation and motivation of the health workforce, and medical education
- expand the application of traditional and alternative medicine for disease prevention and illness healing
- empower primary care with digital technology
- ensure access to medicinal products and appropriate technologies
- strengthen global partnership and international health cooperation.

(Ren et al., 2023)

Primary healthcare services include, but are not limited to, primary medical services.

16.1.2 Primary medical services

Traditionally, primary medical services have been provided by physicians operating out of small facilities based in the community. However, as the demand for primary healthcare has grown, a wide range of delivery models have emerged for primary medical services (Table 16.1).

Primary care physicians often have a role in managing a patient's overall care, which goes well beyond their own medical services. As the needs of an ageing population become more complex, and specialist medicine remains rooted in its clinical specialties, this coordinating role becomes ever more crucial. They maintain a comprehensive medical history for each patient and communicate with other healthcare providers involved in the patient's treatment.

Primary care physicians are often the first point of contact with the healthcare system for patients. They are equipped to diagnose and treat various health conditions and can address a significant portion of their patients' medical needs. Many have a public health role in terms of providing health advice and administering vaccination and other preventative programmes.

They often act as "gatekeepers" in many healthcare systems. Gatekeeping is a healthcare strategy that involves directing patients to seek non-emergency medical care through a designated healthcare provider first, before accessing specialised services or more advanced treatments. This is intended to ensure that individual patients receive the right level of expertise for their specific health issue, whilst managing overall resource allocation.

Whilst the gatekeeping model has advantages in terms of care coordination and cost management, it also has its critics.

Sripa et al. (2019) carried out a systematic review of the impact of gatekeeping on the quality of care and potential delays in accessing specialist services. They argue that it can lead to delayed access to specialised care and potentially hinder patients from receiving timely treatment for certain conditions.

From looking at 25 studies, the review concluded that gatekeeping was linked to reduced healthcare utilisation and costs, along with improved healthcare quality, but it resulted in lower patient satisfaction. Patients with cancer in gatekeeping systems had

Table 16.1 Alternative models of primary medical services

Provision type	Description
Primary care physicians	In many health systems, especially in higher income countries, such as HMOs in the US and the UK NHS, primary care physicians (referred to in the UK as "General Practitioners") provide basic medical service and act as gatekeepers to the rest of the system. They often work in groups located in the community.
Private physician practices	This model involves patients visiting a private physician's office for consultation, diagnosis, and treatment. The physician may have their own practice or be part of a group practice.
Community health centres	Community health centres serve underserved populations and offer a wide range of outpatient services, including primary care, preventive care, and other medical and social services. These centres often focus on promoting health and wellness in the community.
Telemedicine/telehealth	With advancements in technology, telemedicine has emerged as a model of care where patients can receive medical consultations and treatment remotely through video conferencing and other communication tools. Telemedicine is particularly valuable for patients in rural or remote areas and for those with limited mobility.
Retail clinics	Retail clinics are located in pharmacies, supermarkets, or retail stores, offering basic healthcare services for minor ailments and preventive care. These clinics provide quick and convenient access to healthcare services for common conditions like flu, colds, vaccinations, and screenings.

notably lower survival rates compared to those with direct access, although primary care gatekeeping did not lead to delayed patient referrals.

The most commonly cited example of gatekeeping is in the US, where many HMOs require patients to visit a primary care physician before being referred to specialist services from a provider operating within the HMO.

In 2011, Velasco-Garrido and colleagues conducted a literature review to compare healthcare organisations with gatekeeping and those with direct referral systems. Two-thirds of the organisations were from the US, and the rest were from Europe. The findings indicated that there were no significant distinctions in health- and patient-related outcomes between the two approaches. Gatekeepered HMOs were linked to slightly shorter hospital stays, but the results were not statistically significant. Most observations suggested potential cost reductions under gatekeeping, but with a wide variation in the actual saving achieved, ranging from 6% to 80% (Velasco-Garrido et al., 2011).

The results suggested shorter length of stay under gatekeeping, In practice, many of the findings were based on subsets of the whole review, and caution is needed since a lack of evidence does not necessarily reflect an actual finding of no difference, merely a failure to demonstrate a difference.

Gatekeeping is common in systems funded from taxation or from social health insurance. In the UK, upon the establishment of the NHS in 1948, general practice assumed the responsibility for providing comprehensive personal medical care and became the primary entry point for individuals seeking access to hospitals, specialist care, and sickness benefits. However, even during its early years, the absence of clear standards for general practice, limited incentives for medical professionals to become GPs, and a swiftly increasing demand for services were identified as notable challenges (Collings, 1950). Although the history of General Practice in the UK NHS has been one of reform, change, and an almost continuing sense of crisis (Roland, 2020), it remains the case that patients cannot access specialist services in the UK without a GP referral, even if they are paying for private healthcare.

Gatekeeping in Western Europe social health insurance-based systems

In France, in 2005, a gatekeeping reform was introduced to enhance care coordination and reduce the utilisation of specialist services. The reform required patients to select a médecin traitant, typically a general practitioner, as their initial point of contact for healthcare needs and specialist referrals. A crucial aspect of the policy was that patients who directly consulted a specialist faced higher cost-sharing compared to those referred by their médecin traitant.

Dumontet et al. (2017) examined the impact of this policy on the utilisation of physician services using administrative claims data from 2000 to 2008. Their analysis revealed that visits to specialists, which had been increasing before the reform's implementation, declined after the policy took effect. Further evidence from administrative claims and survey data indicated that this reduction was mainly due to a decrease in self-referrals, aligning with the policy's objectives. The decline in visits was seen across all specialties whether targeted by the policy or not.

In Germany, the gatekeeping role of primary care physicians is much more limited. People have the freedom to choose their own general practitioners (GPs) and specialists without any mandatory registration with a family physician or formal gatekeeping function for GPs. However, patients may opt into a family physician care model. This model has demonstrated superior service quality compared to traditional care methods and funds frequently offer incentives to encourage adherence to gatekeeping rules (Tikkanen et al., 2020).

16.1.3 *Private physician practices*

In systems where primary care is privately funded, either out-of-pocket, or via insurance funds not using an HMO model, patients may visit a private physician's office for consultation, diagnosis, and treatment. Such physicians may have their own practice or be part of a group practice. In this model, patients schedule appointments in advance, and the physician provides individualised care based on the patient's condition.

In the US, there was a significant decline in the proportion of physicians working in private practices between 2012 and 2022 (Kane, 2022), decreasing by 13 percentage points from 60.1% to 46.7%.

16.1.4 *Community health centres*

Community health centres (CHCs) serve underserved populations and offer a wide range of services, including primary medical services alongside preventive care, and other medical and social services. These centres often focus on promoting health and wellness in the community. Although community health centres may be found in most healthcare settings, the delivery model varies according to local needs and resources. In African countries, they are usually referred to as community health clinics.

Community health clinics in South Africa

Community health clinics in Africa are often the hub of important primary care interventions in both treatment and prevention and play a vital role in meeting the SDGs. The clinics provide a focus for community outreach clinics.

In 2010–2011, South Africa initiated its primary healthcare (primary care) re-engineering strategy, which included the establishment of community health worker teams. These teams were linked to specific clinics, acting as a bridge between health services and the community (Thomas et al., 2021).

The ideal composition of each primary care outreach team comprised six community health workers who were accountable for 1500 to 2000 households, effectively encompassing around 6000 individuals within a ward (Schneider et al., 2018).

In accordance with national directives, workers were chosen from the local community and overseen by a staff/enrolled nurse or a professional nurse designated as the outreach team leader. These teams received assistance from a variety of district resources including health promoters, primary healthcare-trained clinicians, social workers, and environmental health workers. They were responsible for delivering an extensive array of health and psychosocial services, with a focus on screening, disease prevention, and health education.

The interventions were targeted at specific groups, such as mothers and children, individuals affected by HIV/AIDS or tuberculosis, and those with chronic conditions like hypertension or diabetes, in addition to households headed by orphans. They also conducted contact tracing and ensured patients were not defaulting on their treatments, referring them back to the clinic if needed.

The workers were community members who possess a good understanding of their own communities' language and culture, enabling them to provide culturally appropriate health services. They require shorter training compared to health professionals, making them valuable assets in community healthcare.

In support of the aim of reducing the risk of HIV and sexually transmitted diseases, they provided condoms to members of their communities. Condom distribution saw a significant increase, with male condoms more than doubling and female condoms increasing fivefold. They also provided chronic medications to households with clients having conditions like HIV, TB, hypertension, and diabetes.

Screening activities covered:

- infectious diseases such as TB, HIV, and STIs
- non-communicable diseases such as hypertension, diabetes, and cervical cancer
- mother and child health problems

The workers reviewed the immunisation and nutrition status of children under five, leading to a reduction in malnourished children identified. Pregnancy screening and referrals for antenatal care also improved, leading to better care for pregnant women.

The teams emphasised screening for HIV, TB, and non-communicable diseases, with good rates of referrals and access to care in vulnerable communities. For sexually transmitted diseases and cervical cancer, referrals and access to care were also relatively high. Tracing defaulters and contacts was another important activity, with over 90% of tracing focused on defaulting HIV and/or TB treatment (Thomas et al., 2021).

16.1.5 Community health centres in the US

The Community Health Center (CHC) initiative was founded in the United States in 1965 to deliver comprehensive and excellent preventive as well as primary healthcare to marginalised groups, irrespective of their financial capacity. Since then, the program has experienced substantial expansion, catering to more than 28 million patients by 2019. Within this patient population, CHC services have reached one out of every six Medicaid beneficiaries, one out of every three individuals falling below the poverty threshold, and one out of every four residents in rural areas in the US. The Affordable Care Act (ACA) has led to an expansion of the CHC sector as the resulting insurance expansion has improved CHCs' financial viability by increasing reimbursement and enabling more patients to benefit from their services.

Despite the considerable success of the US CHC program, its patients continue to face significant health challenges. Compared to other low-income patients, individuals receiving care from CHCs generally exhibit poorer health, characterised by elevated prevalence of chronic ailments such as diabetes, hypertension, and asthma. Moreover, they face challenges when seeking specialised medical services and diagnostic tests. Patients attending CHCs are also more inclined to be jobless, lack insurance coverage, possess lower incomes, and belong to non-White racial or ethnic categories in contrast to patients attending non-CHC facilities. These factors further contribute to their overall poorer health status (Tilhou et al., 2020).

The CHCs in the US and their counterparts in Africa differ significantly but share a common purpose in providing healthcare to the poorer members of their societies and those who traditionally find accessing services difficult. In all settings, this model may include mobile health clinics that are housed in vehicles and travel to various locations, such as schools, workplaces, or underserved communities, to provide healthcare services. Mobile health clinics aim to improve the reach of community services to populations with limited access to healthcare facilities.

16.1.6 Telemedicine/Telehealth

Telemedicine has become an increasingly valuable tool in primary healthcare settings especially in remote areas, providing healthcare services remotely through technology. It can enable general practitioners to access specialist advice or services remotely or facilitate communication between patients and primary and community healthcare services (Haleem, 2021).

Traditionally, telemedicine was used to allow patients in remote or underserved areas to access primary and community healthcare services without the need to travel long distances. During and since the COVID-19 pandemic, its use has expanded to remove the need for patients to attend a clinic in person, even when they are closer to the facility. Patients can have virtual consultations with healthcare providers, discuss their symptoms, receive medical advice, and get prescriptions when necessary. Where necessary, a three-way conversation can be facilitated involving a specialist to prevent the need for a patient to attend a hospital.

This use of technology is increasingly reaching low-to-middle income countries, where it may offer cost-effective solutions (Mars, 2013; Mensah et al., 2023).

Telemedicine can facilitate the continuous monitoring and management of chronic conditions like diabetes, hypertension, and asthma. Patients can use wearable devices to track vital signs and health parameters, and this data is transmitted to healthcare providers for remote monitoring. Healthcare providers can intervene if they notice any concerning trends, leading to better disease management. Telemedicine may also be used to remotely review and adjust medication regimens for patients. It ensures medication adherence and reduces the risk of medication errors (Peyroteo et al., 2021).

Telemedicine has been instrumental in expanding access to mental health and counselling services in primary and community healthcare settings. Patients can have confidential virtual sessions with therapists or counsellors, making mental healthcare more accessible and convenient.

16.1.7 *Retail clinics*

Retail clinics are healthcare facilities typically located in retail stores, pharmacies, or supermarkets. They may also be referred to as walk-in clinics or convenient care clinics and are often private businesses where payment is out-of-pocket. They offer a range of basic services and treatments, including:

- Diagnosis and treatment of common illnesses such as cold and flu symptoms, sore throat, cough, sinus infections, earaches, and urinary tract infections.
- Vaccinations and immunisations for flu, tetanus, pertussis, measles, mumps, rubella, and other preventable diseases.
- Treatment of minor injuries like cuts, bruises, sprains, strains, and minor burns.
- Basic physical examinations for school, sports, or employment purposes.
- Screenings for conditions like high blood pressure, cholesterol levels, and diabetes risk assessments. Some clinics also provide rapid strep tests, urine tests, and blood glucose testing.
- Travel Health Services including travel vaccinations and advice on health risks related to specific destinations.
- Treatment of minor skin conditions like rashes, insect bites, and skin infections.
- Health and Wellness services such as smoking cessation programs, weight management counselling, and basic health education.

Bachrach et al. (2015).

Whilst they serve as a convenient option for individuals seeking quick and basic medical care for minor ailments, it is important for patient safety that if a patient's condition requires more extensive evaluation, ongoing care, or management of chronic conditions, they are referred onto a primary care physician or specialist.

16.1.8 Other primary healthcare professionals

Primary healthcare is not confined to medical services, and these days even medical services may be delivered by a multi-professional team, usually overseen by a physician.

Where primary care physicians work in group practices, they are often assisted in the delivery of services by a range of other healthcare professionals. In many cases, they will be co-located with the physicians' offices, in others they may be located elsewhere and patients be referred by their primary care physicians. These professionals include:

- *Nurse practitioners* are advanced practice registered nurses who can assess, diagnose, and treat patients. They often collaborate closely with physicians to manage patient care. They may often have additional training to take on day-to-day case management of long-term conditions such as diabetes. They may have a key role in health education, providing information and resources to patients regarding preventive care, healthy lifestyle choices, and managing chronic conditions.
- *Physician assistants* work under the supervision of physicians, assisting in patient examinations, diagnosis, and treatment. They can free up physicians for more complex cases.
- *Registered nurses* provide a range of healthcare services, including administering medications, performing procedures, and educating patients on managing their health conditions. They may run screening programmes.
- *Nutritionists/dietitians* work with patients to develop dietary plans, educate them on nutrition, and work with other professionals to manage conditions such as diabetes or obesity or ensure that older patients are eating properly.
- *Psychologists, psychiatrists, or counsellors* may be integrated into primary care settings to address mental health concerns and collaborate with physicians on holistic patient care.
- *Phlebotomists* may be employed by primary care practices to take blood to facilitate diagnostic tests to assist in the prevention, diagnosis and management of chronic diseases
- *Podiatrists* may be employed by primary care practices to assist in the care of older patients and those with diabetes.

Beyond primary medical care, there is a range of other primary healthcare services, which may coordinate with primary medical services to lesser or greater extents depending on the local context. These would include community pharmacies, primary care dentists, opticians and ophthalmologists, and audiologists working in the community. In the next section, we shall consider the care provided by nurses and carers in people's own homes and residential care homes.

16.1.9 Knowledge review

Before you move on, can you define the following key concepts:

- Gatekeeping?

16.1.10 Question to think about

Do you have a primary care physician who coordinates your healthcare across a range of providers? If yes, how effective are they in their coordinating role? If not, what are the barriers to achieving this coordination?

16.2 Community and long-term care

At a global level, Rudnicka et al. (2020) argue that "an ageing global population is the most important medical and social demographic problem worldwide" and that "addressing this problem is the highest priority for the care of the ageing population worldwide."

Healthcare services typically focus on addressing acute conditions. As individuals age, the nature of health issues often shifts towards chronic conditions, and it's not uncommon for multiple ailments and diseases to coexist. With advancing age, there is an increased prevalence of physical, sensory, and cognitive impairments. Conditions like urinary incontinence, frailty, and a heightened risk of falling can result in the decline of functional abilities. It is essential to have proper training and adequate tools to effectively assess the medical, psychological, and functional capacities of elderly individuals. This assessment is crucial for developing a comprehensive and coordinated plan for both treatment and long-term care (De Carvalho et al., 2021).

The implementation of such plans inevitably raises the priority of care services provided, on a regular basis, in people's homes. The specific services needed will vary based on factors such as health conditions, functional abilities, and social support. They may be classified as services aimed at keeping people in their own homes and alternative types of accommodation once a person can no longer be supported in their own home. Services that enable people to stay in their homes will include some that are traditionally regarded as social care and some regarded as healthcare:

- in-home care services offer assistance with daily tasks, medication management, and other necessary tasks, allowing older adults to remain in their homes
- meal services ensure older adults have access to nutritious meals
- assistance with transportation for medical appointments, grocery shopping, and other essential activities may be needed for older patients with mobility issues or other impairment
- adaptations to the home environment can enhance safety and accessibility for individuals with mobility challenges
- socialisation and companionship services can combat feelings of isolation and loneliness
- emotional and psychological support, counselling, and mental health services can address the emotional well-being of older individuals
- assistive devices such as wheelchairs, walkers, and hearing aids can enhance independence.
- remote monitoring and telehealth services can be used to track vital signs and connect with healthcare providers to reduce the need for frequent in-person visits

Although many of these needs go well beyond the traditional scope of primary healthcare, the coordinating role of a primary care physician may enable them to co-ordinate and monitor a multi-agency care plan.

Once these are insufficient to enable people to stay in their own homes, then different residential options may need to be considered with varying levels of support:

- assisted living facilities that provide assistance with daily activities while promoting independence
- residential care homes, communal living facilities that provide more assistance with daily activities, and monitor patient's health and well-being

- nursing homes that provide 24-hour skilled nursing care for individuals with complex medical needs or those who require continuous supervision
- specialised nursing homes for individuals with Alzheimer's disease, dementia, or other cognitive impairments
- end-of-life care, based within a hospice that focuses on comfort and quality of life for individuals with terminal illnesses

Caring for an ageing population in China

As a result of China's one-child policy, the average age of the population has increased rapidly since 1970. Over the last five decades, China's population has increased by more than 600 million, leading to a significant change in the age distribution. In 1970, just over half of China's population was under 20 years old, while less than 4% were over 65. During this period, China had a similar proportion of elderly dependents as India, with the majority of the population in both countries being under 20. By 2020, the percentage of children and adolescents in China had decreased to 23.4%, resembling figures seen in the UK, while China's elderly dependency ratio had almost doubled compared to India. Projections suggest that by 2050, China's elderly population (aged 65 and above) will surpass that of the UK and the USA, nearly doubling that of India. By then, China's elderly dependency ratio is expected to be comparable to that of the UK (Lobanov-Rostovsky et al., 2023).

Between one-fifth and one-quarter of adults over 65 are reported to be living with some form of age-related disability. Cardiovascular diseases, particularly strokes, are the primary cause of DALYs in China (Zheng et al., 2022). In 2018, the number of individuals living with cardiovascular diseases in China reached 290 million, which represents an increase of greater than 20% since 2007. Hypertension and diabetes are significant risk factors for vascular diseases and disability. Diabetes prevalence among Chinese adults is approximately 50% higher than the global average, posing a substantial disease burden among both the current and future elderly population (Lobanov-Rostovsky et al., 2023).

In traditional Chinese culture, children are expected to care for their ageing parents(Liu et al., 2015). Family-based care for older people remains based on this principle, enshrined in the 90-7-3 framework. This framework divides elderly care into three categories: 90% are anticipated to receive care within their own homes, 7% with assistance from community-based services, and 3% within institutional settings, such as care homes or nursing facilities, which becomes necessary when familial and community support are insufficient to meet their needs.

However, this does not reflect the reality of modern life in China,. Economic development has led to migration and the dispersal of families. Hu and Peng (2015) report that as long ago as 1990, less than one-fifth of households followed a traditional three-generational pattern. In response, the Protection of the Rights and Interests of Elderly People Law was amended in 2013 to require adult children to offer assistance to their ageing parents, including making regular visits and attending to their emotional and spiritual needs.

Adult children deemed to be inadequately caring for their parents have been warned that they may face consequences such as being placed on a credit blacklist, which could lead to restrictions such as being denied access to a bank account, starting a business, or purchasing a house. The impact of these measures is unclear.

At the same time, there is an increasing number of pilots of long-term care institutions in cities. Financing is provided mostly by universal social health insurance, but co-payment requirements mean that low-income groups may still be excluded.

Early evaluation studies demonstrate some benefits, but highlight challenges due to inconsistent financing, variability, and inequality in eligibility and reduced service capacity (Feng et al., 2020).

16.2.1 *Knowledge review*

Before you move on, can you define the following key concepts:

• Long-term care?

16.2.2 *Question to think about*

• When you reach an age where you need assistance for daily living, how would you ideally like that support to be provided?

16.3 The relationship between primary healthcare and public health

The boundaries of primary care are imprecise. We have already seen how older people requiring support may need primary healthcare as part of a broader package. Some primary care physicians will offer services traditionally provided in hospitals, either for patient convenience, or their own interest, professional development or remuneration.

However, the most fluid boundary is between primary care and public health.

A study of low- and middle-income countries that achieve good health outcomes at modest cost (Bangladesh, Ethiopia, Kyrgyzstan, Tamil Nadu(India), and Thailand) identified the critical role of access to primary healthcare in child and maternal health and for delivery of critical public health interventions: immunisation, oral rehydration for diarrheal disease, and modern contraception.

The WHO (2023) claims that an effective approach to primary healthcare can effectively deliver 90% of the interventions necessary for achieving universal health coverage, and 75% of the anticipated health improvements outlined in the Sustainable Development Goals is only realistic if primary healthcare prioritises preventative health measures and public health activities. White (2015) advocates a wide and inclusive definition of primary healthcare along these lines:

> *Essential healthcare made accessible at a cost that a country can afford, with methods that are practical, scientifically sound and socially acceptable. Everyone should have access to it and be involved in it, as should other sectors of society. It should include community participation and education on prevalent health problems, health promotion and disease prevention, provision of adequate food and nutrition, safe*

water, basic sanitation, maternal and child healthcare, family planning, prevention and control of endemic diseases, immunisation against vaccine-preventable diseases, appropriate treatment of common diseases and injuries, and provision of essential drugs. (White, 2015)

In practice, primary healthcare is a continuum of activities that sits between public health and curative health services.

Public health is focused on promoting and protecting good health, preventing disease, disability and premature death, restoring good health when it is impaired by disease or injury, and maximising the quality of life. Public health requires collective action by a wide range of agencies including primary healthcare, mostly through its role in preventative healthcare and health education.

Curative health services start within primary care dealing with simple illnesses, typically those that can be managed with medications, but are mostly the province of specialist services that deal with more serious conditions.

In publicly-funded primary healthcare systems, primary care is often funded by capitation-based remuneration schemes. In theory, these should incentivise primary care providers to undertake health promotion and education activities in order to keep their patients healthy and reduce their workload.

However, it is noteworthy that many systems operating this payment model, such as the UK, have found it necessary to provide additional incentives beyond basic capitation, in order to encourage primary care providers to carry out health promotion and education activities (Gillam & Siriwardena, 2018).

Globally, for primary healthcare to fulfil its key role in delivering universal health coverage and achieving other sustainable development goals by 2030, an inclusive scope with public health goals at its heart is necessary.

The role of and implications for primary care physicians of the Sustainable Development Goals: A view from Malaysia (after Renganathan & Davies, 2023)

In the Malaysian context, the 12th Malaysia Plan (2021–2025) aims to foster a prosperous, inclusive, and sustainable Malaysia. It prioritises reconfiguring healthcare services to improve their efficiency and affordability. The plan aims to reinforce healthcare policies, address both communicable and non-communicable diseases, enhance healthcare programs for the elderly, and bolster the nation's capacity to handle health crises. These efforts collectively aim to enhance the quality and accessibility of healthcare services. Moreover, the plan sets the stage for a comprehensive transformation of the Malaysian healthcare system through the introduction of a blueprint tailored to this purpose.

Arising from the 12th Malaysia Plan, and guided by a consultative process initiated in 2022, the Health White Paper titled "Strengthening people's health, future-proofing the nation's health system" was formulated and endorsed by the Parliament in June 2023.

It emphasises the primacy of prioritising primary healthcare, transitioning from a model of sick care to one focused on enhancing overall health and well-being. It advocates for fortified and more efficient public-private partnerships to achieve superior health outcomes for the populace. These considerations bear significant importance for primary care physicians and other healthcare workers operating within the primary care domain in Malaysia.

Primary care physicians in Malaysia can contribute to delivery of the SDGs in multiple ways. Firstly, in the clinical setting, primary care physicians play a pivotal role in ensuring the maintenance and restoration of good health among individual patients. They are often the initial point of contact for individuals seeking healthcare services, and much of their daily practice aligns with SDG 3, which aims to "ensure healthy lives and promote well-being for all at all ages." Through activities such as health education, counselling, and early detection and management of diseases, primary care physicians contribute significantly to achieving SDG targets related to maternal and child health, disease prevention, and treatment.

Within the public health domain, primary care physicians actively engage with communities to promote health and prevent diseases. Their close ties to local communities enable them to design and implement health promotion programs tailored to specific community needs, thereby advancing SDGs related to health promotion, disease prevention, and overall well-being.

Furthermore, primary care physicians can contribute to environmental sustainability by adopting practices that minimise their carbon footprint and promote environmentally friendly healthcare delivery methods, thereby supporting SDG 13, which focuses on combating climate change and its impacts and further contributes to the broader determinants of health.

Beyond their clinical and community roles, primary care physicians wield significant influence as advocates for health-related policies and initiatives. Through their involvement in advocacy efforts at local, national, and international levels, they can push for policy changes that align with various SDGs, including those related to gender equality, environmental sustainability, and overall health and well-being.

In conclusion, primary care physicians in Malaysia can play a crucial role in advancing the SDGs through their clinical practice, community engagement, advocacy efforts, and commitment to environmental sustainability. By recognising and leveraging these diverse roles, primary care physicians can contribute meaningfully to the achievement of the SDGs and the overall improvement of population health and well-being.

16.3.1 *Knowledge review*

Before you move on, can you define the following key concepts:

• Public health?

16.3.2 *Question to think about*

In your country, how much of primary care is devoted to public health goals through disease prevention, health promotion and health education? Do you think there should be more or less?

16.4 The business of primary care

Many primary care providers operate as business units within the larger healthcare system. Even in largely public systems, primary care physicians often operate as private contractors to the healthcare funders. They operate as single contractors or often as groups of physicians, allowing them to share costs and premises and collectively offer additional therapeutic services.

This means that in many countries, primary care operates as a business, even if most or all of their income is derived not directly from patients but from funders such as government agencies or insurance funds.

16.4.1 Remuneration for primary care

The manner in which these primary care providers are paid will influence their behaviours and incentivise them to prioritise certain activities over others. Capitation is an important provider-payment mechanism in primary care. It may form the sole payment mechanism or be supplemented by payments designed to incentivise meeting specific targets.

Funding primary healthcare by capitation can offer several advantages. It provides a predictable budget for both funders and providers. This allows for better financial planning and management.

It should encourage healthcare providers to focus on preventive care and cost-effective treatments. Since they are responsible for managing the healthcare needs of their enrolled population within the fixed budget, keeping them healthy should reduce activity and costs whilst minimising administrative costs should further reduce costs and increase the amount left over from the capitation payments.

Capitation-based remuneration should promote a population health perspective rather than a fee-for-service model that may incentivise providers to perform more procedures. Providers are motivated to invest in preventive measures and manage chronic conditions effectively to keep their patients healthy and minimise costly interventions. However, in practice, there are a complex range of factors involved which may negate this incentive.

In fee-for-service models, there may be a tendency for providers to order unnecessary tests or treatments to increase revenue. By contrast, with capitation, the risk of overutilisation is reduced as providers are not rewarded for performing unnecessary procedures.

Capitation encourages a more comprehensive and coordinated approach to healthcare. Providers are motivated to consider all aspects of a patient's health and address preventive, diagnostic, and treatment needs in a holistic manner. Where patients have a choice of providers, capitated providers are incentivised to focus on patient satisfaction and patient-centred care to maintain long-term relationships and patient loyalty.

Finally, capitation-based payment systems can simplify administrative tasks, as there are fewer individual claims to process and reimburse compared to a fee-for-service model.

However, funding healthcare by capitation has disadvantages as well. It may lead to healthcare providers limiting access to services or being selective about the patients they accept to control costs. This can result in reduced access to care for certain patients, especially those with complex or costly medical conditions.

Similarly, since healthcare providers receive a fixed payment per patient, they may have an incentive to provide fewer services or less intensive treatments to reduce costs, potentially compromising the quality of care.

Alternatively, they may seek to reduce costs by avoiding or selecting fewer patients with higher medical risks to minimise expenses. This can lead to "cherry-picking" healthier patients while leaving sicker individuals to other providers or the public health system, leading to disparities in access and care.

16.4.2 *Managing relationships with patients aka customers*

In contexts where primary care providers are competing for patients, they may need to look at optimising their relationships with their customers. For many primary care providers, with a traditional paternalistic medical culture, Customer Relationship Management (CRM) techniques as used in other industries will seem quite alien, but in recent years, and as living standards rise in many low-to-middle income countries particularly, patients have become more demanding and started to see themselves as customers and consumers.

Veber (2009) describes CRM in terms of a process of increasing maturity in the deployment of CRM as shown in Figure 16.1.

In practice, all primary care providers need to establish effective communication channels with patients. This includes sending appointment reminders, follow-up messages, and personalised health information through various channels such as emails, text messages, or patient portals. Prompt and informative communication helps patients stay engaged with their healthcare, leading to better compliance with treatment plans and improved health outcomes.

Patients increasingly expect personalised care plans. Providers can use CRM systems to collect and analyse patient data, including medical history, preferences, and lifestyle choices. With this information, primary care physicians can create personalised care

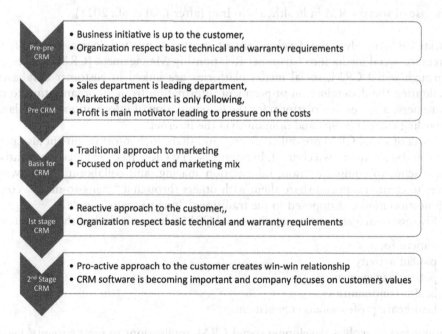

Figure 16.1 Stages of CRM after Veber (2009) Graphic created by the author

plans tailored to each patient's needs, promoting better patient satisfaction and adherence to treatment.

Providers can use CRM systems to simplify their appointments process, helping patients to make appointments online or through mobile applications. Additionally, these systems can help manage patient flow efficiently, reducing waiting times and enhancing the overall patient experience.

Primary care providers can collect feedback from patients through surveys and other means. Understanding patient experiences and satisfaction levels allows healthcare facilities to identify areas for improvement and make necessary changes to enhance the quality of care provided.

Customer support and complaints systems from CRM can be used to manage patient inquiries and resolve issues efficiently. They enable primary care providers to track patient concerns and respond in a timely manner, demonstrating that patient satisfaction and well-being are top priorities.

Building strong relationships with patients through effective CRM strategies can foster patient loyalty. Satisfied patients are more likely to continue seeking care from the same primary care provider and recommend it to others, contributing to patient retention and positive word-of-mouth marketing.

Providers can use targeted marketing and outreach initiatives drawing on CRM data to identify patient populations for targeted outreach and preventive care initiatives. By analysing patient data, healthcare providers can create campaigns focused on promoting health screenings, vaccinations, and other preventive measures.

For those patients with chronic conditions who require ongoing care, CRM can help in tracking appointments, monitoring medication adherence, and providing targeted educational resources to assist patients to manage their conditions and care effectively.

The use of social CRM in healthcare in Iraq (after Jalal et al., 2021)

Social CRM involves the development of strategies, methodologies, and skills to integrate social media into Customer Relationship Management (CRM) processes. Through social CRM, social media platforms are linked to customer databases, facilitating the dissemination of pertinent information from an organisation to its customers. It serves as a platform for the dissemination of information, particularly regarding current events and opinions, via the Internet.

Users of social CRM not only consume and share such information but also generate and share their own content. In essence, social CRM has introduced innovative approaches to communication, information sharing, and collaboration, allowing users to create ideas and share them with others through a "many-to-many" communication mode, as opposed to the traditional "one-to-many" mode.

Five essential features characterise social CRM schemes in the healthcare context:

- patient focus
- patient activity
- patient engagement
- health communities
- healthcare professionals engagement

Patient focus involves developing social CRM applications to meet patients' needs through healthcare specialists. Patient activity entails the structure of CRM systems facilitating patients' active involvement in providing and gathering health-related information directly relevant or interesting to them.

Patient engagement refers to the ability of social CRM systems to empower patients to manage certain aspects of their health issues via social media platforms. Engaging healthcare professionals involves the development of social CRM platforms for information exchange among healthcare professionals, such as setting up discussion boards for discourse on specific healthcare topics. Creating healthcare communities makes use of community healthcare features derived from social CRM applications, enabling the sharing of opinions on individuals, business activities, products, and services.

Jalal et al. (2021) argue that the adoption of social CRM technologies for health-related exchanges offers numerous benefits. Firstly, these technologies allow patients to manage their healthcare through communication with fellow patients, fostering a sense of belonging and support, which can alleviate feelings of isolation and improve patients' coping attitudes towards their medical conditions. Additionally, the use of technological applications by patients can enhance their ability to manage their medical conditions effectively. Moreover, the low implementation costs make social media platforms feasible facilitators for health-related communication and social support exchange activities via the Internet.

However, despite the undeniable benefits of health social media utilisation, its adoption faces several challenges. Concerns about the effectiveness of security measures and the confidentiality of personal health information posted on these platforms, as well as doubts regarding the reliability and quality of information presented, may deter users, providers, and administrators from active involvement in social CRM platforms.

16.4.3 Knowledge review

Before you move on, can you define the following key concepts:

* Customer Relationship Management (CRM)?
* Social CRM?

16.4.4 Question to think about

Do you want your primary care provider to think of you as a patient or a customer? Why?

References

Bachrach, D., Frohlich, J., Garcimonde, A., & Nevitt, K. (2015). The value proposition of retail clinics. *Robert Wood Johnson Foundation, 12*.

Balabanova, D., McKee, M., & Mills, A. (2012). 'Good health at low cost': 25 years on. What makes a successful health system?. *Reproductive Health Matters, 20*(39), 212–214.

Collings, J. S. (1950). General practice in England today. A reconnaissance. *Lancet, 555–585*.

de Carvalho Vieira, B. L., Martins, A. C., Ferreira, R. C., & Vargas, A. M. D. (2021). Quality of care in long-term care institutions: A scoping review of literature. *Research, Society and Development, 10*(8), e17110817117-e17110817117.

Dumontet, M., Buchmueller, T., Dourgnon, P., Jusot, F., & Wittwer, J. (2017). Gatekeeping and the utilisation of physician services in France: Evidence on the Médecin traitant reform. *Health Policy* (Amsterdam, Netherlands), 121(6), 675–682.

Feng, Z., Glinskaya, E., Chen, H., Gong, S., Qiu, Y., Xu, J., et al. (2020). Long-term care system for older adults in China: policy landscape, challenges, and future prospects. *Lancet*, 396(10259), 1362–1372.

Gillam, S., & Siriwardena, A. N. (2018). The Quality and Outcomes Framework: Triumph of evidence or tragedy for personal care? In *The Quality and Outcomes Framework* (pp. 156–166). CRC Press.

Haleem, A., Javaid, M., Singh, R. P., & Suman, R. (2021). Telemedicine for healthcare: Capabilities, features, barriers, and applications. *Sensors International*, 2, 100117.

Hu, Z., & Peng, X. (2015) Household changes in contemporary China: An analysis based on the four recent censuses. *Chinese Journal of Sociology*, 2(1), 1–20.

Jalal, A. N., Bahari, M., & Tarofder, A. K. (2021). Transforming traditional CRM into social CRM: An empirical investigation in Iraqi healthcare industry. *Heliyon*, 7(5). e06913

Kane, C. K. (2022). *Recent changes in physician practice arrangements: Shifts away from private practice and towards larger practice size continue through 2022*. American Medical Association

Liu, H., Han, X., Xiao, Q., & Feldman, M. (2015). Family structure and quality of life of elders in rural China: The role of the new rural social pension. *Journal of Aging & Social*, 27(2), 123–138.

Lobanov-Rostovsky, S., He, Q., Chen, Y., et al. (2023). Growing old in China in socioeconomic and epidemiological context: Systematic review of social care policy for older people. *BMC Public Health*, 23, 1272.

Mars, M. (2013, November 1). Telemedicine and advances in urban and rural healthcare delivery in Africa. *Progress in Cardiovascular Diseases*, 56(3), 326–335.

Mensah, N. K., Adzakpah, G., Kissi, J., Boadu, R. O., Lasim, O. U., Oyenike, M. K., Bart-Plange, A., Dalaba, M. A., & Sukums, F. (2023). Health professional's readiness and factors associated with telemedicine implementation and use in selected health facilities in Ghana. *Heliyon*, 9(3), e14501.

Peyroteo, M., Ferreira, I. A., Elvas, L. B., Ferreira, J. C., & Lapão, L. V. (2021). Remote monitoring systems for patients with chronic diseases in primary health care: Systematic review. *JMIR mHealth and uHealth*, 9(12), e28285.

Ren, M., Zhang, T., Xu, J., Qiao, J., Qiao, J., Zhan, S., ... Huang, Y. (2023). Building quality primary health care development in the new era towards universal health coverage: A beijing initiative. *Global Health Research and Policy*, 8(1), 53.

Renganathan, E., & Davies, P. (2023). Sustainable development goals and the role of and implications for primary care physicians. *Malaysian Family Physician: The Official Journal of the Academy of Family Physicians of Malaysia*, 18, 54.

Roland, M. (2020). Just another GP crisis: The Collings report 70 years on. *British Journal of General Practice*, 70(696), 325–326.

Rudnicka, E., Napierała, P., Podfigurna, A., Męczekalski, B., Smolarczyk, R., & Grymowicz, M. (2020). The World Health Organization (WHO) approach to healthy ageing. *Maturitas*, 139, 6-11.

Schneider, H., Sanders, D., Besada, D., Daviaud, E., & Rohde, S. (2018). Ward-based primary health care outreach teams in South Africa: Developments, challenges and future directions. *South African Health Review*, 2018(1), 59–65.

Sripa, P., Hayhoe, B., Garg, P., Majeed, A., & Greenfield, G. (2019). Impact of GP gatekeeping on quality of care, and health outcomes, use, and expenditure: A systematic review. *British Journal of General Practice*, 69(682), e294–e303. doi:10.3399/bjgp19X702209

Thomas, L. S., Buch, E., & Pillay, Y. (2021). An analysis of the services provided by community health workers within an urban district in South Africa: A key contribution towards universal access to care. *Human Resources for Health*, 19, 22.

Tilhou, A. S., Huguet, N., DeVoe, J., et al. (2020). The affordable care act medicaid expansion positively impacted community health centers and their patients. *Journal of General Internal Medicine*, 35, 1292–1295.

Tikkanen, R., Osborn, R., Mossialos, E., Djordjevic, A., & Wharton, G. A. (2020). *International health care profiles*. The Commonwealth Fund.

Veber, J. (2009). a kol. Management, základy, moderní manažerské přístupy, výkonnost a prosperita. Praha: Management Press. ISBN 978-80-7261-200-0.

Velasco Garrido, M., Zentner, A., & Busse, R. (2011). The effects of gatekeeping: A systematic review of the literature. *Scandinavian Journal of Primary Health Care*, 29(1), 28–38.

World Health Organisation. (1978, September 6–12). *Alma-ata declaration of 1978*. International Conference on Primary Health Care, Alma-Ata, USSR.

World Health Organisation. (2023, November 15). *Factsheet: Primary health care*. World Health Organisation.

White, F. (2015). Primary health care and public health: Foundations of universal health systems. *Medical Principles and Practice*, 24(2), 103–116.

WHO and UNICEF. (2018). *A vision for primary health care in the 21st century: Towards universal health coverage and the sustainable development goals. Special programme on primary health care (primary care)* (WHO/HIS/SDS/2018.15). WHO and UNICEF.

Zheng, P.-P., Guo, Z.-L., Du, X.-J., Yang, H.-M., & Wang, Z.-J. (2022). Prevalence of disability among the Chinese older population: A systematic review and Meta-analysis. *International Journal of Environmental Research and Public Health*, 19(3), 1656.

17 Supporting industries

17.1 Pharmaceutical manufacturing

The pharmaceutical industry develops, produces, and markets drugs and other treatments, licensed for use as medications. They can often deliver better health outcomes at lower cost by preventing or reducing the consequences of disease and eliminating the need for expensive and invasive alternatives such as surgery.

Because of the potential for harm alongside the considerable benefits, the sector is subject to a high degree of regulation regarding the patenting, testing, safety, efficacy, and marketing of drugs.

The pharmaceutical sector includes:

- prescription drugs for treatment or prevention
- OTC drugs for other purposes such as pain management
- vaccines for prevention of disease
- generic drugs, providing cheaper drugs once patents have expired
- food supplements and vitamins
- support services such as packaging and labelling services

17.1.1 Value of the global pharmaceutical industry

By the end of 2021, the total global pharmaceutical market was valued at about 1.42 trillion US dollars, which represents around 450% growth over the last 20 years. Source: (Mikulic, 2021).

The pharmaceutical industry produces medicines to treat a broad range of indications. Based on forecasted global spending for 2026, the four largest indications for pharmaceutical use are oncology (cancer), immunology (auto-immune conditions), antidiabetics (diabetes), and neurology (conditions affecting the nervous system, like epilepsy and Parkinson's disease). With 306 billion USD global spending forecasted for 2026, oncology is by far the largest therapy area, followed by immunology (178 billion USD), antidiabetics (173 billion USD), and neurology (151 billion USD) (IQVIA, 2022).

If we prioritise the therapy areas based on volume of use (defined daily doses) rather than global sales, the picture changes: cardiovascular (heart and blood vessels), diabetes, kidney disease, and musculoskeletal (muscles and bones) disorders dominate in emerging and developed markets (IQVIA, 2021).

The difference between the rankings by sales versus by defined daily doses is because, despite both groups of indications affecting many people, there are many older medicines

DOI: 10.4324/9781003478874-21

available where the originator patents have expired and generic alternatives are offered at a lower price. For those diseases that affect most people, generic pharmaceuticals are available at a low price (lower spend). Disease areas targeted by current innovations affect fewer patients but pharmaceutical prices are very high (high spend).

17.1.2 Regulation of the pharmaceutical industry

Because of the risk to patient safety, drug regulation has historically been rigorously enforced, with governments closely overseeing every aspect, from development to marketing. This oversight extends to pricing and distribution in many cases. Despite the globalisation of the pharmaceutical industry, regulation was primarily the domain of national sovereignty until recently, requiring separate tests, applications, and criteria for each market.

However, since the 1990s, there has been a shift towards greater cooperation among national regulatory agencies. Initiatives like the European Union's centralised drug approval system, increased cooperation by the US FDA with foreign counterparts, and efforts by major economies like the US, EU, and Japan to harmonise approval requirements through the International Conference on Harmonisation of Technical Requirements for the Registration of Pharmaceutical Products (ICH) reflect this trend.

Over the past two decades, the global framework for pharmaceutical regulation has significantly changed, largely due to the implementation of new global standards for intellectual property (IP) rights. This shift has compelled developing countries to establish new institutions to oversee and manage the evolving IP system (Sweet, 2017). Consequently, the pharmaceutical sector has become a focal point for disputes concerning ownership rights, access to medicines, and marketing practices.

Research indicates that alongside the adoption of IP standards, there has been a surge in the regulation of off-patent products. However, pharmaceutical standards and regulatory systems remain fragile and inconsistent across many countries, often relying heavily on aid and technical assistance from international donors. A study by Olsson et al. (2010) focusing on least developed countries revealed that less than half of them publicly funded their pharmaceutical regulatory agencies, with many relying on financing from international organisations. In some cases, regulatory activities were entirely funded by a single international source, such as the Global Fund.

This dependence on external funding underscores the vulnerability and diversity of regulatory models in developing countries. It also contributes to a broader discourse highlighting the link between the quality of regulation and the lack of local democratic control over healthcare systems in these nations. Overall, the involvement of international institutions underscores the challenges faced by developing countries in establishing robust pharmaceutical regulatory frameworks.

17.1.3 The new drug development process

Pharmaceutical companies are often criticised for the high price of new and especially of novel treatments but bringing a new drug to the market is an expensive business and many potential drugs do not get that far.

The innovative force in pharmaceutical care is the research-based pharmaceutical industry. It's research and development (R&D) intensity in 2018 was 15%, much larger than, for example, the automotive sector (4.5%) or technology hardware and equipment

(8.7%) (International Federation of Pharmaceutical Manufacturers & Associations [IFPMA], 2021).

The research-based pharmaceutical industry invests billion of dollars and employs millions of people to develop innovative pharmaceuticals. The industry has high entry barriers:

Specific skills and large funds are required for the development, production, market access, and commercialisation of pharmaceuticals (IFPMA, 2021).

The pharmaceutical industry needs to adhere to strict regulations during drug development.

This aims to ensure that the pharmaceuticals' benefits outweigh its risks and side effects. Only one out of 5,000 to 10,000 screened candidate compounds is promising enough to be included in clinical testing. The testing process may take 10 to 15 years and only a few candidates pass the clinical trial process (IFPMA, 2021). The process of taking a successful drug to market is often described as a drug development funnel as shown schematically in Figure 17.1.

Once a drug is ready for market, then there are several steps the manufacturer needs to pass to get an innovative pharmaceutical from clinical development to its intended use in patients. In Europe, this process includes the following steps (IFPMA, 2021):

- Clinical development: This is R&D with drug discovery and phase I-III clinical trials. The pharmaceutical industry selects the compounds for development based on expected clinical and commercial success.
- Market authorisation: The European Medicines Agency (EMA) evaluates the benefits and risks of the new compound based on the clinical dossiers. Successful applicants receive permission to sell their product in Europe.
- Pricing and reimbursement: National decision-making bodies usually evaluate the new compound, clinical benefits, or cost-effectiveness. They may set a price for the product covered by public health insurance (if applicable).
- Production: The pharmaceutical company will either produce the product itself or out-license it to a partner for manufacturing at a large scale. The product is packaged and labelled according to the requirements set by the target market.

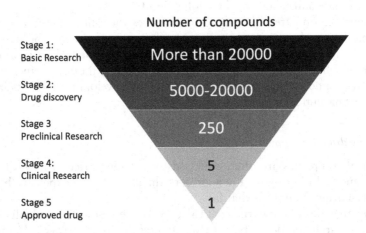

Figure 17.1 The drug development funnel.

- Marketing and distribution: The pharmaceutical is distributed either through wholesale or direct sales to hospitals, clinics, or outpatient pharmacies. Interest and demand for the product is created through collaborations with key opinion leaders, scientific publications, and key conferences, as well as common marketing methods like advertisement or detailing. The scope of permitted marketing is defined by the target market's regulation.
- Treatment decision: Most innovative compounds must be prescribed by a physician. Therefore, to reach a patient, the physician must make a treatment decision with the consent of the patient. This decision is often based on the expected effectiveness of the product.

17.1.4 *Access to pharmaceuticals in low-to-middle income countries*

There is an essential conflict between the need for pharmaceutical companies to achieve a return on their investment in research and development and the need to provide affordable pharmaceuticals especially in LMICs.

Traditionally, the manufacturer gains 20 to 25 years of exclusive rights to market their new drug through patent protection. After this, the patent lapses, and other manufacturers are allowed to produce their own versions, known as generic drugs.

A generic drug is a medication created to be the same as an already marketed brand-name drug in dosage form, safety, strength, route of administration, quality, performance characteristics, and intended use. Generic medicines are designed to be bioequivalent, which means that they work in the same way and provide the same clinical benefit as the brand-name medicine. Because they do not have to incur the cost of the initial development, generic drugs can be much cheaper than the patented original.

Expensive pharmaceutical innovations protected by patents are often beyond the reach of people in lower-income countries. To evaluate whether people have adequate access to pharmaceutical care, the World Health Organisation's (WHO's) Essential Medicines List (EML) may be used as a point of reference. An analysis of access to 469 essential medicines in 13 lower-middle income countries shows that, on average, 68% of these medicines are available. However, the average EML volume share was only 25% of the total drug market in these countries. This indicates that only one quarter of the medicines distributed in these countries were essential medicines. Also, more than 95% of the essential medicine doses distributed are drugs that are greater than 20 years old (IQVIA, 2022).

However, paradoxically, access to lower-cost generic drugs can be more difficult in the poorest countries. Silverman- et al. (2019) claim that:

> In the poorest countries, unbranded generics are only 5% of the pharmaceutical market by volume – in comparison to the US where unbranded quality-assured generics are 85% of the market by volume.

During the 1990s, as part of the negotiations to establish the WTO for the protection of free trade, all the member nations of the WTO signed up to the TRIPS agreement on Intellectual Property Rights. TRIPS plays a crucial role in relation to access to medicines in low- and middle-income countries. TRIPS requires WTO member states to ensure that intellectual property rights are subject to strict protection. Patents must be enforceable for at least 20 years (Art. 33) whereby exceptions to exclusive rights must be limited.

Under the TRIPS agreement, WTO members retained important policy options, flexibilities and safeguards, including the liberty to determine the grounds for issuing compulsory licences and for when to order government use; to allow for various forms of parallel imports; to apply general exceptions, and make use of transition periods for developing countries and a longer, extendible transition period for least developed countries in particular.

The Millennium Declaration in 2001 set the goal to achieve, by 2010, universal access to treatment for HIV/AIDS for all those who need it. This was reaffirmed in the Political Declaration on HIV/AIDS highlighting the flexibilities of the TRIPS Agreement in order to improve access to treatment. WHO Global Strategy and Plan of Action on Public Health, Innovation and Intellectual Property urges governments to consider, using the full range of flexibilities contained in the TRIPS Agreement

One major type of exemption that may be used by national governments to provide access to otherwise patented high-cost medications is compulsory licensing, This grants every WTO member the right to issue compulsory licenses and the freedom to determine their basis. The WTO Ministerial Conference emphasises the importance of interpreting the TRIPS Agreement in a manner supportive of public health, encouraging access to existing medicines and fostering research and development into new medicines.

Discussions on the impact of the TRIPS agreement coincided with significant increases in HIV incidence and deaths, particularly in sub-Saharan Africa. Concerns quickly emerged regarding what the TRIPS agreement would mean for access to antiretroviral drugs for HIV treatment.

Access to antiretroviral therapy in the world's poorest countries

Antiretroviral therapy significantly reduces morbidity and mortality among people living with HIV. As of December 2009, an estimated 5.2 million people living with HIV in low- and middle-income countries were receiving antiretroviral therapy, a 12-fold increase since 2003. The 2010 WHO HIV treatment guidelines for adults and adolescents recommended starting HIV treatment at a lower CD4 count to reduce HIV-related mortality and to prevent opportunistic infections such as tuberculosis.

This increased the number of people estimated to need antiretroviral therapy from 10.1 million to nearly 15 million (Manosuthi et al., 2015).

At the end of December 2021, 28.7 million people were accessing antiretroviral therapy, up from 7.8 million in 2010. In 2021, about 76% of the adults aged 15 years and older living with HIV had access to treatment, as did about 52% of children under 15. Around 81% of pregnant women living with HIV had access to antiretroviral medicines to prevent transmission of HIV to their children in 2021, but access is poorer amongst adult males.

Some governments have used the exceptions available within TRIPs.

In July 2007, Rwanda became the first country to announce its intention to use the WTO 30 August, 2003 decision to import a generic fixed-dose combination of antiviral therapies from a Canadian generic manufacturing company.

Using the threat of compulsory licensing, the Brazilian Government negotiated significant price reductions of key antiviral drugs between 2001 and 2006.

In late 2006 and early 2007, Thailand issued compulsory licences for a number of pharmaceutical products.

The use of TRIPS exceptions to provide cost effective access to HIV anti-virals remains controversial but is a vital tool for low-to-medium income countries with high HIV rates to combat the disease and meet the goals of universal access.

In more recent discussions on COVID-19 vaccines and treatments, debates on patent protection for medical innovations have resurfaced, with arguments advocating that patent protection incentivises research and development. However, existing flexibilities within the TRIPS Agreement are still not widely utilised (Haugen, 2021).

Today, there are worries that the agreement may negatively affect access to medicines in developing countries. It has had both a positive and a negative impact on access to medicines. While the TRIPS Agreement has spurred investment and innovation in the pharmaceutical sector, it has also led to higher medicine prices and increased trade barriers, resulting in a mixed impact on access to medicines in developing countries. Although the treaty has built-in safeguards for the poorest countries, in practice, their use has been very limited.

17.1.5 Emerging technologies in the pharmaceutical industry

The pharmaceutical industry invests very heavily in research and development and this is reflected in the rapid pace of innovation in the industry. Two current trends in pharmaceutical innovation are personalised medicine and biosimilars.

In simple terms, personalised medicine is the process of tailoring treatments to the individual characteristics of the patient. Traditional pharmaceutical interventions are often unsubtle in their effects on the human body, having many effects beyond their intended purpose. Generally, personalised medicine refers to the use of emerging technologies such as DNA sequencing and the monitoring of the impact of interventions through proteomics (the study of certain large proteins), imaging protocols, and wireless health monitoring devices to demonstrate how different individuals respond to the same pharmaceutical interventions.

Examples of personalised medicine (after Goetz & Schork, 2018)

One notable example is warfarin, a commonly used blood thinner. Improper dosing of warfarin can lead to severe adverse reactions. Warfarin interacts with the VKORC1 gene and is metabolised partly by the CYP2C9 gene. Natural genetic variations in these genes result in differences in how individuals respond to warfarin, prompting the US FDA to recommend personalised dosing based on an individual's genotype.

Primaquine (PQ) provides another classic example. While effective against malaria, some individuals develop acute haemolytic anaemia (AHA) after PQ administration. This adverse reaction is associated with genetic variants in the G6PD gene. Current clinical practice involves genotyping patients to determine if they carry relevant G6PD gene variants, which may indicate whether PQ use is advisable.

Imatinib, used in treating chronic myelogenous leukaemia (CML), is another well-known example. Imatinib targets an enzyme called tyrosine kinase, which is elevated due to the fusion of the Abelson proto-oncogene (abl) and the breakpoint cluster region (bcr), known as the bcr-abl fusion or "Philadelphia chromosome." However, not all CML patients exhibit this fusion event. Therefore, imatinib is typically prescribed only to those with the bcr-abl fusion mutation.

Instead of developing a drug and then identifying factors that mitigate its efficacy or side effects through observational studies on individuals who are provided the drug, such as warfarin, PQ, and imatinib, there are now attempts to identify genetic profiles possessed by patients and then craft therapies that uniquely target those profiles.

A notable example is the emerging category of cancer treatments referred to as immunotherapies. The common objective of all immunotherapies is to stimulate or activate an individual's immune system to combat cancer. One approach within immunotherapy focuses on exploiting unique genetic alterations found in a cancer patient's tumour cells, known as neo-antigens. These neo-antigens have the potential to trigger an immune response if correctly recognised by the host's immune cells. Essentially, this form of immunotherapy involves extracting immune-reactive cells, such as T cells, from a patient, then modifying them to specifically identify and target the neo-antigens detected in the patient's tumour. Subsequently, these altered cells are reintroduced into the patient's body to attack the tumour cells emitting the neo-antigen signals (Farkona et al., 2016).

One of the biggest challenges to the adoption of personalised medicine is its expense and specificity. However, the remarkably rapid fall in the cost of genome sequencing offers hope that access to such treatments may increase over time.

Biosimilar drugs are biological drugs that are very similar to another already approved biological medicine, referred to as the "reference medicine." Biosimilars must be approved according to the same standards of pharmaceutical quality, safety, and efficacy that apply to all biological medicines. The European Medicines Agency (EMA) is responsible for evaluating the majority of applications to market biosimilars within the European Union (EU) and approved its first biosimilar drug in 2013.

Biological medicines are used to treat patients with chronic and often disabling conditions such as diabetes, autoimmune diseases, and cancers. They derive their active ingredients from a biological source, such as living cells or organisms (human, animals and microorganisms such as bacteria or yeast) and the extraction often requires advanced technology.

Most biological medicines in current clinical use contain protein-based active substances although these may differ in size and structural complexity from simple proteins like insulin or growth hormone to more complex ones such as coagulation factors or monoclonal antibodies.

The primary advantage of using biosimilar drugs is the potential cost reductions. Biosimilars closely resemble original biologic agents. Like generics, biosimilars are typically less costlier than their originators. The cost-effectiveness of biosimilars compared to the "reference medicine" primarily stems from the fact that biosimilars do not need to undergo the extensive clinical development process required for originator approval. Additionally, biosimilars do not incur substantial expenses related to marketing, market access, and post-marketing research and development. However, because of their long development time and the regulatory requirements to ensure their quality, safety, and efficacy, the price differential of biosimilar drugs compared to their reference medicine is unlikely to be as profound as for chemical generics (Weise, 2012).

Because biosimilars are similar but not identical, the biggest threat is rejection. If the immune system recognises that a molecule is foreign and, thus, produces antidrug antibodies, this may lead to the loss of efficacy or the development of side effects (Feagan, 2017).

17.1.6 *Knowledge review*

Before you move on, can you define the following key concepts:

* Generic drugs?
* Biosimilar drugs?

17.1.7 *Question to think about*

Do you think the high profits of pharmaceutical companies are justified by the fact that the sector has the highest percentage invested in R&D of any comparable business sector?

17.2 Medical products and devices

The global medical devices market was worth nearly 456.8 billion USD in 2020 and is expected to exceed 863 billion USD by 2030 (Business Research Company, 2021).

Like drugs, the manufacture and selling of medical devices are also highly regulated, but the degree of regulation depends on the level of risk associated with the device. Within the European Union, medical devices are regulated by the European Commission (EC).

Similar to pharmaceuticals, medical devices are highly regulated because of the risk to patient safety. Devices vary widely from walking sticks to complex MRI scanners.

MDCG 2019-11 (European Commission, 2019) defines a medical device as follows:

> "medical device" means any instrument, apparatus, appliance, software, implant, reagent, material, or other article intended by the manufacturer to be used, alone or in combination, for human beings for one or more of the following specific medical purposes:
> * diagnosis, prevention, monitoring, prediction, prognosis, treatment, or alleviation of disease,
> * diagnosis, monitoring, treatment, alleviation of, or compensation for, an injury or disability,
> * investigation, replacement, or modification of the anatomy or of a physiological or pathological process or state,
> * providing information by means of in vitro examination of specimens derived from the human body, including organ, blood and tissue donations,

and which does not achieve its principal intended action by pharmacological, immuno-logical or metabolic means, in or on the human body, but which may be assisted in its function by such means.

In order to be legally sold in the European Union (EU), a medical device must obtain a Conformité Européene (CE) marking. The Medical Device Regulation (MDR) 2017/745 categorises medical devices into four classes: Class I, Class IIa, Class IIb, and Class III.

Different conformity assessment routes are established for each class, tailored to the perceived level of risk associated with the device.

Classification of medical devices within the European Union

- *Class I medical devices*, such as stethoscopes, bandages, and glasses, are considered to have the lowest perceived risk. While most Class I devices can be self-certified by manufacturers, certain types, such as Class Is (sterile devices), Class Im (devices with measuring features), and Class Ir (reusable surgical instruments), require assessment by a notified body before the CE marking can be affixed.
- *Class IIa medical devices*, like catheters, hearing aids, and disposable contact lenses, present a moderate level of risk. Manufacturers must submit these devices to regulatory bodies for assessment and obtain a declaration of conformity before market placement.
- *Class IIb medical devices*, including incubators, insulin pens, long-term contact lenses, and ventilators, pose a higher risk compared to Class IIa devices. Therefore, they also require involvement from a notified body for assessment and certification.
- *Class III medical devices*, such as pacemakers, prosthetic heart valves, surgical mesh, and breast implants, represent the highest level of risk as they are implanted in the human body. Consequently, they are subject to the most rigorous requirements. Unlike devices with lower risk, Class III devices must undergo clinical evaluation before market introduction and are subject to more intensive post-market monitoring.

The European Parliament and the Council of the European Union (2017)

The US Food and Drug Administration uses a similar scheme, but does not split class II devices.

Many medical devices are increasingly dependent upon software, which may be external or embedded. MDCG 2019-11 defines medical device software (MDSW) as:

> *Software that is intended to be used, alone or in combination, for a purpose as specified in the definition of a "medical device" in the medical devices regulation or in vitro diagnostic medical devices regulation, regardless of whether the software is independent or driving or influencing the use of a device.*
>
> (European Commission, 2019)

In the US, the Food and Drug Administration (FDA) uses the term Software as a Medical Device (SaMD) instead of MDSW. The definitions are similar, but not identical.

For a device to be classified as SaMD by the FDA, it must operate independently of any hardware medical device. If it drives or influences the device, it is known as Software in a Medical Device (SiMD). This differs from MDCG 2019-11, which makes it clear that software that drives or influences a hardware medical device may still qualify as medical device software in the EU.

The FDA uses the International Medical Device Regulators Forum's (IMDRF's) definition of Software as a Medical Device as:

> software intended to be used for one or more medical purposes that perform these purposes without being part of a hardware medical device (US FDA, 2018).

Examples of Software as a Medical Device (SaMD) include

- Software that allows a smartphone to view images obtained from a magnetic resonance imaging (MRI) medical device for diagnostic purposes
- Computer-aided detection software that performs image post-processing to help detect breast cancer; software that regulates an installed medical device, like a pacemaker
- BMI and body fat calculators
- Treatment software which interprets patient input data to develop a plan of action for a provider and patient
- Sleep data app that uses camera/microphone on a smartphone to transmit back to sleep lab

SaMD may be interfaced with other medical devices, including hardware medical devices, or other software as a medical device software. Where software provides parameters as an input for a different hardware medical device or other SaMD, such as treatment planning software that supplies information used in a linear accelerator, then this is defined as SaMD.

SiMD is software in a medical device. This is any software that helps to run a hardware medical device, for example, by powering its mechanics or producing a graphical interface. Some examples include:

- software that controls the inflation or deflation of a blood pressure cuff
- software that controls the delivery of insulin on an insulin pump
- software used in a closed loop control of a pacemaker

As this software is often embedded within a medical device, it is often referred to as "embedded software" or "firmware."

Digital imaging as an example of the use of software that is part of a medical device

Capturing the image in digital form allows for the possibility for further processing. The first enhanced technique is computerised tomography (CT).

A conventional CT image is similar to a conventional digital X-Ray. However, instead of a single image of the region of interest, multiple passes over the patient are performed, producing multiple scans. The patient is placed within a tubular gantry, and radiation is transmitted through the patient multiple times from multiple angles and recorded by one or more circumferential detector elements. A computer then reconstructs the acquired data sets into different attenuation values for particular locations on an axial slice (Wesolowski & Lev, 2005).

The technology has advanced through a number of innovations. In the late 1980s, slip-ring technology was introduced, allowing the continuous acquisition of a helix of data. This data "ribbon" could then be digitally processed to provide values for each pixel.

Further enhancements were introduced in the late 1990s, with helical scanners that included four or more rows of detectors in the longitudinal (z) direction. Now, instead of a single helical data set, information could be collected in several overlapping helical ribbons at the same time. Modern machines use up to 64 separate data channels (helixes) giving increased coverage in a smaller time.

17.2.1 Knowledge review

Before you move on, can you define the following key concepts:

- Software as a medical device?
- Software in a medical device?

17.2.2 Question to think about

How many types of medical devices can you think of?
How many are critically dependent upon software?

17.3 The digital health industry

Statista (2023) estimates that the value of the digital health market is 193.7 billion USD in 2024. They expect it to grow by over 9% per year reaching 275 billion USD by 2028.

There are a wide variety of digital applications used in healthcare, summarised in Table 17.1, from records systems used by large healthcare providers to personal applications used by individuals on their smartphones or increasingly, smartwatches.

All of these applications are designed to improve the decision-making of either healthcare professionals or patients or both. In spite of the huge potential benefits and the extravagant claims that are made for their realisation, significant issues remain:

- Interoperability is generally poor, meaning that information does not readily follow the patient. This is often due to organisational issues as much as technological barriers
- Records systems are usually owned by specific facilities who will naturally favour their own priorities rather than optimising the systems of the patient journey including multiple providers

Table 17.1 Types of digital health applications

System	Description
Electronic Health Records (EHR)	EHR systems centralise and streamline the processing of patient data for primarily clinical purposes, but the information may also be used for administrative purposes. EHR systems are designed to facilitate efficient record-keeping, enable easy access to patient information, and support decision-making processes for healthcare providers.
Patient Administration Systems (PAS)	PAS help healthcare organisations manage and analyse health information, including patient data, medical records, and administrative data. They integrate various administrative and clinical functions within a hospital. These systems handle tasks such as patient registration, scheduling, billing, inventory management, and resource allocation. They can streamline operations, enhance efficiency, and support effective resource utilisation.
Picture Archiving and Communication Systems (PACS)	PACS are a medical imaging technology used for storing, retrieving, presenting, and sharing digital images and diagnostic reports, such as X-rays, MRIs, CT scans, and ultrasounds.
Laboratory Information Systems	These systems automate the management of laboratory operations, including sample tracking, test ordering, result reporting, and quality control.
Pharmacy information systems	These systems manage medication-related processes, including medication ordering, dispensing, administration, inventory management, and drug interaction checking.
Radiology Information Systems	These systems manage the workflow and operations of radiology departments, including appointment scheduling, image tracking, reporting, and billing.
Clinical Decision Support Systems (CDSS)	These systems help clinicians with decisions about patient care. They can provide warnings to prevent medical errors.
Telehealth systems	Telehealth systems facilitate remote consultations, monitoring, and diagnosis.
Data analytics tools	These tools can enable hospitals to gain insights from large datasets. Analysing clinical and operational data helps identify trends, patterns, and areas for improvement, helping hospital management to make data-driven decisions, enhance patient outcomes, and optimise resource allocation.
Communication and collaboration tools	Applications such as email, messaging platforms, and virtual meeting software enhance communication and collaboration among hospital staff, departments, and external stakeholders. Improved communication streamlines workflows, enhances coordination, and supports effective decision-making processes.
Digital patient portals and mobile applications	These patient-facing applications enable patient engagement and empower individuals to actively participate in their care. They facilitate appointment scheduling, access to medical information, communication with healthcare providers, and self-management of health conditions.

- Data breaches and cybersecurity incidents are sufficiently common to undermine patient confidence in committing their information to digital systems

- Healthcare professionals are not always open to changing their working practices to realise the benefits sometimes due to a reluctance to change, sometimes a lack of competence or confidence in using the technology

---

Case study: Rollout of digital health technology in India after Gopichandran et al. (2020)

The widespread adoption of information and communication technologies (ICTs) in India has led to the emergence of digital health applications, raising significant ethical concerns. Inadequate funding and inefficient resource allocation are key challenges faced by the public health sector in India. Improving existing digital health records aims to enhance the efficiency of healthcare services.

The Aadhaar identification system assigns a unique 12-digit identification number linked to demographic and biometric data of each Indian resident. Its use in welfare programmes ensures targeted benefits reach the intended recipients efficiently. Since 2013, Aadhaar has been integrated into various health programmes, facilitating successful outcomes like incentivising pregnant women to deliver at healthcare facilities. However, concerns about breaches of confidentiality have led to patient dropouts in other programmes, such as tuberculosis and HIV/AIDS treatment.

Linking sensitive private health information with the Aadhaar identification system introduces issues of potential breaches of privacy, data ownership and use, and the autonomy of individuals whose data have become available for analysis. Leaks of the Aadhaar data have been reported; a private telecommunication company in India collected the Aadhaar numbers of many of its subscribers and published them on the internet. According to reports from the Press Trust of India. (2017), over 200 government websites were also found to be inadvertently displaying the Aadhaar data of individuals.

For the first time, in 2023, India passed a comprehensive data protection law, and it is hoped that this will increase protection for sensitive data and increase confidence in the use of digital technology in health. However, unlike the EU GDPR regulations, which provide additional safeguards for special category data including health data, the Indian legislation has no such additional protection for health information.

17.3.1 *Knowledge review*

Before you move on, can you define the following key concepts:

- Unique identifier?

17.3.2 *Question to think about*

How confident are you about the safety and security of your personal health information?

17.4 Global health insurance market

Statista (2024) estimates that the value of the global private health insurance market in terms of premiums written reached 2.32 trillion US dollars in 2023 and forecasted it to rise to 2.62 trillion US dollars by 2028.

The five biggest international markets are the USA, China, the Netherlands, India, and Brazil.

Healthcare inflation, the cost of providing healthcare, is rising faster than general inflation in the key markets for private health insurance. Private insurance providers are seeking ways of keeping premiums affordable through a series of measures:

- There is a growing trend among private health insurers to incorporate telemedicine services into their offerings. This development enables policyholders to receive medical care remotely, thereby enhancing convenience and accessibility.
- Insurers are placing greater emphasis on wellness and preventive health packages. These packages provide policyholders with access to resources such as gym memberships, wellness apps, and preventive health screenings, aimed at encouraging healthier lifestyles.
- There is a shift towards personalised health insurance plans designed to meet individual health needs. Using data-driven underwriting, insurers customise coverage and premiums based on the unique health profiles of policyholders.
- To address the challenge of rising drug prices, insurers are collaborating with pharmacy benefit managers to negotiate lower prices for medications. This collaboration aims to provide policyholders with cost-effective prescription drug coverage.
- As part of their investment in digital technology, insurers are prioritising the security of digital health records and invest in advanced cybersecurity measures to safeguard policyholders' sensitive health information. Aside from the harm to patients, the reputational and financial harm to the insurance provider arising from a security breach is very significant (Statista, 2024).

Private health insurance in the Netherlands

The Netherlands is by far the smallest country amongst the five largest private insurance markets by value. This is because private insurance funds provide coverage for every citizen.

However, the terms of this coverage are determined by the government. Everyone who lives or works in the Netherlands is legally obliged to take out standard health insurance to cover the cost of basic health services, including primary care, hospital treatment, and prescription medications. There is provision for a dispensation from health insurance for citizens with conscientious objections, and they pay equivalent income tax in lieu of insurance premiums.

All insurers offer the same standard package. Healthcare insurers are obliged to accept anyone who applies for the standard insurance package and must charge all policyholders the same premium, regardless of their age or state of health.

People on a low income may be eligible for healthcare benefit to help pay for health insurance.

Children under the age of 18 are insured free of charge. However, employed people pay a percentage of their income as an additional premium for the standard package known as the ZVW contribution. This contribution is deducted by employers and submitted directly to the Health Insurance Fund.

For service beyond those covered by the standard package, citizens may opt to take out additional insurance to cover, for example, physiotherapy or dental care. This additional insurance is not mandatory. Citizens may seek their standard insurance and additional insurance from different insurance companies.

Insurance companies are not obliged to accept everyone who applies for additional insurance. They can refuse to accept clients or can ask questions about their health before accepting them.

In this way, although health insurance is provided by private providers, the funds and coverage operate like the social insurance funds found in neighbouring European countries.

17.4.1 *Knowledge review*

Before you move on, can you define the following key concepts:

• Healthcare inflation?

17.4.2 *Question to think about*

Why would the Netherlands use private health insurance funds whilst France and Germany use social health insurance funds?

17.5 Retail pharmacies

The World Health Organisation (WHO, 1994, p. 10) defines community pharmacists as:

> Community pharmacists are the health professionals most accessible to the public. They supply medicines in accordance with a prescription or, when legally permitted, sell them without a prescription.

Because of their key role and their impact on patient safety, the profession is highly regulated in most jurisdictions. Typically, national laws and regulations stipulate that pharmacists must undergo training at a university. These regulations outlining their education generally lay out the duration of the training (both theoretical and practical components), the subjects to be covered (or a framework of competencies), quality assurance criteria, and in certain countries like France, the maximum annual intake of pharmacy students is also specified (WHO, 2019).

Pharmacies are associated with dispensing pharmaceutical products in hospitals and community settings. However, especially in community settings, they have a wider and increasing role.

In their core role of dispensing medications, pharmacies are responsible for accurately dispensing prescribed medications to patients. They ensure that patients receive the right dosage and formulation of their medications, which is essential for proper treatment.

Pharmacists provide important information about medications, including their proper usage, potential side effects, drug interactions, and storage instructions. They help patients understand their medications and promote safe and effective usage.

Alongside advice on the drugs they prescribe, they may educate patients about their medical conditions, treatment plans, and lifestyle modifications. This helps patients to take an active role in managing their health and encourages adherence to prescribed therapies.

Many pharmacies offer medication therapy management services where pharmacists review a patient's medication regimen, identify potential issues, and work with healthcare providers to optimise therapy. This is especially important for patients taking multiple medications.

Pharmacies help improve medication adherence by offering tools like medication synchronisation (aligning medication refills), blister packaging, and reminder systems. They have a crucial role in ensuring the safety of medications, ensuring medication safety by verifying prescriptions, checking for potential drug interactions, and providing guidance on avoiding medication errors.

In addition to prescribed medications, pharmacists may assist patients in selecting appropriate over-the-counter (OTC) products, and importantly where the same patients are taking prescribed medications, they may advise on potential interactions.

Often, they will offer advice on managing minor health concerns and help patients understand when to seek medical attention, as well as providing support for patients with chronic conditions by offering medication management, monitoring, and guidance on lifestyle changes to improve overall health.

Many pharmacies contribute to disease prevention and public health efforts by offering immunisation services, such as flu shots and vaccinations. They will collaborate with physicians and other healthcare providers to optimise patient care, resolve medication-related issues, and contribute to comprehensive treatment plans. They may perform medication reviews to assess appropriateness, effectiveness, and safety of medications, making recommendations for adjustments if needed.

Additionally, they often provide emergency contraception and advice on family planning, making these services more accessible to the public.

The growing use of technology can be used to facilitate telepharmacy. This may take a number of forms. A patient may submit an online request remotely to a doctor for a repeat prescription, who may approve the request and pass it electronically to a remote dispensing pharmacist who may dispatch the medication directly to the patient without any face-to-face interactions. In other contexts, pharmacies may provide a range of remote services through patients consulting with pharmacists via video or phone calls.

17.5.1 Roles of community pharmacies across the world

In a survey of community pharmacies in European countries, Costa el al. (2017) found that in many European nations, community pharmacists commonly offered extra services and regularly utilised computer software in their interactions with individual patients. Furthermore, there was a significant rise in the proportion of pharmacies with a designated private consultation space in several European countries (such as Northern Ireland, Portugal, Sweden, and Switzerland) compared to the results of a previous study from 2006 (Hughes et al., 2010). However, Costa et al. (2017) still report that the extent of pharmaceutical care offered by community pharmacists continues to be restricted in many European countries. They report that separate research conducted in various countries, such as the United States, Denmark, Spain, Northwest China, and Jordan, has similarly underscored the challenge of inadequate delivery of pharmaceutical care by community pharmacists Fang et al., 2011; Zardain et al., 2009).

The extent to which community pharmacists contribute to overall patient care throughout Europe was linked to several factors including:

- engaging in additional services such as health screening, patient monitoring, medication review, and health education
- active participation in multidisciplinary team meetings
- regular use of digital systems for checking clinical data and drug interactions
- access to clinical data through databases shared with other providers
- working in a pharmacy equipped with a private patient consultation space

Costa et al. (2017)

Mossialos et al. (2015) reported on a range of national initiatives to increase the role of community pharmacists. Since 2003, community pharmacists in Canada have taken on shared responsibilities with doctors, particularly in the realm of prescribing. Since healthcare in Canada falls under the jurisdiction of individual provinces, each province has its own framework for medication management, prescribing, and reimbursement. However, in a common trend across the whole of Canada, pharmacists are taking more responsibility for the renewal, modification, or substitution of prescriptions from physicians, although the degree of this autonomy varies from province to province.

In Alberta, accredited community pharmacists have the autonomy to initiate and oversee drug therapy independently. During the process of independently prescribing medications, pharmacists are obligated to comprehensively document their interaction with the patient, encompassing the reasoning behind the decision, assessment, pertinent drug information, and a follow-up strategy involving other healthcare providers.

In more recent times, three provinces have given community pharmacists legal authority over laboratory tests, and similar initiatives are in progress in three other provinces.

In Australia, community pharmacies routinely provide drug-related information and conduct clinical interventions. They are authorised to engage in emergency prescribing, continued dispensing, and offer supplementary services like medication use reviews. While there is encouragement for Australian community pharmacists to prescribe for minor ailments, this is not formally supported. Community pharmacies and primary care practices frequently collaborate over medication reviews. Studies assessing the impact of these collaborative reviews indicate their positive influence on prescription practices, with potential benefits in terms of reduced healthcare utilisation and medication costs for patients with multiple chronic conditions (Lenaghan et al., 2007).

Furthermore, Australian data reveals that most GPs accept and act on medication changes suggested by community pharmacists within the scope of these collaborative arrangements (Castelino et al., 2010).

Both Australia and Canada have large rural areas that can struggle to provide medical services, and this may be a common driver for an increased role for community pharmacists.

By contrast, a review of Alanazi et al. (2016) found that only one out of the four studies conducted in Saudi Arabia reported pharmaceutical care service beyond simple dispensing. They found a high degree of OTC dispensing, which they attribute to commercial pressures with big discounts to pharmacists offered by the representatives of manufacturers. They highlight weak regulation of the pharmacy sector as a further contributory factor.

Khdour and Hallak (2012) report this domination of dispensing services and associated high degree of OTC in other countries such as Palestine, India, and Pakistan. Universally, community pharmacies can play a wide and increasing role in patient care, but the need for effective regulation remains paramount.

17.5.2 *Knowledge review*

Before you move on, can you define the following key concepts:

• Community pharmacy?

17.5.3 *Question to think about*

What services would you be happy to have provided by a local pharmacy as opposed to a primary care physician?

17.6 The role of laboratories

Clinical laboratories are medical establishments that offer an extensive array of laboratory techniques aimed at assisting doctors in conducting patient diagnosis, treatment, and care. These facilities are staffed by medical technologists (also known as clinical laboratory scientists) who are educated to conduct diverse tests on biological samples taken from individuals. The majority of these clinical laboratories are conveniently located within, or in close proximity to, hospital premises, ensuring convenient access for both medical professionals and their patients.

Laboratories can either be government-operated, typically as components of hospitals and medical centres, in which case they are affiliated with the pathology or laboratory medicine department, or they can be privately owned, functioning as divisions of privately operated medical or healthcare establishments.. In healthcare systems with a strong public ethos such as Canada, private ownership of laboratory can cause concerns.

In the US, 50 major laboratory firms oversee 40% of a divided domestic market. In Australia, resembling British Columbia, Ontario, and Manitoba in how laboratory services are financed and owned, private businesses are employed to offer community laboratory services. These companies are compensated through a national public insurance plan based on service fees. Hospital budgets, funded by individual states, cover inpatient services (Medical Benefits Reviews Task Group, 2011).

The National Health Service in England introduced profit-driven diagnostic service providers, aiming to incorporate market dynamics nearly 20 years ago (Beastall, 2008).

After a period with limited further expansion of private provision within the NHS, the UK Government announced plans for further expansion in 2023.

Sutherland (2012) highlights concerns about the use of for-profit corporations in providing essential medical laboratory services within the Canadian public healthcare system. These concerns revolve around transparency, cost, and the integration of healthcare services.

For-profit corporations often protect their confidential business information, and this may limit public access to data and impede informed debate. This lack of transparency can hinder accountability and public understanding of how taxpayer funds are being used to deliver crucial healthcare services. The need to generate a profit, which may drive up the cost of diagnostic testing.

The integration of healthcare services is crucial for providing comprehensive and coordinated care to patients. For-profit corporations may prioritise profit over collaboration and integration, which could disrupt the seamless provision of healthcare across various medical specialties and services. Similarly, commercial confidentiality may become a barrier to information sharing.

Moving away from fee-for-service funding, where providers are paid based on the number of services they deliver, to other remuneration schemes may help shift the focus from profit maximisation to patient outcomes. However, providers must still be incentivised to deliver high-quality care without the undue pressure of generating more services for revenue.

Integrating laboratory services within public administrative structures can promote better coordination, data sharing, and standardisation of care. This could lead to more efficient and effective delivery of services, as the primary focus would be on patient well-being rather than profit, and there may be less steps in the data flow journey.

Ultimately, advocates for private ownership will argue that the profit motive can drive innovation and efficiency, while critics contend that it can lead to prioritising profit over patient well-being. However, political ideology regarding public ownership will also influence decision-making.

Irrespective of ownership, laboratories may provide a range of common diagnostic laboratory tests or may specialise in providing specific diagnostic and confirmatory tests.

They provide a wide range of tests as outlined in Table 17.2:

Laboratories deploy quality management systems to standardise services and operating procedures. They support testing in a logical and strict manner. Generally. there are three phases of the laboratory testing process: pre-analytical, analytical, and post-analytical (Hawkins, 2012).

Standard operating procedure manuals and job aids are crafted to provide instructions for executing every stage of the process. Although contemporary clinical laboratories are often recognised for their advanced machinery and equipment that handle much of the sample testing, these facilities remain dependent on skilled human professionals who ensure the accuracy and dependability of results.

The administration of laboratory services encompasses the oversight of human and financial resources, training and supervision, budgeting and planning, quality assurance, supply and logistics, biosafety, equipment maintenance, and various other concerns.

In 2018, the World Health Organisation introduced the Essential Diagnostics List (EDL) as a means to narrow the accessibility and availability gap in high-quality clinical

Table 17.2 Laboratory tests by type

Role	Description
Diagnosis	Laboratory tests help healthcare providers accurately diagnose diseases and conditions. Blood tests, urine tests, imaging studies, and genetic tests provide valuable insights into a patient's health status and aid in identifying the underlying causes of symptoms.
Monitoring and treatment	Laboratory tests are used to monitor the progression of diseases and the effectiveness of treatments. For example, blood tests can track changes in cholesterol levels for patients with heart disease or monitor the viral load in patients with HIV to assess the effectiveness of antiretroviral therapy.
Early detection	Certain diseases may not present noticeable symptoms in their early stages. Laboratory tests enable the early detection of these conditions, which can lead to more effective treatment and better patient outcomes. For instance, mammograms and Pap smears are used for early detection of breast and cervical cancers, respectively.
Prognosis	Laboratory data can help predict the course and severity of a disease, allowing healthcare providers to develop appropriate treatment plans and interventions. This is often seen in cancer care, where genetic and molecular testing can help determine the aggressiveness of a tumour and guide treatment decisions.
Preventive care	Laboratory tests are essential in preventive medicine, helping to identify risk factors and assess an individual's overall health. Regular screenings for conditions like diabetes, high blood pressure, and certain cancers can help patients make informed lifestyle changes and reduce their risk of developing chronic diseases.
Infection control	Laboratory services play a crucial role in identifying and monitoring infectious diseases. They help healthcare providers track outbreaks, implement appropriate infection control measures, and guide the use of antibiotics or antiviral medications.
Research and innovation	Laboratory services contribute to medical research by providing data that researchers use to advance our understanding of diseases, develop new treatments, and improve medical technologies.
Transfusion and transplantation	Laboratories are responsible for blood typing, cross-matching, and compatibility testing in blood transfusions and organ transplantation, ensuring the safety and success of these life-saving procedures.
Genetic testing	Laboratory tests, including DNA sequencing and genetic profiling, provide insights into an individual's genetic makeup, helping in diagnosing inherited diseases, predicting disease risks, and personalising treatment plans.
Drug monitoring	Laboratory tests measure drug levels in the body, ensuring that medications are within the therapeutic range and helping to prevent adverse reactions or treatment failure.

laboratory testing, particularly in resource-constrained settings (Waldrop et al., 2019). It is an evidence-based guide that looks at disease prevalence globally and recommends the appropriate laboratory test for each condition and plays a key role in delivery of universal health coverage, a central tenet of Goal 3 within the Sustainable Development Goals.

Lessons from the use of WHO Essential Medicines List (EML) for the WHO Essential Diagnostics List (EDL) (after Nyanchoka et al., 2022)

Nyanchoka and colleagues (2022) conducted a comprehensive review of literature concerning the adoption of the WHO essential lists in Africa to provide insights into the implementation of the recently introduced EDL. The study encompassed a search across eight electronic databases to identify studies focusing on the implementation of both the WHO EDL and the preceding EML in African contexts. Study selection and data extraction were carried out independently by two authors, with any discrepancies resolved through consensus. Themes were extracted using the Supporting the Use of Research Evidence (SURE) framework and synthesised using thematic content analysis. Additionally, the quality of included studies was assessed using the Mixed Method Appraisal Tool (MMAT).

The review revealed many studies documenting the implementation of the EML across Africa. The authors found that a major obstacle faced by both the established EML and the newer EDL was inadequately equipped health facilities, leading to issues such as the unavailability of essential diagnostics and medicines, frequent instances of laboratory reagents running out, and insufficient infrastructure and space to support effective health service delivery. Conversely, and perhaps unsurprisingly, the presence of basic tests and medicines, along with enhanced facility capacity to deliver essential services was associated with a successful implementation

Moreover, the review identified notable successes in interventions aimed at addressing barriers to EML implementation, which could potentially inform strategies for the implementation of the EDL. Interventions such as accredited drug dispensing outlets and the implementation of auditable pharmaceutical services and transaction systems were associated with improvements in the availability of essential medicines. However, it was noted that the effectiveness of interventions could vary depending on contextual factors.

They also found that whilst financial and non-financial incentives may motivate implementation, they can unrealistically raise expectations and hinder implementation in the long run due to sustainability issues.

17.6.1 Knowledge review

Before you move on, can you define the following key concepts:

• The Essential Diagnostics List?

17.6.2 Question to think about

When have you or your family member needed a clinical test to be analysed? What was tested, and how did it inform treatment?

References

Alanazi, A. S., Alfadl, A. A., & Hussain, A. S. (2016). Pharmaceutical care in the community pharmacies of Saudi Arabia: Present status and possibilities for improvement. *Saudi Journal of Medicine & Medical Sciences*, 4(1), 9.

Beastall, G. (2008). The modernisation of pathology and laboratory medicine in the UK: Networking into the future. *Clinical Biochemist Reviews*, 29(1), 3–10.

Beck, A., & Reichert, J. M. (2013, September). Approval of the first biosimilar antibodies in Europe: A major landmark for the biopharmaceutical industry. In *MAbs* (Vol. 5, No. 5, pp. 621–623). Taylor & Francis.

Business Research Company. (2021). Medical devices market 2021 – By type of device (in-vitro diagnostics, dental equipment, ophthalmic devices, diagnostic equipment, hospital supplies, cardiovascular devices, surgical equipment, patient monitoring devices, orthopaedic devices, diabetes care devices, nephrology and urology devices, ENT devices, anaesthesia and respiratory devices, neurology devices, wound care devices), by type of expenditure (public, private), by end-user (hospitals and clinics, homecare, diagnostics centres) and by region, opportunities and strategies – Global forecast to 2030.

Castelino, R. L., Bajorek, B. V., & Chen, T. F. (2010). Retrospective evaluation of home medicines review by pharmacists in older Australian patients using the medication appropriateness index. *The Annals of Pharmacotherapy*, 44(12), 1922–1929.

Costa, F. A., Scullin, C., Al-Taani, G., Hawwa, A. F., Anderson, C., Bezverhni, Z., ... Westerlund, T. (2017). Provision of pharmaceutical care by community pharmacists across Europe: Is it developing and spreading?. *Journal of Evaluation in Clinical Practice*, 23(6), 1336–1347.

European Commission. (2019). Guidance on qualification and classification of software in regulation (EU) 2017/745 – MDR and Regulation (EU) 2017/746– IVDR - 10/10/2019 - Created by GROW.DDG1.D.4

European Parliament And The Council Of The European Union. (2017). Regulation (EU) 2017/745 of the European Parliament and of the Council of 5 April 2017 on medical devices, amending Directive 2001/83/EC, Regulation (EC) No 178/2002 and Regulation (EC) No 1223/2009 and repealing Council Directives 90/385/EEC and 93/42/EEC. Document 32017R0745

Fang, Y., Yang, S., Feng, B., Ni, Y., & Zhang, K. (2011). Pharmacists' perception of pharmaceutical care in community pharmacy: A questionnaire survey in Northwest China. *Health & Social Care in the Community*, 19(2), 189–197.

Farkona, S., Diamandis, E. P., & Blasutig, I. M. (2016). Cancer immunotherapy: The beginning of the end of cancer? *BMC Medicine*, 14, 1–18.

Feagan, B. (2017). Benefits, concerns, and future directions of biosimilars in inflammatory bowel disease. *Gastroenterology & Hepatology*, 13(12), 745–747.

Gibbon, G. A. (1996). A brief history of LIMS. *Laboratory Automation and Information Management*, 32(1), 1–5. doi:10.1016/1381-141X(95)00024-K

Goetz, L. H., & Schork, N. J. (2018). Personalised medicine: Motivation, challenges, and progress. *Fertility and Sterility*, 109(6), 952–963.

Gopichandran, V., Ganeshkumar, P., Dash, S., & Ramasamy, A. (2020). Ethical challenges of digital health technologies: Aadhaar, India. *Bulletin of the World Health Organisation*, 98(4), 277–281.

Haugen, H. M. (2021). Does TRIPS (agreement on trade-related aspects of intellectual property rights) prevent COVID-19 vaccines as a global public good? *Journal of World Intellectual Property*, 24(3–4), 195–220. doi: 10.1111/jwip.12187

Hawkins, R. (2012, January). Managing the pre- and post-analytical phases of the total testing process. *Annals of Laboratory Medicine*, 32(1), 5–16.

Hughes, C. M., Hawwa, A. F., Scullin, C., et al. (2010). Provision of pharmaceutical care by community pharmacists: A comparison across Europe. *Pharmacy World & Science*, 32(4), 472–487.

International Federation of Pharmaceutical Manufacturers & Associations. (2021). *The pharmaceutical industry and global health: Facts and figures 2022*. International Federation of Pharmaceutical Manufacturers & Associations.

IQVIA. (2021). *Global medicine spending and usage trends: Outlook to 2025*. IQVIA.

IQVIA. (2022). *The global use of medicines 2022: Outlook to 2026.* IQVIA.

IQVIA Institute. (2021). *Drug expenditure dynamics 1995–2020.* IQVIA Institute.

Khdour, M. R., & Hallak, H. O. (2012). Societal perspectives on community pharmacy services in West Bank-Palestine. *Pharmacy Practice*, 10(1), 17.

Lenaghan, E., Holland, R., & Brooks, A. (2007). Home-based medication review in a high-risk elderly population in primary care—the POLYMED randomised controlled trial. *Age and Ageing*, 36(3), 292–297.

Manosuthi, W., Ongwandee, S., Bhakeecheep, S., et al. (2015). Guidelines for antiretroviral therapy in HIV-1 infected adults and adolescents 2014, Thailand. *AIDS Research and Therapy*, 12, 12.

Medical Benefits Reviews Task Group. (2011). *Review of the funding arrangements for pathology services: Final discussion paper.* Australian Government, Department of Health and Ageing.

Mossialos, E., Courtin, E., Naci, H., Benrimoj, S., Bouvy, M., Farris, K., ... Sketris, I. (2015). From "retailers" to health care providers: Transforming the role of community pharmacists in chronic disease management. *Health Policy*, 119(5), 628–639.

Mikulic, M. (2021). *Pharmaceutical market: Worldwide revenue 2001-2021.* Statista GmbH.

Nyanchoka, M., Mulaku, M., Nyagol, B., Owino, E. J., Kariuki, S., & Ochodo, E. (2022). Implementing essential diagnostics-learning from essential medicines: A scoping review. *PLoS Global Public Health*, 2(12), e0000827.

Olsson, S., Pal, S. N., Stergachis, A., & Couper, M. (2010). Pharmacovigilance activities in 55 low-and middle-income countries: a questionnaire-based analysis. *Drug Safety*, 33, 689–703.

Patel, D. M., Moyo, C., & Bositis, C. M. (2010). A Review of the 2010 WHO Adult Antiretroviral Therapy Guidelines: Implications and Realities of These Changes for Zambia. Medical journal of Zambia, 37(2), 118–124.

Press Trust of India. (2017, November 19). Over 200 govt websites made Aadhaar details public: UIDAI. *The Times of India*.

Silverman, R., Keller, J. M., Glassman, A., & Chalkidou, K. (2019). *Tackling the triple transition in global health procurement.* Center for Global Development,

Sreelalitha, N., Vigneshwaran, E., Narayana, G., Reddy, Y. P., & Reddy, M. R. (2012). Review of pharmaceutical care services provided by the pharmacists. *IRJP*, 3(4), 78–79.

Statista. (2023, October). Digital health - Worldwide. *Revenue*.

Statista. (2024, February). *Health insurance – Worldwide.* Gross Written Premiums.

Sutherland, R. (2012, December 18). The effect of for-profit laboratories on the accountability, integration, and cost of Canadian health care services. Open Medicine, 6(4), e166–170. PMID: 23687532; PMCID: PMC3654513.

Sweet, C. M. (2017). The politics and policies of regulating generics in Latin America: A survey of Seventeen States. *Journal of Health Politics, Policy and Law*, 42(3), 485–512.

US Food and Drug Administration. (2018). *Software as a Medical Device (SaMD), US FDA digital health center of excellence.* US Food and Drug Administration.

Waldrop, G., Goetz, T. G., Siddiqi, O. K., Koralnik, I. J., Shah, H., & Thakur, K. T. (2019, October 8). The world health organisation's essential diagnostics list: Diagnostics for neurologic disorders. *Neurology*, 93(15), 680–683. doi:10.1212/WNL.0000000000008247. PMID: 31591174; PMCID: PMC7010326.

Weise, M., Bielsky, M. C., De Smet, K., Ehmann, F., Ekman, N., Giezen, T. J., ... Schneider, C. K. (2012). Biosimilars: What clinicians should know. *Blood, The Journal of the American Society of Hematology*, 120(26), 5111–5117.

Wesolowski, J. R., & Lev, M. H. (2005). CT: History, technology, and clinical aspects. *Seminars in Ultrasound, CT and MRI*, 26(6), 376–379. Elsevier, New York ISSN 0887-2171.

World Health Organisation. (1994). *The role of the pharmacist in the health care system.* World Health Organisation.

World Health Organisation. (2019). *The legal and regulatory framework for community pharmacies in the WHO European Region.* World Health Organisation.

World Trade Organisation. (1994). Agreement on trade-related aspects of intellectual property rights. World Health Organisation.

World Trade Organisation. (2001). *Doha WTO ministerial 2001: Ministerial declaration.* World Health Organisation.

Zardaín, E., Del Valle, M. O., Loza, M. I., et al. (2009). Psychosocial and behavioral determinants of the implementation of pharmaceutical care in Spain. *Pharmacy World & Science*, 31(2), 174–182.

Section E

Management and leadership

18 Managing healthcare services and products in global markets

18.1 Risk management and product safety

Healthcare organisations face a broad range of risks:

- laws, regulations, standards, corporate compliance
- avoidable harm to patients
- data protection and confidentiality
- staff malpractice or incompetence
- failure to observe patients' rights
- medication management
- infection prevention and control
- abuse reporting
- environmental safety

Risks may have the potential to cause a variety of types of harm, including:

- Financial: Financial cost may be in the form of the cost of repair or replacement, financial sanctions, failure to get renewed contracts, and/or damages awarded to victims.
- Clinical: Clinical harm is caused by poor clinical outcomes, either from the planned intervention or from unrelated causes, such as hospital-acquired infections, and may range from minor illness or injury to death.
- Reputational: Adverse events will cause reputational damage to the organisation that may have ongoing consequences.

In order to manage risks, organisations are recommended (and may be required) to create a risk register. The register may be created at an organisation-wide level but may also need to take account of variations in different parts of the organisation.

Risk is generally calculated as the product of the likelihood and impact of an adverse event, where:

- likelihood is the probability that an adverse event will occur within a defined period and
- impact is (a measure of) the degree of harm that would be caused if the event occurred

This may be represented either visually or numerically. This is illustrated in Figure 18.1.

DOI: 10.4324/9781003478874-23

Impact	Very low (1)	Low (2)	Moderate (3)	High (4)	Critical (5)
Very unlikely (1)	1	2	3	4	5
Unlikely (2)	2	4	6	8	10
Possible (3)	3	6	9	12	15
Likely (4)	4	8	12	16	20
Very likely (5)	5	10	15	20	25

Figure 18.1 Schematic of risk as the product of likelihood and impact.

Table 18.1 Risk register (schematic)

Risk name	Description	Likelihood	Impact	Risk score	Mitigation measure	Revised risk score

The risk register will provide a list of all identified risks together with an assessment of the risk associated with each. In addition, a risk register should incorporate a mechanism to incorporate mitigation measures and an assessment of the risk after mitigation, as shown in Table 18.1.

The risks in healthcare are considerable. Rodziewicz et al. (2022) report that in the US alone:

- Approximately 400,000 hospitalised patients experience some type of preventable harm each year, of whom approximately 100,000 people die each year from medical errors.
- Medical errors cost approximately 20 billion USD a year.
- Healthcare-related infections add close to 35 billion USD to the annual cost of healthcare.

Simple inexpensive prevention and mitigation measures, such as the WHO surgical checklist (WHO, 2009), designed to improve communication and teamwork have been adopted across the world and shown to be effective.

Managing product safety as an example of risk mitigation

The product safety regime for medical devices is based on the perceived risk of harm and administered by a national agency in most countries such as the Food and Drug Administration in the US.

These agencies regulate the entry of new medical devices into the market. Once they have approved a new product, they undertake market surveillance of medical devices. Based on this market surveillance, and in response to adverse events and near misses, they issue guidance and product recalls. In order to minimise adverse events and near misses, they also support healthcare organisations in the use of medical devices.

Healthcare organisations should have systems in place to report issues with medical devices to the appropriate regulator. These systems should monitor the condition and performance of medical devices including:

- device failures and issues
- utilisation, performance, and maintenance
- repair and calibration history; and the execution of investment, replacement, and disposal plans

Healthcare organisations should have a device management policy in place to minimise or eliminate the risks associated with medical devices by identifying responsibilities in relation to medical device management. The policy should cover the complete equipment life cycle (including selection, acquisition, acceptance, maintenance, repair, decontamination, monitoring, traceability, and disposal/replacement) of all medical devices.

The policy should define how the organisation manages risks, including adverse incident reporting and actions required on alerts, safety messages, and manufacturers' Field Safety Notices. It should also cover

- training and access to manufacturer's instructions
- records, including device inventory
- outsourcing
- equipment deployment, tracking and utilisation
- equipment financing

The policy should be regularly reviewed to ensure that whenever a medical device is used, it is suitable for its intended purpose, used in line with the manufacturer's instructions, traceable (where possible), maintained in a safe and reliable condition, with associated records kept and disposed of appropriately at the end of its useful life (Medicines & Healthcare products Regulatory Agency, 2021).

18.1.1 Knowledge review

Before you move on, can you define the following key concepts:

- Risk?

18.1.2 Question to think about

Think about the last healthcare consultation you attended. How many risks can you identify?

18.2 Health product procurement

Healthcare providers depend upon procuring a wide range of goods to provide their service. In addition to the drugs and medical devices already described, the Covid pandemic has highlighted the need for large quantities of other products such as effective personal protective equipment.

Public procurement is the procurement of goods, services, and works on behalf of a public authority, such as a government agency. There is a need for a procurement process that delivers value for money for the customer and fairness and transparency for the potential suppliers.

Failures in procurement can lead to vital products not being available, procured products not fit for purpose, healthcare facilities or agencies paying higher than necessary prices, and patients not receiving the care that they need or receiving care in an unsafe environment.

The OECD (2017) reports that around the world public confidence in the fairness and probity of procurement is low, with 45% of people surveyed from across the globe rating the health sector as either corrupt or extremely corrupt. The need for rapid procurement during the COVID-19 pandemic has also highlighted the challenges of rapid procurement in response to an emergency situation.

Within Europe, public procurement is dominated by EU procurement directives, which in addition to the core EU treaty principles of the free movement of goods, freedom to provide services, freedom of establishment and non-discrimination, enshrine the principles of equality, transparency proportionality, and mutual recognition (Crown Commercial Service, 2015).

- The principle of equality means that all bidders must be treated equally.
- The principle of transparency means that the success criteria and any exclusion criteria must be available to all bidders.
- The principle of proportionality means that the resources devoted to bidding and bidding selection should be proportionate to the value of the contract.
- The principle of mutual recognition means that goods sold in one EU country can be sold in another EU country on the same basis.

Typically, the procurement process to be used will depend upon the lifetime value of the contract:

> Small contracts up to a threshold of typically €10,000 (or 10,000 GBP in the UK) may be awarded without competitive tendering.

Larger contracts up to a threshold determined by the EU, and varying by the type of contract and size of the contractor, will generally be awarded using a competitive tendering process with a minimum of three bids.

For contracts exceeding the EU threshold, the opportunity must be published in the Official Journal of the European Union, and EU rules must be followed to facilitate bidding from any business within the EU.

Private health businesses are not bound by public procurement rules, although they share a common goal of achieving value for money and fitness for purpose. There is less requirement to be transparent, so they may, for example, value an existing supplier relationship over the lowest price submitted.

All healthcare businesses, whether public or private, must ensure that products procured meet all necessary regulatory requirements.

Looking beyond Europe, the WHO reports that only one-fifth of the countries in the world have effective procurement practices in respect of pharmaceuticals and other medical equipment (Olugbenga, 2014). Many of the countries with inadequate procurement practices are amongst the poorest with the least resources available for healthcare, and corruption facilitated by inadequate procurement processes affects the ability of both citizens and governments to pay for healthcare (Kanavos & Wouters, 2014).

Poor procurement processes may also allow the purchase of counterfeit medicines, with obvious risks to patients. Improved governance in pharmaceuticals in Nigeria demonstrated that this is an effective measure in reducing counterfeiting of medicines (Garuba et al., 2009).

The COVID-19 pandemic with its need for rapid procurement of medical goods and services led to many governments relaxing their rules for procurement with a range of negative consequences (World Bank, 2021).

The World Bank survey indicated that the crisis led to a major relaxation of procurement rules:

- 47% used direct contracting for emergency procurement
- 25% increased their threshold for application of direct contracting
- 36% placed no threshold value on direct contracting
- 42% used accelerated bid times
- 28% put emergency framework agreements in place
- 29% had no requirement for bid security
- 14% used unwritten, verbal, or other informal contracts
- 25% did not apply lowest price bidding
- 31% relaxed checks on firms' technical qualifications

Even in countries regarded as demonstrating acceptable procurement practices by the World Bank, such as the UK, subsequent inquiries and reports have shown that practice was too lax (National Audit Office, 2020, 2022).

Problems with public procurement in the UK during COVID-19

The National Audio Office report (2022) identified the following problems with procurement during the COVID-19 pandemic:

- Out of 394 contracts awarded through the Parallel Supply Chain and UK Make, 115 were awarded to 51 High Priority Lane suppliers. (These were suppliers who were vouched for by MPs, peers, ministers, and senior officials.)
- Contracts through the VIP lane totaled 3.8 billion GBP and were expected to deliver 7.8 billion items of PPE.

- In January 2022, the High Court ruled that the use of the High Priority Lane was unlawful.
- The department's due diligence process evolved over time, with an eight-stage process introduced in May 2020.
- By January 2022, the department had spent 12.6 billion GBP on PPE against total commitments of 13.1 billion.
- 2.5 billion GBP was paid to suppliers through 298 upfront payments, with concerns raised about non-delivery risks.
- Storage costs incurred amounted to 737 million GBP by November 2021, with penalty charges due to insufficient storage capacity.
- 3.6 billion PPE items were deemed unsuitable for frontline services, representing 11% of all PPE received.
- The department identified 1.5 billion items of PPE that expired before use, with an estimated cost of 619 million GBP.
- Inconsistencies were noted between contracted volumes and reported stock counts, with discrepancies in management data.
- Contract disputes on 76 contracts with a total value of 1.8 billion GBP were concluded, involving issues such as product quality and delivery timeliness.

18.2.1 Knowledge review

Before you move on, can you define the following key concepts:

- Public procurement?

18.2.2 Question to think about

In a crisis such as the COVID-19 pandemic, how far should governments relax the rules for public procurement to ensure that healthcare providers have access to the equipment they need?

18.3 Competition parameters (quality, delivery, cost, flexibility)

To measure the effectiveness of healthcare providers, we may use a set of parameters first suggested by Hayes and Wheelwright (1984). They identified four parameters: quality, lead-time, cost, and flexibility. Within these parameters, they and subsequent authors have suggested a number of dimensions with associated metrics to measure effectiveness.

18.3.1 Quality

Quality has many different dimensions (Gillies, 1997), and the most relevant will depend upon the circumstances. One of the challenges with quality is that it is often easier to observe by its absence (Kitchenham & Pfleeger, 1996) than its presence. Thus, there is a tendency to focus on products that fail to meet required specifications and adverse events in the provision of healthcare services.

When assessing the quality of products, the first dimension is often conformance to specification, where a range of parameters are defined to quantify an acceptable range of values for physical dimensions such as composition, purity, mass, size, and so on. When considering the quality of services, then this is often translated into a series of targets for activity such as the number of patient episodes. One of the challenges when measuring the quality of services is that it is often easier to measure activity than outcomes. The consequence is that this can lead to an emphasis on measuring the quality of inputs rather than health outcomes (Gillies, 1997).

Garvin (1984) suggested five primary dimensions of quality. These views still inform research today (Solin & Curry, 2023).

The transcendent view: This view relates quality to innate excellence. Another word for this might be "elegance." This is the classical layman's perception of quality. It is impossible to quantify and is difficult to apply in a meaningful sense to healthcare. An attempt to build a high degree of innate excellence into healthcare is likely to be constrained by resources.

The user-based view: This view may be viewed as fitness for purpose and measured as how well the users' expectations and needs are met. It often has two distinct subdimensions. The first is a consumerist view of the patients' satisfaction with the process: Was it a pleasant experience? Were the staff polite to me? However, this may or may not correlate with whether their long-term needs were met, which are better measured through long-term health outcomes. Many effective treatments may require short-term pain and discomfort, for example.

The manufacturing view: This view measures quality in terms of conformance to requirements. A simple example might be the dimensions of a component. The specification will state both the required dimension and the tolerance that will be acceptable.

The manufacturing view emerges in healthcare in several ways. The first is the introduction of protocols and standards for specific clinical procedures. Protocols can be effective in reducing errors and therefore costs of litigation but tend to limit innovation and improvement.

The value-based view: In a business context, this is the ability to provide what the customer requires at a price that they can afford. Almost all healthcare services are ultimately rationed within a finite budget. A value-based view of quality assesses the outcomes in terms of the cost-effectiveness of a service or treatment. The value-based view is the antithesis of the transcendent view because it links quality to cost. Although there are cases where better healthcare costs less not more, this is often not the case.

The product-based view: This view says that better products and services require more money. There are often calls within public-funded health services for more money to provide more procedures, drugs, and staff to improve the quality of the system, and this is based upon the product-based view. However, taken to an extreme, the US system with its highest costs and some of the poorest outcomes shows that how resources are deployed can also be important.

18.3.2 Lead-time aka delivery

A key measurable and obvious measure of the performance of healthcare systems are the waiting times experienced by patients for appointments and elective and urgent treatments.

Governments often use targets for waiting times as a means to measure the performance of healthcare systems. Examples from the UK NHS include:

- The maximum waiting time for elective, consultant-led treatments is 18 weeks
- The maximum waiting time for an appointment about a suspected cancer is two weeks

(NHS, 2022)

Waiting times are often used as a means to make international comparisons of the performance of healthcare systems. Care is needed in international comparisons to ensure that waiting times are measured in the same way. For example, the starting point can be the first presentation of the patient, or when a diagnosis is made, when a treatment plan is agreed, or when a patient is added to a formal waiting list for treatment.

For businesses supplying health services with drugs, medical devices, and other equipment, delivery times are likely to be a key parameter. Modern business practices are generally built upon the "just-in-time" principle. Just-in-time is the principle that raw materials and finished products should be delivered at the exact time they are needed to reduce the cost of holding stocks.

However, the global pandemic severely disrupted global supply chains and this was subsequently exacerbated by the impact of the conflict in Ukraine. During the pandemic, it was common for governments to seek to buy and store PPE and vaccine supplies to guarantee availability for the population, but this has been shown to be both expensive and wasteful (NAO, 2022).

18.3.3 Cost

Dimensions of costs for products to the supplier include the cost of raw materials, the cost of processing them to create a product, the cost of sales and marketing, and the costs of transportation. They may also include a proportion of research and development costs and the costs of getting the product approved for sale. For the supplier to make a profit, the sales price must be greater than the total of these costs.

Dimensions of costs relating to products for the customer will include the initial purchase price, but may also include additional costs for storage, maintenance, insurance, and depreciation, according to the nature of the product.

Costs of services have many components. In most cases, the highest cost will be the cost of the staff providing the service, but other costs will include premises, heating lighting, cleaning and maintenance, insurance, transportation, and many other costs.

These costs must be covered by the income received, which is generally linked to the number and type of procedures carried out, although the exact mechanism will depend upon their status (public, private for profit, private not for profit, for example) and the purchaser (government, social insurance fund, private insurance fund, or individual contributions).

In wholly or partly publicly funded systems, healthcare providers often receive higher or additional payments as incentives to prioritise the treatments and patient groups that the funder deems to be a priority. For example, value-based programs are used within the US Medicare system (Centers for Medicare & Medicaid Services, 2022).

18.3.4 Flexibility

Healthcare service providers and product suppliers operate within a constantly evolving environment subject to disruptive events such as the COVID-19 pandemic. A key requirement is for them to be flexible and able to adapt to the changing external environment.

Manufacturers need to be able to adapt to: variations in the quality of incoming materials; variations in the required quality of products; the need for new products and to modify existing products; changes in delivery schedules and demand volumes; changes in regulatory requirements; and changes in the product and resource mix.

Healthcare service providers need to be able to adapt to: seasonal changes in the demands for services; unplanned changes in the demands for service; changes in the priorities of funders; changes in the availability of the workforce, especially those with scarce expertise; and unexpected changes in the cost of key resources such as energy.

Reductions in waiting times 2000–2014, after Siciliana et al. (2014)

Siciliana et al. (2014) reported on trends in waiting times and the measures used to reduce them in a number of countries. The study found that waiting times could be reduced significantly by specific initiatives.

OECD nations pursued various strategies to diminish waiting times. Finland, for instance, enacted a National Health Care Guarantee in 2005, ensuring a maximum waiting period of three months for elective treatments with limited exceptions. Hospitals failing to meet this standard faced scrutiny and the threat of fines. The initial years of this guarantee saw increased health expenditure for municipalities, which corresponded with reductions in waiting times.

Waiting times seem to be relatively short in the Netherlands and Denmark. Over the past decade, countries like the United Kingdom (especially England), Finland, and the Netherlands have significantly reduced their waiting times due to various policy efforts. These efforts include increased funding, the implementation of waiting-time target programs, and incentive mechanisms that reward higher activity levels. However, in recent years, this downward trend in waiting times has either slowed or reversed in these countries. The analysis also highlights consistent variations in different waiting-time metrics, particularly between the waiting times of patients who have received treatment and those still on the waiting list.

In the United Kingdom, substantial reductions in waiting times were attributed to sustained growth in health expenditure and the implementation of waiting-time targets. England, in particular, enforced these targets rigorously, introducing heavy sanctions for hospitals failing to comply, a policy colloquially known as "targets and terror." This approach potentially contributed to greater reductions in waiting times in England compared to Scotland, where hospitals faced monitoring and investigation for breaches but not economic penalties.

The Netherlands witnessed reductions in waiting times between 2000 and 2006 due to a significant shift in the hospital financing system from fixed budgets to activity-based funding. Subsequent reductions were facilitated by a reform in specialist payments, transitioning from lump-sum to activity-based payments in 2008, alongside an expansion of price competition. However, concerns were raised about the rapid growth in health expenditure resulting from activity-based financing.

Denmark implemented a policy of "free choice" for patients to select their hospital provider, enabling patients to opt for an alternative hospital if the maximum waiting time could not be met. The maximum waiting time guarantee was initially two months, reduced to four weeks in 2007. However, this policy was temporarily suspended in 2008–2009 due to a hospital personnel strike.

Portugal achieved reductions in waiting times through various policy initiatives, including the implementation of an integrated information system combined with a voucher system for patients nearing 75% of a specified maximum waiting time.

18.3.5 Knowledge review

Before you move on, can you define the following key concepts:

* The user-based view of quality?
* The manufacturing view?
* The value-based view?
* The product-based view?

18.3.6 Question to think about

When you have made use of healthcare services, how have you judged the quality of the services provided?

18.4 Workforce planning

Staff are the most valuable and costliest type of resource for hospitals and the broader healthcare sector. Therefore, effective management of this resource is crucial to the efficient and effective running of healthcare organisations. The foundations of creating an effective workforce lie in managing the basic human resources (HR) functions, which are summarised in Table 18.2.

However, there is a more strategic role in ensuring that the healthcare provider has access to enough appropriately qualified staff. Healthcare professionals are a scarce resource, and the market for their services is increasingly globalised. The shortage of human resources to address current and emerging health needs across the globe has been highlighted by the WHO (2018) as a barrier to progress towards the SDGs.

SDG target 3.c specifically relates to the health workforce:

> *substantially increase health financing and the recruitment, development, training and retention of the health workforce in developing countries, especially in least developed countries and small island developing States*
>
> UN DESA (2023)

UN DESA (2023) reports that the projected global shortfall in healthcare professionals by 2030 has been diminished from 18 million to 10 million. However, despite a notable rise in the total number of healthcare workers worldwide, regions grappling with the greatest disease burden still exhibit the lowest proportion of health personnel available to provide essential services. From 2014 to 2021, sub-Saharan Africa maintained the

Table 18.2 Operational HR functions

Function	Description
Recruitment and selection	HR is responsible for attracting, screening, and hiring qualified individuals to fill vacant positions. This involves creating job descriptions, advertising job openings, conducting interviews, making job offers, and helping new employees with induction.
Employee relations	HR acts as a liaison between employees and management, promoting positive employee relations and aiding communication between staff and leaders. They handle employee grievances, conflicts, and disciplinary issues, in line with hospital policies and procedures.
Compensation and benefits	HR oversees remuneration for employees. They ensure that salary structures, pay scales, and benefit packages are competitive and compliant with legislation. They also manage employee payroll, track attendance, and administer employee benefits.
Training and development	HR is responsibile for identifying training needs and designs or coordinates employee development programs. They may also facilitate career development initiatives, performance management systems, and succession planning within the hospital.
Policy development and compliance	HR must ensure that all policies and procedures are compliant with employment laws and regulations and are kept up to date. They must maintain all required records and documentation related to employee files, contracts, and certifications.
Performance management	HR monitors the assessment of employee performance. This includes establishing performance evaluation systems, providing feedback to employees, collaborating with managers to address performance issues, and recognising and rewarding high-performing employees.
Employee engagement and retention	HR should develop strategies to enhance employee engagement, foster employee satisfaction and retention, and promote a positive work culture. They may implement employee engagement surveys, wellness programs, and employee recognition initiatives.
Compliance and employee safety	HR must ensure compliance with occupational health and safety regulations. They must establish and promote safety protocols, conduct safety training, and address workplace hazards.
HR data management	HR must maintain accurate and confidential employee records, including personal information, employment contracts, and performance evaluations. They will utilise tailored information systems to manage employee data, generate reports, and analyse workforce trends to support decision-making processes.

lowest density of health workers, with merely 2.3 medical doctors and 12.6 nursing and midwifery personnel per 10,000 individuals.

In contrast, Europe boasted the highest density of doctors, at 39.4 per 10,000 population, whereas Northern America led in nursing and midwifery personnel, with 152.1 per 10,000 population. Disparities persist even in nations where national densities appear adequate, particularly evident between rural, remote, subnational, and hard-to-reach regions versus major urban centres and capital cities.

Most European countries have overall shortages in healthcare workers, exacerbated by an uneven distribution. This contributes to unmet health needs, particularly in rural, remote, and underserved areas. Even in areas currently not experiencing shortages, the projected growth in demand, driven by factors like population ageing and rising expectations, poses an ongoing challenge to ensure the skill distribution and sustainability of the healthcare workforce. Effective policies are needed to address issues, such as the work environment, workplace well-being, and the concept of "decent work," to enhance retention, participation, motivation, and the sustainable supply of health workers with appropriate skills and geographic distribution.

Globally, the inequalities and shortages are more stark. The WHO (2018) suggests that low- and middle-income countries will require an additional 274 billion USD spending on health annually by 2030 to progress towards the SDG 3 targets, with a substantial portion allocated to health systems, including healthcare workforce and infrastructure.

The OECD (2022) estimates that between 25% to 32% of physicians in Australia, Canada, the United Kingdom, and the United States are international medical graduates who received their training in countries located in South Asia and Africa. Additionally, in certain medical specialties, the majority of specialists in high-income countries are international medical graduates from low- and middle-income countries, exacerbating the existing shortages of specialists in those regions.

While the unrestricted movement of individuals across borders in pursuit of opportunities and economic advancement is considered a fundamental human right, various factors contribute to the migration of healthcare workers, exacerbating shortages in low- and middle-income countries. In host countries, enticing factors such as lucrative job prospects and improved lifestyles, alongside factors like poor salaries and inadequate resources in source countries, drive this migration phenomenon. This dynamic, characterised by "pull factors" in host nations and "push factors" in source countries, worsens healthcare workforce shortages in low- and middle-income countries (Joshi et al., 2023).

Initially, healthcare workers from low- and middle-income countries may migrate to high-income countries for training or to acquire new skills. Paradoxically, this can lead to further emigration, as these trained professionals may struggle to find opportunities to apply their new-found skills upon returning home. Moreover, immigrant international medical graduates often play a role in facilitating migration for other healthcare professionals from their home countries, including doctors, nurses, and technicians.

Consequently, this trend contributes to a diminished accessibility to healthcare for citizens of low- and middle-income countries. Despite bearing 24% of the global burden of disease, Africa has only 3% of the global healthcare workforce, underscoring the severity of the situation (Collins et al., 2010). Saluja et al. (2020) estimated that doctor migration costs low- and middle-income countries 15 billion USD per year. Migration of skilled health workers results in the loss of access to the health workforce, leading to increases in ill health and consequent mortality.

They report that the greatest total costs are incurred by India, Nigeria, Pakistan, and South Africa (Saluja et al., 2020). However, medical migration can also occur within regions, such as from poorer Eastern European countries to Western Europe and beyond (Suciu et al., 2017).

Since 2010, WHO member states have adopted the Global Code of Practice on the International Recruitment of Health Personnel, with the goal of improving understanding and ethical management of international health personnel recruitment. However, the code is not legally binding and lacks incentives and institutional mechanisms to enable implementation. A review of the code four years after its implementation showed no significant policy or regulatory changes to the recruitment of health workers (Tam et al., 2016).

Medical emigration from Romania (after Suciu et al., 2017)

Romania has a long and proud tradition of medical education and has long trained more doctors than needed for domestic purposes in the knowledge that many graduates will emigrate. Since Romania joined the EU in 2007, international migration has become much more straightforward for Romanian medical graduates.

Iuliu Haţieganu University of Medicine and Pharmacy in Cluj-Napoca, Romania provides medical education in Romanian, French, and English and attracts a significant number of international students. Although these students generally return to their own countries, they provide a valuable source of income for the university. Suciu et al. (2017) surveyed 957 Romanian medical students studying in Cluj from three cohorts from 2014 to 2016 to investigate their intentions regarding emigration.

They found that 84.7% intended to pursue employment opportunities abroad following graduation. This figure is much higher than in other Eastern European countries; for example, only about 50% of Polish students envisioned emigrating. In Lithuania, 60% of medical residents indicated their plans to emigrate, with 15% considering permanent relocation. However, it is worth noting that, these forecasts often overestimated actual emigration rates, with EU accession typically resulting in emigration rates not exceeding 3%.

Regarding the Romanian cohort, a majority of the sample consisted of female alumni, reflecting the higher enrolment of female students in medical studies. Germany emerged as the top destination choice among those considering emigration, with 34.1% expressing a preference for it. The primary reason cited for seeking employment abroad was the prospect of higher wages compared to Romania. Notably, there were no discernible differences based on gender or marital status concerning the importance of higher wages abroad.

Other factors contributing to migration included dissatisfaction with Romania's healthcare and residency system, as well as concerns about the country's societal issues, such as the prevalence of informal payments in healthcare. Regarding postgraduation practice preferences, approximately 33% of medical alumni expressed a preference for working exclusively in the public sector, while 10.1% preferred the private sector. The majority (56.8%) intended to work in both public hospital settings and private practice simultaneously.

The migration of physicians poses significant challenges, including the loss of a highly educated professional workforce, which incurs substantial costs for education and training. Additionally, the societal impact of physician migration, particularly in smaller towns and rural areas with limited access to healthcare, raises concerns. The ease with which physicians can permanently migrate, along with their ability to bring family members, exacerbates the issue. The loss of even a thousand doctors annually in Romania, considering the total number of doctors, underscores the potential vulnerability at the national level.

Physicians cited low salaries, lack of social status, and systemic issues within the healthcare sector as primary reasons for migration. Many students preparing for emigration had already taken steps such as participating in Erasmus mobility programs, language courses, and job searches online.

While migration can address workforce imbalances and contribute to health system performance in destination countries, it also underscores the need for Romania to strengthen data collection on health workforce migration. Policy interventions to retain medical personnel include measures to improve salaries and working conditions, structural reforms in healthcare provisions, and efforts to combat negative perceptions of the medical profession. Additionally, fostering career development opportunities and reintegrating healthcare professionals who have worked abroad are crucial steps for the Romanian healthcare system's sustainability.

Knowledge review

Before you move on, can you define the following key concepts:

• Medical migration?

Question to think about

What incentives could be used to improve implementation of the WHO Global Code of Practice on the International Recruitment of Health Personnel?

References

Centers for Medicare & Medicaid Services. (2022). *What are the value-based programs?* (p. 21244). CMS.

Collins, F. S., Glass, R. I., Whitescarver, J., Wakefield, M., & Goosby, E. P. (2010). Developing health workforce capacity in Africa. *Science*, 330(6009), 1324–1325.

Crown Commercial Service. (2015). *Guidance -public procurement*. HM Government.

Figueroa, C. A., Harrison, R., Chauhan, A., et al. (2019). Priorities and challenges for health leadership and workforce management globally: A rapid review. *BMC Health Services Research*, 19, 239.

Garuba, A. H., Kohler, C. J., & Huisman, M. A. (2009). Transparency in Nigeria's public pharmaceutical sector: Perceptions from policy makers. *Globalisation and Health*, 5(14), 1–13.

Garvin, D. (1984). *What does quality mean?* MIT Sloan Management Review. Reprint #2613.

Gillies, A. (1997). *Improving the quality of patient care*. John Wiley, ISBN 978-0471966470.

Hayes, R. H., & Wheelwright, S. C. (1984). Restoring our competitive edge: Competing through manufacturing. John Wiley, ISBN: 978-0-471-05159-6.

Joshi, R., Yakubu, K., Keshri, V. R., & Jha, V. (2023, July). Skilled health workforce emigration: Its consequences, ethics, and potential solutions. In *Mayo clinic proceedings* (Vol. 98, No. 7, pp. 960–965). Elsevier.

Kanavos, P., & Wouters, O. (2014). *Competition issues in the distribution of pharmaceuticals*. Organisation for Economic Co-operation and Development.

Kitchenham, B. A., & Pfleeger, S. L. (1996). Software quality - the elusive goal. *IEEE Software*, 13(1), 12–21.

Medicines & Healthcare Products Regulatory Agency. (2021). Managing medical devices guidance for health and social care organizations.

National Audio Office. (2020). *Investigation into government procurement during the COVID-19 pandemic, HC 959 Session 2019–2021 18 November 2020*. Cabinet Office.

National Audio Office. (2022). *Investigation into the management of PPE contracts*. Department of Health & Social Care, ISBN: 9781786044235

NHS. (2022). *Guide to NHS waiting times in England, eepartment of health & social care/NHS England*. NHS.

OECD. (2017). *Tackling wasteful spending on health*. OECD Publishing

OECD. (2022, June 19). *Health workforce migration*. OCED.

Olugbenga, O. E. (2014). The politics and pathology of drug service administration in third world countries: Lessons of two drug distribution experiments in Nigeria. *International Journal of Development and Sustainability*, 3(3), 505–519.

Rodziewicz, T. L., Houseman, B., & Hipskind, J. E. (2022). Medical error reduction and prevention. In *StatPearls* [Internet]. Treasure Island (FL): StatPearls Publishing.

Saluja, S., Rudolfson, N., Massenburg, B. B., Meara, J. G., & Shrime, M. G. (2020). The impact of physician migration on mortality in low and middle-income countries: An economic modelling study. *BMJ Global Health*, 5(1), e001535.

Siciliani, L., Moran, V., & Borowitz, M. (2014). Measuring and comparing health care waiting times in OECD countries. *Health Policy*, 118(3), 292–303.

Solin, A., & Curry, A. (2023). Perceived quality: In search of a definition. *The TQM Journal*, 35(3), 778–795.

Suciu, Ş. M., Popescu, C. A., Ciumageanu, M. D., et al. (2017). Physician migration at its roots: A study on the emigration preferences and plans among medical students in Romania. *Human Resources for Health*, 15, 6.

Tam, V., Edge, J. S., & Hoffman, S. J. (2016). Empirically evaluating the WHO global code of practice on the international recruitment of health personnel's impact on four high-income countries four years after adoption. *Globalisation and Health*, 12, 1–12.

UN DESA. (2023). *The sustainable development goals report 2023: Special edition - July 2023*. UN Department of Economic and Social Affairs. https://unstats.un.org/sdgs/report/2023/

World Bank. (2021). *Opportunities and challenges for public procurement in the first months of the COVID-19 pandemic: Results from an experts survey. Equitable growth, finance and institutions insight*. World Bank.

WHO. (2009). *WHO guidelines for safe surgery: Safe surgery saves lives*. WHO, ISBN: 9789241598552

WHO. (2018). *Health workforce: Fact sheet on Sustainable Development Goals (SDGs): Health targets* (No. WHO/EURO: 2018-2366-42121-58038). WHO. Regional Office for Europe.

19   Leadership in healthcare

19.1 Styles of leadership

A leader's style is expressed in how they issue instructions, implement ideas, and motivate others. It is the result of their leader's thoughts, personality, expertise, skills, and experience. Different situations necessitate various leadership styles. For example, autocratic leadership is best in emergency scenarios, when a decision needs to be made on the spot. Alternately, when there is a need to motivate a team and encourage team members to work collaboratively, then a more "democratic" leadership style is more appropriate (Chestnut, 2017).

Typical leadership styles are identified as:

- Authoritarian (also known as autocratic)
- Democratic (also known as participative)
- Free rein (also known as laissez-faire)
- Task-oriented
- Relationship-oriented
- Paternalistic
- Servant.

The characteristics of each leadership style are summarised below.

19.1.1 Authoritarian (also known as autocratic) leadership

In an autocratic leadership style, as with tyrants, all decision-making powers are consolidated in the leader, and subordinates are not consulted by autocratic leaders. Decisions are made solely by the leader and are only disclosed to other people when the leader decides to do so (Harms et al., 2018).

This style of leadership is associated with clarity, decisiveness, and authority. It satisfies the ego of the leader and is unlikely to be challenged until something goes wrong. In a stable situation, where little unexpected happens, and the leader is not faced with unfamiliar or unpredictable problems, it can be quite successful. Democratic (also known as participative) leaders share authority with all the members of their group, promoting a strong team ethos. They openly communicate information about organisational goals, strategies, and decisions, ensuring that team members are well-informed and understand the reasoning behind various choices. They are willing to consider alternative viewpoints, adapt to changing circumstances, and modify their decisions based on new information

DOI: 10.4324/9781003478874-24

or feedback from team members. Their followers feel valued, engaged, and motivated to contribute to the organisation's success.

19.1.2 Free rein (also known as laissez-faire) leadership

Free rein leaders give the task of decision-making to their teams and subordinates (Yang, 2015). Teams and subordinates are given complete power, freedom, and autonomy to set goals, as well as to solve issues and problems. With experienced, capable staff and effective monitoring, it can be effective. With less-experienced staff and leaders, it can rapidly become chaotic and unproductive.

19.1.3 Task-oriented leadership

Task-oriented leaders devise a systematic approach to address particular issues or objectives, impose rigid timeframes, and focus on attaining the desired outcomes. They prioritise attaining a precise solution to meet production targets rather than focusing on team satisfaction, which can lead to meeting deadlines consistently but potentially compromising the welfare of team members. Their focus lies in reaching the objective and distributing responsibilities among team members accordingly (Rüzgar, 2018).

19.1.4 Relationship-oriented leadership

A relationship-oriented leader cares about their teams' satisfaction and well-being. Relationship-focused leaders care about their team's development and the relationships that exist in it, with increased motivation and support for team members being among the advantages of working in this type of environment. However, putting a greater focus on relationships rather than getting work done may cause productivity to suffer (Rüzgar, 2018).

19.1.5 Paternalistic leadership

Paternalistic leadership approaches generally reflect a perspective. Paternal leaders act as a dominant father-figure and treat employees and partners as though they are members of a large, extended family. In exchange, the leader expects loyalty and trust , as well as obedience from employees. The organisation of the team is hierarchical, with the leader being placed above the followers, providing guidance to team members both professionally and personally. According to Aydin (2018), this is a common leadership style in Russia and Pacific Asian countries.

19.1.6 Servant leadership

Servant leadership puts the needs of others at the forefront. Under this leadership philosophy, the more the leader invests in supporting the team members, the more productive the team becomes.

A servant leader fosters an inclusive culture in their team, allowing every person to feel that they belong. This gives them a chance to maximise their contribution.

Servant leaders are themselves focused on the team, more than the customer. However, they create high-performing teams that serve customers better (Parris & Peachey, 2013).

19.1.7 Collaborative leadership

Collaborative leadership is based on the proposition that collaboration delivers greater benefits for the organisation. Collaborative leadership requires transparency and information sharing with employees, patients, and all other relevant stakeholders so that collective decision-making is based upon the best available evidence, facts, and data. Therefore, this type of leadership promotes information sharing, continuous engagement, and communication between all stakeholders. It requires people to acknowledge and understand different worlds and develop shared beliefs and values (Figueroa et al., 2019).

According to Pérez-Sánchez (2021), healthcare workers have been shown to favour leaders that are collaborative in style, offer support, promote continuous development, delegate work and decision-making, and develop strong relations with their team.

19.2 Transactional vs. transformational leadership

To create a positive culture in the workforce, it is necessary to create a culture of effective leadership. This starts with the top of the organisation but requires all staff to recognise that they have a leadership role to play by influencing those around them.

Sfantou et al. (2017) surveyed the academic literature about the importance of leadership style in achieving quality of care measures in healthcare settings. They found that extensive research has been conducted on effective leadership in health services, particularly in recent decades. The literature highlights the urgent need for effective leadership styles in healthcare and social services due to various societal challenges.

Their review emphasised the relationship between leadership and quality care and a range of patient outcomes, such as mortality rates, safety, satisfaction, physical restraint use, and pain. The reviewed articles identified the importance of leadership in achieving well-coordinated and integrated care across various healthcare settings and in providing benefits to both patients and healthcare professionals (Squires et al., 2010; Castle & Decker, 2011).

Moreover, the influence of leadership style on patient outcomes became evident, as effective leadership contributed to a high-quality work environment and a positive safety climate, ultimately resulting in favourable patient outcomes. Conversely, evidence indicated that a lack of effective leadership leading to a subpar work environment could negatively impact patients. The majority of studies in this domain concentrated on nursing leadership, revealing that transformational and resonant leadership styles were associated with reduced patient mortality, while relational and task-oriented leadership showed a connection to higher patient satisfaction. Transformational, transactional, and collaborative leadership styles were also found to enhance patient satisfaction in acute care and home care settings. However, it is worth noting that many studies assessing patient outcomes primarily focused on adverse events related to clinical management, rather than the patient's primary condition (Vogus & Sutcliffe, 2007).

Additionally, leadership was acknowledged as a pivotal element in cultivating a high-quality organisational culture and driving effective performance in healthcare delivery. Empirical studies based upon primary data have demonstrated a robust connection between leadership and various aspects of care, including safety, effectiveness, and equity. Notably, transformational leadership has been found to bring about positive changes in nursing unit organisational culture, structural empowerment, organisational commitment, job satisfaction, productivity, nursing retention, patient safety, and the overall safety climate, resulting in improved health outcomes. It has been associated with enhanced process quality, organisational culture, and favourable patient outcomes, thereby contributing significantly to improved patient safety and overall care quality (Moneke & Umeh, 2013).

The literature underscores the significance of leadership styles and practices on patient outcomes, the healthcare workforce, and organisational culture. Prioritising effective leadership in healthcare organisations should enhance performance in quantifiable ways. As regional and national health systems undergo structural changes to address modern societal, economic, and health challenges, medical leadership plays a crucial role in successful and qualitative priority-setting processes. Engaging non-medical clinical leaders, such as leaders from a nursing or therapy background, ensures that the priority setting is accepted by the broader group of key stakeholders.

The conclusion from this work is that the most effective leadership styles are collaborative and multifaceted, recognising that management is a dynamic process. These characteristics are associated with transformational and employee-oriented leadership.

19.2.1 *Transactional leadership*

Transactional leadership focuses on the exchange or transaction between the leader and the followers. It is based on a system of rewards and punishments and operates on the principle of "give-and-take." Transactional leaders set clear expectations and define measurable standards of performance. In return, they expect obedience from followers and provide rewards or punishments depending on whether those expectations are met. They accept the goals, structure, and culture of their organisations without question. They tend to be directive and action-oriented. They will usually try to solve problems within the existing constraints.

Transactional leadership is primarily passive, and the associated behaviours seek to establish the criteria for rewarding followers and maintaining the status quo. The directness, simplicity, and consistency of transactional management are part of its attractiveness. Within transactional leadership, power is exerted by a carrot-and-stick approach. These leaders use praise and rewards for effort and for good performance as incentives. They use sanctions when staff subordinates do not meet acceptable performance levels and initiate corrective action to improve performance in a system of management-by-exception that maintains the status quo.

Transactional leaders may be active or passive. Active leaders proactively monitor performance and take corrective actions when needed. Passive leaders do not actively monitor follower behaviour and only take corrective action when serious problems arise. Transactional leadership can be beneficial in some situations. Where it is useful, the advantages include rewarding individuals who are self-motivated and follow instructions, creating a rapid impact on productivity and performance, and achieving short-term goals. It tends to be effective in work environments where structure and systems need to be consistently applied, such as in high-volume manufacturing and compliance is important, for example, in safety situations.

On the other hand, it does not work well in flexible work environments; it only rewards workers with perks or money, no other real motivators are used, and it does not reward individuals who take a personal initiative. In terms of a hierarchy of needs such as that defined by Maslow (1970), it will only satisfy workers' most basic needs.

19.2.2 Transformational leadership

Transformational leadership is a type of leadership characterised by a leader's capacity to inspire and motivate their followers, in the belief that this will lead to exceptional results. This style involves crafting a compelling vision, nurturing a sense of purpose, and enabling individuals to unleash their full potential. Transformational leaders are renowned for their charisma, enthusiasm, and the positive impact they have on their teams.

Transformational leaders routinely challenge the way things are done. They create or support new ideas and turn that support into new products, processes, and services adopted. They will seek out challenging opportunities and look for innovative ways to improve their organisations.

They experiment and take risks with new approaches. Learning is a way of life for these people.

Instead of punishing failure, they encourage it so that they can learn from it. They accept responsibility for failures and do not seek to shift the blame. Transformational leadership is based upon the proposition that all staff enabled by those in senior roles in the organisation can act as transformational leaders by influencing their peers. This means that leadership is not a job role but a responsibility of all staff irrespective of their role. The role of HR is to act as role models and facilitators and ensure that training and development and incentives and remuneration schemes are aligned with encouraging transformational behaviours.

In healthcare, professionals also need to show appropriate leadership behaviours towards patients. Transformational leadership of patients can lead to patients adopting healthier lifestyles and complying with treatment regimes, leading to better health outcomes.

Case study: Transformational change in Southcentral Foundation, Alaska, US (after Charlesworth & Jamieson, 2017)

Southcentral Foundation is a non-profit health and wellness organisation owned by Alaska natives serving approximately 60,000 Alaska native and American–Indian individuals. In the 1980s, Alaska's healthcare system faced significant challenges, characterised by inefficiency, long wait times, increasing emergency room visits, and poor health outcomes. By the late 1990s, Southcentral Foundation recognised the need to change and initiated a comprehensive overhaul of its health system. This involved reimagining and redesigning every aspect of care, from recruitment and training to care models and facility design.

Under the new system, known as Nuka, primary care teams led by Southcentral Foundation physicians cultivate long-term relationships with their patients, focusing on well-being and disease prevention. This approach includes addressing issues such as domestic violence, obesity, substance abuse, diabetes, and heart disease. The results have been remarkable, with significant reductions in emergency room visits, hospitalisations, specialty care utilisation, and routine doctor visits. Moreover, community health indicators, such as binge drinking, suicides, strokes, and mortality rates, have shown marked improvements.

The key to Southcentral Foundation's success lies in several factors. First, leveraging tribal authority, they began contracting health services from the federal government in the late 1980s, gradually assuming ownership of the entire healthcare delivery system by the late 1990s. They prioritised consultation with community members and employees, listening deeply to their stories and expectations, which informed the development of a clear vision, mission, and operating principles centred around valuing human relationships.

The transformation was intentionally designed, starting with modest changes and progressively expanding their scope while continuously engaging with the workforce. Despite challenges, such as provider stress and turnover, primary care services steadily expanded over time. Additionally, Southcentral Foundation implemented sophisticated data and performance management systems to provide real-time feedback and performance metrics to identify areas for improvement and support innovation.

These changes required transformational leadership not just of the healthcare workforce but of the whole community.

19.2.3 Knowledge review

Before you move on, can you define the following key concepts:

* Transactional leadership?
* Transformational leadership?

19.2.4 Questions to think about

What kind of leadership styles have you experienced?
    What type of leader do you like to follow?

19.3 Models of transformational leadership

19.3.1 Burns (2012) model of transformational leadership

As early as 1978, Burns had proposed the distinction between transactional and transformational leadership. According to Burns, transformational leadership consists of four components:

* idealised influence
* inspirational motivation
* intellectual stimulation
* individualised consideration

Table 19.1 identifies the characteristics of each component of Burns model of transformational leadership, drawing on a review by Reza (2019).

19.3.2 Kouzes and Posner (2011) model of exemplary leadership

Kouzes and Posner (2011) argue that modern complex organisations require transformational, rather than transactional leadership. Their model of leadership emphasises

Table 19.1 Characteristics of Burns model of transformational leadership, after Reza (2019)

Component	Description of characteristics
Idealised influence	Idealised influence refers to leaders who serve as exemplary role models for their followers by demonstrating exceptional capabilities and adhering to high standards of ethical conduct. They exhibit behaviours that enable them to become role models for their followers, earning admiration, respect, and trust. These leaders are often seen as icons, particularly due to their display of personal qualities such as charisma. Idealised influence encompasses leaders who effectively model desired behaviours for their followers, providing them with a clear vision and mission for their organisation and consequently garnering a high level of respect and trust from their followers.
Inspirational motivation	Inspirational motivation involves leaders' ability to motivate followers so that they are able to exceed their own expectations. They motivate and inspire those around them by giving meaning and challenge to their followers' work. They have a cooperative vision that they can communicate to followers and can align individual and organisational goals, thus making the achievement of organisational goals an attractive way for followers to achieve their personal goals.
Intellectual stimulation	Intellectual stimulation means that transformational leaders stimulate their followers' efforts to be innovative and creative by questioning expectations, reframing difficulties, and encouraging new ideas. They do not publicly criticise individual errors. They guide their followers to think through issues and problems for themselves and thereby develop their own abilities. Reza (2018) states that one of the most stimulating leaders from history is Socrates, although he was viewed as a troublemaker and as troublesome to the status quo. This questioning nature is also associated with transformational leadership.
Individualised consideration	Individualised consideration means that transformational leaders give special attention to each of their follower's needs for achievement and growth by acting as a coach or mentor. They will seek to identify new learning opportunities and create a supportive climate for followers to pursue their own development. They will recognise the differences amongst followers in their strengths and weaknesses, as well as their likes and dislikes.

that leadership is not a position but a set of practices and behaviours. They propose a collection of practices that guide leaders in accomplishing extraordinary things. These practices align closely with the concept of transformational leadership and have been recognised by many researchers as highly effective.

Kouzes and Posner (2011) advise leaders to:

- challenge the process
- inspire a shared vision
- enable others to act
- model the way
- encourage the heart

The meaning of each behaviour is expanded in Table 19.2.

Table 19.2 Behaviours associated with exemplary leadership (after Kouzes & Posner, 2011)

Behaviour	Description
Challenging the process	Challenging the process involves actively seeking opportunities to challenge the existing system, generating new ideas, and supporting innovation to improve the organisation. Transformational leaders are willing to take risks and view mistakes as learning opportunities rather than failures.
Inspiring a shared vision	Inspiring a shared vision is crucial for creating a sense of unity and commitment among individuals in an organisation. Transformational leaders passionately believe in their ability to make a difference and create an inspiring vision of what the organisation can achieve. They use positive language, metaphors, symbols, and personal energy to generate enthusiasm and excitement among their followers.
Enabling others to act	Enabling others to act focuses on fostering collaboration, empowerment, and trust. Transformational leaders involve others in decision-making, provide them with autonomy and freedom of choice, and create an environment where each individual feels capable, powerful, and responsible. They consider the needs and interests of others and promote a sense of ownership within the organisation.
Modelling the way	Modelling the way involves leading by example. Transformational leaders set high standards and demonstrate commitment to excellence through their daily actions. They establish a clear philosophy and principles that guide the organisation and consistently live by the values they advocate. By aligning their words and deeds, they build credibility and inspire others to follow their lead.
Encouraging the heart	Encouraging the heart is about recognising and celebrating individual and group achievements. Transformational leaders have high expectations for themselves and their employees, and they motivate them by attaching rewards and recognition to job performance. They serve as role models and play a prominent role in celebrating successes, fostering a sense of belonging and inspiring improved performance.

Behaviours identified in a study of nursing leaders in European island countries by Hughes et al. (2023)

In 2017, Hughes and colleagues conducted a study involving 19 semi-structured interviews with nurse leaders from various countries, including England, Greece, Republic of Ireland, and Malta. The aim was to investigate their leadership experiences, the strategies they used for personal and professional growth, and the influence of cultural factors on their journeys (Hughes et al., 2023).

Analysis of the interview transcripts using reflexive thematic analysis revealed four key themes: influences, communication, process, and relationships. The study found that the attributes and behaviours exhibited by successful nurse leaders aligned with the exemplary leadership model proposed by Kouzes and Posner (2011).

The interviews showcased nurse leaders who challenged conventional practices and achieved remarkable results, ranging from "excellent to extraordinary" accomplishments (Hughes, 2017). Some focused on fostering healthy work environments, leading to high nurse retention rates, while others concentrated on enhancing patient outcomes through national nursing research, influencing policy changes, and creating new nursing leadership roles. Additionally, some nurse leaders secured positions in national governments to drive significant changes in nursing education and the scope of practice for advanced practice nurses. Furthermore, the study participants emphasised the importance of empowering nurses to think independently and shared credit for successes.

These findings support Kouzes and Posner's assertion that successful leaders demonstrate exemplary leadership practices regardless of cultural context. The authors also referenced other research indicating that transformational nursing leadership positively correlates with patient care outcomes and nursing in various international settings. Benefits include improvements in patient satisfaction, mortality rates, healthcare utilisation, and patient safety, as well as enhanced nurse retention, reduced workplace incivility, and increased nurse commitment to their profession (Hughes, 2019).

19.3.3 Knowledge review

Before you move on, can you define the following key concepts:

• Exemplary leadership?

19.3.4 Question to think about

Consider the two models of transformational leadership. What are the similarities? What are the differences?

19.4 Public leadership

Hartley (2018) defines public leadership as, "mobilising individuals, organisations and networks to formulate and/or enact purposes, values and actions which aim or claim to create valued outcomes for the public sphere." Her focus goes beyond individual actors to include the processes and practices that shape attention and resources on societal goals and actions. It is not solely about those who are public office holders but also those who influence public debate and action. Hart and Uhr (2008) argue that the aim of public leadership is to attain social objectives within the realms of society, administrative organisation, and political governance. Typical social objectives would include those enshrined within the Sustainable Development Goals, both objectives related directly to health and those related to the social determinants of health such as poverty and the environment.

In the context of political administration, public officials face challenges in a dynamic environment under high levels of governmental scrutiny. As a result, there is a need for public leaders capable of steering leadership through collaboration, deeply connected to societal dynamics, and possessing specific qualifications to ethically serve societal interests, while continuously navigating the complexities of the health system. These leaders guide, inspire, and make principled decisions based on these competencies (Hart & Uhr, 2008).

In the complex landscape of political administration characterised by uncertainty, public leaders need the capacity to provide organisational direction as a symbolic figure and catalyst for values, to inspire, and to take decisive stances. They need to be able to handle paradoxes, respond promptly with appropriate interventions, and maintain their composure. The organisational context and objectives, alongside the diversity within the team, influence the requisite leadership style to foster critical reflection, constructive disagreement, and ultimately, excellence. The team must demonstrate administrative proficiency and domain expertise (Hart & Uhr, 2008).

As public involvement grows, civil society assumes a more prominent role. In this "participation society," there is a heightened emphasis on co-creation, with the government positioned as a network partner. Citizens seek active engagement with the civil service, moving away from traditional top-down approaches, towards more inclusive and participatory methods (Martson et al., 2020).

Politicians and civil servants operate under constant scrutiny, persuasion, evaluation, and accountability from society, amplified by the media's expanded role and focus on incidents. This has fostered a political trend where the emphasis lies on achieving political influence through rapidly demonstrable results. In such a scenario, senior civil servants and officials must anticipate long-term repercussions and embody a consistent and reliable government structure that addresses the evolving needs of the community. For effective "implementation," policy dynamics must remain adaptable yet manageable. Achieving political accountability necessitates clear vertical lines of responsibility (Vogel & Werkmeister, 2021).

The role of women leaders in the COVID-19 pandemic (after Aldrich & Lotito, 2020)

Aldrich and Lotito (2020) claim that "Media outlets have reported that women leaders around the globe are managing the COVID-19 crisis better than their male counterparts, responding faster and communicating better about pandemic policies."

They analysed empirical data from the Coronavirus Government Response Tracker to investigate potential differences in policy responses to the pandemic between countries led by women and those led by men. Specifically, they examined the timing of policy adoption regarding mandatory stay-at-home orders, school closures, and coordinated public information campaigns.

Their analysis did not uncover any evidence suggesting that the gender of the leader influences the speed of implementing containment policies. Likewise, they did not observe a significant impact of female representation in legislative bodies on the timing of stay-at-home orders or information campaigns. These inconclusive findings do not support the widespread assertion that female leaders exhibited greater competence and effectiveness in responding to the COVID-19 pandemic compared to their male counterparts. They concluded that they "found little definitive statistical evidence that women are making different choices than men in terms of time stay-at-home orders or information campaigns" although they also stated that "have shown that the decisions related to school closings may vary based on the preferences across genders." They "caution against making broad generalisations about women or men in leadership during this unprecedented time."

It should also be remembered in a statistical analysis, that a lack of evidence of an effect is not the same as evidence of a lack of the effect, merely the inability to be able to demonstrate it.

19.4.1 Knowledge review

Before you move on, can you define the following key concepts:

• Public leadership?

19.4.2 Question to think about

Do you think that gender plays a role in the preferred leadership styles of either leaders or followers?

19.5 Levels of leadership and governance

Leadership in healthcare systems is often dispersed, with several levels of leadership both in terms of public governance and the characteristics of the leader themselves.

Governance is distributed, both in a vertical manner across municipal, local, regional, and international governments and in a horizontal manner between the government and other stakeholders such as semi-governmental organisations, civil society groups, and NGOs (Cairney, 2022).

Multi-level governance is distinct from the concept of multi-level government. While the scope of multi-level government includes the sharing or delegation of responsibilities among different governmental bodies like ministries, multi-level governance includes the interactions among various levels of government and other significant actors (Schiller, 2018).

Within a framework of multi-level leadership and governance, policies may originate at the local government level and then permeate through to other tiers. Conversely, certain policies may originate at the international or global level and subsequently influence local or municipal policies.

Multi-level governance encompasses both vertical and horizontal dimensions. The vertical dimension includes the institutional, financial, and informational connections between lower and higher levels of government. Studies indicate that enhancing the capacity of local governments, such as municipalities, significantly enhances the quality of subnational public policymaking. Additionally, offering incentives, including monetary incentives, can further bolster subnational public policymaking (Bache, 2019).

The horizontal dimension of multilevel governance involves cooperation and collaboration agreements within and between local governments, municipalities, and regions operating at the same level of government, as well as other non-governmental actors. These agreements are increasingly prevalent due to their positive effects on the quality and efficiency of healthcare services delivered by local governments and other local governing entities (Bache, 2019).

In the increasingly complex landscape of healthcare, governments globally are striving to find a balance between public expectations and the rights of healthcare providers, all while ensuring efficient resource utilisation. Within federal systems, these challenges are addressed through political arrangements mandating the involvement and collaboration of multiple levels of government in shaping and implementing health policies (Hueglin & Fenna, 2015). Existing literature has examined how different federal systems manage the complexities of multi-level governance and the impact of federalism on healthcare service provision (Putturaj et al., 2020).

While there are significant historical, political, and governance disparities among global governance structures, such as federal and unitary systems, their approaches to multi-level governance exhibit notable similarities in addressing policy and political issues (Touati et al., 2019). A comparative perspective offers a robust foundation for assessing the healthcare policy implications of diverse political frameworks. Often, analysts and observers attribute their own political leaders' inability to address significant healthcare policy challenges to deficiencies in their country's political structures and procedures (Hueglin & Fenna, 2015).

Case study: Multi-level governance during COVID-19 pandemic (after Fonseca, 2021)

Health systems confronted huge problems and demands in 2020 as a result of the COVID-19 outbreak. It became apparent that the existing approaches were inadequate to combat this pandemic. The COVID-19 pandemic made the global public realise the importance of local health organisations in general (authorities, hospitals, and local primary healthcare providers). It compelled healthcare systems worldwide to adjust their services to meet the needs of the population. Some national policymakers adopted public policies based on the prevailing traditional world view. Isolation and social distancing, as well as the installation of public health measures, such as the wearing of masks and other personal protective equipment, quickly emerged as key methods for fighting such a pandemic.

As a result of social isolation and other subsequent measures for social distancing, such as employees working from home or online, the connection between healthcare professionals and their patients evolved. National policies were surpassed by WHO rules, which constrained public health policies. A multi-level governance approach was used to mitigate the consequences of this pandemic.

In Portugal, for example, the WHO, which acts at an international level, and the Direço Geral de Sade-DGS (the national health administration of Portugal), which acts at the national level, collaborated in formulating and implementing a public health response to the pandemic. Citizens were aware that scientists provided precise facts, studies, scenario analyses, and solutions to legislators in the current healthcare situation. Meetings were held frequently on both local and national levels, and information was made available to the public on a regular basis (Fonseca, 2021).

Table 19.3 The five levels of leadership according to Maxwell, 2013.

Level	Description
1. Position	At this foundational level of leadership, individuals are merely in authoritative positions without truly embodying leadership. They rely on rules, regulations, and organisational structures to exert control over subordinates. Followers comply with directives solely due to the authority vested in the leader, rather than any actual leadership prowess. These roles are interchangeable and serve as starting points, urging aspiring leaders to progress beyond this basic level.
2. Permission	Transitioning from position to permission marks a leader's first step into authentic leadership. At this stage, leaders start to master the art of influencing others. Their ability to foster genuine connections allows them to inspire individuals and to go above and beyond mere compliance. People are more willing to follow because of the rapport and trust established by the leader. When individuals feel valued, respected, and included, they willingly engage in collaborative efforts, potentially transforming the entire organisational culture. Put simply, people follow leaders they like (although this does not mean that an effective leadership should strive simply to be liked!)
3. Production	Leaders at this level are distinguished by their ability to deliver tangible results. Effective leaders consistently achieve success, making significant contributions to their organisation's objectives. They not only excel individually but also facilitate others to deliver personal and team accomplishments. Authentic leadership is evident through concrete outcomes, as productivity becomes the hallmark of level three leaders. It is not possible to operate as a level three leader without demonstrating substantial contributions to the organisation's bottom line. Advancement requires a proactive approach and a focus on delivering results.
4. People development	Progression to level four leadership requires an emphasis upon productivity, both at the individual and organisational levels. Leaders transition from being mere producers to developers, aiming for higher levels of leadership excellence. Recognising human resources as the most valuable asset, level four leaders prioritise the personal and professional growth of others. They shift their attention from solely focusing on production to nurturing the potential of individuals within the organisation. Typically, they will allocate 20% of their efforts to production and dedicate the remaining 80% to cultivating and guiding others to harness and maximise the overall productivity of the group.
5. Pinnacle	In Maxwell's model, level five leadership represents the pinnacle of leadership excellence, characterised by rare individuals with exceptional expertise and innate leadership abilities. These leaders invest considerable time and effort in developing other leaders, aiming to elevate them to level four. They leave a lasting legacy within the organisation and are remembered fondly for their contributions. Level five leaders transcend ordinary leadership, bringing success and positivity to their roles. Their influence extends beyond their immediate sphere, benefiting the entire healthcare sector. While often achieved later in their careers, leaders at the pinnacle seize opportunities to mentor others, tackle challenges, and drive positive change within their organisation and sector.

19.5.1 The Maxwell model of five levels of leadership

Maxwell (2013) argues that developing leadership qualities can help one improve certain professional abilities, develop and retain relationships, and boost earning potential. He offers a five-level model of leadership. He advocates for the following five levels:

1. Position
2. Permission
3. Production
4. People development
5. Pinnacle

Maxwell (2013)

Table 19.3 provides more information on each level:

19.5.2 Knowledge review

Before you move on, can you define the following key concepts:

• Multi-level governance?

19.5.3 Question to think about

Think about the leaders you have known – where do they fit in Maxwell's model?

References

Aldrich, A. S., & Lotito, N. J. (2020). Pandemic performance: women leaders in the Covid-19 crisis. *Politics & Gender*, 16(4), 960–967.

Aydin, B. (2018). The role of organisational culture on leadership styles. *MANAS Sosyal Araştırmalar Dergisi*, 7(1), 267–280.

Bache, I. (2019). How does evidence matter? Understanding 'what works' for wellbeing. *Social Indicators Research*, 142(3), 1153–1173.

Burns, J. M. (2012). *Leadership*. Open Road Media. ISBN 9781453245170.

Cairney, P. (2022). The myth of 'evidence-based policymaking' in a decentred state. *Public Policy and Administration*, 37(1), 46–66.

Castle, N., & Decker, F. (2011). Top management leadership style and quality of care in nursing homes. *Gerontologist*, 51, 630–642. doi:10.1093/geront/gnr064

Charlesworth, K. E., & Jamieson, M. (2017). New sources of value for health and care in a carbon-constrained world. *Journal of Public Health*, 39(4), 691-697.

Chestnut, B. (2017). *The 9 types of leadership: Mastering the art of people in the 21st century workplace*. Simon and Schuster. ISBN 978-1-68261-148-7.

Figueroa, C. A., Harrison, R., Chauhan, A., & Meyer, L. (2019). Priorities and challenges for health leadership and workforce management globally: A rapid review. *BMC Health Services Research*, 19(1), 1–11.

Fonseca, M. (2021). Risk Management and Risk Governance in NGOs. In Wiedemann, A., Stein, V., & Fonseca, M. (Eds.). (2022). *Risk governance in organizations: Future perspectives*. universi-Universitätsverlag Siegen, p.329.

Harms, P. D., Wood, D., Landay, K., Lester, P. B., & Lester, G. V. (2018). Autocratic leaders and authoritarian followers revisited: A review and agenda for the future. *The Leadership Quarterly*, 29(1), 105–122.

Hart, P., & Uhr, J. (2008). *Public leadership: Perspectives and practices* (p. 283). ANU Press. ISBN 9781921536304.

Hartley, J. (2018). Ten propositions about public leadership. *International Journal of Public Leadership*, 14(4), 202–217.

Hueglin, T. O., & Fenna, A. (2015). *Comparative federalism: A systematic inquiry*. University of Toronto Press.

Hughes, V. (2017). Standout nurse leaders... What's in the research? *Nursing Management*, 48(9), 16–24.

Hughes, V. (2019). Nurse leader impact: A review. *Nursing Management*, 50(4), 42–49.

Hughes, V., Wright, R., Taylor, J., Petchler, C., & Ling, C. (2023). A qualitative descriptive study of effective leadership and leadership development strategies used by nurse leaders in European island countries. *Nursing Open*, 10(2), 1071–1082.

Kouzes, J. M., & Posner, B. Z. (2011). *The five practices of exemplary leadership* (2nd ed.). John Wiley & Sons.

Marston, C., Renedo, A., & Miles, S. (2020). Community participation is crucial in a pandemic. *The Lancet*, 395(10238), 1676–1678.

Maxwell, J. C. (2013). How successful people lead: Taking your influence to the next level. Hachette UK.

Maslow, A. H. (1970). *Motivation and personality*. Harper & Row.

Moneke, N., & Umeh, O. (2013). Factors influencing critical care nurses' perception of their overall job satisfaction: An empirical study. *Journal of Nursing Administration*, 43, 201–207. doi:10.1097/NNA.0b013e31828958af.

Parris, D. L., & Peachey, J. W. (2013). A systematic literature review of servant leadership theory in organisational contexts. *Journal of Business Ethics*, 113, 377–393.

Pérez-Sánchez, S., Madueño, S. E., & Montaner, J. (2021). Gender gap in the leadership of health institutions: the influence of hospital-level factors. *Health Equity*, 5(1), 521–525.

Putturaj, M., Van Belle, S., Criel, B., Engel, N., Krumeich, A., Nagendrappa, P. B., & Prashanth, N. S. (2020). Towards a multilevel governance framework on the implementation of patient rights in health facilities: A protocol for a systematic scoping review. *BMJ Open*, 10(10), e038927.

Reza, M. H. (2018, July). Use of customer satisfaction in total quality improvement of Malaysian use of customer satisfaction in total quality improvement of malaysian automotive (car) manufacturing industry. *IOSR Journal of Business and Management (IOSR-JBM)*, 20(7), 47–51.

Reza, M. H. (2019). Components of transformational leadership behaviour. *EPRA International Journal of Multidisciplinary Research*, 5(3), 119–124.

Rüzgar, N. (2018). The effect of leaders' adoption of task-oriented or relationship-oriented leadership style on leader-member exchange (LMX), in the organisations that are active in service sector: A research on tourism agencies. *Journal of Business Administration Research*, 7(1), 50–60.

Schiller, M. (2018). The local governance of immigrant integration in Europe: The state of the art and a conceptual model for future research. In Caponio, T., Scholten, P., & Zapata-Barrero, R. (Eds.) *The Routledge handbook of the governance of migration and diversity in cities* (pp. 204–215). Abington: Routledge.

Sfantou, D. F., Laliotis, A., Patelarou, A. E., Sifaki-Pistolla, D., Matalliotakis, M., & Patelarou, E. (2017). Importance of leadership style towards quality of care measures in healthcare settings: A systematic review. *Healthcare (Basel, Switzerland)*, 5(4), 73.

Squires, M., Tourangeau, A., Spence-Laschinger, H., & Doran, D. (2010). The link between leadership and safety outcomes in hospitals. *Journal of Nursing Management*, 18, 914–925. doi:10.1111/j.1365-2834.2010.01181.x

Touati, N., Maillet, L., Paquette, M. A., Denis, J. L., & Rodríguez, C. (2019). Understanding multilevel governance processes through complexity theory: An empirical case study of the Quebec health-care system. *International Journal of Public Administration*, 42(3), 205–217.

Vogel, R., & Werkmeister, L. (2021). What is public about public leadership? Exploring implicit public leadership theories. *Journal of Public Administration Research and Theory*, 31(1), 166–183.

Vogus, T., & Sutcliffe, K. (2007). The impact of safety organising, trusted leadership, and care pathways on reported medication errors in hospital nursing units. *Med Care*, 45, 997–1002. doi:10.1097/MLR.0b013e318053674f

Yang, I. (2015). Positive effects of laissez-faire leadership: Conceptual exploration. *Journal of Management Development*, 34(10), 1246–1261.

20 Risk management in healthcare

20.1 Risk management

A healthcare organisation must develop the culture, organisational structure, and processes that support the identification, assessment, and treatment of risks in a timely manner. The program should be consistent with the organisational vision, mission, and values. Risk-based thinking is essential to achieve an effective quality management system throughout the organisation and to establish criteria, assessment, treatment, and proposals for improvement. Risk management may be considered in a number of stages:

- defining risk criteria
- identifying risk
- analysing risks
- assessing risks
- mitigate or eliminate risks

First, the organisation should define their risk criteria and consider the level of risk that is acceptable in relation to meeting their goals, both clinical and non-clinical objectives. This includes defining the criteria for assessing the importance of each risk and the balance between the likelihood of an adverse event and the harm that would follow from such an event. Patient safety should always be paramount in such considerations.

Next, using these criteria as a basis, the organisation should identify the risks present in the operation of the healthcare facility. There are many tools available to help in the process of risk identification, and they are summarised in Table 20.1.

Once potential and actual risks have been identified, they need to be analysed.

The analysis should determine the probability of occurrence of events. It should consider the consequences, not only for patients or workers but for all the relevant stakeholders of an event occurring and the magnitude of those consequences. For each risk identified, the analysis should determine the complexity of the risk and the interconnectedness of the risk and its potential for further consequences and harm through knock-on effects.

To inform subsequent decision-making, the organisation should assess the level of risk associated with each potential risk source. This analysis should then be compared to the previously established risk criteria.

This comparison should enable the healthcare provider to either not address the risk, consider options to address the risk, initiate additional analysis to further study the risk, or consider rethinking or modifying objectives. This decision should be documented and

DOI: 10.4324/9781003478874-25

Table 20.1 Tools and techniques for risk identification

Tool/technique	Description
Failure Mode and Effects Analysis (FMEA)	Failure mode and effects analysis (FMEA) is a step-by-step approach for identifying all possible failures in a design, a manufacturing or assembly process, or a product or service. Failures are prioritised according to how serious their consequences are, how frequently they occur, and how easily they can be detected. The purpose of the FMEA is to take actions to eliminate or reduce failures, starting with the highest-priority ones.
Strengths, Weaknesses, Opportunities, and Threats (SWOT) analysis	By identifying internal strengths and weaknesses, as well as external opportunities and threats, organisations can make more informed choices. The threats and weaknesses represent risks, but the strengths and opportunities offer means of mitigation. This method provides a structured approach to assess and mitigate risks, ultimately enhancing the likelihood of successful outcomes in various ventures.
Delphi Technique	The Delphi technique in risk management involves consulting field experts to predict how risky a certain action would be. The key feature of the technique is the use of a panel of experts through several rounds of feedback and response modification, enabling a conclusion to be reached by the panel.
"What-if" questions	What–If Analysis is a structured brainstorming process for identifying risks. The answers to these questions form the basis of the level of potential risks and aid in determining a recommended course of action to prevent or mitigate them. An experienced risk assessment review team can effectively discern major issues concerning a part of a process or system. Led by a facilitator, each member of the review team participates in assessing what could go wrong based on their past experiences and knowledge of similar situations.
Hazard and Operability Study (HAZOP)	A Hazard and Operability (HAZOP) study is a structured and systematic examination of a planned or existing process or operation in order to identify and evaluate problems that may represent risks to personnel or equipment or prevent efficient operation. It consists of four stages; definition, preparation, examination, documentation, and follow-up. The technique is qualitative and aims to stimulate the imagination of the participants to identify potential hazards and operability problems within a structured standardised process.

used to plan further analysis, implement controls, and possibly reconsider objectives. It is important to communicate risk assessment outcomes to top leadership.

Once risk criteria are defined and risks are identified, analysed, and assessed, actions should be implemented to address the risk most effectively. Healthcare organisations should choose actions to address risks, including the following:

- avoid the risk
- assume the risk
- eliminate the source of risk
- mitigate the risk
- modify the likelihood of the risk
- modify the consequences of the risk

- share the risk
- maintain the risk
- transfer the risk

After the organisation determines what it will do to address the risk, it must create and implement risk management plans, which address how the measure will be integrated with the quality management of the healthcare organisation. Measures taken should be proportionate to the potential impact on healthcare delivery.

The healthcare organisation should conduct a periodic review to assess the effectiveness of its risk management framework and ensure that it continues to evolve and meet the needs of the care process. Reviews are planned as part of the risk management process, with clearly defined responsibilities. Results of risk monitoring and evaluation must be incorporated into all performance management, measurement, and reporting activities of the organisation.

Once the organisation outlines its approach to mitigating risks, it needs to develop and execute risk management strategies that outline how these measures align with the healthcare organisation's quality management. Actions taken should be commensurate with the potential impact on healthcare provision. It's essential for the healthcare organisation to regularly review its risk management framework to gauge its efficacy and ensure ongoing adaptation to meet care process requirements. These reviews should be scheduled as integral components of the risk management process, with clearly delineated responsibilities. Findings from risk monitoring and assessment must be integrated into all performance management, measurement, and reporting endeavours of the organisation.

Using the Delphi method to identify risk factors contributing to adverse events in residential aged care facilities in China after Shi et al. (2020)

Shi et al. (2020) carried out a study using the Delphi method to pinpoint the factors contributing to adverse events within residential aged care facilities in China.

By initially compiling a comprehensive list of potential risk factors through detailed interviews with residential aged care facility managers, a Delphi method, conducted over three rounds, was used to achieve a consensus among experts.

The identified risk factors were presented to the expert panel multiple times using a Likert scale to validate responses.

A total of 67 items were identified as risk factors for adverse events, categorised into four primary indexes: environmental facility, nursing staff, older adults' characteristics, and management factors.

Through the Delphi method employed in this study, a consensus was reached regarding the risk factors contributing to adverse events, leading to the development of a risk assessment framework applicable in aged care practice and research. This compiled list serves as a valuable tool for prioritising risk reduction efforts and evaluating intervention or education strategies aimed at preventing adverse events in residential aged care facilities.

The study found that nursing staff and management factors emerged as key contributors to adverse events, emphasising their pivotal role in fostering a secure and error-free environment. The resultant list will be used by managers and nursing supervisors to improve their decision-making and ultimately reduce preventable adverse events.

20.1.1 *Knowledge review*

Before you move on, can you define the following key concepts:

• Delphi Technique?

20.1.2 *Question to think about*

As a patient, how would you assess what an acceptable level of risk would be, when asked to give your consent for a procedure?

20.2 How the aviation industry has influenced healthcare

In 2011, Dekker argued that healthcare was almost unique in safety-critical fields in relying on individual competence rather than systemic data-driven approaches to preventing adverse events (Dekker, 2011). He goes on to argue that:

> *Medicine has retained a unique subculture with its own rules, norms, mythologies, social structures, hierarchies, clothing and tools, and other markers of status and specialisation and identity. Physicians have generally resisted the notion that their relationship with patients is anything like a commercial or contractual one, relying rather on what they and society see as status-determined duties, sometimes invoking a "sacred calling"* (Dekker, 2011, p. 28).

However, even by the time of Dekker's book, there were attempts to learn lessons from other disciplines. By the end of the 20th century following a number of tragedies, there was a recognition that errors arose not just from individual incompetence but from a range of systemic factors. Inquiries on inquests following tragedies in paediatric cardiac surgery failures in Bristol in the UK (Kennedy, 2001) and Winnipeg in Canada Provincial (Court of Manitoba, 1999) highlighted the fact that errors arose from systemic failures as much as individual incompetence.

In the past, in reaction to negative aircraft incidents, test pilots from the Army-Air Corps created a set of aircraft checklists in 1935 to ease the pilot's workload in managing complex aircraft systems and instruments. These checklists and procedures have since been widely embraced by the aviation community, not only in military, but also in commercial and civilian aviation operations. The primary objective has consistently been the safety of both passengers and aircraft.

Healthcare researchers have looked to aviation to find ways of adopting a more systemic approach to safety. For example, a Canadian Medical Association Journal editorial in 2001 made the link in relation to the surgical failures in Winnipeg:

> *As in other complex activities such as aviation, the identification of error should be active, not passive, focusing not just on catastrophic events, but on near misses that could have been catastrophic but were not   CMAJ (2001).*

Schelkun (2014) describes how aviation flight planning consists of four distinct steps and then goes on to compare them to stages in surgery, as shown in Table 20.2.

Dekker (2011) points out that aviation is capable of generating immediate and almost exhaustive evidence about the effects of any procedural or technological intervention. Modern airliners are equipped with flight data monitoring systems capable of recording

Table 20.2 Comparison of safety procedures between aviation and surgery (after Schelkun, 2014)

Aviation	Surgery
1. Plan the flight using aviation charts to determine how to get from point A to point B.	Plan the operation. First of all, understand the patient, the injury, the goals of the operation, and choose a surgical procedure to get you there. In orthopaedic trauma surgery, this is where templating of the fracture with the surgical implants will help better understand the fracture, understand the goals of reduction and alignment as well as determine the type, location, and size of the implant that are needed.
2. File a flight plan with the FAA providing pertinent details of the aircraft, altitude of flight, route, aircraft fuel capacity, endurance and time enroute. This step also includes defining an alternate plan (i.e., alternate airport) in case the airplane cannot safely land at the intended destination.	Develop a detailed surgical tactic by thinking through the operation chronologically, one step at a time. Decide what operating table, patient position, drape pack, prepping technique, and the surgical approach will be used. This is a good time to review the details of a less frequently used approach. Be prepared for obstacles along the way in the way of important anatomic structures and have an alternate "Plan B" to handle potential problems along the way.
3. A detailed pre-flight equipment and instrument check of the aircraft itself, engine and navigation instruments, and fuel, oil and aircraft systems to ensure that all systems are working properly.	Develop a surgical instrument checklist to let the operative team know what is needed. Every fracture can have different nuances that may require a different instrument and implant set from the inventory of over 85 fracture sets in my hospital. The surgical team cannot be expected to know what I need nor pull the proper sets unless they are told specifically. Pre-printed surgeon preference cards do not work well in trauma surgery due to the variability of cases and the number of sets.
4. Standardised communication with ground control, the tower, and constantly along the route of flight with Air Traffic Control.	Communicate all along the way with the operative team. The team is there to help achieve the goals for the patient. They are professionals as well and want to be part of a successful team. Discussing with them the patient's problem, the goals, and intended plan of approach, teamwork will be improved and the outcomes enhanced. When given the equipment and instrument list before the case, the team can prepare alongside the surgeon. When the patient is in the room, positioned on the table, and the entire team is assembled, a "Time Out" may be called. Each member of the team has a specific task. The surgeon should stand at the foot of the bed with the checklist and address the items one at a time, requiring a verbal reply, the "readback" in aviation terminology, for each item on the list.

hundreds of parameters related to the aircraft and the flight every second and contrasts this with the lack of data in many clinical scenarios, especially in real-time.

Airline pilots are constantly in communication with both co-pilots and air traffic controllers. Schelkun (2014) also highlights the need for open communication and immediate debriefing after surgery in a similar manner to aviation. He states that:

Each member should be given the opportunity to ask questions or express any concerns about the patient's condition, the plans, or completeness of the preparations.

As a formal "debriefing" at the end of each case, he describes how he places the post-operative x-rays next to the pre-op x-rays and the pre-operative planning template and compares the results, looking for any discrepancies.

He describes a formal debriefing session with the team based around two questions:

1. "What went well with this operation?"
2. "What could I do differently next time to improve the results?"

Schelkun (2014) argues that this methodical debriefing process confirms sound decisions and provides insights into areas for improvement in the future. Pre-operative planning is about more than mere procedural steps such as marking the site and reviewing checklists to ensure antibiotic administration; it creates a mindset geared towards the success of the operation. It is a conscientious process that, when executed diligently, enhances surgical proficiency, fosters teamwork, and ultimately leads to better surgical outcomes and increased patient safety.

Paediatric surgery deaths in Winnipeg (after Provincial Court of Manitoba, 1999)

In 1994, in Canada, 12 babies who underwent cardiac surgery at Winnipeg's largest hospital died. The inquest, presided over by Judge Murray Sinclair, aimed to identify ways to prevent similar tragedies rather than assigning blame. Sinclair expanded the scope of the investigation to scrutinise the hospital's paediatric cardiac program since its inception in 1978. The resulting 516-page report, issued in November 2000, included 36 comprehensive recommendations, such as discontinuing high-risk cases, which had already ceased following the complete shutdown of the paediatric cardiac program.

Before the arrival at the hospital of the surgeon responsible for the unsuccessful procedures, the paediatric cardiac surgery program was already facing significant challenges. A decade before, the program showed a mortality rate of 50%, leading to a strike by anaesthetists against the previous cardiac surgeon, which ultimately resulted in the closure of the program by the province. This predecessor resigned after seven years due to frustrations stemming from inadequate staff dedicated to the program, as well as insufficient administrative support and funding.

By 1994, the mortality rate among high-risk patients requiring bypass surgery was almost three times higher than the Canadian average, prompting the hospital to suspend its cardiac program in February 1995. However, this time, a local medical reporter led to public outrage and inquiries, ultimately resulting in the longest inquest in Canadian legal history.

Whilst the inquest did draw attention to the lack of experience of the principal surgeon, it also identified that the province population was too small to sustain surgical teams' skills, in contrast to the average population base for Canada's paediatric cardiac units. Poor communication, inadequate hiring practices, and a lack of oversight contributed to the surgeon being overwhelmed. Concerns raised by surgical nurses regarding his performance were disregarded, and despite pressure from various quarters, the program persisted until its eventual suspension after multiple fatalities and refusals from Intensive Care Unit (ICU) staff to refer patients. The hospital's reluctance to acknowledge the program's shortcomings, amid ongoing restructuring and public scrutiny, underscored a broader pattern of negligence and institutional failure.

Healthcare has adopted several safety measures from aviation including:

- a no-blame culture
- safety checklists
- critical incident reporting systems

20.2.1 Knowledge review

Before you move on, can you define the following key concepts:

- systemic data-driven approaches?

20.2.2 Question to think about

How far would you travel to give your (hypothetical) sick child the best chance of surviving complex surgery?

20.3 A no-blame culture

The WHO (WHO, 2021) defines patient safety as

> a framework of organised activities that creates cultures, processes, procedures, behaviours, technologies and environments in healthcare that consistently and sustainably lower risks, reduce the occurrence of avoidable harm, make errors less likely and reduce the impact of harm when it does occur (WHO, 2021, p. vii).

To ensure that patient safety efforts are successful, it is paramount that the organisation creates a culture of patient safety. Creating this culture involves strong leadership and management commitment. It requires policies, training, the support of healthcare workers, and a no-blame culture. Only when healthcare workers feel safe in reporting a potential or actual safety incident will a patient safety program be effective.

In a rapid policy review into the issues relating to gross negligence manslaughter in UK healthcare, Professor Sir Norman Williams argues that what is needed is a just culture that "considers wider systemic issues where things go wrong, enabling professionals and those operating the system to learn without fear of retribution."

This is not simply a "no-blame" culture but a "just" culture. For lessons to be learnt and improvements in safety to be made, he argues that health workers should be treated with respect and encouraged to speak out if they observe something that is wrong, as exemplified in the WHO Safe Surgery approach (WHO, 2009).

To achieve a culture of patient safety, healthcare workers must believe that their organisation is committed to identifying the root systemic causes of patient safety lapses and be prepared to implement changes to address these fundamental causes.

According to Wolvaardt (2019), this kind of culture is dependent on a number of key factors including "leadership, joined-up thinking, collaboration with policy makers and professional bodies, good record-keeping, and human resources and administrative processes that reward quality, courage and honesty."

No-blame cultures tend to be driven by specific organisational characteristics, including:

- A collective comprehension of complexity: No-blame cultures invest effort in ensuring employees grasp the intricate nature of organisations, enabling them to attribute errors more effectively to systemic factors.
- Respect for others: Industries like air traffic control expose workers to the challenges faced by their colleagues. Consequently, when mistakes occur, there's a greater inclination towards understanding the root causes rather than assigning blame solely to individual performance.
- Emphasis on honesty: Honesty is essential for organisations to have an accurate assessment of their status, facilitating effective decision-making. Therefore, no- blame cultures prioritise and reward honesty among their members.
- Regular debriefing practices: Critical analysis is integral to the success of no-blame cultures, allowing processes to be thoroughly examined, refined, and improved. Debriefing sessions serve to identify shortcomings, suggest improvements for the future, and ensure alignment among team members.
- Deference to expertise: Operational decision-making in normal organisations tends to follow the organisational chart, even though subject-matter experts are often in a better position to make informed decisions. In no-blame cultures, the hierarchy is loose enough that experts are able to lead on operational issues where appropriate.
- Focus on behavioural standards: In complex environments, achieving desired outcomes is challenging due to numerous variables. Consequently, evaluating individuals based solely on outcomes can be unfair. Instead, emphasising behavioural expectations promotes alignment with organisational values.
- Realistic view of human nature: While maintaining high standards can boost performance, it is crucial for organisations to recognise the inherent imperfections of human beings. Noblame cultures embrace this reality, acknowledging that individuals are fallible yet valuable components of a larger system.

Parker and Davies (2020) offer a note of scepticism about the no-blame culture approach and argue that professionals need to share some responsibility for errors and adverse events. They distinguish between blame and responsibility and suggest that it is possible for professionals to take responsibility for their part in an adverse event without them being blamed for an event in which they had a minor role.

Whilst the inquest report from Winnipeg (Provincial Court of Manitoba, 1999) acknowledged a whole range of systemic factors, the surgeon's failure to accept almost any responsibility and to blame colleagues did lead to a great deal of anger.

All professionals have a responsibility to know the limits of when they can operate safely and to not go beyond these limits; for example, the UK Nursing and Midwifery

Council's professional code of conduct (2015) states that nurses and midwives have a responsibility to

> *work within the limits of your competence, exercising your professional 'duty of candour' and raising concerns immediately whenever you come across situations that put patients or public safety at risk.*
> *Introduction to Sections 13-19, UK Nursing and Midwifery Council*

It is also crucial that organisations create an environment in which concerned professionals can report concerns without fear of reprisal.

Whistle blowing in the Australian healthcare system (after Jackson et al., 2010)

The freedom for healthcare professionals to act as whistle blowers is crucial to patient safety. Many enquiries after adverse events highlight attempts by whistle blowers to highlight problems at an early stage that are ignored, and often the whistle blower is vilified and has to leave their place of work.

Jackson et al. (2010) carried out a qualitative study of the experiences of 11 whistle blowing by nurses in the Australian healthcare system. They found that whistle blowing was extremely stressful.

The interviewees believed that in whistle blowing, they were taking steps to promote patient safety, optimising clinical practice and patient management. Their narratives frequently revealed a tension in their perception of themselves as patient advocates, which is valued and accepted and as whistle blowers – a role that is stigmatised and looked upon negatively.

They describe a culture of silence and work practices and systems designed to enforce this. They described how colleagues who did speak out were ostracised by colleagues. This led some to report that they had been changed by the experience of whistle blowing and in future would remain silent.

Once they had become whistle blowers, most reported feeling unsafe and unprotected by their employers.

The findings of this study align with existing literature suggesting that whistle blowing has a significant impact on all involved parties. Despite awareness of the vulnerability of whistle blowers and the introduction of supportive measures, whistle blowing remains a highly stressful phenomenon. Theoretically, highlighting areas of poor practice should not cause stress if due process is followed and healthcare sectors are genuinely dedicated to improving practice. However, pressure to remain silent and maintain the organisational status quo was evident in this study.

The study highlights the dilemma faced by healthcare professionals regarding the conflict between their duty to expose poor quality care and the potential personal and professional repercussions of whistle blowing. Similar concerns have been identified in other studies.

The authors argue that there is a need for changes in leadership styles to promote patient safety, as complaints made by staff are not always appropriately addressed. Greater support for whistle blowers is necessary at all levels to ensure personal safety and job security. Opportunities for healthcare professionals to voice concerns as a team regarding patient safety or organisational wrongdoing should be created to prevent individual blame and harassment. Collaborative approaches to addressing such issues can lead to earlier and more effective resolutions and contribute to a more transparent and supportive working environment in healthcare (Jackson et al., 2010).

20.3.1 Knowledge review

Before you move on, can you define the following key concepts:

- A "just" culture?

20.3.2 Question to think about

What would you do in a professional situation where you observed something causing distress or harm to another person?
What measures would give you the confidence to report it?

20.4 Patient safety checklists

In a review by Weerakkody et al. (2013) of adverse event incidence during surgery, the median adverse incident rate was 9.2%, where 43.5% were deemed to be potentially preventable. At the other end of the scale, 7% of adverse events were identified as leading to permanent disabilities.

In an attempt to reduce the level of harm to patients, one of the key measures to be introduced was a surgical safety checklist, developed by the WHO Patient Safety Program team (WHO, 2009).

The WHO Patient Safety Program team who developed the Surgical Safety Checklist drew upon experiences from the aviation industry. This was then developed with an aim to support clinical practice without disrupting clinical judgments. The checklist was created as a simple sample of checks and not as an algorithm, focusing on items that were agreed upon by clinicians to be of high risk or deadly if omitted or overlooked.

At the outset, the WHO stated very clearly that the checklist should not be comprehensive, encouraging modifications and additions to make it fit into local practice. Further development included tailoring the Surgical Safety Checklist to specific surgical procedures, especially those with a high degree of complexity, as in robotic surgical technology.

The WHO checklist before local customisation has three stages:

1. Before induction of anaesthesia
2. Before an incision is made
3. Before the patient leaves the operating theatre

It is summarised in Table 20.3:

Table 20.3 The WHO surgery safety checklist (after WHO, 2009)

Before induction of anaesthesia	Before an incision is made	Before the patient leaves the operating theatre
Has the patient confirmed his/her identity, site, procedure, and consent? Is the site marked? Is the anaesthesia machine and medication check complete? Is the pulse oximeter on the patient and functioning? Does the patient have a: • Known allergy? • Difficult airway or aspiration risk? • Risk of >500ml blood loss (7ml/kg in children)?	Confirm all team members have introduced themselves by name and role. Confirm the patient's name, procedure, and where the incision will be made. Has antibiotic prophylaxis been given within the last 60 minutes? Anticipated Critical Events To Surgeon: What are the critical or non-routine steps? How long will the case take? What is the anticipated blood loss? To Anaesthetist: Are there any patient-specific concerns? To Nursing Team: Has been confirmed? Are there equipment issues or any concerns? Is essential imaging displayed?	Nurse Verbally Confirms: • The name of the procedure • Completion of instrument, sponge and needle counts • Specimen labelling (read specimen labels aloud, including patient name) • Whether there are any equipment problems to be addressed. To Surgeon, Anaesthetist and Nurse: • What are the key concerns for recovery and management of this patient?

In surgery, equipment-related failures contribute to a substantial part of errors in the operating room. Preoperative use of checklists has been found to significantly reduce equipment errors.

Impact of safety checklists in healthcare

One of the first large-scale studies on checklists in healthcare (the Keystone project) was mostly carried out in 108 Michigan intensive care units (Hales and Provonost, 2006). The interventions included a checklist to improve communications. The interventions reduced venous catheter-related bloodstream infections after 18 months from 2.7 to 0. However, these Michigan results were not replicated in a large-scale United Kingdom intervention program.

In a global study of eight hospitals in eight countries, introduction of the WHO Surgical Safety Checklist reduced complications from 11.0 to 7.0% (P < 0.001), with a mortality drop from 1.5 to 0.8% (P = 0.003).

Use of the checklist resulted in improved patient outcomes, such as reduced infections, wound rupture, respiratory complications, bleeding, blood transfusions, and cardiac complications, through better care processes in the operating room.

The use of checklists in anaesthesia and surgery delivers improvements where their use impacts upon the work processes in the operating room (Haugen et al., 2019).

A study by Johns Hopkins Hospital claimed that the introduction of a simple five-step safety checklist reduced the rate of bloodstream infections caused by intra-venous lines by 67%, while, on average, intensive care units cut their infection rates from nearly 3% of patients treated to zero. During the 18 months of the study, an estimated 1,500 lives were saved due to the implementation of safety checklists (John Hopkins, 2011).

In a broader review of the literature, Haugen et al. (2019) found a range of studies on the impact of checklists. Following the introduction of safety checklists, they found various studies that explored their effects on morbidity and mortality beyond the Surgical Safety Checklist. Systematic reviews indicated positive outcomes associated with checklist use, including reduced complications, wound infections, blood loss, and mortality rates. Checklists were also shown to have the potential to improve outcomes in high-risk paediatric surgery in developing countries and enhancing information transfer and communication during different phases of surgery.

Although few studies report negative patient outcomes with checklist use, they have shown that implementation requires considerable time and effort. The implementation of comprehensive checklists, such as the Surgical Patient Safety System checklists, requires input from multiple care providers across disciplines and emphasises the importance of a "culture of safety." Nonetheless, some studies have found no reduction in complications or mortality rates. A recent publication indicated a decrease in mortality rates but no change in complication rates.

Whilst it has been shown that poor implementation processes can negatively impact teamwork, studies have reported improved communication and coordination, better decision-making, and enhanced team cohesion as benefits of checklist use. Barriers to effective checklist use may adversely affect operating room efficiency, although the checklist itself does not appear to increase operation time or same-day cancellations.

20.4.1 Knowledge review

Before you move on, can you define the following key concepts:

- Patient safety checklist?

20.4.2 Question to think about

Why do you think checklists are generally effective in reducing errors?

20.5 Critical Incident Reporting Systems

A Critical Incident Reporting System (CIRS) is a structured mechanism used in health-care and other safety-critical industries to report and analyse critical incidents or adverse events. Its primary purpose is to promote a culture of safety, learning, and improvement within the organisation.

In healthcare, a CIRS allows healthcare professionals to report incidents or near misses that have resulted in, or could potentially result in, harm to patients, staff, or visitors. These incidents can include medication errors, surgical complications, falls, infections, or any other adverse events.

Key features of a CIRS typically include:

- Reporting mechanism: A user-friendly system for healthcare professionals to report incidents easily and anonymously if desired.
- Incident classification: Standardised categories or classifications for incidents to aid in analysis and reporting trends.
- Analysis and feedback: Review and analysis of reported incidents to identify underlying causes, contributing factors, and patterns. Feedback is provided to staff to promote learning and prevent future occurrences.
- Action planning: Developing and implementing strategies or interventions to address identified issues and prevent recurrence.
- Confidentiality and anonymity: Ensuring confidentiality and anonymity of reporters to encourage open reporting without fear of reprisal.
- Continuous improvement: Ongoing monitoring and evaluation of the effectiveness of interventions implemented to improve patient safety and quality of care.

By implementing a CIRS, healthcare organisations can identify areas for improvement, implement targeted interventions, and ultimately enhance patient safety and quality of care.

In addition, a CIRS may be used to foster a culture of transparency, trust, and accountability among healthcare professionals. After researching the best reporting practices, the WHO (2018) defined the Minimal Information Model for Patient Safety (MIM PS). The model was validated across many European countries.

They created two options: the Basic MIM PS for organisations without a current reporting system and the Advanced MIM PS for organisations with already established reporting systems. The contents of each are compared in Table 20.4.

Since incident reporting takes place in multiple settings – hospitals, clinics, health outposts, and high- to low-income countries – resources available for reporting systems differ greatly. Reports may be made on paper, written on paper and then later transferred to an electronic record by administration, or input directly into an electronic system.

It is imperative that the CIRS be embedded in the organisation's culture and supported by top management.

A just culture will increase the odds of employees actually completing reports. Employees should be trained to ensure that they know how to access the form, how to complete each section of the report, and where to submit it. The reports are essential for gathering data that reduce risks, improve processes, and prevent patient harm.

In the 1990s, the English National Health Service was rocked by a series of high-profile failures in patient safety from poor care in paediatric surgery in Bristol (Kennedy, 2001) to mass murder in Greater Manchester by a general practitioner (The Health Foundation, 2005).

Table 20.4 The information collected by the WHO Basic and Advanced Minimal Information Models for Patient Safety (after WHO, 2018)

Basic MIM PS	*Advanced MIM PS*
Patient Information	Patient Information
• Age	• Age
• Sex	Sex
Incident Time	Incident Time
Incident Location	Incident Location
Agent(S) Involved	Causes
• (Suspected) Cause?	Contributing Factor
• Contributing Factor?	Mitigating Factor
• Mitigating Factor?	
Incident Type	Incident Type
Incident Outcome(S)	Incident Outcome(S)
Resulting Action(S)	Resulting Action(S)
Reporter's Role	Reporter's Role
Free Text	Free Text

In response, in June 2000, the government accepted all recommendations from Dr. Liam Donaldson, the Chief Medical Officer, entitled "An Organisation with a Memory." This report recognised a historical lack of systematic learning from adverse events and service failures within the NHS, highlighting the significant issue of potentially preventable events causing unintended harm to patients.

The proposed solutions in "An Organisation with a Memory" centred on fostering a culture of transparency, reporting, and safety awareness within NHS establishments. It suggested implementing a new national system to identify adverse events and near misses in healthcare, with the aim of gathering comprehensive information on their causes and utilising this knowledge to mitigate risks and prevent similar incidents in the future.

The NPSA (National Patient Safety Agency) improved patient safety through several key strategies:

- collecting and analysing information on adverse incidents from various sources including local NHS organisations, NHS staff, patients, and caregivers
- incorporating other safety-related data from existing reporting systems
- learning from these incidents and ensuring that the lessons learned were integrated back into healthcare practices and service delivery
- addressing identified risks by developing solutions to prevent harm, setting national objectives, and establishing mechanisms to monitor progress

Through its initiatives and the implementation of a new national reporting system, the NPSA aimed to

- eliminate instances of patients dying or becoming paralysed due to incorrectly administered spinal injections
- reduce by 25% the occurrence of harm in obstetrics and gynaecology resulting in litigation

- decrease by 40% the number of serious errors in the prescription and use of medications
- eliminate suicides by mental health patients resulting from hanging on non-collapsible bed or shower curtain rails in ward settings

---

Using data to improve patient safety in the English NHS

In 2003, the National Reporting and Learning System (NRLS) was established as a central national database of patient safety incident reports for the English NHS. The system forms the heart of the national CIRS. Reports are available for each NHS organisation, but the published results currently only go up to about four years before the present.

However, through reviewing recorded patient safety events, the NHS National Patient Safety Team identified a risk of harm from green anaesthetic swabs obstructing the patient's airway.

A post-operative patient had a device used to secure a patient's airway removed in the recovery room. Upon removal, the patient began to struggle to breathe. On investigation, a green anaesthetic swab was found in the upper airway and removed. The swab had reportedly been inserted to help obtain a seal in the patient's oropharynx.

A review of the NRLS identified 11 incidents over a three-year period relating to green swabs in or around the mouth, causing (or with the potential to cause) an airway obstruction.

The NHS Team liaised with professional bodies. They agreed to strengthen guidance in this area. The recently revised National Safety Standards for Invasive Procedures that are used across the NHS to reduce misunderstandings or errors and to improve team cohesion now include a standard for the "Reconciliation of Items in the Prevention of Retained Foreign Objects" which states "The mouth represents a danger zone. Green gauze should never be used to stabilise an airway."

20.5.1 *Knowledge review*

Before you move on, can you define the following key concepts:

- Critical Incident Reporting Systems?

20.5.2 *Question to think about*

What major adverse events have occurred in the healthcare system in your country or region?

Are you aware of anything changing as a result?

References

Canadian Medical Association Journal. (2001). Error and blame: The Winnipeg inquest. *CMAJ: Canadian Medical Association Journal/journal de l'Association medicale canadienne*, 165(11), 1461–1463.
Dekker. (2011). *Patient safety: A human factors approach*. CRC Press, ISBN-13: 978-1-4398-5226-2

Hales, B. M., & Pronovost, P. J. (2006). The checklist—a tool for error management and performance improvement. *Journal of Critical Care*, 21(3), 231–235.

Haugen, A. S., Sevdalis, N., & Søfteland, E. (2019). Impact of the WHO surgical safety checklist on patient safety. *Anesthesiology*, 131, 420–425

Jackson, D., Peters, K., Andrew, S., Edenborough, M., Halcomb, E., Luck, L., ... Wilkes, L. (2010). Understanding whistleblowing: Qualitative insights from nurse whistleblowers. *Journal of Advanced Nursing*, 66(10), 2194–2201.

John Hopkins. (2011, January 31). Safety checklist use yields 10 percent drop in hospital deaths. *Press Release*.

Health Foundation, The. (2005). *Shipman inquiry*. Policy Navigator.

Kennedy, I. (2001). *Learning from Bristol: The report of the public inquiry into children's heart surgery at the Bristol royal infirmary: 1984–1995*. Presented to Parliament by the Secretary of State for Health by Command of Her Majesty July 2001, CM 5207(I)

The Nursing and Midwifery Council. (2015). *Professional standards of practice and behaviour for nurses, midwives and nursing associates*. The Nursing and Midwifery Council.

Parker, J., & Davies, B. (2020). No blame no gain? From a no blame culture to a responsibility culture in medicine. *Journal of Applied Philosophy*, 37(4), 646–660.

Provincial Court of Manitoba. (1999). *Inquest, manitoba pediatric cardiac surgery*. Manitoba, ISBN 0771115164.

Schelkun, S. R. (2014). Lessons from aviation safety: "Plan your operation – and operate your plan!". *Patient Safety in Surgery*, 8, 38.

Shi, C., Zhang, Y., Li, C., Li, P., & Zhu, H. (2020). Using the Delphi method to identify risk factors contributing to adverse events in residential aged care facilities. *Risk Management and Healthcare Policy*, 13, 523–537.

Weerakkody, R. A., Cheshire, N. J., Riga, C., Lear, R., Hamady, M. S., Moorthy, K., Darzi, A. W., Vincent, C., & Bicknell, C. D. (2013). Surgical technology and operating-room safety failures: A systematic review of quantitative studies. *BMJ Quality & Safety*, 22, 710–718.

Williams, N. (2018, June). Gross negligence manslaughter in healthcare: The report of a rapid policy review. Department of Health and Social Care.

Wolvaardt, E. (2019). Blame does not keep patients safe. *Community Eye Health*, 32(106), 36.

WHO. (2009). *WHO guidelines for safe surgery: Safe surgery saves lives*. WHO, ISBN: 9789241598552.

WHO. (2018). *Minimal information model user guide* (WHO/HIS/SDS/2016.22). WHO.

WHO. (2021). *Global patient safety action plan 2021-2030: Towards eliminating avoidable harm in health care*. WHO.

21 Quality assurance in healthcare

21.1 What is quality?

Institute of Medicine (2001) defined six domains of quality in healthcare:

- person-centredness
- timeliness
- efficiency
- effectiveness
- safety
- equity

Over the last two decades, following the Institute of Medicine's (IOM's) establishment of quality standards in healthcare, there has been a notable growth in the field of quality enhancement and patient safety. This expansion has encompassed both academic exploration of theory and methodology, as well as the practical implementation of these findings. While there has been some progress, it falls short of what could be considered a resounding success. Critiques suggest that there is insufficient evidence to support the effectiveness of quality improvement efforts, indicating a need for further research. A recent evaluation by the National Quality Task Force in the United States underscores persistent deficiencies in achieving consistent, high-value, person-centred care. The focus on measurement alone has not produced the desired outcomes. Consequently, we aim to revisit and redefine the fundamental framework of quality, drawing upon the insights gained over the past two decades. This endeavour seeks to address the shortcomings identified by the task force and delineate the necessary steps for effecting meaningful change.

Present-day healthcare delivery struggles to adequately meet the health needs of individuals. Historically, the emphasis has been on addressing failures in disease management rather than on promoting overall health and well-being. There appears to be a tendency to prioritise standardised protocols and interventions for disease management over a more holistic approach that values the relational aspects essential for maintaining health. Furthermore, significant advancements in health outcomes have predominantly arisen from preventive measures in public health, such as immunisation and improvements in sanitation and housing. Additionally, the methods used to evaluate the impact of quality improvement initiatives have not been well-suited to the complex nature of healthcare interventions or the shift towards enhancing overall health rather than just managing diseases.

DOI: 10.4324/9781003478874-26

The ongoing improvement efforts in healthcare have adopted various theories, methodologies, and interventions from other industries that have demonstrated positive results in terms of quality, cost-effectiveness, and safety (Lachman et al., 2021) .

Many quality improvement techniques trace their roots back to the Plan-Do-Check-Act first described by Shewhart in the 1930s, but popularised by Deming (2018) later in the 20th century. The basic PDCA cycle is shown in Figure 21.1:

One of the most influential models in healthcare quality is the Structure-Process-Outcome model of Donabedian (2005). The three components are structure, process, and outcomes. Measurement for improvement has an additional component – balancing measures.

Donabedian argued that structural measures influence procedural measures, which subsequently impact outcome measures, forming the foundational elements necessary for a robust set of metrics. Each type of measure serves a distinct purpose in evaluating the success of improvement initiatives.

- Outcome measures signify the effects on patients, revealing the culmination of improvement efforts and the extent to which goals have been attained. Examples include decreased mortality rates, shortened hospital stays, diminished instances of hospital-acquired infections, reduced adverse events, fewer emergency admissions, and enhanced patient satisfaction.
- Process measures delineate the functioning of systems and processes in achieving desired outcomes. For instance, they assess factors like wait times for clinical reviews, adherence to care standards, hand hygiene compliance among staff, incident reporting and response protocols, and communication with patients regarding appointment delays.

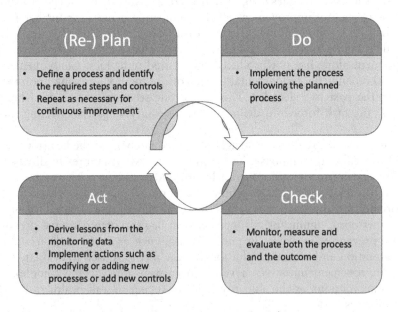

Figure 21.1 Plan-Do-Check-Act cycle after Shewhart (1931) and Deming (2018).

- Structural measures characterise the attributes of service providers or facilities, such as staffing ratios and operational hours, also known as input measures.
- Balancing measures account for unintended or broader consequences of change, which may be either positive or negative. It involves acknowledging and monitoring these effects, aiming to mitigate any adverse impacts if necessary. For instance, monitoring rates of emergency readmissions post-initiatives aimed at reducing hospital stays serves as a balancing measure.

According to Donabedian, outcome measures serve as the ultimate validation of healthcare effectiveness and quality, albeit they may be challenging to define and exhibit time delays. Process measures are pivotal in quality improvement efforts as they gauge the proper application of clinical care protocols, ensuring alignment with established standards. From an improvement standpoint, process measures bridge the gap between behavioural modifications and desired outcomes.

Use of Donabedian's framework to improve healthcare in South Africa (after Ameh et al., 2017)

Ameh et al. (2017) conducted a study examining the effectiveness of the Integrated Chronic Disease Management (ICDM) approach in primary care in South Africa starting from 2011. Their aim was twofold: first, to gauge the satisfaction of patients and operational managers with various aspects of ICDM services and second, to assess the quality of care within the ICDM model using Donabedian's framework, which considers the interplay between structure (available resources), process (clinical activities), and outcome (desired healthcare results) as indicators of quality.

Their research illustrated the applicability of Donabedian's framework in assessing healthcare quality broadly and specifically within the context of the ICDM model. Patients' perceptions regarding the quality of care within the ICDM model suggested that the provision of adequate resources directly influences positive healthcare outcomes, with the relationship between resource availability and outcomes being mediated by the quality of clinical processes. Specifically, patients believed that the availability of equipment, medications, and accessibility of chronic disease services enabled nurses to fulfil their duties professionally, foster friendly interactions with patients, and address their healthcare needs effectively. When nurses fulfilled these responsibilities, patients expressed confidence in their competence and perceived a coherence in the services provided.

21.1.1 Knowledge review

Before you move on, can you define the following key concepts:

- Plan-Do-Check-Act cycle?
- Structure-Process-Outcome model?

21.1.2 *Question to think about*

Do you think that Donabedian's assertion that the premise that improvements in the structure of care will lead to improvements in clinical processes that should in turn improve patient outcomes, is necessarily true in all cases?

21.2 Measuring quality

Deming asserted that "without data, you are just another person with an opinion," emphasising the crucial role of objective evidence (Deming, 2018). Scientific method is based upon achieving demonstrable measured effects under controlled or at least randomised conditions. The application of the scientific method has led to significant advancements across various fields. In today's digitally connected world, vast amounts of data, including "big data," are readily accessible. While opinions on any topic abound, distinguishing between mere opinions and factual information is essential. Objective evidence is now more critical than ever to safeguard consumers and promote responsible and sustainable practices.

The importance of measuring quality data stems from several factors:

- the costliness of rework or re-providing services
- the expense incurred during downtime
- various significant costs associated with losing customers, such as damage to brand reputation, diminished trust, and actual revenue loss
- the expenses involved in acquiring new customers
- the principle that what cannot be measured cannot be controlled
- the ability of reliable data to establish benchmarks, baselines, and goals for improvement
- the role of data in strategic planning and design
- the use of data as evidence to support arguments and advocate for causes
- the facilitation of strategic financial and resource allocation decisions by organisations
- the requirements imposed by many customers and regulatory bodies for organisations to measure their performance (Deming, 2018; Crosby, 1978)

Data play a crucial role in identifying risks. For instance, when process control statistics reveal a common error occurrence at a specific point in a process, it signals the need for measures to control that error, thus minimising the associated risks.

One of the latest trends in healthcare quality assurance is the use of so-called "big data." Big data refers to very large data sets that are difficult to manage due to their volume, velocity, and variety. Big data analytics are advanced techniques that enable healthcare organisations to analyse vast volumes of structured and unstructured data from various sources, including electronic health records, medical imaging, wearable devices, and patient feedback, among others.

These tools and techniques can provide valuable insights and actionable intelligence to drive continuous quality improvement initiatives.

One significant example is in predictive analytics. By analysing historical data and patterns, predictive analytics can forecast potential adverse events, identify high-risk patients, and pre-emptively intervene to prevent complications. For example, predictive models can help identify patients at risk of hospital readmission, allowing healthcare teams to implement targeted interventions to mitigate risks and improve outcomes.

Big data analytics can also play a role in identifying trends and patterns in clinical workflows and outcomes. By analysing large datasets, healthcare organisations can identify areas for improvement, streamline processes, and enhance efficiency. For instance, analysing data on medication adherence rates can highlight opportunities to optimise medication management protocols and improve patient compliance.

Additionally, big data analytics enables healthcare organisations to benchmark performance against industry standards and best practices. By comparing their performance metrics with those of peer institutions, healthcare providers can identify areas of excellence and areas needing improvement, facilitating informed decision-making and resource allocation.

Finally, continuously monitoring key performance metrics, such as infection rates, medication errors, and patient satisfaction scores, healthcare organisations can identify emerging issues promptly and implement corrective actions to address them proactively.

Using data to manage risks associated with the use of indwelling urinary catheters

An example of using data to manage risk within the healthcare environment involves the use of indwelling urinary catheters among hospitalised patients and the incidence of catheter-associated urinary tract infections (CAUTIs).

Research conducted in the early 2000s prompted significant alterations in evidence-based nursing practices regarding the prolonged use of indwelling urinary catheters. Traditionally, hospitalised patients were often fitted with catheters for extended periods, presuming it would enhance patient comfort, safety and offer solutions for those with urinary system-related conditions. Additionally, catheterisation proved more convenient for hospital staff, eliminating the need for assistance with toileting or bedpan use. However, findings from hospital studies revealed that catheters posed a significant infection risk, contributing to elevated rates of morbidity and mortality.

According to the Centers for Disease Control (CDC, 2015), estimates suggest that "17% to 69% of CAUTI cases could potentially be prevented through recommended infection control measures, potentially averting up to 380,000 infections and 9,000 CAUTI-related deaths annually" (para. 1).

21.2.1 Knowledge review

Before you move on, can you define the following key concepts:

• Big data?

21.2.2 Question to think about

Do you think that all aspects of quality are measurable?

21.3 Auditing

ISO 19011:2018 provides a definition of an audit as a systematic, independent, and documented process aimed at obtaining audit evidence – such as records, factual statements, or other relevant and verifiable information – and objectively evaluating it to assess the extent to which the audit criteria are met. These criteria typically consist of a set of policies, procedures, or requirements.

The standard outlines three primary types of audits:

1. Process audit: This audit type assesses whether processes operate within defined limits by comparing operations or methods against predetermined instructions or standards to gauge compliance and effectiveness. It involves verifying conformance to specified requirements, evaluating resources applied, examining process controls, and assessing overall performance.
2. Product audit: This audit examines specific products or services, such as hardware, processed materials, or software, to determine adherence to requirements, including specifications, performance standards, and customer needs.
3. System audit: Conducted on a management system, this audit involves evaluating documented activities to confirm that relevant system elements are suitable, effective, and aligned with specified requirements. Examples include quality management system audits, which assess compliance with company policies, contractual commitments, and regulatory mandates.

Furthermore, audits can be classified into three categories based on the relationship between the auditing organisation and the organisation being audited.

- First-party audits are conducted internally within an organisation to evaluate its strengths and weaknesses against internal procedures or external standards.
- Second-party audits are performed externally on a supplier by a customer or contracted organisation on behalf of a customer, with audit results influencing purchasing decisions.
- Third-party audits are carried out by an independent audit organisation unrelated to the customer–supplier relationship, often resulting in certification or recognition of compliance with standards or regulations. In practice, third-party audits are often based upon scrutinising the rigour and validity of internal first-party audits rather than direct assessment of activities.

In industries requiring adherence to specific standards, such as those involving high-risk products, certification through third-party audits may be necessary. For instance, in order to bring a medical device to market in the European Union, the device must have received a CE mark and the organisation must be accredited to a quality management system standard like ISO 13485:2016 (ISO, 2016) with certification verified by third-party audits.

Additionally, audits can serve various purposes beyond mere compliance, such as assessing organisational performance and driving continual improvement. Follow-up audits may be conducted to verify corrective or preventive actions taken in response to audit findings.

The audit cycle typically involves four phases:

1. Audit planning and preparation: Involves planning activities conducted by relevant parties to ensure alignment with the audit objectives.

2. Audit execution: Comprises on-site data gathering and verification activities, including interactions with auditees and team communication.
3. Audit reporting: Communicates audit findings effectively to aid management in addressing organisational issues.
4. Audit follow-up and closure: Includes verification of corrective and preventive actions taken and may involve subsequent audits to ensure resolution of identified issues.

Corrective action aims to eliminate existing nonconformities or defects, while preventive action targets potential issues to prevent their occurrence. Both actions contribute to improving organisational processes and outcomes.

The Dutch Institute for Clinical Auditing (DICA) (after Beck et al., 2020)

The Dutch Colo-Rectal Audit (DCRA) in the Netherlands was a pioneering initiative providing medical teams with benchmarked, hospital-specific performance information, leading to improved care. Launched in 2009 by the Association of Surgeons of the Netherlands, it served as a model for subsequent audits carried out by the Dutch Institute for Clinical Auditing (DICA).

DICA, a non-profit organisation, was established in 2011 and has since expanded its audits to cover various diseases and treatments. Up to December 2017, 21 nationwide audits had been initiated, resulting in the registration of more than 700,000 patients. Initially, audits were monodisciplinary and treatment-specific, mainly focusing on cancer surgery. Over time, this has expanded to include non-malignant diseases, nonsurgical treatments, and evaluation of the entire multidisciplinary care pathway. The audits focus on developing meaningful quality indicators, collecting and validating data through a certified processor and providing internal feedback to hospitals via a secure online platform.

National audits identified a comparatively high utilisation of radiotherapy before rectal cancer surgery in the Netherlands in 2011 compared to other nations. Consequently, guidelines were revised in 2014. The adaptation was swiftly implemented, resulting in a reduction in radiotherapy utilisation from 84.2% to 64.4% within a span of two years, while maintaining oncologic efficacy.

Audits in cancer care have facilitated various other enhancements. For instance, the proportion of patients undergoing lung cancer surgery with a preoperatively recorded clinical cancer stage surged from 75.4% to 98.3% between 2012 and 2016. Consequently, the degree of variation decreased from 0 to 100% to 82% to 100%. Additionally, numerous process indicators, including time to treatment, witnessed improvement at the national level, leading to a reduction in inter-hospital disparities. The percentage of patients receiving treatment within specified timeframes increased for surgical interventions addressing carotid stenosis (63%–79%) and lung cancer (41%–71%), as well as radiotherapy for lung cancer (60%–71%), and any form of treatment for ovarian cancer (77%–86%), rectal cancer (49%–56%), and oesophageal cancer (31%–47%).

These achievements are attributed to factors such as centralisation, specialisation, and the introduction of new techniques, with the audits playing a crucial role in providing reliable data for continuous improvement in the healthcare system.

21.3.1 Knowledge review

Before you move on, can you define the following key concepts:

- First-party audits?
- Second-party audits?
- Third-party audits?

21.3.2 Question to think about

Audits are necessarily based on snapshots. How can you ensure that performance is maintained between audits?

21.4 Certification and accreditation

Both certification and accreditation signify that an organisation, known as the auditee, has demonstrated to an external body, referred to as the auditor, that it meets specific criteria established by standards, policies, frameworks, guidelines, or a combination thereof. The terminology used may vary depending on the preferences of the organisations or industry groups developing these documents, which may be either public or private entities.

According to the International Standards Organisation (2023a):

- Certification is the provision by an independent body of written assurance (a certificate) that the product, service, or system in question meets specific requirements.
- Accreditation is the formal recognition by an independent body, generally known as an accreditation body, that a certification body operates according to international standards.

Some certification/accreditation bodies receive authorisation from their national governments, while in certain countries, any company can act as a certification body without regulation. The landscape of certification and accreditation can be intricate, as each country has its own set of laws and regulations governing which institutions are permitted to certify or accredit healthcare organisations. Therefore, it is imperative for the quality manager or responsible function to be well-versed in the certification and accreditation norms applicable to their country or region.

Once certified, the organisation is permitted to assert its certification status, provided it adheres to the guidelines outlined in the certification agreement. However, organisations must ensure they do not mislead the public regarding the scope of their certification. For instance, if only one hospital within a network is certified, the organisation should refrain from advertising that all hospitals within the network hold the same certification status.

Furthermore, alternative models of healthcare certification and accreditation exist that do not conform to government-based models.

A prominent example is the Joint Commission International (JCI), a non-profit organisation offering both accreditation and certification services, predominantly in the US. While the JCI provides accreditation for hospitals, home care facilities, and laboratories, it also offers certification for specialised functions such as perinatal care, healthcare staffing services, community-based palliative care, and advanced cardiac and stroke care.

Unlike government-regulated bodies, the JCI operates as a private enterprise and is not granted authority by governmental or regulatory agencies to confer certifications.

21.4.1 Benefits of accreditation and certification

Many healthcare organisations opt for certification due to its associated benefits, while others may pursue certification as a mandatory requirement. Accreditation and certification are intended to offer several advantages, including demonstrate compliance with legal and regulatory standards. The process can provide expert feedback from external auditors to drive process changes and enhancements and provide additional data for improvement by supplementing internal audits with external audits,

They can also improve business performance by creating a competitive advantage in a healthcare market dominated by private providers, potentially securing price reductions from hospital insurance companies, which gain confidence in better risk management practices and increasing stakeholder confidence in the organisation's quality of care.

Internally, they may boost employee morale and foster cohesion through the attainment and maintenance of certified status.

Despite these benefits, the certification and accreditation process can be lengthy, costly, and resource-intensive. Alternatively, organisations may choose to assert compliance with established guidelines without seeking external validation. Compliance entails adhering to established standards or requirements, although it lacks external verification from accreditation or certification agencies. Nonetheless, compliance declarations still offer numerous advantages.

External audits, conducted by second- or third-party organisations, verify adherence to standards, policies, and procedures. While some healthcare organisations pursue accreditation or certification to gain recognition in the marketplace and evidence regulatory compliance, others may opt to self-identify as compliant with specific standards. Regardless of the approach chosen, a robust audit program remains essential for the success of the quality management program.

21.4.2 Certificates

A certificate serves as tangible proof of an organisation's certification status, offering objective evidence of compliance. The validity period of a certificate varies depending on the certification or accreditation program, with some programs requiring annual audits and a three-year recertification cycle. Typically, a certificate includes the following details:

- Name and address of the certified organisation
- Name of the certifying or accrediting agency
- Title of the standard or norm, along with its date if applicable
- Scope of the certification, specifying its applicability to a particular hospital, department, etc.
- Issue date and expiration date of the certificate
- A unique identifier, such as a number or alphanumeric combination

Most certifying and accrediting agencies maintain online registers where individuals can verify the authenticity of a certificate. Given the prevalence of falsified certificates, agencies must offer mechanisms to validate the legitimacy of issued certificates.

Certification of Jordanian hospitals (after Algunmeeyn et al., 2020)

Jordan's healthcare system has been developed with greater relevance to the needs of the nation, compared with most other Middle Eastern countries. Day et al. (2013) observe that Jordan has a relatively advanced healthcare. Moreover, its healthcare system is divided into two sectors: private and public. With regard to public health-care institutions, there are 1,245 healthcare centres operated by the Jordanian Ministry of Health, 27 of these being hospitals that provide 37% of all hospital beds across the country. All kinds of preventive, therapeutic, organisational, and management services are provided in Jordan's public and private health sectors. Conversely, in the private sector, 56 hospitals provide 36% of the total number of hospital beds in the country, along with primary, secondary, and tertiary services.

To meet international standards and obtain accreditation, hospitals in Jordan, both public and private, are actively working to improve their healthcare services. Staff members undergo education regarding accreditation standards, and self-assessments are conducted to ensure compliance. The Jordan Health Care Accreditation Council has played a crucial role in defining quality responsibilities within health facilities. Additionally, initiatives like the US Agency for International Development of Healthcare Projects in Jordan have been established to strengthen partnerships with the Ministry of Health.

Recent efforts have seen a growing adoption of TQM processes in Jordanian hospitals, aiming to elevate the quality of care provided. Algunmeeyn et al. (2020) carried out a qualitative study involving nurses and doctors from public and private hospitals in Amman, Jordan's capital. Semi-structured interviews were conducted to gather data on participants' backgrounds, experiences, and perspectives on accreditation benefits, focusing on areas such as patient safety, satisfaction, cost-effectiveness, and quality improvement.

The interviewees observed that the implementation of accreditation had increased patient safety in two Jordanian hospitals. It had led to an increase in the quality of healthcare services delivered, specifically by standardising service delivery, enhancing local healthcare culture and improving teamwork and co-operation across Jordanian hospitals. The findings also show that the implementation of accreditation improved cost-effectiveness in Jordanian hospitals.

The authors claim that hospitals that apply accreditation deliver excellent care services, meeting patients' needs by applying national and international healthcare standards. This leads to reduced errors, shorter hospital stays, reduced waiting times and, as a result, lower costs. Overall, the interviewees saw improved patient satisfaction, increased patient safety, enhanced quality of services delivered, and improved reputation amongst Jordanian hospitals.

21.4.3 Knowledge review

Before you move on, can you define the following key concepts:

- Certification?
- Accreditation?

21.4.4 Questions to think about

How much confidence would you have in the accreditation of a hospital? What factors might influence that confidence?

21.5 International healthcare standards

21.5.1 International healthcare standards

While each country may write its own set of healthcare-related policies, guidelines, and standards, increasingly the most important standards are internationally recognised.

The European Foundation for Quality Management (EFQM) and the International Organisation for Standardisation (ISO) are highly significant organisations that operate across all business sectors, but are prominent in healthcare. The Joint Commission International (JCI) and the International Society for Quality in Health Care (ISQua) operate solely in the healthcare sector.

21.5.2 European Foundation for Quality Management (EFQM)

Established in 1988, the European Foundation for Quality Management (EFQM) advocates quality as a catalyst for continuous improvement within organisations. The EFQM Model, widely acknowledged globally but primarily utilised in Europe, embodies European values and is rooted in Total Quality Management (TQM) principles. Its latest iteration, the 2020 version, delineates three fundamental areas: direction (why), execution (how), and results (what). EFQM employs a method called RADAR to evaluate organisations against the scheme's requirements. The RADAR diagnostic tool enables assessors to assign points to organisations based on the effectiveness of EFQM scheme implementation.

RADAR comprises the following components:

- Results: Organisations should delineate the results (objectives and targets) they aim to achieve.
- Approaches: Organisations must define and cultivate the processes necessary to attain the specified results.
- Deploy: Once results and approaches are established, processes should be put into action.
- Assess and Refine: Processes should be monitored and evaluated to ascertain whether they meet the predetermined results. If not, processes should be refined, and enhancements should be implemented.

In the assessment scheme, a total of 1,000 points are available. Depending on the number of points awarded, organisations receive recognition in one of three categories: validated, qualified, or recognised EFQM. Within the recognised category, EFQM assigns a three-to-seven-star rating based on performance. The EFQM mark can play a pivotal role in attracting new customers and securing contracts for work bids.

21.5.3 The International Organisation for Standardisation (ISO)

Established in 1946, ISO is an independent, non-governmental entity dedicated to formulating voluntary consensus standards. With a membership comprising 165 national standards bodies representing 165 countries, ISO has developed over 24,115 International Standards as of 2021, covering a broad spectrum from manufactured products to services, circular economies, information technology, and environmental management systems. One of ISO's most widely recognised and implemented standards is ISO 9001: Quality Management Systems (QMS) – requirements, boasting certification by over one million companies and organisations across more than 170 countries.

While ISO 9001 serves as a generic quality management system standard, many hospitals have adopted it as the foundation for their quality management systems. Research findings suggest that implementation of an ISO 9001 quality system can result in heightened patient satisfaction, cost containment, and enhanced patient safety. Additionally, ISO-certified hospitals have reported advantages, such as increased patient focus, error reduction, and improved safety protocols, attributed to the standard's emphasis on process identification and performance indicators facilitating continuous improvement.

Studies analysing the relationships between ISO 9001 certification, hospital accreditation, and quality management have shown positive associations with clinical leadership, patient safety systems, and clinical review processes. ISO-certified or accredited hospitals have demonstrated superior performance and safety compared to their non-certified counterparts, particularly excelling in areas such as patients' rights.

The benefits of ISO certification extend beyond organisational improvements, providing consumers and stakeholders with added confidence and assisting regulators in ensuring compliance with health, safety, and environmental standards.

In 2023, ISO published ISO 7101:2023 healthcare organisation management - management systems for quality in healthcare organisations – requirements.

ISO 7101:2023 (ISO, 2023b) is claimed to be the first international consensus standard for healthcare quality management. It prescribes requirements for a systematic approach to sustainable, high-quality health systems, enabling organisations of any scale, structure, or region to:

- create a culture of quality starting with strong top management
- embrace a healthcare system based on people-centred care, respect, compassion, co-production, equity, and dignity
- identify and address risks
- ensure patient and workforce safety and well-being
- control service delivery through documented processes and documented information
- monitor and evaluate clinical and non-clinical performance
- continually improve its processes and results

The core areas of ISO 7101 are:

- leadership
- service user focus
- access to care
- planning
- risk culture
- risk management processes
- communication
- healthcare facilities management and maintenance
- contingency planning for facilities and services
- environmental responsibility
- emerging technologies

- service design in healthcare
- people-centred care
- service user experience
- compassionate care
- inclusivity and diversity
- health literacy
- co-production
- workforce well-being
- patient safety
- monitoring, measurement, analysis, and evaluation
- internal audit
- management review
- improvement
- nonconformity and corrective action

The DIN EN 15224 Quality Management System is a sector specific standard of quality management for healthcare organisations. It is based on the ISO 9001 standard, and it includes tangible requirements for patient safety and management of clinical risks in the planning, realisation, and management processes. The DIN EN 15224 standard seeks to brings together the advantages of ISO 9001 with comprehensive healthcare quality requirements. It defines issues ranging from the effectiveness and suitability of care to the safety and reliability of care processes. In DIN EN 15524, there are 11 quality features which characterise the quality of healthcare and must be verified as part of a certification. They are

- appropriate, correct care
- availability
- continuity of the care
- effectiveness
- efficiency
- consistency
- evidence-based, knowledge-based care
- patient care, including physical and psychological integrity of the care
- integration of the patient
- patient safety
- timeliness and accessibility

Unlike ISO standards, EN 15224 is not internationally approved through the ISO process. Instead, it has been adopted as a European Norm (EN) via the European Committee for Standardisation (CEN), the European Committee for Electrotechnical Standardisation (CENELEC) members, and national standardisation bodies across 34 countries. However, the extent of implementation and utilisation of EN 15224 has not been extensively documented, and it is likely to be overtaken by ISO 7101:2023 in due course.

ISO 13485: 2016 (ISO, 2016) is a prerequisite for medical device manufacturers wishing to supply the European Union market and many others. It is a stand-alone QMS standard, based on ISO 9001. It retains the ISO 9001 process model concepts of "Plan, Do, Check, Act," but is designed for medical devices QMS. It focuses on patient safety by ensuring the consistent quality throughout the entire lifecycle of medical devices, from design and production to disposal.

It outlines the requirements needed for organisations to establish a QMS that demonstrates their capability to consistently and safely deliver medical devices and related services to meet customer and regulatory requirements. It covers various aspects of the manufacturing process, including risk management, regulatory compliance, traceability, and documentation.

21.5.4 The Joint Commission International (JCI)

Originally known as "The Joint Commission" in the United States where it originated, the Joint Commission International (JCI) is a specialised not-for-profit organisation dedicated to enhancing healthcare quality and patient safety. Established in 1951, The Joint Commission is one of the oldest and largest creators of standards and accreditation agencies in the US healthcare sector. Leveraging its success nationally, it expanded its reach by establishing JCI in 1994–1995 to cater to international needs.

JCI's overarching mission is "to continuously enhance the safety and quality of care globally through education, advisory services, and international accreditation and certification."

One notable aspect of JCI is its dual role as both a standards creator and an accreditation provider. This sets it apart, as not all bodies responsible for creating standards also conduct audits and accreditation and vice versa. While some industries and organisations use "accreditation" and "certification" interchangeably, JCI distinguishes between the two and offers an extensive range of standards against which organisations can undergo assessment and audit.

JCI offers a diverse array of accreditation standards covering various healthcare settings, including home care, hospitals, primary care, long-term care, medical transport organisations, ambulatory care, and clinical care. Additionally, JCI has developed guidelines and standards focusing on specific clinical functions and specialties, such as certified stroke centres, cardiac and orthopaedic rehabilitation centres, primary heart attack centres, and thrombectomy-capable stroke centres. Whether a healthcare organisation seeks accreditation, certification, or aims to implement clinical best practices, JCI provides abundant resources to enhance healthcare quality.

More than 1,000 healthcare organisations in over 70 countries have achieved the Gold Seal of Approval as JCI-accredited organisations.

Impact of JCI accreditation (after Tomblin, 2021)

Tomblin (2021) carried out a literature review to investigate the impact of JCI accreditation. 19 articles met the inclusion criteria for the review with most (5) coming from Saudi Arabia, 3 from UAE, and 2 from Japan. Other countries represented were Belgium, Brazil, Colombia, Italy, Jordan, Palestine, Singapore, and South Korea.

The author used the Donabedian model to classify possible improvements described in the literature. Structure metrics, or those relating to physical resources in the hospital, were found to be mostly positively influenced by the accreditation process. The review found improvements to staff-turnover, finances, and branding in at least one study, although only one study actually described a demonstrable positive impact on financial performance. On the negative side, studies showed accreditation had a negative impact on nursing workloads leading to a lowering of morale and a scepticism towards accreditation from the nursing workforce.

In terms of process improvements, the review found improvements in medical documentation and reporting with increased compliance, completeness, and quality of medical records.

Improvements in measurable outcomes were the most inconsistent across the reviewed studies. For example, two studies found accreditation to be correlated with an improvement to mortality rates while two others found no significant difference. Similarly, Halasa et. al. found a reduction in the readmission rate of the ICU supported by accreditation but not the readmission rate of the hospital.

21.5.5 *International Society for Quality in Health Care (ISQua)*

ISQua is a non-profit international organisation that operates on a membership basis, aiming to catalyse and facilitate enhancements in health, as well as the safety and quality of healthcare globally. While ISQua doesn't directly generate standards for hospitals or engage in certifying healthcare organisations, it holds significance due to its substantial role in advancing knowledge on high-quality healthcare worldwide. The organisation boasts an extensive networking and resource platform, offering education and fellowship opportunities. ISQua's experts and surveyors are dispersed across the globe, contributing to its widespread influence.

ISQua maintains a liaison relationship with the World Health Organisation (WHO), with many WHO publications benefiting from substantial input from ISQua experts. In 2018, ISQua established the ISQua External Evaluation Association (EEA), tasked with providing third-party external evaluation services to healthcare and social care evaluation organisations, as well as standards-developing bodies globally. Through this mechanism, ISQua set standards for certification and accreditation bodies responsible for auditing healthcare organisations. These standards encompass various aspects, including:

- guidelines and standards for quality and patient safety training programs
- guidelines and principles for the development of health and social care standards
- guidelines and standards for external evaluation organisations
- guidelines and standards for surveyor training programs
- guidance on designing healthcare external evaluation programs, including accreditation

21.5.6 *Knowledge review*

Before you move on, can you define the following key concepts:

- The RADAR model?

21.5.7 Question to think about

What are the advantages and disadvantages of using global standards compared with national standards?

References

Algunmeeyn, A., Alrawashdeh, M., & Alhabashneh, H. (2020). Benefits of applying for hospital accreditation: The perspective of staff. *Journal of Nursing Management*, 28(6), 1233–1240.

Ameh, S., Gómez-Olivé, F. X., Kahn, K., Tollman, S. M., & Klipstein-Grobusch, K. (2017). Relationships between structure, process and outcome to assess quality of integrated chronic disease management in a rural South African setting: applying a structural equation model. *BMC Health Services Research*, 17, 1-15.

Beck, N., van Bommel, A. C., Eddes, E. H., van Leersum, N. J., Tollenaar, R. A., & Wouters, M. W. (2020). The Dutch Institute for Clinical Auditing: Achieving Codman's dream on a nationwide basis. *Annals of Surgery*, 271(4), 627–631.

Centers for Disease Control and Prevention. (2015). *Guideline for prevention of catheter associated urinary tract infections (2009)*. Centers for Disease Control and Prevention.

Crosby, P. (1978). *Quality is free: The art of making quality certain*. McGraw-Hill Education, ISBN: 9780070145122.

Day, S. W., McKeon, L. M., Garcia, J., Wilimas, J. A., Carty, R. M., de Alarcon, P., Antillon, F., & Howard, S. C. (2013). Use of joint commission international standards to evaluate and improve pediatric oncology nursing care in Guatemala. *Pediatric Blood & Cancer*, 60(5), 810–815.

Deming, W. E. (2018). *Out of the crisis*. MIT Press.

Donabedian, A. (2005). Evaluating the quality of medical care. *The Milbank Quarterly*, 83(4), 691–729.

Halasa, Y. A., Zeng, W., Chappy, E., & Shepard, D. S. (2015). Value and impact of international hospital accreditation: A case study from Jordan. *Eastern Mediterranean Health Journal*, 21(2), 90–99.

Institute of Medicine. (2001). *Committee on quality of health care in America: Crossing the quality chasm: A new health system for the 21st century*. National Academies Press.

ISO. (2015). *Quality management systems -Requirements* (ISO Standard No. 9001). ISO.

ISO. (2016). *Medical devices - Quality management systems - Requirements for regulatory purposes* (ISO Standard No. 13485). ISO.

ISO. (2018). *Guidelines for auditing management systems* (ISO Standard No. 19011). ISO.

ISO. (2023a). *Glossary guidance on selected words used in the ISO 9000 family of standards*. ISO.

ISO. (2023b). *Healthcare organization management - Management systems for quality in healthcare organizations – Requirements* (ISO Standard No. 7101). ISO.

Lachman, P., Batalden, P., & Vanhaecht, K. (2021). A multidimensional quality model: An opportunity for patients, their kin, healthcare providers and professionals to coproduce health. *F1000Research*, 9, 1140.

Shewhart, W. A. (1931). *Economic control of quality of manufactured product*. Van Nostrand.

Tomblin, B. T. (2021). *Effect of joint commission international accreditation on hospital performance: A systematic literature review* (Doctoral dissertation). University of Pittsburgh.

Section F

Information and innovation

22 Using information to improve clinical care

22.1 Record keeping

Good record-keeping is an essential part of healthcare and the responsibility of every clinician. The Health and Professions Council that regulates a wide range of health professions in the UK states that "once you are registered with us, you have a professional responsibility to keep full, clear and accurate records for everyone you care for, treat or provide other services to."

They go on to say that the purpose of these records is to:

- safeguard continuity of care by providing information to colleagues involved in care and treatment
- ensure service users receive appropriate treatment that is in their best interests
- meet legal requirements or respond to Freedom of Information or Subject Access Requests
- evidence your decision-making processes if later queried or investigated
- what records you need to keep, in what format, and for how long, varies depending on the setting you are working in and the subject matter of those records

(Health and Care Professions Council, n.d.)

All other health-related professional bodies place a similar obligation on the healthcare professionals registered with them.

Medical records serve several important purposes in healthcare. They serve as a comprehensive account of a patient's medical history, including diagnoses, treatments, medications, test results, surgeries, and other pertinent information. This documentation is crucial for healthcare providers to track a patient's progress over time and make informed decisions about their care.

Medical records facilitate communication and collaboration among healthcare providers involved in a patient's care, ensuring that everyone has access to up-to-date information about the patient's condition and treatment plan. This helps to coordinate care and avoid medical errors. They are essential for meeting legal and regulatory requirements, including documentation of informed consent, adherence to privacy regulations (such as HIPAA in the United States), and compliance with billing and coding guidelines.

Medical records play a critical role in the billing and reimbursement process by documenting the services provided to a patient, supporting claims for payment from insurance companies or government healthcare programs. They may (with the patient's consent) be used for research purposes to advance medical knowledge and improve

DOI: 10.4324/9781003478874-28

patient care. They also serve as valuable educational tools for training healthcare professionals.

In legal proceedings, such as medical malpractice cases or disability claims, they may be used as evidence. Accurate and thorough documentation is essential to support legal arguments and defend against allegations of negligence.

Many clinicians feel comfortable with paper-based records, but there are a number of disadvantages to paper-based records. Free-text language can be ambiguous, and handwriting can be illegible.

Paper records are difficult to transmit, and methods such as fax are very insecure. They are very bulky and vulnerable to damage from wear and tear, fire, water, coffee, etc.

If the purpose is more than a simple aide-memoire for an individual physician, they will often need to be sorted or searched. Paper records can only be organised one way at a time, usually alphabetically. Looking for information can be a time consuming business. In the context of integrated care, paper records often leads to incomplete data sharing across multiple agencies and even within teams.

There are a number of barriers to the adoption of electronic medical records. Physicians cherish their independence, viewing the imposition of electronic medical records as a threat to their autonomy. Training deficiencies have been highlighted by Beasley and Girard (2016) and Mason et al. (2017) including a lack of comprehensive assessments and feedback to ensure users' proficiency. These problems stem from a shortage of skilled trainers among other factors.

Ancker et al. (2013) posit that support issues, either technical or financial, are a barrier. Technical challenges include interoperability problems necessitating more assistance in migrating data from previous systems or sharing with other platforms, as well as basic technical support for daily operational hurdles. Kruse et al. (2016) emphasise the ongoing maintenance costs alongside the initial implementation expenses.

Some physicians are resistant, especially where it impacts their clinical practice: clinicians' willingness to integrate the technology into their clinical routines is influenced by various factors such as age, work environment, computer literacy, technical expertise, and perceptions of its impact on the patient–doctor relationship.

Ethical and legal concerns include security breaches, liability worries, and compromised patient confidentiality (Ben-Zion et al., 2014). Menon et al. (2014) reported findings from a web-based survey by the American Society for Healthcare Risk Management and the American Health Lawyers Association, where just over half of the 369 respondents claimed to have witnessed an adverse event related to electronic records. One-tenth of respondents reported witnessing over 20 such events in the past five years. However, it is worth noting that the sample and methodology of this survey might not be fully representative (Kruse et al., 2016).

Problems can be most obvious at the interface between parts of the system. Consider discharge from the hospital. Discharge summaries can take a while to emerge. Whilst working with a local hospital, the staff told the author that they had a target of typing discharge summaries within two weeks. To make matters worse, they had no target for how soon the typed summary would reach the patients' general practitioners, but they weren't hitting their own internal target anyway. And to make matters even worse, because they recognised this was inadequate, faxes were used to transmit information in a very insecure fashion.

Community-based health professionals may be further distanced as information may have to reach them via the general practice introducing a further delay. Electronic records have their own benefits and challenges, summarised in Table 22.1.

Table 22.1 Benefits and limitations of electronic records

Benefits of electronic records	Limitations of electronic records
Electronic records are precise and legible.	Clinical information often comes with a degree of inbuilt uncertainty. Electronic records can be inflexible.
Electronic records are simple to transmit and provide inbuilt protection methods such as encryption.	The ease of transmission of electronic data can pose a threat to confidentiality and offer potential routes for attack from hackers and computer viruses.
Electronic records are compact and can be backed up readily to protect from damage from wear and tear, fire, water, coffee, etc.	Although looking after electronic records is facilitated by the technology, many users don't do it, leaving records vulnerable.
Electronic records can be sorted in any number of ways.	The technology itself can provide a barrier to the information.
Looking for information is facilitated by the use of structured coding schema and query languages.	Electronic systems are generally owned by organisations who have little incentive to help the information they contain follow the patient seamlessly.
In integrated care, electronic records can facilitate data sharing across multiple agencies and even within teams.	

One of the major potential benefits of using information technology is the prevention of adverse events by prompting the clinician when a potential adverse event is about to happen. Many people suffer adverse events within the healthcare system contravening the principle of non-maleficence, which states that the first responsibility is not to do harm.

However, electronic records are not just about preventing harm; it can actively improve patient care. Where patients with specific characteristics are at risk from certain conditions, they may be identified and targeted for preventative interventions. Without electronic records, it is difficult to identify such groups of patients within the overall population.

Predicting diabetes mellitus in pregnant women based upon their electronic records (after Artzi et al., 2020)

Gestational diabetes mellitus (GDM) increases the likelihood of both immediate and long-term complications for mothers and their children. Although it is typically diagnosed between 24 and 28 weeks of pregnancy, earlier detection could help prevent or significantly reduce negative pregnancy outcomes. In their study, Artzi et al. (2020) used a machine-learning approach to predict GDM using retrospective data from 588,622 pregnancies in Israel, supported by comprehensive electronic health records. Their models demonstrated high accuracy in predicting GDM even at the onset of pregnancy (area under the receiver operating curve (auROC) = 0.85), significantly surpassing a baseline risk score (auROC = 0.68).

They validated their findings using both a future validation set and a geographical validation set from Jerusalem, reflecting real-world application. Analysis of the model revealed new risk factors such as the results from previous pregnancy glucose challenge tests. Additionally, they developed a simpler model based on nine patient questions, which maintained a high accuracy (auROC = 0.80). These models could enable early intervention for high-risk women and offer a cost-effective screening method that may reduce the need for glucose tolerance tests by identifying low-risk women.

Although the authors of the study focus upon their novel use of machine learning, this technique is only possible because of a comprehensive set of reliable electronic records.

22.1.1 Knowledge review

Before you move on, can you define the following key concepts:

- Electronic health record system?

22.1.2 Question to think about

Last time you visited a doctor, did they use electronic or paper records?
    What do you think are the pros and cons of each, as a patient?

22.2 The role of structured terminologies

For computers to effectively manage and process electronic records, the information needs to be stored in a structured manner.

It has been calculated that on average, most words in the English language have four distinct meanings: and this is too much for the poor computers. They need everything to be black and white. They have to be able to reduce everything to ones and zeros ultimately. So, for example, you might use the word "heart" to mean:

- the organ that pumps blood
- the essence of the matter
- courage or spirit

This would leave a computer thoroughly confused. And it works the other way, too. A doctor might talk about a myocardial infarction, a patient about a heart attack. Unless you tell the computer, it doesn't know that these are the same.

This is the reason why we have to use codes to describe diagnoses, drugs, treatments, etc. for the computer to tell it precisely what we mean. This may help the computer but it leaves us with three distinct problems:

- We have to make sure that everyone is using the same coding system.
- We have to make sure everyone is using the same codes for the same things.
- The real world is ambiguous, and this is why clever humans have developed ways of handling ambiguity. The poor stupid computer has not.

They need their information in a particular form; at a fundamental level, a computer's processor is just a collection of switches that are on or off. This means what may make perfect sense to you appears to the computer as complete rubbish. Even the slowest human brain by comparison is capable of all sorts of interpretative tasks that computers don't understand.

So if a nurse writes "astma" on the record of a child whose mother had brought them to see you because they were wheezing, a colleague would assume that they meant "asthma." The computer would look at "astma" and say, "This Is Not Asthma!" True but unhelpful.

But once you operate in the computer's world, the roles are reversed. If six clinicians coded "asthma" on a child's electronic record, they might use different codes to reflect subtleties about the condition; the computer sees six codes, six conditions. Unless we specifically tell the computer that each code represents the same thing, then it will assume that they are not. It will only search for the specific codes that you tell it to, so you must make sure that those are the same codes that were used to store the data.

One of the first structured terminologies deployed on a mass scale in electronic health records systems were the Read Codes first used in primary care across the UK in the 1990s and still used in Scotland, Wales, and Northern Ireland.

For example, if a primary care physician wishes to find which of their patients have asthma, the computer will select the records that contain the corresponding Read Code H33.

The Read Code terminology is hierarchical with additional characteristics providing more detail, as shown in Table 22.2.

Structured terminologies are easy to search. However, the structured terms carry no context with them so are vulnerable to error. If a single letter is misplaced from a free text description, a human will likely still see the correct meaning. If a computer finds a string of alphanumeric characters and one is misplaced, it will record the information as something completely different.

Two modern structured terminologies of global significance are ICD-11 and SNOMED-CT.

22.2.1 ICD-11

The first version of the International Classification of Diseases (ICD) dates back to the 19th century and long predates electronic medical records. The 11th revision (ICD-11) was adopted for global use in 2022 (WHO, 2022).

The ICD is generally dominant in the field of population-based health where it is used for a variety of purposes. It is used globally to inform practitioners and research about the prevalence, causes, and consequences of human disease and death worldwide. However, as it takes a while for the latest versions to be adopted, much of the data may be in ICD-10 or even ICD-9. Therefore, each new update retains backwards compatibility.

Clinical terms coded with ICD provide a common structured format for health recording and statistics on disease across all levels of healthcare and is used to record the cause of death on death certificates. These data and statistics inform decision-making on health remuneration, demand forecasting, and the planning of services, the quality of services, and the safety of issues, as well as a broad range of health services research.

The previous version of the ICD, ICD-10, provided a hierarchical set of codes with a single code for each condition, so "stroke" was, for example, listed in the cardiovascular

Table 22.2 Read codes for asthma

Read Code	Term
H33	Asthma
H33.11	Bronchial asthma
H330	Extrinsic (atopic) asthma
H330.11	Allergic asthma
H330.12	Childhood asthma
H330.13	Hay fever with asthma
H330.14	Pollen asthma
H3300	Extrinsic asthma without status asthmaticus
H330011	Hay fever with asthma
H3301	Extrinsic asthma with status asthmaticus
H330111	Extrinsic asthma with asthma attack
H330z	Extrinsic asthma NOS
H331	Intrinsic asthma
H331.11	Late onset asthma
H3310	Intrinsic asthma without status asthmaticus
H3311	Intrinsic asthma with status asthmaticus
H331111	Intrinsic asthma with asthma attack
H331z	Intrinsic asthma NOS
H332	Mixed asthma
H333	Acute exacerbation of asthma
H33z	Asthma unspecified
H33z0	Status asthmaticus NOS
H33z011	Severe asthma attack
H33z1	Asthma attack
H33z111	Asthma attack NOS
H33z2	Late onset asthma
H33zz	Asthma NOS
H33zz11	Exercise induced asthma
H33zz12	Allergic asthma NEC
H33zz13	Allergic bronchitis NEC
9hA1.	Excepted from asthma quality indicators: Patient unsuitable
9hA2.	Excepted from asthma quality indicators: Informed dissent
9OJ2	Refuses asthma monitoring

chapter. In order to make ICD-11 fit for computerised analysis, it uses a computable knowledge framework designed to be interoperable across varied digital health information environments (Harrison et al., 2021).

Though ICD-11 can be used in paper-based systems, the tools and capabilities made possible by the framework are designed to encourage its use with computer systems. Because ICD-11 is not easier to use without computers than previous versions, it is likely that ICD-10 will remain the dominant version in many countries with limited access to digital technology for years to come.

ICD-11 allows for derived classification schemes. The first of these is known as ICD-11 for Mortality and Morbidity Statistics (ICD-11-MMS). It can be used to classify data to ICD-11 standards but retains backward compatibility with ICD-10. Thus, the stroke, which is located in the neurology chapter of ICD-11-MMS, also appears in the cardiovascular chapter because this is where it was located in ICD-10. The secondary location comes with a note that its primary location in ICD-11 is elsewhere (Harrison et al., 2021).

ICD-11 allows for clustering of code; for example, the code for type 2 diabetes mellitus is 5A11 and the code for proliferative diabetic retinopathy is 9B71.01. Proliferative diabetic retinopathy in type 2 diabetes mellitus may, therefore, be recorded as 5A11/9B71.01. ICD-11. CODE CA23.32: UNSPECIFIED ASTHMA, UNCOMPLICATED.

This code indicates a diagnosis of asthma that is unspecified, meaning the specific type or severity is not specified, and that the condition is uncomplicated, meaning there are no associated complications. The "J45" portion of the code refers to the chapter for diseases of the respiratory system, and the ".909" extension represents the specific diagnosis within that chapter (WHO, 2022).

22.2.2 SNOMED CT

SNOMED CT is a structured terminology that represents coded terms in a form that may be used within electronic health records (EHRs) to capture, record, and share clinical data for use in healthcare organisations. It has been designed for use in the records of individual patients as opposed to the population-based uses of the ICD.

It facilitates retrieval of meaningful clinical information from electronic record systems. It was created by a collaboration of the English NHS and the US College of American Pathologists (CAP) who agreed to merge SNOMED with read codes to produce a single joint clinical terminology – SNOMED CT (clinical terminology). The first release of SNOMED CT was in 2006 (Gillies, 2006).

SNOMED CT terms were not widely adopted until they were mandated by governments. In 2013, the US federal government required EHR systems to include the terminology in their systems to be compliant with the regulations that apply to government mandated EHRs. In England, although the UK mandated the use of SNOMED CT in 2019, the other parts of the UK are yet to adopt SNOMED CT as a standard.

SNOMED CT has

> three core building blocks: concepts, descriptions and relationships. Each concept represents a single specific meaning; each description associates a single term with a concept (any concept may have any number of descriptions or names); and each relationship represents a logical relationship between two concepts (Benson, 2005).

SNOMED CT is much more detailed than ICD-10. It includes over 300,000 concepts, over a million descriptions, and a million and half relationships. ICD-10 has only 10,760 distinct disease classifications. The SNOMED codes are connected in the dictionary to establish connections between different concepts. For example, the concept "fracture of the fibula" has an explicit relationship with the concept "fibula" to define where the fracture is located. "Relationships are also used to build expressions within patient records. For example, the concept of fracture of shaft of tibia can be qualified by laterality [left or right] … and fracture type" (Benson, 2005).

SNOMED CT was arguably the first terminology designed exclusively for use in computer systems – it cannot be used manually. Its scale means that it is practically unmanageable without a computer. More significantly, it is structurally different from earlier coding schemes, such as ICD-10 or the read codes. "In these schemes the relationships between concepts is specified within the code itself" (Benson, 2005), whereas SNOMED CT relies on its three distinct building blocks.

Its distinct relationships depend on computer software to work. This makes it more complex than a single code-dependent hierarchy but, in turn, delivers more power and flexibility, which can be exploited by computers. In this way, it is much closer to ICD-11 than ICD -10, as both have been designed to take advantage of computerised processing and analysis. Unlike ICD-11, it does not have a derived classification to maintain backward compatibility

---

The importance of context (reported to the author)

Once structured electronic records were started to be shared between different primary care physicians across the UK, it became important to ensure the quality of the clinical data contained within them.

A national quality assurance audit was ordered, and the sample of the records scrutinised to establish their quality. The auditors noticed a cluster of cases of pigeon fancier's lung in the East Midlands of England. The cluster was associated with young women in their 20s and some younger. This was odd because pigeon fancier's lung is a disease which is associated with the sport of pigeon racing almost exclusively practised by men in middle age and above.

On further investigation, the local primary care physicians admitted that they had deliberately miscoded these cases. In practise, they used this code to represent patience with a sexually transmitted disease chlamydia. They said they did not wish to embarrass their female patients by adding the correct code to their record. They added that all the local doctors understood what it meant and therefore they didn't see the problem. However, once a patient moved out of the area and took that electronic record with them, the local context was lost and the true meaning of the code was obscured.

22.2.3 Knowledge review

Before you move on, can you define the following key concepts:

- Structured clinical terminology?

22.2.4 Question to think about

How precise do you think clinical diagnosis is? How well does it fit structured classification?

22.3 Clinical decision support

One of the major potential benefits from using information technology is the prevention of adverse events by prompting the clinician when a potential adverse event is about to happen. Many people suffer adverse events whilst within the healthcare system, contravening the principle of non-maleficence, which states that the first responsibility is not to do harm.

Clinical decision support systems can prompt a clinician to act in a number of cases:

Where records hold information that show that a proposed action would contra-indicate with an existing therapy, the computer can post a suitable warning to the clinician. Most commonly, this is used with medication, because this is the area where there is the most evidence. However, there is considerable potential to extend its use to a wide range of therapies.

Clinical decision support built into an electronic health records system may also warn the clinician where the records hold information that shows that a proposed action would contra-indicate with this particular patient due to an allergy or existing condition.

Some warnings are based on information about the drugs to be prescribed irrespective of the patient. These may relate to checking the dosage to prevent an over- or underdose.

Table 22.3 summarises the prescribing process, the associated risks, and how an electronic health records system with built-in decision support can help to reduce risks:

The use of technology can help reduce the risk of errors at each stage and therefore risk to the patient at the time of taking the drug:

- More information about medications available more quickly can help clinicians make better decisions about the right medication.
- Electronic records can store allergies and flag potential problems.
- Electronic records can store existing medications and flag potential problems.
- Electronic records can identify at-risk patients and suggest proactive prescribing, e.g., aspirin in relation to cardiovascular problems.
- Electronic systems can not only improve legibility, they can check dosage and other information at the point of entry to the system, preventing some types of errors.

Table 22.3 The prescribing and dispensing process (after Gillies, 2006)

Drug selection	Prescribing	Dispensing	Administration
Risks			
• Inappropriate medication chosen • Patient allergic to medication • Patient taking contraindicating medication • Patients need for medication not detected	• Writing difficult to read, leading to errors in medication or dosage	• Dispensing error in dosage or type	• Any of the prior potential errors could lead to adverse event at this point
What electronic records with decision support can do to help			
• Decision support to prevent inappropriate medication choice • Flag up patient allergies • Flag up contra-indicating medications • Suggest need for medication	• Clarity of information	• Flag up potential errors in dosage or type	• Prevention of errors increases chance of safe use of medication

- If the consultation venue and dispensing pharmacy are linked electronically, then the steps in the chain are reduced, reducing the chance of human error in writing or reading the prescription.
- Electronic systems can also check dosage and other information at the point of dispensing, preventing some types of errors.

Reducing prescribing errors (after Manias et al., 2020)

Manias et al. (2020) carried out a systematic review to compare the effectiveness of different interventions in reducing prescribing, dispensing, and administration medication errors in acute medical and surgical settings. They reviewed a total of 34 articles and identified 12 different intervention types, of which 5 involved electronic systems:

1. Pharmacists identify the most accurate list of medications and provide patients with the correct medications in hospital. This is usually conducted at admission and/or discharge.
2. Electronic systems are used to identify the most accurate list of medications and provide patients with the correct medications in hospital. This is usually conducted at admission and/or discharge.
3. Electronic systems are designed to automate the medication order process with the use of standardised and complete order. Sometimes this is complemented with the availability of clinical decision support, providing information on medication dose, route, and frequency.
4. Pharmacists are involved as part of the team. This can include ward rounds, providing monitoring service and/or prescription reviews.
5. Educating the prescribers through online modules or pharmacist-led sessions
6. Patient education especially on the medical terms on how to take the medication; this is usually conducted by pharmacists.
7. Collaboration with various healthcare discipline groups for better medication management
8. Experts who were trained in medication administration
9. Electronic systems designed to facilitate medication administration
10. Electronic systems designed to facilitate medication administration via automating drug distribution
11. Electronic records that comprise tools for medication prescription and administration
12. Different methods of medication cart filling methods to facilitate administration, for example, medications arranged by round time or by their names

The authors found that prescribing errors were reduced by pharmacist-led medication reconciliation, computerised medication reconciliation, pharmacist partnership, prescriber education, medication reconciliation by trained mentors, and computerised physician order entry as single interventions.

They also found that medication administration errors were reduced by computerised physician order entry and the use of an automated drug distribution system as single interventions. Combined interventions were also found to be effective in reducing both prescribing and administration medication errors.

22.3.1 Knowledge review

Before you move on, can you define the following key concepts:

• Clinical decision support?

22.3.2 Question to think about

Last time you or a family member received a prescription, was electronic prescribing used? What risks were (or would have been reduced) by electronic prescribing?

22.4 Patient communication and education

The purpose of clinical information is to improve decision-making. Decisions may be made by healthcare professionals, patients, or both together. Before treatment can start, a patient must be able to provide informed consent. The use of the term "informed" implies that the patient has sufficient information to agree to the proposed treatment.

Hall et al. (2012) argue that informed consent means different things in different contexts. They identify distinct legal, ethical, and administrative compliance contexts.

Legally, basic consent safeguards patients from unwanted medical interventions, preventing assault and battery. However, the legal standards for obtaining informed consent vary by jurisdiction and are subject to ongoing interpretation. Many countries uphold a higher standard of informed consent to further protect patients' rights to autonomy and self-determination. Thankfully, legal interpretations are typically pragmatic, often deeming a good-faith effort to inform as sufficient.

Ethically, informed consent aims to respect patient autonomy by ensuring that treatments align with the patient's desires and are chosen by them. It seeks to shift decision-making from physician-centred to more patient-centred approaches. In the ethical realm, informed consent is viewed as a process rather than a single event, preceding the formal signing of documents and continuing as long as the decision remains relevant. Therefore, consent for ongoing treatments like dialysis or chemotherapy is continually reviewed and may change. The consent form merely documents this process; it should not be seen as the primary outcome of the consent process. Other parts of the patient's medical records, such as clinic or operative notes, should support the details of the consent process.

From an administrative standpoint, the informed consent document serves as a system-level check to ensure that the consent process has taken place. For example, patients typically cannot proceed to surgery without a signed consent form. However, there is a risk that pressures for efficiency may prioritise obtaining a signature over meaningful conversation during the informed consent process. Better information can improve patient decision-making in a variety of ways:

• Patients who have access to comprehensive information about their health conditions and available treatments can better understand their options. This understanding enables them to actively participate in discussions with healthcare providers, ask relevant questions, and make decisions aligned with their preferences and values.
• Information about the risks associated with different health conditions, treatments, and lifestyle choices allows patients to assess their personal risk factors more accurately. This knowledge helps them make decisions about preventive measures, such

as lifestyle changes or screening tests, to reduce their risk of developing certain health issues.

- Knowledge about various treatment options, including their benefits, potential side effects, and success rates, empowers patients to weigh the pros and cons of each option based on their individual circumstances. This enables them to make informed decisions about their treatment plans in collaboration with their healthcare providers.
- Informed patients are better equipped to engage in shared decision-making with their healthcare providers. By actively participating in discussions about their health and treatment options, patients can express their preferences, values, and concerns, leading to decisions that are more personalised and aligned with their goals.
- Access to information about managing chronic conditions or recovering from illnesses empowers patients to take an active role in their own care. Patients who understand how to monitor their symptoms, adhere to treatment plans, and make lifestyle modifications are better equipped to manage their health effectively between healthcare visits.
- Providing clear, accessible health information improves health literacy levels among patients. Health literate individuals are more likely to understand health-related information, navigate the healthcare system more effectively, and actively engage in behaviours that promote their well-being.
- Access to reliable information can alleviate anxiety and uncertainty among patients facing health-related decisions. By understanding their conditions and treatment options more thoroughly, patients may feel more empowered and confident in their decision-making process.

There are an increasing number of mobile phone apps available that are designed to facilitate self-care by providing advice, recording symptoms, or sometimes by direct measurement, with or without the aid of additional sensor services.

Hosseini et al. (2023) carried out a quasi-experimental longitudinal single-group study in Iran between October 2020 and March 2021 with the participation of 60 dialysis patients. The authors used simple random sampling to select the patients. The intervention included an educational application, and participants completed questionnaires on self-efficacy and self-care performance at four points including baseline and at one, three, and six-month intervals post-intervention. The study showed significant improvements in these patients' self-care behaviours and self-efficacy over time, when they had access to the educational app. However, the structure of this study means that it shows that the patients with access to the educational app got better at self-care over time; it does not demonstrate that this is due solely to the app or that patients might not have accessed the information in a different way.

DeSousa et al. (2023) developed a mobile application called "Tum Tum" aimed at supporting self-care for individuals with heart failure (HF). The research was conducted in a teaching hospital in Paraíba, Brazil, known for specialised cardiology care. The study followed a three-step protocol: analysis, design/development, and validation.

In the analysis phase, literature reviews were conducted to identify educational content relevant to HF self-care. Remote scientific meetings were held to discuss and select educational topics based on scientific evidence and clinical experience. In the design/development phase, the instructional content was created, emphasising accessible language and intuitive interface design. The application was developed using React Native to ensure compatibility with both Android and iOS platforms.

The content and interface were validated by an expert committee, followed by face validation with HF patients. The application, evaluated using the Suitability Assessment of Materials (SAM) instrument, scored high, indicating superior quality. Feedback from experts and patients led to adjustments, including improvements in typography size for better readability.

The application, "Tum Tum," offers educational content on HF, including causes, symptoms, diagnosis, and treatment. The prototype of the application, called "Tum Tum," has an interface and free navigation screens covering the concept of heart failure, its causes, symptoms and signs, diagnosis, and treatment. It has a mosaic with educational guidelines, resources for early recognition of signs of clinical decompensation, registration for body weight control, and reminders for medication use, consultation and exam schedule. The interface is user-friendly, with clear information and interactive elements.

The authors argue that the study demonstrates the potential of mHealth technology in supporting self-care for individuals with chronic conditions like HF. The "Tum Tum" application provides a valuable resource for patients and healthcare professionals, aiding in education and self-management of the disease.

Table 22.4 summarises some of the key advantages and disadvantages of using phone apps to assist with self-care.

Table 22.4 Key advantages and disadvantages of using phone apps to assist with self-care

Advantages	Disadvantages
Mobile apps provide convenient access to self-care tools and resources anytime and anywhere, allowing users to engage in self-care activities at their own pace and schedule.	Not all self-care apps undergo rigorous testing or regulation, raising concerns about the accuracy and reliability of the information and advice provided. It can be difficult for users to verify the credibility of the app and its content.
Apps can make self-care resources more accessible to a wider audience, including individuals who may have difficulty accessing traditional healthcare services due to geographical or logistical barriers.	Mobile apps may collect sensitive personal data, such as health information, raising privacy and security concerns regarding data protection and unauthorised access. Users should review the app's privacy policy and take precautions to safeguard their personal information.
Many apps offer personalised features tailored to individual needs and preferences, allowing users to track their progress, set goals, and receive customised recommendations for self-care activities.	Relying solely on self-care apps for health management may lead to overdependence and a lack of engagement with healthcare professionals, potentially delaying or neglecting necessary medical treatment or interventions.
Self-care apps often include educational content and resources that can help users learn more about their health conditions, symptoms, and treatment options, empowering them to make informed decisions about their care.	While many self-care apps are free or offer basic features at no cost, some may require a subscription or payment for access to premium features or content, which can be a barrier for individuals with limited financial resources.
Some apps include features that facilitate peer support and community engagement, allowing users to connect with others who share similar experiences and challenges, providing a sense of belonging and social support.	Maintaining long-term engagement with self-care apps can be challenging, as users may lose interest or motivation over time, leading to decreased adherence to self-care activities and goals.

The problem with informed consent: a personal anecdote

Some time ago, the writer underwent an ordeal with kidney stones. For those unfamiliar with them, kidney stones can induce excruciating pain. After enduring several bouts of agonising but temporary pain, the situation reached a critical point one night. Following numerous calls to a nurse advisory service, it was advised that the writer seek help at the local hospital's emergency department. The severity of the pain was evidently clear, as the standard triage procedure was swiftly bypassed, and the writer was promptly admitted.

It was determined that the first priority was to alleviate the pain, so morphine was to be administered. However, to mitigate the risk of nausea, an anti-nausea injection was administered first, causing a significant delay before the morphine could be given. Eventually, the morphine took effect, easing the pain. After nearly 12 hours of intense suffering, the relief was profound.

A few hours later, as the initial dose began to wear off and the pain returned, the clinical team approached the writer and offered another dose of morphine. Recalling the recent agony, the writer readily accepted, desperate to avoid such torment again. However, upon reflection, it became apparent that this decision was heavily influenced by the distorted judgment caused by the intense pain. Further evidence of his questionable judgement was the writer's prior action of driving himself to the hospital despite his driving ability being severely impaired by pain.

The concept of informed consent is admirable, yet in reality, even if patients possess the cognitive ability to understand the implications of their decisions, other factors, particularly pain, can impair their capacity to weigh evidence effectively.

22.4.1 Knowledge review

Before you move on, can you define the following key concepts:

- Informed consent?

22.4.2 Question to think about

Under what circumstance would you trust and make use of ,a phone app to manage your own care?

References

Ancker, J. S., Singh, M. P., Thomas, R., Edwards, A., Snyder, A., Kashyap, A., & Kaushal, R. (2013). Predictors of success for electronic health record implementation in small physician practices. *Applied Clinical Informatics*, 4(1), 12–24. http://10.4338/ACI-2012-09-RA-003

Artzi, N. S., Shilo, S., Hadar, E., Rossman, H., Barbash-Hazan, S., Ben-Haroush, A., ... Segal, E. (2020). Prediction of gestational diabetes based on nationwide electronic health records. *Nature Medicine*, 26(1), 71–76.

Beasley, S., & Girard J. (2016). *Office-based physician EHR adoption and use in Southern US States*. SAIS 2016 Proceedings, 26.

Benson, T. (2005, June 2). *Code of practice*. Digital Health.

Ben-Zion, R., Pliskin, N., & Fink, L. (2014). Critical success factors for adoption of electronic health record systems: Literature review and prescription analysis. *Information Systems Management*, 31(4), 296–312.

de Sousa, M. M., Lopes, C. T., Almeida, A. A. M., Almeida, T. D. C. F., Gouveia, B. D. L. A., & Oliveira, S. H. D. S. (2023). Development and validation of a mobile application for heart failure patients self-care. *Revista da Escola de Enfermagem da USP*, 56.

Gillies, A. C. (2006, February 15). *The clinician's guide to surviving IT* (1st ed.). CRC Press, ISBN: 978-1857757972

Hall, D. E., Prochazka, A. V., & Fink, A. S. (2012). Informed consent for clinical treatment. *CMAJ: Canadian Medical Association Journal = journal de l'Association medicale canadienne*, 184(5), 533–540. https://doi.org/10.1503/cmaj.112120

Harrison, J. E., Weber, S., Jakob, R., & Chute, C. G. (2021). ICD-11: An international classification of diseases for the twenty-first century. *BMC Medical Informatics and Decision Making*, 21, 1–10.

Health and Care Professions Council. (n.d.). *Meeting our standards record keeping.* https://www.hcpc-uk.org/standards/meeting-our-standards/record-keeping/

Hosseini, A., Jackson, A. C., Chegini, N., Dehghan, M. F., Mazloum, D., Haghani, S., & Bahramnezhad, F. (2023). The effect of an educational app on hemodialysis patients' self-efficacy and self-care: A quasi-experimental longitudinal study. *Chronic Illness*, 19(2), 383–394.

Kruse, C. S., Kristof, C., Jones, B., Mitchell, E., & Martinez, A. (2016). Barriers to electronic health record adoption: A systematic literature review. *Journal of Medical Systems*, 40(12), 252.

Manias, E., Kusljic, S., & Wu, A. (2020). Interventions to reduce medication errors in adult medical and surgical settings: a systematic review. *Therapeutic Advances in Drug Safety*, 11, 2042098620968309.

Mason, P., Mayer, R., Chien, W. W., & Monestime, J. P. (2017). Overcoming barriers to implementing electronic health records in rural primary care clinics. *The Qualitative Report*, 22(11), 2943–2955.

Menon, S., Singh, H., Meyer, A. N., Belmont, E., & Sittig, D. F. (2014). Electronic health record-related safety concerns: A cross-sectional survey. *Journal of Healthcare Risk Management*, 34(1), 14–26.

WHO. (2022). *International statistical classification of diseases and related health problems (ICD).* WHO.

23 Using information to improve the management of hospitals

23.1 Hospital management information systems

Hospitals collect and use many different types of data in order to carry out their purpose of providing healthcare services, including clinical data, demographic data, and administrative data. This data can be used for various purposes such as patient care, research, and public health surveillance. Medical data is typically sensitive and subject to privacy regulations such as the Health Insurance Portability and Accountability Act (HIPAA) in the United States. Protecting patient privacy while allowing for the sharing and analysis of medical data is a critical challenge in healthcare.

A key purpose of information management in hospitals is to improve their performance by more effective management.

23.1.1 Patient Administration Systems (PASs)

The role of a Patient Administration System (PAS) is to capture and store non-clinical information about patients, including their name, date of birth, home address, and emergency contact details.

Initially, PASs were developed to automate administrative tasks in hospitals and care facilities. However, with the advancement of healthcare technology, these systems have transitioned into much more comprehensive digital platforms and are ideally integrated with other information systems including electronic patient record systems. Modern healthcare software now stores not only the basic patient details but also tracks their interactions and activities across various care settings.

PASs are designed to reduce errors and save time by automating processes, replacing manual data entry with electronic communication, simplifying and accelerating key tasks, reducing unnecessary repetition to use, and developing consistent and efficient practices. For example, they make it easier to put in place measures to reduce do-not-attend rates and to send reminders to patients. These days, PAS are designed to integrate with other systems, including EHR systems.

Patient Administration Systems (PASs) help hospitals manage and analyse health information, including patient data, medical records, and administrative data. They integrate various administrative and clinical functions within a hospital. These systems handle tasks such as patient registration, scheduling, billing, inventory management, and resource allocation.

DOI: 10.4324/9781003478874-29

They can streamline operations, enhance efficiency, and support effective resource utilisation. They may provide tools for data integration, analysis, and reporting, allowing hospital management to make informed decisions based on real-time data.

Many of the management benefits are derived from the use of structured workflows in the organisation. These are standardised, repeatable processes used to implement core administrative and management tasks within the hospital. The PAS will guide the user through the standard process and ensure that all of the information needed is collected on the way.

A typical modern PAS will have modules to support a range of management functions.

The system will help to manage patient registrations through the capture of patient demographic information, contact details, insurance information, and other relevant data necessary for creating patient records in a standardised data collection process.

It will support workflows for the scheduling of appointments for patients with healthcare providers, specialists, or diagnostic services, ensuring efficient allocation of resources and minimising wait times. These will be linked to workflows for the admission, transfer, and discharge processes for patients, including bed allocation, room scheduling, and tracking patient movement within the hospital. Where necessary, this will include functions for managing waiting lists for those patients unable to be seen immediately.

The system will process billing, invoicing, and payment processing for healthcare services provided to patients, tailored to the types of funding mechanism and sources of funding available to the hospital.

The system will support workflows for quality improvement initiatives by capturing clinical quality measures, monitoring compliance with regulatory requirements, and generating performance reports for internal analysis and external reporting purposes.

Many systems will provide patients with secure access to their health information, appointment scheduling, communication with healthcare providers, educational resources, and online bill payment, promoting patient empowerment and engagement in their care. The system may issue automatic reminders by SMS text or other electronic messaging.

The functions of the PAS will be available for scrutiny and analysis through comprehensive reporting facilities to facilitate monitoring, evaluation, compliance, and improvement.

The system will include robust security measures, user authentication, role-based access control, and auditing capabilities to comply with privacy regulations and ensure the confidentiality, integrity, and availability of patient information.

A modern PAS will normally be at the heart of a hospital information system interfacing with other systems for more specialised purposes, as shown in Figure 23.1.

In addition to links to the hospital's electronic patient records system, the system will interface to other systems used in the management of the hospital.

23.1.2 Decision Support Systems (DSS)

Decision Support Systems (DSS) are used to support management decision-making in hospitals as well as for clinical decision-making. They can use data drawn from both the EHR system and the PAS system to assist decision-making in several areas of financial and risk management.

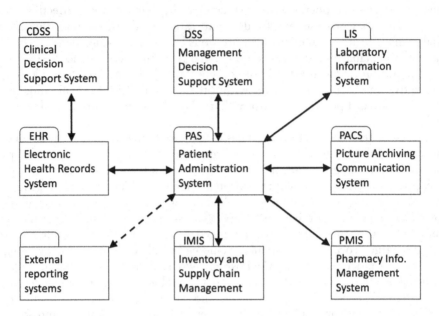

Figure 23.1 A modern PAS is at the heart of a hospital's information systems.

DSS can help hospitals analyse financial data, such as revenue, expenses, and profitability. It can generate reports and dashboards that provide insights into financial performance, identify trends, and highlight areas of concern. This information can help hospital administrators make informed decisions about resource allocation, cost reduction, and revenue enhancement strategies.

DSS can support the budgeting and forecasting processes by integrating financial data from various sources and allowing administrators to create accurate and detailed financial plans. They can facilitate scenario analysis and "what-if" simulations to assess the potential impact of different budgetary decisions or external factors on the hospital's financial position. They can help manage costs by providing cost analysis and cost driver identification. By analysing expenses across departments, services, or procedures. They can identify cost-saving opportunities, inefficiencies, and areas where process improvements can be made. By providing real-time cost information and alerts for potential cost overruns, they can also help monitor and control costs.

They can assist hospitals in optimising revenue generation by analysing patient data, reimbursement rates, and billing information. It can help identify opportunities for maximising reimbursement, improving coding accuracy, and reducing claim denials. Additionally, they can support decision-making related to pricing strategies, contract negotiations, and the development of new revenue streams.

They can monitor key performance indicators (KPIs) related to financial management, such as revenue growth, profitability ratios, cash flow, and operational efficiency. By tracking these metrics over time and comparing them against industry benchmarks or internal targets, they can identify areas where performance is lagging and support the development of improvement initiatives.

They provide tools to manage financial risks by providing tools for evaluating the potential impact of financial decisions, market fluctuations, or regulatory changes. They can be used to simulate the financial implications of different risk scenarios and help administrators develop strategies to mitigate risks and ensure financial stability. By varying input parameters, such as staffing levels, patient volumes, or equipment failures, the systems can be used to assess the sensitivity of the hospital's performance to different risk factors. This enables hospitals to develop risk mitigation strategies and contingency plans to minimise the negative effects of potential risks.

To do this, DSS aggregate and analyse data from various sources within the hospital, such as patient records, incident reports, regulatory information, and external databases to identify potential risks. By applying data mining and predictive analytics techniques, they can identify patterns, anomalies, and emerging risks that may not be readily apparent. This can help hospitals proactively identify and address potential risks before they escalate.

They can assist in assessing and quantifying risks by providing tools and models for risk analysis. It can incorporate historical data, benchmarks, and probabilistic methods to estimate the likelihood and impact of identified risks. The systems can generate risk scores, heat maps, and risk profiles to help hospitals prioritise and allocate resources based on the severity and potential consequences of each risk.

They may be used to continuously monitor risk indicators and alert hospital staff to potential risks in real-time. By integrating with hospital information systems and data streams, these systems can analyse data patterns, identify deviations from normal behaviours, and trigger notifications or alerts when predefined thresholds are exceeded. This enables hospitals to take timely action and implement preventive measures before risks escalate.

They can assist hospitals in managing compliance with regulatory requirements and industry standards. By monitoring changes in regulations, updating compliance frameworks, and providing guidance on adherence, they can help hospitals stay compliant and minimise the risk of penalties or legal issues.

23.1.3 Laboratory Information systems (LMSs)

Modern computerised LMSs first introduced in the 1980s are key to the effective management of laboratory services (Gibbon, 1996). They were initially focused on tasks like data reduction, analogue-to-digital conversion, and radioimmunoassay analysis. These days, they are sophisticated digital systems with a wide range of capabilities and functions. An LMS helps track and manage samples from the moment they are collected to their final disposal. It records sample details, location, storage conditions, and movement, ensuring proper organisation and minimising the risk of errors.

An LMS can be used to automate workflows, including test ordering, sample processing, and result reporting. This reduces manual intervention, reduces errors, enhances accuracy, and accelerates turnaround times. Many LMS platforms can interface with laboratory instruments, enabling seamless data transfer and reducing manual data entry errors.

Use of an LMS centralises data storage, allowing easy retrieval and secure management of test results, patient information, quality control data, and other relevant data. This aids in maintaining a comprehensive record of laboratory activities. It facilitates the implementation and management of quality control processes, ensuring that tests and procedures adhere to predefined standards and regulations. It helps in tracking instrument calibration, control samples, and proficiency testing.

LMS systems implement robust security measures to safeguard sensitive patient data and maintain compliance with data protection regulations.

The system helps monitor and manage laboratory supplies, reagents, and equipment. This prevents shortages, optimises inventory levels, and reduces wastage. It can be programmed to generate accurate and standardised reports for test results, aiding healthcare providers in making informed decisions. It may also provide analytical tools to identify trends, monitor performance, and support decision-making.

It maintains an audit trail of all activities, ensuring accountability and traceability. This is crucial for regulatory compliance and accreditation requirements.

The LMS provides a central communication facility among laboratory staff, clinicians, and other stakeholders. It may include features for result notifications, data sharing, and collaboration on complex cases.

Finally, an LMS helps allocate resources efficiently, including staff scheduling, equipment utilisation, and workload distribution, leading to improved operational efficiency.

23.1.4 *Picture Archiving Communication System (PACS)*

PACSs (Picture Archiving and Communication Systems) are a crucial component of modern hospital management systems. Digital images represent very large amounts of data and they require different processing techniques from text-based data. The information contained in a digital image is represented not just by the numerical values attached to the individual pixels, but by their relative positions and the relationships between them that form the patterns that make up the meaningful information content of the image.

Skyquest (2024) forecast that the global market for these systems by 2030 will be worth US$3.4 billion. However, this is an increase of only 6.25% from 2021, suggesting that this is a well-established technology in traditional markets in high-income countries, and increases in usage are more likely to be seen in emerging economies.

These systems are primarily used for storing, retrieving, distributing, and presenting digital medical images. Digital images generally offer significant benefits in terms of resolution for clinicians, but the systems that help to manage them provide significant benefits to hospital managers. The systems streamline the process of storing, retrieving, and sharing medical images, reducing the time required to access patient data and increasing operational efficiency.

By digitising and centralising image storage, PACS reduces costs associated with film, storage space, and maintenance of physical archives and eliminates the need for expensive film processing equipment and chemicals and removes potential environmental risks associated with the chemicals needed for developing physical films. Quicker access to medical images leads to faster diagnoses and treatment, improving productivity, patient outcomes, and reducing the chance of misdiagnoses in turn reducing medical errors.

PACS enables healthcare providers to access historical images, aiding in the comparison of current and previous conditions for better treatment planning.

However, these systems are complex and provide challenges as well as opportunities for management. Implementing PACS requires significant upfront investment in infrastructure, software, and staff training. Integration with existing hospital systems is essential to maximise the benefits of the system, but can be complex and may require adjustments to workflows. Similarly, ensuring interoperability between PACS and other healthcare systems and imaging devices from different manufacturers is vital but can be challenging. The very large amounts of data processed can mean that PACS and interconnected systems are at a higher risk of technical glitches, server failures, or network issues leading to downtime and preventing access to critical medical images.

Impact of PACS systems on five dimensions of user effectiveness (after Montazeri & Khajouei, 2022)

Montazeri and Khajouei (2022) evaluated the impact of the PACS on different dimensions of users' work:

*   external communication
*   service quality
*   user intention to use the PACS
*   daily routine
*   complaints on users

They carried out a questionnaire survey of all PACS users in two academic hospitals of Kerman University of Medical Sciences in Iran, including radiologists, radiology staff, ward heads, and physicians. The users were drawn from two hospitals having different PACSs and medical specialties where the PACSs are available in all clinical wards of the hospitals.

The survey used questions based upon a Likert scale to investigate the impact of the PACS. It found that the respondents believed that PACS improves external communication, enhances service quality, streamlines daily routine, and reduces user complaints. Users who had used PACS would be more likely to use it again.

23.1.5 Pharmacy Information Management Systems (PIMS)

PIMS help hospitals and their pharmacists manage prescriptions more efficiently. It stores patient information, prescription details, dosage instructions, and refill history. It also ensures compliance with regulatory requirements and helps prevent medication errors.

These systems track medication inventory in real time, including stock levels, expiration dates, and reordering needs. They help optimise inventory levels, reducing wastage and stockouts. They may also offer automated ordering and inventory replenishment features.

The maintain comprehensive patient profiles, including medical history, allergies, and insurance information. Pharmacists can access this data to ensure safe medication dispensing and provide personalised care.

They facilitate billing processes, including insurance claims processing and reimbursement. It verifies insurance coverage, calculates co-payments, and generates invoices. Integration with insurance databases streamlines the claims submission process.

They will automatically check for potential drug interactions and contraindications when processing prescriptions. They will alert pharmacists to potential risks, enabling them to intervene and prevent adverse reactions.

They will help pharmacies comply with regulatory requirements, such as record-keeping, prescription tracking, and privacy regulations like the Health Insurance Portability and Accountability Act (HIPAA) in the US and the General Data Protection Regulations (GDPR) in the EU and the UK. They can provide evidence and audit trails to demonstrate compliance in the event of challenges or complaints.

Finally, they generate reports and analytics to help pharmacy managers monitor performance metrics such as prescription volume, inventory turnover, and revenue. These insights inform strategic decision-making and process improvement efforts.

They may interact with CDSSs to provide evidence-based recommendations for medication selection, dosing, and monitoring based on patient characteristics and medical history.

Although PIMS can provide benefits as stand-alone systems, they provide most benefits when integrated with other hospitals' systems. Once again, this creates a need for effective interoperability with other hospital management systems.

23.1.6 Inventory and supply chain management systems

Healthcare institutions have the responsibility of coordinating the planning, procurement, administration, supervision, monitoring, and transportation of various stocks, such as medications, medical tools, and supplies. These tasks are crucial for their day-to-day functions. The management of inventory and supply chains primarily aims at enhancing operational efficiency, cost control, and ensuring timely acquisition and distribution of necessary resources to enhance patient care (De Vries, 2011).

Efficient supply chain management plays a pivotal role in streamlining workflow and monitoring inventory levels, procurement processes, orders, and financial transactions. Effective supply chain management within healthcare facilities necessitates proficiency in cost management, inventory prediction, and space optimisation, whereas inventory management requires a deep understanding of logistical and financial aspects associated with stock (Dwivedi & Kothiyal, 2012). These management frameworks are instrumental in safeguarding organisations against both material and financial losses by maintaining precise and efficient records of items and supplies.

The sheer quantity of data and the need for real-time analysis means that hospitals are dependent upon inventory and supply chain management systems.

As with other management systems, hospitals gain benefits by defining and implementing structured and standardised workflows which are then facilitated by the management systems that guide users to follow the correct procedures and collect the required data.

Hospitals use software systems to monitor inventory levels in real-time. These systems track items as they are used, received, or expire, helping to prevent stockouts or overstock situations. Automated alerts can be set up to notify staff when inventory levels reach reorder points, ensuring timely replenishment.

Supply chain management systems streamline the procurement process by automating purchase orders, tracking deliveries, and managing vendor relationships. They may also incorporate features for price negotiation and contract management to optimise purchasing decisions.

Once supplies are received, inventory management systems facilitate efficient distribution within the hospital. They track the movement of items from central storage areas to various departments or units, ensuring that supplies are delivered to where they are needed when they are needed. This involves optimising logistics to minimise transportation costs and reduce delivery times.

The more advanced inventory and supply chain management systems use historical data and predictive analytics to forecast demand for medical supplies accurately. By analysing usage patterns, seasonal variations, and other factors, hospitals can anticipate their future needs and adjust inventory levels accordingly, reducing the risk of stockouts or excess inventory.

Hospitals must adhere to strict quality standards and regulatory requirements when managing their inventory and supply chains and management systems can assist with this. They include features for tracking expiration dates, lot numbers, and product recalls to ensure compliance with regulatory agencies such as the Food and Drug Administration (FDA) in the US. They also facilitate quality control processes, such as regular inspections and audits to maintain the integrity and safety of medical supplies.

Finally, effective inventory and supply chain management systems help hospitals control costs by optimising inventory levels, negotiating favourable contracts with suppliers, and minimising waste. These systems provide insights into spending patterns, budget allocation, and financial performance, enabling hospital administrators to make informed decisions to optimise resource utilisation and reduce expenses.

Use of Just in Time (JIT) procurement in hospitals (after Balkhi et al., 2022)

JIT is an innovative stock management strategy: a supply–demand system that attempts to precisely match the demand for care with supply. It was originally developed by the Toyota Motor Company in Japan and was then applied in a variety of industries worldwide, including healthcare.

It works by suppliers delivering small quantities of supplies as they are needed, which avoids the problem of overstocked inventory and eventually lowers operational costs. It reduces waste and eliminates non-value-added item, but requires a very effective inventory and supply chain management system and effective communications with suppliers.

One of the major concerns with JIT systems is the uncertainty and unpredictability of the volume of hospital work, which can pose a serious risk to hospital operations when the demand unexpectedly increases and the current inventory is insufficient.

For example, the COVID-19 pandemic substantially increased global demand whilst simultaneously disrupting global supply chains and therefore the flow of supplies, increasing demand for key materials.

As a result, many hospitals have adopted a buffered approach to JIT following the pandemic, where a small inventory is maintained in reserve to cope with variations in supply and demand.

23.1.7 *External reporting systems*

Hospitals have a range of external stakeholders for whom they may need to provide information.

Where that information is required on a continual basis, aggregated anonymised data may be shared directly between the hospital management information systems and the systems of the external stakeholders. These exchanges may include the regulators that set standards and regulations for healthcare facilities. Hospitals must provide management information to demonstrate compliance with these regulations, including data on patient care quality, safety, staffing levels, and financial performance.

Hospitals share management information with funding agencies such as governments or health insurance providers to facilitate billing, claims processing, and reimbursement. This includes patient demographic data, treatment codes, and billing details necessary for insurance claims.

Hospitals often report other management information to government agencies responsible for healthcare oversight, public health surveillance, and funding allocation. This may include data on patient outcomes, infectious disease outbreaks, healthcare disparities, and utilisation rates.

Accrediting organisations, such as the Joint Commission, set standards for healthcare quality and safety. Hospitals share management information with these bodies to undergo accreditation surveys and maintain their accreditation status.

Hospitals collaborate with research institutions to conduct clinical trials, research studies, and data analysis aimed at advancing medical knowledge and improving patient care. They may share management information such as patient demographics, treatment protocols, and outcomes data for research purposes.

Whilst security and privacy are always important, where personally identifiable information is exchanged or personal identification of individuals may be possible by combination with other data, hospitals must comply with all data protection regulations, ensure that they have the correct permissions in place, and that their security is commensurate with the sensitivity of the information exchanged.

23.1.8 Knowledge review

Before you move on, can you define the following key concepts:

- Patient Administration System (PAS)?
- Interoperability?

23.1.9 Question to think about

Which of these systems (if any) have you interacted with as a patient?

Did they make your life easier? If you have interacted with any of them, which do you think would improve the service offered by your healthcare provider?

23.2 Big data and data analytics

Data analytics techniques are increasingly used to analyse and derive insights from large healthcare datasets for management as well as research purposes. The term "big data" is applied to data sets that are not simply large but have a number of characteristics which make their analysis difficult. Different writers have characterised big data in terms of a variety of criteria.

According to Kaisler et al. (2013), Laney articulated one of the first definitions of big data in 2001 in terms of three Vs: Volume, Velocity, and Variety:

Oguntimilehin and Ademola (2014) presented big data in terms of five Vs: Volume, Velocity, Variety, Variability, and Value and Complexity. Other authors have defined up to ten different criteria. In practice, many of these additional criteria are not unique to big data but merely desirable characteristics of any data set.

Kapil et al. (2016) define the original core characteristics of big data as:

- Volume – the quantity of collected and stored data
- Velocity - the transfer rate of data between source and destination
- Variety – number of different types of data such as pictures, videos, audio, etc.

These characteristics render big data difficult to analyse suing conventional methods and so new methods have been devised and implemented, often referred to as data analytics or advanced analytics.

Advanced analytics, including machine learning and artificial intelligence, can identify patterns, predict outcomes, and support decision-making. The use of data analytics as a model for predicting risks and targeting care requires a structured process (Figure 23.2).

The stages of the process are described in more detail in Table 23.1 below:

The use of analytics is often classified in terms of four distinct types:

- Descriptive Analytics: What is happening?
- Diagnostic Analytics: Why is it happening?
- Predictive Analytics: What is likely to happen?
- Prescriptive Analytics: What do I need to do?

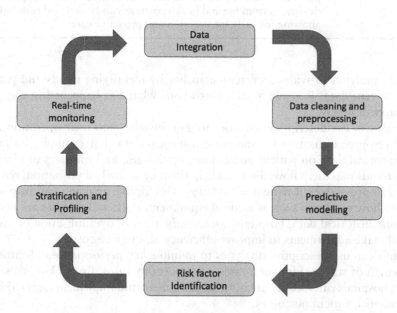

Figure 23.2 Use of data analytics predicting risks and targeting care as a structured cyclical process.

Table 23.1 Use of data analytics predicting risks and targeting care as a structured cyclical process

Phase	Description
Data Integration	Data analytics starts with integrating various sources of healthcare data, such as electronic health records (EHRs), medical imaging, laboratory results, genomics, wearable devices, and demographic information. By combining these diverse datasets, a more comprehensive view of patients' health can be established.
Data Cleaning and Pre-processing	Once the data is collected, it undergoes a process of cleaning and pre-processing. This involves removing duplicates, correcting errors, handling missing values, and standardising formats. Data quality is essential to ensure accurate and reliable analysis.
Predictive Modelling	Data analytics employs predictive modelling techniques to identify patients at high risk. By applying machine learning algorithms, patterns and correlations within the data can be discovered. Historical patient data is used to train models that can predict the likelihood of developing specific diseases based on various risk factors.
Risk Factor Identification	Data analytics can help identify the risk factors associated with particular diseases. By analysing large datasets, patterns can emerge, indicating factors such as genetics, lifestyle choices, environmental exposures, comorbidities, and demographic characteristics that contribute to disease development. These insights enable healthcare providers to assess the risk of individual patients.
Stratification and Profiling	With the help of data analytics, patients can be stratified into different risk groups based on their individual characteristics and risk factors. This allows healthcare providers to prioritise resources and interventions for patients at higher risk, ensuring timely preventive measures and early interventions.
Real-time Monitoring	Data analytics can integrate real-time data streams, such as wearable devices, continuous monitoring, and patient-reported data, to monitor patients' health status. By continuously analysing this data, any deviations from normal health patterns can be detected promptly, allowing for early intervention and proactive care.

Descriptive analytics provides a current snapshot by identifying trends and patterns of past and current data. It answers questions about what has happened in the past and what is happening now.

Hospitals can use descriptive analytics to gain insights into their operations, patient care, and resource utilisation by analysing historical data. For example, hospitals can analyse historical data on patient admissions, discharges, and transfers to identify patterns and trends in patient flow. This can help them optimise bed utilisation, reduce wait times, and improve overall patient satisfaction. Descriptive analytics can help hospitals understand how resources such as medical equipment, staff, and supplies are being used. By analysing historical data, hospitals can identify areas of overutilisation or underutilisation and make adjustments to improve efficiency and reduce costs.

Hospitals can use descriptive analytics to monitor key performance indicators (KPIs) such as length of stay, readmission rates, and mortality rates. By tracking these metrics over time, hospitals can identify areas for improvement and implement targeted interventions to enhance patient outcomes.

Descriptive analytics can be used to analyse historical data on inventory levels, procurement cycles, and supply chain disruptions. Hospitals can identify patterns and trends in supply usage and demand to optimise inventory levels, reduce stockouts, and minimise waste.

Hospitals can use descriptive analytics to analyse financial data such as revenue, expenses, and reimbursement rates. By tracking financial metrics over time, they can identify opportunities to improve revenue cycle management, reduce costs, and enhance financial performance.

Descriptive analytics can be used to analyse clinical data such as patient outcomes, adherence to clinical guidelines, and compliance with quality metrics. Hospitals can identify variations in care delivery and implement quality improvement initiatives to standardise care practices and improve patient outcomes.

Diagnostic analytics focuses on the reasonings behind trends and patterns that are identified in the previous stage, helping to discover the factors for past performance. Diagnostic analytics can provide hospitals with valuable insights into various aspects of their operations, clinical practices, and financial performance, enabling them to make data-driven decisions to optimise efficiency, improve patient outcomes, and enhance overall performance.

For example, by analysing historical patient data, including demographics, medical history, and diagnostic tests, hospitals can develop predictive models to identify patients who may be at higher risk for diseases such as diabetes, heart disease, or sepsis. This enables hospitals to implement targeted interventions and preventive measures to improve patient outcomes and reduce healthcare costs.

Diagnostic analytics can help hospitals identify operational inefficiencies and bottlenecks in processes such as patient flow, resource allocation, and staffing. By analysing historical operational data, hospitals can identify patterns and root causes of inefficiencies and implement targeted interventions to improve workflow, reduce wait times, and enhance overall operational performance.

Hospitals can use diagnostic analytics to analyse billing and claims data to identify patterns of denials, coding errors, and reimbursement delays. By identifying the root causes of revenue cycle issues, hospitals can implement corrective actions to improve billing accuracy, reduce denials, and optimise revenue capture.

Diagnostic analytics can be used to analyse financial data to identify patterns indicative of fraudulent activities, such as billing for services not rendered or upcoding. Hospitals can use advanced analytics techniques, such as anomaly detection and predictive modelling, to detect suspicious patterns and prevent fraudulent behaviour, thereby safeguarding financial resources and maintaining compliance with regulatory requirements.

Hospitals can use diagnostic analytics to analyse patient feedback data from surveys, social media, and online reviews to identify trends and patterns in patient satisfaction and experience. By understanding the factors influencing patient satisfaction, hospitals can implement targeted initiatives to improve the patient experience and enhance overall satisfaction levels.

Predictive analytics enables the identification of specific risk factors for different groups, employing techniques such as remote personalised health monitoring and artificial intelligence in healthcare IT. For instance, it can identify diabetes patients who are at a high risk of being hospitalised by considering factors like age, concurrent chronic diseases, medication adherence, and previous patterns of personalised home care. By predicting the occurrence of diseases and chronic illnesses through this research, early treatments can be initiated to reduce emergency department visits and hospital readmission rates.

Rather than relying on routine check-ups, proactive treatment can be provided by sending reminders via email or phone calls to encourage patients to come in, visit a specialist, or undergo specific screenings or imaging tests. Moreover, patients can be made aware of various health concerns through targeted email campaigns, such as the effects of smoking, and assistance can be offered to those who wish to quit.

In the realm of risk assessment and threshold warnings, predictive healthcare IT analytics solutions can assist patients as well as the hospital in making informed decisions. This technology facilitates personalised messaging to remind patients about medication refills and offers support in case they encounter difficulties in obtaining refills or visiting the pharmacy.

The ultimate goal is to reduce readmissions, emergency department visits, and other undesirable events in the future. Those responsible for care can receive notifications from AI systems when patients deviate from their treatment plans, enabling targeted outreach. Such seamless patient experiences foster better adherence to care pathways and, consequently, lead to improved health outcomes.

Prescriptive analytics uses machine learning, algorithms, and business rules to provide specific solutions and recommendations on what to do next to achieve a desired outcome.

By utilising predictive analytics, practitioners can optimise treatment strategies and enhance patient outcomes. AI algorithms can leverage information about a patient's existing illnesses, medications, and personal history to identify similar individuals within a population cohort.

Machine learning algorithms can then identify patterns in electronic medical record (EMR) data to group patients with similar characteristics and develop therapeutic strategies that yield the best patient outcomes. The treatment plans derived from aggregating data are then presented to physicians for review, aiding them in making the most appropriate choices for their patients. To date, this kind of use of data analytics still requires human supervision because AI technology lacks self-awareness and cannot check its own results.

**Real world applications of data analytics after
Raghupathi and Raghupathi (2014)**

Premier, a healthcare alliance network operating in the United States, has used its extensive network of more than 2,700 members, which includes hospitals, health systems, non-acute facilities, and physicians, to establish a sizable repository of clinical, financial, patient, and supply chain data. This wealth of data has allowed Premier to generate comprehensive and comparable measures of clinical outcomes, resource utilisation reports, and detailed cost data. These insights have informed decision-making processes and led to improvements in healthcare processes across approximately 330 hospitals. As a result, it is estimated that Premier's initiatives have saved around 29,000 lives and reduced healthcare spending by nearly $7 billion (IBM, 2013).

North York General Hospital in Toronto, Canada has employed real-time analytics within its operations to enhance patient outcomes and gain valuable insights.

By implementing a scalable real-time analytics application, the hospital can examine clinical, administrative, and financial perspectives simultaneously (IBM, 2013).

Columbia University Medical Center is harnessing big data analytics to examine real-time physiological data from patients with brain injuries to promptly provide vital information to medical professionals for aggressive complication treatment. The advanced analytics used have enabled the early detection of serious complications, up to 48 hours sooner than traditional methods, in patients who suffered a bleeding stroke from a ruptured brain aneurysm (IBM, 2013).

Meanwhile, the Rizzoli Orthopaedic Institute in Bologna, Italy, is employing advanced analytics to gain a comprehensive understanding of clinical variations among families. This approach has led to a notable 30% reduction in annual hospitalisations and a substantial 60% decrease in the number of imaging tests for individual patients with varying symptom severity. The institute also aims to use these insights to explore the impact of genetic factors, aiming for more effective treatment approaches in the future (IBM, 2013).

Lastly, the Hospital for Sick Children (Sick Kids) in Toronto is leveraging analytics to enhance outcomes for infants at risk of life-threatening "nosocomial infections." By analysing data from bedside monitoring devices in real-time using advanced analytics, Sick Kids can now identify potential signs of infection as early as 24 hours before previous methods allowed (IHTT, 2013).

Brigham and Women's Hospital in Boston and the University of Michigan Health System have employed personal experience and big data analytics research to standardise surgical procedures and blood transfusion practices, respectively, resulting in improved outcomes and reduced costs. The National Institute for Health and Clinical Excellence (NICE) in the UK and the Italian Medicines Agency use clinical datasets to explore the effectiveness of new drugs and treatments. The Department of Veterans Affairs (VA) uses its extensive data set to comply with performance-based accountability frameworks. Kaiser Permanente successfully associated clinical and cost data, leading to the identification of adverse drug effects and the withdrawal of Vioxx from the market (IHTT, 2013).

Analytics has also demonstrated its potential in predicting flu-related emergency room visits using data from Google Flu Trends, tracking the spread of cholera in Haiti through Twitter updates and predicting outcomes for diabetes patients based on panel data linked to physicians and population health management averages and outperformed traditional surveillance methods (Raghupathi & Raghupathi, 2014).

Blue Cross Blue Shield of Massachusetts integrated analytics into its business processes to provide decision-makers with insights into financial and medical data. This enabled medical directors to identify high-risk disease groups and introduce preventive treatment protocols, leading to improved patient outcomes. Additionally, BCBSMA could generate complex health informatics reports significantly faster, aiding in more effective client servicing (IHTT, 2013).

23.2.1 Knowledge review

Before you move on, can you define the following key concepts:

- Data analytics?

23.2.2 *Question to think about*

- As a patient or carer, have you seen any examples of the use of data analytics in your own experiences?
- If so, how do you think they improved (or would improve) the service provided to patients? If not, how could data analytics have improved the service or outcomes if they had been available?
- Are there any disadvantages for patients that you can see?

References

Balkhi, B., Alshahrani, A., & Khan, A. (2022). Just-in-time approach in healthcare inventory management: Does it really work?. *Saudi Pharmaceutical Journal: SPJ: The Official Publication of the Saudi Pharmaceutical Society*, 30(12), 1830–1835.

De Vries, J. (2011). The shaping of inventory systems in health services: A stakeholder analysis. *International Journal of Production Economics*, 133(1), 60–69.

Dwivedi, S., & Kothiyal, P. (2012). Inventory management: A tool of identifying items that need greater attention for control. *The Pharma Innovation*, 1(7, Part A), 125.

Gibbon, G. A. (1996). A brief history of LIMS. *Laboratory Automation & Information Management*, 32(1), 1–5.

IBM. (2013). *Data driven healthcare organisations use big data analytics for big gains*. IBM.

IHTT. (2013). *Transforming health care through big data strategies for leveraging big data in the health care industry*. IHTT.

Kaisler, S., Armour, F., Espinosa, J. A., & Money, W. (2013). Big data: Issues and challenges moving forward. *Hawaii International Conference on System Sciences*, 46, 995–1003.

Kapil, G., Agrawal, A., & Khan, R. A. (2016). A study of big data characteristics. In 2016 *International conference on communication and electronics systems (ICCES)* (pp. 1–4). IEEE.

Montazeri, M., & Khajouei, R. (2022). Determining the effect of the picture archiving and communication system (PACS) on different dimensions of users' work. *Radiology Research and Practice*, 2022(1), 4306714.

Oguntimilehin, A., & Ademola, E. O. (2014, June). A review of big data management, benefits and challenges. *Journal of Emerging Trends in Computing and Information Sciences*, 5, 433–437.

Raghupathi, W., & Raghupathi, V. (2014). Big data analytics in healthcare: Promise and potential. *Health Information Science and Systems*, 2, 3.

SkyQuest. (2024). *Global VNA and PACS market size, share*. Growth Analysis, Report ID: SQMIG35A2153

24 Innovative technologies for healthcare

24.1 Telemedicine

Telemedicine is the provision of healthcare services remotely, typically through the use of telecommunications technology such as video conferencing, phone calls, text messaging, or secure messaging platforms. It allows patients to consult with healthcare professionals without the need for an in-person visit to a medical facility. Telemedicine encompasses a wide range of healthcare services, including diagnosis, treatment, monitoring, and education.

Traditionally, telemedicine was used to allow patients in remote or underserved areas to access primary and community healthcare services without the need to travel long distances. During and since the COVID-19 pandemic, its use has expanded to remove the need for patients to attend a clinic in person, even when they are close to a facility. The use of telemedicine accelerated rapidly during the COVID-19. However, it continues to be deployed because of a number of benefits:

- Telemedicine improves access to healthcare services, particularly for individuals in rural or underserved areas who may have limited access to medical facilities.
- Patients can consult with healthcare providers from the comfort of their own homes, reducing the need for travel and time spent in waiting rooms.
- It can be more cost-effective for both patients and healthcare providers, as it reduces overhead costs associated with in-person visits.
- It can streamline healthcare delivery by enabling quicker consultations and reducing the need for physical paperwork.
- It allows for ongoing monitoring and follow-up consultations, promoting continuity of care for patients with chronic conditions or those in need of regular check-ups.

Despite the benefits, there are also challenges and limitations, including issues related to data privacy and security, technological barriers for some patients, and limitations on the subtler clinician-patient interactions and in the types of medical services that can be effectively delivered remotely.

Telemedicine can enable general practitioners to access specialist advice or services remotely or facilitate communication between patients and primary and community healthcare services (Haleem, 2021). Patients can have virtual consultations with healthcare providers, discuss their symptoms, receive medical advice, and get prescriptions when necessary. Where necessary, a three-way conversation can be facilitated involving a specialist to prevent the need for a patient to attend a hospital.

DOI: 10.4324/9781003478874-30

This use of technology is increasingly reaching low-to-middle income countries, where it may offer cost effective solutions (Mars, 2013; Mensah et al., 2023).

Alternatively, telemedicine is useful for post-treatment or post-surgery follow-up appointments. Patients can communicate their progress and recovery to healthcare providers through virtual visits, reducing the need for unnecessary in-person visits.

Telemedicine can facilitate the continuous monitoring and management of chronic conditions like diabetes, hypertension, and asthma. Patients can use wearable devices to track vital signs and health parameters, and this data is transmitted to healthcare providers for remote monitoring. Healthcare providers can intervene if they notice any concerning trends, leading to better disease management. Telemedicine may also be used to remotely review and adjust medication regimens for patients. It ensures medication adherence and reduces the risk of medication errors (Peyroteo et al., 2021).

Telemedicine has been instrumental in expanding access to mental health and counselling services in primary and community healthcare settings. Patients can have confidential virtual sessions with therapists or counsellors, making mental healthcare more accessible and convenient.

Telemedicine helps in triaging patients and determining the urgency of care needed. Healthcare providers can remotely assess patients' symptoms and decide whether they require immediate attention in a community or hospital setting or can manage their conditions at home. Patient telephone advice services can combine basic triage facilities with general health advice and signposting. This model of telemedicine is not new; it has been operating since at least 1996 in the UK (Lattimer et al., 1996).

In some community health centres, telehealth monitoring stations are set up to allow patients to perform basic health checks under the remote guidance of a healthcare professional. These stations are equipped with necessary devices to measure vital signs like blood pressure, heart rate, and temperature, and the data is sent to healthcare providers for review.

Telemedicine can be used for remote monitoring of patients' vital signs, health indicators, or specific health conditions. Patients have the option to make use of wearable devices, mobile applications, or other connected tools to collect and transmit data, such as blood pressure, heart rate, glucose levels, or activity levels. Healthcare providers can then review this data and intervene as necessary. With the widespread use of smartphones, mobile apps have gained popularity in telemedicine. These apps enable patients to schedule appointments, communicate with healthcare providers through messaging or video calls, access electronic health records, receive medication reminders, track health metrics, and more. This provides an effective telemedicine platform in low-to-middle income countries where digital infrastructure is poor and mobile phones are how most people access the Internet (Mahmoud et al., 2022).

Many healthcare providers offer online portals or web-based platforms where patients can securely access their medical records, test results, appointment scheduling, and communicate with healthcare professionals via messaging or email. These portals enhance patient engagement, streamline communication, and may be integrated with mobile applications.

Telemedicine also enables other services such as triage, allowing patients to remotely consult with healthcare professionals to assess the urgency and severity of their condition. Based on this assessment, appropriate recommendations for further care or referrals can be made. Additionally, telemedicine facilitates remote pharmacy services, allowing patients to consult with pharmacists, ask medication-related questions, receive medication counselling, and even obtain prescription refills without visiting a physical pharmacy.

Implant telemetry, a method of remotely monitoring implanted medical devices like pacemakers, defibrillators, neurostimulators, and implantable cardiac monitors, may be used for passive monitoring but is increasingly used for active management of devices. This can improve patient care, convenience, and outcomes by reducing the need for frequent in-person visits and enabling timely interventions.

Implantable devices equipped with sensors and communication capabilities can collect and store data on device performance and patient health. Telemedicine enables secure transmission of this data to remote monitoring centres or healthcare providers. The data transmitted may include parameters like heart rate, device battery status, pacing thresholds, and arrhythmia events. Automated systems can monitor this data in real-time, triggering alerts for healthcare providers in case of abnormal events, allowing for timely interventions to ensure patient safety.

Furthermore, healthcare providers may use the technology to remotely adjust device settings when appropriate and clinically safe, avoiding the need for patients to visit medical facilities for minor adjustments. Associated telemedicine systems facilitate remote consultations and follow-up appointments, allowing patients to discuss their symptoms, concerns, or questions with healthcare providers through video conferencing or telephonic consultations. This ensures regular monitoring and ongoing management of the implanted device without frequent in-person visits.

The data collected from implantable devices can be presented directly within video consultations, facilitating informed discussions between patients and healthcare providers. Additionally, healthcare professionals can remotely analyse this data using specialised software or platforms to monitor trends, track treatment effectiveness, and make informed decisions regarding patient care.

Telemedicine technology also supports patient education and support, allowing healthcare providers to remotely educate patients about their implanted devices, functionalities, and care instructions. This empowers patients to understand and manage their devices effectively, with access to information, resources, and support to troubleshoot common issues.

The uptake of implant telemetry is growing, with the global market projected to increase from 1.27 billion USD in 2022 to 1.75 billion USD in 2031, reflecting increasing recognition of its benefits and adoption in healthcare settings (Research Reports World, 2023).

Within home care services, telemedicine can enhance services for older adults, promoting independence and overall well-being by reducing barriers to care access, ensuring regular monitoring, and enhancing communication between older adults, healthcare providers, and caregivers. Telemedicine platforms enable older individuals to consult with healthcare providers without the need for travel, facilitating regular check-ups, medication management, and monitoring of chronic conditions.

Telemedicine helps with medication management for older adults by allowing healthcare providers to remotely review medication lists, prescribe or adjust medications, and provide guidance on usage. It also enables medication reminders and remote monitoring of vital signs and health parameters using wearable devices or mobile apps. Additionally, telemedicine can support fall prevention through virtual assessments, home safety evaluations, and personalised exercise or physical therapy programs, as well as monitor patients living alone and trigger an alarm in the event of a fall.

Telemedicine can also be used to provide mental health support and counselling for older individuals through remote therapy sessions, promoting their emotional well-being and reducing the risk of cognitive decline. At the same time, it can improve care coordination among healthcare providers, caregivers, and family members through virtual meetings, facilitating care planning and coordination of services.

However, older adults face barriers to accessing digital technology, such as age-related declines in online service use and digital competence. Cognitive abilities, motivation, physical limitations, and perceptual problems also hinder successful engagement with digital platforms. Concerns about privacy, security, limited technology access, and financial constraints may further impede adoption among older adults, whatever their level of motivation to use information technology.

In hospital settings, within operating theatres, telemedicine may be used to enhance surgical care by providing remote assistance, tele-mentoring, and real-time monitoring of patients during and after surgery. Surgeons can seek guidance from remote experts during complex procedures, improving patient outcomes. Robotic surgery systems offer advanced technology and precision, minimising trauma, blood loss, and recovery times. The technology allows remote surgeons to perform procedures, particularly useful in scenarios with limited access to specialised surgical expertise or in emergency situations requiring immediate intervention.

Robots integrated with imaging technologies provide real-time, high-resolution images during surgery, enabling accurate navigation and precise interventions while minimising damage to healthy tissues. In gastrointestinal and thoracic surgeries, robotic systems perform endoscopic procedures, offering improved visualisation and manoeuvrability for precise interventions.

Advanced applications of telemedicine and robotics in surgery offer many potential advantages but represent significant risks, and so are subject to regulatory oversight to ensure patient safety. All tools impacting patient care are subject to medical device regulation, with the highest-risk tools subject to rigorous regulations.

Barriers to use of telehealth technologies amongst older people

In spite of the benefits, significant obstacles exist for older individuals in adopting digital technology. Research conducted by Heponiemi et al. (2022) examined the interplay between age and digital proficiency in the utilisation of online health and social care services. Their results demonstrated that as individuals age, there is a diminishing likelihood of engaging in online activities such as accessing test results, renewing medical prescriptions, or scheduling appointments. This decline was particularly pronounced among individuals aged approximately 60 and older. Nonetheless, those with strong digital skills were able to partially counteract this decline in online service utilisation, although this effect waned among the oldest participants, typically around the age of 80.

Heponiemi et al. (2022) highlighted the risk of older adults being marginalised from digital platforms, corroborating earlier research indicating a decline in Internet and online service usage with increasing age (Vasilescu et al., 2020). Previous studies often categorised participants into age groups, complicating the identification of when this decline begins and its progression. Heponiemi et al. (2022) revealed a non-linear relationship between age and online service utilisation, with no discernible pattern before the age of 60, but a notable decrease in usage as individuals advance in age. Another study echoed these findings, indicating reduced interest in health-related technology among individuals over 75 compared to those aged 50 to 64 (Cherid et al., 2020).

24.1.1 Knowledge review

Before you move on, can you define the following key concepts:

- Telemedicine?
- Implant telemetry?

24.1.2 Question to think about

How could telemedicine improve your access to healthcare services?

24.2 Technology-enhanced medical education

24.2.1 Technology-enhanced learning

Technology-enhanced learning (TEL) has become increasingly important in medical education, offering various advancements and benefits. One example is the flipped classroom approach, where learners are provided with video-based information before class, allowing class time to be dedicated to problem-solving activities. Problem or team-based learning sessions enable instant retrieval and sharing of information among peers and faculty through portable devices.

High-fidelity simulation and computerised mannequins provide a safe environment for learners to participate in clinical scenarios, gaining knowledge and skills for real-life patient interactions. Computer-based instruction has also transformed assessment practices, with exams being delivered electronically, providing instant feedback (Sharma et al., 2017).

The accessibility of the internet via portable devices has empowered doctors to access clinical information instantly, both in the ward and clinic settings. Platforms that offer expert knowledge and medical journals are increasingly available through apps. Online knowledge-based modules allow doctors to further their learning, incorporating assessment and providing immediate feedback. This is particularly valuable since formal examination feedback is often limited.

Technology has facilitated the documentation of learners' progress through online portfolios. Trainees and specialists can record their competency across various domains and engage in reflective writing to document their experiences. With the introduction of revalidation in the UK and the American Board of Medical Specialties (ABMS) Portfolio Program in the US, electronic portfolios have become essential for record keeping and performance distribution.

However, despite the positive impact of technology in medical education, a key concern is the lack of recognition of individual learners' needs. TEL is currently delivered uniformly to a large cohort, disregarding individual knowledge, understanding, and skills. Learners progress at different rates and have varying knowledge gaps. Large-scale lectures and seminars often limit individual engagement due to time constraints. To fully realise the potential of TEL, it is crucial to address learner diversity and engagement by leveraging technology for personalised and adaptive learning experiences.

24.2.2 Adaptive learning

Adaptive learning (AL) offers an individualised learning process through technology that identifies learners' strengths and weaknesses. By recognising strengths, the learning material can be modified to focus more on individual limitations. For instance, The University of New South Wales implemented AL in a massive open online course (MOOC), "Learning to Teach Online," where personalised learning content was generated based on learners' responses and self-reflection information. Research on the use of AL has shown increased pass rates and decreased course withdrawals (Zimmer, 2014).

Adaptation in AL extends beyond content customisation. It also includes an adaptive system interface that meets learner preferences for navigation and course structure. Additionally, content discovery and assembly from multiple sources, such as web-based learning repositories, and the use of discussion forums connect learners with peers and faculty based on individual learner profiles and requirements.

Massive Open Online Courses (MOOCs) emerged in the second decade of this century. MOOCs are typically offered by universities, educational institutions, or online learning platforms. They provide free or affordable access to high-quality educational content on a wide range of subjects, including medicine and healthcare. They have a number of defining characteristics.

They are designed to accommodate a large number of participants simultaneously. They can attract thousands or even hundreds of thousands of learners from diverse backgrounds. They are open to anyone who wishes to enrol. There are usually no prerequisites or admission requirements, making them accessible to learners worldwide.

They are delivered entirely online through a learning management system or a dedicated online platform. Participants can access course materials, watch video lectures, participate in discussions, and complete assignments remotely. They often incorporate various multimedia elements, including video lectures, interactive quizzes, readings, and discussion forums. These resources aim to enhance the learning experience and cater to different learning preferences.

Typically, MOOCs offer flexible learning schedules, allowing participants to learn at their own pace. Learners can access course materials and complete assignments according to their availability and preferences. They often include discussion forums or other means of communication that enable learners to interact with each other. This fosters collaboration, knowledge sharing, and the opportunity to engage in meaningful discussions with fellow participants.

MOOCs may provide assessments or quizzes to evaluate learners' understanding of the course material. Some MOOCs also offer certificates of completion or achievement for those who successfully meet the course requirements. Certificates may be free or available for a fee, depending on the MOOC provider.

When MOOCs first emerged, there was much optimism about them (Harder, 2013). However, by 2019, initial hopes had not been realised. Reich and Ruipérez-Valiente (2019) conducted an analysis of data encompassing all the MOOCs offered by MIT and Harvard University up until May 2018. The dataset included more than 12 million course registrations from approximately 5.6 million learners. The findings revealed that the majority of MOOC learners do not continue their studies beyond the first year, and a significant portion of registrants tend to disengage soon after enrolling. The majority (52%) of those who sign up for a course do not even access the course materials.

High dropout rates and low completion rates can be ascribed to several factors, including uninspiring MOOC content, limited interactivity, insufficient personal motivation, and the challenge level of courses. Since the majority of MOOC content is designed to be accessible without charge, the expenses involved in development are typically minimised. Consequently, numerous courses consist merely of electronic pages that fulfil the basic criteria for earning CME credits or meeting compliance stand-ards. This passive form of learning fails to capture learners' interest or encourage deep engagement, ultimately leading to limited retention of knowledge in the long term. (Setia et al., 2019).

Shortly after this study was published, the COVID-19 pandemic arrived and this trig-gered a massive growth in technology-assisted education in medicine and health care. However, this technology has often been deployed within more traditional frameworks and the MOOC model has not achieved the disruption of mainstream medical and health education that was predicted

24.2.3 *Virtual reality in medical education*

Virtual reality (VR) has gained significant traction in medical education due to its abil-ity to create immersive and realistic learning experiences. It is still an emerging field and there are a variety of definitions:

The US Department of Defense (2018, p. 40) defines VR as:

> The use of computer technology to create an interactive three-dimensional world in which the objects have a sense of spatial presence; virtual environment and virtual world are synonyms for virtual reality.

Lopreiato et al. (2016, p. 40) defined VR as:

> A wide variety of computer-based applications commonly associated with immer-sive, highly visual, 3D characteristics that allow the participant to look about and navigate within a seemingly real or physical world. It is generally defined based on the type of technology being used, such as head-mounted displays, stereoscopic capa-bility, input devices, and the number of sensory systems stimulated.

VR offers a range of applications that enhance medical training and education in various ways. Here are some prominent uses of virtual reality in medical education.

VR technology can help students to learn about anatomy. It allows students to explore virtual anatomical models in three dimensions. They can examine detailed structures, manipulate organs and tissues, and gain a deeper understanding of complex anatomical relationships. VR provides a more engaging and interactive learning experience com-pared to traditional methods, such as textbooks or cadaver dissection.

VR enables medical students and surgeons to practice surgical procedures in a safe and controlled virtual environment. They can manipulate virtual instruments, perform intricate procedures, and interact with realistic anatomical models. This immersive train-ing helps develop surgical skills, hand-eye coordination, and decision-making abilities without the risks associated with live surgery.

Virtual reality can be used to simulate patient encounters, enabling medical students to practice communication, empathy, and bedside manner. VR scenarios can present a variety of challenging situations, such as breaking bad news or dealing with diffi-cult patients, allowing students to develop crucial interpersonal skills in a controlled environment.

VR can enhance the interpretation of medical imaging, such as MRI or CT scans. Students can immerse themselves in a virtual radiology suite, examine virtual patient cases, and learn to interpret scans more accurately. This technology helps improve diagnostic skills and aids in understanding complex imaging modalities.

For complex surgeries, VR can be used to create a simulation of the procedure to allow even more experienced surgeons to rehearse a procedure before carrying out the procedure on a live patient.

VR is being widely adopted and investment in this technology is increasing. Fortune Business Insights forecast that the global VR in healthcare market size will grow from $3.11 billion in 2023 to $25.22 billion by 2030, at an annualised growth rate of 34.9% (Fortune Business Insights, 2023).

Virtual reality in medical education and clinical care (after Dhar et al., 2023)

Dhar et al. (2023) conducted a comprehensive review of recent advancements in VR)applications within therapeutic care and medical education, specifically focusing on training medical students and aiding patients. Initially, they identified 3743 studies, from which 28 were ultimately chosen for inclusion in their review. Of these, 11 studies concentrated on medical education, assessing various aspects including knowledge, skills, attitudes, confidence, self-efficacy, and empathy. The remaining 17 studies centred on clinical care, with a particular emphasis on mental health and rehabilitation. Notably, 13 of these studies also explored user experiences and feasibility alongside clinical outcomes.

Eight rehabilitation studies included in the review were primarily centred on therapy using VR and examined its effects on motor performance. Within these studies seven VR-based training programs exhibited enhancements in patients' physical capabilities, such as fine motor recovery, upper extremity function, dexterity, gait speed and resistance, balance, gripping strength, mobility, walking duration, and the degree of independence in performing daily activities. While the other trial did not achieve statistical significance, it still showcased the potential of the VR system to expand access to care.

Their findings indicate that healthcare professionals are increasingly using VR to enhance patient care and to provide more effective training for both medical practitioners and students. The literature underscores the widespread adoption of VR as a tool for educating medical students and for managing the health and rehabilitation of patients across various medical conditions. In the realm of medical education, nine out of eleven studies reported positive outcomes in terms of knowledge acquisition, skill development, confidence building, and empathy enhancement. Moreover, VR has emerged as a promising asset in clinical care, with 13 out of 17 studies in this domain demonstrating positive results, particularly in the context of rehabilitation programs and mental health interventions.

24.2.4 *Knowledge review*

Before you move on, can you define the following key concepts:

- Massive open online courses (MOOCs)?

24.2.5 *Question to think about*

How do you like to learn?
    How do you use technology to improve your learning?

24.3 Personalised Medicine

Personalised medicine is an approach to medical treatment and prevention that takes into account individual variability in genes, environment, and lifestyle for each person. It involves tailoring medical decisions, practices, interventions, and treatments to the characteristics of each individual patient.

Personalised medicine involves analysing an individual's genetic makeup, including variations in genes (such as single nucleotide polymorphisms (SNPs), gene expression profiles, and other molecular markers to understand the individual's disease susceptibility, progression, and response to treatment.

Personalised medicine often relies on identifying specific biomarkers that can predict how a patient will respond to a particular therapy or how their disease is progressing. Biomarkers are measurable indicators of biological processes, disease states, or responses to treatment.

Personalised medicine requires the integration and analysis of diverse types of data, including genomic data, clinical data, imaging data, and patient-reported outcomes. Advanced computational and analytical techniques are often used to derive insights from these data and make personalised treatment recommendations.

Personalised medicine may be used for treatment or prevention. Based on the individual's genetic and molecular profile, personalised medicine aims to develop tailored treatment strategies that maximise therapeutic efficacy while minimising adverse effects. This may involve selecting the most appropriate medication, dosage, or treatment regimen for each patient.

Personalised medicine can also be used to develop preventive strategies based on an individual's genetic and environmental risk factors. By identifying individuals who are at increased risk of developing certain diseases, personalised medicine aims to implement targeted interventions to prevent or delay disease onset.

Personalised medicine offers a range of advantages over traditional approaches to healthcare, shown in Table 24.1

While personalised medicine has great potential, it also creates challenges (Kasztura, et al. (2019):

> One of the primary challenges of personalised medicine is the cost associated with genetic testing, data analysis, and tailored treatments. These technologies and interventions can be expensive, limiting access for certain populations, particularly those in low-income or resource-limited settings. Although costs of genetic testing are falling all the time, the costs of many specialised treatments remain high.

Personalised medicine relies on the integration and interpretation of vast amounts of genetic, molecular, and clinical data. Analysing this complex information requires specialised expertise and sophisticated computational tools, which may not be readily available in all healthcare settings.

Table 24.1 Advantages of personalised medicine over traditional approaches to healthcare.

Benefit	Explanation
Improved Treatment Efficacy	By tailoring medical interventions to the individual characteristics of each patient, personalised medicine can enhance treatment efficacy. This means that patients are more likely to receive therapies that are optimised to target their specific disease pathways, leading to better outcomes.
Reduced Adverse Effects	Personalised medicine aims to minimise the occurrence of adverse effects by selecting treatments that are better tolerated by individual patients. By considering genetic factors, biomarkers, and other patient-specific variables, healthcare providers can avoid prescribing medications that may be ineffective or harmful to certain individuals.
Optimised Drug Selection	Personalised medicine enables healthcare providers to select the most appropriate medications for each patient based on their genetic and molecular profile. This can help avoid the trial-and-error approach often associated with medication prescribing, leading to faster symptom relief and improved patient satisfaction.
Targeted Preventive Interventions	By identifying individuals at increased risk of developing certain diseases, personalised medicine allows for targeted preventive interventions. This may include lifestyle modifications, screening programs, or prophylactic treatments aimed at reducing disease incidence and improving long-term health outcomes.
Potential Cost Savings	Although initial implementation costs may be higher due to the need for genetic testing and data analysis, personalised medicine has the potential to generate cost savings over the long term. By reducing the likelihood of treatment failures, adverse events, and unnecessary medical interventions, personalised medicine can lead to more efficient use of healthcare resources.
Empowerment of Patients	Personalised medicine empowers patients by involving them in their healthcare decisions and providing them with personalised information about their health risks and treatment options. This can lead to greater patient engagement, adherence to treatment plans, and overall satisfaction with healthcare services.

The use of genetic and molecular data in personalised medicine raises ethical concerns related to privacy, informed consent, and the potential for discrimination based on genetic information. Safeguarding patient privacy and ensuring the responsible use of genetic data are critical considerations in the implementation of personalised medicine.

While genetic and molecular markers can provide valuable insights into disease risk and treatment response, they do not always have perfect predictive power. Many diseases are influenced by a complex interplay of genetic, environmental, and lifestyle factors, making it challenging to accurately predict individual outcomes based solely on genetic information. Further, reaching genuinely informed patient consent may be difficult due to both the complexity and uncertainties associated with decisions about personalised treatments. Human biology is inherently variable, and individuals may respond differently to the same treatment based on factors such as genetic background, disease stage, and environmental exposures. Personalised medicine must contend with this variability and the inherent uncertainty in predicting individual responses to treatment.

Botham et al. (2021) found that members of the public were largely unfamiliar with the term personalised medicine and its implications in respect of cancer treatments. Smittenaar et al. (2016) suggest this lack of awareness is a major barrier to the integrating personalised medicine within healthcare systems. Public difficulties in understanding personalised medicine are not confined to cancer. In a study of parents with a child undergoing personalised medicine testing, Zhang et al. 2014). reported that a proper explanation of genomic testing from healthcare professionals is the most important issue that needs to be addressed.

Despite a lack of knowledge, a systematic review by Holden et al. (2019) found that the public are keen to integrate personalised treatments into standard clinical practice. They found that this was particularly true in studies of conditions such as asthma and depression

Personalised medicine encompasses a wide range of technologies, tests, and treatments, which may lack standardisation and regulation. The variability in quality and reliability across different personalised medicine interventions can pose challenges for healthcare providers and patients in evaluating their efficacy and safety, and in ensuring regulatory compliance.

Vicente et al. (2020) outline a vision proposed by the International Consortium for Personalised Medicine on how personalised medicine will influence healthcare by 2030.

Their vision is based upon five perspectives:

- individual and public engagement
- involvement of health professionals
- implementation within healthcare systems
- health-related data, and
- the development of sustainable economic models

They argue that this will depend upon four pillars: data and technology. synergies between healthcare and research, a shift in focus from treatment to risk definition, patient stratification, and personalised health promotion and disease prevention strategies, and finally changes in medical and other healthcare provider education.

The International Consortium for Personalised Medicine's vision of healthcare in 2030 driven by personalised medicine (after Vicente et al., 2020)

In their vision of the future, by 2030, digital technology has become an integral part of maintaining the health and well-being of individuals. A shift in attitudes towards digital technology and data sharing has occurred, primarily driven by a new generation that seamlessly integrates digital tools and social networks into their daily lives. This generation exhibits greater control over their health data, leading to increased involvement in healthcare decisions and willingness to share data for research purposes. Regulatory frameworks and data management protocols have evolved to meet international standards, prioritising the protection of personal rights concerning data security, accessibility, storage, and curation.

Comprehensive personal health data is easily accessible through Electronic Health Records Wearable devices, mobile apps, and biomarker technology enable continuous and real-time monitoring of health parameters and behaviours.

Advancements in understanding genomic variations allow for the identification of individual genomic risk profiles for common diseases, emphasising preventive measures. Additionally, other biological information such as epigenomics, proteomics, and metabolomics complement genomic-risk assessments, offering monitoring tools for individuals at risk. The continuous evolution of data generation necessitates innovative IT solutions to address the storage, management, access, safety, and sharing needs of personalised medicine models. Interoperability and harmonisation concepts are integrated into healthcare and research systems through standardised data collection tools. Substantial investments in artificial intelligence facilitate the efficient integration and interpretation of data from diverse sources, supporting clinical decision-making.

Synergies between healthcare and research sectors leverage routine healthcare data for research purposes, enabling patient stratification and personalised clinical trials. Alignment between healthcare providers, researchers, and patients promotes user-driven biomedical and clinical research, facilitating the translation of research findings into clinical practice. The integration of various parameters influencing health outcomes, including lifestyle, socioeconomic status, and environmental exposure, enriches personal health data, fostering inter-sectoral synergies for health promotion and disease prevention.

Collaboration with the private sector is driven by the mutual benefits of technological advancement and novel business opportunities. personalised medicine stimulates innovation, particularly in digital technology, biomarker detection, and drug development. Partnership with the pharmaceutical industry enhances patient access to innovative treatments by providing data from clinical trials. Health technology assessment helps evaluate the true value of technologies, incentivising personalised medicine implementation.

Healthcare systems prioritise risk assessment, patient stratification, and personalised strategies, especially for aging populations. Economic sustainability and societal benefits are integral to personalised medicine implementation, with economic analyses considering broader societal perspectives and equity of access. Adequate reimbursement models support equitable healthcare delivery, acknowledging the long-term value of technology-based approaches.

Substantial investments in technological infrastructure and digital platforms maximise the economic value of public data ownership, necessitating new skills and professional profiles. Health professionals are trained in digital technologies, biomarker analysis, and data interpretation, working in multidisciplinary teams to make informed clinical decisions. Lifelong education and training are essential to keep pace with technological advancements.

Education and literacy initiatives focus on empowering citizens with personalised medicine knowledge, including ethical, regulatory, and data control aspects. Healthcare providers receive comprehensive training to become informed and responsible practitioners, emphasising digital literacy and multidisciplinary collaboration. Healthcare managers and policymakers have access to ample evidence supporting the benefits of PM, enabling the establishment of political frameworks to address effectiveness, efficiency, equity, and ethical concerns surrounding personalised medicine implementation.

24.3.1 *Knowledge review*

Before you move on, can you define the following key concepts:

- Personalised medicine is an approach to medical treatment and prevention that takes into account individual variability in genes, environment, and lifestyle for each person

24.3.2 *Question to think about*

How would you feel about your genetic profile being taken to provide you with access to personalised treatments?
What privacy safeguards would you wish to see?

24.4 Artificial Intelligence (AI) in Healthcare

IBM define AI, as a technology that enables computers and machines to simulate human intelligence and problem-solving capabilities.

In the last few years, the term "artificial intelligence" has been very prominent in the popular media due to the emergence of technologies such as ChatGPT. You can type questions into Chat GPT so when I asked ChatGPT, "What are you?" it replied:

> "*I am an artificial intelligence language model created by OpenAI called ChatGPT. My purpose is to assist users like you with a variety of tasks, including answering questions, providing information, generating text based on prompts, and engaging in conversation on a wide range of topics. If you have any questions or need assistance, feel free to ask!*"

When asked for more information, the system responds by saying that it belongs to the family of models known as Generative Pre-trained Transformers (GPT), specifically based on the GPT-3.5 architecture, and that it is trained on a vast amount of text data and is capable of generating human-like text responses based on the input it receives. The model is designed to understand and generate text in a conversational manner, making it useful for a wide range of natural language processing tasks, such as answering questions, providing explanations, generating creative content, and engaging in dialogue with users.

Its apparently human-like behaviour and informal style has made this form of artificial intelligence very attractive, but it is one example of this type of technology which has been around for about 50 years. The earliest forms of the technology were rule-based so-called expert systems, such as MYCIN. MYCIN (Shortliffe & Buchanan, 1975), was an expert system developed in a computer Language known as LISP to identify bacteria causing severe infections and to recommend antibiotics. It was never used in clinical routine, probably because of its stand-alone character and the high effort in maintaining its knowledge base (Holzinger et al., 2019).

These early expert systems such as MYCIN were the subject of fierce criticism by authors such as Dreyfus (1992) who were able to point to many of the limitations of these systems. (Gillies & Smith, 2022). One of the key limitations was the characteristic described as "brittleness", the inability to cope with a problem outside of their competence.

As early as 1960, there had been dramatic examples of brittleness in heuristic-based systems:

In 1960 there was an indication, in the recently installed early warning system in Greenland, of a massive impending Soviet missile attack. It was an error, of course; it turned out that the system's radar signals had bounced back off the moon.

How did this happen? It turned out that moonrises hadn't been thought of by the designers, so they weren't in the system's model (Davis, 1989), Disaster was averted when the humans in charge applied a degree of common sense.

Their first thought was to contact the US Government in Washington, but an iceberg had cut the telegraph cable and communication was impossible. When they considered the situation, various factors suggested that this might be a false alarm. For one thing, the whole system was new. In addition, they realised that Kruschev happened to be in New York, and it seemed unlikely that the Soviets would have chosen such a time for an all-out attack. It turned out that the system had been confused by a rising moon and moonrises hadn't been considered by the designers, so they weren't in the system's model.

Although MYCIN surpassed a typical doctor's ability to diagnose meningitis in patients but could easily produce false results if asked to diagnose beyond its area of expertise.

Kilov (2020) asserts that human expertise can be brittle as well as computer systems:

"Experts are often unable to transfer their proficiency in one domain to other, even intuitively similar domains. Experts are often unable to flexibly respond to changes within their domains."

One of the purposes of professional codes of conduct is to govern the brittleness of human experts operating in a professional context. All codes of conduct applying to healthcare professionals emphasise that they should always practice only within their areas of expertise.

The limitations of rule-based expert systems led to alternative technologies based around machine learning. Machine learning is a branch of artificial intelligence and computer science that focuses on using data and algorithms to enable AI to imitate the way that humans learn, gradually improving the accuracy of results.

The earliest machine learning applications were artificial neural networks. They were designed to model the neural networks of the human brain and learn from examples offering the potential to incorporate implicit knowledge as well as explicit knowledge, although Savain argues that at a fundamental level they are less different from rule-based systems than might appear.

"A deep neural network is actually a rule-based expert system. AI programmers just found a way (gradient descent, fast computers and lots of labelled or pre-categorised data) to create the rules automatically. The rules are in the form, if A then B, where A is a pattern and B a label or symbol representing a category." (Chougrad et al., 2018)

One medical example of the use of such systems to assist human clinicians is in the interpretation of mammograms for the detection of breast cancer. (Ahn et al., 2023). Their review covers AI used as a second opinion for a human radiographer or as an autonomous system in various configurations. Shortages of human radiographers and increased workloads make the use of AI an attractive option. Human radiographers are not perfect and error rates tend to increase with workloads and the studies reviewed by Ahn et al. (2023) suggest that AI errors can match or exceed human rates, and are likely to improve over time as the systems learn from more examples. However, ethical considerations mean that AI systems are most likely to be used as a second opinion, at least initially.

Additionally, the results of such automated analysis are acknowledged to be highly dependent upon effective optimisation by the authors and studies in other fields have shown their fragility and demonstrated their susceptibility to contamination of images or even deliberate manipulation. (Heaven, 2019)

Koteluk et al. (2021) state the current situation as:

> Machine learning enables human doctors to save their time, hospitals to save money, and patients to receive highly personalised and more accurate treatment. However, the progressing implementation of machine learning in medicine has many technical and ethical limitations.
>
> The main technical issue that machine learning needs to overcome is the number of potential manipulations of input data that can influence the system's decisions. For example, a simple action as adding a few extra pixels or rotating the image can lead to misdiagnosing and cancer misclassification as malignant or benign.

Further, the inability of such systems to communicate what they have learnt, and justify their conclusions (Holzinger et al., 2019), limits their ability to be deployed without human supervision and this suggests that they would not meet the requirements of a professional code of conduct for a professional. In spite of the major developments in big data and processing power which we have witnessed over the last few decades. Gillies and Smith (2022) argue AI systems still cannot meet ethical standards of the codes of conduct which govern human professionals, and therefore should only be used as decision aids in healthcare and not as autonomous decision-makers.

The integration of AI into clinical healthcare presents significant opportunities for improving patient care, but it also introduces broader ethical challenges that need to be addressed that require careful consideration of topics such as informed consent, transparency, safety, fairness, and privacy (Gerke et al., 2020).

One major concern is the application of informed consent in the context of AI-assisted care. As AI systems become more prevalent in tasks like imaging, diagnostics, and surgery, it raises questions about how clinicians should educate patients about the complexities of AI, including the types of machine learning used, data inputs, and potential biases. Furthermore, transparency becomes crucial, especially when AI operates using "black-box" algorithms that are difficult for clinicians to interpret fully. Balancing patient privacy with the effectiveness of AI algorithms is another challenge, particularly when dealing with sensitive data like genetic information.

AI-driven health apps and chatbots also pose ethical dilemmas regarding user agreements and informed consent. Unlike traditional consent processes, user agreements are often agreed upon without full understanding by the individual, raising concerns about transparency and accountability (Cohen et al., 2014).

Additionally, ensuring the safety and effectiveness of AI systems is paramount, as highlighted by cases like IBM Watson for Oncology, which faced criticism for providing incorrect treatment recommendations due to inadequate training data (Ross & Swetlitz, 2018). Reliable and valid datasets, along with transparency in algorithmic processes, are essential for building trust among clinicians and patients.

Algorithmic fairness and biases are significant concerns in AI-driven healthcare, as biased algorithms can lead to unjust outcomes, particularly for underrepresented populations. Efforts to mitigate biases should be made throughout the development process, including careful selection of training data and algorithmic procedures. Transparency in AI decision-making is crucial for detecting and addressing biases, although achieving transparency in "black-box" algorithms remains challenging (Obermeyer et al., 2019).

Data privacy is a fundamental issue in the use of AI in healthcare, highlighted by cases such as the breach of patient data by the Royal Free NHS Foundation Trust to Google DeepMind (UK ICO, 2017). Adequate patient education and transparency are necessary to build trust and ensure the ethical use of patient data. Questions regarding data ownership, patient consent, and protection against misuse of data underscore the need for robust privacy regulations and ethical guidelines.

As the amount of data available to businesses and public organisations increases, the growing demand to derive value from "big data" increases in parallel. Very often, the sheer quantity of data renders it impossible to analyse by human means and AI is used. Worldwide business spending on AI was predicted to be around $50 billion in 2020 and $110 billion annually by 2024 (Pazzanese, 2020).

Clinical applications of artificial intelligence and machine learning in cardiac intensive care (after Jentzer et al., 2023)

The depth and breadth of data produced in cardiac ICUs poses challenges to clinicians and researchers. AI and machine learning (ML) methodologies have been increasingly used to provide insights into this complex patient population. Major analytical tasks where ML methodology can be applied in the cardiac ICU and other critical care settings include mortality risk stratification, prognostication, non-fatal event prediction, diagnosis, phenotyping, identification of occult heart disease from the electrocardiogram, and interpretation of echocardiographic images.

The process of assessing mortality risk in cardiac ICUs is complex and challenging due to the diverse patient population and varying conditions. Although several risk prediction scores are available, they often lack accuracy and calibration when applied to cardiac ICU patients. Traditional statistical methods have limitations, and there is a growing interest in using Machine Learning techniques for real-time mortality prediction. However, as of 2023, there are few viable machine learning techniques for predicting cardiac ICU mortality.

In certain patient subgroups like acute coronary syndrome or heart failure, machine learning techniques, such as penalised regression and deep learning, have shown promise in developing improved mortality risk prediction models compared to conventional methods. Machine learning methods have also been used to predict nonfatal events in critical care, which could potentially help through early intervention and lead to improved patient outcomes.

Phenotyping through unsupervised ML clustering methods offers insights into underlying patterns within the cardiac ICU population, potentially leading to tailored treatments and improved prognostication. Machine learning is also being applied to automate echocardiographic and electrocardiographic analysis, facilitating quicker and more accurate diagnoses.

Looking to the future, Jentzer et al., 2023 argue that machine learning models integrated into Electronic Medical Records (EMRs) could revolutionise cardiac ICU practice by providing real-time risk assessment, disease-specific predictions, and personalised treatment recommendations. However, further research and validation are needed to ensure the effectiveness and applicability of these methods across different cardiac ICU populations and settings.

At the time of their review, in 2023, the promise of the technology still exceeded the practical applications and benefits.

24.4.1 Knowledge review

Before you move on, can you define the following key concepts:

- Artificial intelligence?
- Machine learning?

24.4.2 Question to think about

Would you trust your treatment to AI used as an autonomous decision maker?

Do you think that using AI as a decision aid for human clinicians can improve the quality of decision making?

References

Botham, J., Shilling, V., & Jones, J. (2021). Patient and public understanding of the concept of 'personalised medicine' in relation to cancer treatment: A systematic review. *Future Healthcare Journal*, 8(3), e703–e708.

Botham, J., Shilling, V., & Jones, J. (2021). Patient and public understanding of the concept of 'personalised medicine' in relation to cancer treatment: A systematic review. *Future Healthcare Journal*, 8(3), e703–e708.

Cherid, C., Baghdadli, A., Wall, M., Mayo, N. E., Berry, G., Harvey, E. J., ... Morin, S. N. (2020). Current level of technology use, health and eHealth literacy in older Canadians with a recent fracture – A survey in orthopedic clinics. *Osteoporosis International*, 31, 1333–1340.

Chougrad, H., Zouaki, H., & Alheyane, O. (2018). Deep convolutional neural networks for breast cancer screening. *Computer Methods and Programs in Biomedicine*, 157, 19–30.

Cohen, I. G., Amarasingham, R., Shah, A., Xie, B., & Lo, B. (2014). The legal and ethical concerns that arise from using complex predictive analytics in health care. *Health Affairs*, 33(7), 1139–1147.

Davis, R. (1989). Expert systems: How far can they go? A report on a panel session at the 1985 international joint conference on artificial intelligence in Los Angeles. *AI Magazine*, 10(2) (AAAI). https://ojs.aaai.org/index.php/aimagazine/article/download/745/663/0

Dhar, E., Upadhyay, U., Huang, Y., Uddin, M., Manias, G., Kyriazis, D., ... Syed Abdul, S. (2023). A scoping review to assess the effects of virtual reality in medical education and clinical care. *Digital Health*, 9, 20552076231158022.

Dreyfus, H. L. (1992). *What computers still can't do: A critique of artificial reason*. MIT press.

Fortune Business Insights. (2023, May). *Virtual reality in healthcare market | revenue statistics [2023-2030]* (Report ID FBI 101679). Fortune Business Insights.

Gerke, S., Minssen, T., & Cohen, G. (2020). Ethical and legal challenges of artificial intelligence-driven healthcare. *Artificial Intelligence in Healthcare*, 295–336.

Gillies, A., & Smith, P. (2022). Can AI systems meet the ethical requirements of professional decision-making in health care?. *AI and Ethics*, 2(1), 41–47.

Haleem, A., Javaid, M., Singh, R. P., & Suman, R. (2021). Telemedicine for healthcare: Capabilities, features, barriers, and applications. *Sensors International*, 2, 100117.

Harder, B. (2013). Are MOOCs the future of medical education?. *BMJ* (Clinical research ed.), 346, f2666.

Heaven, D. (2019, October 10). Deep trouble for deep learning. *Nature*, 574, 163–166.

Heiberg Engel, P. J. (2008). Tacit knowledge and visual expertise in medical diagnostic reasoning: Implications for medical education. *Medical Teacher*, 30, e184–e188.

Heponiemi, T., Kaihlanen, A.-M., Kouvonen, A., Leemann, L., Taipale, S., & Gluschkoff, K. (2022). The role of age and digital competence on the use of online health and social care services: A cross-sectional population-based survey. *Digital Health*, 8, 20552076221074485.

Holden, C., Bignell, L., Mukhopadhyay, S., & Jones, C. (2019). The public perception of the facilitators and barriers to implementing personalised medicine: A systematic review. *Personalised Medicine*, 16(5), 409–420.

Holzinger, A., Langs, G., Denk, H., Zatloukal, K., & Müller, H. (2019). Causability and explainability of artificial intelligence in medicine. *Wiley Interdisciplinary Reviews: Data Mining and Knowledge Discovery*, 9(4), e1312.

Jentzer, J. C., Kashou, A. H., & Murphree, D. H. (2023). Clinical applications of artificial intelligence and machine learning in the modern cardiac intensive care unit. *Intelligence-Based Medicine*, 7, 100089.

Kasztura, M., Richard, A., Bempong, N. E., Loncar, D., & Flahault, A. (2019). Cost-effectiveness of precision medicine: a scoping review. *International journal of public health*, 64(9), 1261–1271.

Kilov, D. (2020). The brittleness of expertise and why it matters. Synthese, 199(1–2), 3431–3455.

Koteluk, O., Wartecki, A., Mazurek, S., Kołodziejczak, I., & Mackiewicz, A. (2021). How do machines learn? Artificial intelligence as a new era in medicine. *Journal of Personalized Medicine*, 11(1), 32.

Lattimer, V., & George, S. (1996). Nurse telephone triage in out-of-hours primary care. *Primary Care Case Management*, 6, 3–6.

Lopreiato, J. O. (Ed.), Downing, D., Gammon, W., Lioce, L., Sittner, B., Slot, V., Spain, A. E. (Associate Eds.),and the Terminology & Concepts Working Group. (2016). *Healthcare simulation dictionary* (p. 40). http://www.ssih.org/dictionary

Mahmoud, K., Jaramillo, C., & Barteit, S. (2022). Telemedicine in low-and middle-income countries during the COVID-19 pandemic: A scoping review. *Frontiers in Public Health*, 10, 914423.

Mars, M. (2013, November 1). Telemedicine and advances in urban and rural healthcare delivery in Africa. *Progress in Cardiovascular Diseases*, 56(3), 326–335.

Mensah, N. K., Adzakpah, G., Kissi, J., Boadu, R. O., Lasim, O. U., Oyenike, M. K., Bart-Plange, A., Dalaba, M. A., & Sukums, F. (2023). Health professional's readiness and factors associated with telemedicine implementation and use in selected health facilities in Ghana. *Heliyon*, 9(3), e14501.

Obermeyer, Z., Powers, B., Vogeli, C., & Mullainathan, S. (2019). Dissecting racial bias in an algorithm used to manage the health of populations. *Science*, 366(6464), 447–453.

Pazzanese, C. (2020, October 26). Ethical concerns mount as AI takes bigger decision-making role in more industries. *The Harvard Gazette*.

Peyroteo, M., Ferreira, I. A., Elvas, L. B., Ferreira, J. C., & Lapão, L. V. (2021). Remote monitoring systems for patients with chronic diseases in primary health care: Systematic review. *JMIR mHealth and uHealth*, 9(12), e28285.

Research Reports World. (2023). *Global "telemetry implant market" (2023-2031) research report*. Research Reports World.

Reich, J., & Ruipérez-Valiente, J. A. (2019). The MOOC pivot. *Science*, 363(6423), 130–131. doi:10.1126/science.aav7958

Ross, C., & Swetlitz, I. (2018). *IBM's Watson supercomputer recommended 'unsafe and incorrect' cancer treatments, internal documents show*. STAT.

Setia, S., Tay, J. C., Chia, Y. C., & Subramaniam, K. (2019). Massive open online courses (MOOCs) for continuing medical education–why and how?. *Advances in Medical Education and Practice*, 10, 805–812.

Sharma, N., Doherty, I., & Dong, C. (2017). Adaptive learning in medical education: The final piece of technology enhanced learning?. *The Ulster Medical Journal*, 86(3), 198–200.

Shortliffe, E. H., & Buchanan, B. G. (1975). A model of inexact reasoning in medicine. *Mathematical Biosciences*, 23(3–4), 351–379.

Smittenaar, C. R., Petersen, K. A., Stewart, K., & Moitt, N. (2016). Cancer incidence and mortality projections in the UK until 2035. *British Journal of Cancer*, 115(9), 1147–1155.

UK Information Commissioners Office. (2017). *ICO. Royal Free—Google DeepMind trial failed to comply with data protection law*. UK Information Commissioners Office.

US Department of Defense. (2018, August 1). *DoD modeling and simulation glossary*. US Department of Defense.

Vasilescu, M. D., Serban, A. C., Dimian, G. C., Aceleanu, M. I., & Picatoste, X. (2020). Digital divide, skills and perceptions on digitalisation in the European Union – Towards a smart labour market. *PLoS One*, 15(4), e0232032.

Vicente, A. M., Ballensiefen, W., & Jönsson, J. I. (2020). How personalised medicine will transform healthcare by 2030: The ICPerMed vision. *Journal of Translational Medicine*, 18, 1–4.

Zhang, S. C., Bruce, C., Hayden, M., & Rieder, M. J. (2014). Public perceptions of pharmacogenetics. *Pediatrics*, 133(5), e1258–e1267.

Zimmer, T. (2014, October 22). Rethinking higher education: A case for adaptive learning. *Forbes*.

Glossary of Terms

Accreditation is the formal recognition by an independent body, generally known as an accreditation body, that a certification body operates according to international standards.

Advocacy groups are a group of people whose members support a common political, social, or economic cause. They educate and fight for issues that impact the lives of individuals or larger groups of people, and this may include lobbying officials or other policy maker.

The **affordability of health care (at a national level)** is the ability of governments to fund healthcare and is typically measured as the proportion of GDP devoted to healthcare.

Agenda setting is the mechanism by which issues are brought to a government's attention. Problems in health and healthcare are identified, and stakeholders propose potential solutions. It is the first stage of the policy making process.

Allocative efficiency is the optimal strategic resource allocation to achieve the best population health.

Antimicrobial resistance is the development of resistant strains of bacteria, viruses, parasites, and fungi due to the misuse and overuse of antibiotics and other antimicrobial drugs.

Artificial intelligence, or AI, is a technology that enables computers and machines to simulate human intelligence and problem-solving capabilities.

Automatic healthcare coverage means that a person's residency or citizenship entitles them to access to healthcare, and the funds are drawn from non-specific taxation.

Big data refers to very large data sets that are difficult to manage due to their volume, velocity, and variety. However, it is this complexity and scale that potentially provide greater insights, better operational efficiency, and higher revenue growth.

Biosimilar drugs are copies of an approved original biologic medicine whose patent protection has expired. They are derived from living cells or organisms and consist of relatively large and often highly complex molecules that may be difficult to fully characterise.

Catastrophic health expenditure occurs when medical spending of a household exceeds a certain level of capacity to pay, often in response to a sudden unexpected illness.

Certification is the provision by an independent body of written assurance (a certificate) that the product, service or system in question meets specific requirements.

Co-payments are contributions required to pay a portion of the cost for healthcare services at the point of use.

Community pharmacies are retail businesses situated in accessible locations. Their traditional role of dispensing medications have expanded in recent years in many countries.

Complementary health insurance provides coverage for contributions towards services where the main taxation-funded or social insurance coverage requires a contribution.

Complex problems are defined by the interrelationship between multiple players and factors. There is no simple relationship between inputs and outputs, and no simple cause and effect and no simple cause and effect associated with interventions to address them.

Complex adaptive system is a model from systems theory used to describe a collection of individual agents or components that interact with each other and their environment, leading to emergent behaviours and properties that cannot be predicted from the characteristics of the individual agents alone.

Complicated problems have linear, step-by-step solutions, and tend to be predictable. They can be solved by breaking them down into a series of steps..

Compulsory healthcare coverage requires a specific contribution from or on behalf of the individuals covered.

Conflicts of interest arise where decisions about patient care, treatment options, or medical research may be influenced by financial considerations rather than the best interests of patients or public health. They occur in health policymaking when competing interests influence the research methods, data interpretation, and conclusions used to form health policy.

Contact tracing is the process of identifying, assessing, and managing people who have been exposed to someone who has been infected with an infectious disease, such as the COVID-19 virus.

Coronavirus disease (COVID-19) is an infectious disease caused by the SARS-CoV-2 virus, that was responsible for a global pandemic in 2020.

Cost containment is concerned with reducing costs in ways that minimise the impact on patient care.

Cream skimming is the selection that occurs because health providers or purchasers plans prefer low-risk consumers to high-risk consumers.

Critical Incident Reporting Systems (CIRS) are structured mechanisms used in healthcare, and other safety critical industries to report and analyse critical incidents or adverse events.

Curative care is treatment and therapies provided to a patient with the main intent of fully resolving an illness and the goal of returning the patient to their status of health before the illness presented itself.

CRM (customer relationship management) is the combination of practices, strategies and technologies that businesses use to manage and analyse customer interactions and data throughout the customer lifecycle to improve customer service relationships.

Data analytics is the use of data, techniques and tools to identify patterns and trends, from which actionable insights are generated that support informed decision-making.

Decentralised healthcare governance is the transfer of planning, management, and decision-making authority from the national level to sub-national entities, such as regional, state, or district/municipal levels.

The **Delphi Technique** uses several rounds of feedback and response modification, to enable a panel of experts to arrive at a consensus conclusion concerning a specific proposition or problem.

The **Demographic dividend** is the accelerated economic growth that begins with a decline in a country's mortality and fertility and the subsequent change in the age structure of the population.

The **Determinants of health** are a diverse range of social, economic and environmental factors which influence people's mental and physical health.

Diagnosis-Related Groups (DRG) is a Provider payment mechanism that categorises patients with similar clinical diagnoses in order to better control hospital costs and determine provider reimbursement rates.

Disease prevention consists of specific, population-based and individual-based interventions for both the prevention of and early detection of (otherwise known as secondary prevention), diseases to minimise the burden of diseases and their associated risk factors.

Disembodied globalisation is the global interchange of intangible things and processes, such as ideas, language, visuals, meanings, knowledge, sounds, data, electronic texts, software programs, and innovative digital assets like blockchain-encoded cryptocurrencies.

Duplicate cover is private health insurance that provides access to services that are also available in the publicly funded system. This may offer faster access to services and greater choice to those who can pay.

Environmental sustainability in healthcare refers to the responsible management of natural resources to fulfil current healthcare needs without compromising the ability of future generations to meet theirs.

Evidence-Based Resource Allocation is the allocating of resources based on scientific evidence helps to ensure that interventions and treatments are effective and have a proven impact on health outcomes.

The **Extreme poverty line** is a level of income defined by the World Bank as living in extreme poverty. As of 2023, it is defined as $2.15 per day, and 700 million people are living at or below this level.

Fee-for-service is a provider payment mechanism in which healthcare providers are remunerated according to the number and type of services provided.

Financial risk protection is defined by the WHO as being able to utilize an essential health service without falling into financial difficulty.

First-party audits are conducted internally within an organisation to evaluate its strengths and weaknesses against internal procedures or external standards.

Fiscal space may be defined as room in a government's budget that allows it to provide resources for a desired purpose without jeopardizing sustainability. This may be defined as room in a government's budget that allows it to provide resources for a desired purpose without jeopardizing sustainability.

Fixed payment system is a provider payment mechanism where the healthcare providers are remunerated with a fixed amount irrespective of the number and type of services provided.

Gaming the system occurs when healthcare providers exploit resource rules' ambiguity and flexibility to bypass the rules, whilst ostensibly honouring them, to benefit themselves, their organisation or one specific patient group.

Gatekeeping is the requirement that patients visit a primary care physician to gain access to more specialist services.

GATT - The General Agreement on Trade and Tariffs is a trade treaty designed to boost its member nations' economies, by reducing tariffs and promoting global free trade. Since 1994, it has been overseen by the World Trade Organisation.

Generic drugs are medications created to be the same as an already marketed brand-name drug in dosage form, safety, strength, route of administration, quality, and performance characteristics, thereby providing the same clinical benefit as the brand-name medicine.

Genomics is an interdisciplinary field of biology focusing on the structure, function, evolution, mapping, and editing of genomes that are made up of a person's complete set of DNA, including their genes and their three-dimensional structural configuration.

Global health policy is a subset of health policy that concentrates on the global and national health systems, encompassing both healthcare and public health services .

Globalisation describes how trade and technology have made the world into a more connected and interdependent place. It has also come to represent the economic and social changes that have come about as a result.

Gross Domestic Product per capita is the sum of gross value added by all resident producers in the economy plus any product taxes (less subsidies) not included in the valuation of output, divided by mid-year population.

Healthcare is the efforts made to maintain, restore, or promote physical, mental, or emotional well-being, particularly when carried out by licensed professionals.

Healthcare inflation refers to an increase in the average and unit cost of healthcare services over time .

Health policy is an articulation of objectives aimed at enhancing the health situation, the priorisation of these objectives, and the primary direction for achieving them.

Health policy analysis is the use of various methods to assess health policies, identify their strengths and weaknesses, and provide evidence-based recommendations for improvement

Health promotion is the process of empowering people to increase control over their health and its determinants through health literacy efforts and other actions to increase healthy behaviours and decision-making.

Health system A health system includes all elements that work together to improve health, which could involve organisations, people, and resources.

A **Hierarchy of evidence** ranks different types of research or evaluation study design based on the rigour of their research methods.

Implant telemetry is a method of remotely monitoring implanted medical devices such as pacemakers, defibrillators, neurostimulators, and implantable cardiac monitors.

Informed consent is the process in which a health care provider educates a patient about the risks, benefits, and alternatives of a given procedure or intervention. The patient must be competent to make a voluntary decision about whether to undergo the procedure or intervention.

Interoperability is the degree to which a software system, devices, applications or other entity can connect and communicate with other entities in a coordinated manner without effort from the end user.

Interpretivism is a research philosophy based on the assumption that reality is subjective, multiple and socially constructed. Within this world-view, we can only understand someone's reality through their experience of that reality, which may be different from another person's shaped by the individuals' historical or social perspective.

A **Just Culture** considers wider systemic issues when things go wrong, enabling professionals and those operating the system to learn without fear of retribution.

Linear management is characterised by breaking down the overall system into individual components and determining the required inputs and desired outputs for each component, then representing the whole as a summation of all the components, without taking into account the interactions and relationships between the components.

Lobbying is the act of lawfully attempting to influence the actions, policies, or decisions of government officials, most often legislators or members of regulatory agencies, but also judges of the judiciary.

Long Covid describes the observation that after recovery from acute COVID-19, a substantial proportion of patients continue to experience symptoms of a physical, psychological, or cognitive nature.

Long-term care includes a broad range of personal, social, and medical services and support that ensure people with, or at risk of, a significant loss of intrinsic capacity (due to mental or physical illness, disability or infirmity) can maintain a level of functional ability consistent with their basic rights and human dignity.

Long-term conditions are illnesses that cannot be cured. They can usually be controlled with medicines or other treatments. Examples include diabetes, arthritis, high blood pressure, epilepsy, asthma and some mental health conditions.

Machine learning is a branch of artificial intelligence and computer science that focuses on using data and algorithms to enable AI to imitate the way that humans learn, gradually improving the accuracy of results.

Malnutrition is an imbalance between the nutrients your body needs to function and the nutrients it gets, and as defined by the WHO includes under- and overnutrition.

A **Mission Statement** is a succinct statement of not more than one or two sentences describing the purpose of the organisation.

Mental health policy (at a national level) is a specifically written document of the government or Ministry of Health containing the goals for improving the mental health situation of the country, the priorities among those goals, and the main directions for attaining them.

Massive open online courses (MOOCs) are online courses designed to be open to a large number of participants from around the world.

mRNA vaccines deliver the instructions for making a harmless piece of protein identical to one found in a particular virus or bacterium, to the cells of a human body. Once the instructions have been decoded and the protein assembled, the immune system recognises it as a foreign body and starts to produce antibodies that can attack the protein if it encounters it again in the form of the 'real' virus.

Multilevel governance has both vertical and horizontal dimensions. The vertical dimension includes the institutional, financial, and informational connections between lower and higher levels of government. The horizontal dimension of multilevel governance involves local governments, municipalities, and regions operating at the same level of government, as well as other non-governmental actors.

Need-Based Allocation is the allocation of resources based on the healthcare needs of the population. This involves prioritising interventions and services that address prevalent health issues and contribute to the overall well-being of the community.

Out of pocket expenditure is any direct outlay by households, including gratuities and in-kind payments, to health practitioners and suppliers of pharmaceuticals, therapeutic appliances, and other goods and services.

Overnutrition is an imbalance between the nutrients your body needs to function and the nutrients it gets, where the body receives more than it needs.

Palliative health services improve the quality of life of patients (adults and children) and their families who are facing problems associated with life-limiting illness, usually progressive. It prevents and relieves suffering through the early identification, correct assessment and treatment of pain and other problems whether physical, psychosocial or spiritual.

A **Patient Administration System (PAS)** is a computerized system designed to handle mostly non-clinical data for management purposes.

Pay-for-performance is a type of PPM that rewards health care providers for meeting pre-defined targets for quality indicators or efficacy parameters to increase the quality or efficacy of care.

Personalised medicine is an approach to medical treatment and prevention that takes into account individual variability in genes, environment, and lifestyle for each person.

Preventable mortality is defined as causes of death amongst people aged under 75 years that can be mainly avoided through effective public health and primary prevention interventions (i.e. before the onset of disease/injury, to reduce incidence).

Philanthropy is a form of altruism that consists of private initiatives for the public good, focusing on other people's quality of life.

Public procurement is the procurement of goods, services and works on behalf of a public authority, such as a government agency.

Leveraged funding is funding obtained because other funders have also put in money to the project.

A **Policy** is a set of principles or guidelines that direct decision-making to follow a specific course of action in order to achieve a particular goal or goals.

Policy formulation is the second stage of policymaking. This involves considering, examining, and defining different policy options.

Population-based health services is an approach to identifying and managing the health and care risks of the local community, segmenting the risks based on needs, and designing services and other interventions to best meet these needs.

Positivism is a research paradigm that relies on measurement and reason, that knowledge is revealed from a neutral and measurable (quantifiable) observation of activity, action or reaction. Within this world-view, we can only know for certain what we can measure.

A **Power-interest grid** is a technique used to categorise stakeholders based on their power or influence and interest in a project.

Preventive healthcare, is treatment and therapies provided to a patient to prevent them becoming ill, keeping them healthy and avoiding the need for curative interventions.

Procurement is the strategic, multi-step process that a healthcare organisation follows to obtain supplies and services. It encompasses the entire buying process within a health care organisation, from finding the right suppliers to ensuring timely and correct payment of vendors.

Progressive taxation is a taxation system where higher-income groups contribute a greater percentage of their income, in contrast to low-income groups.

Proportional taxation applies a uniform percentage across all income brackets.

Prospective payment systems, such as capitation, pay providers in anticipation of services to be provided.

Provider payment mechanisms are the methods by which purchasers of health care pay providers for the services they provide.

Public health is the art and science of promoting and protecting good health, preventing disease, disability and premature death, restoring good health when it is impaired by disease or injury, and maximizing the quality of life.

Public health policy is a comprehensive term denoting the laws, regulations, actions, and decisions implemented in society to promote health and achieve specific health objectives.

Public–private partnerships are agreements between one or more public and private entities, usually of a long-term nature, which reflects mutual responsibilities in the promotion of common interests.

Quantitative research uses objective measurements with statistical methods, mathematics, economic studies or computational modelling to enable a systematic, rigorous, empirical investigation.

Qualitative research describes a range of data collection methods, for example interviews, focus groups, observation, recordings (audio or video) and documents, that collect non-numerical data to explore in-depth a problem or phenomenon, to gain a deeper understanding and greater insight.

Undernutrition is an imbalance between the nutrients your body needs to function and the nutrients it gets, where the body receives less than it needs. Be aware that some authors use the term "malnutrition" in this way but this book uses the WHO convention of including under- and overnutrition as malnutrition.

A **Patient Safety Checklist** is a list of actions to be performed in a given clinical setting, in order to ensure that no step will be forgotten, and no safety check omitted.

The **Plan-Do-Check-Act cycle** is a four-step model for carrying out change used for the control and continual improvement of processes and products. It forms the basis for any standards, models and techniques designed to improve the quality of healthcare.

Politics has multiple definitions. *Politics as government* is primarily associated with the art of government and the activities of the state. *Politics as public life* takes the view that politics is primarily concerned with the conduct and management of community affairs. *Politics as conflict resolution* emphasizes the expression and resolution of conflicts through compromise, conciliation, negotiation and other strategies. *Politics as power* views politics as the process through which desired outcomes are achieved.

Population health has been defined as "the health outcomes of a group of individuals, including the distribution of such outcomes within the group".

The **Private Finance Initiative** was a specific form of Public –private partnership used by the UK Government to renew public infrastructure, introduced in the 1990s, but expanded rapidly after the turn of the century.

Public health encompasses "refers to all organized measures (whether public or private) to prevent disease, promote health, and prolong life among the population as a whole. Its activities aim to provide conditions in which people can be healthy and focus on entire populations, not on individual patients or diseases.".

The **RADAR model** is a diagnostic tool used by assessors from the European Foundation for Quality Management (EFQM) to assess organisation's performance against the EFQM model. It looks at Results, Approaches, Deployment, Assessment and Refinement (monitoring and evaluation).

Regressive taxation places a higher burden upon low-income individuals, as it takes a larger percentage of their income compared to high-income individuals.

Relative poverty line is defined as when a household income is 60% of the average household income in their own country, so represents a much lower income level in the poorest countries relative to high-income countries.

Retrospective payment systems, such as fee-for-service, pay providers after the services have been provided.

Revenue raising is the collection of funds from various sources for the purpose of funding healthcare activities.

Risk is generally calculated as the product of the likelihood and impact of an adverse event, where likelihood is the probability that an adverse event will occur within a defined period; and the impact is (a measure of) the degree of harm that would be caused if the event occurred.

Risk pooling is the accumulation and management of revenues in such a way as to ensure that the risk of having to pay for health care is borne by all members of the pool and not by each contributor individually. The larger degree of pooling, the less people will have to bear the health financial risks.

Scarce resources in healthcare are those resources which are in short supply relative to demand. They may include drugs, staff, or equipment. They may short because of a shortage of supply or because demand increases either due to a short-term emergency situation or a longer-term trend.

Second-party audits are performed externally on a supplier by a customer or contracted organization on behalf of a customer, with audit results influencing purchasing decisions.

The **SERVQUAL** model of customer service quality is a widely used framework for assessing and measuring service quality across a wide range of industries in five dimensions   : tangibles, reliability, responsiveness, assurance and empathy.

Sin taxes are excise taxes specifically levied on certain goods deemed harmful to society and individuals, such as alcohol, tobacco, and drugs to discourage consumption and/ or help to pay for treatment needed as a result of consumption.

Social CRM is the development of strategies, methodologies, and skills to integrate social media into Customer Relationship Management (CRM) processes.

Social determinants of health are the conditions in which people are born, grow, live, work and age, and people's access to power, money and resources.

Social health insurance Under this model, people (and usually their employers) pay compulsory contributions to non-governmental bodies, separate from the tax system, in return for a predetermined set of services and treatments available to all based on need.

Software as a medical device is software intended for one or more medical purposes that perform those purposes without being part of a hardware medical device.

Software in a medical device is software intended for one or more medical purposes that drives or influences a hardware medical device, and is embedded in the device.

Solidarity (in health care) is the idea that healthcare is a fundamental human right and a collective responsibility.

Stakeholder analysis is the process of collecting information about any person that will be impacted by (or can impact) your healthcare project or program.

The **Structure-Process-Outcome model** is a quality improvement model based upon the premise that improvements in the structure of care should lead to improvements in clinical processes that should in turn improve patient outcomes.

Structured clinical terminologies are structured collections of descriptive terms which are stored in (usually electronic) health records and used in clinical practice at the point of care. On computers, they are generally stored as alphanumeric sequences meaningless to humans but with plain English terms attached to them.

A **Systemic data-driven approach** is based upon the systematic collection, management, analysis, interpretation and application of data to solve a problem

Supplementary health insurance provides coverage for health services that are excluded from taxation-funded or social insurance schemes.

The **Sustainable Development Goals** are a collection of seventeen interlinked objectives designed to serve as a "shared blueprint for peace and prosperity for people and the planet, now and into the future" that form a major driver for global health policy.

Technical efficiency is about the optimal use of resources within healthcare facilities.

Telemedicine is the provision of healthcare services remotely, typically through the use of telecommunications technology such as video conferencing, phone calls, text messaging, or secure messaging platforms.

Third-party audits are carried out by an independent audit organization unrelated to the customer-supplier relationship, often resulting in certification or recognition of compliance with standards or regulations.

Transactional leadership is a style of leadership where leaders seek to gain compliance from their followers by the use of rewards and punishments.

Transformational leadership is a style of leadership where leaders engage with followers, seek to inspire them and change their expectations, perceptions, and motivations to work towards shared goals.

Treatable mortality is defined as causes of death that can be mainly avoided through timely and effective health care interventions, including secondary prevention and treatment (i.e. after the onset of disease, to reduce case fatality).

Triage is a risk assessment process to classify patients arriving at hospital in order to allocate medical care efficiently and effectively, and ensure that the most critically ill or injured patients receive immediate attention.

Total health expenditure refers to the sum of public and private expenditures. The expenditures considered are those spent for preventive and curative health services, family planning, nutrition, and emergency aid. Activities that are generally classified as part of water provision and sanitation are not included.

Universal health coverage means that all people and communities receive the full spectrum of health services from health promotion to prevention, treatment, rehabilitation and palliative care across the life course that they need and of sufficient quality to be effective while also ensuring that the use of these services does not expose the user to financial hardship.

Variable payment systems are provider payment mechanism in which healthcare providers are remunerated a variable amount, usually according to the number and type of services provided.

A **Vision Statement** describes where the hospital should be aiming to get to. It should be broad and descriptive rather than detailed, and it should be about the destination, not how to get there.

The **WHO Essential Diagnostic List** is an evidence-based guide that looks at disease prevalence globally and recommends the appropriate laboratory test for each condition.

Index

Printed in the United States
by Baker & Taylor Publisher Services

Printed in the United States
by Baker & Taylor Publisher Services